ESSAYS IN MEDIEVAL HISTORY

From a photograph by Lafayette.

T F Tout

ESSAYS IN MEDIEVAL HISTORY

PRESENTED TO

THOMAS FREDERICK TOUT

EDITED BY

A. G. LITTLE

AND

F. M. POWICKE

Essay Index Reprint Series

BOOKS FOR LIBRARIES PRESS, INC.

FREEPORT, NEW YORK

First published 1925
Reprinted 1967

THESE papers, many of which are concerned with problems in the administrative history of England during the Middle Ages, are presented by his colleagues, pupils and many other friends, on the occasion of his seventieth birthday, to Thomas Frederick Tout, M.A., LL.D., Litt.D., Fellow of the British Academy, in grateful recognition of his work as teacher, scholar and counsellor during the thirty-five years of his tenure of a Chair of History in the Victoria University and the University of Manchester.

MANCHESTER,
September 1925.

CONTENTS[1]

[1] In the descriptions of the authors, an asterisk is attached to the names of Mr. Tout's former pupils. When no University is named, the teaching posts, fellowships, etc., are or were held in the University of Manchester.

PLANS

The Editors are indebted to Messrs. Lafayette of Manchester and London for their kind permission to use the photograph of Professor Tout, which appears as a frontispiece to this volume.

I

THE FAMILIA AT CHRISTCHURCH, CANTERBURY, 597–832

THE question whether S. Augustine founded at Christchurch, Canterbury, a monastery of Benedictine monks or a normal episcopal familia has for long remained uncertain. The facts that Augustine and his Italian companions were monks, that Christchurch after the Norman Conquest was a Benedictine house, that many archbishops of Canterbury subsequent to Augustine were monks, that many early Christchurch documents long regarded as genuine spoke of the familia at Christchurch as monks, all suggested that Christchurch had been in origin a Benedictine house. Certain indications in the records that the familia there did not at all periods live as Benedictine monks were thought evidence only of laxity and indiscipline. Modern scholars, especially since the work of Dr. Armitage Robinson on the early familia at Worcester, have suspected that the early familia at Christchurch might prove as "secular" as that at Worcester; but the origin of the sees was different, the interval between the foundation of the see and the first authentic charter longer in the case of Christchurch than of Worcester, and other circumstances rendered it difficult to argue from one case to the other. The first indisputable grant to Christchurch is that of the Mercian Offa in 774; the first to which the signatures appended probably include the more important part of the familia, that of Archbishop Wulfred in 813. It is therefore impossible to prove the nature of the familia between 597 and 813 from the signatures to charters, as Dr. Armitage Robinson did in the case of Worcester, from the charter of Headda in 798 onwards. Nevertheless, an attempt will here be made to show that the familia founded at Christchurch was secular, by considering the authentic English evidence in the light of contemporary custom, and particularly of the disciplinary canons of contemporary continental councils. Mention of the spurious documents and charters will be omitted for the sake of clearness, though the motive for their composition is often interesting.

When Gregory the Great sent S. Augustine to England the most important duty of any bishop was to train and provide for his episcopal familia. In Italy episcopal sees were frequent and small; the bishop and his familia served the basilica of the civitas, and there might be, as in the see of Populona,[1] three churches served each by a presbyter and a small familia in the bishop's "rus" or "territorium" (his see outside the bounds of his civitas). "Parochia" was normally used of the bishop's see, and continued so to be used for hundreds of years; but it was in the time of Gregory the Great also beginning to be used for the sphere of the small presbyteral churches in the *rus*, where the presbyter "ruled" his own endowments as rector. Earlier, all the clergy of the see had been accounted the bishop's familia, and had been paid stipends by him from the general endowments of the see. Sees differed in size, those in south Italy, Sicily, and central and north Gaul having a much larger "rus" or "pagus" than the older ones of central and north Italy and the Rhone valley; but the point for emphasis is, that in all sees about 600 the episcopal familia which served the civitas and cathedra was still the larger and more important part of the whole clergy of the see. Sometimes it was still, in newly converted districts, co-extensive with the clergy of the see, and there were no separately endowed presbyteral "parishes". The nucleus of the familia was the bishop's domus, close to his cathedra; here the bishop lived, ate, and slept with the secular clergy in training. He received them, often at the age of seven, sheared and blessed them, and admitted them to the first three grades or orders of the "celestial militia", ostiarius, exorcist, and lector. These boy lectors were drawn in large numbers from the serfs or freedmen of the episcopal "praedia" or lands; such boys might rise to the higher orders, but probably in most cases married and remained in minor orders, practically as the domestic servants and sacristans of the cathedra, and the caretakers of small chapels and martyria in the civitas and in the rus. Every episcopal familia contained a large proportion of such inferior clergy, though the children of freemen and nobles were also sent to be trained by the bishop as lectors. While the young clerks still remained in close touch with the bishop, it had become the special duty of the first presbyter of the familia, the capischola or magister scholarum, to teach them to recite the canonical hours, with as much grammar and rhetoric as possible. They received the other orders at intervals of several years, and could not be ordained presbyter before they were "provectioris aetatis", generally about forty years old. Except in Italy there were no secular schools, so that the training of the future clergy in the familia was a vital part of the bishop's office.

As to the maintenance of the familia,[2] while some clerks would be eventually ordained "to a title", to the service of some chapel or basilica, others might receive holy orders and continue to serve

[1] Migne, *P.L.* 77. 461; Homes Dudden, *Gregory the Great*, 1905, I. 360.

[2] See article on "Partage" in Migne, *Dictionnaire de discipline ecclésiastique*, 1856, II. 411-45. The *Patrimony of the Roman Church*, by E. Spearing, 1918, is enlightening as to the maintenance of the Roman familia, though his interpretation of the letter to Paschasius of Naples, p. 121, about the familia, seems to the writer more than doubtful.

the cathedra. While it was canonical that at least two presbyters should be retained by the bishop to live with him, as " witnesses of his life ", it lay with the bishop to decide which presbyters to retain in his domus, and to apportion to his clergy their stipends.[1] All the clergy, even the young lectors, received stipends, both in kind and in money ; but to a few of the higher clergy of the familia—the magister scholarum, the archdeacon, and possibly one or two of the presbyters—the bishop often granted for life a piece of land or vineyard, in lieu of the frequent small payments in money and kind which the other clergy received. Such clergy generally lived in houses of their own and were men of some patrimony, which the canons allowed them to retain. Thus an ordinary episcopal familia would be housed in the bishop's domus, and close by in his xenodochium (hospitium or almshouse, for the lodging of the poor, and " clerici peregrini "), in the small houses of his married lectors and exorcists, and in a few separate houses for his superior clergy. In Gaul, where the bishops were often hastily-elected married nobles, the bishop often maintained his wife and children on the villa of his patrimony, while he was supposed to live continently with the clerks of his familia in the domus of his cathedra. The Council of Tours, 567, ordered that :

> The bishop should have his wife as his sister, and thus govern his whole house in holy conversation, both his ecclesiastical house and his own house, so that no suspicion for any reason arise. And although, by God's help, he shall live chastely by the testimony of his clerks, because they live with him both in his " cella " and wheresoever he is, and the priests and deacons and moreover the crowd of young clerks, by God's help, preserve him : nevertheless, for zeal to God, let them be so far distant from his " mansio " that those who are being nourished in hopes of being received into the clerical servitude be not polluted by the contagious neighbourhood of the women servants.[2]

A similar enactment (to secure celibacy) was made about the heads of the small presbyteral familiae, generally " ruled " in Gaul by archipresbyters (or where the familia included no other presbyter, by a presbyter).[3] Both in Gaul and Italy at the time of Augustine's mission the familia was still a large unit of clergy ; it was not till the ninth century that the familia of a rural parish became reduced to a presbyter and a single clerk. The area of a rural parish in late sixth-century Gaul was of course more comparable to the modern rural deanery than the modern rural parish ; many sixth-century rural parishes soon became bishops' sees, while others persisted as the extensive parishes of great collegiate churches.

It should be noted that though the life of a large part of the familia

[1] For Gregory the Great's minute and explicit directions about stipends see Mansi, *Sacrorum Conciliorum . . . Collectio*, 1763, IX. 1163 ; X. 90, 268, 371-2.

[2] Mansi, IX. 795, xii. ; Hefele and Leclercq, *Histoire des Conciles*, 1910, **3.** i. 187.

[3] Mansi, IX. 797, xxix. ; Hefele and Leclercq, **3.** i. 189.

was communal, and much more closely shared by the bishop than in the Carolingian and later period, when the bishops became royal ministers and feudal lords, yet the communal element in the life was due to economic motives of convenience, and not enjoined on the clergy universally by the canons. Nevertheless, many stricter spirits had interpreted the verse in Acts IV., "*No man called anything his own, but they had all things in common,*" of the clergy, as descendants of the apostles, and had argued that they ought to lead a communal life in imitation of the apostles. S. Augustine of Hippo had made the best-known attempt to enforce such a communal life on all his clergy, not drawing up any rule, but constraining all his familia to live with him, without money stipends, in the house next his cathedra, which he called in his letters his "domus" or his "monasterium" indifferently. But the remonstrance of his fellow bishops had made him finally withdraw his refusal to ordain any clerk who would not promise to lead this "apostolic" or communal life. A lesson in S. Augustine's office connected his name with the apostolic life in the minds of all medieval clerics; "he instituted a family of religious, who had common food and common worship, and he taught them diligently the discipline of the apostolic life and doctrine". Certain zealous bishops later copied this manner of life for their familia from S. Augustine, without drawing up any specific rule; and the members of such familiae, like his, lived in a domus or monasterium, and were spoken of as "monachi".

The mission sent by Gregory to England consisted of forty monks, certain slave boys bought for missionary purposes, and certain Frankish presbyters as interpreters. It was led by Augustine, who had been the alumnus or "nutritus" (the technical word for one trained in an episcopal familia) of Felix, bishop of Messina, and who had joined and finally become prior of Gregory's own monastery of S. Andrew.[1] He had probably at some time been taken from the monastery to accompany Gregory, either in Constantinople or when pope, since he is spoken of as his "syncellus"; he was not then without experience of the life of both an episcopal and the papal familia, as well as of that of a great monastery. He was not a Benedictine monk, for there were neither in east nor west at the time monastic "orders"; in Greek monasticism none were developed later. Certain rules and holy treatises were read and honoured; but the founder of each house adapted the manner of life of his monks from these as it pleased him, usually without making a written rule. S. Andrew's was not a Benedictine house, nor could it, situated in a town, have copied the Benedictine life as closely, for instance, with regard to agricultural labour, as the other monasteries Gregory had founded in Sicily. The lack of definition about contemporary monachism should be taken

[1] Homes Dudden, II. 105.

into account for the study of Augustine's mission, and the history of English monasticism thereafter till the time of Dunstan. When Isidore of Seville, roughly contemporary with S. Augustine, wished to draw up a Latin rule for monks, *c.* 582, he used the Benedictine rule but composed his own, as did other Spanish leaders. In Gaul in the mid-seventh century Bishop Donatus of Besançon drew up a rule in which he fused together the Benedictine rule, the Columban, and that of Cesarius of Arles. In seventh-century Gaul it was quite usual to found monasteries, enjoining on them the observance both of the Columban and Benedictine rules, without any fusion. A joint copy of the two rules dating from the year 630 is found to have belonged to the great Celtic house of Luxeuil; and in 631 a monastery was founded at Limoges where the observance of the two rules was prescribed "according to the practice of the men of Luxeuil".[1] It was not till the year 670 that the synod of Autun first made the Benedictine rule obligatory on monasteries for at least part of France, and the use of the term "vel" [*or* or *and* ?] makes even this clause not quite clear. "Abbots and monks . . . ought to fulfil and keep in all matters whatever the order of the canons [conciliar decrees] and [vel] the rule of S. Benedict teaches."[2] Probably monks were here ordered to observe the frequent conciliar decrees dealing with the monastic state, together with the rule of S. Benedict; but in view of the contemporary use of "monks and abbot" for an episcopal familia and its head, leading the stricter communal life, the clause might be translated "the order of the canons *or* the rule of S. Benedict". It was an important part of the work of the synods of 742 and 743, presided over by Carloman and Boniface, to make the rule of S. Benedict the norm for all men's and women's cloisters among the Franks. The work of Benedict of Aniane and Louis the Pious was directed not only to the restoration of Benedictine discipline in houses which had become laicised and relaxed, but to the reduction of houses which had never explicitly professed the Benedictine rule to its observance.

A study of the letters of Gregory the Great and the works of Gregory of Tours (*d.* 594) yields some points of interest with reference to Augustine's mission. It shows that the grades of the clerical militia were still more honourable than the title of "monachus". S. Augustine of Hippo had lamented that it was scarcely possible out of even a good monk to make a clerk, but the Italian monks of 597 were so much more civilised than the African solitaries that Gregory found in the monks his best missionary material. Still, even monasteries in the Benedictine tradition would have had but one or two presbyters; and sometimes, when they had no inmate,

[1] For references see Herzog-Hauck, *Realencyklopädie*, II. 583.

[2] Mansi, XI. 124, XV.; Hefele and Leclercq, **3.** i. 307.

even the abbot, sufficiently learned to be ordained to the presbyterate, bishops were asked to appoint a secular presbyter as their chaplain. Contemporary descriptions appended to the signatures of charters, or in papal correspondence, specified that a man was both " presbyter et monachus ", " presbyter et abbas " ; and the description of a man simply as " monachus " can be taken as a sure sign that he was neither presbyter nor deacon. With regard to the monks whom Augustine, as their abbot, led to England, it is unlikely that any besides Augustine and Lawrence (who is so described) were presbyters. This would be in accordance with contemporary proportions, and is supported by what we know of the missionaries' later history. It is likely that Augustine would send the most capable of his band as his emissaries to Gregory ; he sent Lawrence the presbyter and Peter the monk. Lawrence succeeded him at Canterbury ; Peter (later spoken of as presbyter) became first abbot of the monastery of SS. Peter and Paul at Canterbury.[1] Contemporary conditions, the provision about ordination to titles, etc., render it extremely improbable that other of Augustine's monks of whom we know nothing were presbyters. Some were doubtless ordained by Augustine after his consecration as bishop.

The more important point which is shown by Pope Gregory's correspondence is that he considered the clerical and monastic professions incompatible. A man might be taken from his monastery, with his abbot's consent, and ordained to the grades of the clerical militia, as Gregory had been himself ; but thereafter he was under no obligation of obedience to his former abbot or rule, but to the bishop who had ordained him.

> No one can serve as a clerk and persist under order in the monastic rule, nor can he be bound by the restraint of the monastery, who is forced to remain in the daily service of the church. . . . The duties of each office separately are so weighty that no one can rightly discharge them. It is therefore very improper that one man should be considered fit to discharge the duties of both.[2]

It is thus quite clear that Gregory would consider that when Augustine ordained certain of his monks to the various grades of clerkship to form his episcopal familia, the central work of his whole mission, these clerks would be no longer under the restraint of their earlier rule.

Bede's evidence about Augustine's mission is especially valuable, because he died before Boniface and Chrodegang of Metz (see *infra*) persuaded their contemporaries that only the communal life for the clergy was really canonical. Before their work to make monasticism entirely Benedictine, Wilfrid of Ripon claimed that he had been the first to introduce the Benedictine rule into England ; Bede was reared

[1] Homes Dudden, II. 122.
[2] *Ibid.* II. 191, 192 ; cf. Migne, *P.L.* 77, col. 112.

in a monasticism more sharply Benedictinised by Wilfrid and Benedict Biscop than that planted originally by S. Augustine in the monastery of SS. Peter and Paul. Bede's sympathies were therefore Benedictine; but he in no case suggests that Christchurch was a "monastery" in the same sense as that of SS. Peter and Paul. He says that king Ethelbert gave the missionaries "a mansio in the civitas of Canterbury" and supplied them with sustenance; "as soon as they entered the dwelling place assigned to them they began to imitate the apostolic manner of life in the primitive church".[1] They used the old basilica of S. Martin, on the east side of the city, as their oratory, rededicating it to the "holy Saviour, our divine lord Jesus Christ", and soon after, the king gave them "the place for a see, suitable to their degree in the metropolis", and "such possessions of divers sorts as were necessary to them", *i.e.* praedia and serfs. Ethelbert also built (but probably after an interval, as the Church was not ready for consecration by Augustine) "a monastery not far from the city to the eastward", dedicated to SS. Peter and Paul.[2]

Gregory's answer to Augustine's query: "Concerning bishops, what should be their manner of conversation towards their clergy?"[3] shows plainly that the familia at Christchurch was to be secular, although in deference to the monastic training of all its original personnel, a communal life was to be followed similar to that enjoined by Augustine of Hippo. Gregory replied that the apostolic see usually enjoined on bishops the division of their revenues into fourths, one of which was for the bishop and his household, and another for the clergy (which would have been subdivided into individual stipends or portions); but Augustine, having been instructed in monastic rule, must not live apart from his clergy.

You must establish the manner of conversation of our fathers in the primitive church, among whom, *None said that ought of the things which they possessed was his own, but they had all things in common.* But if there are any clerks not received into holy orders who cannot live continent, they are to take wives and receive their stipends outside the community. . . . Care is also to be taken of their stipends, and provision to be made, and they are to be kept under ecclesiastical rule, that they may live orderly and attend the singing of psalms. . . . [All this was the usual provision for the married lectors.] But as for those that live in common, there is no need to say anything of assigning portions [or stipends], or dispensing hospitality and showing mercy [making regular provision for a xenodochium].

Gregory probably guessed that the comparative slenderness of Augustine's endowments would render the payment of individual stipends difficult; but it is notable that Gregory laid down no direction that this communal organisation was to be permanent, or even extend

[1] Plummer, *Ven. Baedae Op. Hist.* I. 46.
[2] *Ibid.* I. 47, 70.
[3] *Ibid.* I. 48 *et seq.*

beyond the first generation. The choice of the young clerks as to whether they wished to marry was both normal and formal. The Council of Toledo, 531, had provided for such a choice.

Of those whom the will of their parents sets free from the years of their first infancy for the clerical office, we decree that immediately they have received the tonsure they shall be handed over to the ministry of the lectors; they ought to be taught in the house of the church, in the bishop's presence, by his deputy. But when they shall have completed their eighteenth year, their wishes concerning the taking of a wife ought to be scrutinised by the bishop in the presence of clerks and people.[1]

It is quite clear that Gregory did not contemplate Augustine's reception of children as Benedictine oblates; both because it was not yet the custom to receive such young monks, and also because oblates were not allowed afterwards to marry. Augustine was to train native boys as lectors; the serfs from his praedia would often choose to marry; children of nobles would promise chastity in the expectation of attaining at length to the sacerdotium. The first native Englishman to be made archbishop of Canterbury would have been about the canonical age for ordination to the episcopate, if he were received by Augustine at the age of seven as lector.

The principle of individual stipends had been allowed at Christchurch from the first, in the case of the married lectors; there can be little doubt that it was soon extended to the other members of the familia, after the normal continental fashion. The grants of Ethelbert to Christchurch were verbal only, or have not survived; but his endowment of the closely connected see of Rochester was attested by a written grant, which points to a purely secular familia. There was, in fact, no need for written grants till the last half of the eighth century,[2] when synods enacted that bishops must keep a record of their endowments and privileges, and synodal decisions concerning them; after this both genuine and spurious charters began to be produced.

The first Christchurch charter reflects the reform movement begun by Boniface on the continent. This was essentially and professedly an effort to return to canonical directions in all Church matters, and particularly in the life of the clerical militia. The preface to the Council of Ver, 755, shows this most clearly: "The rules of the early fathers of the holy catholic church, and these righteous norms afforded for mental correction, would indeed suffice if their holy authority had remained intact. . . ." As it had not, Pepin had summoned the bishops "desiring to recover in some measure the canonical teaching, to observe the sacred canons more fully and more perfectly, and to

[1] Mansi, VIII. 785, i.; Hefele and Leclercq, **2.** ii. 1082. All these canons are of great interest for the familia.

[1] Mansi, XII. 851; Hefele and Leclercq, **3.** ii. 956.

establish their authority firmly and completely".[1] Two hundred years had elapsed between the synod of Tours, 567, and the work of Boniface, and in that interval the number of bishops had increased, and the number of rural parishes and chapels also; more presbyters were ordained, and though it was still uncanonical to ordain to the presbyterate before thirty, this was ten years earlier than had been normal in the earlier period. The old canonical arrangement of many years of marriage before a late ordination was becoming unworkable; the increase of clergy and earlier ordination were to make it quite unworkable later. In addition, the Frankish church suffered many irregularities from a largely untrained married clergy, dominated by the lay nobles. To Boniface the marriage of presbyters seemed a root evil; he conceived it as alone canonical that they should (largely to ensure celibacy) live in a monastery with their bishop, or the praepositus he set over them.[2] Large non-episcopal familiae should lead a similar life, and small ones as far as possible. He did not conceive of himself as founding a new order of canons, but as reducing all clerks as far as possible to a life in accordance with the canons. "Let each bishop take heed in his parochia, that where there is a monastery of monks, they shall live regularly and monastically; but where the canonical life is found, they shall live well and canonically."[3] The Council of Aschaim enacted also: "About clerks or nuns; let them either live in a monastery, or let them live regularly with the consent of the bishops to whom they are credited".[4] Boniface's conception was shared by all the stricter bishops. Rigobert of Reims (*d.* 743) "restored the canonical religion to his clerks, and appointed them sufficient victuals and praedia, which he conferred on them, and he instituted a common chest for their use", *i.e.* he gave his chapter a separate endowment and required them to live communally. Above all, Bishop Chrodegang of Metz furthered the reform by drawing up a rule, "a form of instruction . . . how prelates ought to live and rule their subjects". In the preface to this rule for canons he apologised for its superfluity, since the canons had already sufficiently dealt with the life of the clergy; he had composed this little "decretulum" in times of negligence and disobedience for convenience.[5] Chrodegang's rule gradually became the norm for the life of all the larger familiae, and at the Council of Aix-la-Chapelle, 817, a few chapters were added, and it was made (as the Regula Aquisgranensis)

[1] MGH, *Leges*, Boretius, p. 53; Mansi, XII. 579; Hefele and Leclercq, **3**. ii. 934, and see can. xi. The preface of the council of Aschaim (in Bavaria) is similar: Mansi, XII. 668; Hefele and Leclercq, **3**. ii. 947.

[2] Certain seventeenth-century historians upheld this view. See the interesting *Histoire des chanoines*, Paris, 1699, by R. Chabonel.

[3] Hartzheim, *Concilia*, I. 74, can. xii.; and cf. can. xvii.; Hefele and Leclercq, **3**. ii. 947.

[4] Mansi, XII. 669, ix.

[5] Napier, A. S., *Enlarged Rule of Chrodegang*, E.E.T.S. Orig. Ser. **150**. I.

obligatory on all cathedral and collegiate churches of the Carolingian empire. By the rule, all the familia were to lead a communal life in dormitory and refectory, young lectors were to be trained by a brother of proven life, the canons (among whom the young lectors are included) were allowed to retain the disposition of their patrimony, and in certain cases to receive special stipends.

Boniface's canonical renaissance reacted on England. The two legates of Hadrian I. visited England and presented twenty capitula for acceptance to two English synods in 787. One canon enjoined: " Let bishops provide . . . that all their canons live canonically, and their monks and nuns regularly "; their habit was to be that of the continental canons and monks.[1] The Christchurch charters of the period give no indication that the familia were as yet living canonically or communally. In 774 Offa of Mercia made one grant of land to Archbishop Iamberhtus (Lambert), and another grant to him " ad ecclesiam Christi ", for the endowment of the familia.[2] In 805 Archbishop Ethelheard made another grant specifically to the familia: " sanctae ecclesiae Christi in propria possessione donabo ", and recalled to its proper use an earlier grant which a lay thegn of Canterbury " fratribus nostris ad mensam tradidit ", of which the familia had been unjustly deprived. The signatures to the charter, which are probably those of the familia, included two " praepositi ", eight presbyters, one archdeacon, one deacon, and two clerks of lower rank.[3] It was usual for at least one or two of the inferior clerks to sign charters and privileges, both as representatives of their order, and probably because as young men their witness would be longer available; the mention of these two does not preclude the existence of a much larger number of their grade in the familia. The chapter had now obtained an endowment separate from that of the see; Archbishop Wulfred added to this endowment in 811.[4] In 813 Wulfred also completed the assimilation of the life of his familia to the ideals of Boniface and Chrodegang:

For the honour and love of God I have caused to be rebuilt, renewed, and restored the holy monastery of the church of Canterbury, for the presbyters, deacons, and all the clergy serving God there together. [The " rebuilt " need not be pressed into meaning more than that Wulfred believed that all cathedral clergy used to live " canonically " in a monastery, and that he knew that S. Augustine and his companions were " monachi ".] I, Wulfred, give and grant to the familia of Christ to have and enjoy the houses which they have built for themselves at their own cost by the perpetual right of inheritance, during their own lifetimes, or of those descendants to

[1] Haddan and Stubbs, III. 450, iv.

[2] Kemble, *Codex Diplomaticus Aevi Saxonici*, I. pp. 149, 150; Birch, *Cartularium Saxonicum*, I. p. 300.

[3] Kemble, I. 231; Birch, I. 447.

[4] Kemble, I. 239; Birch, I. 461.

whom each shall have free power to leave or grant them within the said monastery, but not to any external person without the congregation [*i.e.* the possibly married canons who have received stipends, and lived in their own houses, may bequeath them to sons or relations trained in the Christchurch familia, as the canons had probably received them themselves, but not to their other children]. But under this condition, that they sedulously frequent the canonical hours in the church of Christ. . . . And that they frequent together the refectory and dormitory, and that they observe the rule of the discipline of life in a monastery. But if any of them . . . dare to gather together feasts for eating and drinking or even sleeping in their own cells (houses), let him know, whoever he be, that he shall be deprived of his own house and it shall be in the power of the archbishop to hold and to grant to whomsoever it shall please him.[1]

The charter is signed by Wulfred, one "presbyter abbas", eight presbyters, and three other clerks. The "praepositi" of the earlier charter are now replaced by the "presbyter abbas", for the enforcement of the communal, canonical life, and the signatures to other cathedral charters suggest that the title was in fairly common use, for headship of a house of canonical, or monasterial, clerks. This charter may fairly be said to apply the ideals of Boniface and Chrodegang to the Christchurch familia.

Though this charter speaks of the canons of Christchurch as leading a "vita monasterialis" it does not call them "monachi", although "monachi" could lawfully be used at the time of those who lived in a monasterium. In another charter of Wulfred, probably later in date, while the Christchurch clergy are spoken of in the older phraseology as the "familia", a certain Dodda, probably one of their number, is spoken of as a "monachus". Wulfred granted[2] some of his own land to the familia, and "since our common congregation has been by God's grace established, I will appeal to my familia" to aid him with their prayers and masses, with the condition that he grants them this said land, land which Cynehard the archdeacon had held and granted to him, certain other hereditary estates, and "the house and garden [curtem, *infra*, villam] which Dodda the monk held within the monastery as his own possession". This house they may use as they think fit, for feeding the citizens at suitable or necessary times, or "when a presbyter or deacon of the familia is weighed down with corporal infirmity, he may rest there with suitable honour". That is, the rigours of monasterial life shall not be enforced on sick or aged canons.

The grant of Earl Osulf to the "holy congregation" of Christchurch, Canterbury, in 806, was confirmed by Wulfred, and suggests

[1] Kemble, I. 251; Birch, I. 478.

[2] Kemble, I. 290; Birch, I. 522. The charter is signed by two "presbyteri abbates", possibly the successors of the two earlier praepositi, nine presbyters, three deacons, six clerks.

a communal life there,[1] and a grant of Werhard the presbyter in 832 expressly calls the Christchurch familia "monachi". The grant shows that the efforts of Wulfred had been successful. Werhard's will arranged for the disposal of the

> substance and lands which, by God's grace, and the help of Archbishop Wulfred my kinsman, I have acquired. I give back to Christchurch, and the monks my brothers who serve God there, all the lands within Kent and without which I have heretofore held by the grant of the said archbishop and the consent of the aforesaid familia of Christchurch. [Lands in lieu of stipend, such as Cynehard the archdeacon is mentioned to have held earlier. Such lands were not as yet called a "prebend", although bishops were technically said to "praebere" their stipends to their clerks. The lands "given back" included a house on the northern wall of Canterbury.] I also grant . . . to Christchurch . . . thirty-two hides of my patrimony, which I may grant to whom I will in the city of Canterbury. . . . And another land . . . which Ceolnoth the archbishop and the monks of the aforesaid Christchurch gave me, I give back to the said church. . . . Let the monks of Christchurch remember my soul, because I have freely restored what I ought to restore, and I have offered to Christ devoutly what was my own.[2]

The communal nature of the familia is also indicated by the presence of a "presbyter abbas" among the signatories to the charter of Abba the Reeve in 835.[3] It is clear that the "monasterial" life which S. Augustine had planted at Christchurch had been restored.

The indisputable points in the history of Christchurch up to this date may be thus summarised. Those of Augustine's companions whom he ordained as clerks formed his episcopal familia at Christchurch, and were free from their former monastic obligations. But they lived a communal life with him, as the clergy of S. Augustine of Hippo had done. Nevertheless, from the first, boys were trained who were allowed to marry, remain in minor orders, and receive stipends. After two hundred years the presbyters of the familia are found to have been living in separate houses and receiving stipends, as was normal on the continent. At what point the familia had lapsed from the stricter to the normal mode of life is not known; but such a change was not in itself uncanonical. From Frankish analogies the present writer would suspect it to have been made early. Archbishop Wulfred was responsible for re-introducing the communal life at Christchurch, and his action was inspired by the theory of Boniface

[1] *Select English Historical Documents of the Ninth and Tenth Centuries*, ed. Harmer, 1914, I. These charters are of great interest for the other Kentish "monasteries" or churches of canons. The A.S. "higan, hiwan", belonging to these churches, is the equivalent of the Latin "familia", which it would be better to use than to translate "community".

[2] Kemble, I. 297; Birch, I. 558.

[3] Kemble, I. 312; signed also by Archbishop Ceolnoth, six presbyters, three deacons, and three subdeacons.

and Chrodegang that such a life accorded more perfectly with the canons. Charter evidence shows that the communal life persisted at Christchurch at least in the first half of the ninth century. A contemporary churchman would have described the history by saying that under S. Augustine, and under Wulfred, the clerks of the familia led the " vita canonica ", and that during at least the latter part of the interval, they did not.

MARGARET DEANESLY.

II

THE SOUTH-WESTERN ELEMENT IN THE OLD ENGLISH CHRONICLE

NONE among all the materials for English history possesses authority for a longer period than the series of annals which it is convenient to call the Old English Chronicle. From the age of the Saxon migration to the Anarchy of Stephen's reign, they continue to offer information which may be rejected but cannot be ignored. The criticism of the Chronicle is the basis of Early English historiography. Pursued at times with too little regard for the probable mental processes of an early annalist; at others, with too much regard for minute differences of style and syntax, it has at least revealed in outline the conditions under which the successive sections of the Chronicle were composed. It seems clear that the central years of the ninth century mark a turning-point in its development. It is highly probable that soon after king Alfred's accession in 871 the archetype of the Chronicle which we possess was brought down to the death of king Æthelwulf in 858, that after a brief interval another hand began the series of entries which end with the annal for 891, and that from this point different copies of the Chronicle developed an independent life which increases the evidence for the history of the period but also greatly complicates its criticism.[1] The present paper is not concerned with the complex development of the Chronicle after the annal for 891, nor with the sources which may have lain before the annalist who wrote the long section which ends with Æthelwulf's death. Recent analysis has made it probable that he possessed an older set of annals bringing the history to the middle of the eighth century,[2] but there is hardly material for speculation as to the place or date of their composition. The annals between 750 and 891 have a different character. At many points they record an amount of local detail which is in strong contrast to their normal brevity. They ought therefore to offer at least a sugges-

[1] It would probably be generally accepted that the long West Saxon genealogy which follows the entry of Æthelwulf's death was intended to form the termination of a Chronicle. On the other hand, it is hard to believe that the statement in the annal for 853 that pope Leo " hallowed " Alfred as king was written before Alfred's accession in 871. The exact point at which the original Saxon Chronicle ended is hardly relevant to this paper.

[2] Cf. Chadwick, *Origin of the English Nation* (ed. 2), pp. 24-25.

tion as to the district in the history of which the successive annalists were especially interested. The persons for whose instruction or entertainment the annals were composed may not be beyond all conjecture. The annals themselves will always remain anonymous, but it may be possible to extract from them some clue as to the particular part of the wide West Saxon kingdom in which they were first set down.

It might, perhaps, be answered that such a clue is unnecessary in view of the reasons which suggest that both the original Chronicle which extends to the death of Æthelwulf and its continuation to 891 were written in what is often regarded as the West Saxon " capital ", namely Winchester. In his authoritative survey of Early English literature, Professor Brandl suggests that the origin of the original Chronicle to Æthelwulf's death can only be sought in Winchester, the political and ecclesiastical centre of Wessex, and he would also assign to Winchester the annals which were subsequently composed in Alfred's reign.[1] Mr. Plummer, in the introduction to his edition of the Chronicle, suggests that the annals " which led up to the full development of historical writing under Alfred " were kept at Winchester.[2] This opinion, which does not seem to have been seriously challenged, really rests on the assumption that Winchester was the West Saxon capital, and the grounds for such an assumption are, to say the least, slender. Apart altogether from the extreme improbability that Wessex in the ninth century possessed anything that can be called a capital, the importance of Winchester in this age may easily be exaggerated. It contained the seat of one of the two West Saxon bishoprics. Coins bearing Alfred's name were struck there, but Exeter was also a West Saxon minting place in Alfred's time. Alfred was at Winchester when he ordered the execution of a number of Danish raiders who had been captured in the last of his wars, but there is no evidence that he commonly resided there. His burial at Winchester should certainly not be taken to imply that he had regarded the town as the centre of his kingdom. That he proposed to found a monastery at Winchester is probable, but the project belongs to his last years, and the monasteries of which he actually completed the foundation were placed at Athelney and Shaftesbury. In all this there is little either to connect Alfred with Winchester or to indicate the pre-eminent importance of the town in his time. That Winchester had become the largest town south of Thames before the Norman Conquest is certain, but its demonstrable importance belongs to the tenth and eleventh centuries, not to the ninth.

It is much more significant that an analysis of the annals between 754 and 891 gives little support to the assumption that they were written at Winchester. If they are read without any antecedent

[1] " Geschichte der altenglischen Literatur " in Paul's *Grundriss* (ed. 2), iii. 1057, 1071.
[2] *Two Saxon Chronicles*, II. cxii.

assumption as to their provenance, they certainly do not suggest that their compiler had any especial interest in Winchester or in Hampshire. The long annal for 755 mentions incidentally that king Sigebeorht was murdered at or near Privett in Hampshire, but the circumstances of the king's death must have been known throughout the whole of Wessex. For the rest, the annals record under 755 that king Cynewulf was buried at Winchester; under 799, that bishop Cyneheard of Winchester accompanied archbishop Æthelheard on a journey to Rome; under 833, that bishops Hereferth and Wigthegn of Winchester died; under 837, that ealdorman Wulfheard fought at Southampton with thirty-five ships' companies of Danes. Under 855, they state that king Æthelwulf's body "lies at Winchester", a statement which may have been true at the date at which this section of the Chronicle was composed, but ignores the fact, recorded by a good authority,[1] that the king was originally buried at Steyning. The only other annal which specifically relates to Hampshire asserts that Winchester was stormed by the Danes in king Æthelbeorht's reign. There is no attempt during this period to give a list of the bishops of Winchester, no indication of especial interest in the successive ealdormen of Hampshire. What is far more suggestive, these annals entirely ignore an event which must have excited lively apprehension in Winchester, the Danish descent upon Southampton in 842, recorded by a contemporary Frankish writer.[2] And it cannot be through accident that when in this period the annals break out into local detail, it never relates to the region of which Winchester is the geographical centre.

This meagre record of events in the region around Winchester contrasts strongly with the abundant information which the Chronicle affords with reference to the country further west. It has indeed little to tell about Wiltshire beyond the fight between the Hwicce and the Wilsatan, which it assigns to 800, Ecgbeorht's victory at Ellandun, entered under 823, and the events which followed the Danish occupation of Chippenham at the beginning of 878. But the number and variety of the entries which relate to Somerset and Dorset suggest, at the very least, a much more definite interest in this region than is generally recognised. They begin with the curiously detailed annal for 787, which records the first coming of the Danes. Even if it stood alone, this annal would prove that the compiler of the Chronicle was drawing on information preserved in the district which the Danes then visited, and the still fuller version of the annal preserved by Æthelweard identifies this district with the Dorset coast. No stress can be laid on the annal for 812, which records the pilgrimage of Wigbeorht of Sherborne to Rome, and the fights between king Ecgbeorht and the

[1] The Annals of St. Neots, which at this point seem to be following a lost manuscript of Asser's *Vita Alfredi*. See Stevenson's note in his edition of this work, pp. 213-14.
[2] Nithard, IV. c. 3.

Danes at Carhampton and between the men of Dorset and the Danes at Portland might perhaps have been recorded by an annalist anywhere in the south. But the suspicion that the chronicler's interest lay in the south-western shires is materially strengthened by the annal for 845, which tells how the ealdormen of Somerset and Dorset defeated the Danes at the mouth of the Parret, and by the annal for 851, which opens with the record of a victory won at Wigborough in the west of Somerset [1] by Ceorl the ealdorman of Devon. The suspicion grows when the annal for 867 is compared with other entries in the Chronicle which relate to similar events. It recites that bishop Ealhstan died in that year, that he had held his bishopric at Sherborne for fifty years, and that his body lies there *on tune.* Ealhstan had been an important figure in Wessex for a long time, but there was no reason for an annalist who was not much interested in bishops to record the length of Ealhstan's episcopate, nor need he have gone out of his way to state that the bishop's body lay *on tune.* The only probable explanation of this precision is that the annalist was especially interested in the circumstances of Ealhstan's burial, and that he wished to record that the bishop was buried, not in his cathedral church, but in the enclosure, the *tūn,* which surrounded it. And it may with some confidence be conjectured that an annalist who was careful to preserve this detail did not live many miles from Sherborne.

But if this conjecture is well founded, it at once becomes easy to understand the far more remarkable annal for 878 which deals with the Danish descent on Chippenham and the events which centred round Alfred's victory at Edington. Nothing in Early English history is more familiar than the story of Alfred's retreat to Athelney, Guthrum's baptism at Aller, and his crism-loosing at Wedmore. It is not easy to reconcile the preservation of these names with the assumption that the Chronicle was composed at Winchester, and it is still harder on this assumption to explain the annalist's care to record the obscure names of the stages by which Alfred moved from Athelney to Edington, Ecgbryhtes stan, and Iglea. It is no doubt possible that an annalist at Winchester might have derived these names from some one who had taken part in the war of 878. Wherever he lived, the annalist certainly drew his information about the earlier struggle which followed the Danish occupation of Reading in 871, the war of Ashdown and Basing, from some one who had been intimately concerned in it. But Athelney, Aller, and Wedmore, Ecgbryhtes stan and Iglea, were not, like Ashdown and Basing, the sites of battles. Apart from Alfred's retirement on Athelney, the events associated with these places were not of such importance as to compel insertion in a very concise set of annals. The fact that the annalist chose to record them suggests at

[1] On this identification see Stevenson's note in his edition of Asser's *Vita Alfredi*, pp. 175-76.

once that the names of the places where they occurred were already familiar to him and to the men for whom he was writing, that he knew the west country, and allowed himself to reveal his interest in incidents which happened within the region of which he had personal knowledge.

That the extant texts of the Chronicle between 750 and 891 are all very imperfect reproductions of their archetype would now be universally admitted. And if the suggestion is well founded that the centre of interest for the compiler of these annals lay in the south-west, it should be possible to obtain further evidence to this effect from later writers who have followed versions of the Chronicle which have been lost since their time. Among such writers, Æthelweard, ealdorman of the south-western shires under Æthelred II., and himself a descendant of Æthelred I., is by far the most important. Patricius Consul Fabius Quaestor Æthelweard is not an attractive writer. He still awaits an interpreter who will grapple with the heart-breaking task of editing a Latin text of which a great part cannot be construed. But he certainly possessed and according to his limited power translated a version of the Chronicle different from any which is now extant, and he has preserved much authentic information of which there is no other record. It is, perhaps, not generally recognised how much of this information relates specifically to the south-west. In translating the annal for 787, which records the first coming of the Danes, Æthelweard gives the name of Beaduheard the reeve who wished to arrest them, and the name of Dorchester, the town to which he wished to drive them. Under the year 823, Æthelweard states that Hun, the ealdorman of Somerset, was killed at Ellandun and buried at Winchester. Under 867, Æthelweard records the death of Eanwulf, the next ealdorman of Somerset, and his burial at Glastonbury. Like the Chronicle, Æthelweard records the death of Heahmund, bishop of Sherborne, but it is only Æthelweard who states that the bishop was buried at Keynsham in Somerset. Under 876, Æthelweard states that the greater part of the country round Wareham was depopulated by the Danes. In the great annal for 878 he makes an appreciable contribution to the abundant south-western detail preserved by the Chronicle. He does not refer to Ecgbryhtes stan, Iglea, or Aller, but he gives the name of Odda, the ealdorman of Devon whom the Danes besieged in that year, and he records that Æthelnoth, the ealdorman of Somerset, held out in a forest with a small band when Alfred had retired to Athelney, and that the same ealdorman was present at Guthrum's chrism-loosing at Wedmore. It seems certain that either Æthelweard himself or the annalist who composed the text of the Chronicle which he followed was interested in the history of the south-west, and more particularly in the successive ninth-century ealdormen of Somerset.

It is therefore an important question whether the south-western detail in Æthelweard's Chronicle was taken by him from an earlier and fuller version of the annals or merely represents the information which he himself had been able to gather regarding the history of the country of which he was ealdorman. In every way the former is the more probable. Æthelweard undoubtedly found little to record about events which happened after the death of Edward the Elder. His work ends meagrely with entries recording the succession of kings, with notices of the battle of Brunnanburh, the expulsion of Ragnald and Anlaf, the death of king Edmund's wife, and with bad poems about king Edgar's coronation and death. If he had been at pains to discover information not contained in his copy of the Chronicle about south-western ealdormen of the ninth century, he would certainly have found something to relate about the men of his own youth and the previous generation. Dangerous as is the argument from silence, it is strong enough in the present case virtually to prove that Æthelweard made no attempt at independent investigation, that if he tells little of English history in the reigns of Æthelstan and his successors it is because he was relying on a version of the Chronicle which ended or almost ended with the death of Edward the Elder.

There is, moreover, definite evidence that some at least of the additional information supplied by Æthelweard was drawn by him from a version of the Chronicle fuller than any that is now extant. Under 882 and 885, he states that the Danes upon the Continent wintered respectively at Elsloo and Louvain. The Chronicle is less precise; under 882 it states that the Danes moved "far into Frankland", under 885, that they moved "eastwards". On the other hand, Æthelweard certainly derived from the Chronicle the statements that in 883 the Danes moved up the Scheldt to Condé and that in 884 they moved up the Somme to Amiens, and his precision in naming the place of their winter quarters in 882 and 885 can only be explained by his dependence upon a text of the Chronicle in which these names were recorded. But the most convincing evidence that Æthelweard's version of the Chronicle was fuller than any that is now known is afforded by the continuation of the annal for 885. The text of the Chronicle may be translated:

> In this year the afore-mentioned army divided into two parts. One part went east, the other part to Rochester and besieged the town and made another fortress around itself, but those (within the town) defended it until Alfred came out with the fyrd. Then the army went to their ships and abandoned their fortress, and they were there deprived of their horses, and soon, that same summer, went over sea. And that same year king Alfred sent a ship host to the East Angles, and as soon as they came to the mouth of the Stour they met sixteen ships of vikings and fought with them.

Æthelweard's version of this passage does not admit of an exact translation. He records the division of the Danish army, deriving from his version of the Chronicle the statement that those who remained upon the Continent wintered at Louvain. He then relates the siege of Rochester, and through the cloud of his verbiage can be seen translating the extant text of the Chronicle down to the passage which records that the defeated Danes went over sea. At this point he inserts a passage which does not correspond to anything in the Chronicle :

> Cursu in eiusdem anni presentis obsidatum cum renouant Anglis omissi bisque numerant fraude praedas in anno telluris in condenso adhaerenti Notheas fluuio partes Tamesi. Petias sub dant plebs immunda quae tum Orientales continebat Anglos. Repente extraneum petunt uestigio cursum ad locum Beamfleote ibique lurido motu partitur socia manus. Quidam manent quidam petunt ultra partes marinas.

The information supplied by this passage is important.[1] It explains the expedition which Alfred sent against the East Anglian Danes later in the year, and it suggests that one of the motives for his occupation of London in 886 was the wish to prevent communication between the East Anglian Danes and any army which in future might be raiding south of Thames. A passage like this, fitting so naturally into its ninth-century context, cannot be an invention of a tenth-century ealdorman. It must come from the Alfredian annals which Æthelweard follows before and after this point, and its omission from all existing texts of the annals can easily be explained. The uncouth phrase which ends the passage, *petunt ultra partes marinas*, is used by Æthelweard earlier in the annal to translate the Old English words *ofer sæ gewiton*, which in all surviving texts of the Chronicle conclude the sentence recording the departure of the Danes who had besieged Rochester. In the fuller text which Æthelweard followed, this sentence must have been followed by an entry, of which Æthelweard's translation has been quoted, also ending with the words *ofer sæ gewiton*. It seems evident that the scribe who wrote the text from which all existing versions of the Chronicle descend was misled by the occurrence of the same words at the end of two contiguous or almost contiguous sentences, and omitted all that lay between them. Here, at least, there can be no question that a lost version of the Chronicle is the source of information peculiar to Æthelweard.

From the nature of the case, evidence of this kind is rare. All that can safely be said is that the portion of Æthelweard's work dealing with the period between 750 and 891 records no facts which may not have been drawn from an early version of the Chronicle, and that in particular there is no reason to assume any different origin for the information which he alone gives about men who had been important

[1] Lappenberg saw that this passage makes a notable addition to the information supplied by the Chronicle, but did not follow out its implications. The charred fragments of the unique manuscript of Æthelweard's work do not include this passage, which depends on Sir Henry Savile's edition.

in the south-western shires. If so, the theory that this section of the Chronicle originated in the south-west becomes at once highly probable. Even in its extant form the Chronicle contains much to suggest that it arose at some point not far from the boundary between Somerset and Dorset. It can hardly be through chance that nearly half the places in Wessex mentioned in the Chronicle between 750 and 891 lie within a radius of thirty-five miles around Somerton.[1] If the facts recorded by Æthelweard alone—the unique information, for instance, which he gives about ealdorman Æthelnoth of Somerset—come from a version of the Chronicle more nearly original than any that is now extant, it becomes very difficult to frame any intelligible history of the Chronicle which does not imply its origin in one of the south-western shires.

A nearer approach to the place of its origin is perhaps impossible. It is easy to consider too closely, to attach too much weight to the incidental local reference. Nevertheless the field of conjecture is limited by certain obvious facts. It seems evident that the section of the Chronicle with which this paper is concerned was a secular work. Its compilers were not sufficiently interested in the bishops of either Sherborne or Winchester to give the order of their succession, nor does their work reveal anything to connect them with any particular monastery. It may be assumed that they did not live at Sherborne, Glastonbury, or any of the smaller religious houses of the west country. The problem in their case is rather to identify the patron for whose pleasure they wrote than to discover the religious house of which they were inmates. Their outlook on the world was wide, but there is nothing that can be called evidence to connect them with the body of learned men who gathered round king Alfred, and there are peculiarities of style and syntax which place their work apart. There is much to suggest that their patrons should be sought among the West Saxon nobility. And reticent as they were in their manifestations of personal interest, it can at least be said that they have allowed themselves to give slightly more prominence to the successive ealdormen of Somerset than strict historical justice required.

If, indeed, the information about this period which is preserved by Æthelweard is inserted in the existing text of the Chronicle, it is hard to avoid the impression that the fuller annals which result were composed for an ealdorman of Somerset, or at least for some prominent thegn of this region. Moreover, the theory that the chronicler wrote under the patronage of a great Somerset noble provides a natural explanation of one of the worst enigmas presented by the whole Chronicle. There can be no doubt that when king Æthelwulf returned from the land of the Franks in 856, he was confronted by a conspiracy

[1] Wareham lies just beyond this radius to the south-east, but is far outside the Winchester country. The battles of Galford and Kingstondown were fought outside the Somerton area, but belong to the history of the south-west.

which led to his relinquishment of the West Saxon kingdom, and his retirement to its eastern provinces, Sussex, Surrey, and Kent. Asser, who as bishop of Sherborne and at the same time king Alfred's friend was compelled to write carefully, gives the two versions of the conspiracy which were current in his time.[1] Most people, he says, attributed it entirely to Ealhstan bishop of Sherborne and Eanwulf ealdorman of Somerset, but many people ascribed it to the *insolentia* of Æthelbeald the king's son. Asser's words are carefully guarded, but they prove a wide-spread opinion that the bishop and the ealdorman were in some especial degree responsible for the conspiracy, and they are quite definite as to the considerable measure of success which it attained. It is therefore highly remarkable that the author of the Chronicle not only ignores the conspiracy, but uses words which, read naturally, are incompatible with its existence. According to him, Æthelwulf " came to his people, and they welcomed him ".[2] The chronicler, in fact, was disingenuous. But it is easy to forgive him if he was writing in the very region where the conspiracy arose. And if he was writing for the successor of the ealdorman whom general opinion regarded as a chief mover in the business, or for some powerful thegn of that ealdorman's shire, he really deserves the sympathy of modern readers for the embarrassment which he must have felt.

It should be said in conclusion that there is no *a priori* reason why such a work as the Chronicle should not have been written for an ealdorman or thegn of the ninth century. King Alfred cannot have stood alone in his regard for letters, and a nobility which respected the ideals of courtesy and honour which give dignity to Early English heroic poetry cannot be dismissed as uncivilised. Personal reasons, not now to be discovered, may have led some particular noble of the ninth century to wish for a vernacular rendering of earlier English history. The ramifications of the West Saxon royal house were wide, and among the first readers of the Chronicle there may well have been some who regarded the wars of the old West Saxon kings as matters of family interest.[3] The west country family from which Dunstan sprang could claim kindred with the king of Wessex,[4] and there is much to suggest that it was in the head of such a family, a man primarily interested in the south-western shires, but capable of a wider view, that the West Saxon annalists of the ninth century found their patron. No definite proof of the circumstances under which the Chronicle arose is ever likely to be forthcoming. It contains no dedication to any

[1] *Vita Alfredi*, c. 12. [2] *Sub anno* 855.

[3] It is at least probable that the version of king Æthelwulf's pedigree given by Æthelweard, which traces the king's descent from Scyld and Scef, preserves the text of the original Chronicle, and that the descent from Adam which occurs in all versions of the Chronicle at this point, was substituted after the work had passed into monastic hands.

[4] On this family see the letter of Edmund Bishop quoted by the dean of Wells in *The Times of St. Dunstan*, pp. 94-96.

patron, nor is its text marked by any peculiarities of dialect which define the region within which it arose. But it may at least be said that the theory of its origin which is here proposed agrees with its secular character and with the indications of local interest which it displays, that it explains the chronicler's enigmatical silence about the conspiracy against king Æthelwulf in 856, and his curious particularity in regard to bishop Ealhstan's burial. And it may not be through accident that the two writers who first made the Chronicle the basis of a historical work, Asser, bishop of Sherborne, and Æthelweard, ealdorman of the western provinces, are each associated with the south-western region to which the origin of the Chronicle is here assigned.

F. M. Stenton.

III

NENNIUS
THE AUTHOR OF THE *HISTORIA BRITTONUM*

1. Dedication. 2. Nennius knows Lucius from Bede. 3. Supposed conversion A.D. 167. 4. Nennius not Bede's source. 5. He depends on him. 6. Also in the *Genealogiae*. 7. Run Map Urbgen. 8. No *Historia Brittonum* existing before A.D. 800. 9. It is coeval with Nennius, 800–830. 10. Nennius denies pre-existent British History and proclaims the *Historia's* sources as his own. 11. Peculiar style of the *Historia*. 12. Vocabulary of *Prologus* identical with that of *Historia*. 13. Prologue and appendices belong to Nennius. 14. Variations in the MSS. explained by several recensions. 15. Pedigree of MSS. 16. Nennius's method of working. 17. What did he borrow from the lost *Liber S. Germani* ? 18. Faustus of Riez. 19. Celtic procedure of forcing a debtor to pay. 20. The British prince's sin of incest. 21. Vortigern. 22. His Saxon marriage ; treachery at the British banquet. 23. Nennius's date of Saxon landing. 24. Aurelius Ambrosius. 25. Horsa. 26. Hengist. 27. Germans in the north-east of Britain in the fifth century. 28. Nennius as a source for the 5th/6th and the 8th/9th centuries. 29. His Cymric nationalism. 30. His narrow horizon. 31. He was not confined to Radnorshire. 32. He prepares the Cymro's re-entry into Latin civilisation.

1. THE introduction of Christianity into Britain, the English conquest of the island, and the appearance of the paramount Celtic hero [1] of European romance are treated together in no earlier book than Nennius's compilation. Though not entitled to the name of history in the higher sense, it may therefore hope to arouse the interest of our present revered leader of historical research on Britain's Middle Ages.

2. The unreality or the origin [2] of the fable [3] about King Lucius's conversion by Pope Eleutherius need not be discussed here. But was Nennius,[4] besides the Roman *Liber pontificalis*, Bede's authority for it ? If so, the Northumbrian would have managed to avoid all the four erroneous deviations [5] from the Roman text by which the Brython [6] has changed the impossible story for the worse.[7]

[1] Cf. Windisch, *Kelt. Britan. bis Arthur* [1912], 52 ff., 142.

[2] Harnack's hypothesis is excerpted in my *Gesetze der Agsa*. ii. 574. Thurneysen in *Zeitschr. deut. Philol.* 28 [1896], 92, suspects an Irish invention. I cannot agree with Anscombe in *Miscell. pres. to K. Meyer* [1912], 1-17.

[3] The omission in MS. Z is not decisive, as Z is full of gaps.

[4] So Mommsen in his edition *Mon. Germ. hist., Auct. antiq.* xiii. [1898], 111, 113, 116, 132, 228, and *Gesamm. Schr.* vi. 638.

[5] (1) Conversion *cum omnibus regulis totius Britannicae gentis* ; (2) Mission initiated from Rome ; (3) it comes *ab imperatore Romanorum* ; (4) The Pope's name is corrupt.

[6] " Welshman " might be wrong ; see below § 31. I adopt from J. Rhys the name for the insular Celtic branch different from the *Scoti*, *i.e.* Goidhels.

[7] Against Bede's acquaintance with the *Historia Britt.* several *argumenta ex silentio* could be adduced : would he, who filled so many pages with St. German's miracles and introduced Vortigern and Hengist and Horsa into English history, have omitted

3. The supposititious date, viz. the year 167, is the only addition to the fable that occurs both in Bede and Nennius without earlier authority. Bede, however, clearly had his misgivings. Hence his inconsistency. In his *Chronicle* he dates the event between *a. mundi* 4122–44,[8] *i.e.* A.D. 170–193 ; in his *Historia* he assigns it at first *temporibus* of Emperors Marcus and Verus (161–9) and of Pope Eleutherius (174 [?]–189) ; and, finally, in the *Recapitulatio* he wrongly commences in 167 Eleutherius's pontificate, ascribing to it, in accordance with his Roman source, a duration of fifteen years and the conversion of Britain, which in this passage bears no fixed year. Now consider the strange way of dating the conversion *POST* 167 *annos post C.* in Nennius. The first *Post* must remain enigmatical, if it does not refer to Eleutherius's first pontifical year taken from Bede.[9]

4. Ferd. Lot,[10] in an essay of deep and far-sighted criticism,[11] points out several other passages in Nennius doubtless going back to Bede.[12] Verbal coincidences there are but few. Nennius seems rather to have written from memory after having read Bede either from excerpts or from an intermediate epitome.[13] The Northumbrian and the Cymro, if independent of each other, could not have commenced their history with a similar sentence, nor would they—in an age when the two races were still bitterly hostile—agree about the English conquest of Britain in the following historical particulars :

5. *Bedae Hist. eccl.*[14]		*Nennius ed. Mommsen.*
i. 1. Brittania [Christianitatem] 5 gentium linguis confitetur : Anglorum, Brettonum, Scottorum, Pictorum et Latinorum.	P. 147.	In Brittania habitant 4 gentes Scotti, Picti, Saxones atque Brettones.
ii. 5. Hengist cum filio invitatus.[15]	179.	" Invitabo filium."
Saxonum gens a rege locum suscipit.[16]	171.	[Rex] suscipit.
Segnitia Brittonum.	177.	Re[x] iners, gen[s] sine armis utebatur.[17]
Mittitur classis, praemissae adiuncta cohorti [Saxonum].	177.	" Mittemus ad patriam et invitemus."
Ut pro patri[a] militarent [Saxones].[18]	176.	Promiserunt expugnare inimicos.

St. German's connection with Vortigern, the king's fall in consequence of pagan sins, and the battles of Hengist and Horsa ?

8 Ed. Mommsen, *Auct. ant.* xiii. 288.

9 *Liber pontificalis*, therefore, must no longer range among Nennius's sources.

10 " Hengist " in *Mélanges Bémont* [1913], 4-14.

11 Mommsen himself did not conceal being at a loss to explain why Bede here omitted to quote his authority and picked a solitary date out of a large collection.

12 Zimmer, *Nennius vindicatus* [1893], 61, thinks both independent of each other.

13 With an Anglo-Saxon trace ? Below, note 160. Cf. § 16.

14 I leave out irrelevant words.

15 Plummer, *Bede*, ii. 23, suspects the influence of Gerontius's history.

16 All the rest of these parallels come from one chapter, i. 15 !

17 *Sine armis utebantur Brittones*, 158.

18 This sentence and the next come from Gildas, whom Nennius may have used here as elsewhere.

Bedae Hist. eccl.	*Nennius ed. Mommsen.*
[Brittones Saxonibus] stipendia conferrent.	P. 176. Promisit rex victum.
Angulus usque hodie desertus.	178. Venerunt de insula[19] Oghgul: [180] insula[e],[19] ad[20] quas venerunt[21] absque habitatore.
Duces: fratres Hengist et Horsa.	171. Hors et Hengist fratres.
Horsa occisus in bello hactenus in Oriental[i] Canti[a] monumentum habet suo nomine insigne.	187. In secund[o] bell[o] cecidit Hors; tertium iuxta lapidem tituli super mar[e]. Cantia tradebatur paganis.
Grandesce[ns gens Saxonum] indigenis terrori.	177. "Numerus vester multiplicatus: recedite!" [180] [Saxonum] gens crevit.

Though Nennius does not quote Bede he need not be charged with fraudulent reticence, since *annales Saxonum*, which he cites as his authority, may include historical writings generally,[22] not only annalistic year-books.

6. The genealogies of five English dynasties, excluding the Kings of Wessex, Sussex, and Essex, constitute one of the integral elements[23] of the *Historia Brittonum.*[24] They merely represent one branch,[25] with peculiar excrescences, of the well-known collection of name lists of English bishops and princes. This was begun possibly when Offa tried to unite England. The Mercian branch, of about A.D. 812,[26] is near akin to Nennius;[27] he, however, mingles with the bare names several historical notes, partly North-Cymric,[28] partly derived from Bede. Let us compare the following excerpts:

Bedae Hist. eccl.	*Nennius.*
iii. 6 = iii. 16. [Bamborough] urb[s] ex Bebbae reginae vocabulo cognominatur.	206. Uxori [regis] Bebbab . . . ; et de nomine[29] uxoris suscepit nomen Bebbanburth. . . .
ii. 9-v. 24. Eanfled filia Ædwini baptizata cum 12 de familia die pentecostes.	Eanfled filia illius 12. die post pentecosten baptismum accepit cum suis.

[19] Nennius's own error.

[20] Celto-Latin for *a quibus.*

[21] Nennius alone calls Angeln the home of *all* the Anglo-Saxons.

[22] *Annales Romanorum, Scotorum* must be interpreted in the wider sense. See note 67.

[23] Though printed by Mommsen separately as Part V., they must not be mistaken for an appendix.

[24] They appear in the most archaic class of MSS. (hk) and partly in the youngest (cdgl), but not in Class II. (zmn) or III. (CDpq); see below, § 15.

[25] Zimmer's hypothesis of a North-Cymric *Continuatio Gildae ad* a. 680, adopted by Mommsen, has been refuted by Duchesne, Thurneysen, F. Lot, and van Hamel, *De oudste Kelt. en Angelsaks. geschiedbronnen*, 35.

[26] Ed. Sweet, *Oldest Engl. Texts*, 167.

[27] Thurneysen, 80.

[28] Theodric's British struggle may contain his enemy's true name (206); but the details are borrowed from Gildas!

[29] *A nomine suo accepit nomen G.* 190.

Bedae Hist. eccl.	*Nennius.*
ii. 14. Accepit rex Ædwini cum plebe perplurima fidem; baptizatus die paschae.	Eadguin in pascha baptismum suscepit et 12000[30] cum eo. . . .
Paulinus praedicabat, credebantque. . . . 36 diebus baptizandi officio deditus.[33]	Per 40 dies[31] non cessavit baptizare genus Ambronum[32]; per praedicationem crediderunt.

While the 40 days and 12,000 seem exaggerations according to the common hagiological form, the twelfth day after Whitsuntide looks like a perversion of the number of Eanfled's companions. That this amounted to 12 is very probable by the analogy with legal oath-helpers.

In all these three points where we find Nennius at variance with Bede we unhesitatingly decide in Bede's favour. Nor must we forget that the Northumbrian conversion interested the English church more intimately than Cymric antiquarians.

7. If we find in Nennius the contention that *Rum*[34] *map Urbgen baptizavit* princess, king, and people, I cannot but suspect this to be the invention of a Cymric nationalist, possibly Nennius himself. Some critics, indeed, assume Urien to be identical with the prince fighting against Kings Hussa and Theodric (*d.* 586) and Run with the grandfather of the first wife of King Oswiu (born *c.* 612, *d.* 671),[35] whose second wife was Eanfled. These identifications *may* be not quite irreconcilable with chronology, and Run *may* have been a father before taking holy orders. But could a bishop of princely descent and related to the Northumbrian king's wife, after having given Christianity to the Northumbrians be completely forgotten by their truly great historian only three generations after? Others have attempted to solve the riddle by overbold assumptions. Haddan[36] proposes to consider *Rum* as a corruption from *Romanus*,[37] Eanfled's chaplain, who led Northumbria to the Roman Easter-rite (not to Christianity!) in 663 (a generation after the conversion!), and was neither Urien's son nor a Cymro!

In his latest recension Nennius identifies Run map Urbgen with Paulinus. Now, it is true, the name of Paulinus[38] does not exclude the

[30] *Patricius* 12000 *convertit*, 196.

[31] *Germanus* 40 *diebus orabat*. *Patricius* 40 *diebus ieiunavit*, 191 f.

[32] Also 203 = *Humbrorum*; Plummer, ii. 261. Gildas uses *ambrones* for "robbers"; Nennius possibly intended a pun. Zimmer and Mommsen do not recognise the name of a tribe.

[33] As a further similarity may be mentioned that Nennius, 208, speaks of S. Cuthbert and King Egfrid in the same sentence, just as does Bede, iv. 26.

[34] Correctly *Run*.

[35] Nennius, 203, 206 f.; above, § 6.

[36] *Councils and eccles. doc.* 124.

[37] Another Romanus, Paulinus's predecessor at Rochester, could hardly be confused with this prelate acting at York.

[38] I find it in Haddan, 164, 168, once for a bishop.

British nationality of its bearer, and Run map Urbgen may have been a preordination name.[39] But is there any other example of history preserving the vulgar barbaric name of a man combined with his feat of eternal fame if this had been officially achieved under his ecclesiastical designation? So Cymric Run—invented or historical—is a figure to be kept distinct from Paulinus. He may, on the other hand, be identical with another being not less shadowy, also occurring in Nennius alone. His oldest MS.,[40] though not the archetype, begins thus: *Incipiunt exberta fili*[41] *Urbacen de Libro S. Germani inventa et*[42] *origine et gene*[*a*]*logia Britonum*. This rubric betrays Nennius's own Latin in the words *experta*[43] and *inventa*. A scribe must have dropped the Christian name[44] before *filii*. If the original text offered here *Run*,[45] Nennius intended to quote a *writing* of that bishop founded on the *Liber*, because later on he confesses having inquired about the identity of the man long since dead. Elsewhere, however, he refers to the *Liber* as his direct authority without an intermediate source. Finally, Nicholson, supported by Alcuin's glorification of Paulinus as *civis urbis Romanae*,[46] and by the explanation of the name *Urbaghen*[47] as *Urbi-genus*,[48] *i.e.* born in Rome, tried to excuse the identification[49] of Paulinus with Urien's son as an unconscious confusion. But why was Paulinus called *Run* and *son* of a Roman? To me the assumption seems simpler that *Run*[50] as the apostle of Northumbria was a Cymric invention, and that Nennius trying to reconcile it with his later better information[51] fraudulently identified two persons.

8. Are there any traces of a *Historia Brittonum* of the seventh century recognisable among Nennius's sources? All the leading scholars before Zimmer assumed this, and Mommsen, in spite of his well-deserved admiration for his predecessor, returned[52] to the exploded view. In his edition he limits Nennius's authorship to the meagre

[39] Nicholson in *Zeitschr. Celt. Philol.* iii. (1901) 104.

[40] Not "saec. 9/10", but *c.* 1050, according to Nicholson.

[41] Not *fu*; *ibid.*

[42] Supply *de*.

[43] The emendation *excerpta* was rejected by Mommsen, 119, and *experta* [see note 88] was proposed by Traube in *Neues Archiv f. Dt. Gesch.* 24, 721. I find some analogies for *p* being replaced by *b*: *Gebidi, Bartholon, Eobba,* all in Nennius; *ebibatus* for *epibates* in a Cymric canon (Wasserschleben, *Bussordn. abendl. Kirche*, 102, 10); and since this text Z may have wandered through continental scriptoria before reaching Chartres, I may adduce many examples in Gregory of Tours, *stibulatio* in *Lex Ribuariorum*, and *Batherbrunn* (for Paderborn) from St. Gall.

[44] Mommsen did not fail to remark this, but unluckily sought the name in *Exberta*.

[45] van Hamel "Nennius" in Hoops, *Reallexikon germ. Altert.* iii. (1916) 302.

[46] *Pontif. Ebor.*, ed. Raine, *Histor. abps. York*, i. 353.

[47] From * *oirbo-genos*; Max Förster in *Festg. Liebermann*, 190.

[48] Windisch, 170.

[49] Repeated by *Ann. Cambriae*, where, however, Nennius's sources are also used.

[50] Renchid, whom Nennius refers to as his authority, was "possibly bishop of St. Asaph" (Haddan, 144).

[51] Most likely from Bede, above, § 6.

[52] F. Lot in *Moyen Âge*, 8 (1895), 179, opposed him at once in Zimmer's favour.

second[53] column containing merely afterthoughts, alterations, and additions, which, originally having their place on the margin, appear in the text only in the latest recension.

9. If a *Historia Brittonum* of older date[54] were hidden behind Nennius, it would appear strange indeed that no line of the work betrays the slightest trace of having been received into his compilation *before*[55] a. 800, while half-a-dozen allusions to the *ensuing* generation have been stigmatised by critics as interpolations.[56] Such persons or events incidentally alluded to by the author can be dated some time after[57] 766, 796,[58] *c.* 795–815,[59] 820,[60] 826[61] and *ab*[62] *incarnatione* a. 831.[63] No critic without the preconceived imagination of a much older *Historia* would have ascribed all the above entries to a second revising hand.[64] And the so-called original author, though ending the main thread of his narrative about 520, nowhere tries to make us believe he was born in the seventh century, as he is anxious continually to cite old writings or traditions even for an event as late as A.D. 627; he therefore could not be much older than the reviser.

10. Moreover, Nennius uses the same sources as the supposed previous *Historia*. His short prologue[65] begins thus: *Ego Nennius excerpta coacervavi* from the chronicles of Jerome,[66] Prosper, and Isidore, from *annales*[67] *Romanorum, Scotorum Saxonumque*, and from *traditio veterum nostrorum*. Now these seven elements, and almost they alone, constitute the contents of the *Historia*. If Nennius were a merely revising copyist of an anonymous predecessor, he would—like some skilful students of more modern schools of history—have sorted and labelled the separate jewels of his stolen treasure, in order to make us believe

[53] The third, inscribed *Nennius interpretatus*, is Zimmer's Latin translation of the old Irish Nennius-version.

[54] No hint is left in Nennius of the struggle of the Celtic church against Rome's Easter term or tonsure, while many words and local names, possibly even some institutions, are borrowed from England (see below, note 200).

[55] The end of the Mercian genealogy in 796 marks only the *terminus post*, p. 204.

[56] See Mommsen's Introduction, not referred to in the text.

[57] *Ecgbirth fuit primus* [!] *episcopus* of York *de natione* [*Anglorum*], an error hardly contemporary (p. 205).

[58] See note 55.

[59] *Fernmail modo in Buelt*, 192.

[60] a. 4, *Mermini* (158), altered to a. 838 in MS. L, pp. 127, 131.

[61] a. 421 + 405, p. 159.

[62] P. 145. A couple of Cymric poets of the seventh century could not before the eighth be mentioned as *having* flourished (F. Lot, 13).

[63] Thurneysen doubts Zimmer's identification of *Catel Durnluc* with the prince who died in 810.

[64] Later interpolations seem to me the entries about a. 858–9 (ascribed by Thurneysen and van Hamel to Nennius), 910 and 945: they are wanting in three MSS. classes. Nennius has been used by Asser (ed. Stevenson, 186) and (possibly also *c.* a. 900) in the *Officium de S. Germano* (ed. Hardy, *Descr. catal. of MSS.* i. 48; below § 17), which, however, cannot be early, as it calls *Germanus a S. Gregorio missus*! The Irish Nennius-translation is now considered to date not necessarily earlier than 1100.

[65] Some words from it occur in the letters of *Nemnivus* quoted by Kingsford (*Nennius* in *Dict. Nat. Biogr.*).

[66] Eusebius (translated by Jerome) is quoted after him.

[67] See above, note 22, and below, 75.

the more readily that it was his property : is there a medieval analogy for such a plagiarism ? Secondly, he flatly denies having known a British history ;[68] nay he blames the *hebetudo*[69] *gentis Britanniae* for neglecting to commemorate their antiquity, and informs us that many learned countrymen of his had indeed attempted but relinquished as too difficult a work like his *Eulogium*[70] *Brittaniae*. Scholars clinging to the hypothesis of a previous *Historia Brittonum* give Nennius the lie and, moreover, charge him, the glowing patriot, with a gross injustice against his nation.

11. The *Historia* is the work of an artist commanding but few colours on his pallet. It is in almost identical words[71] that he narrates the German invasion twice or the two catastrophes by each of which a sinful prince with all his court and castle was burned at night by heavenly fire.[72] Thus we have all the more right to detect the same stylist in the short prologue,[73] together with the notes added in Nennius's latest recension, on the one hand, and on the other hand, in the main body[74] of the work formerly ascribed to an anonymous predecessor. The following peculiarities are common to both :

12. Prologue and *Historia* design by *annales*[75] all sorts of historical writings. In the prologue the work is called *brevissimum* ; the author of the *Historia* says : *pro compendio volui breviare*, 198. *Congregare*, a favourite word throughout the book, is used not only for men and ships,[76] but means in the prologue " to compile " [a treatise] and in the *Historia* " to bring together " [all sorts of building material, a castle, and waves' crests].[77] According to the prologue Britain *deiecerat* [rejected] the conservation of her historical

[68] He therefore does not reckon Gildas among historians, nor must he be called his continuator ; he borrows many sentences and rare words from him, *e.g. ciula*, " ship."

[69] *Hebetudo* is given as the character of the Bavarians in *De malis naturis gentium* (ed. *Mon. Germ. Auct. Antiq.* xi. 390), a tract of the early Middle Ages, copied in the Nennius MS. C (ed. Petrie, *Mon. Hist. Brit.* 81) ; Mommsen, 125.

[70] I.e. *sermo, dictio quaevis* ; Ducange. Cf. *Eulogium histor. mon. Malmesbur.*, 1366, ed. Haydon, and Joh. Cornubiensis, *Eulogium ad Alexandrum III*. The inscription *Historia* or *Gesta* generally given to Nennius's work may be due to copyists.

[71] I subjoin here a few curiosities, leaving out common Celto-Latin, as *Saxo* for " Englishman " or *sinister* for " northern " (cf. Stevenson, *Asser*, p. lxxvii) : *ad* for *a, de*, 180 ; *addo* for *audeo*, 203 ; *in aeternum* (*non*), " ever (never) ", 182, 183, 188 ; *ciula*, see note 68 ; *epi-Romanus*, 145, 149 ; *exosus*, " hostile ", 150 f., 191 ; genitive for accus. : *nescire originis*, 151 ; *iudicare*, " to govern ", 148, 159 ; *usque*, superfluous before *ad, in*, 153, 155, 158, 167, 175 f., 183, 186 f., 208, 214 ; *ut*, for infin. after *audeo, coepi*, 167, 185, 203 ; *uti sine*, " not to employ ", see note 17 ; mere flourishes : *si quis scire voluerit*, 149, 156, 206, 207 ; *repetendus est sermo*, 168 ; *redeam ad id de quo digressus sum*, 162 ; *flectendus est articulus*, 170.

[72] 175, 191 f. ; below, § 20.

[73] Kingsford calls the longer prologue, found only in the late MS. L (see below, note 196), a forgery. It seems to me to belong to an Anglo-Norman monk on account of its smooth Gallo-Latin (cf. *duellum, c.* 42), together with the long list of chapters (mentioning Hengist's daughter Romwenna[*sic*] (below, note 159) from [?] Geoffrey of Monmouth) and the subjoined *computus* quoting Huntingdon, who died after 1157. Mommsen prints all these late elaborations, pp. 126-31.

[74] The Latin of the body of the work seems worse than that of the prologue to Jos. Stevenson and Heeger in *Götting. gel. Anz.*, 1894, 405. But the verses at the end of the short prologue baffle the skill of interpreters, even of Zimmer and Mommsen.

[75] Above, note 67. [76] 181, 188 f. [77] 182, 214, 217.

treasures; in the *Historia*, a. 409, *Britones deiecerunt regnum Romanorum neque reges illorum acceperunt*, and try to *deicere Anglos trans mare*; elsewhere *deiecit* means "expelled".[78] *Ego Nennius* are the first words of the prologue, and the first person singular (never plural) is oftener heard throughout the book than in any similar compilation. *Id est* means not only "that is", but several times rather "namely, viz."[79]: *tibi, Samuel, id est infans magistri mei, id est B.; magistro meo, id est B.; insula a [Bruti] nomine accepit nomen, id est Brittania; iunxit duas regiones in una, id est D. et B.*[80] By *inveni* or *repperi* the author in all parts of the work emphasises certain information as founded on written authority.[81] The *lector* is addressed in both parts.[82] The word *mas*, quite like a synonym of *vir*, means "husband" in an additional note and "heroical ancestor" in the text.[83] *Scribere*, narrower than "to write", signifies "to narrate", "to hand over historically".[84] As a pompous rhetorician Nennius prefers to simple *scripsi* the periphrastic forms *scribere curavi* (*volui*), *scribenda decrevi, explicare curabo, melius mihi videtur narrare*.[85] *Traditio veterum nostrorum* (or a synonym) is often referred to.[86] In order to emphasise an expression he characterises it as one of a class designated by the same word in plural; *nullo Brittone Brittonum; deus deorum; miraculum de miraculis; os de ossibus; rex inter reges*.[87] Finally, *peritia, experimentum, experta, peritus* bear the special sense of knowledge or information "about the past, in history".[88]

13. The whole work, therefore—the short prologue and the six sections into which Mommsen divided it, in both the columns assigned by him to two writers,—belongs to Nennius alone. It may be solely in the prologue that he is aspiring to the rank of a freely conceiving author; and he sinks to the humble task of a slavish copyist in the list of *Civitates*[89] which seems too systematic and rational for his confused brain.[90] The chapter on Patrick, agreeing verbally with whole sentences of an Iro-Scottish *Vita S. Patricii*,[91] proclaims itself as an abridgement, repeats some lines from Prosper or Bede,[92] employs the same allegation *ut dicunt Scoti* as other sections of the work, and intends to continue without a break the life of Saint German. This latter could quite as well claim a section for itself, because Nennius expressly quotes it from a *Liber S. Germani*.[93] So could the passage about the 7 or 9 emperors holding sway over Britain, which betrays a Cymric hand in the name *Caer Segeint*.[94] The different parts[95] of the whole

[78] 167, 186, 185.

[79] Max Förster's kind letter informs me that frequently *ipse est* is a Cymricism, meaning "namely"; he quotes Owen, *Pembrokeshire*, iii. 224.

[80] 152, 207, 205; similarly, 148, 156, 192, 216.

[81] 119, 149, 152, 155, 159, 161, 172, 191.

[82] 144, 178.

[83] 157, 171.

[84] 143 f., 152, 172, 207.

[85] 143, 147, 172, 207, 215.

[86] 143, 147, 159, 161, 167.

[87] 172, 171, 174, 178, 192, from the Vulgata.

[88] 143 f., 147, 149, 159, 161; above, note 43.

[89] The arrangement being different in various MSS., he seems to have tampered even with this piece.

[90] About *Genealogia*, see above, § 5.

[91] Bury, *Life of S. Patrick*, 277.

[92] Ed. Mommsen, 302.

[93] Below, § 17.

[94] Possibly *Seoint*, opposite Anglesey; Windisch, 44; see *Civitates*, 210 f. [More correctly *Seiont*, now *Saint*. Förster.]

[95] *Sex aetates* are referred to p. 158.

compilation are indeed but loosely bound together, but they must not appear as later additions to an imaginary previous *Volumen Britanniae.*

14. It is the multiplicity of Nennius's revisions of his book that partly explains numberless verbal variants, the transformation of entire paragraphs, the changing arrangement of the sections, the omission of whole chapters,[96] and some glaring contradictions in the various texts. Four editions of the work ought to be distinguished. Mommsen justly prefers the HK class to all the rest of MSS. and reserves a separate column for the latest text; but he hides the readings of classes II and III partly among the variants, partly in the subject notes; and the index [97] unluckily pays no regard to these two batches of variations below the line. Many a reader, therefore, might overlook important entries, even of the oldest codex [98]; for instance about the year when *Saxones pervenerunt, sicut Libine* [99] *abas İae in Ripum civitate invenit vel reperit.* Here, and often in the readings of Z or mn, we detect Nennius's own style.[100]

15. The following diagram, founded only on Mommsen's variants, pretends no more than to serve as a working hypothesis until the definitive edition of Nennius appears, which ought to give a separate column to class zmn [101] as well as to cdglpq.[102]

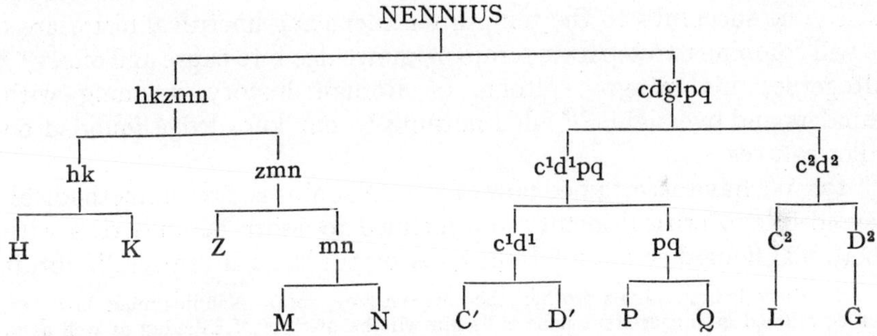

[96] Copyists not interested in Cymric place-names, *genealogia*, or *mirabilia* may be responsible for their omission. The annotators and the Irish translator are too prone to mingle passages from Bede, i. 14 f., with Nennius. As to the reconstruction of the text Zimmer overrates the Irish version (see Heeger, 405) and Mommsen the Chartres MS. Z.

[97] *Militis filii* is wanting because not recognised as proper name. The names, as far as edited before Mommsen, are indexed in Petrie's *Mon. Hist. Brit.* It is only here that one can easily find some highly interesting passages in MS. L, annotated even after 1550 [Melrose, *quondam monasterium*], about the Roman wall and Snowdon [cf. San Marte, *Galfrid*, 329], the name of the Aremorican Bretons [p. 167; cf. Plummer, *Saxon Chron.* ii. 98, and my deviation from Steenstrup in *Histor. Zeitschr.* 150 (1924), 159], Arthur's voyage to Jerusalem, etc. Mommsen omits the explanations of former editors, even of Petrie.

[98] Above, note 40.

[99] I find an abbot Leofwine in *Liber vitae Dunelmensis.* Anscombe (in *Zeitschr. Celt. Philol.* i. [1897] 274) proposes [*S*] *libine*, abbot of Hy (Iona), *c.* 752–67; Nicholson (*ib.* iii. [1907] 104) agrees with it. As the year is calculated *ab incarnatione*, the entry cannot be earlier than Bede.

[100] Above, note 81.

[101] Its Latin is much smoother and clearer than that in hk.

[102] The majuscules are the names of the MSS. in Mommsen's edition; minuscules signify missing hypothetical exemplars. I suppress my arguments for want of space.

Only one branch, viz. c^2d^2 of the second stem, preserves Nennius's name, while the sister branch is inscribed *Gildas*, no doubt by some rubricator's fault.

16. Many inconsistencies, nay self-contradictions,[103] disfiguring the work as early as in the original draft, result from Nennius's low level as an author; he chiefly wants to collect antiquarian lore for posterity. Not attempting to bring afterthoughts into harmony with his first conception, nor to reconcile conflicting materials, nor to select between two stories of one event the more likely, he modestly confesses that different authorities told it variously.[104] It is also this diversity of the sources that explains several repetitions on the same page (166 f. 169 f.). Faint traces of criticism appear but rarely.[105] Sometimes he seems to write from disjointed excerpts or from his recollection of books read long ago. So he perverts names of persons[106] and places,[107] blends two *Marcus*[108] into one, splits one person into two[109] and attributes an action to a wrong subject or to a wrong century.[110] Though he calculates a great many periods of time in his introductory and concluding passages, and notes not a few dates throughout his book, his chronology has proved incurable, in spite of the most skilful doctoring.[111] For the mythical and legendary parts of the work dates did not exist; but neither does Nennius avail himself of the correct Roman annals. Lastly, he succumbs to the temptation menacing uncritical historians: he will combine two separate scraps of knowledge into cause and effect.[112] Altogether his meagre epitome of Roman history, teeming with blunders and oversights,[113] adds nothing to our knowledge founded on other sources.

17. We have ascertained how careless Nennius is, how unmethodical, devoid of any critical faculty and inclined to adorn his materials with rhetorical flourishes or to fill out gaps by the sheer invention[114] not, it

103 Ældric is first Adda's brother, then his son (202, 206). Nennius must, however, not be blamed as inconsistent if he calls himself the disciple of Elbodug as well as of Beulan.

104 *Alii, aliter, aliud*, 147, 149, 159, 191; *traditione*, 7; *Romani autem*, 9, p. 167; *bifaric*, 149. Cf. above, note 13.

105 *Fertur*; *nulla certa*, 155.

106 *Bellinus filius Minocanni*, 162; cf. Mommsen, 118, for a quantity of similar mistakes.

107 Below, § 18.

108 Trajan and Antonine.

109 Emperor *Severus*, *Silvius Posthumus*, 153; above, note 66, below, 177.

110 The British colonisation of Armorica, 167.

111 He dates Vortigern and the German invasion a. 374, 391, 400, 428, long before 448, 447; pp. 158, 172, 191, 201, 209. See below, § 23.

112 Carausus is said to have avenged Severus, murdered [!] by the Britons, and the Romans did not return to Britain on account of such murders.

113 See Mommsen's notes, 164^5, 166^1, 166^3, 168^4, etc.

114 Suggested by Roman poetry (chiefly Vergil), the Vulgate (see below, note 135) saints' legends, Celtic mythology, popular tales, folk-lore, heroic story (Arthur), dynastic and national traditions. The numbers 3, 7, 12, 30, 40, 12,000 are frequently employed at random, but Nennius is not wholly responsible for them; the three ships (Gildas, 23) of the English invaders are parallel to those of the Goths (Jordanes, 17); Welsh triads offer another example of 3 as a common form. See above, note 30 f.

is true, of an epical poet, but of a widely informed collector of manifold antiquarian lore.[115] Now only we may venture to guess how much rubbish we can impute to himself in those passages where he refers either to oral tradition or to some treatises lost to us. He quotes repeatedly[116] the *Liber S. Germani*.[117] To judge from his excerpts it had nothing in common with German's almost contemporary biographer, Constantius, Bede's source. But it was read[118] also by Nennius's countryman and younger contemporary, Mark, who after being educated in Ireland had been a British bishop for a long time and was now living in old age as a hermit near Soissons. There he told, about 859–76, to Heiric of Auxerre,[119] the author of *Miracula S. Germani*, one miracle[120] perpetrated by German which materially and in part even verbally agrees with Nennius. Mark, however, seems to me not to follow him, but rather his lost source, the *Liber*, since Heiric would hardly have failed to propagate German's miracles connected with Vortigern, if Mark had read them in Nennius. The proper names and two particular incidents in that tale, which are wanting in Heiric, seem to me to be added by Nennius[121] to the *Liber*. This lost treatise is attributed to an Iro-Scot[122] by Lot; and Scottish monks have indeed preserved to us *Officia de S. Germano*.[123]

18. It may be the same now unknown *Liber* to which Nennius owes his knowledge of Saint Faustus.[124] This famous theologian, author, and letter-writer was a Briton.[125] *Condidit*,[126] says Nennius, *locum magnum super ripam fluminis quod vocatur Renis; et manet usque hodie.* With the river Rhine[127] some other name seems here to be contaminated. Is it, as Zimmer thought, Riez, where Faustus was a bishop for thirty or forty years? To me a monastery seems to be meant rather than a cathedral, the continued existence of which since

115 Personal and place-names in Nennius are highly valuable for Celtology. Thanet's older name (172) seems to recur in a Kentish forgery with Birch, *Cartul. Saxon. n.* 86.

116 P. 119, 171, 191.

117 It does not seem necessary to refute S. Baring-Gould (*Lives of Brit. Saints* [1911], ii. 407, iii. 1) identifying Vortigern's adversary with bishop German of Man and Vortigern's bastard with Edeyrn.

118 *Apud Britanniam litteris contineri*, quoted 173. The *Liber*, interested in miracles only, may have omitted the saint's chief historical part, his victory over Pelagianism.

119 Cf. Traube, *Mon. Germ., Poet. Carol.* iii. 422.

120 Quoted by Mommsen, 172; cf. p. 120.

121 Mark his style; *tyrannus* and *os de ossibus*, above, note 87.

122 See below, §§ 19, 31.

123 See above, note 64. Narbey (*Étude crit. sur S. Germain d'Auxerre*, 1884) does not mention Nennius, whom the Bollandists (*Acta sanct.* Jul. vii. [1868] 195) also refuse to acknowledge; see below, note 145.

124 *Faustinus*, for whom MSS. mn mistake him, but not *Faustus*, occurs in British calendars; Haddan, i. 27-34.

125 His best biography is by Krusch (*Mon. Germ. Auct. Antiq.* viii. [1887] liv.). Engelbrecht (*Fausti Rei. opp.*, Wien, 1891) and Koch (*Der hl. Faustus*, 1895) ignore Nennius.

126 Mommsen, 192, prints this as if German were the subject: put a stop or brackets after *docuit*.

127 Mayence is in Lombardy according to Nennius!

its erection would hardly appear remarkable. In fact the second class of MSS. speaks of *monasterio non parvo* instead of *locum*. If so, at the bottom of this confusion appears to be Lérins (Lirinus); the first syllable of the name might erroneously be taken for an article. Here Faustus became under the founder of the house before 426, a monk, and in 433 its abbot.[128] This celebrated school of theology reckoned also German among its disciples, according to an early Iro-Scottish liturgist.[129] Moreover, German (as well as his predecessor Amator of Auxerre) entertained relations with Patrick's mission,[130] a fact Nennius does not fail to mention.[131] It is, therefore, not without analogy if we assume Faustus, another young Celtic monk eager to serve his church in her Gallic form, to have applied to German who came to Britain in 428. *Germanus Faustum nutrivit et docuit* are Nennius's words which need not be doubted.[132] Faustus, possibly recommended to Lérins by German, continued as a Gallic prelate the correspondence with his native country,[133] where his memory was kept alive for two centuries. Faustus as a child is said to have brought *novacula[m] cum forcipe pectineque ad patrem carnalem: "caput meum tonde!"* Monastic tonsure, as generally understood, perhaps by Nennius too, is most likely not, or not alone, meant by the first inventor of the legend, because those three instruments play a peculiar part in Celtic folk-lore.[134]

19. Nennius refers expressly to *Liber b. Germani* for one of the two reports about Vortigern's end,[135] and this is indissolubly connected with miracles of the saint, which we presume to have formed the chief contents of the *Liber*. The Irish character of this source seems to manifest itself if German, after having tried to induce the sinful prince *ut ab illicita coniunctione se separaret*, at last (in the form of legal procedure) *causaliter*[136] *ieiunus tribus diebus mansit* in front of the sinner's castle, before it, with all its inmates, sinks into ashes by avenging fire from heaven. So in oldest Celtic law the creditor was fasting before the debtor's door in order to force him to fulfil his obligation.

20. What Nennius calls Vortigern's "illicit" carnal intercourse comprises not only polygamy[137] but the incest with his own daughter,

128 Engelbrecht, viii.; he finds no British traces in Faustus's Latin, xxxiii.

129 *De cursu liturgiae Scotorum* (ed. Haddan, i. 139), using Constantius.

130 Bury, *Early Patric. doc.* in *Eng. Hist. Rev.* 19 (1904), 497.

131 195. German's British mission had been promoted by Palladius; Prosper a. 429, not copied by Nennius.

132 *Baptizavit* seems incredible.

133 Aviti Epist. 6 (ed. *Mon. Germ. Auct. Antiq.* vi. 2. 30); Sidon, *ib.* (1887), 157.

134 Windisch, 136.

135 The other report uses Vulgate words (*Num.* 16. 80), and is perhaps shaped after this Biblical pattern.

136 P. 191, *litigiose*, Ducange; cf. above, note 122.

137 *uxoribus*, 191, Hengist's daughter is not mentioned in this connection; see below, note 156.

whose offspring is Faustus.[138] The prince instigates her to calumniate, before a national assembly, Saint German as the child's father; the saint, though spiritually adopting the boy, causes him to manifest his true carnal father. This story, intertwined with the former miracle, seems to go back to the same *Liber*.[139] Only the *magna synodus clericorum ac laicorum* before the king, in the shape of a supreme court of law, and his condemnation *ab omni Britonum concilio* look like the invention of the British neighbour of an Anglian kingdom after the pattern of a *witena gemot* about 800. A saint maliciously suspected and miraculously proved innocent and an infant giving witness before the court are common requisites of saints' legends. But by whom were these pre-existing forms combined with Vortigern? I strongly suspect Nennius, by one of his numberless confusions, to have defamed the unlucky prince.[140] It was *Vorteporius* whom Gildas inveighed against by the following apostrophe: "*In throno adulteriis constuprato culminis malorum omnium stupro impudentis filiae*[141] *pondere animam oneras!*" It seems to me more than a casual coincidence if Nennius blames Vortigern's incest also as his crime *super omnia mala*.[142] A saint of theological renown like Faustus could hardly vanish from the memory of his native church without some special reason. I find it in the official condemnation of Faustus's semi-Pelagian tenets. Possibly orthodox zeal tried now to degrade his authority by the rumour that he was the offspring of incest, a scandal which we would fain disprove, if we could with certainty ascribe its natural sense to a verse of Sidonius: here the poet thanks Faustus for the permission *ut sanctae matris sanctum quoque limen adirem*.[143] Did the bishop's old mother, honoured like a saint, live in the son's city?[144] Krusch prefers to understand *mater* figuratively as the cathedral of Riez.

Both the British princes, whom S. German,[145] according to Nennius, had warned from their unchristian behaviour, perish in the same way. Only Vortigern's fate, however, is quoted from *Liber S. Germani*. Nennius may have transposed it to the other prince too, whom he alone calls Benli. While, therefore, German's connexion with these two persons remains extremely doubtful, his twofold mission to Britain, though it had an ecclesiastical purpose, can hardly be conceived without some

138 P. 180.

139 The *Liber* need not be much older than Nennius, nor can it enhance the credibility of these fables.

140 Windisch, 166, adduces this incest as an example of Celtic barbarism in sexual relations.

141 *privignae* variant; ed. Mommsen, p. 43.

142 P. 180. F. Lot, 14, however, does not believe in this explanation.

143 *Carm.* xvi. 83; cf. Krusch, *Mon. Germ. Auct. Antiq.* viii. 241.

144 So Engelbrecht, vii., and the Bollandist *Acta sanct. Sept.* vii. [1867], 609-67.

145 His most competent biographer, W. Levison, dismisses Nennius from the sources as *inutilis*; *Mon. Germ., SS. Meroving.* vii. (1919) 228, *sqq.*; cf. above, note 123. As the British church devoted a saint's cult to German, most likely on account of his British achievements, her writer must not remain unheard.

attempt to bring the secular authorities on his side. Nor must critics [146] absolutely reject his Hallelujah-victory told by his almost contemporary biographer: its historical germ may have been a British skirmish with an invading band, fought under the blessing of a saintly bishop, whose presence would presuppose some understanding with the military leader of the half Romanised Celts. Among the several dates given by Nennius for the English invasion, quite independently of German's history, one, viz. a. 428,[147] fits exactly in with German's first stay in Britain.

21. Vortigern's *name* seems not to have been recorded by any writer before 700. The monarch under whom the Germans landed is reviled by Gildas as *superbus tyrannus*, but without his proper name.[148] Oral tradition, then, being the only source of Vortigern's name, has been first transmitted to posterity by Bede [149] among the Teutons and by Nennius among the Celts. Nennius seems, in this case independent of Bede,[150] to have known the name from a lost Cymric source.[151] I cannot adopt Lot's ingenious explanation [152] that *Vortigern's* name originated from a Cymric gloss, superscribed on *superbus tyrannus* (see above), because none of our numerous Gildas MSS. bears such a Cymric gloss; moreover, it could have taken only one of two shapes: either it was a complete interlinear version, which would not have given occasion for mistaking an adjective and a substantive for one proper name, or, if only rare words were interpreted, those two expressions would have appeared too common to require a gloss.[153]

22. The German marriage of Vortigern, told by Nennius alone, is in my opinion no more than a romance. History, it is true, offers everywhere, also in Britain's Middle Ages,[154] analogies enough of two hostile peoples trying to get reconciled by a dynastic match.[155] Here, however, the bride's father was a barbarian and a heathen too. We learn nothing of her later position in the British harem [156] or of her

[146] Narbey, 13. I do not believe the historical germ of the tradition to consist in German's protection offered to Aremorica, a region called *Brittania* only two generations later, against a king of the Alans.

[147] Accepted by Thurneysen, *Wann sind Germanen nach Engl. gekommen?* in *Eng. Studien*, 22 (1896), 163. More than one landing may have been epoch-making!

[148] *Vortigernus* is interpolated only in late Gildas MSS.; Mommsen, 8, 38.

[149] *Hist.* i. 14 f., ii. 5; *Chron.* ed. Mommsen, 303.

[150] While Mommsen supposed Bede to have taken the name from the *Hist. Brittonum*, Lot, 15, assumes the reverse.

[151] P. 193. I do not adduce the Cymric form of the name as an argument for Nennius's originality, as he or his copyist is cymricising even Anglo-Saxon *w* to *gu*.

[152] Lot, 18.

[153] According to another hypothesis, Gildas intended to hide the prince's name under the Latin equivalent of the composed word; but no analogy appears in his style.

[154] Cnut, Henry I.

[155] Celtic names occur among the earliest ancestors of English dynasties, most likely from Celtic mothers.

[156] Above, note 137.

offspring; nor did a national reconciliation follow.[157] Could Kentish tradition, though expressly connecting the first German colony in Britain with a spontaneous action of Vortigern, remain silent about the first Kentish king's sister on the British throne? Nennius, or oral tradition before him, here seems to have drawn from the rich fountain of Celtic love tales.[158] Another element of the fable of Hengist's daughter [159] may be found in the same Cymric patriotism that seems to have engendered the story of the British chieftains treacherously murdered by the Saxons at their banquet; defeated people, too vain to perceive the cause of their fate in their own shortcomings, will explain it by their leaders' infatuation or the enemy's deceit. To Nennius's own imagination we may safely ascribe the cry he gives in Anglo-Saxon language: "Saxons,[160] take your *seaxas* (*i.e.* knives, short swords)!" This playing upon the homophonous words, impossible for Hengist, whose followers were Jutes, sounds like the pun not of a Cymric folk-tale, but of a philological scholar, proud of his knowledge of the Teutonic tongue. Now the episodical figure of an interpreter [161] mastering the Saxon idiom appears at Vortigern's court, without being required by the main thread of Nennius's narrative. The rarity and the importance of a Briton understanding English are so remarkably emphasised [162] by Nennius that I cannot but suspect that he himself held the post of official interpreter at his prince's court near the English frontier.

23. Nennius dates [163] the beginning of Vortigern's reign, and his fourth year when *Saxones ad Britanniam venerunt*, by means of the names of the Roman consuls of A.D. 425 and 428 [164] respectively. The latter year, he says, was 400 years *ab incarnatione*, corrected by modern critics to *passione*.[165] The year 428 agrees with Saint German's victory [166]

[157] The Scoto-Irish fable, which he received into his collection, may have been Nennius's pattern to some extent: a prince is helped by a foreigner expelled from his home and the alliance confirmed by marriage; *Scozza* proves the *Īro*-Scottish origin.

[158] The Norwegian parallel of a king marrying the foreign girl who presented him drink is later than the twelfth century; cf. Matter, *Engl. Gründungsagen Geoffrey of Monm.* 191.

[159] The name *ron* ("long hair") *-gwen* ("white") seems older than Geoffrey; Förster, 190. Cf. above, note 73.

[160] P. 189. A trace of Anglo-Saxon, see above, § 5: *Oghgul.*

[161] To *Ceretic*, his personal name, *Elmet* is added by a later recension. With *Ceretic regem Elmet*, living five generations later, possibly the annotator did not intend to identify him, as ancestors' names recur sometimes in British genealogies; he possibly chose this territorial name because Elmet fell under Anglian sway.

[162] *Nullo Brittone sciente Saxonic[u]m; stude[a]t qui legit, quo eventu evenit viro intelligere Saxonicum*, 178. [The Cymro borrowed the word for "interpreter" from A.-S. *wealhstod*. Förster.]

[163] P. 209; see, however, above, note 111.

[164] I do not agree with Anscombe ("Date of Settlement of Saxons", in *Zeitsch. celt. Philol.* iii. [1901] 492), who explains a. 428 and 450 (= Bede's a. 449 properly [?] interpreted) to be identical, the former being calculated according to the Welsh era, the latter to the Northumbrian.

[165] *Passio* = A.D. 28; Poole, "Beginning of Year", in *Proc. Brit. Acad.* x. (1922) 16[3], 19[2].

[166] Above, note 147.

and with another calculation [167] found in Nennius. His chapter about the date of the invasion ends thus: *Ab anno quo Saxones venerunt usque ad Decium* [486] *sunt* 69; modern critics correct this number to 59 and so come to 427. I therefore assume Nennius's date to go back to a lost Romano-British treatise ending in, and possibly penned soon after, 486, which dated Vortigern's first regnal year or the English landing, or both, by means of the consul-names; some later writer may have compared these Roman years with the Christian era. The invasion here meant need not be identical with the colonisation of Kent, and therefore contradicts neither the year 441 noted for the conquest in the only contemporary annals [168] nor Bede's year 449.

24. About Aurelius Ambrosius our compiler serves us with a nauseous farrago attached, not without self-contradiction and impossible miracles, to a hero whose real position he seems to know from Gildas [169] only. It consists of folk-lore, national prophecy, magicians' tales,[170] and bardic legend. Judging from his sins committed in Roman history, I venture to charge Nennius with blending the half druidical boy of miraculous origin with the historical prince. Three single bits, however, look historical,[171] viz. the monarch's fear of Aurelius,[172] Aurelius's possession of a stronghold formerly Vortigern's, and the lordship, under Aurelius, of Vortigern's son over Buelth.[173] Local reminiscence, therefore, seems here to have preserved Aurelius's final success in the struggle between two British princes about the British hegemony in the fifth century. We are not told how far they, and Arthur later on, were Brythonic chieftains only, or inherited Roman magistracy too.

25. Whether Nennius possesses any information about Horsa [174] independent of Bede's words,[175] or simply dupes us by combining them with a disfigured local name, remains in doubt. *Super vadum Episford*,[176] he says, *cecidit Hors*: can this be a confusion of Ayles*ford* and *Ebbs*fleet, the landing-place possibly mentioned in the lost embryonic Anglo-Saxon annals? Bede's Kentish correspondent, but hardly the Cymro, may have known the stone believed to be Horsa's grave.[177] Such a place-name has, indeed, engendered more than one shadow of a

[167] *Occisio Maximi tyranni* + 40 *annos sub metu*, p. 171; Thurneysen in *Zeitschr. deut. Philol.* 28 (1896), 87.

[168] *Chron. Gall.*, ed. Mommsen, *Mon. Germ. Auct. Antiq.* xiii. 660.

[169] C. 25, used also by Bede, *Chron.*, ed. Mommsen, 306.

[170] He brings in similar fables about Brutus's ancestors.

[171] *Discordia Guitolini et Ambrosii a regno Guorthigirni* 12 years later seems another genuine scrap; p. 209. It must not (with Windisch, 130) be explained from Geoffrey.

[172] P. 171.

[173] P. 192.

[174] Is *Ebissa*, Hengist's nephew, a mere Cymric fiction? cf. the name *Ebisar* in Haddan, i. 168 f.

[175] See above, § 5; on the site of the tombstone, see Plummer, *Saxon Chron.* ii. 11.

[176] *Rithergabail*, given as its Cymric name by Nennius, may be one of the forging translations from English syllables, sagaciously remarked by F. Lot (cf. below, note 185), if we change *p* to *o*, *eoh* meaning "horse" in Anglo-Saxon.

[177] The battle at *Lapis tituli* (above, § 5) seems to be split in two; cf. above, note 109.

pseudo-historical person;[178] if the probability of Horsa's reality rises slightly above it, it is by his distinct connexion with the Kentish king.

26. Conscientious Bede confesses relying on oral traditions[179] only for the names of Hengist and Horsa. Hengist's name is rare. The same man, therefore, seems to be the hero Hengist in an epical tale[180] of about the same chronological and geographical circle. This assumption will not go to weaken our belief in Hengist having commanded the German invaders of Kent, if we remember the abundant analogies of historical heroes being glorified by features of epical fiction, while none exist of an important historical event being fathered on an invented figure in the poet's own age.[181] Moreover, a slight variation, *Anschis*[182] is testified as the chief's name by the geographer of Ravenna. And the earliest genealogy[183] of the Kentish kings, though they called themselves *Oiscingas*,[184] did not fail to remember *Hengist* as their ancestor. That it was a pre-existing principality that, as Nennius tells us, fell under Hengist's sway, seems plausible from the name of Kent as a separate region in Roman times. Last, not least, a Canterbury annalist, the predecessor of our Saxon Chronicle, seems to me to have transmitted independently of Bede those few short sober notes about Hengist which the Chronicle contains and which he drew from Romano-Celtic easter-tables of the fifth and sixth centuries where contemporary monks used to put down important events now and then.

27. Did Germans colonise the Humber in the fifth century? Nennius asserts it more than once with elaborate details and without nationalist or moralising tendency. Still, present criticism justly pauses before believing a sole witness of this quality. The sway of a South-British defender of Kent over the North-east as well as the extension of Hengist's tribe from Kent to Northumbria will not fit in with the scant knowledge we possess of those times. Northumbrian historiography, Bede before all, dates the beginning of German colonisation in those regions much later, and no traces of Jutes have occurred in the north-east. A local legend, perhaps resting on a place-name, and an archaic tomb may have engendered the assumption of Vortigern's son being buried at Lincoln, the possible germ of Nennius's story.[185]

[178] Lot, 17.

[179] *Duces fuisse perhibentur* (above, § 5); if he had followed a written source he would have said *fuerunt*; cf. Plummer, ii. 28.

[180] Heusler in Hoops, ii. (1915) 505, dates the Finsburg-tale before 600.

[181] Lot, 15, opines the epical name to be transferred to the unknown conqueror of Kent.

[182] Anscombe (*Zeitschr. celt. Philol.* iii. 492) proposes to identify the name with *Oisc*, Hengist's son [?].

[183] One branch is preserved by Bede, another by Nennius and a Mercian; this reaches as high up as *Geat*; cf. Plummer, *Saxon Chron.* ii. 4. 384.

[184] Pippin's offspring was called Carlovingian.

[185] F. Lot (*Emreys* in *Romania*, 28 [1899], 337) tries to explain it by Nennius's erroneous interpretation of place-names; cf. note 176.

28. So the output of Nennius's contributions to historical knowledge is but slight, as the principal writings used by him are still in existence. He represents to posterity only some few sources otherwise lost, viz. *Liber S. Germani*, *Vita S. Patricii*, *Civitates*, a tract on Scoto-Irish origins, Cymric and English genealogies of dynasties, and short single notes akin to one of the earliest elements of the *Annales Cambriae* and *Anglo-saxonici*. The remaining information about the time before 520, not reducible to written sources, but depending on oral tradition of an age three hundred years past or on the author's own imagination, valuable[186] as it may appear for archaic institutions, folk-lore, epical motifs, and Celtic philology, offers to serious history extremely few separate ascertained facts and no comprehensive view. A dozen short incidental allusions, however, to the author's lifetime and a century before throw welcome sidelights on events, persons, or places chiefly of Wales or north-western England. One stray note possibly illustrates Kent's earliest supremacy[187] over neighbouring Saxon tribes.

29. If we then must lower Nennius's rank as a historian we are all the more ready to praise his patriotic heart. For more than five hundred years between Gildas and Geoffrey, Nennius alone in Latin literature testifies the idealistic belief of the Brythons[188] in a distant future, when their former sway over all the island will be restored. This hope, not clad in the garb of dynastic loyalty or faded imperial tinsel, rests on genuine national feeling alone. Confiding in God's returning grace,[189] it cherishes no realistic projects of mundane policy. It was in the twelfth century that the Welsh church, as we read in Geoffrey and Gerald, aspired to metropolitan dignity according to forged privileges; Nennius, however, claims for her no higher glory than the gift of Christianity to Northumbria. Arthur figures with him[190] not yet as the world conqueror, the model sovereign, the pattern of chivalry, or the gracious lord of feudal vassals; he does the bloody war work on foot with his own hands; beating the Saxon enemy he achieves no more than the persistence of the Cymric nation. Nennius's political insight does not reach far enough to perceive the possible advantage for his country's foreign aspirations from the internecine struggles between the English states, let alone the continual internal strife in every kingdom. Of the supremacy of Mercia or Egbert, nay of Wessex at all, not so much as a mention occurs. While the author was working, the northern vikings had landed on the British Isles;

[186] See above, notes 136, 140 f., 146, 170, 176; a building is cemented by human blood (p. 182); an incubus engenders *Ambrose* (p. 183).

[187] Hengist's followers gain (p. 190) *regiones plurimas: Eastsexe, Suðseaxe, Middelseaxe*: an echo of the age before West-Saxon or Mercian hegemony; see my *Gesetze*, iii. 68.

[188] Opposed to the Scoti, Picts, and English.

[189] Pp. 167, 188.

[190] In contradistinction to the scribe of MS. L, above, notes 73, 97.

he, however, fails to suspect the danger threatening the English, whose expulsion from Britain he would fain see; nay, he propagates as an uninfringed prophecy Saint Patrick's privilege afforded to the Irish *ne a barbaris consumantur in aeternum*.

30. The horizon of our antiquarian busily copying Trojan, Roman, and Frankish pseudo-history is limited as to his own times like that of a cave-dweller. He does not visualise the foreign powers influencing all European civilisation, viz. the Roman papacy and the Frankish empire. His narrowness only exemplifies the general distance of the Cymric mind from the spiritual and intellectual movement of the Occident: the Christian mission since the sixth century and the literary renaissance since Charlemagne were led by many Iro-Scots and from about 675 by Anglo-Saxons, but by no Cymro. The people Nennius wished to address was in the main Cymric, including Cumbrians, but hardly Cornish or Bretons, not Iro-Scottish or Teutonic. Two generations later his countryman Asser writes for all England and about 1130 Geoffrey for all Europe.

31. On the other hand, we must not narrow overmuch the local field commanded by our author's view. His life was not spent in Builth only; he knew the regions in or near Anglesey[191] and south-western Northumbria, the home, according to former scholars, of a pretended previous writer now identified with Nennius. Judging from his *Mirabilia* he liked to travel and saw nature with open eyes. He felt the interest of a *confrère* in the figure of an interpreter mastering English at the Brythonic royal court. If, as I venture to assume, he filled the same official post with his prince, he had also, as was then usual,[192] to serve him as a clerical messenger to Teutonic neighbours. Iro-Scottish[193] is the origin or character of several of the writings or traditions he has used; the form of his name[194] as well as a peculiarity of his Latin[195] is said to be Gaelic. He boasts being the disciple of the romanising bishop of Bangor and betrays in his artificial verses, teeming with rare, far-fetched words and puzzling difficult forms, a long grammatical schooling. The collection of at least fifteen Latin books of Roman, Cymric, Iro-Scottish, and Anglo-Saxon writers used by Nennius must not be looked for, considering that age and country, in a village church, but in a conventual library. And his verse *Nos omnes precamur*[196] points distinctly to a collegiate church as

[191] See above, note 94.

[192] Above, note 161. The priest in *Archenefelde* took royal letters to Wales; *Domesday Book*, i. 179^2.

[193] See above, § 10, notes 122 f. Though the Brythonic missionaries who first converted the *Scoti* no doubt became acquainted with their pagan and pre-Roman traditions, Nennius knows their ancient lore only after its mingling with the matter of monastic schools.

[194] van Hamel in Hoops; Geoffrey uses *Nennius* as a Welsh name.

[195] *inter . . . et*, "as well as"; Windisch, 288.

[196] Hence Nennius appears as *obtemperans iussionibus seniorum* (p. 126) in the forged preface; see above, note 73.

his spiritual home. We should guess it was Bangor, his master's cathedral.[197]

32. Though living in the same island and almost in the same century with the greatest historian and with the supreme epic poet of the Anglo-Saxons, Nennius compiled but little of his historical matter from Bede and ignored Beowulf completely. He condemned the origin of the English conquest as immoral and devoutly wished the Teutonic invaders to be expelled. Still, he could not help recognising the real power of their kingdoms, and, far from preaching a war of revenge, thought it worth while to teach his country their history, which he had learnt from at least three Anglo-Latin books.[198] He was proud of such knowledge of English as he possessed[199] and introduced into his fables one or two features from Teutonic institutions.[200] He nourished no jealousy against the Anglo-Roman church which for more than five generations had waged a bitter conflict with his fathers, a conflict settled only by his own revered master. He approached very near the door of Anglo-Latin civilisation, and paved the way for his greater countryman, the biographer of Alfred.[201]

F. LIEBERMANN.

[197] In Saint David's, it is true, MS. H, one of his best codices, and the source he and the *Annales Cambriae* commonly drew from were written; but from this fact his school or home must not be deduced.

[198] Bede, Genealogies, Annals.

[199] See above, notes 13, 160 *sqq*.

[200] Above, § 20. A symbol of adoption may lurk in the words *daret filium in sinum Germani, quod ipse erat pater* (p. 180); cf. my *Gesetze*, ii. 369, *n.* 4 f.

[201] Asser, above, note 64.

IV

LONDON LANDS AND LIBERTIES OF ST. PAUL'S, 1066–1135

IN 1913 I was able, through the kindness of the Dean of St. Paul's, to search the manuscripts of the Dean and Chapter for unpublished charters of the Anglo-Norman kings. Some of the material which I collected there has been utilised in this paper. It was found chiefly in the form of copies which are included in the following compilations: (*a*) the twelfth-century Roll of Liberties (A. 69), which Sir Henry Maxwell Lyte described in his report,[1] but did not analyse, having reason to believe that Stubbs would make them the subject of a monograph; (*b*) the Liber A sive Pilosus (W.D. 1), mainly written in 1241; and (*c*) the earlier part of Liber L (W.D. 4), dating from the twelfth century. Though the royal charters do not throw as much light as I had hoped upon the government of London, or even on the succession of sheriffs and justiciars, they give certain clues which led me to believe that much of the history of twelfth-century London might be disinterred by a patient study of the deeds relating to the London lands of the Dean and Chapter. Some of these deeds have been printed by Sir Henry Maxwell Lyte; but it is no easy matter to determine their approximate dates without a patient dissection of witness-lists, printed and unprinted, and the following up of the history of many properties. I believe, however, that the results would be well worth the trouble, and that, if a considerable number of these charters were once dated approximately, not only would our knowledge of London government be enlarged, but we should have a firm basis for a study of social conditions in mediæval London. An enquirer might do worse than take as his starting-point the Survey (*c.* A.D. 1128) of the London lands of St. Paul's. Here we have a list of tenants, holdings and rents, arranged geographically by wards and sokes. A certain number of these tenants and their ancestors or descendants are traceable in the deeds already printed; and amongst the tenants are members of important civic families. The aldermen of many wards are named in the Survey, and in some instances we have also the names of their fathers who preceded them in office.

[1] Appendix to Part I. of the *Ninth Report of the Hist. MSS. Commission* (1883), pp. 1-72.

In the following pages I have attempted to show: (1) the enquiries which the Survey suggests, particularly as to the dynasties of aldermen and the organisation of the wards and sokes; (2) the light thrown by royal charters upon the privileges of the lands of the bishop and of the chapter; (3) the relations of the chapter with Bishop Maurice and Bishop Richard I. de Belmeis. My materials are fragmentary and I have put them together simply to indicate what might be expected as the fruit of an investigation which is not, as mine has been, incidental to another enquiry.

I

The Survey is to be found in Liber L of the chapter muniments, and is in a hand of the twelth century. A facsimile has been published in a *Descriptive Account of the Guildhall* by J. E. Price (1886), issued by the City Corporation;[1] but the document has hardly been studied with the attention that it deserves, except by Mr. William Page, whose recent book, *London, its Early Origin and Development* (1923), contains some valuable comments upon the topographical problems which the document raises. I print the text in an appendix to this paper.

The document was compiled not later than 1132. This appears from the description in § 23 of the lands held by Meinbod, one of the tenants of St. Paul's. At the time of the Survey his land was adjoined by a vacant tenement lying in the demesne of the dean and canons. This was granted to Meinbod by deed in 1132.[2] That the document is not earlier than 1123 may be inferred from the reference to land given by Gerold de Stratfort. This land was given to the canons in 1115 with the stipulation that it should be held for eight years from the preceding Michaelmas at a rent of 3s. 6d. by one Ailbrith or his heir. In the Survey (§ 11) we find that certain land given by Gerold is granted in fee-farm at a rent of 8s.[3] The doubt occurs whether the Survey and the deed of 1115 refer to the same parcel of land, the deed referring to Gerold's grant as *in soca episcopi*, and the Survey stating that the land of Gerold, which is there in question, lies *in warda Radulfi filii Liuiue.* But the land mentioned in the deed is *apud Cornhillam*, and the land in the Survey has a frontage on the road leading to St. Peter's, Cornhill. We may then infer that the same land is intended in both documents, and that, while it lay geographically in Ralph's ward, legally it was in the bishop's soke.[4] The Survey also refers to the soke of the Earl of Gloucester (§ 15). As Mr. Round has shown, Robert received his earldom between April 1121 and June 1123.[5]

[1] Mr. Price also supplies a translation; but this is not always accurate.
[2] *9th Report* App., p. 67*b*.
[3] *Ibid.* 61*b*.
[4] Mr. Page concludes that Ralph held the Cornhill Ward (*London*, p. 176).
[5] *Geoffrey de Mandeville*, p. 433.

Having narrowed down the limits of date to this extent we may notice that the death of Bishop Richard de Belmeis at the beginning of 1128 might cause the dean and canons to take stock of their lands. We find in the Liber Pilosus (fo. 18) a precept by Henry I. to barons and sheriffs, commanding that the Church of St. Paul is to hold its lands and tenants, rights and customs, in borough and out of borough, as the King and his father commanded by their charters, and as they held in the time of any former king.[1] This writ, which makes no reference to any bishop of London, appears to have been issued during a vacancy of that see, that is either in 1107–8 or in 1128. But during the vacancy of 1107–8 the canons did not enjoy the freedom which this precept ascribes to them. Immediately after the election of Richard de Belmeis in 1108 we find the King *restoring* to the canons of St. Paul the right of holding and disposing of their prebends and lands in the city of London.[2] We may, I think, connect the Survey with the precept mentioned above, and refer both documents to the year 1128 as the most probable date.

The wards which are mentioned in the Survey are usually though not invariably denoted by the name of an alderman.[3] No name of a soke or ward is attached to the first section of the Survey, and it is possible that the first leaf of the original document was missing or mutilated; the land of Hubert here mentioned was near the market (*iuxta forum*).[4] Each subsequent section is headed by the name of a ward or soke, the list being as follows:

§ 2 Ultra Fletam. § 3 Warda Episcopi.[5] § 4 Warda Haconis. § 5 Vicus Judeorum.[6] § 6 Warda Alwoldi. § 7 Aldresmanesberi. § 8 Warda Fori.[7] § 9 Warda Edwardi Parole. § 10 Warda Algari Manningestepsune. § 11 Warda Radulfi filii Liuiue. § 12 Warda Alegate.[8] § 13 Warda Godwini filii Esgar. § 14 Warda Brichmari Bordarii. § 15 Warda Brichmari Monetarii. § 16 Warda Sperlingi. § 17 Warda Eilwardi filii Wizeli. § 18 Warda Herberti.[9] § 19 Warda Osberti Dringepinne.[10] § 20 Warda Liuredi. § 21 Warda Brocesgange.[11] § 22 Warda Hugonis filii Ulgari.[12] § 23 Warda Reimundi. § 24 Warda Radulfi filii Algodi.

[1] *9th Rep.*, p. 61*a*, for the text.

[2] *9th Rep.*, *loc. cit.* This writ is addressed to Abp. Anselm and Bp. Richard and dated at Windsor. These three facts fix its date as May-July 1108.

[3] This was the ancient usage according to the *Liber Albus*, p. 34.

[4] See the grant in *9th Report* App., p. 61*a*.

[5] Castle Baynard Ward, according to Mr. Page, who, however, elsewhere assigns this ward to a lay alderman (p. 180, *note*).

[6] Old Jewry.

[7] Ward of Cheap.

[8] By this time in the hands of the priory of Holy Trinity.

[9] Bread Street, according to Mr. Page (p. 176).

[10] Mr. Page reads "Dringewinne", and identifies this ward with the Vintry (p. 176).

[11] Walbrook Ward.

[12] Mr. Page conjectures Queenhithe Ward (p. 176).

About some of the persons named in this list we have a little information from our printed sources. Osbert Dringepinne or Dringewinne was a member of the Cnihtengild; so were Hugh son of Ulgar and Ralph son of Algod. Liuiua (§ 11), daughter of Colsuen, made an agreement with the canons of St. Paul's in 1103, concerning half a hide of land formerly held by her husband Ailward in Sandon.[1] Esgar, the father of Godwin (§ 13) may be Esgar the Staller. Brichmar the moneyer (§ 15) can be identified with Brihcmar of London whose name appears on one coin of Henry I.[2] Ulgar the father of Hugo (§ 22) was a contemporary of Hugh of Bochland, the sheriff of London who died, as Mr. Farrer has shown, in 1116 or 1117;[3] Ulgar *aldermannus* and Hugh of Bochland join in attesting a grant to St. Paul's which is printed in the appendix to the Ninth Report (p. 62*b*). Hugh the son of Ulgar attests a grant of 1115, and may be identified with Hugo *aldermannus* who attests a convention respecting St. Michael's, Queenhithe, in the time of Dean William, that is before 1138.[4] The alderman Reimund (§ 23) witnesses in 1132 the grant made by the canons to Meinbod of land lying in his ward.[5]

That a ward was regarded as a kind of soke is clear from certain passages in the twelfth-century documents of St. Paul's. Aldgate, described in § 12 as a ward, is called a soke in a charter of Henry I.[6] A deed of the year 1111 refers to a plot of land *versus Tamisiam* which was in the soke of the bishop, and for which Leuricus agreed to pay 12*d.* annually to the canons.[7] This land is mentioned in the Survey (§ 3) as lying *in warda episcopi*. The wards held by laymen tended to be hereditary if they were not so by right. We have already seen how Hugo succeeded his father Ulgar. Reimund (§ 23) was similarly succeeded within a few years of the compilation of the Survey by his son Azo.[8]

What was the nature of the jurisdiction enjoyed by the alderman? In the *Leges Anglorum* it is said to be that of a hundred-reeve. It is therefore covered by the traditional formula *sac et soc, toll et team et infangthief*.[9] This is the formula employed by Henry I. when he confirms the soke of the Cnihtengild to the priory of the Holy Trinity.[10] We gather that the alderman's jurisdiction was neither more nor less than that of the lord of an ordinary soke within the city. Some of the highly privileged sokes of religious houses (*e.g.* Holy Trinity Aldgate)

1 *9th Rep.* App., p. 65*a*.

2 G. C. Brooke, *Catalogue of English Coins, Norman Kings*, ii. p. 325, No. 241.

3 *Itinerary of Henry I.*, Nos. 361, 376.

4 *9th Rep.* App., pp. 61-2 and 63-4.

5 *9th Rep.* App., p. 67*b*.

6 Sharpe, *Cal. of Letter Book C.*, p. 73.

7 *9th Rep.* App., p. 26*a*.

8 *9th Rep.* App., p. 67*b*, where in a deed of 1132 Azo attests as *filius Reinmundi* and in another of 1142 as *aldermannus*. Mr. Page (*London*, p. 180).

9 Liebermann, *Gesetze*, i. 655.

10 Ballard, *Borough Charters*, i. 128. They are also the privileges of the soke of Cripplegate as confirmed by Henry I. to St. Martin le Grand (Lansdowne MS. 170, fo. 162).

were free from the hustings-court; but the soke of the Cnihtengild, which seems to be more typical, was only exempt *de warda*. In the fifteenth century the ward-moot met once a quarter. It made presentments of breaches of the peace, and of infringements of various assizes, such as those relating to bread and houses, and of offences against the Statute of Winchester and the Statute of Labourers. It enrolled in frank-pledge those residents in the city who had not the freedom; it provided for watch and ward; and it elected the officials of the ward from the aldermen down to the beadle.[1] Some of these duties were imposed on the ward after the twelfth century. But it is clear that at all times the ward-moot was expected to fulfil the ordinary duties of a hundred court.

References to the wards in the St. Paul's documents, so far as can be judged from the Ninth Report, are not very numerous or important. But there are several twelfth-century deeds referring to transfers of land which are witnessed by a single alderman and a small group of other persons in whom we may perhaps detect the suitors of a ward-moot. The best example is a grant, to John the physician, of land in Aldermanbury, in the time of William the Deacon.[2] This is a grant in fee; the land in question had belonged to Wlured the canon, who gave it to the chapter. The grant to John is witnessed by Walter son of Terri, the alderman, his brother Milo, his nephew Terri, Rainer of Aldermanbury and his son, the parish priest and several other laymen. There are in all fourteen witnesses apart from those who attest on behalf of St. Paul's. It appears from the Survey (§ 6) that the land in question owed a quit-rent of three-farthings to the soke of Aldermanbury. Similar cases of an alderman appearing at the head of a group of witnesses are Leuric's grant to St. Paul's in 1111, and Godwin's grant in Aldermanbury which was made some time before the compilation of the Survey.[3]

The aldermen of the wards acted as judgment-finders in the hustings court; and a jury of the ward might be required to appear and make recognition before the sheriff, as appears from the following writ of Henry I. The writ shows incidentally the value of causing transfers of land to be witnessed by the ward.

> H. rex Angl' vicecomit' London' salutem. Precipio quod recognosci faciatis per probos homines de warda in qua est hieda illa de Fleota quam Henricus Arborarius tenet, ubi naves Sancti Pauli solent cum petra applicare, an illa hieda sit Sancti Pauli an Henrici; et si naves Sancti Pauli solent et debent ibi esse quiete de theloneo et consuetudine. Et quod Sanctus Paulus et episcopus iuste ibi habere debuerunt, secundum quod recognitum fuerit, sine

[1] *Liber Albus*, pp. 277, 337-8. [2] *9th Rep.* App., p. 67*b*.
[3] *9th Rep.* App., pp. 26*a*, 62*b*. Godwin's land is mentioned in § 6 of the Survey.

dilacione eis faciatis habere in omnibus rebus, ne super hoc audiam inde clamorem. T. Willelmo de Pont.' Apud Wintoniam. (*Liber Pilosus*, fo. 18*b*; and in the Roll of Liberties, A. 69.)

The hustings-court, according to the charters of Henry I. and Henry II. and the *Leges Anglorum*, was accustomed to meet once a week;[1] but in later times the practice was to hold the court once a fortnight, and to observe the harvest season—from Aug. 1 to Oct. 13—as a legal vacation.[2] In the *Lei as Lorengs* it is expressly called a royal court, and in it were promulgated all royal ordinances which affected the city.[3] But it might meet in a private house. We have a Ramsey deed of the years 1123–8 which was executed "coram omni Hustengo de Londiniis in domo Alfwini filio Leofstani".[4]

From twelfth-century documents we learn something of the organisation of the hustings-court. The sheriff, at a full session, was accompanied by an under-sheriff and one or more clerks. In the Ramsey deed to which we have just referred there appear John the under-sheriff and Gervase the sheriff's clerk. A St. Paul's deed of the reign of Stephen gives the names of the officials who received fees when the deed was executed. The sheriff Gilbert Prutfoot took 2s., Vitalis his clerk 4d., Azo the alderman of the ward 2s., the beadle of the ward 4d. Hugo son of Ulgar, the alderman of another ward, received 3s., but in what capacity is not clear. The duties of the under-sheriff are described in the *Liber Albus*. He was expected to summon juries of inquest, to keep the record of pleas, to collect customary dues and amercements and to see to the serving of writs (p. 317).

II

For business purposes, when they were buying or selling lands, the Dean and Canons of St. Paul's gladly accepted the services of the hustings-court. But we have evidence that they were jealously on their guard against encroachments on the part of the civic authorities. The following writ of William II., which belongs to the year 1097, shows them appealing for help to the King against the sheriffs of Essex and London:

W. rex Angl' Rad[ulfo] de Marceio et Vlurico de Holeburna et omnibus vicecomitibus in quorum vicecomitatibus canonici mei de Sancto Paulo Londonie habent terras salutem. Precipio vobis ut dominicas terras canonicorum Sancti Pauli predicti permittatis et faciatis sic esse quietas et solutas ab omni geldo et ab omni opere et castelli Londonie et muri et pontis et balii et carreti sicut precipit

[1] *Liber Custumarum*, i. 32; Liebermann, *Gesetze*, i. 657.
[2] *Liber Cust.* i. 334.
[3] *Op. cit.* i. 63, 188, 214.
[4] *Hist. Rameseiensis* (R.S.), p. 248.

breuis patris mei. Et si quid propter hoc captum est sine mora reddatur et videte ne aliqua iniuria illis amodo fiat. Et si amplius inde clamorem audiam pro penuria iusticie mihi displicebit et quisque vestrum mihi x libris emendabit. Quia volo ut res suas pacifice et honorabiliter teneant. T[estibus] W. episcopo et W[illelmo] cancellario et Ran[ulfo] capellano. Apud Herefort de Walia.[1]

The following charter (of William I.) is less easy to date, but illustrates the same point:

W. rex Angl' iustic' vicecom' et omnibus baronibus suis London' et Middelsexe salutem. Clāmo quietas imperpetuum xxiiij hidas quas rex Athelb[ertus] dedit Sancto Paulo iuxta murum London' de siris et hundretis et omnibus aliis consuetudinibus. Teste Eudone dapifero.[2]

The customs from which these hides were released are more explicitly defined in another charter of William I., "de danageldis et omnibus aliis geldis et ab omni expedicione et ab omni opere".[3]

The 24 hides were specially privileged. The general privileges attaching to all the lands of St. Paul's are defined in an English writ of the Conqueror as sac and soc, toll and team and infangthief.[4] This writ appears to have been issued in 1075 during the vacancy of the see of London. There was another vacancy in 1085, with which we may connect a similar English writ declaring the canons of St. Paul's to be worthy of sac and soc, in borough and out of borough, by strand and by land; also of toll and team and infangthief, fihtwite and ferdwite and grithbrice.[5] These writs show that St. Paul's was well protected by the Conqueror. But William II. appears to have been an even better friend. He confirmed to St. Paul's (1093–5) all the lay-fee which Bishop Maurice had held of him, and gave to these acquisitions all the liberties pertaining to the older endowment of the bishopric:

W' rex Angl' Ansell[mo] archiepiscopo et omnibus baronibus suis Anglie salutem. Sciatis me concessisse Deo et ecclesie Sancti Pauli de Londonia totum feudum quod Mauricius London' episcopus de me tenuit pro salute anime patris mei matrisque mee et mee. Ita ut ipse et omnes successores sui in episcopatu istam terram teneant sicut illam que prius fuit in episcopatu. T. Walch. episcopo et episcopo Roberto Lincolie et episcopo Johanne et Comite de Mell[ent] et Comite Henrico et Comite de Molbr[aio]. (*Liber Pilosus*, fo. 17*b*.)

[1] *Liber Pilosus*, fo. 17*b*; Roll of Liberties, A. 69.
[2] *Liber Pilosus*, fo. 17*b*; Roll of Liberties, A. 69; Davis, *Regesta*, i. No. 246.
[3] *Liber Pilosus*, fo. 17*b*; Liber L. fo. 13. *Regesta*, i. No. 274.
[4] *Liber Pilosus*, fo. 17.
[5] *Liber Pilosus*, fo. 17.

In the last months of his life we find Rufus energetically defending the liberties of Bishop Maurice and the canons of St. Paul's against the encroachments of Sweyn the sheriff of Essex.[1] One of these writs shows that the bishop had established the exemption of his lands from the jurisdiction of the shire-court.

> W. rex Anglorum Sueno de Essexia salutem. Precipio tibi ut dimittas terras et homines et omnes res Mauricii Londoniensis in pace et in quietudine esse de warpennis et placitis et omnibus aliis rebus sicut dirationatum fuit apud Writtle ante iusticiarios meos per cartas et breves suos ubi tu ipse fuisti unus ex iudicibus. Teste Ranulfo Dunelmensi episcopo. Apud London' post Pentecost'.[2]

Henry I. was not backward in confirming to Maurice the favours granted by his brother and father. The following writ, issued within a few weeks of his coronation, is remarkable for the statement that Maurice is to have the full benefit of the king's coronation charter.

> Henr' (Dei gratia) [3] rex Angl' omnibus baronibus et omnibus vicecomitibus suis in quorum vicecomitatibus Mauricius Londoniensis episcopus terras habet et homines salutem. Sciatis quod ego concedo Mauricio Londoniensi episcopo episcopatum suum et omnes terras suas et homines et omnes consuetudines suas episcopales et laicales, sicut antecessores sui melius eas habuerunt tempore regis Edwardi, et sicut pater meus illi concessit per breves suos et frater meus per suos, cum illis emendacionibus lagarum et consuetudinum quas ego dedi illi et aliis baronibus meis. Quapropter volo et precipio ut ipse pacifice et honorifice teneat. Et videte ne aliquis vestrum sibi super hoc aliquam iniuriam faciat. T. Rob[erto] episcopo de Cestra. Apud West[monasterium]. In exaltatione Sancte Crucis.[4]

A little later in the autumn of 1101 the king issued a precept on behalf of the canons to all barons and sheriffs in whose shires and jurisdictions they held lands :

> Henr' rex Anglorum omnibus baronibus et vicecomitibus in quorum vicecomitatibus vel potestate canonici Sancti Pauli terras habent salutem. Precipio firmiter ut canonici Sancti Pauli omnes consuetudines habeant in omnibus terris suis in ciuitate et extra ciuitatem sicuti testantur breuia regis Edwardi et patris mei. Et defendo ne quis eis super hoc quicquam forisfaciat ; et eis defendo ne cuiquam super hoc respondeant vel quicquam faciant. Et si quis eis quicquam super hoc fecerit, contradictionem precepti mei

[1] *Liber Pilosus*, fo. 18, and Roll of Liberties, A. 69.
[2] *Liber Pilosus*, fo. 18. The date is 1100.
[3] An interpolation of the copyist.
[4] Roll of Liberties, A. 69. The date is 14 Sept. 1100.

michi emendabit secundum iudicium curie mee. Teste Rogero Cancellario et Eudone dapifero. Apud Westm[onasterium]. Post festiuitatem Sancti Michaelis.[1]

At some date in the years 1103–6 the King issued a special injunction to Hugh of Bochland, the sheriff of London, that the twenty-four hides granted by King Æthelbert should be free from the present geld and from all other gelds and services.[2] Again, between 1110 and 1123, possibly in 1111, he issued a prohibition to the lord of Baynard's Castle,[3] on behalf of the Bishop, the canons of St. Paul's and the burgesses of London, which is sufficiently unusual to be quoted in full:

H. rex Angl' Roberto filio Ricardi et hominibus suis salutem. Prohibeo ne aliquis vestrorum hospitetur in terra vel domibus episcopi Lond' vel in domibus canonicorum suorum et burgencium donec diracionatum sit si potest hospitari an non. Teste Roberto episcopo Linc'. Apud Portesmudam.[4]

In the latter part of his reign the King received a complaint from the canons of St. Paul's concerning a demand for geld on four hides and one virgate. The shire is not named, but the writ is addressed to Aubrey de Vere, as sheriff, and the land therefore presumably lay in Middlesex or in Essex or both.

H. rex Angl' Alberico de Ver salutem. Fac cito recognosci per homines comitatus utrum canonici de Sancto Paulo London' habeant terram unde requiritur ab eis geld' de quatuor hidis et de una virgata terre an non. Et si habent eam tunc volo quod acquietent eam. Sin autem illi qui eam habent acquietent eam. T. episcopo Sar'. Apud Wintoniam.[5]

This order is not improbably to be connected with a curious list of wrongs inflicted on the canons by Ralph de Marceio, Peter de Valognes, Otto the goldsmith and Herbert the Chamberlain. The list was compiled in the lifetime of two of these culprits, Peter and Otto, and therefore belongs to the first half of the twelfth century. These plaints enumerate four and a half hides of land which have been misappropriated, partly in Essex, partly in Middlesex.[6]

III

The canons of St. Paul's became involved in acute controversies with Bishop Maurice and Bishop Richard de Belmeis respecting the rights

[1] Roll of Liberties, A. 69 (two copies); *Liber Pilosus*, fo. 18; *Liber L.*, fo. 14.
[2] *9th Rep.* App., p. 45*a*.
[3] See Armitage Robinson, *Gilbert Crispin*, p. 39. The writ which we give seems to confirm the tradition, there referred to, that Robert fitz Richard acquired Castle Baynard in 1111.
[4] Roll of Liberties, A. 69; *Liber Pilosus*, fo. 18*b*.
[5] *Liber Pilosus*, fo. 18*b*.
[6] *9th Report* App., fo. 65*b*.

of the chapter. The *Liber Pilosus* contains renunciations by each of these bishops of rights which they had unjustly usurped. Maurice's offence, according to his own account, consisted in interfering with elections and the distribution of prebends. Richard appropriated and imparked the wood in the Essex soke of Edulvesnasa. Both made handsome amends, although Richard extenuated his fault by the transparent excuse that he had enclosed the wood " bona intentione, scilicet ut canonicis melius custodiretur ".[1] His letter on the subject is addressed to Aubrey de Vere, sheriff of Essex, and must have been written towards the year 1128, possibly at the time of the bishop's death. The letter of Maurice has more interest, as it bears witness to the exceptional independence of the dean and chapter.

> Mauricius sancte London' ecclesie vocatus sacerdos U[lstano] decano et archidiaconis et Sancti Pauli canonicis, salutem et paternam benedictionem. Consilio fratris mei et coepiscopi Hereberti Norwic' amonitum penitet me de malis que feci et maxime contra ecclesiam Sancti Pauli et contra vos. Quapropter precor vos ut ea que iniuste commisi in vos mihi indulgeatis, eo pacto ut deinceps consuetudines vestre ecclesie et statuta et elecciones et potestates in dandis prebendis, in stabiliendis maneriis sicut eo die, quo in episcopali sede fui positus, possidebatis habeatis.[2]

This has all the air of a deathbed repentance and may therefore be ascribed to the year 1107. That the dean and chapter were within their rights in withstanding Maurice may be inferred, not only from this confession, but also from a writ of William I. which appears to have issued in the period 1075–1083.

> Willelmus rex Anglorum omnibus primatibus suis ac fidelibus salutem. Notum sit vobis canonicos Sancti Pauli in manu mea esse ita libere ut fuerunt melius in manu regum antecessorum meorum. Et volo et precipio ut ita liberi sint et ita libere locent et disponant prebendas suas et omnia sua ut locauerunt et disposuerunt tempore Willelmi episcopi et aliorum episcoporum. T. Odone Baioc' episcopo.[3]

A similar writ was issued by Henry I. at Westminster in 1101 or 1102.[4] The best commentary on these three documents is to be found in the early pages of Archdeacon Hale's introduction to " The Domesday of St. Paul's ". He points out that there are no traces of any of the bishop's lands having belonged at any time to the cathedral, or of his possessing at any time the right to participate in the cathedral's revenues. This separation of endowments made it possible for the

[1] A. 41, No. 1488, misdated (original) 1154 in *9th Report*.
[2] *Liber Pilosus*, fo. 21. [3] *Liber L.*, fo. 13*b*.
[4] Roll of Liberties (A. 69).

dean and canons to negotiate separately with the crown for grants or confirmations of liberties. Three writs of the Conqueror in favour of the canons exist in copies; one has been given above, and the other two (in the English language) are in the *Liber Pilosus* (fo. 17). These are general confirmations of the rights of sac and soc, toll and team and infangthief, fihtwite, fyrdwite and grith-breach, and they threaten any man who wrongs the canons with loss of the king's friendship. William II. issued two writs to protect the canons against particular depredations. These are in the Roll of Liberties (A. 69). Henry I. issued (including those already mentioned) no less than six writs in favour of the canons. There are, however, writs issued by this sovereign in favour of the bishop and the canons jointly; they suggest that, in the royal mind at least, the *ecclesia Sancti Pauli* was a legal person superior to, and embracing these not always concordant partners. There was in this period, so far as our records show, no instance of a lawsuit between the bishop and the canons, although the latter had good cause to complain of the conduct of Bishop Maurice and Bishop Richard. Were there special reasons which prevented the canons from going to law? Or was the king's court unwilling to recognise the corporateness of the canons to this extreme degree? As to these questions we can only say that Bishop Richard had to deal with a Dean who was a near relative, but that Maurice, a worse offender, was more probably protected by his services as the Conqueror's chancellor, and by the fact that the Dean of his time was Wulfstan, an Englishman.

H. W. C. Davis.

APPENDIX

De Mensuris Terrarum Sancti Pauli intra ciuitatem Lund' (Liber L., fo. 47-50*b*)

§ 1. Terra Bugie est latit. xxxviij ped' longitudinis in profundum lxij ped'. Porta Huberti in introitu habet latitudinem viij pedum et dimidii et hoc tantillum huius est longitudinis cuius et Bugi. De eadem tenet etiam Hubertus et est longitudinis in profundum ab aquilone ciij pedum et a meridie lx pedum et dimidium et latitudinis in medio lviij pedum. Et hee mansure reddunt ij solidos in festo Sancti Michaelis.

§ 2. Ultra Fletam Teobaldus iij solidos et dimidium. Ex his redduntur regi in festo Sancti Martini xvj d. Latitudinis cxxxij ped', longitudinis clxxxj ped'.

Terra Wlurici loremarii est latitudinis xxxviij ped' longitudinis clxxxi ped'. Habet et alteram cuius latitudo est xxvi ped' longitudo clxxxi ped'. Pro his duabus mansuris reddit iij solidos.

Willelmus filius Fulcredi pro terra Liuingi diaconi quam Teobaldus dedit cum filia sua Fulcredo. Latitudinis xlvij ped' longitudinis clxxxi ped'. Et reddit xvj d.

Terra Deringi ij solidos. Latitud' lii ped'. Longitud' in profundum ccxlix ped'.

§ 3. In Warda episcopi. Terra Wulframni reddit ij sol. in pascha. Latitud' est liij ped'. Longitud' c ped' iij minus. Et erit nostra quieta post obitum matris et filie.

Terra Leurici prepositi reddit in feudo xij d. et est latitudinis secus uiam xxj ped' longitud' lxiii ped' et dimid' et ij pedes sunt purpris'.

Terra Hugonis de Verli viij d. pro socagio in pascha reddit. Latitudo eius est xxxij ped' et longitudo lxvii ped'. De retro xxx ped'.

Terra quam tenet Decanus est latitud' xxx ped' longit' in profundo lxxxvij ped'. De retro xiij ped'.

Terra Noriot lata est secus uiam xxxiiij ped' longit' liij ped' et dimid'. De retro xxxij ped' et dimid'. Et reddit in festo Sancti Pauli xij d.

Terra Gubaldi reddit viij d. de socagio in pascha.

Terra Episcopi Dunelmensis quam tenet Helyas reddit ij solidos in Pascha et in festo Sancti Michaelis. Latitud' est lxxxvij ped'. Longitud' ab aquilone cvij ped. ; a meridie uero cxv ped'. De retro cij ped'. Introitus porte est latitud' xij ped'. Longitudo eiusdem introitus lxvj ped'.

Terra Theodorici latitudinis est xlix pedum. Longitud' iuxta murum liiij ped'. Reddit iij solidos in Pascha et in festo Michaelis.

Terra Osberti Masculi latitud' lxij ped' longitud' lxvii ped'.

Terra Brichtrici reddit xij d. Latitud' xliiij ped' ; longitudinis lxvj pedum.

§ 4. In Warda Haconis. Terra Alberti Loteringi, quam tenet Rannulfus canonicus, reddit xviij d. in festo Sancti Michaelis. Et hec quidem mensuranda est.

Terra quam tenet Alueva uxor Edwardi Ceci reddit iij solidos in pascha et in festo Sancti Michaelis, et libram piperis in festo Sancti Pauli. Latitudinis est in fronte iuxta uiam xxxv pedum ; in fine xl pedum. Longum cc ped. xiij ped' minus. Et altera terra quam Gilbertus Prutfot nobis diffortiat vij d. de socagio de eadem terra.

§ 5. In uico Iudeorum. Terra Lusberti in fronte ex parte occidentis est latitud' xxxij ped'. Versus Sanctum Olauum longit' quater xx et xv pedum. Iterum uersus Sanctum Olauum long' lxv ped'. In fronte xiij ped'. Terra in fronte lxxiij ped'. In profundo xli ped'. Et reddit x solidos.

§ 6. In Warda Alwoldi. Terra Brichtrici est latit' liij ped', longit' cvj pedum. Et reddit in feudum v solidos. Ex parte Sancte Margarete xij pedibus minus lata. Ex parte aquilonali longit' breuior vj pedibus.

Terra Radulfi Britonis est latitudinis xxviij pedum, longitudinis lx ped'. Et reddit ij solidos in feudum.

Terra Alsi in fronte lxij pedum, in profundo quater xx pedum et reddit iij solidos in feudum.

Terra Goldwini clerici latitudinis xxx pedum, longit' c et quater xx et iiij pedum. In fine eiusdem ex parte orientali uirgultum latitudinis xxxiij pedum, longitudinis lxxxiij pedum et reddit in feudo ij solidos in festo Sancti Michaelis, xij d. operi et xij d. canonicis. Socce Aldremanesberi iij ob. et i d. Regi in media quadragesima.

Terra Edrici clerici est longitudinis quater xx pedum ij minus. In fronte latitudinis xl pedum. Et reddit in feudo xij d. in festo Sancti Edmundi. Regi de soccagio j d. Ex parte orientali terra latior est viij pedibus.

Terra Edmari reddit ij solidos in Natiuitate Sancte Marie. Ex his redduntur Regi iij d. in Ramis Palmarum. Long' quater xx. ix ped', latitudinis lxxj ped'.

§ 7. In Aldresmanesberi. Terra Wluredi reddit iij solidos in feudo et iij ob. socce. In fronte longitudinis cxxxiij pedum, latitudinis xlj pedum.

§ 8. In Warda Fori terra Goduini Scat reddit in feudo xx solidos. Longitudinis c et xj pedum. Latitud' quater xx et ij ped'. De retro similiter quater xx et ij ped'.

§ 9. In Warda Edwardi Parole. Terra Sprot quam tenet Godardus filius Haroldi reddit iij solidos. Hec est in fronte latitudinis lvii ped' et usque ad moram protendit longitudo.

Ante domum Taisonis tres mansure reddunt xviij d. et una iij in festo Sanctorum Petri et Pauli. Quam terram tenent Stephanus, Martinus, Eilwinus et Godid mater Huuiet. Longitudinis secus uiam c et xv pedum. Latitudinis cj pedis ex occidente, lx pedum ex oriente.

§ 10. In Warda Algari Manningestepsune. Terra quam tenet Adam reddit iiij solidos et viij d. in pascha et in festo Sancti Michaelis. In fronte secus uiam habet latitudinem lv pedum longitudinem cxlvj pedum.

Terra Ascilli latitudinis secus uiam ab aquilonali parte clj pedis ; longitudinis c et quater xx et j pedis tendens ad meridiem. Et ex eadem terra secus uiam ex occidente longitudinis c et xxxiiij, latitudinis lxiiij pedum.

§ 11. In Warda Radulfi filii Liuiue. Terra quam dedit Geroldus de Stratfort reddit in feudo iiij solidos in festo Sancti Johannis et in Natali Domini. Longitudo eius est cxx pedum ab aquilone ; xxxj pedis in fronte, secus uiam uersus ecclesiam Sancti Petri de Cornhilla xliij pedum et dimidii.

§ 12. In Warda Alegate. Terra Edwini Atter reddit xvj d. Latitudo eius ccxxij pedum. In fronte iuxta murum latitudo lj pedis ; in medio lviij pedum ; in meridie xxxij pedum.

§ 13. In Warda Godwini filii Esgari. Terra Brichmari Manci reddit xx d. In fronte iuxta uiam latitudinis xxxiiij pedum et dimidii. Longitudo eius est clj pedis. Ex oriente xxxvij pedum.

§ 14. In Warda Brichmari Bordarii. Terra Gialle ij solidos et est latitudinis lij pedum, longitudinis cxxxij pedum. In fine xxx pedum et dimidii.

§ 15. In Warda Brichmari monetarii. Terra Nortune Edmundus et Caperun de ij mansuris vij solidis et x d. reddunt in Pascha et in festo Sancti Michaelis. Longitudinis ccxix pedum. In fronte iuxta uiam lxxv pedum. In fine quater xx et vj pedum.

Terra Radulfi aurifabri quam tenet Eilwinus reddit canonicis feudaliter xxxd. ; et viij d. socce Comitis Gloecestrie. Longitudinis l pedum, latitud' xxxvj pedum.

§ 16. In Warda Sperlingi. Terra Anskeri quam tenet Rannulfus reddit iij solidos. Longitudinis in fronte iuxta uiam lxxviij pedum ; latitudinis lxxv pedum. Iterum de terra Nortune quam Paganus tenet ij solidos. Latitudinis lj pedis, longitudinis lxxiii pedum.

Terra quam tenuit Eduinus filius Golduini ij solidos reddit ad Vincula Sancti Petri. Latitudinis xliiij pedum et dimidii, longitudinis lvj pedum media mansura. Superior mansura latitudinis xxxvj pedum, longitudinis xlj pedis. Inferior mansura quater xxiij pedum. Ex aquilone xxxv ped', a meridie xxx ped'.

§ 17. In Warda Eilwardi filii Wizeli. Terra Brichmari Manci reddit v solidos in Pascha et in festo Sancti Michaelis. Latitudinis xxj pedum, longitudinis xxxiij pedum. Johannes filius Radulfi filii Euerardi xxxij d. in festo Sancti Michaelis. Latitudo eius xxxvij pedum, longitudo lxxiiij pedum ; de retro xliij pedum.

§ 18. In Warda Herberti. Terra quam tenet Willelmus de Pontearch' reddit xxx d. Et monachi Sancti Salvatoris xij d. de Socagio.

§ 19. In Warda Osberti Dringepinne. Terra Wakerilde xxij d. reddit in festo Sancti Pauli. Latitudo xlix pedum, longitudo iuxta uiam lxv pedum ; iuxta ecclesiam ex altera costa lx pedum.

Terra quam tenet Wlwinus Juvenis xxviij d. reddit. Latitudinis iuxta uiam xxxiij pedum, longitud' lxj pedis. Fabrica ante domum Willelmi de Arundel ij solidos. Latitud' xxij ped', longitud' L pedum.

§ 20. In Warda Liuredi. Terra Suetmanni presbiteri quam tenet Robertus de Uruilla xij d.

Terra monialis vij solidos et viij d. reddit in Pascha et in festo Sancti Michaelis. Latitudinis xxxvij pedum, longitudinis liiij pedum.

§ 21. In Warda Brocesgange. Terra Willelmi nepotis Hulboldi xviij solidos in Pascha et in festo Sancti Michaelis. In fronte latitudinis xxv pedum et durat usque Tamisiam.

Terra Bretelli reddit xxxiiij solidos in Pascha et in festo Sancti Michaelis. Latitudinis xxix pedum et durat usque Tamisiam.

Terra quam tenet Robertus frater Fulcredi xij solidos reddit. Latitudinis xvj pedum et durat usque Tamisiam. Et habet inde Robertus iiij solidos de superplus.

§ 22. In Warda Hugonis filii Ulgari. Terra Ragenilde reddit xl d. in Pascha et in festo Sancti Michaelis. In posteriori c pedum iij pedibus minus. Versus domum Eustacii latitudinis xlv pedum.

Terra Willelmi filii Simeri unam marcam argenti reddit. Et est longitudinis cxx pedum et dimidii ; latitudinis xxxvj pedum. De eadem terra Robertus filius Willelmi filii Terri iij solidos reddit in festo Sancti Pauli.

Terra Wluardi ij solidos reddit et tenent eam Willelmus Malet et Eustacius nepos Fulcredi. Et de hac terra habet Willelmus Malet longitudinem xxx pedum et latitudinem xx pedum et reddit iiij d. Est autem totius terre longitudo lxiiij pedum, latitudo xliiij pedum.

Terra Willelmi de Colecestria dimidiam marcam argenti reddit in Pascha et in festo Sancti Michaelis. Longitudinis lxxj pedum, latitudinis xliij pedum est.

§ 23. In Warda Reimundi. Terra Fabri iij solidos reddit in festo Sancti Pauli. Longitud' xxxv ped' et dimidii ; latitud' xxxj pedum est.

Terra Trenchemarche iiij solidos reddit. Latitud' in fronte xliiij pedum, longitud' lix pedum. Et de superplus habet Odo ij solidos.

Terra Meinbodi in fronte uersus Sancta Margaretam. Latitudinis lxi ped', longitudinis lxxxvj pedum, et uirgulti longitudo lvij ped', latitudo xlij pedum.

Terra Fulcheri Nain in fronte secus uiam latitud' habet xxvj ped' et dimid', longitud' lxxviij ped', et reddit ij solidos et iij d. et j quadrantem.

Terra quam tenet Eua in uadium secus uiam latitud' lvij ped., longitud' lxxx ped' habet. Et reddit in feudo xv solidos. Item Meinbodus in posteriori tenet duas mansuras, latitudinis in fronte xliiij pedum, longitudinis lij pedum.

Terra uacua in dominio est latitud' xvij ped' et dimidii, longitud' xxxiiij pedum. Item terra Meinbodi iuxta uacuam terram latitud' xxiij ped', longitud' xxxiiij pedum.

Terra Edild. Latitud' xxiij ped', longitud' xxxiiij ped'. Modo nichil reddit. Post obitum erit nostra. Iuxta tenet Meinbodus terram latit' xxiiij ped', longit' xxxiiij ped'. Alwinus Scot tenet terram latit' xxiij ped', longit' xxxiiij pedum.

Terra Clausag. Latit' cellarii xix pedum et dimidii, longit' liij pedum.

Terra quam tenet Robertus de Auco, latit' xxxviij ped', longitud' lx pedum. Item Robertus de Auco terram tenet in fronte latit' xxxix ped', longitud' lx ped' et he ij terre reddunt xij solidos.

§ 24. In Warda Radulfi filii Algodi terra Eduini de Sancto Augustino reddit feudaliter ij solidos et xij d. operi, et xij d. canonicis. Longitud' c et iij ped', latit' xxxix ped'.

De terra Osberti thesaurarii Willelmus de Draitona reddit iiij solidos in Pascha et in festo Sancti Michaelis. Latit' xxvij ped', longitud' lxxiij ped'. De eadem Waco presbiter habet latit' xx pedum et dimidii, longitud' lxxiiij ped' et reddit xxxij d. De eadem Willelmus filius Gosberti tenet latit' xxxix ped' et dimidii et reddit viij solidos. De eadem in eodem uico Robertus filius Gosberti reddit xxvj solidos in Pascha et in festo Sancti Michaelis; latit' xxj ped' in uico piscario; longit' lxxiiij pedum. De eadem tenet Theodoricus in eodem uico piscario et reddit xx solidos; longitud' lxxxiij pedum et dimidii; latit' xxiiij pedum et dimidii. De eadem in uico fori Robertus filius Gosberti ij mansuras tenet, latit' lx pedum et dimidii, longit' lxxxiij pedum et dimidii. De eadem Robertus filius Berneri tenet latitud' xvj ped', long' xxxj pedum et reddit feudaliter vij solidos in festo Sancti Michaelis. De eadem in stricto uico iuxta domum Herlewini in fronte latitud' xxviij pedum. De eadem Deremannus latit' xlv pedum et dimidii tenet. De eadem Winebertus latit' xxxij pedum. Harum trium longitud' xlvj ped' preter hoc quod uie exposuerunt inter domos et polum, scilicet xvj ped'. Item de eadem terra quam tenuit Ranulfus Paruus, long' lxxxj ped', latit' lxxij ped'. Item de eadem terra quam tenuit filius Passeluuet in uiculo secus uiam longit' xxxvij ped' in profundum xxiij pedum et reddit ij solidos.

Item in foro iuxta domum Herlewini terre latitudo est in fronte iuxta uiam xvj ped', longit' xxiiij ped' et j palm'.

Terra quam tenet Gaufridus canonicus latit' in fronte secus uiam xxxij ped', longit' liiij pedum in profundum uersus curiam.[1]

§ 25. (*Added in a later hand.*) In Warda Osberti Drinkepinne terra quam tenuit Wulwinus Juvenis reddidit canonicis Sancti Pauli xxviij d. Et est latitudinis iuxta uiam xxxiiij pedum, longitudinis lxj pedum.

[1] Geoffrey held the church of St. Mary Magdalen in Milk Street (Cripplegate Within).

V

THE EARLY LIVES OF ROBERT PULLEN AND NICHOLAS BREAKSPEAR

WITH NOTES ON OTHER ENGLISHMEN AT THE PAPAL COURT ABOUT THE MIDDLE OF THE TWELFTH CENTURY

THE visit of five bishops and four abbots from England to the Lateran Council of 1139 might have been expected to lead to closer and more frequent relations between the Church in England and Rome. But if this was the result, it did not immediately take effect; for the first Englishman to be given office in the Roman church was not appointed until 1144, and he was called to Rome, not from England, but from Paris.

I. This was Robert Pullen, of whom John of Hexham[1] speaks under the year 1146 as eminent in the Roman church. After referring to his wisdom and learning, he says that Robert refused a bishopric offered to him by Henry I., being content with having enough to live upon (*victum et vestitum habens*). A rhymester who wrote about 1140 calls him, in distinction from a namesake, Robertus Amyclas, a favourite term in those days to indicate a poor man.[2] As Robert was without influential connexions, we may presume that he was not offered a bishopric at an early age and may therefore place his birth in the last quarter of the eleventh century. Not long before the end of Henry's reign we have a definite record of his activity as a teacher. In the Annals of Oseney Abbey, just outside the walls of Oxford, we read under the year 1133:

> Magister Rob' pulein scripturas divinas que in Anglia obsoluerant aput Oxoñ legere cepit. Qui postea, cum ex doctrina eius ecclesia tam Anglicana quam Gallicana plurimum profecisset, a papa Lucio secundo vocatus et in cancellarium sancte Romane ecclesie promotus est.[3]

Of this there is an expanded version in a manuscript known as the Continuatio Bedae, which was written for Robert Wyvill, bishop of Salisbury, 1330–1375. This book, Bodl. MS. 712, contains a compilation chiefly from Walter of Hemingburgh but including a number

[1] Contin. of Simeon of Durham, ii. 319, ed. T. Arnold, 1885.
[2] See my article in the *English Historical Review*, xxxv. (1920) 339 *seqq.*
[3] Cotton MS., Tiberius A. 9, fo. 54 A.

of notices relative to Oxford and Oseney manifestly derived from the Oseney Annals. Here it is said that—

> Eodem anno [1133] venit magister Robertus cognomento pullus de civitate Exonia Oxenfordiam ibique scripturas divinas, que per idem tempus in Anglia [1] absolute erant et scolasticis quippe necglecte fuerant, per quinquennium legit. Omnique die dominico verbum Dei populo predicavit; ex cuius doctrina plurimum profecerunt. Qui postea ob eximiam doctrinam et religiosam famam a papa Lucio vocatus et in cancellarium Romane ecclesie promotus est.[2]

Dr. Rashdall, who quotes this passage,[3] rightly calls attention to the suspicious resemblance to the forged Continuation of Ingulf bearing the name of Peter of Blois, in which we hear of one Master Gilbert *omnibus dominicis diebus . . . verbum Dei ad populum praedicans.*[4] But it is not certain which of the two writers was the borrower. What seems plain from the Bodleian manuscript is that the compiler was here putting together his information from two sources, one of which spoke of Oxford and the other of Exeter, and that he endeavoured to reconcile them by making Robert come from Exeter to Oxford.

Now in the Oseney Annals, the words *oxon̄* and *exc̄n* are written extremely alike. In two instances *oxon̄* is certainly a mistake: the siege in 1135 was of Exeter not Oxford Castle, and there were no bishops of Oxford (fo. 32*b*) in the Middle Ages. It may be observed that the form *Oxonia* given in Luard's *Annales Monastici* is due to the editor. In the fourteen places in which the word occurs between 1133 and 1209 we find *oxon̄* or *oxen̄* nine times, *oxon'* (under 1135, meaning Exeter) once, and *oxeneford'* or *oxenf'* four times. The manuscript from which the edition is printed is a copy made in the fourteenth century from an older book, Vitellius E. 15, which was destroyed in the fire at the Cottonian library in 1731. Of this only a few fragments are preserved; but from these we may be certain that Robert's teaching was in it placed *ap. ox.*, and the erroneous entry of 1135 is correctly assigned to *exonie* (written in full). Still *exon* and *oxon* were very similar, and an Oseney scribe would almost automatically presume that a word so written really meant Oxford.

Whether Robert in fact taught at Oxford or Exeter involves a balance of probabilities. On the one hand there is no well-attested instance of any teaching or of any literary activity at Oxford between the isolated appearance of Theobald of Étampes, probably in the first decade of the twelfth century, and some time after 1167.[5] Exeter, on

[1] MS. *Angliam.*
[2] Bodl. MS. 712, fo. 275.
[3] *The Universities of Europe*, ii. 335, note, Oxford, 1895.
[4] *Rerum Anglic. Script.* i. 114 [ed. W. Fulman], 1684.
[5] The statement of Gervase of Canterbury that Vacarius taught law at Oxford may be dismissed as an excusable mistake in a chronicler who wrote at the very end of the century.

the other hand, about the time that Robert taught, must have been a centre of learned study. The pupils of 1133 would be mature masters twenty years afterwards, and charters drawn up under Bishop Robert Warelwast (1155–1160) contain the witness of not a few. In one of them we read of Mr. Bartholomew the archdeacon, of Mr. Peter the bishop's brother, and of Mr. Joseph.[1] In another dated on 1st March 1159/1160 there is a larger list. Among the bishop's clerks are Mr. Ralph, Mr. Baldwin, Mr. Richard. The clerks of the choir include one *magister*, Algar, and there are nine *scholares*.[2] Archdeacon Bartholomew won renown as a divine and was made bishop of Exeter in 1161. Mr. Baldwin had a greater career before him, for he rose to the archbishopric of Canterbury. Master Joseph became famous as a Latin poet. No one can read the earlier letters of John of Salisbury without the persuasion that Exeter about 1160 was a place of studious activity. Exeter had also a literary tradition. From the time at least of Bishop Leofric books were written there, and of the eighty-one manuscripts which the dean and chapter presented to the Bodleian library in 1602 not a few belong to the twelfth century, and some of them are unquestionably written by English hands. If then there is to be a choice between Exeter and Oxford as the place where Robert Pullen taught, I should not hesitate to support Exeter.

According to the Continuatio Bedae, Robert pursued his teaching for five years, that is, until about 1138. He is next found as archdeacon of Rochester. The date of his appointment cannot be fixed, for there is no notice of any preceding archdeacon after 1123. It is unlikely that he was appointed by Bishop John of Rochester, who died in June 1137, and there is no certain record of any bishop having been consecrated to that see until 1142. Most scholars suppose that during the interval the diocese was administered by Bishop John of Séez; but the Profession Rolls at Canterbury are defective, and there are some traces of a namesake, also of Séez, having held the bishopric until Ascelin was consecrated in 1142. In either event Rochester was brought into relations with the Norman see, and it was a Norman prelate who made Robert archdeacon, and by whose permission Robert left England and established himself as a teacher of theology at Paris. He was certainly there in 1142, when John of Salisbury attended his lectures.

That same year a new bishop, Ascelin, was appointed at Rochester, and a dispute arose between him and Archdeacon Robert about certain rights, into the particulars of which we need not enter.[3] That it was also connected with Robert's continued non-residence may be gathered from the fact that St. Bernard wrote to the bishop urging that the

[1] Hist. MSS. Comm., *Report on Various Collections*, iv. (1907) 47.
[2] *Ibid.* p. 49.
[3] See a letter by Mr. J. H. Round in the *Athenæum*, October 31, 1896.

archdeacon might be allowed to remain at Paris.[1] Bishop Ascelin brought his suit before the pope and Robert failed to appear. This was in November 1143. Sentence was therefore given against him in default, and the bishop was directed to summon Robert to appear next Whitsuntide and to order him to reside. Now it so chanced that while the suit was in process a new pope was elected, in September 1143. Had Innocent II. been still alive, he would probably have followed the counsels of St. Bernard, and Robert would have been left at Paris. But the change of pope meant a change of policy. Robert was a conservative divine, while Celestine II. was reputed to favour the views of Abailard. Hence it was natural that he should wish to remove Robert from his position as a teacher at Paris and send him back to the obscurity of his archdeaconry.[2] Celestine, however, died in a few months, and one of the first acts of his successor, Lucius II., was to call Robert to Rome as cardinal. Lucius was elected in March 1144, and by the following November Robert was engaged in doing business at Rome; he was almost immediately appointed chancellor.[3] From this time down to 2nd September 1146 he was active at his post; but from the 18th his duties at the chancery were performed by a subdeacon. No chancellor appears until the 17th December. We may therefore presume that Robert either died or his health failed early in September. He certainly did not accompany Pope Eugenius III. on his journey to France in 1147.

2. I come next to Nicholas Breakspear, afterwards Pope Adrian IV. What little is known of his early life is recorded by Cardinal Boso and William, canon of Newburgh, who both wrote rather more than thirty years after his death. Boso, an Englishman, who was his devoted friend, wrote his life as pope and passed by his earlier career briefly. Nicholas, he says,[4] was by nation an Englishman, *de castro sancti Albani*, who left his country as a youth in order to improve himself in the study of letters. He went to Arles, where while he was still engaged in the schools, it was the Lord's will that he should go to the church of St. Rufus and there make his profession as a canon. He advanced to the dignity of prior and then of abbot. Afterwards it happened that he went to Rome on business connected with the church, and having accomplished his task prepared to return. But Pope Eugenius kept him with him and made him bishop of Albano. Here we have only to note that Nicholas was not born at St. Albans but at a village belonging to the abbey, and that he did not go to the city of Arles but to Avignon which lay in its province.

William of Newburgh, as an Austin canon, was careful to collect

[1] Ep. 205.

[2] J. Thorpe, *Registrum Roffense* (1769), pp. 39 *seq.*

[3] Here and elsewhere I take the dates of cardinals' subscriptions from the second edition of Jaffé's *Regesta Pontificum Romanorum.*

[4] *Liber Pontif.* ii. 388.

all the information he could find about a member of his order who became famous. He tells us[1] that Nicholas' father was a clerk of moderate estate who became a monk at St. Alban's. The boy was too poor to become a scholar and sought for subsistence from the monastery; but his father drove him away, and he went to seek his fortune abroad. He found little success in France, and passed on beyond the Rhone into Provence, where he was admitted to a minster of regular clerks known as that of St. Rufus. This was on the outskirts of Avignon: in 1158 it was removed to Valence,[2] a fact which explains some discrepancies in later accounts.

To fill in the details omitted by our early witnesses we have to rely on the materials collected by Matthew Paris about the middle of the thirteenth century. He says that Nicholas, *de quodam viculo abbatis, scilicet Langele oriundus, cognomento Brekespere,* besought Abbot Robert to admit him to the monastery;[3] but he was rejected on account of his insufficient learning. In the hamlet of Bedmond in Abbot's Langley, Hertfordshire, there is a farmhouse called Breakspear's, which may have borne its name from Nicholas' family.[4] But a confusion has arisen from the fact that there is another Breakspear, not far off, in the parish of Harefield on the northern border of Middlesex, and this place has been conjectured to be the place from which Nicholas' family came. For this supposition there is no foundation. In another notice Matthew adds the information that Nicholas was the son of Robert de Camera, who, *honeste vivens in saeculo, litteratus aliquantulum,* became a monk at St. Alban's.[5] The father was thus a clerk in the king's chamber, a department of finance which was becoming overshadowed by the exchequer. Matthew's statement that Nicholas was refused admission to St. Alban's by Abbot Robert is a manifest mistake, for Robert was not elected until 1151. The further statement that Nicholas went to Paris, where he worked so strenuously that he surpassed all his fellows and was made a canon of St. Rufus, looks like the account which a writer of the thirteenth century would take to be natural and obvious. But Matthew alone mentions Paris. William of Newburgh says that it was after prospering ill in France that the poor young man went on to St. Rufus, where he obtained means for his subsistence. This is not what one would expect of a scholar who had won laurels at Paris; he would rather have gone on to a place where

[1] *Hist.* ii. 6.

[2] *Gallia Christ.* xvi. (1865) 355.

[3] *Gesta Abbat.* i. 112 *seq.*; cf. *Chron. Maj.* ii. 204. The statement in Onuphrius Panvinius' *Epitome Pontificum Romanorum* (Venice, 1557), p. 121, that Nicholas came from Malmesbury, a town of St. Alban's in the diocese of Bath, was repeated in Ciaconius' *Vitae Pontificum,* with various misspellings, and the additional information that Langley is the same as Malmesbury, in the edition of 1601, pp. 443, 453; in that of 1630, pp. 542, 555; and in that revised by Oldoinus in 1677, i. 1044, 1057.

[4] *Victoria Hist. of Hertfordshire,* ii. (1908) 325.

[5] *Gesta Abbat.* i. 124 *seq.*

he could find a famous master to sit under. St. Rufus was not such a place. It seems to me much more probable that he was sent to the Austin canons there by a house of the same order to which he was attached in some humble capacity in England. That he had not risen high may be inferred from the later Life of Adrian IV. by Bernard Guidonis,[1] where we read that he was first a poor clerk—*pauper clericus sive clericus pauperculus*—in the church of St. James at Melgueil in the diocese of Maguelonne, and at length (*tandem*) a brother at St. Rufus. This church had been confirmed to the abbot and canons of St. Rufus by Urban II., 19th September 1095.[2] It would seem, therefore, that the canons sent him for a time to serve in the church at Melgueil.[3]

I believe it is possible to identify the English house from which Nicholas was sent beyond seas. There is a letter of John of Salisbury,[4] in which he brings a petition of the canons of Merton in Surrey before this same Nicholas when he had become Pope Adrian IV. He ends with the words, *May it be of advantage to the men of Merton that when you were in the church of St. Rufus their sweet savour reached you, and that your worship was wont to speak* [*of it*] *in conversation with me your servant.* The priory of Merton was a young foundation, and like other newly founded houses in that age it rapidly grew in favour. From about 1120 one Bernard, a writer in the king's court, was acquiring lands which he bequeathed to Merton ;[5] and we may well suppose that official association led Robert, a clerk in the chamber, to send his son there. Merton had a school which was attended by Thomas Becket about 1128 ;[6] and the priory was in such good repute that Archbishop William of Canterbury, who was himself an Austin canon, shortly before his death in 1136, directed the bishops of Rochester and St. David's to reconstitute the secular house of St. Martin's at Dover on its pattern.[7]

A great difficulty in tracing the biography of Nicholas arises from the total absence of any dates to guide us until he became pope. We do not know when he was born or when he went to St. Rufus, when he was elected abbot or when he was made a cardinal. All that can be said is that the dates commonly given are in every instance wrong.[8]

[1] Muratori, *Scriptores*, III. i. 440 *b*.

[2] The bull is printed by Jacques Petit, *Poenitentiale Theodori Archiepiscopi* (Paris, 1677), p. 615, where the date is wrongly given as 1096.

[3] It is possible that he had recommendations from northern parts, for Bishop Walter of Maguelonne, who is known as a poet, came from Lille (Devic and Vaissete, *Hist. de Languedoc*, iii. 575) : he died in 1129.

[4] Ep. 28.

[5] Round, " Bernard, the King's Scribe ", in the *Engl. Hist. Rev.* xiv. (1899) 417-30.

[6] W. FitzStephen in Robertson's *Materials*, iii. 14.

[7] Gervase of Canterbury, i. 97, ed. W. Stubbs, 1879.

[8] In A. H. Tarleton's *Nicholas Breakspear* (1896) the future pope is supposed to have been born about 1100 (p. 18), to have gone abroad about 1120 (p. 19), and to have been made abbot in 1137 (p. 40) and cardinal towards the end of 1146 (p. 45). The *Dictionary of National Biography*, *s.v.* Adrian IV., also dates this last appointment in 1146.

William of Newburgh is not helpful in this matter. He says that Nicholas quitted England when he was growing up (*adolescentiam ingressus*), and that after failing to find a home in France he went on to Provence, where he was given maintenance at the monastery of St. Rufus and afterwards made a canon of the house. Thus he lived for very many years (*annis plurimis*) and was in time elected abbot. Now one William is mentioned as abbot about 1133;[1] but Nicholas did not succeed him for many years if we are right in identifying him with the Nicholas, canon of St. Rufus, who in 1140 wrote a charter at Barcelona which is still preserved.[2] Our first definite notice of him as abbot occurs at the beginning of 1147, when Eugenius III. travelling towards France granted at Vico[3] in the Val d'Elsa, between Poggibonsi and San Miniato, a bull addressed to N. abbot of St. Rufus, conferring a privilege on his monastery.[4] According to William of Newburgh, after Nicholas had been abbot for some time (*aliquandiu*), his canons rose up against him and brought a petition to Pope Eugenius III., no doubt for his removal. The pope succeeded in arranging a reconciliation, but peace was not long preserved (*non diu quievit nescia quietis malitia*). The canons soon renewed their appeal, and the pope heard their allegations. The issue was unexpected. Eugenius calmly said, *I know, brethren, where is the seat of Satan; I know what has roused this storm among you. Go forth: elect you a father with whom ye can or will live in peace; for he shall no longer be a burthen to you.* And he forthwith consecrated Nicholas to the bishopric of Albano, and thus made him not only a cardinal but also a member of his intimate council. This was the form in which the story reached Newburgh. The discreet Cardinal Boso speaks only of the ability with which Nicholas conducted the business of his house at the papal court, and Matthew Paris says that he thrice had occasion to repair thither, each time with more conspicuous success. Whichever account be true, it is evident that two or three suits at the papal court require a considerable length of time. We have no information when they began, except that it was when Eugenius was pope, and therefore not earlier than 1145. His absence from Italy for fifteen months from the beginning of 1147 must have delayed business at his court. He did not take up his residence at the Lateran until the end of November 1149, and Nicholas first makes his appearance as cardinal on the 30th January 1150. It would seem, therefore, likely that he was nominated at Christmas 1149.

But the question remains to be considered, how it was that an

[1] Hauréau, in *Gallia Christ.* xvi. 359.

[2] Villanueva, *Viage literario a las Eglesias de España*, xi. (1850) 199 *seq.* Nicholas probably accompanied Archbishop William of Arles, who went as legate to Barcelona late in 1139: *ibid.* xvii. 317.

[3] Not Vienne in Dauphiny, as Hauréau supposed.

[4] Jaffé, *Regesta Pontif.* 8998, ed. 2.

abbot of a comparatively obscure monastery in Provence, coming to the papal court to answer accusations made against him by his canons, or possibly merely in connexion with some title to lands, was at once preferred to one of the highest and most desirable posts in the pope's gift. Here we are left to conjecture, and I propose only an hypothesis. The see of Albano had been vacant since the spring or summer of 1145, and the chancellor of the Roman church was then the Englishman, Cardinal Robert Pullen. Robert is understood to have been appointed archdeacon of Rochester about 1137 by Bishop John of Séez, who a year before had been actively engaged in treating Merton as a model priory.[1] There are indications that Bishop John was well acquainted with Merton long before. I suggest that in this way he knew of Nicholas' merits, and recommended him to the archdeacon for future advancement. When he became cardinal Robert found his opportunity, and through him, though after his death, Nicholas was made cardinal bishop of Albano.

If this hypothesis is favourably regarded, the dates in Nicholas' biography need reconsideration. He was sent on his long mission to Scandinavia in 1152, and did not return until late in 1154. So onerous a task would hardly be imposed on a man past middle life. I incline to think that Nicholas was born much later than is generally supposed, and that he went abroad some time after 1130. He would then be well remembered at Merton seven years later, and the interest of Bishop John might well have been employed in bringing his name before Archdeacon Robert. When Robert was made cardinal and chancellor, he would have a natural desire to promote a fellow-countryman, and I think it likely that he recommended Nicholas for high preferment so soon as an opportunity presented itself. The distractions of the time and the pope's long visit to France sufficiently explain the fact that the appointment was not made until several years after Robert's retirement or death.

3. I can here add only a few brief notes about some other Englishmen who appear at the papal court under Eugenius III.

(*a*) There can be little doubt that it was Cardinal Robert who brought John of Salisbury thither, as I believe towards the end of 1146.[2] John continued the pope's clerk until after the death of Eugenius in 1154.

(*b*) Another man owed his advancement to Bishop Henry of Winchester. This was his clerk Hilary, who was dean of Christ Church at Twynham in Hampshire—the name of the church has now supplanted that of the town—about 1140.[3] He went to Rome, that is to the papal

[1] See above, p. 66.

[2] See my article on "John of Salisbury at the Papal Court" in the *Engl. Hist. Rev.* xxxviii. (1923) 323 *seqq.*

[3] See Mr. Round's paper in the *Athenæum*, January 23, 1897.

court, probably at Viterbo, and acquired a great reputation for his ability in dealing with litigious business.[1] He came to England at the beginning of 1145, presumably in attendance on the legate Cardinal Imar, and took part in a suit of the monks of Rochester against Bishop Ascelin.[2] It was Eugenius himself who directed Hilary's appointment to the see of Chichester in August 1147. The learning which he had acquired in Italy made him an important accession to Henry II.'s strength in his later contest with Archbishop Thomas.

(*c*) Boso, said, on what authority I cannot discover, to have been a nephew of Nicholas Breakspear, became personally acquainted with Thomas Becket from the time of Guido Pisanus.[3] Now this cardinal succeeded Robert Pullen as chancellor at the end of 1146, and Boso had probably belonged to Robert's staff. When Guido ceased to hold the office in the spring of 1149, Boso was employed in the chancery until May 1152. After this, in 1156, he was sent on business into England;[4] and it was then probably that Thomas introduced him to Archbishop Theobald.[5] On his return he was made cardinal deacon of SS. Cosmas and Damianus by Adrian IV. before the 4th January 1157, and promoted cardinal priest of the title of St. Pudentiana by Alexander III. in 1166. He was chamberlain of the Roman see. To him we owe important biographies of these two popes, and probably a revised edition of the Roman Provinciale.

(*d*) Baldwin, the future archbishop of Canterbury, we have mentioned as clerk to the bishop of Exeter in 1160.[6] It has not, I think, been noticed that nearly ten years earlier his learning must have been well known, because when he was presented to Eugenius III. at Ferentino the pope appointed him as instructor (*institutor*) to Gratian,[7] a nephew of Innocent II. Eugenius was at Ferentino from November 1150 to the following summer. Among the Englishmen who then attended his court were Cardinal Nicholas of Albano and the two clerks, John of Salisbury and Boso. When Baldwin returned to Exeter he became clerk, as I have said, to Bishop Robert Warelwast; and the next bishop, Bartholomew, who was consecrated in 1162, made him archdeacon, an office which he held at least as late as 1168.[8] That he afterwards entered the Cistercian order and became abbot of Ford, and many years later was made bishop of Worcester and then archbishop, are facts which lie beyond the range of the present notice.

(*e*) From John of Salisbury's words it might appear that another

[1] John of Hexham, ii. 321.

[2] Thorpe, *Reg. Roff.* p. 41.

[3] See the archbishop's letter in Robertson's *Materials*, vi. 58.

[4] See John of Salisbury, ep. 31. In my paper on *The Early Correspondence of John of Salisbury* (1924), p. 15, I inclined to date this letter in 1157, but I now think it was probably written in the autumn of 1156.

[5] *Materials*, l.c.

[6] See above, p. 63.

[7] John of Salisbury, ep. 292.

[8] Hist. MSS. Comm. *Report on Various Collections*, iv. 51.

contemporary at the papal court, Gratian, was also an Englishman. John says:

> Desiderabam autem revera meum videre cognominem et (quod magis est) compatriotam et quodammodo fratrem Gratianum. . . . Illum fratrem dixerim confidenter, cum quo mihi fidei et societatis sunt iura communia; et, licet nos non ediderit una civitas, patriam tamen nobis unam esse non ambigit, qui patriam fortium, quae nobis individua est et quam ostendit Carmentis, reducit ad mentem.

One might suppose that Gratian's mother, a sister of Innocent II., married into England. But on closer inspection we see that John is amusing himself with elaborate allusions. Gratian is his namesake, because John, that is Johanan, means *gratia Domini*.[1] He is a compatriot, because all brave men are of one country; as Carmentis said to her son Evander,

> Omne solum forti patria est.[2]

In 1169 Gratian was sent on a mission to appease the controversy between Henry II. and Archbishop Thomas, and was made cardinal deacon of SS. Cosmas and Damianus in 1178. Twenty years later he aspired to the papacy when Innocent III. was elected.

I invite other writers to continue this list. At the end of the twelfth century the English chancery came to classify its documents on a method evidently derived from Rome. The papal rules of *dictamen* were by that time also well known in England. One wishes to find out to whom was due this penetration of the English system, both on its external arrangement and on its internal diction.

REGINALD L. POOLE.

[1] Cf. ep. 291.

[2] Ovid, *Fasti*, i. 493.

VI

HENRY II. AS A PATRON OF LITERATURE

"The mediæval writer", says Professor Samuel Moore,[1] "was not a professional, but an occasional author. He gave to literary work only a part of his time, and did not depend upon it for a living; the making of books was not his vocation, but his avocation." The most voluminous of monastic historians were historians but incidentally; the authors of the great academic tomes were first of all professors; even court poets were courtiers first and poets second. Except at the universities of the later period, there was no book-trade; and in the absence of a market for books writing could not be a profession. The writer required an independent source of income, whether of a permanent sort as monk, chaplain, teacher, or civil servant, or from such casual bounty as an occasional patron might provide. To a degree which has prevailed at no other period in history, writers and scholars in the Middle Ages were dependent on courts, royal, feudal, or ecclesiastical, either directly as members of the household or indirectly for the appointments which courts could bestow elsewhere.[2]

In the earlier Middle Ages, evidence of literary patronage is found chiefly in dedications and sporadic references, whereas later the growth of bureaucracy produced new types of official records which have been eagerly searched by investigators of the writers and artists of the fourteenth and fifteenth centuries. Even the discovery of a new world left its mark in the £10 which Henry VII. bestowed upon "hym that founde the new Isle"! True, literature never became a department of government, and thus does not enter directly into that administrative history of which Professor Tout is the master; but it was at least a phase of the larger life of the mediæval court, and thus not without its contacts with actual administration. In the twelfth century it is significant that the two most advanced states from the point of view

[1] "General Aspects of Literary Patronage in the Middle Ages", in *The Library*, 3rd series, iv. 369-392 (1913). Compare, from another angle, Miss Marian P. Whitney, "Queen of Mediæval Virtues: Largesse," in *Vassar Mediæval Studies* (New Haven, 1923), pp. 183-215.

[2] Karl Holzknecht, *Literary Patronage in the Middle Ages* (University of Pennsylvania thesis, Philadelphia, 1923), collects a wide variety of interesting material, but needs editorial revision. England has the first place in the plan, and there is a special chapter on "Literary Patrons in England". The author's historical equipment is defective: for example, he accepts the Pseudo-Ingulf without suspicion.

of administrative organisation, England and Sicily, should be precisely those in which literature and learning are most fully developed in relation to the royal court.[1]

That the reign of Henry II. was " an age of great literary activity; of very learned and acute men, and of culture enough to appreciate and conserve the fruits of their labours ", was made clear by Bishop Stubbs in the two entertaining lectures which still constitute the best sketch of learning and literature at Henry's court.[2] When this sketch, as some day it should be, is expanded into a volume, one of the points requiring elaboration and closer definition is the share of the king in the intellectual life of his realm, and the relative importance of the *curia* as compared with local centres of culture. The recent tendency has perhaps been in the direction of exaggeration, particularly on the part of those who claim that the whole romantic movement had its genesis in Henry's reign, and build upon the doubtful mentions of later manuscripts a whole theory of the royal encouragement of Celtic legend as the literary basis for a new British imperialism.[3] Yet Henry grew up in the household of that patron of British history and romance, his uncle Robert of Gloucester, where he also appears to have studied the exact sciences under Adelard of Bath;[4] he knew the languages of the world from the Channel to the Jordan;[5] according to Peter of Blois, he was a far better scholar than William II. of Sicily, occupying himself with private reading and encouraging " constant conversation of the best scholars and discussion of questions ".[6] We know, too, that his court was an important centre of international relations, both intellectual and political.[7] Still the *curia regis* is a vague term, in a literary as well as in an institutional sense, and greater precision is desirable.

[1] For Sicily see my *Studies in the History of Mediæval Science* (Harvard University Press, 1924), chapters ix., xii.-xiv.

[2] *Seventeen Lectures on Mediæval and Modern History*, chapters vi., vii. (1900).

[3] Cf. *Cambridge History of English Literature*, i. 258, 272, and its references; Joseph Jacobs, *Fables of Æsop* (London, 1889), i. 180 f.; Miss Norgate, *Angevin Kings*, ii. 446-448. The connection is generally sought through Walter Map, on whose pretended discovery and translation of Arthurian legends see Ferdinand Lot, *Étude sur le Lancelot en prose* (Paris, 1918), pp. 126-9. On the report that Henry instituted a search for King Arthur's bones at Glastonbury see R. H. Fletcher, *Arthurian Material in the Chronicles* (Boston, 1906), pp. 190 f., 279. For the latest summary of Arthurian problems see James Douglas Bruce, *The Evolution of Arthurian Romance* (Göttingen, 1923).

[4] *English Historical Review*, xxviii. 515 f.; *Studies in Mediæval Science*, pp. 28 f.

[5] Walter Map, *De nugis*, ed. James, p. 237.

[6] Ep. 66 (ed. Giles, i. 194; Migne, ccvii. 198). Aristippus, on the other hand, praises William I. to an English friend, probably Robert of Cricklade (*Hermes*, i. 387; *Studies in Mediæval Science*, p. 166).

[7] Besides the summary in Stubbs, pp. 142 ff., see, for Scandinavia, Henry Goddard Leach, *Angevin Britain and Scandinavia* (Harvard University Press, 1921); and for Sicily my articles in *English Historical Review*, xxvi. 433-47, 641-65. For Henry the Lion see F. Philippi, " Heinrich der Löwe als Beförderer von Kunst und Wissenschaft ", in *Historische Zeitschrift*, cxxvii. 50-65 (1922). J. H. Round's introductions to the later Pipe Rolls list many new facts on international relations.

If Henry II. had left to us any records of his chamber or wardrobe, such as Professor Tout has illuminated for later periods, we should be likely to discover there some traces of the intellectual side of the *curia*. Only by exception could such relations find their way into the Pipe Rolls, where a fortunate accident has preserved the mention of Adelard of Bath in 31 Henry I. Here we must know our man before we seek him, and even then we cannot be sure of identifying him. Still, a Maurice *fabulator* slips into the roll for 1166;[1] besides occasional harpers earlier,[2] Henry *cytharista* is entered each year after 1176; Walter Map and Roger of Hereford, probably the astronomer of this name, appear here as itinerant justices in 1185;[3] while Daniel of Morley, late a student of astrology at Toledo, is mentioned in a lawsuit with a Jew, 1184–87.[4] So a foreign ecclesiastic may appear, like the Norwegian Archbishop Eystein, who has a corrody of 10s. a day in the rolls of 1181–82; but we realise that the king had other resources at his command when we read in Jocelin of Brakelonde that these 10s. were from the funds of St. Edmund's Abbey and that the archbishop abode in the abbot's house.[5] The Queen of Spain's clerk has a grant while at school in Northampton in 1175–76,[6] while the *magistri* of Prince Henry and the king's grandson William are duly recorded.[7] If the preface in the name of Elie de Borron were not fraudulent, a King Henry gave him two castles for his romances.[8]

Besides actual grants from his own purse, the king had chaplaincies at his court and the whole royal influence in the preferment of favoured clerks. Until some one has given us a study of ecclesiastical elections and appointments under Henry II., we cannot penetrate far into this field. We know, however, that two of the most prolific writers of the reign were royal chaplains, Giraldus Cambrensis and Peter of Blois; that Wace received a canonry at Bayeux, apparently in reward for his *Roman de Brut*; and that the king used all his influence to secure the see of London for the eminent Gilbert Foliot—though doubtless not primarily as the author of a commentary on the Song of Solomon! We must remember that literature was often only a subordinate element in the services which kings rewarded.

Patronage also may be prospective, "the lively hope of favours

[1] Pipe Roll 12 Henry II. p. 32 (Norfolk and Suffolk).

[2] Galfridus cytharedus in Pipe Roll 18 Henry II. p. 4; Radulfus citharedus in Pipe Roll 21 Henry II. p. 204.

[3] Pipe Roll 31 Henry II. p. 146. Walter goes to Rome for the king in the Pipe Roll of 24 Henry II. p. 106. On Roger see *English Historical Review*, xxx. 66 f.

[4] Pipe Rolls 31-33 Henry II. pp. 40, 64, 55 (Norfolk and Suffolk). Daniel's patron was John, bishop of Norwich (*English Historical Review*, xxx. 68, xxxvii. 540).

[5] Leach, pp. 89-95.

[6] Pipe Roll 22 Henry II. p. 47.

[7] Pipe Rolls 2, 3, 4 Henry II. pp. 66, 101, 180; Pipe Roll 5 Henry II. p. 58; Pipe Roll 32 Henry II. p. 49.

[8] H. L. D. Ward, *Catalogue of Romances in the British Museum*, i. 364-9; Bruce, *Arthurian Romance*, i. 486 f., ii. 21.

to come". Both Giraldus and Wace complain that Henry did not fulfil their legitimate expectations; or, as Wace puts it,

> Mult me dona, plus me pramist,
> E se il tot done m'eust
> Co qu'il me pramist, mielz me fust.[1]

Such favour is often foreshadowed in eulogies and dedications, and in the absence of connected evidence of other sorts, the works dedicated to Henry are a source of considerable importance for the literary relations of the reign. The following list is doubtless incomplete, but it is offered for what it is worth as a contribution to the subject:

1. Adelard of Bath, *On the Astrolabe*, addressed to Henry as "regis nepos" *c.* 1142–46. See the preface printed in *English Historical Review*, xxviii. 515 f.; and in my *Studies in Mediæval Science*, pp. 28 f.

2 (?). William of Conches, *De honesto et utili*, printed in Migne, clxxi. 1007-1056, as of Hildebert of Le Mans, was ascribed to William by Hauréau (*Notices et extraits des manuscrits*, xxxiii. 1, pp. 257-63), and declared to be dedicated to the young Henry. The evidence is doubtful, though William's connection with the family is shown by the dedication of his *Dragmaticon* to Geoffrey as duke of Normandy and count of Anjou in an introduction which praises his care for the education of the young princes (R. L. Poole, *Illustrations of the History of Mediæval Thought*, edition of 1920, pp. 298 f.).

3. Osbert of Clare. Ninety-seven lines, beginning:

> Dux illustris Normannorum et comes Andegavorum

addressed to Henry in 1153–54 between the treaty of Wallingford and his coronation. Henry is hailed as a Maecenas. Published by Stevenson, *Scalacronica*, pp. 242-4; and by Anstruther, *Epistolae Herberti de Losinga, Osberti de Clara, et Elmeri*, pp. 205-11. On Osbert, see now Marc Bloch, "La Vie de S. Édouard le Confesseur par Osbert de Clare", in *Analecta Bollandiana*, xli. 1-131 (1923).

4. Ailred of Rievaulx. (*a*) *Genealogia regum*, or *De prosapia Henrici*, dedicated to Henry as duke, 1153–54. Twysden, *Decem Scriptores*, coll. 347 ff.; Migne, cxcv. 711. Cf. Powicke, in *Bulletin of the John Rylands Library*, vi. 344 f., 478 f. (1921–22). (*b*) *Vita et miracula Edwardi regis*, dedicated to Henry as his descendant at the translation of October 13, 1163. Twysden, coll. 369 ff.; Migne, cxcv. 737. Cf. Marc Bloch, *loc. cit.*

4*a*. Henry of Huntingdon, *Historia*, final edition of 1154.

5. Wace. (*a*) *Roman de Brut*, written in 1155 and, according to Layamon, dedicated to Queen Eleanor. (*b*) *Roman de Rou*, begun in 1160 with a eulogy of Henry and Eleanor, but not completed in its present form until 1174. Native of Jersey and clerk of Caen, Wace followed the court in Normandy, as we see in 1162, and was rewarded by a cathedral prebend at Bayeux. He later complains that the king assigned to Benoit the task of a history of the dukes of Normandy.[2]

[1] *Roman de Rou*, ed. Andressen, lines 11488-11490; Giraldus, *Opera*, vi. 7.

[2] The fundamental study is a review of Andresen's edition of the *Rou* by Gaston Paris in *Romania*, ix. 592-614 (1880). For Wace's use of monastic sources cf. my *Norman Institutions*, pp. 268-72; for his relation to Arthurian romance, Bruce, *Arthurian Romance*, i. 56 ff. Thomas, who used Wace's *Brut* for his *Roman de Tristan* (ed. Bédier, Paris, 1902–1905) before 1170, can be connected only conjecturally with the court.

6. Benoit, *Chronique, c.* 1180. See the eulogies and references to Henry as patron cited in Michel's edition (Paris, 1836), i. pp. xxii-xxv.[1] Formerly ascribed to Benoit de Sainte-More, author of the *Roman de Troie,* which appears to have been dedicated to Queen Eleanor, the *Chronique* is now attributed to another Benoit. See L. Constans, *Le Roman de Troie* (Paris, 1904–12), vi. 165-91.

7. Jordan Fantosme, *Chronicle.* Addressed to Henry between 1173 and 1183 : Howlett, *Chronicles of Stephen,* iii. 202-377 ; Liebermann, in *Monumenta Germaniae Historica, Scriptores,* xxvii. 53 ff.

8. John of Marmoutier, *Gesta consulum Andegavensium.* See his preface, 1164–73, calling Henry's attention to the deeds of these ancestors, in Halphen and Poupardin, *Chroniques des Comtes d'Anjou,* p. 162, and cf. their introduction.

9. Robert of Torigni, abbot of Mont-Saint-Michel, *Chronicle,* presented to Henry in the redaction of 1184. See Delisle's edition, i. p. xlvi.

10. Robert of Cricklade, *Defloratio Plinii,*[2] in nine books. The dedication to Henry, anterior to 1172, probably by several years, celebrates the king's devotion to the study of letters, and declares it unfitting that the lord of so large a part of the earth should be ignorant of its different regions.[3] It is published by Wright, *Biographia literaria,* ii. 186, both dedication and preface by Rück in *Sitzungsberichte* of the Munich Academy, phil.-hist. Kl., 1902, pp. 265 f., where the treatise is specially studied and extracts printed. For Robert's biography, see *Harvard Studies in Classical Philology,* xxiii. 162-4 ; *Studies in Mediæval Science,* pp. 168-71. In the process of condensing Pliny, the author omits many places important to the Roman taxgatherer, but " from which tribute can no longer be collected ". Few of the author's marginal notes survive. In the Eton MS. (No. 134) the following note occurs opposite Bk. iii. c. 44 :

> *Rob.* In nostra etate reperta est mulier Matildis regis filia regis etiam uxor que filium suum quoque vidit regem potentissimum, et quod etiam additur miraculo unusquisque Henrici sortitus est nomen.

11. Richard the Treasurer, bishop of London, *Dialogue on the Exchequer,* 1178–79, with a well-known preface addressed to the king. That such a description of administrative processes should be written—and then published by the king's licence—Maitland declares " one of the wonderful things of Henry's wonderful reign ".[4]

12. Glanvill (?), *Tractatus de legibus et consuetudinibus regni Anglie,* 1187–1189. Henry's governance is eulogised at length in the preface.

14. Peter of Blois. Consult provisionally Kingsford in *Dictionary of National Biography,* and J. Armitage Robinson, *Somerset Historical Essays* (London, 1921), pp. 100-140, and the editions of Giles and Migne (ccvii) ; a critical study is much needed. (*a*) *Epistole,* collected, according to Ep. 1, at the king's request. (*b*) *Compendium in Job,* written, we are told, at the king's order. (*c*) Dialogue between Henry II. and the abbot of Bonneval.

[1] The *Draco Normannicus* of Étienne de Rouen, though not specifically dedicated to Henry, centres about his deeds.

[2] Apparently the *Pliny* ascribed to Robert of Torigni by d'Achery, *Guiberti Opera,* p. 716 ; Delisle, *Robert de Torigni,* ii. pp. xviii, 343.

[3] Cf. the letter on the geography and curiosities of Britain which Henry is said to have sent Manuel Comnenus (Giraldus Cambrensis, *Opera,* vi. 181).

[4] *History of English Law,* i. 162 ; cf. R. L. Poole, *The Exchequer in the Twelfth Century,* pp. 3 f. ; Liebermann, *Einleitung in den Dialogus* (1875).

No specific dedication. (*d*) (?) *Quales sunt.* Attack on the bishops of Saintes and Limoges written for the king. (*e*) *De prestigiis fortune.* Lost eulogy of the king.

15. Giraldus Cambrensis, " curie sequela et clericus regis ". (*a*) Verses addressed to Henry II., *Opera,* i. 361: (*b*) *Topographia Hibernica,* 1188, *Opera,* v. 20. The *Expugnatio Hibernica* is dedicated to Richard as count (*ibid.* v. 222).

16 (?). Marie de France, *Lais.* Dedicated to a " noble king ", usually identified with Henry II., who would be the author's half-brother if we accept the further identification with Mary, abbess of Shaftesbury. See on this point Miss Edith Rickert, *Marie de France* (New York, 1901), p. 143; and J. C. Fox, *English Historical Review,* xxv. 303-6, xxvi. 317-26; and for recent publications on Marie, Bruce, *Arthurian Romance,* i. 56 ff.; L. Foulet, in *Romania,* xlix. 127-34 (1923). E. Levi in *Archivium Romanicum,* v. 448-93 (1921), identifies the king of the dedication with the Young King.

17 (?). John of Tilbury, to whom a treatise on shorthand entitled *Ars notoria,* composed soon after 1174, is ascribed by V. Rose, in *Hermes,* viii. 303. The dedicatory epistle which the heading addresses to Henry II. is on internal grounds probably to be transferred to some ecclesiastic. John of Tilbury, " scriba doctus et velox ", was a follower of St. Thomas (Herbert of Bosham, in *Materials,* iii. 527); one wonders if he was related to Gervase of Tilbury, who dedicated his lost *Liber facetiarum* to the Young King.

18 (?). One MS. of John of Tilbury (Royal 12 C. vi. ff. 11v-12) also contains forty-three lines of moral maxims addressed to a King Henry, who cannot be distinguished by internal evidence. Cf. Warner and Gilson's *Catalogue,* ii. 23 f.

19 (?). Treatise on falconry. In the Provençal poem of Daude de Pradas on falconry, written early in the thirteenth century, we find this citation:[1]

En un libre del rei Enric
d'Anclaterra lo pros el ric,
que amet plus ausels e cas
que non fes anc nuill crestias,
trobei d'azautz esperimens
on no coue far argumens.

This lost work may have been written by Henry or dedicated to Henry. Either Henry I. or II. is possible; Henry II. was well known for his devotion to falconry.[2]

20. The *Panegyricum ad Henricum* of Joseph of Exeter mentioned by Bale is probably the passage on the Young King in the *De bello Troiano.* See Jusserand, *De Josepho Exoniensi* (Paris, 1877), pp. 45, 96; and the *Dictionary of National Biography.*

Such a list of dedications, even if it were complete, would not, of course, register the entire literary production of Henry's court. It omits the unknown author of the official *Gesta Henrici* and such

[1] Ed. Monaci in *Studî di filologia romanza,* v. 65-192, lines 1930-35. Cf. *Romanic Review,* xiii. 20; *Studies in Mediæval Science,* p. 348.

[2] See Giraldus Cambrensis, ii. 161, v. 274 f.; and the numerous entries in the Pipe Rolls, of which those concerning Norway falcons have been collected by A. Bugge, *Diplomatarium Norvegicum,* xix., Nos. 35 ff. See the indexes to the Pipe Rolls, especially under " accipitres ", " aves ", and " falconarii ".

clerici regis as Roger of Hoveden, the historian, as well as many whose attachment to the court was of a looser sort; nor has it a place for a work like Walter Map's *De nugis curialium*, written at odd moments in the *curia* itself,[1] or for lost books like the Treasurer's *Tricolumnis* or the roll of Thomas Brown. The circle of the Young King [2] must also be noted, as well as the Provençal friends of Richard and his mother. Moreover, the Becket controversy set against Henry the whole group of the *eruditi Sancti Thome*, and doubtless others who had been in relations with the king. Still the list is significant, both for its length and its subjects. Little theology, some science and miscellany, vernacular poetry, probably some sport, much recent history, both in Latin and French, and two distinctive works on the administration of justice and finance—the whole represents not unfairly the tendencies of the king's mind. And if some of these books might have been written at any court and dedicated to any sovereign of the period, the historical works show the converging tendencies, English, Celtic, Norman, Angevin, which came together in the Angevin empire. Still more significant are those unique works, Glanvill and the *Dialogus*, which could have been written only at the court whose procedure they minutely describe. In this sense the most characteristic products of Henry's court are those with the least literary pretensions —the Treasurer's *Dialogue, non . . . luculento sermone compositum set agresti stilo*, Glanvill's compilation of writs, the amorphous entries of the Pipe Rolls—no courtier's trifles these but the rude records of administration. Their style, however, is suited to their purpose, like the documents of the king's chancery, whose clearness and conciseness drew unstinted admiration from Léopold Delisle.[3] The " solid and severe elegance " of these documents " shows a high degree of culture in the clerks of the chancery, which agrees well with what we know of the talent of which many Anglo-Norman writers have left examples in their works, both in prose and verse; their habit of accuracy is manifest in the smallest details and recalls the method of the great English annalists of the period ". *Parum litteratus et multum occupatus*,[4] if one is to accept the unfavourable characterisation of Giraldus, Henry's very occupations created literature. He was first and foremost an administrator, and his clearest impression on literature is seen in the literature of administration.

CHARLES H. HASKINS.

[1] Ed. James, p. 140. On its composition see James Hinton in *Publications of the Modern Language Association of America*, xxxii. 81-132 (1917).

[2] On the vernacular literature centring about the young Henry see Olin Moore, " The Young King, Henry Plantagenet, in Provençal and Italian Literature " in *Romanic Review*, iv. 1-26, v. 45-54 (1913–1914). Cf. the eulogy by Thomas Agnellus (Ralph of Coggeshall, ed. Stevenson, pp. 263-73) and the " Planctus " in *English Historical Review*, v. 315 f. (1890).

[3] *Recueil des actes de Henri II*, Introduction, p. 151.

[4] *Opera*, vi. 7.

VII

LIBER BURGUS

THE formulae used by the royal chancery and by feudal lords in early town charters in this country have never been thoroughly studied, and there is good reason to believe that much needed light upon certain obscure problems of the borough has thereby been missed. A case in point seems to be afforded by the well-known clause which granted the status of "free borough" (*liber burgus, liberum burgum*). Its sudden appearance in charters at the very end of the twelfth century, though the term is known to have been already well understood and applied to many boroughs which never received the formal grant,[1] has not been satisfactorily explained. The difficulty would be less pressing had the grant been made to new boroughs only, but this was not the case.

The absence of any definition of the term, save in one obscure seignorial charter, and its application to every degree of chartered town from manorial boroughs like Altrincham and Salford to the greatest cities of the realm, have led to some bad guessing on the one hand, and on the other to difference of opinion and misunderstandings among those who have seriously searched the evidence for a definition. Lawyers, with their too common indifference to historical facts, used to explain a grant of free borough as conferring "a freedom to buy and sell, without disturbance, exempt from toll, etc." [2] It is more surprising to find so well equipped a scholar as Mr. E. A. Lewis identifying as the essential attributes of the *liber burgus* "the non-intromittat clause exempting them from the sheriff's control as well perhaps as the grant of the *gilda mercatoria* ".[3]

Even Maitland's well-known interpretation has led to some misapprehension, because it has not been kept in mind that he was dealing only with new boroughs, to whose charters the free borough clause is mostly confined, and in particular with that relatively simple type of new borough which was created by a mesne lord. What happened, Maitland asked himself, when a manorial vill was converted into a

[1] See the frequent references to *liberi burgi nostri* in the Ipswich charter of 1200 (Gross, *Gild Merchant*, ii. 116).

[2] Jacob, *Law Dictionary*, ed. 1782, *s.* " Borough ".

[3] *Mediæval Boroughs of Snowdonia*, 39.

borough with a grant of *liber burgus*? His answer was that a free borough of that type was one whose lord had abolished villein services, heriot, and merchet, and instead thereof took money rents.[1] In other words, burgage tenure of land was the essential feature of the *liber burgus* of this kind. Ballard agreed that it was essential, but considered that a court for the borough was also a fundamental requisite. These two features, and these only, were, he considered, common to all boroughs, and he could find no difference between a borough and a free borough,[2] the adjective merely emphasising the freedom of the borough as contrasted with the manorial world outside. His definition of *liber burgus* is therefore a complete one, applicable to the older and larger boroughs as well as to the new creations of the feudal period to which Maitland's *obiter dictum* was confined. But Maitland himself has incidentally made it clear that he regarded burgage tenure as at least the most fundamental, though not an original, feature of the older and more complex boroughs, and (along with French *bourgs*) providing precedents for this tenure in the newer boroughs.[3]

On Ballard's view, a grant that a place should be a free borough, with or without the addition, "with the liberties and free customs pertaining to a free borough", conveyed no more in any case than burgage tenure and a special court with the liberties and customary law that had become appurtenant to them in existing boroughs. It did not include any of those further rights and exemptions which were being steadily accumulated by charter either from the crown or in a less degree from mesne lords, such as the gild merchant and exemption from tolls without the borough. Here, though without naming him, Ballard is challenging the extreme opposite view developed by Gross in his *Gild Merchant*. In the notion of free borough, according to Gross, was comprehended every privilege that was conferred on boroughs up to and including the *firma burgi* and the return of writs which together secured the almost complete emancipation of the borough from the shire organisation. But as these privileges did not come into existence all at once, and were granted in very varying measure to boroughs that differed widely in size and importance, *liber burgus* was necessarily "a variable generic conception".[4] Burgage tenure is regarded in this view as a very minor ingredient of the conception and relegated to a footnote, because it does not appear in the charters of the greater boroughs; in their case it is taken for

[1] *Hist. of English Law*, i. 640 (2nd ed.). Heriot was by no means always forgone (*British Borough Charters*, i. 76, ii. 95).

[2] *The English Borough in the Twelfth Century*, 76.

[3] *Op. cit.* i. 639; *Domesday Book and Beyond*, 217.

[4] *Gild Merchant*, i. 5. His view is accepted in the latest discussion of the term by Mr. T. Bruce Dilks in *Proc. Somerset Archaeol. and Nat. Hist. Soc.* lxiii. (1917), 34 ff. Mr. Dilks was, however, misled by my insufficiently qualified reproduction of Maitland's *dictum* in *Mediæval Manchester* (p. 62) into regarding it as intended as a general definition.

granted. Things that are taken for granted are apt to be among the most fundamental, and a variable conception offends the logical mind, but it would certainly be strange if the extensive privileges won by the great towns in the twelfth and thirteenth centuries formed no part of the contemporary conception of a borough. We say borough simply because, as will be seen later, Ballard was right in denying that "free borough" implied any class distinction between boroughs. All boroughs were free, though their share of privilege varied within very wide limits. A decision between the opposing views propounded by Ballard and Gross can only be reached by a close scrutiny of the charters of the thirteenth century, and to this we now proceed.

I

The free borough clause is first found in extant royal charters at the beginning of the reign of King John. A month after his accession in 1199, John granted to the burgesses of Dunwich: "quod burgum de Dunwichge sit liberum burgum nostrum",[1] and in 1200 to William Briwerr, lord of Bridgewater, that that town should be a "liberum burgum". In the next eight years the same clause was granted in the case of six other towns.[2] Of three of these, Helston (1201), Stafford (1206), and Great Yarmouth (1208), the king was lord, three, Wells (1201), Lynn (1204), and Chesterfield (1204), belonged to mesne lords. Lynn, Stafford, and Yarmouth received the grant *inperpetuum*. Dunwich, Stafford, Great Yarmouth, Wells, and possibly Helston were old boroughs, the rest new creations. The Bridgewater and Wells charters not only conceded that the borough should be free, but that the burgesses should be free too (*sint liberi burgenses*).[3]

The most instructive of these cases, because the best documented, are those of Lynn (now King's Lynn) and Wells. Lynn's promotion to burghal rank required, or at least produced, three charters, two from the king and one from its lord, the bishop of Norwich. They enable us to retrace every step in the transaction. The bishop first asked that the vill should be a free borough. John acceded to his request in a charter of a single clause, recited in the *Quare volumus*, with the addition: "and shall have all liberties and free customs which our free boroughs have in all things well and in peace", etc.[4] This was less vague than it seems, for the bishop tells us, in the charter he proceeded to grant to the vill, that it gave him the option of choosing

[1] *Rot. Litt. Chart.* 51 b. The passage is incorrectly given in Ballard, *British Borough Charters*, i. 3. (The title of this work is abbreviated *B.B.C.* hereafter.)

[2] Seven, if Totnes should be included, but its charter is spurious as it stands, though Ballard believed it to be based on a genuine grant (*ibid.* i. xxxviii.).

[3] *B.B.C.* i. 101. This clause was used alone in John's charter to Hartlepool (1201) in place of the *liber burgus* one.

[4] *Ibid.* 31.

any borough in England as a model for his own.[1] He chose Oxford, and his charter is a grant that Lynn should be a free borough with the liberties of Oxford.[2] As authorised by the king's charter, he reserved his own rights in the vill of Lynn. The final step was a second charter from John, in which he repeated, to the burgesses and their heirs this time, the grant of a free borough and appended a number of specific franchises, some of which (including a merchant gild) but not all are found in Henry II.'s charter to Oxford. As Oxford enjoyed the liberties of London, the fullest record of her privileges would be found in the charters of London. The Lynn clauses relating to crown pleas and to land suits specially prescribe the law and custom of Oxford, and there is general provision for reference to the mother town in case of doubt or contention as to any judgement (*de aliquo judicio*).

The free borough clause no doubt authorised those fundamental changes of personal status and land tenure on which Maitland and Ballard lay such stress, and presumably also the borough court which the latter regards as equally fundamental, but, if Gross be right, it was meant to authorise a great deal more. It remained indeterminate until it was individualised by the grant of the status of an existing free borough, the choice of which was left to the mesne lord. The gild merchant and general exemption from toll, which the king conferred, *inter alia*, on the new borough as Oxford privileges, were as much part of the conception of free borough as burgage tenure and borough court.

Why did John grant the privileges of Oxford in detail immediately after the bishop, with his licence, had granted them in general terms? As the king granted the liberties of Nottingham to William Briwerr for his new borough at Chesterfield[3] without a further charter, the reason probably was that the burgesses of Lynn secured the great advantage of a direct grant to themselves and their heirs from the ultimate authority and in the fullest terms.

Wells in Somerset belonged, like Lynn, to episcopal lords, but it had been a borough by their grace for some time. Bishop Robert (1136–1166) had granted that it should be a borough (not called free) for ever. Bishop Reginald had confirmed his charter with slight additions, and a second confirmation was issued by Reginald's successor Savaric in or before 1201. He states that his predecessors had conceded the liberties and free customs " of burgesses and boroughs enjoying full liberties " and ordains that the whole territory of Wells shall be a free borough and enjoy these liberties.[4] There is nothing to show that either Reginald or Savaric added anything vital to Robert's creation. Savaric's " free borough " seems to have been Robert's

[1] Stafford received the same right of selection in the less ambiguous form: " All liberties, etc., which any free borough in England possesses," which in the case of Liverpool (1207) was restricted to maritime boroughs.

[2] *B.B.C.* i. 32. [3] *Ibid.* 33. [4] *Ibid.* 2.

"borough" and no more. No royal licence for a grant of borough privileges is so far mentioned, but a charter was obtained from John in 1201 which granted that Wells should be a free borough and the men of the vill free burgesses, and confirmed its market and fairs, but, save for a fifth fair, made no express addition to its liberties. The *Quare volumus* clause runs: "that they and their heirs shall have all the liberties and free customs of a free borough (*liberi burgi*) and of free burgesses, and (those) pertaining to such a market and fairs".[1] The first part of this clause, like the second, may only have been a royal confirmation of existing privileges, but the almost identical formula which closes the very similar charter to William Briwerr for Bridgewater (1200): "with all other liberties and customs pertaining (*pertinentibus*) to a free borough (*ad liberum burgum*) and to a market and fair", was used to confer liberties, etc., on a new borough.[2] What liberties, we ask, for we know that there was no fixed set of privileges which every free borough enjoyed. The subsequent history of the Bridgewater formula "liberties and free customs pertaining to a (free) borough", which came to be almost regularly associated with grants of (free) borough in the thirteenth century, shows that its effect was to give the grantee the right of choosing the borough which was to serve as a model, just as a grant of the liberties of all free boroughs or of any free borough to Lynn and Stafford respectively had conceded that right.[3] Thus John's charter to the abbot of Burton empowering him to make a borough at Burton-on-Trent with all liberties, etc., pertaining to a borough was used by him to grant to his burgesses all the liberties, etc., which it was in his power to give, "like the free burgesses of any neighbouring borough",[4] and a similar grant by Henry III. to a later abbot for a borough at Abbots Bromley (1222) was his authority for his gift of the liberties of Lichfield to that borough.[5] Abbot William, in his charter to the men of Burton, did not, like the bishop of Norwich at Lynn, begin with the *liber burgus* clause, but with one assuring free tenure to those who took up burgages and to their heirs. As we descend in the scale of boroughs, the primary feature of free tenure naturally receives greater emphasis.

John's charter, or rather writ, to those who were willing to take up burgages at Liverpool, granting them the liberties and free customs of any free borough by the sea[6] is likewise without the *liber burgus* formula. Liverpool's second charter (1229) containing that formula with specified privileges has been hitherto regarded as raising the status of the borough, but a town which was given the liberties of the most highly privileged maritime borough (for such was the effect of

[1] *B.B.C.* i. 31. [2] *Ibid.* 176.

[3] In the case of Lynn it was definitely *royal* free boroughs, but as it was merely "any free borough" in the Stafford charter, it would be unsafe to infer that the Bridgewater formula imposed any restriction of choice.

[4] *B.B.C.* i. 21 (cf. 42). [5] *Ibid.* ii. 18, 45. [6] *Ibid.* i. 32.

the grant of 1207) was already a free borough. It would seem therefore that Henry III.'s grant was merely one of those confirmations by regrant which were common in the years which followed the close of his minority.

The appearance of the free borough clause in charters granted to existing boroughs, some of which are registered as such in Domesday Book, whether mesne or royal, presents a difficulty on any interpretation of the formula, but it is perhaps less serious if we adopt Gross's view than if the meaning of the term is definitely restricted to the fundamental requisites of a borough. The Wells case may possibly be one of confirmation by regrant, a procedure usual before the method of *inspeximus* came in, though this seems the only occasion on which the borough court could have formally received the hundredal status which it possessed later. None of the royal boroughs which got the clause had any earlier charter, as far as is known, and as they seem to be receiving new privileges (Dunwich, *e.g.* hundredal status [1]) as well as a confirmation of old ones, a formal recognition of their position as royal free boroughs of the highly privileged type would not be unnatural. But practice varied, for the charter which gave Huntingdon the *firma burgi* and the privileges of royal free boroughs has no *liber burgus* clause.[2]

Objection may be taken to Gross's view of the comprehensive implications of " free borough " on the ground that the Wells and Bridgewater charters agree in granting the liberties pertaining to market and fairs separately from those of a free borough. It will be best to deal with this difficulty in the next section when the evidence becomes fuller.

II

Under Henry III. and Edward I. grants of *liber burgus* status became much more common. They were made to twenty-four royal boroughs and to a slightly larger number of mesne boroughs.[3] Most of these were new foundations, Edward I.'s new boroughs in Wales and elsewhere figuring largely in the list. The old boroughs which received the grant were Liverpool (1229), Bridport (1253), Berwick (1302), possibly Windsor (1277), and in Ireland the two Droghedas, the only instances of the use of the *liber burgus* clause at all in that country. The " free burgess " clause was now much more frequently associated with that of " free borough ".[4]

Grants by mesne lords sometimes refer to a royal or other licence, as at Abbots Bromley (1222), Stockport, *c.* 1260 (earl of Chester), Ormskirk (1286), and Kirkham (1296), but more usually there is no record of licence or early confirmation.

[1] *B.B.C.* i. 124.
[2] *Ibid.* 15.
[3] *Ibid.* ii. 2-7. Altrincham has been accidentally omitted.
[4] *Ibid.* 132.

In the case of Abbots Bromley the licence was for a borough simply, but as the abbot was able to bestow upon it the liberties, etc., of Lichfield, we have here clear evidence, if that were still needed, that the epithet was descriptive, not restrictive. The charter of Weymouth (1252) affords corroboration by referring in the common tallage clause to the king's *free* boroughs where the adjective is rare in this context.[1]

In the case of three new boroughs, Lydham and Clifton (1270), and Skynburgh (1301), we have only the royal charter to the lord granting free borough, etc., and no evidence that the latter issued one of his own. In the Agardsley charter (1263) there is no express grant of free borough, but the new foundation is incidentally so described in the first clause of its charter.[2] The experimental character of the formulæ used in John's reign for the conveyance of "liberties and free customs," where no borough was prescribed as a model, is somewhat mitigated in this period. Grantees are no longer referred to the privileges of "any free borough" or those of "a free borough", and only in a single case (Windsor) to those "used by the burgesses of our other boroughs in our realm".[3] The formula now in general use is that first employed in John's Bridgewater charter: "libertates et liberae consuetudines ad (liberum) burgum pertinentes (spectantes)".[4] Sometimes a mesne lord would bestow the liberties, etc., "quas debet (decet) liber burgus (burgenses) habere,"[5] and this might be qualified by an "et quas mihi licet conferre,"[6] such lords having no power to give certain privileges for which they had not a royal grant. The Abbots Bromley charter shows that one way at least, perhaps the usual way, of using a grant expressed in these terms was to copy the liberties and customs of a neighbouring borough.

It is by examination of cases in which this formula is employed or implied that the validity of Gross's "variable generic conception" must be tested. The crucial instances are found in the case of three royal foundations towards the close of the century. They have their difficulties, it will be seen, but cumulatively they seem to establish the main point on which Gross insists.

When Edward I., in 1284, wished to found a borough at Lyme (Regis) in Dorset, which should have a gild merchant along with the liberties of Melcombe in the same county, which did not include the gild, he used the free borough and free burgess clauses followed by these words:

Ita quod Gildam habeant mercatoriam cum omnibus ad hujusmodi Gildam spectantibus in burgo predicto et alias Libertates et liberas Con-

[1] *B.B.C.* ii. 117. The adjective does not appear to be used in any but municipal documents.

[2] *Ibid.* 47.

[3] *Ibid.* 24.

[4] Above, p. 83.

[5] *B.B.C.* ii. 16 (Carlow), 22 (Yarmouth (I.W.)).

[6] At Carlow. Cf. the Burton charter above, p. 83.

suetudines per totam Angliam et Potestatem nostram quas Burgensibus de Melecumbe . . . nuper concessimus.[1]

Although the liberties of a free borough are not directly mentioned, the wording of the charter certainly seems to imply that a gild merchant and the liberties of Melcombe were not a mere addition to, but part and parcel of the free borough then created.

More decisive, though not without its difficulties, is the charter which Edward gave to the new borough of Caerwys in Flintshire in 1290.[2] In its brevity and the disposition of its parts, it closely resembles that of Lyme, falling into three divisions: (1) free borough and free burgess clauses; (2) grant of a gild merchant (but introduced by "et quod"); (3) grant of the liberties of a specified borough (two, Conway and Rhuddlan are mentioned but their charters (1284) were identical). Here, as in the case of Lyme, much parchment and labour were saved by a general reference to the privileges of boroughs which had recently received comprehensive charters. But it is the differences rather than the likenesses of the Lyme and Caerwys charters which concern us here. In the latter the liberties granted are definitely described as "liberties and free customs pertaining to a free borough such as (*quales*), namely, our free burgesses of Conway and Rhuddlan have in their boroughs". Thus the many privileges granted in identical charters in 1284 to these and five other new castle boroughs in North Wales, including gild merchant, general exemption from tolls, a free borough prison, and a number of liberties which had only been given to boroughs in comparatively recent times, are clearly labelled as privileges belonging to a free borough. There was nothing novel, as we have seen, in giving a new borough the liberties of an older one by the grant of the privileges pertaining to a free borough, but in the case of Bridgewater and Abbots Bromley the choice of the model was left to the grantee, here it is prescribed, and we are thus enabled to identify a definite set of fairly advanced liberties as comprised in the conception of free borough.

The separate grant of gild merchant to Caerwys despite its inclusion among the liberties of Conway and Rhuddlan is hard to understand and runs directly counter to the inference one seemed entitled to draw from the Lyme charter. But the difficult question of the relation of gild to borough must be reserved for the moment.

Further light is thrown upon the conception of free borough by the documents relating to Edward I.'s foundation of the borough of Hull (Kingston-on-Hull), and this was the case on which Gross mainly relied. The actual charter (1299) might indeed seem incompatible with his view. It opens with the *liber burgus* clause to which is attached

[1] Gross, *Gild Merchant*, i. 14 *n*.

[2] *Ibid.* ii. 356. Newborough in Anglesey received a charter in exactly the same form in 1303 (Lewis, *Mediæval Boroughs of Snowdonia*, 283).

the grant of the liberties pertaining "ad liberum burgum" usually reserved for the *Volumus* clause, with a proviso (*ita tamen quod*) that the borough should be kept by a warden appointed by the king, *i.e.* not by an elective mayor. Eight liberties and customs are then separately granted: the right of devise, return of writs, freedom from external pleading, an elective coroner, a royal prison and gallows (for judgement of infangenethief and utfangenethief), freedom from tolls throughout the king's dominions, lot and scot in tallages by all enjoying the liberties, and two markets and a fair. The free borough and liberties clause and each of these grants are individually recited in the *Volumus* section.[1] On the face of it, there seems to be a distinction made between the liberties pertaining to a free borough and those which are specified. Fortunately, there has been preserved and printed by Madox[2] the petition from the men of Kingston on which the charter was granted, and this contains the substance of its clauses in practically the same order. The inclusion of the proviso about the warden shows that the petition was not uninfluenced from above, but it may well be that the anxiety of the applicants to have their most important privileges set out in full accounts for their separate position in the charter. At any rate, we have a definite statement in the report of an *ad quod damnum* inquiry before the royal council (which has preserved the petition), that these were free borough privileges. The petitioners, it is stated, asked to be allowed to use and enjoy "quibusdam Libertatibus ad Liberum Burgum in Regno vestro pertinentibus". For any liberties and customs not specified but authorised by the general clause of their charter the new burgesses perhaps used Scarborough as their model, since they asked for exemption from toll as enjoyed by the burgesses of that town.

Still further confirmation of Gross's interpretation of *liber burgus* comes from a charter of Edward which does not found a new borough, but enlarges an old one. In 1298 he annexed the lands of Pandon to the borough of Newcastle-on-Tyne and ordained that they should be one vill and one borough.[3] The charter goes on to grant that the burgesses of Newcastle should have in the lands and tenements of Pandon "liberum burgum sicut habent in predicta villa Novi Castri cum omnibus libertatibus et liberis consuetudinibus ad liberum burgum pertinentibus".[4] Here *liber burgus* must certainly carry more than the mere conversion of the Pandon lands and tenements into Newcastle burgages, for that is the subject of a special clause.[5]

The apparent use of *liber burgus* in this charter as an abstract term could perhaps be explained as due to the awkwardness of applying an old conception to a new and rather different case. But it is

[1] Madox, *Firma Burgi* (1726), 272-3.
[2] *History of the Exchequer*, i. 423.
[3] *B.B.C.* ii. 41.
[4] *Ibid.* 6.
[5] *Ibid.* 52.

also possible that it reveals a tendency of the term at the end of the thirteenth century to take on a narrower and more technical meaning. For the number of *liberi burgi* was certainly decreasing. This was the inevitable result of the extension of higher franchises to the more advanced boroughs and the differentiation produced by the reorganisation of the police system culminating in the Statute of Winchester (1285) and by the introduction of a higher borough rate in national taxation. The smaller mesne boroughs whose privileges did not extend much beyond burgage tenure were losing burghal status and descending into the new category of *villae mercatoriae*. The process was somewhat slow, and was not complete until the fourteenth century was well advanced, but its causes lay far back. Among the boroughs which suffered this fate was Manchester. Recognised as a borough in royal inquisitions as late as 1322, and having a charter of 1301 closely following that of Salford (a *liber burgus*), it was judicially declared in 1359 not to be held by its lords as a borough but as a *villa mercatoria*.[1] No reasons are given, but it is evident that by that date mere burgage tenure and portmoot or borough court was not considered a sufficient qualification for borough rank.

The earlier and more comprehensive application of the term " (free) borough " is well illustrated by another judicial decision. In 1270 Penryn in Cornwall was decided to be a free borough, though its charter from a bishop of Exeter (1236) did not use the term, and gave it only free tenure and a low judicial amercement.[2] At Higham Ferrers the conversion of some eighty villein tenements into burgages was sufficient to constitute a free borough (1251).[3] This limited conception of *liber burgus* is seen also in the only really contemporary definition of the term with which we have met. In granting that status to Welshpool, between 1241 and 1286, Gruffydd ab Gwenwynwyn explains : " so that the aforesaid burgesses and their heirs shall be free of all customs and services pertaining to me and my heirs in all my lands, wherever they may be ".[4] This case is the more notable that, Welshpool being in the March of Wales, Gruffydd was able to give his new borough such unusual privileges for a mesne borough as the right to imprison and try homicides as well as thieves, and the old year and day clause for villeins settling in the borough, in addition to a gild merchant and the law of Breteuil as enjoyed by Hereford. Here it is the fundamental liberty of burgesses as contrasted with the manorial population without that is referred to the grant of *liber burgus* and not the whole body of liberties and customs granted, as in the royal charters we have examined.

It was natural that in seignorial boroughs of a simple type emancipation from manorialism, more or less complete, and the new burgage

[1] Harland, *Mamecestre*, iii. 449.
[2] *B.B.C.* ii. 46, 216.
[3] *Ibid.* 47, 142.
[4] *Ibid.* 6.

tenure should overshadow everything else, while in the great boroughs of immemorial origin and high franchises, in important mesne boroughs like Lynn, whose lords obtained similar franchises for them from the crown, and in royal castle boroughs in Wales which were English garrisons in a newly conquered country, burgage tenure, though vital, was subordinated to the extensive liberties enjoyed by them. The ordinary feudal lord who founded a borough without a special royal charter could indeed add little to the initial boon of free borough tenure. Unless in his manor which in whole or part became a borough he already possessed by grant or prescription, as was perhaps often the case, such franchises as market and fairs, the right of trying thieves and the enforcement of the assize of bread and ale, these had to be sought from the king or palatine lord. It must be kept in mind, however, that burgage tenure in itself involved a very considerable body of legal custom, much of it peculiar to the boroughs, the scope and importance of which has been fully revealed in Miss Bateson's volumes on *Borough Customs*.[1] Thus, when Bishop Poore of Salisbury created new burgages at Sherborne in 1227–1228, he granted them "with all liberties and free customs pertaining to burgages of this kind".[2] A comparison of the phrasing here with that of Edward I.'s charter annexing Pandon to Newcastle-on-Tyne[3] is instructive, because chartered liberties unconnected with tenure had to be included in the latter case.

As the lord had often a manorial market and fairs available for his new borough, so he had always a manorial court, with or without franchises, which could be used as it stood or divided according as the whole manor or only a part of it was included in the borough. The extent to which this court became a really independent borough court depended on the will of the lord. As a definite grant of a borough court by charter was excessively rare,[4] and some charters of creation contain no reference even to the lord's court, we must infer that this requisite of a borough was either taken for granted as already there or implied in the grant of burgage tenure. It seems clear, in any case, that if we look only at the humbler boroughs, which had but partially escaped from manorial fetters, their court was less distinctive and less fully developed a burghal feature than was burgage tenure.

As regards a large class of mesne boroughs, then, Maitland's explanation of the effect of a *liber burgus* clause would appear to be sufficiently confirmed. It does not profess to be a general definition of the term. Ballard's interpretation, on the other hand, which does make that profession, overstresses the jurisdictional aspect of the humbler borough, though admitting that its court was inferior to the hundredal court of the greater towns, and ignores the higher non-tenurial liberties of the latter.

[1] Selden Society. [2] *B.B.C.* ii. 45. [3] Above, p. 87. [4] *B.B.C.* ii. 146.

There is one class of mesne boroughs which we have reserved for separate consideration. It comprises those which were either founded by royal licence and seignorial charter or by royal charter to the lord, which apparently dispensed with the necessity of a charter from him. In some instances of the former kind, *e.g.* Ormskirk and Kirkham, there are indications that the licence must have specified the particular privileges to be conferred.[1] Among those contained in the Kirkham charter (1296) are two which are specially referred to the conception of the free borough: "prison, pillory, ducking stool and other judicial instruments *pertaining to a free borough* by which malefactors and transgressors against the liberties of the said borough may be kept in custody and punished",[2] and "assize of bread and ale *as pertains to a free borough*".[3]

More commonly in both kinds of royal charter brevity was secured by coupling the grant of (free) borough with a general grant of liberties in the formula now familiar to us in connection with greater boroughs: "liberties and free customs pertaining to a (free) borough". The case of Abbots Bromley shows that this was a licence to copy the institutions of some neighbouring borough.[4] Unfortunately, we do not know under what conditions, not expressed in the licence, such permission was given. It is improbable, of course, that the grantee was empowered to invest his borough with all the liberties enjoyed by a highly privileged royal borough that were relevant to its mesne status. Even in the case of royal boroughs, we have seen the vague general formula elucidated either by specification of the higher franchises as at Hull or by mention of the borough to be copied as at Caerwys. Possibly, the feudal lord who got a licence for a borough in this form had to submit his choice for approval. This hypothesis would hardly be so necessary if the formula when unqualified gave no title to certain important franchises. For this there is some evidence. That markets and fairs were excluded may be asserted with a certain measure of confidence. It will be remembered that in two of John's charters, a market and fairs were granted separately from the liberties pertaining to a free borough. Now, this distinction recurs in the charter of Richard, king of the Romans, to Camelford, confirmed by Henry III. in 1260,[5] and in that of Edward I. to the abbot of Holme Cultram for Skynburgh (1301).[6] Moreover, Henry III.'s licence to the abbot of Burton for a borough at Abbots Bromley (1222) grants a fair (there was doubtless a market already) separately from the liberties.[7] The lucrative right of authorising markets and fairs, which in England were not confined to boroughs as they were in Scotland, was a jealously guarded prerogative of the crown and the possessors of palatine powers.

[1] *B.B.C.* ii. 5, 283.
[2] *Ibid.* 170.
[3] *Ibid.* 223.
[4] See above, p. 85.
[5] *B.B.C.* ii. 4.
[6] *Ibid.* 28, 247, 249.
[7] *Ibid.* 45.

In many cases the founder of a borough had a market or fair or both by their grant in his manor long before he thought of making a borough there. Where this was not the case, a bare general grant of borough liberties would not, it appears, include this franchise. But, when once granted, it could be described as one of the liberties pertaining to a free borough in the particular case. Thus the borough of (High) Wycombe was granted in fee farm to the burgesses by its lord in 1226, "with rents, markets and fairs and all other things pertaining to a free borough", and at Hull in 1299 the market and fairs, though granted separately in the charter, are included, as we have seen, in another document among liberties pertaining to a free borough.

Another privilege which can hardly have been conveyed by a general formula, but must surely have required a specific grant, is that most valuable one of exemption from tolls throughout the kingdom and the other dominions of the king. It is inconceivable that a petty borough such as Abbots Bromley should have been able to acquire this great liberty by *verba generalia*.[1]

The wording of some charters seems almost to suggest that a general grant of liberties did not entitle the grantee to set up a gild merchant. Edward I.'s charter to Caerwys (1290), already referred to,[2] granted "a gild merchant with hanse and with all liberties and free customs pertaining to a free borough", though the constitution of Conway and Rhuddlan, which was named as a model for the new borough, included the gild. In the Kirkham charter, six years later, a free gild was granted "with the liberties which pertain to a free borough and to a free gild".[3] Gross remarked long ago that in charters gild and borough are often treated as distinct conceptions, which indeed they were. Though peculiar to boroughs and *quasi*-boroughs,[4] the gild was absent in many of them, including some of the greatest; where it existed it sometimes came into conflict with the purely burghal organism, successful conflict in certain cases, and it often comprised non-burgesses as well as burgesses. On the other hand, the wording of the Lyme Regis charter (p. 85) seems to imply that the gild was granted as a liberty of free borough in that case. It is true also that mesne lords could apparently grant the gild without any licence, and it may therefore seem unlikely that they were debarred from doing so under a general licence. Stress has also been laid upon the fact that the gild at Bridgewater has no known creation unless it was authorised by John's general grant of the liberties pertaining to a free borough.[5] One

[1] We may quote here, though no royal licence for it is on record, Baldwin de Redvers' charter to Yarmouth (I.W.) between 1240 and 1262: "de omnibus libertatibus, etc. quas liber burgus habere debet, *necnon* de libertate et quietancia de teolonio", etc. (*B.B.C.* ii. 22). The exemption was only for his own lands.

[2] Above, p. 86.

[3] *B.B.C.* ii. 283.

[4] *E.g.* Kingston-on-Thames, which, though it had burghal features, was never called a borough, and was taxed as part of the royal demesne.

[5] Dilks in *Proc. Somerset Archaeological and Natural History Society*, lxiii. (1917), 44.

is prepared, too, for the suggestion that in the Caerwys charter the gild is only singled out as the most important of the borough liberties, just as it is occasionally specially mentioned among the liberties and customs of existing boroughs. But with the exception of the Lyme Regis case, none of these arguments seem strong. A mesne lord might have the power to allow the gild, but not as a burghal liberty in the strict sense. The lords of Bridgewater may have used their power to set up a gild independently of John's grant and even without a charter. If the gild in the Caerwys charter were included among the liberties mentioned in close association with it, we should have expected the sentence to read: "with hanse, and with all *other* liberties", etc. The singling out of the gild among the liberties and customs of established boroughs is capable of interpretation in just the opposite sense. However liberties were classified in grants to new boroughs, whether as strictly burghal or otherwise, they were all privileges of the free borough which had received them, and if one of them was given special mention, the inference is perhaps rather that it was felt to be different in kind from the rest than that it was presented merely *exempli gratia.*

If this line of reasoning be sound, and if we were correct in our suggestion (p. 87) that the men of Kingston-on-Hull copied Scarborough for the liberties which were not granted to them specifically (which did not include the gild), it might explain why there was no merchant gild at Hull, though Scarborough had one. However this may be, we shall see in the next section that in the first half of the twelfth century a clear distinction between gild and borough liberties was made in an important charter of creation (p. 95).

There are more "ifs and ans" here than one could wish, but it may be hoped that detailed investigation of the municipal history of particular boroughs will some day show exactly what was obtained under these general powers.

We are now in a position to summarise the main conclusions to which our inquiry, so far as it has gone, appears to have led: (1) In the thirteenth century as in the twelfth any place, large or small, old or new, royal or mesne, which had the specific burgage tenure could be described as a borough, or free borough, for the epithet merely emphasised the contrast with manorial unfreedom, but beyond this there were wide differences in the privileges enjoyed by them. (2) A simple grant that a place should be a (free) borough and its inhabitants free burgesses involved liberties and free customs appurtenant to burgage tenure, but new creations usually contained also an express grant of such liberties and customs either (*a*) by specification, or (*b*) by gift of the liberties, etc., of some borough which was named in the charter, or (*c*) by a general grant of the liberties pertaining to a free borough, with or without partial specification. (3) As there was no single standard of borough liberties, the effect of (*c*) certainly, and of (*a*) probably, was to allow some freedom of choice in regard to the borough whose institutions were to be followed. (4) The limitations under which this freedom of choice was exercised in the case of mesne boroughs remain at present uncertain, but there is good reason to believe that markets and fairs, if not already possessed by the manorial lord, and general exemption from toll required a special grant. (5) In the case of royal creations and of established boroughs generally the " liberties, etc., pertaining to a free borough " included these and any other privileges enjoyed by the individual borough, irrespective of their nature and origin, though such distinctions may be still occasionally recognised in a formal way. Thus the connotation of " free borough " varied from the privileges of London or Winchester to the mere burgage tenure of the humblest seignorial borough. (6) By the close of the thirteenth century the administrative and financial policy of the crown was drawing a line which ended in the denial of burghal status to a large number, perhaps the majority, of mesne boroughs.

Clumsy as this variable conception of free borough and its liberties may appear to be, especially in its application to the creation of new boroughs, it represents a real attempt on the part of the royal chancery to introduce some form and order into a very intractable set of facts due to earlier want of system and to the great outburst of feudal borough making, which was only partly under the control of the crown. This will become clearer in the next section, where we trace the antecedents of the *liber burgus* formula in the twelfth century.

So far we have been testing the modern interpretations of that formula by the light of charter evidence, some of which has not hitherto been taken into consideration. The result seems to show that Gross was right in asserting that *liber burgus* was a variable conception, but did not observe, or failed to make clear, that in a general grant of that status to a mesne borough the term seems to exclude those privileges which only royal power could grant and to be more or less limited to liberties involved in the primary fact of burgage tenure, even when some of these higher privileges were conceded. Maitland and Ballard, on the other hand, by concentrating their attention too exclusively on this simpler type of borough, missed the fuller conception of *liber burgus* in the case of the greater towns where the higher privileges overshadowed burgage tenure. Maitland did not attempt a general definition, and is substantially correct as far as he goes. Ballard's definition is scientific in its elimination of every feature which was not common to all boroughs, from the greatest to the least. But contemporaries were less concerned with scientific definition than with a terminology which would represent actual facts. If we give a rather wider interpretation to " burgage tenure " than Ballard seems to do,[1] there had doubtless been a time when his definition was approximately

[1] See below, p. 95.

true of all boroughs, and traces of the old restricted meaning of "borough" are, as we have seen, clearly visible in the charters of the lesser boroughs of the thirteenth century. What he failed to notice was that the conception was an elastic one, and was expanded in that century to include the great franchises of the more important towns.

None of these writers seems to have observed the device which enabled a brief general grant of borough liberties to be made, despite the absence of a common standard among boroughs. In the next section, too, it is hoped to show, what has not been yet noticed, that the *liber burgus* formula was not an absolutely new conception of John's chancery, but merely an adaptation of an older and less convenient formula.

III

If we could trust the text of a charter which Reginald, earl of Cornwall, granted to the canons of Launceston between 1141 and 1167,[1] we should have to admit that *liber burgus* and "liberties pertaining to *liber burgus*" were terms already in use about the middle of the twelfth century and perhaps much earlier. But their absence from all other known charters before 1199 and the use of less advanced formulae down to that date throw grave doubt on this feature of Reginald's charter. Proof of the second objection will now be adduced.

New boroughs were rare in the twelfth century as compared with the thirteenth and were created by the concession of the liberties and free customs of some one town or by a grant of specified liberties and customs. Bishop Hugh de Puiset prefaces his grant of the liberties of Newcastle-on-Tyne to his borough of Durham with a single clause which rather closely anticipates Maitland's description of the effect of a later grant of *liber burgus* in the case of a mesne borough: "Quod sint liberi et quieti a consuetudine quod dicitur intoll et uttoll et de merchetis et herietis".[2] Intoll and uttoll were dues on the transfer of tenements. For our present purpose, however, it is the formulae of the royal chancery that we are seeking. The most instructive of these appears in the very interesting charters by which the borough of Beverley was founded. About the year 1125 probably, Thurstan, archbishop of York, with leave from Henry I., granted to the men there the liberties (later described as free customs) of York with hanshus or gildhall, farm of the town tolls, free entrances and exits and exemption from toll throughout Yorkshire.[3] The king's confirmation took the form of a grant to them of "*liberum burgagium* secundum liberas leges et consuetudines burgensium de Eboraco", with their gild, toll, and all their free customs and liberties as bestowed

[1] *B.B.C.* ii. 379-380.
[2] *Ibid.* i. 192. The clause is out of place here.
[3] *Ibid.* 23; Farrer, *Early Yorkshire Charters*, i. 90.

by Thurstan.[1] An interesting variation of the royal formula appears in the confirmation issued twenty years later by archbishop William, where it reads: " liberale burgagium juxta formam liberalis burgagii Eboraci ".[2] The points of importance for us here are: (1) That in the twelfth century as in the thirteenth an ordinary vill could be raised to borough rank by the gift of the liberties, etc., of some existing borough without an express formula of creation. (2) That the royal chancery has found a formula which remedies this omission by the introduction of the abstract notion of *liberum burgagium*, which is applicable to all creations but is individualised by reference to the liberties and customs of a particular town. In archbishop William's charter the abstract idea takes on a concrete shape. The laws and customs of York are the *liberale burgagium* of that city. (3) That certain liberties, those of gild merchant and of toll are made the subject of specific grant, though enjoyed by the city which served as model. (4) That a clear distinction between liberties and free customs is not preserved, in Thurstan's charter at least, and that " laws " might be used to cover both.

In the use made of *liberum* (*liberale*) *burgagium* in two of the three Beverley charters, and especially in that of archbishop William, we have a clear anticipation of the *liber burgus* formula which expressed the same idea in concrete form. It is usual to translate *burgagium* in this sense by " burgage tenure ", but " borough tenure " would be preferable as avoiding confusion with the derivative use of *burgagium* for the individual burghal tenement and leaving room for a good deal of " liberty " or " law " or " custom " which was not all tenurial, though the free tenement at a money rent was the most fundamental element in the borough. It was not merely the individual tenement which was held in free burgage, but the town as a whole with all its liberties, etc. An instructive case is that of Drogheda in Meath, which vill with its newly created burgages and the law of Breteuil was granted to the burgesses in 1194 by Walter de Lacy *in libero burgagio*.[3]

" Free burgage ", like the later " free borough ", was a " variable generic conception ". The gild merchant and exemption from toll, however, were not, apparently, regarded as included in this conception, but as supplementary to it. This is important in view of some evidence already discussed that these privileges may not have been included in general grants of the liberties of a free borough.[4]

There is ample proof that the formula of " free burgage ", though rarer than the later " free borough ", continued to be used in the

[1] Farrer, *Early Yorkshire Charters*, i. 92; *B.B.C.* i. 23.

[2] *Ibid.* 24; Farrer, 100. Cf. the " juxta formam legum burgensium de Eboraco " in Thurstan's description of the king's original licence.

[3] *B.B.C.* i. 48.

[4] Above, p. 91.

foundation of new boroughs during the reign of Henry II. Henry himself between 1167 and 1170 made a grant of *liberum burgagium* in Hedon (Holderness) to William, earl of Albemarle, and his heirs, in fee and inheritance, " so that his burgesses of Hedon may hold freely and quietly in free burgage as my burgesses of York and Lincoln best and most freely and quietly hold those [? their] customs and liberties ".[1] Reginald, earl of Cornwall, gave to his burgesses of Bradninch their burgary and their tenements (*placeas*) before 1175,[2] and somewhat later abbot Richard granted Whitby for ever *in liberam burgagiam* (sic), and to the burgesses dwelling there " liberty of burgage and free laws and free rights ".[3] As late as 1194 Roger de Lacy founded a borough at Pontefract by the gift to his burgesses of " liberty and free burgage and their tofts to be held of me and my heirs in fee and inheritance ".[4]

If more direct proof of the equivalence of this formula with the later one of " free borough " be needed, it is not wanting. Dunwich, for instance, which was the first town to receive the *liber burgus* clause, had a later charter from John in 1215, in which that clause did not appear and was replaced by a grant of free burgage.[5] Much later still, in the parallel statements of their baronial privileges made by two Cheshire magnates, Henry of Lancaster claims to hold Halton and Congleton as free boroughs and to have there free burgesses,[6] but Hamon de Massey claims to hold the vill of Altrincham *libero burgagio* and to have free burgesses there.[7] As Massey's charter (*c.* 1290) had made Altrincham a free borough, the two phrases are clearly identical in meaning even at the end of the thirteenth century.

The Beverley town charters show that the privileged status of a great and ancient town like York could be summed up in the same term " free burgage " as was applied to new mesne boroughs, though in the first case no grant to that effect was producible. Madox has adduced clear evidence that in the fourteenth century royal towns, including York and London, were accounted as held of the crown by free burgage (*in liberum burgagium*).[8] He restricts this status to those boroughs which had grants of fee farm and so paid their rents, etc., in a fixed sum to the Exchequer. But the validity of this limitation may perhaps be questionable. We have already seen the burgesses of a mesne borough, Drogheda in Meath, enfeoffed for themselves and their heirs with that vill as well as their individual burgages and the customs of Breteuil *in libero burgagio*, though here the money service was a render from each burgage, not a lump sum from the town. If we may argue from this case and from general

[1] *B.B.C.* i. 38.
[2] *Ibid.*
[3] *Ibid.* 39.
[4] *Ibid.* 41.
[5] *Ibid.* 45.
[6] Ormerod, *Hist. of Cheshire*, i. 703.
[7] *Ibid.* 526.
[8] *Firma Burgi*, 21-23.

probabilities, any grant to the burgesses of a new borough in fee and inheritance, with reservation of a money rent only, must have been in free burgage.

The motive which dictated the substitution of *liber burgus* for *liberum burgagium* in charters of creation from John's reign onwards is sufficiently obvious. The same idea was expressed in a more concise and concrete form and the grant of borough liberties by a general formula, which did not tie the grantee to a particular model, was made possible. We ought perhaps to note that Ballard had already suggested that "the term (*liber burgus*) was introduced by the lawyers of John's reign to shorten the verbiage of charters", but verbiage is too strong a word in this connection, and he did not realise that the term had a definite predecessor not much longer, though less convenient for practical use.

JAMES TAIT.

VIII

QUERIMONIAE NORMANNORUM

I

COMMENT s'est formée, du point de vue administratif, l'unité française ? Quelles décisions le roi et ses conseillers ont-ils prises, et quelle politique les gens du roi ont-ils suivie sur place, pour incorporer et absorber les nouvelles provinces, à mesure que les grands fiefs ont disparu ou que les frontières du royaume se sont élargies ? Comment les populations ont-elles réagi et accepté la domination capétienne ? C'est un sujet qui a été rarement abordé de front et qui a suscité peu de travaux d'ensemble. Il y aurait, par exemple, un beau livre à faire, qu'on intitulerait : *Comment la Normandie est devenue une province française.*

Un des maîtres de l'école historique de Manchester, le Professeur F. M. Powicke, auteur d'une excellente étude sur la conquête de la Normandie par Philippe Auguste, a écrit un chapitre de cette synthèse.[1] Léopold Delisle, toute sa vie, avait travaillé à la préparer. A la fin de sa carrière, il avait notamment publié, dans son édition monumentale des Enquêtes de St. Louis, un document de premier ordre, les *Querimoniae Normannorum* de 1247,[2] où l'on trouve l'écho de quarante années de domination française. Je me propose ici de présenter en ordre les renseignements les plus intéressants que les *Querimoniae* contiennent sur la tâche accomplie en Normandie par Philippe Auguste, Louis VIII, St. Louis et leurs baillis. Je ne saurais naturellement me dispenser d'en chercher le commentaire dans d'autres textes. Pour apprécier les *Querimoniae* à leur valeur exacte, il serait bien imprudent, comme on le verra, de les lire isolément.

II

Quelles étaient les conditions générales du gouvernement de la Normandie à l'époque où St. Louis y envoya ses enquêteurs ?

Ces conditions avaient été fixées dès le lendemain de la conquête par Philippe Auguste. Sa conduite se modela sur deux principes : il voulut garantir sa conquête contre un retour offensif, et empêcher

[1] *The Loss of Normandy* (1189–1204), 1913. Voir notamment les chapitres ix et x.

[2] *Recueil des historiens de la Gaule et de la France* (=H. F.), t. xxiv, 1ère partie, 1904, pp. 2-73 (551 articles).

des connivences entre la noblesse et la bourgeoisie normandes et le roi d'Angleterre ; d'autre part, il voulut posséder, exploiter et gouverner la pays aussi complètement que l'avaient fait les ducs-rois descendants de Guillaume le Bâtard.

Il maintint donc le système des tenures " ad usus et consuetudines Normanniae ", formule qui reparaît à tout instant dans les actes du *Cartulaire normand* ; les dispositions du droit privé ne furent que très exceptionnellement modifiées.[1] Des enquêtes furent faites pour fixer les droits traditionnels.[2] Le roi respecta la liberté des élections ecclésiastiques, si souvent violée par les Plantagenets,[3] et il empêcha ses agents de molester le clergé ;[4] il confirma et augmenta les privilèges des villes.[5] Mais il ne permit point aux nobles et aux villes de rester, sauf autorisations spéciales, en relations avec l'Angleterre. Les terres appartenant aux seigneurs anglais furent confisquées, de même que celles des Normands qui se rallièrent au parti de Jean sans Terre ;[6] celui-ci usa de la réciproque ; le cas de Guillaume le Maréchal[7] et de quelques autres,[8] qui, en bons finauds normands qu'ils étaient, surent garder leurs domaines des deux côtés de la Manche, fut exceptionnel, et la grande réputation du vieux Maréchal n'empêcha point qu'il ne fût taxé de trahison. Grâce à ces confiscations, Philippe Auguste put enrichir le domaine ducal[9] et établir dans le pays de nouvelles familles dont la fidélité lui paraissait assurée ; des baillis, des officiers et chevaliers de la *Curia Regis*, de simples sergents ou arbalétriers, reçurent ainsi des dotations plus ou moins importantes.[10] Bien entendu, les points stratégiques furent particulièrement garantis, et les forteresses furent, ou bien gardées par les baillis en personne, ou bien confiées à des nobles qui promirent de les rendre à la première réquisition.[11]

L'Échiquier des ducs, avec ses attributions judiciaires et financières,

[1] Guillaume le Breton, *Philippide*, l. viii, vers 221 et suiv. (édit. Delaborde, t. ii. p. 219), a exposé avec justesse la politique suivie à cet égard par Philippe-Auguste.

[2] On en trouvera bon nombre dans le *Cartulaire normand* publié par L. Delisle (*Mém. de la Soc. des Antiq. de Normandie*, t. xvi., 1852). Voici le début bien caractéristique d'une d'elles : " Quando rex Philippus conquisivit Normanniam, tradidit balliviam Archiarum Johanni de Roboreto, et precepit illi ut terram illius ballive tractaret sicut tractata fuerat quando ad manum suam pervenit. Idem autem Johannes inquisivit de hoc. . . ." (*Cartul. norm.* no. 167 ; H. F. t. xxiv, 1ère partie, p. *286.)

[3] *Philippide, loc. cit.*, vers 241 et suiv., pp. 219-220.

[4] L. Delisle, *Catalogue des actes de Phil. Aug.*, 1856, nos. 827, 839, 844, 863, 886, 899 etc.

[5] *Ibid.* nos. 829, 830, 903, 904, etc. Giry, *Établissements de Rouen*, t. i., 1883, p. 31 et suiv., p. 47 et suiv.

[6] Voir notamment *Cartul. normand*, no. 113.

[7] *Cartul. normand*, nos. 74, 1120 ; cf. no. 254. *Hist. de Guillaume le Maréchal*, édit. Paul Meyer, t. ii., 1894, pp. 99-101, 105-110 ; t. iii., 1901, pp. 176-178, 179-181.

[8] Voir Powicke, *ouvr. cité*, p. 431 et suiv., 482 et suiv.

[9] *Cartul. normand*, no. 113 déjà cité ; no. 209, etc.

[10] *Ibid.* nos. 66 et suiv., 76, 78, 85 et suiv., 135 et suiv., 153, 159 et suiv., 182, 184, etc.

[11] *Ibid.* nos. 97, 174, 209, 259, 1106, etc.

fut maintenu,[1] et, loin de le déprécier, les gens du roi vinrent y étudier des pratiques plus savantes et y prendre des leçons d'administration.[2] Mais l'Échiquier fut surveillé par ces délégués que le roi y envoyait en mission. Les baillis qui venaient y rendre leurs comptes y siégaient aussi pour les procès, de même qu'à la *Curia Regis*. Tous ces " justiciarii regis ", venus à Rouen, à Caen ou à Falaise pour les sessions de l'Échiquier, rendirent aux Capétiens les mêmes services que les juges itinérants aux Plantagenets. Du reste la Cour de France, la *Curia gallicana*, s'occupa directement de certaines affaires et devint la Cour suprême pour la Normandie comme pour les autres pays soumis au roi. Lorsque Philippe-Auguste, en 1211, reconnut la haute justice à l'abbé de Fécamp dans ses domaines, il déclara que si l'abbé faisait défaut de justice, il l'amenderait " ad juditium curie gallicane ".[3]

Les Plantagenets avaient en Normandie un représentant, un vice-roi : le Sénéchal. Cet office, apres quelques hésitations, fut supprimé et démembré : des " grands baillis " [4] furent envoyés en Normandie comme dans les autres parties du domaine royal. Ce fut là une décision d'importance capitale. Elle était toute naturelle, puisque, depuis quinze ans, Philippe Auguste avait laissé vacant en sa propre cour l'office de Sénéchal, considéré comme dangereux, et qu'il avait généralisé l'institution des baillis.[5]

Dès le début, les attributions politiques, militaires, administratives et financières des baillis sont complètes. De cela nous sommes certains. Mais l'histoire primitive de cette institution est loin d'être encore tout à fait éclaircie. Elle s'estompe dans un brouillard qui, par la nature même des choses, ne pourra jamais être tout à fait dissipé. La documentation que Léopold Delisle a minutieusement réunie concernant les premiers baillis de Normandie [6] confirme bien ce que nous savons par ailleurs [7] sur le caractère encore imprécis de cet office. Les circon-

[1] Voir L. Delisle, *Recueil des jugements de l'Échiquier au XIIIe siècle* (1207–1270), 1864, et *Mém. sur les recueils des jug. rendus par l'Échiq. de Norm.*, dans les *Mém. de l'Acad. des Inscr.* t. xxiv., 2e part., notamment pp. 380-381.

[2] Ch. V. Langlois, *De monumentis ad priorem Curiae regis judiciariae historiam pertinentibus*, 1887, p. 12.

[3] *Cartul. normand*, no. 725. Voir aussi le no. 493. *Le Recueil des jug. de l'Échiq.* mentionne plusieurs fois l'intervention de la Curia Regis, dès le règne de Phil. Aug. Voir notamment les nos. 108, 274.

[4] " Ballivi capitales " (Charte de l'archevêque de Rouen, 1217 : *Cartul. normand*, no. 251).

[5] On remarquera qu'il y avait des baillis en Normandie à l'époque anglaise. Voir Powicke, *ouvr. cité*, p. 66 et suiv., 71 et suiv. Le terme apparaît dès le temps d'Henri Ier. Il correspond sans doute à l'envoi en Normandie d'administrateurs tout dévoués à la cause royale. Henri II semble avoir adopté une division du duché en baillies, correspondant généralement aux vicomtés de l'âge précédent. Cette institution n'a-t-elle pas influé sur la création des baillis dans le royaume de France ? La question mériterait d'être creusée. Mais en Normandie, à l'époque de Jean sans Terre, le vicomte paraît avoir repris son autorité, et il n'y a pas lieu de penser que les grands baillis de Philippe-Auguste aient simplement remplacé des baillis anglais.

[6] *Chronologie des baillis et des sénéchaux royaux*, dans H. F. t. xxiv., 1ère partie, p. *97 et suiv.

[7] Voir H. Waquet, *Le Bailliage de Vermandois aux XIIIe et XIVe siècles*, 1919, chap. i.

scriptions territoriales ne sont pas fixées et telle baillie qu'on voit apparaître dans les textes disparaît ensuite. Dans les documents officiels de la première partie du siècle, on ne voit guères de baillie portant un nom géographique ; c'est l'officier qui donne son nom à sa circonscription : ainsi, dans les *Scripta de feodis*, le pays de Caux ne s'appelle point baillie de Caux, mais " baillie de Geoffroi de La Chapelle" et le Vexin ne s'appelle point baillie de Gisors, mais " baillie de Guillaume de Ville-Thierry ". Le bailli, de son côté,[1] est intitulé tout simplement " bailli du roi " ou " bailli et justicier " ou " bailli en Normandie " ou encore " châtelain " de telle ville forte, Rouen, Arques ou Gisors, ou même " sénéchal de Normandie ", bien que jamais il n'administre tout le duché. Parfois, comme dans d'autres provinces, une même baillie est gérée par plusieurs baillis à la fois. Enfin ceux d'entre eux que le roi considère comme des collaborateurs spécialement remarquables reçoivent des missions de toutes sortes. Ainsi Guillaume de la Chapelle et son fils Geoffroi administrent la baillie de Caux, mais sont appelés hors de Normandie, non seulement pour siéger à la cour du roi, mais pour faire des enquêtes et terminer comme arbitres des différends. Ce sont vraiment des lieutenants du roi. En somme, de très grands personnages, dont le prestige explique que les populations n'aient pas osé se plaindre de leurs abus de pouvoir, jusqu'au jour où les enquêteurs de St. Louis ont délié les langues.

Au dessous d'eux, nous voyons agir des vicomtes, des sergents, des fermiers. On sait que les vicomtes, à l'époque anglo-normande, étaient les représentants du duc, mais que certains d'entre eux avaient conservé leur office à titre héréditaire.[2] Comment cette institution a-t-elle évolué après l'annexion ? Achille Luchaire estime que le vicomte normand à l'époque capétienne est un prévôt [3] et Léopold Delisle le considère comme un " véritable fonctionnaire placé tout à fait en dehors de la hiérarchie féodale ".[4] La vérité est plus complexe, car le prévôt distinct du vicomte existe en Normandie ; le fermier du domaine s'y appelle tantôt *prepositus*, tantôt *firmarius* : les *Querimoniae* nous le prouvent ; et d'autre part la vicomté, après la conquête française, était parfois encore héréditaire.[5] Un acte de 1236 concernant le rachat de la vicomté d'Avranches [6] me fait croire que les rois de

[1] Les exceptions sont rares. Renaud de Cornillon, premier des baillis de Cotentin, s'intitule dans une lettre, " baillivus domini regis in Constantino " (Delisle, *Chronologie des baillis*, p. *146). Au moins pour la Normandie, il semble bien, d'après les divers textes cités par Delisle, que des expressions comme *bailli de Caen, bailli de Bayeux* ou *bailli de Gisors*, appartiennent au parler courant, longtemps avant de pénétrer dans la terminologie officielle. Sur les noms donnés aux baillis créés en Normandie par Henri II, voir Powicke, *ouvr. cité*, p. 72 et note 2.

[2] Powicke, *ouvr. cité*, p. 62 et suiv.

[3] *Manuel des instit. françaises*, 1892, p. 543 et note 1.

[4] *Chronologie des baillis*, p. *97.

[5] Voir des jugements de l'Échiquier rendus en 1207 et en 1239 : *Recueil des jug.* nos. 25 et 658.

[6] *Cartul. normand*, no. 429.

France, ayant trouvé en Normandie des vicomtes officiers du duc, en ont fait des agents du bailli ; de même, le viguier fut conservé dans le Midi, entre le sénéchal et le baile ; les familles normandes qui prétendaient à des vicomtés héréditaires, ont été désintéressées et ont renoncé à leurs droits. Peu à peu, à mesure que les baillages se sont fixés et précisés, ils se sont trouvés divisés en vicomtés, partagées elles-mêmes en sergenteries.[1] Les sergents étaient des agents exécutifs avec des attributions de police,[2] tandis que les prévôts et les fermiers avaient surtout la charge de percevoir les revenus royaux.

Baillis, vicomtes, sergents, à n'en pas douter, s'acquittèrent strictement du mandat qu'ils avaient reçu. Philippe Auguste donnait l'exemple de la raideur et de la méfiance.[3] Ses baillis eurent la poigne dure. Lorsque Jean de Rouvrai, vers 1204, reçut le château d'Arques et la baillie de Caux, il commença par faire une enquête, " afin de traiter ce pays comme il avait été traité avant de parvenir entre ses mains ". Il maintint au profit du roi toutes les prérogatives ducales, garda bien le pays et tira rançon des seigneurs attachés à la cause anglaise. Les bourgeois de Dieppe avaient arraché des mains de ses sergents un homme arrêté pour avoir osé pêcher dans l'eau de Dieppe, qui est au roi jusqu'à la mer ; il ajourna les vingt-quatre plus riches bourgeois de la ville ; ceux-ci refusèrent de comparaître ; alors il priva la ville d'eau potable et les bourgeois se résignèrent à payer au roi une amende de 400 livres.[4]

Louis VIII et Louis IX étaient des hommes pieux et justes. En parcourant leurs actes [5] et les chroniques locales,[6] on a l'impression que de plus en plus l'administration de la Normandie, sous ces deux règnes, se stabilisa ; que les petites gens se détachèrent complètement et très vite de la cause anglaise ; que la bourgeoisie des villes, après la rupture de fructueuses relations avec l'Angleterre, trouva de nouveaux débouchés en se tournant vers les marchés français, et rechercha les faveurs royales ; que la noblesse locale, traitée avec bienveillance,[7] se plia aux obligations féodales et fournit à la royauté, avec plus ou moins de bonne humeur, les guerriers qu'elle demandait ; qu'enfin les églises et les abbayes, comblées de donations et de privilèges, s'attachèrent aux Capétiens par des liens de plus en plus cordiaux et sincères.

[1] Voir dans H. F. t. xxiv. p. *143, une liste des vicomtés et sergenteries du bailliage de Caen à l'époque de Philippe-le-Bel.

[2] Signalons d'excellentes pages de H. Waquet sur les sergents et leurs rapports avec les baillis et les prévôts : *ouvr. cité*, p. 123 et suiv.

[3] Voir notamment *Cartul. norm.* nos. 1080 et 414.

[4] H. F. t. xxiv. 1ère part, *Preuves de la Préface*, no. 62, p. *286.

[5] Aux sources déjà citées, ajoutez mon *Catalogue des Actes de Louis VIII*, dans : *Étude sur la vie et le règne de Louis VIII*, 1894 ; cf. pp. 370-371 ;—pour les jugements de la Curia Regis sous St. Louis, la collection des *Olim* (édit. Beugnot, t. i., 1839), très riche en arrêts concernant la Normandie.

[6] Dans H. F., t. xxiii. Le ton en est remarquablement objectif.

[7] Comme dans le Midi, Louis IX consulta la noblesse et fit convoquer des assemblées locales en certaines occasions. Voir *Cartul. norm.* nos. 414, 425-426.

Sans doute il y eut des querelles,[1] et surtout des conflits entre juridictions rivales ; [2] mais il y en avait dans toute la France.

Les chroniques normandes, les chartes de la Chancellerie royale et des cartulaires, les jugements de la Cour du Roi et de l'Échiquier, contredisent, en somme, les conclusions de M. Élie Berger, qui considère que la Normandie, durement traitée, restait suspecte et malheureuse.[3] Ce que nous savons de l'histoire politique et militaire des règnes de Philippe Auguste et de Louis VIII et l'exposé que M. Berger nous fait lui-même de la première partie du règne de St. Louis n'autorisent pas une telle allégation. La coalition de Bouvines, les guerres continuelles soutenues par Louis VIII, les troubles de la régence de Blanche de Castille, les expéditions d'Henri III en France, furent des pierres de touche de la fidélité normande. On voit bien un certain nombre de Normands passer à l'ennemi en 1214, le seigneur de la Haye-Pesnel se déclarer pour Pierre Mauclerc en 1229, des marins prêter leurs navires à Henri III ; [4] les faits de ce genre demeurent exceptionnels. Guillaume le Breton paraît donner la note juste, lorsqu'il déclare que les Normands grognent contre leur nouveau maître, mais l'acceptent :

> Neustria fida satis, immo fidissima regi,
> Parcere mordaci si lingue vellet in illum . . .[5]

Reste à savoir si les plaintes présentées aux enquêteurs de St. Louis doivent modifier cette première impression.

III

Nous venons de voir comment la Normandie était administrée, lorsqu'en 1247 y apparurent les enquêteurs de St. Louis. Aucun fait grave, particulier à la Normandie, n'était l'occasion de ces tournées. Louis IX les avait ordonnées par toute la France pour soulager sa conscience, au moment de prendre le chemin de la Terre Sainte.[6]

On sait que, malgré les patientes recherches de Léopold Delisle, nous ne connaissons qu'une faible part des enquêtes de St. Louis. Pour la Normandie, nous n'avons que des enquêtes de 1247 et elles sont loin de comprendre toute la province. Des plaintes présentées par les

[1] Par exemple, sous Louis VIII, à propos du service d'ost personnel, auquel répugnaient les évêques normands (*Louis VIII*, p. 409).

[2] Le plus violent fut dû au caractère intransigeant de l'archevêque de Rouen, Thibaut d'Amiens, et de Blanche de Castille. Voir E. Berger, *Hist. de Blanche de Castille*, 1895, pp. 101-102. En 1258, l'Échiquier intervint pour calmer le bailli du Cotentin, en conflit avec l'évêque de Coutances (*Jugements*, nos. 804 à 809). Voir également le *Chronicon Rothomagense*, dans H. F. t. xxiii. p. 332 et suiv., et p. 339. Cf. aussi les *Olim*, t. i. notamment p. 101.

[3] *Ouvr. cité*, p. 289-290.

[4] *Ibid.* pp. 76, 128, 161, 167, 172 et suiv.—Powicke, *ouvr. cité*, p. 395 et suiv.

[5] *Philippide*, l. x, vers 499-500 (édit. Delaborde, t. ii. p. 302).

[6] Sur l'ensemble de la question, voir Ch. V. Langlois, *Doléances recueillies par les enquêteurs de St. Louis*, dans *Rev. historique*, t. 92, 1906.

habitants de la haute Normandie et du Cotentin, il ne nous reste rien ; de la Normandie centrale, il ne nous est parvenu que les *Querimoniae* recueillies dans le pays d'Auge et la vicomté de Pont Audemer, les vicomtés de Bernay, de Falaise, d'Exmes, de Breteuil, de Verneuil et de Bellême-et-Corbon :[1] bref, le pays dont nous connaissons les doléances ne représente guères qu'un quart de la Normandie. C'est dire d'avance que les conclusions à tirer d'un tel document doivent être présentées avec modestie.

Qui fait les enquêtes en Normandie ? Nous l'ignorons. Ce sont évidemment des hommes d'Église. En 1247, St. Louis confia cette tâche de préférence à des Dominicains et des Franciscains. Est-il téméraire de supposer que le Franciscain Eude Rigaud, qui devait être élu archevêque de Rouen l'année suivante, figure parmi les enquêteurs ? Quant aux plaignants, ils appartiennent à toutes les classes de la société ; depuis les évêques jusqu'aux paysans et aux lépreux,[2] tous peuvent déposer librement. Il arrive souvent que trois ou quatre villageois se présentent et se plaignent " pour eux-mêmes et pour tous les hommes de la paroisse " ;[3] nous ne savons pas s'ils avaient reçu régulièrement mandat pour cela.[4]

Quels sont les griefs du Clergé ? Il n'a pas été forcé comme la noblesse laïque de renoncer à ses propriétés d'Angleterre et ne subit, de ce fait, que des incommodités,[5] dont il n'est point parlé dans notre document ; à peine voyons-nous le petit neveu d'un prêtre réclamer à titre d'héritage un quart de fief, confisqué parce que ce prêtre, qui le possédait et était en même temps pourvu d'un bénéfice en Angleterre, est mort outre Manche, l'année même où la Normandie " a passé au roi ".[6] Depuis ce temps, le régime appliqué au clergé s'était fort adouci. En somme, en 1247, une demi-douzaine de couvents, St. Hymer, St. Pierre de Préaux, St. Évroult, La Trappe, Bernay, Silly, se plaignent d'avoir perdu, qui un manoir, qui un bois, ou des droits d'usage, des redevances, des dîmes de bois, de pêcheries ou de moulins, ou bien d'avoir été dépouillés des compensations que leur avaient accordées Philippe Auguste et Louis VIII.[7] Dans un cas, celui de Préaux, nous voyons nettement qu'il s'agit d'une mesure prise après un procès en Parlement de Paris. D'autres, les prêtres de Falaise et les moines de St. Martin du Vieux-Bellême, se lamentent d'être obligés de payer, pour leurs victuailles, des droits de marché, comme de simples

[1] Pour la vicomté de Séez, nous ne possédons qu'une seule doléance (*Querimoniae, édit. citée*, no. 339), j'ignore pour quel motif.

[2] Réclamations des lépreux de St. Antoine de Condé-sur-Risle (no. 66) et de Lieurey (no. 79).

[3] Exemples : nos. 222, 236, etc.

[4] Il y a eu évidemment des meneurs. Des courants de doléances spéciales selon les régions sont assez visibles ; l'exemple le plus frappant est celui des plaignants de Bellême (voir plus loin).

[5] Voir Powicke, *ouvr. cité*, pp. 425-426.

[6] No. 41.

[7] Nos. 45, 47, 76, 237, 273, 326, 481.

laïques.[1] Les frères de l'Ordre de Grandmont, de la Bellière, sont tracassés par les gens du roi, qui s'opposent à leur droit d'avoir dans chaque paroisse du diocèse, un collecteur d'aumônes " quitte de tout sauf du cornage " : de ce fait ils perdent cent livres par an.[2] Ajouter à cela quelques griefs individuels de peu d'importance.[3] C'est à peu près tout, si l'on met à part l'éternelle question de l'excommunication, qui a mis si souvent en conflit le pouvoir spirituel et le pouvoir temporel.

Le conflit portait notamment sur l'abus de l'excommunication, prodiguée contre des laïques pour des raisons laïques,[4] ou contre les officiers du roi, et sur la prétention qu'avait le clergé d'obliger ces derniers à sévir contre les excommuniés. Philippe Auguste avait obtenu et fait des concessions, pour avoir la paix.[5] Louis IX, en des cas de ce genre, défendait peut-être plus énergiquement que son grand-père les droits du pouvoir temporel. Une *Querimonia* de 1247 nous apprend qu'en 1233 un bourgeois de Verneuil, ayant été excommunié par l'évêque d'Évreux à la suite d'une rixe, reçut du roi la défense de comparaître devant l'évêque, de peur que le droit du roi et de la ville de Verneuil n'en fût atteint ; le bourgeois dut rester ainsi excommunié trois ans et demi, par ordre du roi, et son commerce en souffrit ; ses fils, ingénument, réclament une indemnité aux enquêteurs.[6] Mais voici une plainte que leur adresse l'évêque de Séez lui-même. Lui et ses officiaux, au temps de Philippe Auguste et de Louis VIII, jouissaient du droit de mander au bailli de faire justice des excommuniés : par contrainte de corps et de biens, ils étaient forcés de rentrer au giron de l'Église. Mais quand le roi actuel a passé à Bellême, des chevaliers de ce pays sont allés le trouver ; ils ne voulaient pas être ainsi contraints et voulaient que leurs hommes mourussent excommuniés, pour que les biens meubles des excommuniés décédés revinssent à leur seigneur ; Louis IX, au lieu de se méfier d'eux, les a crus et a défendu au bailli de Corbon-et Bellême de contraindre les excommuniés à obtenir leur absolution. Et ainsi nombre de crimes restent impunis. L'évêque en est plus dolent que si le roi lui avait soustrait la moitié des biens temporels de son église.[7] On ne sait ce que Louis IX a dit de cette plainte. Cinq ans après, pendant qu'il était en Terre Sainte, Blanche de Castille eut à négocier avec l'archevêque de Rouen Eude Rigaud,

[1] Nos. 395, 135. Les moines de St. Martin se plaignent aussi des dommages subis à l'occasion du siège de Bellême.

[2] No. 489.

[3] Nos. 2, 5, 14, 203, 272, 545.

[4] Voir un jugement de l'Échiquier (*Recueil des jugements*, no. 51), en 1209, contre un chanoine d'Avranches.

[5] Jugement de 1210 (*Recueil des jugements de l'Échiq.* no. 61), prescrivant aux baillis du roi de forcer les excommuniés à se soumettre et défendant aux évêques d'envoyer les excommuniés en prison. Promesse de l'archevêque, en 1217, de ne pas excommunier les " grands baillis du roi," sous certaines réserves (*Cartul. normand*, no. 251). Mandement de 1218 aux baillis de Normandie, contre les usuriers excommuniés ; concession faite aux évêques normands, mais pour quelques semaines seulement. (*ibid.* no. 253).

[6] *Querimoniae*, No. 256.

[7] No. 537.

grand ami du roi d'ailleurs, au sujet des clercs excommuniés dont le bailli de Caux devait, selon l'archevêque, assurer le transport en prison. Elle ordonna simplement une enquête sur les précédents.[1]

Toute la question était, pour la royauté capétienne, de maintenir les droits que les Plantagenets avaient exercés à l'égard de l'église normande. En 1207, les chanoines de Rouen, à l'occasion d'un conflit où ils avaient obtenu satisfaction, faisaient part en ces termes aux évêques de Normandie d'une visite que leur avaient faite Barthélemy de Roie, Guérin, et le bailli Jean de Rouvrai : " Ils sont venus de la part du roi et nous ont dit que le roi voulait la complète observation des droits et libertés des églises de Normandie et des autres, et nous ont demandé de ne rien réclamer que nous n'eussions au temps du roi Henri, du roi Richard et du seigneur roi de France ".[2] A condition que l'église normande ne voulût pas profiter de l'annexion pour augmenter ses droits, elle put vivre tranquille et fut honorée, protégée et enrichie par Philippe Auguste et ses descendants.

Les laïques eurent à présenter des griefs plus nombreux aux enquêteurs, et certaines de leurs plaintes,—je ne dis point toutes, tant s'en faut,—dévoilent de pénibles vicissitudes que les autres documents permettent bien rarement de soupçonner. Le fait le plus saillant, ce sont les confiscations et leurs répercussions. Sur 551 articles très divers, les *Querimoniae* en comprennent plus d'une centaine sur ce sujet. S'il faut en croire les plaignants, ce régime des confiscations, dont nous avons dit un mot plus haut, a été appliqué dès 1205, en ce qui concerne les laïques, avec une extrême rigueur. Les Normands passés en Angleterre reçurent l'avis de revenir et de se présenter à la justice du roi Philippe avant la Noël (de l'année 1204, évidemment) et ceux qui se présentèrent après cette date perdirent leurs biens ;[3] de même ceux qui, les années suivantes, passèrent en Angleterre.[4] Si, à l'ouverture d'une succession, l'héritier le plus proche était en Angleterre, les autres héritiers ne pouvaient pas entrer en possession.[5] Sous le règne de Louis VIII, la terre de Guillaume Boutevilain fut confisquée à son décès, parce que l'aîné de ses sept fils avait passé en

[1] *Cartulaire normand*, no. 502 ; supplément, p. 326.

[2] H. F. t. xxiv. 1ère part, *Preuves de la Préface*, p. *274. Cf. l'enquête de 1205 : *Cartul. norm.* no. 124. Remarquer qu'il n'est jamais question du roi Jean ; Philippe Auguste a affecté de le considérer comme un usurpateur, et ses successeurs ont fait de même.

[3] Réclamation de Richard le Bourgeois, de St. Pierre-sur-Dives (no. 100) : son oncle revint d'Angleterre le 23 juin, mais ne se présenta qu'après la Noël ; alors ses terres furent confisquées par le bailli et vendues en 1222 à l'abbaye de St. Pierre-sur-Dives, qui les revendit. Cf. *Hist. de Guill. le Maréchal*, t. ii. p. 99, sur les larmes versées par ceux " qui a tens n'i vindrent ".

[4] Nombreux exemples. Voir notamment le no. 330 : " . . . . amisit terram suam . . . eo quod ivit in Angliam nec postea comparuit." No. 353 : " . . . ivit in Angliam tempore pacis cum quodam mercatore, ut ibi panem suum lucraretur, ibique fuit mortuus. . . ." Voir aussi les *Olim*, t. i. p. 122, 123, etc. . . .

[5] Nos. 4, 46, 53, 61 ; nos. 349 (cf. nos. 1, 91, 93), 410. *Recueil des jugements de l'Échiquier*, nos. 332, 343 (anneés 1222 et 1223).

Angleterre au moment de la Conquête.[1] Un père de famille résidant en France et voulant conserver sa fortune à ses deux filles n'eut même pas la liberté d'établir l'une dans ses biens d'Angleterre et l'autre dans ses biens de Normandie ; en ce cas, à sa mort, la moitié de ses biens de France était confisquée.[2] Une femme qui avait été emmenée par son mari en Angleterre ne pouvait garder ses biens.[3]

Des erreurs ou des applications trop dures du système se produisirent, qu'expliquent évidemment l'ignorance des gens du roi et la crainte qu'ils inspiraient : avant l'institution des tournées d'enquêteurs, bien des gens n'osaient point réclamer. La fuite du plus proche héritier en Angleterre n'était pas toujours un fait incontestable.[4] Des femmes qui n'avaient pas accompagné leur mari dans leur fuite, perdirent tout de même leur dot au moment de la confiscation.[5] On vit même une terre saisie à la mort de celle qui la tenait, parce que la sœur de la défunte avait passé en Angleterre au temps du roi Henri II.[6] Marie la Guibée, de Verneuil, perdit sa terre, parce que son régisseur avait pris parti contre Philippe Auguste ; elle la récupéra au bout de longues années, mais sans obtenir les revenus déjà touchés par le Trésor.[7] Une jeune héritière fut privée de son fief parce que son suzerain avait passé en Angleterre.[8] Il arriva souvent que les terres confisquées n'étaient qu'à titre de gages dans les mains des gens qui refusaient de se soumettre à Philippe Auguste ; les ayant-droits se plaignirent aux enquêteurs.[9] Ceux-ci écoutèrent aussi de pauvres familles dont les terres avaient été saisies par le seigneur avant l'annexion, parce que les redevances ou les droits de transmission n'avaient pas pu lui être payés ; il avait pris le parti du roi d'Angleterre et ces terres étaient maintenant dans le domaine du roi.[10]

Le système de la confiscation continua d'être appliqué pendant tout le règne de Philippe Auguste et jusque sous le règne de St. Louis. Les chevaliers normands qui accompagnèrent Louis de France pendant son expédition en Angleterre (1216–1217) purent s'apercevoir eux-mêmes qu'il était imprudent de s'attarder outre Manche.[11] Il était également défendu de quitter la Normandie pour aller en Poitou, pays dont la condition politique était mal définie.[12] Encore en 1238, le roi ayant autorisé une dame normande à se rendre en Angleterre, le bailli de Rouen confisquait la terre d'un sénéchal qui l'avait accompagnée dans

[1] Nos. 246, 258.
[2] No. 54. Cf. no. 263.
[3] Nos. 64, 73.
[4] Voir notamment nos. 392, 422, 429.
[5] Nos. 60, 358, 360.
[6] No. 65.
[7] No. 257.
[8] No. 78.
[9] Nos. 75, 314, 319, 320, 324, 476, etc., et la série des réclamations des tenanciers de Duranville : nos. 277, 292, 294, 297, 298, 302, 303, 318.
[10] Nos. 18, 26, 81, 337, 348, 408.
[11] No. 248. Autre exemple de 1217 : no. 333.
[12] No. 80 : cas de deux jeunes Normands qui avaient dû quitter la maison paternelle parce qu'ils avaient rossé la maîtresse de leur père et avaient terminé leur vie en Poitou.

son voyage.[1] La même année, Richard de Glanville ne pouvait entrer en possession d'un héritage, à cause de l'absence suspecte de son frère.[2] En 1243, les terres d'un marchand d'Aclou, près Brionne, furent saisies par le bailli de Rouen, parce qu'il était allé en Angleterre, croyant les hostilités finies.[3] Bien entendu, pendant les troubles du début du règne, la confiscation avait frappé les Normands soupçonnés d'intelligence avec l'ennemi ;[4] notamment, des frères habitant à Échauffour, qui avaient passé en Bretagne, et leur mère, soupçonnée d'être allée dans ce pays " comme messagère et même comme espionne contre le roi ".[5]

On a l'impression, en lisant les doléances inspirées par ces mesures, que la plupart du temps les baillis s'étaient simplement conformés aux principes commandés par la conservation de la conquête. La modération de la politique capétienne apparaît mieux encore, à la lecture des jugements de l'Échiquier qui nous sont parvenus. De 1207 à 1223 nous voyons, à plusieurs reprises, l'Échiquier restituer des terres confisquées, parce qu'il s'agit d'une dot, d'un douaire, d'une terre mise en gage ou donnée en fief, etc. . . . et que les ayant-droits sont lésés.[6]

Sous le règne de St. Louis, en tous cas, le régime des confiscations s'atténua de plus en plus, grâce, certainement, aux interventions personnelles du roi. Louis IX qui avait un esprit droit et net, s'accommodait mal de certaines équivoques que Philippe Auguste avait tolérées. Mathieu de Paris assure qu'en 1244, les Anglais que Philippe Auguste avait laissés libres de faire hommage à la fois aux rois de France et d'Angleterre, furent obligés par Louis de choisir.[7] C'est ce même besoin de clarté qui le conduisit à conclure, à tout prix, un traité avec l'Angleterre, traité éminemment favorable à la pacification des esprits en Normandie. Dans la même intention, il poussa, en 1261, l'abbé de St. Martin de Troarn à échanger avec le prieur de Brewton, en Somerset, les possessions qu'ils avaient, le premier en Angleterre, le second en Normandie, et dont ils ne pouvaient jouir sans périls et embarras de toutes sortes.[8] Cette politique de simplification et de franchise dans les rapports entre peuples ne pouvait avoir que d'heureuses conséquences. D'autre part les mesures de bienveillance qu'il prit en 1255 en faveur de Raoul de Meulan,[9] les restitutions de terres normandes

[1] No. 15.—Sur la " licentia in Angliam transfretandi " à cette époque, voir *Recueil des jugements de l'Échiquier*, no. 613, ann. 1237.

[2] No. 50. Il est vrai que Richard ajoute que cette terre appartenait à leur oncle, " qui obiit cum iret ultra mare ". Sur cet oncle, qui devait porter aussi le nom de Richard de Glanville, voir le *Catal. des Actes de Ph. Aug.* no. 1446. Cf. le no. 52 des *Querimoniae* et le no. 680 des *Jug. de l'Échiquier*.

[3] No. 295.

[4] Nos. 342, 415, 439, 492. Cf. *Jug. de l'Échiquier*, nos. 470, 623, 635.

[5] No. 340.

[6] *Jug. de l'Échiquier*, nos. 7, 18, 20, 30, 171, 174, 246, 339.

[7] *Chronica majora*, édit. Luard, t. iv. p. 288.

[8] Confirmation de l'échange par Louis IX : *Cartul. normand*, no. 673.

[9] *Ibid.* no. 536.

" dictées par sa conscience ", dont il parle dans des chartes fameuses de juin 1248 et qu'il accomplit en effet,[1] et tout ce que nous savons de son gouvernement pendant la seconde partie de son règne, nous persuadent qu'il fit ce qu'il pouvait pour panser les plaies produites par le système des confiscations.

Mais il fut sans doute impossible de réparer tous les dommages causés. Une bonne partie des *Querimoniae* relate des répercussions qui atteignent des tiers. Les seigneurs de terres forfaites déclarent qu'elles auraient dû leur revenir : ils sont lésés.[2] D'autres ont perdu une rente constituée sur une terre qui a été saisie.[3] Un autre qui avait pris à ferme une terre avant qu'elle fût forfaite, réclame une indemnité.[4] Un autre assure que son père avait acheté tel pré, confisqué ensuite parce que le vendeur avait passé en Angleterre.[5] Enfin, les rois de France auraient, dit-on, consacré des usurpations commises au temps de Jean sans Terre. Ainsi le sénéchal de Normandie, Guillaume le Gras, à l'époque anglaise, avait dépouillé de leurs terres, sous différents prétextes, ou même sans raison et " en vertu de sa puissance ", nombre de gens du pays de Falaise et les avait ensuite forfaites pour avoir pris le parti de Jean sans Terre ; les enquêteurs enregistrent les réclamations de ses victimes.[6] Il ne fut sans doute pas toujours aisé de savoir la vérité. Les *Querimoniae* font allusion à de longs procès qui avaient eu lieu pendant les années précédentes et n'avaient pas donné satisfaction aux plaideurs.[7]

On ne se plaint pas seulement des confiscations qui n'auraient dû atteindre que les ennemis du roi et qui ont lésé des sujets soumis et fidèles. De nombreux Normands déclarent avoir été spoliés de terres, de redevances, de droits traditionnels, sans que le motif de forfaiture pût, même indirectement, être invoqué.[8] Pour ce qui concerne les dépossessions immobilières, il est rare que le texte même de la doléance n'en dévoile point la cause. Très souvent la terre a été saisie parce que le tenancier est considéré comme n'accomplissant pas ses engagements ou qu'il refuse de céder aux injonctions des officiers royaux.[9] Ou bien

[1] *Cartul. normand*, nos. 473, 1185. L'interprétation donnée du no. 473 par L. Delisle est erronée. Cf. Powicke, *ouvr. cit.* p. 397.—*Querimoniae*, no. 16, jugement de la cour du roi ordonnant restitution, en 1241.

[2] Par exemple : nos. 40, 131, 258, 404, 456, 471.

[3] Nos. 6, 59, 68, 93, 306, 349, 370 à 372, 450, 472.

[4] No. 263.

[5] No. 271. Voir aussi no. 251.

[6] Nos. 382, 399, 406, 407, 412, 427, 430 à 432, 434, 440, 441, 448, 449, 452, 454, 455, 459, 462. Guillaume le Gras avait été nommé sénéchal en août 1203.—Autres réclamations du même genre : nos. 7, 94.

[7] " Diu in curia regis laboravit " (no. 4). " Prae paupertate non valens sequi curiam . . . " (no. 73). Voir aussi nos. 20, 289.

[8] Nos. 8, 10, 22, 23, 51, 58, 215, 252, 291, 329, 336, 344, 361, 366, 373, 374, 376, 385, 389, 393, 403, 418, 421, 437, 469, 541, etc.

[9] Nos. 25, 29, 39, 283, 284, 345, 356, 362, 380, 397, 405, 414, 434, 440, 493, 495, 506, etc.

le relief n'a pas été payé.[1] Ou bien le tenancier laissait sa terre inculte.[2] Ou bien la terre avait été, sans doute, donnée par le roi à ferme.[3] Ou bien la terre avait été livrée en gage, par exemple à un Juif ; or les terres des Juifs ont été confisquées par Philippe Auguste.[4] Ou bien il y avait contestation de limites entre un domaine privé et le domaine royal,[5] notamment en région boisée ; et les gens du roi, toujours jaloux de conserver la " Forêt ", ont maintenu ou peut-être outrepassé les droits qu'ils ont à défendre.[6] Plus fondées sont les réclamations des gens qui ne sont pas en possession de certaines terres auxquelles ils croient avoir droit, et paient tout de même des redevances pour les susdits biens.[7] Fréquemment, on se plaint du sans-gêne des officiers, quand ils exécutent des travaux publics ; s'ils élèvent des fortifications, creusent des fossés ou le bief d'un moulin royal, bâtissent " la maison où se tient la Justice ", créent des carrières pour se procurer des matériaux, il arrive que des propriétaires ne soient pas indemnisés pour les parcelles prises.[8] La possession du droit d'usage des forêts, des pâturages et des eaux suscita partout au moyen âge d'innombrables conflits. Elle fait l'objet de beaucoup de *Querimoniae* ;[9] quelques-unes sont d'une touchante ingénuité : ainsi les habitants de Bons Moulins gémissent, non seulement de n'avoir plus le droit de bois mort et sec dans la forêt du lieu, depuis dix ans, mais de ne plus pouvoir emporter le bois qu'ils ont frauduleusement coupé, lorsqu'ils sont surpris et condamnés à l'amende (18 sols pour avoir coupé un arbre, 3 sols pour une branche) ; jadis, une fois qu'ils avaient payé l'amende, ils pouvaient emporter le bois.[10] Ou bien encore, ce sont des réclamations pour des redevances qu'on ne peut plus toucher, par exemple sur les moulins de Pont-Audemer, qui ont brûlé.[11]

L'augmentation des impôts est un grief, dans toute la France ; les Normands s'en plaignent amèrement. On incrimine tantôt les " firmarii regis " et les prévôts, les sergents, les forestiers, tantôt le vicomte ou le bailli. C'est que les baillis, en raison notamment des guerres soutenues contre les Anglais et dans le Midi albigeois et en vue de la croisade que Louis IX a juré d'entreprendre, ont dû certainement hausser les prix d'adjudication des fermes, en Normandie comme ailleurs, et les fermiers doivent retrouver leurs débours. On a donc augmenté, en certaines terres du domaine, les redevances[12] ou la

[1] No. 238.
[2] Nos. 402, 510.
[3] Nos. 424, 435.
[4] Nos. 56, 67, 69, 388, 416.
[5] Cf. la plainte caractéristique de Robert et Hugue Tison, de Damblainville, contre les fermiers du roi, no. 394. Voir aussi nos. 379, 433, 485.
[6] Nos. 21, 125, 140, 205, 214, 304, 309, 321, 458, 497, 505, 507, 513, 547.
[7] Nos. 27, 30, 315, 402.
[8] Nos. 31, 34, 164, 234, 260, 411, 419, 420, 451, 517, 544.
[9] Nos. 12, 139, 159, 182, 208, 209, 221, 222, 229, 235, 236, 241, 243, 265, 266, 269, 276, 281, 327, 347, 468, 474, 484, 490, 498, 504, 508, 511, 515, 518, 522, 538, 540, 551, etc.
[10] No. 236.
[11] No. 74 ; Nos. 35, 208, 213, 226, 232.
[12] Nos. 57, 92, 288, 297 à 299, 313, 317, 322, 369, 438, 442, 444, 446 ; voir surtout le no. 384.

rétribution des banalités,[1] si on les a jugées trop faibles. Ici, on a violé les privilèges de gens exemptés de certaines coutumes ; [2] là, on a introduit des charges toutes nouvelles : les habitants de Corneville-la-Fouquetière prétendent que la corvée pour moissonner le blé du roi ne date que de vingt ans.[3] Des redevances, des tailles, des coutumes sur les marchandises, sont créées.[4] A Argentan, l'amende qui frappait certains débitants de boissons faisant fausse mesure s'est transformée en une coutume que les taverniers de la ville, sans distinction, paient tous les trois ans.[5] A Montpinçon, le marché n'existe plus, mais les droits de marché sont perçus tout de même.[6] Enfin on se plaint des réquisitions opérées, soit pour les constructions et les réparations des édifices royaux,[7] soit à l'occasion des séjours du roi en Normandie, soit pour les guerres. Les enquêteurs enregistrent patiemment les doléances de gens qui ont perdu des paniers ou des coussins.[8] Des charrettes et des chevaux ont été emmenés pour la croisade de Louis VIII en Albigeois et les propriétaires n'ont reçu aucune indemnité ; [9] de même pour les campagnes de 1234 en Bretagne et de 1242 en Poitou.[10] Mais ce sont surtout les habitants de Bellême et des environs qui réclament compensation : lorsque l'armée royale est venue assiéger le château en 1229, elle a détruit des maisons, des moulins, des arbres, des moissons en herbe, réquisitionné du blé, du foin, du vin, du bétail, des chariots, et les habitants, traités en ennemis du roi,[11] n'ont pu rien réclamer. Si l'on fait l'addition de toutes les sommes énumérées de ce chef, on obtient un total d'environ 8000 livres tournois.[12] Il est évident que les paysans de Bellême n'ont pas dû obtenir réparation de tous les " dommages de guerre " qu'ils évaluaient si libéralement.

Ces doléances proviennent presque toujours de petites gens. Quelques nobles viennent réclamer aux enquêteurs des héritages sur lesquels ils prétendent avoir des droits et que le roi ne croira pas toujours équitable de leur attribuer.[13] D'autres réclament des patronages d'églises [14] ou déclarent que les gens du roi, en exerçant le droit de garde sur un manoir, l'ont " dissipé extraordinairement et en partie

[1] No. 287 : la banalité du moulin royal de Fontenelles (Eure) rapporte maintenant 11 l. t., au lieu de 100 s. Voir aussi nos. 95, 268.

[2] Nos. 207, 225, 239, 244, 270, 351, 354, 548.

[3] No. 275.

[4] Nos. 149, 160, 219, 224, 261, 262, 266, 363, 367, 378, 401, 425, 436, 453, 461, 475, 477, 487, 488, 519, 535.

[5] No. 479. Plainte contre l'augmentation du taux des amendes, no. 270.

[6] No. 355.

[7] Nos. 55, 227.

[8] Nos. 103 à 110. Voir aussi no. 528.

[9] Nos. 17, 38, 77, 117, 157, 168, 230, 282, 543.

[10] Nos. 206, 242, 249.

[11] Sur ce point, voir nos. 152 et 218.

[12] Nos. 113 et suiv., jusqu'au no. 202 ; no. 211.

[13] Voir notamment la réclamation de Raoul de Meulan, no. 286, et les termes de la charte royale de 1255 : *Cartul. norm.* no. 536. Réclamation de Jacques de Château-Gontier, *Querimoniae*, no. 121 ; cf. son désistement en 1257 : *Cartul. norm.* no. 587. Le *Recueil des jugements de l'Échiquier* montre que la justice royale en Normandie avait constamment à s'occuper de ce genre de procès.

[14] Nos. 13, 352. Cf. des jugements dans les *Olim*, t. i. pp. 242, 649, etc.

détruit ".[1] Une douzaine de chevaliers ont perdu des droits de chasse ; [2] l'extrême rareté des doléances relatives à la chasse royale montre qu'en passant sous la domination française, les Normands, à cet égard, n'avaient point perdu au change.

Notons enfin que les baillis veillent à ce que les roturiers n'entrent point dans la classe noble en se faisant conférer la chevalerie sans l'autorisation du roi. Nos *Querimoniae* contiennent, à ce sujet, un texte digne d'être signalé. Le bailli de Rouen, Jean des Vignes, a détenu dix-sept semaines en prison, vers 1235, Robert de Beaumont, qui s'est fait armer chevalier " sine licencia regis " ; le bailli disait qu'il était de famille bourgeoise, et Robert prétendait être de famille noble ; la reine Blanche et Barthélemy de Roie, en 1237, l'ont fait comparaître et il a dû verser cent livres d'amende, sans pouvoir obtenir de Jean des Vignes l'enquête qu'il réclamait.[3]

Ce ne sont pas seulement les administrés qui viennent demander justice aux enquêteurs. Ce sont aussi des administrateurs. Des fermiers, des prévôts, présentent une foule de griefs. Ils se plaignent, par exemple, qu'on les force à garder des fermes trop chères ; on devrait leur décompter telle somme en raison des circonstances ; les guerres ont amené des réquisitions de charrettes, les marchés ont diminué d'importance faute de moyens de transport et les prévôts sont lésés ; un d'eux, qui a la mémoire longue, incrimine à ce propos la campagne de Bouvines. D'autres se plaignent de n'avoir pas la sergenterie héréditaire [4] à laquelle ils ont droit. Ou bien c'est un sergent auquel on a enlevé sa sergenterie fieffée, sous prétexte qu'il avait la goutte, ou dont le bailli a remanié la circonscription " parce qu'elle était trop dispersée et causait des vexations et des fatigues aux pauvres gens " : avouons que le bailli avait raison.[5] Enfin des chevaliers, des sergents, des charretiers, des ouvriers, réclament des gages qui ne leur ont pas été payés, quand ils ont servi à la guerre [6] ou travaillé à construire une tour.[7] Un architecte demande qu'on lui paie un dépassement de devis.[8] A la lecture de ces doléances, souvent puériles, on se prend à croire que tous les Normands dont la famille

[1] Nos. 85, 428. Sur le droit de garde et ses abus, voir aussi nos. 86, 89, 90, 240, 307, 325, 483, 529, 536. Cf. *Olim*, t. i. pp. 533, 613, 625, etc.

[2] Nos. 163, 208, 209. Plainte d'un paysan qui a perdu son cheval, réquisitionné pour porter la *venatio regis*, no. 254. Voir aussi no. 216. Si l'on s'en fie aux *Olim*, les nobles normands ont engagé peu de procès à ce sujet sous le règne de St. Louis ; en revanche, ils réclament souvent contre l'application du droit de tiers et danger ; voir t. i. pp. 147, 159-160, 179, 207, 211, 226, 241, 665, etc.

[3] No. 19. Voir des contestations du même genre dans les enquêtes de Touraine, nos. 42, 122, 153 ; H. F. *vol. cité*, pp. 100, 108, 112.

[4] L'Échiquier reconnaissait les sergenteries héréditaires ; voir le *Recueil des jug. de l'Échiq.* nos. 184, 495, 504, 730.

[5] Nos. 9, 44, 87, 141, 217, 220, 223, 228, 267, 280, 300, 334, 338, 343, 364, 460, 467, 470, 473, 482, 514.

[6] Nos. 301, 391, 464, 500. Réclamations pour pertes de chevaux, nos. 531, 539. Gens au service du comte du Perche en 1216, nos. 119, 123.

[7] No. 233.

[8] No. 24.

avait subi quelque tort depuis cinquante ans, fût-ce du fait du roi d'Angleterre,[1] sont venus allonger la liste des plaignants.

L'impression que l'administration capétienne a été en somme honnête, équitable et douce en Normandie, se trouve singulièrement fortifiée, si l'on fait le compte des accusations précises portées contre les gens du roi et si on compare, à cet égard, les *Querimoniae Normannorum* avec les enquêtes faites dans d'autres régions. Les enquêteurs ont invité les habitants à tout dire sans crainte et ceux-ci ne se gênent point pour porter plainte contre " le roi Philippe d'illustre mémoire " et contre Blanche de Castille en personne. Le maire et les pairs de Verneuil exposent en effet que le roi Philippe a violé le serment qu'il avait fait, au moment de la reddition de la ville, de maintenir les us et coutumes dont les bourgeois jouissaient auparavant ; dix ans après, " ému et irrité d'une sottise dite par feu le maire de Verneuil, il a ordonné de lever un fouage sur les bourgeois et de détruire les créneaux de la ville ".[2] Quant à Blanche de Castille, elle a commis un abus de pouvoir par affection pour une de ses filleules : cette jeune fille ayant épousé le fils de Guillaume de Minières, le roi, à l'instigation de sa très chère mère, a forcé Guillaume à payer cinq cents livres tournois pour son fils et, afin de l'y contraindre, a envoyé chez lui des garnisaires qui ont dévasté ses biens.[3] Ces abus de pouvoir qu'on reproche à un roi et à une reine, on n'a certainement pas hésité à les signaler quand ils ont été commis par des baillis et leurs subordonnés. Les accuse-t-on souvent d'arbitraire, d'actes brutaux, de concussions ? Fort rarement.[4]

On assure que Renaud de Ville-Thierry, bailli de Caen et de Bayeux, a fait pendre pour vol, sans jugement, vers 1226, un habitant de Briouze-St.-Gervais ; or, il n'était pas coupable : ce sont ses héritiers, fort désireux de rentrer en possession de ses biens confisqués, qui l'affirment.[5] Jean de la Porte, bailli de Rouen, et Pierre de Thillai, bailli de Caen, au temps de Philippe Auguste, ont " extorqué " de grosses sommes (200, 100, 60, 40, 13 livres tournois) à des gens accusés d'être des usuriers ou bien à leur famille ; ces amendes ont, du reste, été versées au trésor ; cependant, une fois, Jean de la Porte a pris dix livres pour lui et pour le vicomte, et Pierre de Thillai a exigé un tonneau de vin de 8 livres.[6] Notez que Pierre de Thillai, le plus considérable peut-être des baillis de Philippe Auguste, avait une immense fortune, qu'il fit de grandes fondations pieuses, notamment l'Hôtel-Dieu de Gonesse, et qu'après sa sortie de charge, il se retira au Temple de Paris.[7]

[1] Torts causés par le roi Jean et son sénéchal de Normandie, nos. 250, 457, 516, 523.

[2] No. 253.

[3] No. 255.

[4] L'extrême rareté d'actes de St. Louis rappelant à l'ordre ses officiers de Normandie procure la même impression. Évidemment il ne recevait pas beaucoup de réclamations contre eux. En 1247, on s'est plaint de l'administration royale en général, *de domino rege*. Voir plus loin une note à ce sujet.

[5] No. 447.

[6] Nos. 33, 96, 98, 99, 101.

[7] L. Delisle, *Chronologie des baillis*, déjà citée, p. *134 et suiv. ; *Fragments de l'Hist. de Gonesse*, dans *Bibl. de l'Éc. des Ch.*, 1859, 4e série, t. v., p. 114 et suiv.

En réalité, le seul bailli normand contre lequel on relève quelques charges sérieuses est Lambert Cadoc, ce capitaine de routiers que Philippe Auguste, ne sachant sans doute comment se débarrasser de lui, improvisa administrateur ; châtelain de Gaillon et bailli de Pont-Audemer, pendant une quinzaine d'années, il finit par se faire mettre en prison vers 1220, pour avoir gardé devers lui 14,200 livres parisis dûes au Trésor ; il resta sept ans captif et mourut vers 1231.[1] Certains des griefs formulés contre lui ressemblent aux réclamations que nous avons déjà notées et n'impliquent pas improbité de sa part ; [2] mais d'autres mentionnent expressément l'esprit de rapine qui inspirait l'ancien chef de bande : d'après Pierre de Cracouville, son père a été spolié de biens valant 140 livres tournois de revenus, parce qu'il n'avait pas consenti à faire présent à Cadoc d'un faucon ; [3] une autre fois, Cadoc a dépouillé un propriétaire qui ne voulait pas lui donner un moulin ; [4] un autre a perdu 15 livres de revenus sur la prévôté de Pont Audemer, parce qu'il n'a pas accepté d'épouser la niece de Cadoc ; [5] un autre, pour avoir refusé de donner ses filles en mariage à deux sergents du bailli, a été accusé faussement de voyage en Angleterre et a perdu un domaine considérable.[6] Tantôt le bien confisqué était annexé au domaine royal, tantôt Cadoc le gardait pour lui.[7] Une enquête que Léopold Delisle a datée de 1230 nous atteste un fait analogue : apprenant qu'un certain Pierre Chapon réalise ses biens pour aller en Terre Sainte et a de l'argent liquide, Cadoc lui demande 20 livres tournois à titre de prêt et est repoussé ; après le départ du croisé, il confisque un bois lui appartenant, pour se venger.[8]

Dans les *Querimoniae* de 1247, un seul vicomte, Guillaume Faiel, vicomte de Bernay en 1212, est incriminé d'un abus de pouvoir du même genre : une vengeance contre un administré qui n'avait pas voulu épouser sa fille.[9] Les prévôts et les fermiers du roi sont très rarement accusés de concussions.[10]

[1] *Cartul. norm.* nos. 118-119, 132, 247, 363, 1084. *Querimoniae*, no. 305. L. Delisle, *Chronologie*, p. *130 et suiv.

[2] *Querimoniae*, nos. 32, 70, 84, 102, 279, 316, 494, 501, 503, 512.

[3] No. 278. Cf. no. 491.

[4] No. 71.

[5] No. 72.

[6] No. 62.

[7] Terre " extorquée par force " et gardée par Cadoc, no. 496.

[8] *Cartul. normand*, no. 1143. Au nom de Cadoc, il faudrait peut-être ajouter, d'après les *Querimoniae*, no. 245, celui de Raoul Arondel, qui fut bailli de Gisors et de Verneuil sous St. Louis, et qui aurait été incarcéré à Paris.

[9] No. 346.

[10] " Non habebat pecuniam quam posset dare famulis dicti regis " (no. 28). Un des officiers auxquels il est reproché le plus d'abus de pouvoir est Girard de la Boiste, dont il est souvent question dans les enquêtes de la vicomté de Falaise, pour des faits de la période 1239–1245 (nos. 356, 359, 377, 385, 388, 421, 461, 468, 475). Girard de la Boiste est qualifié, une fois seulement (no. 377), *ballivus*. Delisle, *Chronologie*, p. *137, croit qu'il s'agit d'un bailli de Caen, de ce nom, qui figure comme tel en 1246. Mais on voit nettement, au no. 385, que, au moins en 1239, Girard n'est pas *capitalis ballivus* : il est le subordonné de Jean des Vignes, alors bailli de Rouen ; voir aussi no. 461. Quoi qu'il en soit, tous les reproches qui lui sont adressés n'accusent que son zèle excessif pour les intérêts du roi.

Cette liste d'accusations paraît bien anodine, quand on a lu le reste des Enquêtes de St. Louis. Dans le Midi, les Enquêtes [1] nous montrent les sénéchaux de Beaucaire et de Carcassonne presque indépendants, souvent tyranniques, assistés de bailes et de sergents brutaux et chapardeurs, qui exaspèrent la population par leur arbitraire et leurs extorsions. On se rit des lettres royales qu'obtiennent les plaignants. L'aventure de ce Durand de la Bastide, dont le baile Pierre d'Auvergne emplit la bouche de fumier,[2] est symbolique. Les graves insurrections de 1240–1242 sont le fruit de cette politique, qui ne laissait aux populations méridionales que la ressource de la révolte ; le Languedoc ne sera assimilé que lorsque la communication sera établie régulièrement entre les sujets et le roi. Mais n'allons pas si loin : feuilletons les enquêtes faites en 1247 dans les provinces de la Loire et de l'Ouest nouvellement annexées, Maine, Anjou, Touraine, Poitou, Saintonge.[3] Nous y trouvons ce qu'on ne rencontre pas dans les *Plaintes des Normands*, c'est-à-dire des enquêtes faites spécialement sur l'administration de tel bailli ou de tel prévôt, accusé d'énormes abus de pouvoir et de concussions. Par exemple, Philippe Coraud, châtelain de Tours, est l'objet de 188 plaintes, auxquelles s'ajoutent " aliae multae querimoniae examinandae " ; Mathieu de St. Venant, prévôt de Tours, doit répondre à 137 plaintes, et Léonard de Benais, prévôt de Chinon, à 254. Aux frontières mêmes de la Normandie, dans le Maine, le prévôt de la Flèche, Étienne Mocart, est représenté comme un tyran cynique et brutal. A Angers, à Langeais, à Château Chinon, à La Rochelle, etc. . . . on se plaint des baillis, des prévôts, des sergents, des bedeaux, des forestiers, et on les incrimine nommément.[4]

IV

En résumé, que l'on examine les chartes des rois et des baillis, les documents juridiques, les chroniques, ou bien qu'on lise—avec l'attention nécessaire—les *Querimoniae Normannorum* de 1247, en les comparant avec les autres enquêtes, l'impression totale est la même : la Normandie était bien administrée et les souffrances de l'annexion se réduisirent au minimum.

Les raisons de cette différence entre le sort de la Normandie et celui des autres provinces rattachées au domaine par Philippe Auguste et ses successeurs est évidemment la position géographique de la Normandie. Les Capétiens avaient un intérêt de premier ordre à

[1] H. F. t. xxiv. 1ère et 2ème part, p. 296 et suiv.
[2] *Querimoniae Nemausensium, ibid.* p. 433, no. 147.
[3] H. F. *vol. cit.* 1ère part, p. 73 et suiv.
[4] C'est à peine si nous relevons, dans les *Querimoniae Normannorum*, une demi-douzaine de *Querimoniae de ballivis* (nos. 96-102), où d'ailleurs il ne s'agit pas de concussions ni d'actes de brutalité. Les doléances normandes s'intitulent presque toujours *Querimoniae de domino rege*.

se concilier une population limitrophe de l'Île de France, et il leur était facile de la visiter eux-mêmes, de contrôler sans cesse la gestion des officiers qu'ils lui envoyaient. Le Poitou, et à plus forte raison le Midi, leur paraissaient des terres lointaines, difficiles à gouverner. Nous en avons une preuve bien intéressante dans des instructions données vers 1206 par Philippe Auguste à un émissaire qu'il chargea de négocier avec un baron poitevin, Raoul de Lusignan, sire d'Exoudun et comte d'Eu. Philippe désirait que Raoul acceptât de gérer pendant cinq ans le domaine royal en Poitou et lui livrât, pendant le même temps, ses terres et ses forteresses de Normandie ; " le Poitou, devait ajouter l'émissaire, est si lointain, que le roi ne peut y aller ni y envoyer comme il le faudrait ".[1] La trahison du vicomte de Thouars, sénéchal de Poitou, lui avait montré que sa domination dans ce pays était précaire, et il croyait avoir trouvé une combinaison merveilleuse pour s'assurer la fidélité d'un nouveau gouverneur ; mais on voit ici combien la Normandie lui tenait plus à cœur, et combien il était décidé à " y aller et y envoyer ". En fait, il ne se passa pas une seule année, depuis 1204 jusqu'à sa mort, sans qu'il fît séjour dans quelqu'une de ses résidences favorites de Paci, Pont de l'Arche, Gisors, Vernon.[2] Il plaça en Normandie ses meilleurs baillis et se servit de l'Échiquier pour les contrôler et les tenir en haleine. Les deux hommes qui eurent la plus grande autorité dans le conseil royal à la fin du règne de Philippe Auguste et pendant celui de Louis VIII, furent l'évêque de Senlis, Guérin, qui faisait fonctions de vice-chancelier, et le chambrier Barthélemy de Roie ; or Guérin assista à toutes les séances de l'Échiquier de 1216 à la fin de 1225, et Barthélemy de Roie y figura presque constamment depuis 1218 jusqu'à sa mort.

Les successeurs de Philippe Auguste suivirent ses errements. Un des plus fidèles amis de St. Louis, le Franciscain Eude Rigaud, devint archevêque de Rouen en 1248, et s'employa avec zèle au gouvernement de la province ; [3] il fut un des négociateurs du traité de paix entre la France et l'Angleterre, et ce fut lui qui, le 4 décembre 1259, donna solennellement lecture à Paris, dans le jardin du roi, de ce pacte fameux, selon lequel Henri III renonçait au titre de Duc de Normandie.[4] Pendant les dernières années de son règne, St. Louis, malgré le délabrement de sa santé, fait de nombreux voyages en Normandie, y visite les pauvres, et depuis le Vexin jusqu'au Mont-St. Michel, les abbayes le reçoivent solennellement ; il les comble de donations et de faveurs de

[1] Pièce publiée dans le *Cartul. normand*, no. 1082, et dans le *Catal. des Actes de Ph. Aug.* pp. 510-511. Cf. Cartellieri, *Philipp II August*, t. iv. 1ère part, 1921, p. 229. Cette négociation n'aboutit pas.

[2] *Tableau chronologique des séjours de Phil. Aug.*, dans l'*Introduction* du *Catal. des Actes*, p. cvii. et suiv.

[3] Voir une charte de non-préjudice de St. Louis : *Cartul. normand*, no. 615, et la note de L. Delisle.

[4] M. Gavrilovitch, *Étude sur le traité de Paris de 1259*, 1899, pp. 37 et 67.

toutes sortes.[1] Les chartes de Philippe le Hardi nous montrent que le fils de St. Louis et ses conseillers suivent la même politique ; la Normandie est tranquille, les droits acquis sont respectés ; le Parlement de Paris défend, au besoin, les particuliers contre les abus de pouvoir et intervient de plus en plus activement dans les affaires de la province.[2] L'arbitraire fantaisiste et les concussions d'un vicomte de Pont Audemer, Jean de Neuvi, font l'objet d'une longue et minutieuse enquête.[3] La Normandie est maintenant devenue une province française.

Les documents dont nous nous sommes servis sont fragmentaires et des réserves s'imposent. Mais nos *Querimoniae* elles-mêmes, faites pour ne signaler que les abus, sont bien significatives par la rareté des griefs graves, qu'on trouve si nombreux dans la plupart des Enquêtes. Jointes aux autres textes, elles contribuent à prouver, jusqu'à nouvel ordre, que la Normandie, qui jusqu'alors n'avait jamais appartenu aux Capétiens et avait été le berceau des glorieux conquérants de l'Angleterre, se détacha très facilement et très vite de ses anciens princes. Les fautes qu'ils avaient commises, la communauté de langue et de civilisation qui reliait le pays à la France, l'esprit positif et pratique des Normands, ne suffisent pas à en rendre compte. Nous avons essayé de prouver que l'administration de Philippe Auguste et de ses descendants fut ferme, mais attentive et sage ; et sans doute faut-il imputer surtout ce succès politique aux vertus morales de St. Louis, à son esprit de charité, de justice et de paix.

CH. PETIT-DUTAILLIS.

[1] Voir le *Cartul. norm.*, et les notes de L. Delisle ; notamment les nos. 543 et suiv., 566 et suiv., 573 et suiv., 670, 695, 727, 749, 752 ; le *Registrum visitationum* d'Eude Rigaud, édit. Th. Bonnin, 1852, pp. 241, 272, 273, 401, 402, 479, 601 ; la *Chronique du Bec*, extraits publ. dans H. F. t. xxiii. pp. 454-455.

[2] *Cartul. norm.*, notamment les nos. 854, 897, 950, 951, 992, 1014, 1015, 1021, 1049. *Olim*, édit. Beugnot, t. i. pp. 377, 831, 833, 835, etc. . . et t. ii., *passim*. *Arresta communia Scaccarii*, édit. E. Perrot, 1910, no. 137.

[3] *Cartul. norm.* no. 664, et *Supplément*, no. 1229. Cf. Charles V. Langlois, *Le Règne de Philippe III le Hardi*, 1887, pp. 331-333.

IX

SOME OBSERVATIONS ON THE BARONIAL COUNCIL (1258–1260) AND THE PROVISIONS OF WESTMINSTER

THE London chronicle of mayors and sheriffs, generally cited as the *Liber de antiquis legibus*, tells us that an affair of much solemnity took place in Westminster Hall on Friday, October 24, in the year 1259. King Henry sat in state, in the presence of earls and barons and a crowd of people. At his command a document was read to the assembly in a loud, clear voice; and then the Archbishop of Canterbury and the bishops present, in pontifical array, declared sentence of excommunication upon all who might seek to make the execution of the decree of no effect.

The document was the Provisions of Westminster, the most enduring monument of the baronial revolution. A few days later it was enrolled,[1] and the official preamble preserves the appearance of royal initiative which had been so evident in Westminster Hall:

> Convenientibus apud Westmonasterium in quindena Sancti Michaelis (October 12) ipso domino rege et magnatibus suis in communi consilio et consensu dictorum regis et magnatorum factae sunt provisiones subscriptae per ipsos regem et magnates et *publicatae* in hunc modum.

The provisions were the outcome of discussions in the Michaelmas parliament; they were drawn up on October 12, the eve of the feast of St. Edward the Confessor, Henry's patron saint; and they were published twelve days later at the session in Westminster Hall, where the king received formal permission to go to France for the final settlement of the dispute which had alienated the two countries since the days of King John. The lord king, says the London chronicler, took leave to cross to France ("cepit licentiam transfretandi"), and entrusted the kingdom to the Archbishop of Canterbury, the Bishop of Worcester, the lord Roger Bigod, Hugh Bigod, and Philip Basset.[2]

This is history from public documents and pageants; but, just as

[1] The new regnal year began on October 28, and the Provisions are enrolled on the Close Roll for that year, 1259–1260; Close Roll 44 Henry III. part 1, m. 17 d.; printed in *Statutes of the Realm*, i. 8, and thence in the *Select Charters*; also in Shirley, *Royal Letters of the Reign of Henry III*. (Rolls Series, 1866), ii. 394-8.

[2] *Chronica majorum et vicecomitum* (Camden Soc., 1846), 42.

months of discussion and a bewildering number of drafts and agreements lay behind the final ratification of the Treaty of Paris and prepared the way for the meeting between St. Louis and King Henry, so the publication of the Provisions of Westminster concealed much more than it disclosed. The London chronicler had no illusions, for he describes the document as a "compositionem factam per barones super usibus et legibus regni emendandis". Every word of this pithy description is significant. For reasons which will appear, the phrase suggests to my mind that the document was read in French, and that it contained a good deal more than the Latin version entered on the Close Roll. Again, it suggests that the writer was aware of the discussions at Westminster, of the pressure brought to bear by the "bachelors" of England; when we find the words *compositio, compromissum,* describing ordinances and provisions, in these years, we may be sure that arbitration of some sort has been at work. It may be worth while, therefore, to go behind the scenes a little way.[1]

The previous history of the Provisions of Westminster is part of the history of the Council of Fifteen which was elected in July 1258. The circumstances of the election and early activities of the Fifteen have been obscured in some measure by our traditional attitude to the famous parliament of Oxford. We are generally told that a Council of Twenty-four, comprising twelve royalists and twelve of the baronial party, was set up at Oxford, and, in its turn, proceeded to set up a constitution whose terms are precisely defined in a systematic state paper known as the Provisions of Oxford. In reality, we cannot be sure what exactly happened at Oxford. The Twenty-four had probably been at work for a month before this adjourned parliament met; the Provisions of Oxford, which were never officially enrolled, are a series of memoranda rather than a formal state paper, and make no reference to the one decision taken at Oxford which disturbed the course of its proceedings. They contain the names of the Council of Fifteen, and we know that the Council was not chosen before June 26.[2] On that day the king, who was still at Oxford, ordered the four electors to proceed, but we cannot be sure that they performed their delicate task then and there.

If we wish to find the right point of view, it is safer to regard the period between May 2 and August 4 as a whole. On these days the king issued two important letters patent. On May 2 he declared that he and his son had sworn to observe whatever the Council of Twenty-

[1] For some of the material used in this paper, see the interesting article by Dr. E. F. Jacob, "What were the Provisions of Oxford?" in *History*, October 1924, ix. 188-200. In some respects my reading of the events of these years differs from that of Dr. Jacob, but I owe much to his kindness in allowing me to refer to unpublished material which he has collected.

[2] *Royal Letters*, ii. 127-8. This letter was enrolled under the date June 22 (*Cal. Pat. Rolls*, 1247–1258, p. 637).

four, of which his own nominees had already been chosen (*iam electos*), might decide; on August 4 he issued letters, a copy of which was handed to the earl marshal by king and council, promising to observe what the council, *i.e.* the Fifteen, might decide.[1] The revolution took place during this interval, and was decided by June 26, when Henry ordered the four electors, chosen by the Twenty-four, to elect the Council of Fifteen. During May and June the Twenty-four worked out its plan, presented it at Oxford, and crushed the opposition of the Poitevin relatives of the king. Then it drops out of view, and by the end of July the new permanent council is finding its feet. The new council must have had in writing a record of the decisions and programme accepted at Oxford, but no coherent statement has come down to us. The terms of the oaths to be sworn by new castellans were enrolled in the Patent Roll, and, later, stitched as a schedule into a Memoranda Roll of the Exchequer[2]; the chancery officials, in the spring of 1259, found it convenient to write down the list of the council and of the twelve barons who, with them, formed the three annual parliaments[3]; but if the Burton annalist had not preserved a copy of the haphazard memoranda, known as the "Provisions of Oxford", we should find it hard to say what it was that the king had sworn to observe. These memoranda, I imagine, were drawn up in July as a guide to the Council of Fifteen.[4]

The Burton annalist also preserved an anonymous report upon the proceedings at Oxford, which may well have been written by the man from whom he got the "Provisions". The writer was well informed, acquainted both with the work of the Twenty-four and with the intentions of the barons. He is described as "somebody at court", and was presumably one of the clerks who, as members of the royal and baronial households, must have done so much to shape the ideas

[1] *Foedera*, i. 371; *Royal Letters*, ii. 129. The wording of the second letter, which is in French, suggests that the council had but recently been elected.

[2] *Cal. Pat. Rolls*, 1247–1258, p. 637; K.R. Mem. Roll, No. 32, 42-43 Henry III. The castellans' oath appears in the Provisions, and was probably drawn up at Oxford, since the castles were then entrusted to other hands (cf. *Ann. Mon.* i. 443 at foot, also p. 453; and, for a rather different list, *Cal. Pat. Rolls*, 637-9). Another schedule in the same memoranda roll contains the sheriffs' oath, "Secundum provisionem et disposicionem magnatorum iuratorum de consilio domini Regis". This was drawn up at the Michaelmas parliament, 1258, and was imperfectly copied in the royal charter of October 20 (*ibid.* pp. 454-5; cf. *Cal. Pat. Rolls*, p. 655), and Annals of Dunstable (*Ann. Mon.* iii. 210).

[3] Close Roll 43 Henry III. m. 12 d. John fitzGeoffrey's name was omitted, and at the end the names of Hugh Bigod, justiciar, and Henry de Wengham, chancellor, were added to the list of the council. W. Bardolf had taken John de Verdun's place on the committee of twelve.

[4] Dr. Jacob has discovered another text of the "Provisions of Oxford" in Cott. MS. Tib. B 4 ff. 213-14. Verbal discrepancies with the Burton text are numerous, but the only serious difference is in the list of the twenty-four to treat of an aid, a short-lived body of which nothing more is known. Not twenty-four but twenty-five names are given, three of which are new. As one of the three new names is that of Master William of Powick, who was not a baron but a king's clerk and future justice, it may be that we have here the man who was to treat on behalf of the king. William had experience, for he was royal proctor at the Council of Lyons in 1245.

of their masters. That great king's clerk, John Mansel, one of the Twenty-four, one of the four electors, one of the Council of Fifteen, was the chief of them, and rose far above most of them in importance; but there must have been many more. It is almost certain, for example, that an obscure John Sackville, who appears at this time as a clerk of the Earl of Gloucester, was no less a person than the John Sackville, an Englishman of noble birth, who had recently been rector of the University of Paris.[1] If this was the case, we may be sure that the learned controversialist would not be kept in the background. These men were not necessarily partisans; they would differ from each other, just as the Twenty-four or the Fifteen might, in sympathy rather than in policy. A new effort had been made after so many vain attempts,[2] and it was the duty of everybody to make it a success. The king was suspicious and resentful, no doubt, but acquiescent; he might feel that his dignity had been rudely disregarded, and fear the Earl of Leicester more than the hostile elements of nature, and even be outraged by the sworn association of barons with their implicit assertion of the right of resistance[3]; yet he had not been quite isolated. His own friends had agreed that nothing less than this new constitution would meet the case, and there was any amount of work to be done in which all parties and all varieties of administrative experience could take part. The royalist witness of the Oxford parliament, at all events, writes not as a partisan, but as a man interested in the transaction of business. And, once the Poitevins were out of England and the young lord Edward had given his word, this was the prevalent note in all quarters.

The "litera cuiusdam de curia regis" begins with a reference to the recent changes made at Oxford, the appointment of Hugh Bigod as justiciar, a summary of the oath which he had taken, and the distribution of the royal castles among new castellans who were Englishmen. The Twenty-four, he proceeds, then proposed a general act of resumption of alienated domain on the ground of the king's poverty. This measure led to the crisis which was only ended with the departure of the Poitevins from England on July 14. The writer gives a spirited account of this. He next mentions the submission of the young lord Edward, who, it may be observed, had lately (June 18) completed his

[1] For Sackville (*Secheville, Sacqueville*) and his writings see Matthew Paris, v. 599; *Calendar of Papal Letters*, i. 415; *Calendar of Patent Rolls*, 1258–1266, p. 10; *Catalogue of the Royal MSS.* ii. 60 (12 E. xxv.); Pits, *Scriptores*, p. 339 (*s.v.* Driton).

[2] The least known of these was the reorganisation of the king's council in 1257. The Burton annalist gives the text of an oath by the new counsellors, the barons of the exchequer, and the justices (*Ann. Mon.* i. 395-7). The oath contains a clause against the alienation of ancient demesne, which was perhaps the excuse for one of the charges made against the Earl of Leicester in 1260 (Bémont, *Simon de Montfort*, p. 345). For the use made of the oath in later times see Baldwin, *The King's Council*, pp. 346-7.

[3] *Ann. Mon.* i. 447-8; cf. Matthew Paris, v. 696-7. Wykes fastens upon the significance of the political theory underlying this oath (*Ann. Mon.* iv. 119).

nineteenth year, and he concludes with a forecast of the baronial programme:

In brevi vero providebunt de statu hospitii ipsius (Edwardi) et hospitii domini regis. Saepius autem rogavit eos dominus rex, quod nullus moraretur cum eo nisi Anglicus; et ita erit. Magna et ardua habent ipsi barones providenda, quae non possunt cito vel facile consummari et effectui mancipari. Providebunt etiam in brevi una cum domino regi apud Londonias plura tangentia alienigenas, tam Romanos, quam mercatores, camsores et alios. . . . Ferociter procedunt barones in agendis suis; utinam bonum finem sortiantur.[1]

The date of the letter would seem to be the end of July, or, if Edward's adhesion was only secured about the time when his father announced it (August 4), the beginning of August.

By this time the members of the council had come to London. Earl Simon is known from an incident related by Matthew Paris [2] to have lived in July in the house of the Bishop of Durham between the Temple and Westminster, and, as the Temple was the headquarters of the council, it is probable that, as later in the spring of 1260, other houses in the vicinity were occupied by his colleagues.[3] They deliberated apart, and did not follow the king as a body, for although Henry left Westminster early in August only to return for the feast of his patron saint, St. Edward the Confessor, on October 13, the barons sat in council daily at the New Temple or elsewhere.[4] They had, as our letter-writer says, much arduous business before them. They were engaged, says the London chronicler, "super usibus et consuetudinibus regni in melius conformandis". It would be absurd to suggest that the whole body remained at Westminster; some would be with the king, others had public duties or private business to consider; but the evidence does suggest that this council, unlike any previous council in English history, was not regarded and did not behave as an expression of the Curia Regis.

The first parliament of the official year was to meet in the octaves of Michaelmas and would thus coincide with the gathering of English society about the king at the feast of St. Edward. The business which at this time aroused most public interest was undoubtedly the reform of local government. Some progress was made during the summer on the lines laid down at Oxford, but a royal proclamation of October 20 shows that anxiety had found expression in the shires lest necessary changes and remedies should be delayed.[5] Two days

[1] *Ann. Monast.* i. 445.
[2] *Chronica majora* (ed. Luard), v. 706.
[3] See the interesting description of the way in which the barons who attended the April parliament of 1260 were lodged, in the London chronicle, *Chr. majorum et vicecomitum*, pp. 44-5.
[4] *Chr. majorum et vicecomitum*, p. 39.
[5] *Royal Letters*, ii. 130-32, from the Patent Roll; also in Burton, *Ann. Monast.* i. 453-5.

earlier, in the presence of the whole council and many more gathered in this time of parliament, King Henry had issued, in French and English, the decree which called upon all true men to swear that they would hold and help each other to hold and defend the arrangements made by the council. This famous decree may be regarded as the first public ratification of the revolution, giving it the character of a national enterprise. In the first parliament of the new order, on the eve of a new regnal year, the king brought his people into partnership with him in the adhesion which he had promised in his letters patent of May 2 and August 4. The word used to describe the acts of the council is significant: it is not provisions but *establissements*, in English *isetnesses*.[1] As we shall see, this word is sharply distinguished from the word " provision " in the Provisions of Westminster.

What these *establissements* were, or what steps were taken to execute them, falls outside the scope of this paper. No collection of them has yet been found, although some record was doubtless kept.[2] But we have the sketchy programmes in the so-called Provisions of Oxford and in the anonymous letter already quoted; we have the long list of grievances presented by the whole body of barons at Oxford; and we have, in the plea rolls and the records of chancery and exchequer, a great deal of scattered evidence about the actual work done by council and parliament. When this evidence has been collected and discussed, no doubt will any longer be possible about the reality and the wide range of council rule during the years 1258–1260.[3] In any discussion of the Provisions of Westminster, the work of the second Michaelmas parliament held under the new régime, we should not lose sight of the fact that the council, with the parliamentary committee of Twelve, was no sham, but the seat and source of actual government throughout the year 1259. It controlled the use of the Great Seal, co-operated with the justiciar and judges, supervised the exchequer.

This general statement requires some explanation. In his *Chapters in the Administrative History of Medieval England* Professor Tout has shown again and again how slightly baronial revolutions interrupted the transaction of normal administrative business or the royal control of the king's household. His description of wardrobe, chancery, exchequer is smooth and continuous for the whole period between the reigns of John and Edward II. In 1258 the baronial leaders, even if we take no account of the professions of mutual loyalty between king

[1] *Foedera*, i. 377-8. The insistence upon a particular oath to be taken by castellans —one of the " Provisions " of Oxford—was described at the time as an *établissement*.

[2] Cf. the reference in October 1259 to the " roules de ces establissimenz " (*Ann. Mon.* i. 476) and the comment on this passage below.

[3] The researches of Dr. E. F. Jacob, to whom I am deeply indebted, have had especially notable results; and we may expect much from the investigations of two Manchester graduates, Mr. Treharne and Mr. Tyson.

and baronage, had no intention of changing the machinery of government. They made comparatively few changes in its personnel, and, once the Poitevins were removed, pursued no vendetta. Yet the most casual survey of the records for the year 1258–59 is sufficient to show that the new council kept a tight hold of the daily administration. The councillors regarded themselves as jointly responsible, working, as Earl Simon put it in 1260, for " la commun emprise ". Deeds done or words said in council (*devant le conseil*) must be attacked and defended in council.[1] A leading member of the council could go to the exchequer, apparently in the course of business, break open the chests and take away a record which he required.[2] If we take the letters patent for the forty-third year of King Henry (October 28, 1258, to October 27, 1259) we find that, while presentations to churches, letters of protection, most of the pardons, and many grants were issued without reference to the council, the authentication of the council or of one or more of its members was carefully noted by the chancery clerks when they enrolled all letters of importance. The chancellor had sworn his oath that this should be done.[3] On one occasion the justiciar and council deprived one of their own number of the custody of Dover Castle because, acting on letters patent issued under the Great Seal and, so the king assured him, authorised by the council, he had admitted a papal nuncio to England. He had broken his oath, Bigod argued, for before taking such important action he should have sought further instructions.[4] It was the whole council which authorised the fortification of castles and houses, the payment of royal debts or important grants, the appointment of escheators, wardens of bishoprics, forests, or of royal demesne, the issue of loans. It carefully regulated the finances of the bishopric of Winchester vacated by the bishop's exile, dealt with valuable wardships, appointed castellans, and exacted the castellans' oath, treated with Llywelyn ap Gruffydd, controlled the movements of royal agents abroad, gave its support to the king in his disputes with ecclesiastical authorities like the dean and chapter of York. And the justiciar or one or two members of council similarly authorised the issue of letters on more technical and less important matters which did not fall within the limits of routine business. King Henry might well say, as he said a

[1] See Simon's defence in Bémont's *Simon de Montfort*, pp. 343-353.

[2] L.T.R. Memoranda Roll, No. 34, 42-43 Henry III. m. 1. " Memorandum quod R. comes Glovern' venit ad scaccarium primo die Octobris (1258) hoc est die martis proximo post festum sancti Michaelis et de consilio J. fil. Galfridi et baronum de scaccario, fractis sigillis Hugonis le Bigod justiciarii et Ph. Lovel thesaurarii que erant apposita magnis forulis, ac extracto rotulo anni XL, signavit predictos forulos signo suo."

[3] " E ke il ne ensele hors de curs par la sule volunte del rei, mes le face par le cunseil ke serra entur le rei."

[4] On the circumstances which led to Richard de Gray's removal from Dover in September 1259, see Mr. R. F. Treharne's paper in the *English Historical Review* for July 1925, vol. xl.

year or so later, that the three sources of government, seal, exchequer, the law, had been under rigid control.[1]

The council reached its decisions by a majority vote, and few things would be more interesting than an account of one of its debates. Peter of Savoy and John Mansel, who were friends of the king, would not always agree with Gloucester and Mortimer, nor the archbishop with his brother of Worcester, and as time went on the justiciar, with his store of new experience, would see difficulties where the other barons would see none. Moreover, Gloucester and Leicester differed widely in temperament and outlook. The first serious clash between them, indeed the first crisis in the history of the council, came in the second or Candlemas parliament of the year 1258–59 and lasted through February and March 1259. It arose over the alleged abuses within the baronial franchises. Historians generally imply that legislation upon this matter had from the outset been an item in the baronial programme. Except for a passage in the annals of Dunstable,[2] I can find no evidence of this. The Petitions of the Barons refer to the rights of baronial courts and the disabilities to which they were subjected, but only one clause could possibly refer to the abuse of baronial privileges.[3] Yet the problems caused by the growth of baronial franchises were always present, and, as they affected the crown and local officials no less than the tenants, they inevitably became an important issue in the period of legislative and administrative revision. After long disputes, the council, again sitting at the Temple, issued a provision sometime in March upon the subject of baronial courts. This *providentia*, as it is styled, is a first draft of the later Provisions of Westminster. It was not enrolled, but a copy came to Matthew Paris and was added by him to his document book or Liber Additamentorum. It will be edited before long, I hope, by Dr. E. F. Jacob.[4] The title says that it was published (*publicata*), but there is no evidence that it was issued to the shire courts. About the same time, however,

[1] Cotton. MS. Tib. B. iv. ff. 214-18. On this document see below, p. 132. Cf. Henry's remark in February 1261, perhaps taken by the St. Albans chronicler from this very document: "me non quasi dominum, sed quasi ministrum, vestrae subjugasse custodiae" (*Flores Historiarum* (R.S.), ii. 464).

[2] *Ann. Mon.* iii. 209. The passage reads like an expansion of the more vague terms of the oath sworn by the baronage as a whole (*le commun de Engleterre*).

[3] The last clause, on the intervention of superior lords in local courts in cases transferred to the local courts under a writ of right. Even here the grievance was primarily that of the immediate lord whose judicial rights were threatened by the claim of the overlord.

[4] Cott. MS. Nero D. i. f. 82: "Provisio magnatum Anglie publicata apud Novum Templum mense marcii anno regni regis Henrici xliij". Luard gives the title and the opening clauses in the appendix to the Additamenta (*Chr. maj.* vi. 696 and note). Dr. Jacob has discovered another and longer text of the same document in Camb. Univ. MS. Mm. i. 27, f. 73v-74: "Providencia baronum Anglie anno regni regis Henrici xlii de sectis curiarum". The date xlii is, I think, merely a scribal error for xliii. The MS. belongs to the end of the century. Dr. Jacob, however, is inclined to think that this is actually a series of provisions drafted in the summer of 1258, and afterwards taken up in part in the spring of 1259.

the king was authorised to issue throughout the country, to be read in every shire and hundred, a formal promise by the parliament, that is by the council and the committee of Twelve, that the whole programme of inquiry and reform, hitherto confined to the royal administration, would be applied in the franchises, and that justices would be appointed to investigate abuses. The following clause is particularly suggestive, for it shows that during the next six months the council proposed also to continue its work upon matters affecting the judicial and financial rights of the crown. The Fifteen and Twelve promise that "what the King's Council should establish between that date (March 28) and the feast of All Saints then next (November 1) with respect to the king and his subjects, as to suit of courts and amercements and socage wards and his farms and other manner of franchises, and the ordinances which should be for the relief of the state of the kingdom, they would keep with respect to them[selves] and their subjects for themselves and their heirs ".[1]

When we turn to the Provisions of Westminster, we find that this is precisely what happened. At the Michaelmas parliament the Fifteen and Twelve took up and revised the provisions which they had made at the Temple in March,—this is the document enrolled on the Close Roll and included in the Statutes of the Realm,—and they *also* drew up a very important series of decrees relating to every aspect of the royal administration. This part of their work, as a description of baronial control, is even more illuminating than the "Provisions of Oxford". The true facts have been obscured for the simple reason that only the first document, translated into Latin, was enrolled on a chancery roll. In its original form this was written in French and was part of a much longer series of clauses. Stubbs, as one would expect, called attention to this, but dismissed it because he interpreted the additional clauses in such a way as to give an impression entirely opposite of the true one. In his view they were omitted from the Latin provisions on the Close Roll because the Council felt that they had been forced to go too far.[2] If Stubbs had studied them more closely he would have seen that they were omitted because they did not deal, as the other provisions deal, with matters which were daily causing trouble in the courts, and upon which the justiciar and his colleagues were anxious for instructions. The Provisions of Westminster in the narrow and usual sense of the term dealt in the main with problems of the franchises and their relation to the royal courts—problems which had perplexed the judges in the eyres of 1258–9 but would, in the eyres of 1259–60, be decided in accordance

[1] Pat. Roll 43 Henry III. m. 10, printed in the *Foedera*, i. 381. I quote the version given in the Lords Reports on the Dignity of the Peerage (1826), i. 130, first report, of 1820. The discussion of our parliamentary history during 1259–1260, contained in this report, is still very helpful.

[2] *Const. History*, ii. 84 (fourth edition).

with the decision of parliament.[1] The long French document of which the Latin provisions originally formed part covered much more ground and was no more suitable for this kind of publication than the Provisions of Oxford had been. So far from weakening the power of the Council it elaborated and strengthened its control. In part doubtless it was, as the London chronicler says, a *compositio*. The arrangement for the future election of sheriffs by the shire courts and the exchequer increased the power of the knights. But this clause was not, as Stubbs supposed, a stringent attempt to limit the power of the council. It gave more power to the government than the Provisions of Oxford had given. It was to come into force, and may have been enforced, at Michaelmas 1260, and when, in 1261, the king joined issue with the barons on the appointment of sheriffs, it was this very *compromissum* which he succeeded in setting on one side.[2] The other clauses of the additional provisions of 1259 explicitly define the control of the council over the judges, exchequer, and household.

Both the St. Albans chronicler and the Burton annalist had copies of the original. A document in the *Liber Additamentorum* gives an abbreviated version of the "administrative" clauses, but it is significant that in this copy these were separated from the rest and were written before them.[3] The Burton annalist gives the document as one, the administrative clauses at the end. He then copied out a Latin version of the "legislative" provisions which differs from that on the Close Roll and seems to be an earlier and incorrect, though official, translation.[4] The French document ends with a clause defining very precisely the authorship of the Fifteen and the Twelve:

> Ces sunt les purveances et les establissimenz fetz a Westmoster al parlament a la saint Michel par le rei et sun conseil et les xii par le commun conseil esluz par devant la communance de Engletere, ke dunke fu a Westmuster le an del regne Henri le fiz le roi Johan quarantime terz.

If we set this passage beside the references in the chronicles, and notably beside the London chronicler quoted at the beginning of this paper, its phrases become very significant.

In the first place, we must clearly revise our conception of the rôle played by the "communitas bacheleriae Angliae", at whose instance,

[1] My friend, Mr. R. F. Treharne, who has examined the Assize Rolls in the Public Record Office for the period August 1258 to October 1259 (Nos. 362, 873, 1187, 1188), tells me that he has found cases brought before the justiciar and his associates which raised issues dealt with by about seventeen clauses in the Provisions of Westminster.

[2] See Annals of Osney in *Annal. Monast.* iv. 128-9; *Royal Letters*, ii. 198; *Foedera*, i. 415. Cf. Dover Chronicle in Gervase of Canterbury (R.S.), ii. 213.

[3] Cott. MS. Nero D. i. f. 137b. Luard did not print this part of the manuscript, and I owe the statement given above to Dr. E. F. Jacob.

[4] *Ann. Monast.* i. 480-84. This translation deserves more attention than it has received. It looks like a rather careless draft by a clerk who did not follow the original intelligently, or who wrote it from dictation.

says the Burton annalist, this long document was compiled. The bachelors, whoever they were, could have done no more than hasten the deliberations of the Council of Twelve, and their intervention was intended to strengthen the hands of their champions in the Council in the framing of those clauses of the Provisions which had been drafted over six months before. The Council did exactly what it had intended to do, and what we might have expected it to do. It is worth noting that an outburst of impatience, very similar to that of the bachelors, may very well have provoked the royal proclamation a year before, also at a Michaelmas parliament, about the reforms in local administration. We must remember that the parliament, on each occasion, met at Westminster at the time of the feast of St. Edward, and also of the Michaelmas session of the exchequer. Westminster was crowded, not only with great ecclesiastics and barons gathered for a great ceremony of church and state, but also with local juries, accountants, and others who had business at the exchequer or were retainers of the great men. The latter were in the main substantial men, tenants of lands worth from ten to twenty pounds a year, liable to distraint of knighthood, or actually knights. They had long experience of the abuses, alike in shire, hundred, or baronial courts. Nothing is more likely than that a group of these persons formed themselves into a temporary association, perhaps a sworn association, and seeking out the young lord Edward, a lad of twenty, asked him to see that justice was done by the great men as the great men had seen that justice was done by the king. The style "communitas bacheleriae Angliae" was not invented by the annalist; he must have had it from a correspondent who had access to documents, perhaps the same man as wrote the letter describing the proceedings at Oxford in the previous year. The presumption is that the writer was in close touch with Edward, and that otherwise he would not have troubled to report an incident unknown to any other chronicler.[1]

Secondly, the words "les xii par le commun conseil esluz par devant la communance d'Engletere, ke dunke fu a Westmuster" seem to imply that the Committee of Twelve was elected annually, just as the justiciar, treasurer, and chancellor were. "Le commune

[1] The reader will observe that I am more conservative in my interpretation of the famous phrase "communitas bacheleriae Angliae" than Professor Tout has taught us to be (*Eng. Hist. Review*, 1902, xvii. 89-92). The evidence which he has collected shows how vague the term "bachelor" was; but at this period it was certainly used to describe those members of a baronial household who, while belonging to the "knightly" class, *i.e.* the landholders liable to distraint of knighthood, had not been knighted. Cf. the list of the Earl of Gloucester's followers in 1267; see *Calendar of Patent Rolls*, 1266–1272, pp. 145-7. One of these, John de Traylei, appears in 1256 among the men holding fifteen librates of land, not yet distrained to knighthood (Chancery Miscellanea $\frac{1}{7}$, inquiry of 40 Henry III.). Men of this class had not the social position of the young aristocrats who were sometimes called bachelors. They belonged to the class from which local juries were chosen, the good and law-worthy men of substance in the shires.

de la tere ", " communance ", or " commune d'Engletere " are phrases always used in these years of the baronage as a whole, and the baronage always gathered about Henry III. at this particular time of the year. In Latin the last words would run : " duodecim communi consilio electi a communitate baronum Anglie ". The bachelors may have intended to parody this when they called themselves the "communitas bacheleriae Angliae ".

Lastly, I would call attention to the words " les purveances et les establissimenz ". As a rule it is wrong to distinguish sharply general legislative terms, statute, ordinance, provision, establishment, and the like.[1] They are used indifferently, and some confusion has been caused in our legal history by attempts to give them rigid and separate meanings. Yet in this case I am inclined to think that a distinction was intended between the legislative and administrative clauses of the Westminster document, and I fancy that, if we had the original title, we might find that a similar distinction was made in the decisions taken at Oxford in 1258.[2] The " Provisions " of Westminster, as we have seen, were divided into two parts, the one mainly legislative, the other administrative, and it would be natural to find names for them. The latter would be the matters " set " or established. Two bits of evidence go to confirm this view. The phrase used by the London chronicler, " usus et leges ", is a fairly good translation of the French phrase, and suggests that the whole document was read at the great meeting in Westminster Hall, and that it was read in French. The barons wished to give publicity to all that they had done to define their administration, not only to their provisions about baronial courts. Again, two or three clauses in the document itself, unless they are a confused jumble of words, make it clear that the provisions and the establishments were distinguished from each other. The justices and their baronial assessors are to see that the establishments made or to be made for the profit of the realm shall be sent to the shires ; provisions made since the beginning of these establishments are to be maintained ; the rolls of the establishments are to be read and confirmed.[3] The last words suggest that a separate record had been kept of the various changes established at or since the Oxford Parliament. However all this may be, it will be convenient to refer to the administrative clauses of the settlement of 1259 as the Establishments of Westminster, and to keep the word Provisions for the document which usually goes by that name.

[1] See Plucknett, *Statutes and their Interpretation in the First Half of the Fourteenth Century* (1922).

[2] In Latin *provisio* covers everything, and much of the so-called " Provisions of Oxford " is in Latin. It has not been noted, however, that in the series of notes and memoranda given by the Burton annalist, only the first, regarding the local investigation into the rule of the sheriffs, is definitely called " provisio facta apud Oxoniam ". As I have already pointed out, the castellan's oath is called an *établissement*.

[3] *Ann. Monast.* i. 476.

The Establishments recognised the fact that the whole council could not sit together permanently. Some members, Leicester, Gloucester, and Mansel among them, were going with the king to France. It was decided that, during the king's absence, the justiciar should be assisted by the Archbishop of Canterbury, the Bishop of Worcester, the Earl Marshal, the Earl of Warwick, Philip Basset (one of the Committee of Twelve), and Roger Mortimer. We may see this body at work in an interesting writ, ordering the sheriffs to come together on November 19 with four knights from each shire

ad audiendum et faciendum precepta Regis dicto vicecomite et eis ore plenius exponenda per H. le Bigod justiciarium et alios quos ei Rex adjunxit ad custodiam regni sui dum moram traxerit in partibus transmarinis secundum provisionem factam per magnatos de consilio Regis.[1]

The justiciar had the disposal of the exchequer seal, which was in the keeping of Walter de Merton, the great seal having gone to France with the king.[2] He directed the judiciary and finance with the aid of other assessors, chosen from the Fifteen or the Twelve. The exchequer and the court of Common Pleas or Bench at Westminster each had two baronial assessors, the justices on eyre had one, *i.e.* one for each of the six circuits into which the country was divided.[3] In August, earlier in the year, the council had provided that a select group of seven judges should alone be qualified for the more responsible judicial work (*speciales justiciarie*),[4] and these men seem henceforth to have had precedence in the judicial body. Two of them, Roger of Thurkelby and Henry of Bath, were now closely associated with the administration. They were to act with the justiciar, the treasurer, and Master Thomas of Wymondham as a finance committee for the sale of wardships, the settlement of the vexed question of the queen's gold, an investigation at the exchequer into the tallages levied during the reign, and the possible revenue which might be anticipated from this source, and for the direction of pleas regarding services. Also, they were to assist the justiciar and exchequer in the appointment of

[1] K.R. Mem. Roll, No. 33, m. 4. The business was doubtless connected with the inquiry by four knights of each shire into the local administration, a measure repeated in the establishments of 1259, though originated in 1258. It may be observed that the word *establissement* is not used in any Latin equivalent.

[2] K.R. Mem. Roll, No. 33, m. 4 d. The use of the great seal by the king in France is mentioned in *Cal. Pat. Rolls*, 1258–1266, p. 67.

[3] Close Roll 44 Henry III. m. 18 d. (November 1259). The provision entered here shows some elaboration of the original proposal. One councillor, one of the body of Twelve, and one judge were to go into each circuit: " Provisio de illis qui de consilio una cum justiciariis itinerabunt per diversa loca ad inquisiciones faciendas et transgressiones corrigendas, videlicet quod sex de concilio Regis eligantur quorum quilibet una cum aliquo de duodecim et aliquo de justiciariis ad hoc eligandis in uno sex locorum per Angliam, que deberit dividi per comitatus, eat et inquirat de transgressionibus factis secundum articulos quos habebunt ordinatos per consilium ", etc.

[4] Close Roll 43 Henry III. 7 d.; see Maitland, *Bracton's Note-Book*, i. 20. The seven were Thurkelby, Bath, Bracton, Erdinton, Preston, Wilton, Wyvil.

sheriffs for the coming year.[1] King Henry bitterly resented the loss of his control over the sale of wardships, and, a year or so later, made a great point of it in his disputes with the council. The reply of the council shows that the justiciar had hoped to make the profits of wardships and escheats the basis of a financial reform for the payment of the king's debts and the maintenance of the royal household.[2]

The Establishments contemplated a permanent system of delegation apart from these more or less temporary measures. At each succeeding parliament two or three members of council were to be appointed to be with the king, without prejudice to the rights of the other members to sit as councillors if they should be summoned or happen to be at court on public or private business. If business of serious and urgent importance were to arise between the dates of parliament the whole council was to be summoned by writ, and, unless secrecy were necessary, the occasion of the summons was to be put in the writ. We may see here an anticipation of the later constitution of 1264, which made Earl Simon the actual, though not nominal, head of affairs. Another step in the same direction was taken in the Michaelmas parliament of 1260, when the council delegated the election of the justiciar, treasurer, and chancellor to a committee of five.[3]

By the autumn of 1260, however, the new constitution had already begun to totter. The council kept unity and control until the end of the year, and was strong enough, after Bigod's resignation or rejection, to elect Despenser as justiciar; but internal division had shaken it, and with the troubles of this year we have already entered upon a new phase in the history of the revolution. The king had begun to call the constitution in question. He had tried to prevent the meeting of the Candlemas parliament in February; he had put Earl Simon formally on the defensive in July; and then, gaining confidence from his reliance on French gold and his understanding with the Pope, he entered upon a dispute with the council as a body. One of the first results of these events was the disappearance of the parliamentary committee of Twelve. It is mentioned early in 1261,[4] and we may assume that it acted in the three statutory parliaments of 1260; but it has not been noticed, I think, that in April of this year 1260, between the parliaments of February and July, the justiciar, acting on royal instructions, took the responsibility of summoning a parliament

[1] The new method of appointment was not to come into force until Michaelmas 1260. One of Henry of Bath's last appearances in the records was on October 28, 1260, when he authorised letters to the sheriff of Somerset on behalf of the priory of Witham, "Per Henricum de Bathonia et Henricum de Bratton et per totum consilium" (Close Roll 44 Henry III. m. 1).

[2] This very illuminating discussion, which can be dated early in the year 1261, has been found by Dr. Jacob in the Cottonian MS., Tiberius B. iv. ff. 214 b-218. A critical edition of this text will shortly be published by Dr. Jacob.

[3] *Ibid.* f. 215 b.

[4] In the answers of the council to the king's complaints (see above).

in the older sense—a *generale parlamentum*,[1] or meeting of the great council of the baronage. Rumours were abroad that the lord Edward, inspired by Earl Simon, was trying to seize the throne before Henry's return from France. The story was probably false, but a quarrel between Edward and the Earl of Gloucester was real enough, and caused serious alarm to Bigod and Earl Richard, King of the Romans. In order to allay anxiety the justiciar did what the king commanded. A memorandum in the Close Roll gives the names of those to whom the writ was sent, and we find in the same record a lively picture of the haste with which the writs were despatched. Walter de Merton, Keeper of the Seal, was at his manor of Malden, in Surrey, when on the Thursday before Easter (March 30) he received Bigod's instructions :

De summonicione servicii regis usque London' a die Pasch' in tres septimanas.

Memorandum quod die Iovis proximo ante Pasch' Dominus W. de Merton mandatum H. le Bygod justiciarii regis Anglie recipit in hec verba : H. le Bygod justiciarius regis Anglie dilecto et speciali amico suo domino W. de Merton salutem quam sibi. Mandatum domini regis recepimus in hec verba hoc die Mercurii ante Pasch' :

H. dei gracia etc. Hugoni le Bygod justiciario Anglie salutem. Mandamus vobis quod omnes illos quorum nomina inseruntur in cedula presentibus inclusa summoneri faciatis quod sint London' a die Pasch' in tres septimanas cum serviciis que nobis debent, audituri ibidem mandatum nostrum et facturi quod eisdem injunxeritis ex parte nostra. Et hoc sicut honorem nostrum diligitis nullatenus omittatis. T. me ipso apud sanctum Audomarum xxvii die Marcii anno regni nostri xliii^to^.

Et ideo vobis mandamus ex parte domini regis quatinus visis litteris istis brevia domini regis fieri faciatis per que omnes contenti in eadem cedula, quam vobis presentibus inclusam mittimus, mandentur quod sint London' ad terminum predictum et sicut predictum est, et eadem brevia sine dilacione mitti faciatis per nuncios cancellar[ie] sicut moris est, providentes ob amorem nostri quod taliter fiat istud negocium quod de pignicie [*sic*] seu infidelitate redargui non debeamus nec possimus. Datum apud parcum Windesor die Mercurii predicto. *Cedula custodiatur secreciori modo quo potest.*

The schedule, drawn up in France and despatched by King Henry three days before, follows. It contains the names of three bishops, Salisbury, Exeter, and Norwich, of the abbots of Bury St. Edmunds and Glastonbury, of seven earls (*excluding* the earls of Cornwall, Leicester, and Derby), and of no less than ninety-nine barons. Then comes the note of the chancery clerk :

Sciendum est quod die Jovis proximo ante Pasch' ut predictum est recepit

[1] *Chr majorum et vicecomitum*, p. 44. The omission of Simon de Montfort's name from the list of those summoned (see below) is significant. Gloucester, who had accompanied the king to France, was summoned. The episode goes to confirm the chronicles, and perhaps prepared the way for the formal attack on Earl Simon in the July parliament. See the Dunstable Annals (*Ann. Monast.* iii. 215) and the documents published by Bémont (*Simon de Montfort*, pp. 343-53) and Jacob (*Eng. Hist. Review*, 1922, xxxvii. 80).

dictus dominus W. de Merton mandatum predictum et eodem die in mensa. Et eodem die et in mane conscripta fuerunt et consignata brevia Regis ad singulas personas supradictas in forma predicta apud Maldon. Et die sabbati (Easter Eve) post missam et mensam statim tradita fuerunt deferenda per nuncios illis quibus diriguntur una cum brevibus ad vicecomites ut ipsi propter brevitatem temporis ea deferri facerent incontinenti per nuncios diversos.[1]

The writs summoned the parliament for April 23, three weeks later. They were dated [the phrase is added in a later hand on the Close Roll], "teste H. le Bygod justitiario nostro apud Westmonasterium xxix die Marcii". The incident shows that, by means of the messengers of chancery and the sheriffs, it was possible to collect the baronage of England within three weeks.[2] It illustrates the method of attestation: the keeper of the seal had gone with the seal to spend Easter at his country house, and there, acting on the written instructions of the justiciar from Windsor, prepared and sent out writs dated a day or two before at Westminster.

And, to conclude, the incident shows that the justiciar was prepared to disregard the new constitution in order to avert a crisis. His action may have brought his great career as head of the baronial party to a close; it certainly marks a turning-point in the history of the revolution. A year or so later Henry was strong enough to defy Bigod's successor and occupy the Tower of London. The Provisions, not the Establishments, of Westminster were destined to win permanence. In the nature of things a joint administration of barons, royal servants, justices, and exchequer under the direction of a justiciar and council who had control of the great seal, in accordance with the decrees of a parliament whose powers were delegated to it by the whole body of tenants-in-chief, could not endure. I hope that I have said enough to show that it was a reality for more than two years, and that the more closely the records of its work are studied, the more remarkable the experiment will be seen to have been. No other period of medieval history can show so long an episode of fruitful co-operation between a revolutionary baronage and a reluctant king.

F. M. Powicke.

[1] Close Roll 44 Henry III. m. 16 d. The writer, as often, treats *dies* as feminine or masculine, indifferently. I have corrected this.

[2] Wykes says (*Ann. Mon.* iv. 124) that Henry delayed his return until the justiciar had sent him assurances, based on the sealed letters of Edward and the *magnates*. Unless these were given only by the council, the barons must have reached London before April 23, for Henry landed at Dover on that very day.

X

THE KEEPER OF PAPAL BULLS

THE brief list of Papal Bulls which is printed here is apparently to be assigned to A.D. 1269 or a little earlier. It was found recently among other miscellanea and fragments of little value, most of which seem to have come from the Tower of London, and to have been regarded for that reason as records of the Chancery. Their character agrees well in most cases with such an origin, but it must be remembered that the Tower contained some records of other departments, for instance, early records of the Exchequer, and therefore single documents found there cannot be assigned with certainty to the Chancery.[1]

The list appears to have been made in order to justify the collection by Henry III. of a tenth of ecclesiastical property estimated according to the "Norwich" taxation of 1254. It was not a complete list of the Bulls in the possession of Henry III., but a special return made by the keeper of them and preserved for reference. The endorsements show that he used it as a place for notes of the production and replacement of the documents in his custody.

The keeper, John of St. Denis, was one of the king's clerks. We first hear of him in 1268, when he was appointed to hold a financial inquiry in Yorkshire, where there seems to have been some uncertainty whether or not the sheriffs appointed since the Provisions of Oxford had accounted at the Exchequer for all the sums raised by them in the county. In the same year he was acting as collector of a clerical tenth, and was employed in the taxation of benefices. In the next year he was appointed to tax ecclesiastical temporalities in the diocese of Norwich. It seems probable that his appointment as Keeper of Papal Bulls and Privileges, of which I have found no record, was closely connected with his activities in the collection of the tenth. In 1270 he was appointed to the custody of the goods of Roger le Bigod, earl of Norfolk, who had just died. In the next year he acted jointly with John of Kirkby, keeper of the Rolls of the Chancery, as judge in an action relating to a prebend of Rouen the corpus of which was in England. A letter of the dean and chapter to the two judges is preserved in the class of *Ancient Correspondence* (viii. 95).

In 1271 John of St. Denis is found witnessing a deed with John of

[1] See below, pp. 231 ff.

Kirkby and William of Hamilton, afterwards Chancellor. We have therefore no hesitation in assigning him, in spite of his financial mission, to the regular staff of the Chancery. It seems likely that the Exchequer was weak at this time, since we find that the next treasurer, Kirkby, came from the Chancery. In February 1272 St. Denis was appointed Keeper of the House of Converted Jews in succession to Adam of Chesterton. He retained his office as Keeper of Bulls, since he is called by that title in 1275, the year in which he lengthened the chapel of the House of Converted Jews, afterwards the Rolls Chapel. He became archdeacon of Rochester in 1278, and died in 1288. He had administered the House of Converted Jews by deputy since 1283. We may probably assign to the previous winter a letter addressed to Burnel, as Chancellor (*Ancient Correspondence*, xxiv. 78), begging him to urge the Exchequer to let him have money to maintain his "starving and shivering" converts.

The Bulls mentioned in the list and endorsements cannot now all be identified with certainty. One or two have probably been lost, but most of them seem to be in the Public Record Office, and to have come there from the Treasury of the Receipt of the Exchequer at Westminster, the proper place of deposit. It is not clear when they were deposited there, but it seems certain that in the early years of Edward I. they were in the custody of a clerk of the Chancery, and most probably either in Chancery Lane or at the Tower. It seems possible that the Exchequer may have reclaimed them on his death. At all events there is on the Close Roll for 1305 an order to the treasurer and chamberlains to deliver all Papal Privileges concerning the estate of the King and the Realm to Robert of Cottingham, controller of the Wardrobe, to be kept at the Tower of London under his seal and that of Adam of Osgodby, Keeper of the Rolls of the Chancery. If this order was carried out, we may presume that these Bulls remained at the Tower at all events until 1320, and possibly later.

CHARLES JOHNSON.

APPENDIX

(1) P.R.O. *Miscellanea* (*Chancery*) *Ble.* 32, No. 1 (16)

DE SUBSIDIO REGI CONCESSO IN SUBSIDIUM TERRE SANCTE PRO NEGOCIO CRUCIS EI ASSIGNANDO CUM ITER ARRIPUERIT TRANSMARINUM

LITTERA Innocencii pape quarti de decima Regi concessa per quinquennium in Anglia et in aliis terris Regis.

Item alia littera de redempcionibus votorum indistincte legatis relictis et aliis in subsidium terre sancte deputatis.

Item alia littera ejusdem de decima danda Regi de maneriis episcoporum et prelatorum.

Item alia littera de vicesima regni Scocie Regi assignanda in subsidium terre sancte per triennium.

Item alia littera de pecunia redempcionis votorum legatorum relictorum et aliorum crucesignatis jam mortuis vel inhabilibus ad transfretandum liberata Regi assignanda, etc.

Item alia littera quod Abbas Westmonasteriensis faciat assignare Regi pecuniam de usuris et illicite adquisitis si non sint qui ea possint repetere juste in regno Anglie et in aliis terris Regis.

(*A space of 2 in. is here left blank.*)

Item alia littera Alexandri pape de vicesima Scocie per aliud triennium.

Item alia de redempcionibus votorum legatis et aliis concessis in subsidium terre sancte Regi assignandis [1] in regno Scocie.

Item alia littera ejusdem pape de fructibus beneficiorum non residencium Regi assignandis nisi sint in scolis vel apud Sedem apostolicam vel in peregrinacione vel in negociis ecclesiarum ubi habent beneficia.

Item alia littera de decima habenda secundum veram estimacionem non obstante antiqua estimacione.

Item alia littera quod Abbas Westmonasteriensis compellat collectores pecunie redempcionis votorum legatorum relictorum in subsidium terre sancte ante crucesignacionem Regis ad reddendum ei racionem.

Item alia quod bona ab intestato decedencium colligantur et Regi assignentur pro negocio crucis.

Item alia littera ejusdem pape directa Archiepiscopo Cantuariensi et magistro Rostando de decima colligenda et de redempcionibus votorum crucesignatorum legatis indistincte ac fructibus beneficiorum vacancium et de quibuscumque aliis obvencionibus regi concessis pro sui voti prosecucione coligendis.

De negocio Sicilie

A domino Innocencio quod ecclesie Anglie et aliarum terrarum Regis obligari possint pro mutuo contrahendo pro negocio Sicilie.

Item ab eodem quod promisit Regi solvere centum millia librarum Turonensium ad prosequendum negocium illud.

A domino Alexandro de voto regis Anglie et Regis Norwagie et voto crucesignatorum Anglie et regni Norwagie commutandis in negocium Sicilie et quod pecunia debilium et defunctorum pro redempcione votorum suorum assignetur una cum pecunia a crucesignatis recepta et eis assignata in prosecucionem voti sui regi restituatur nisi ipsi personaliter transfretaverint.

Item redempciones votorum relicta et le[g]ata et alie obvenciones deputate in subsidium terre sancte tam in Anglia quam in aliis terris Regis convertantur in execucionem negocii Sicilie, vel ipsi crucesignati personaliter exequantur votum suum.

Item multe alie gracie concesse fuerunt Regi pro negocio crucis que non faciunt mencionem de negocio Sicilie set mutato voto crucis videtur quod omnes gracie ille in mutacionem illam debeant converti eo quod ante mutacionem illam regi concesse fuerunt pro voto crucis.

(*Endorsed.*)

Memorandum quod dominica proxima post translacionem beati Thome martiris anno gracie m°.cc°.lxix°. extraxit Johannes de Sancto Dionisio privilegium de retinendis episcopis sibi ad suum consilium assistentibus.

[1] MS. assignanda.

Idem extraxit quoddam privilegium super capellanis Regiis cum ejusdem conservatoriis in crastino animarum anno LIIII°.

Et eadem restituit in coffro in crastino Sancti Martini.

Item Johannes extraxit privilegium super confirmacione Jurium regiorum in ecclesiis, etc.

Item privilegium de Anglis non trahendis extra regnum in causa, etc., die Lune post festum Sancti Andree.

(2) P.R.O. *Ancient Correspondence*, vol. xxiv. No. 78

[Reverendiss]imo domino suo se totum semper humillimum et devotum. Dominacioni vestre supplico devocione qua possum quatinus de conversis vestris [pauperibus] qui jam fame pariter et frigore cruciantur memoriam habere dignemini, precipientes si placet quod breve regium [de Liberacio]ne dictis conversis ad suam sustentacionem de termino sancti Michaelis proximo jam preterito a Domino nostro Rege deputata Thesaurario [et Camerari]is de Scaccario sine difficultatis incomodo dirigatur. Licet enim multa Domino Regi et vobis hiis diebus in[cumb]ant in partibus ubi estis, propter hoc tamen non sunt omittenda si placet ex hac parte que spiritu dei aguntur et divino [aux]ilio sunt concessa. Quia non solum viribus hominum et virtute armorum, set elemosinis et oracionum suffragiis bella [vi]ncuntur et hostium fortitudo conteritur. Nec credo quod sit locus in Anglia ubi saluberrius fiant oracionum et laudum sacrificia pro Domino Rege et suis quam in hac minima Domo sua et vestra. Et novit deus quod nisi eisdem conversis, ut dictum est, subveniatur ad presens, non restat nisi, quod absit, in dispersione sua deficiant et cum confusione mendicent. Super quibus credatis si placet R. clerico meo et Johanni de Norwico clerico et converso, quem nostis, presencium portitoribus. Ego ad vos personaliter accessissem si status corporis, qui nondum ad tot viarum discrimina sufficeret, aliquatenus permisisset. Super quo meam si placet habere velitis absenciam excusatam. Supplico insuper Dominacioni vestre devocione qua possum quatinus litteram regiam deprecatoriam una cum vestra si placet juxta tenorem quem vobis modo transmitto domino Norwicensi episcopo dirigendam concedere dignemini mihi vestro. Valeat salus et prosperitas vestra per tempora diuturna.

Addressed on back]

Domino Bathoniensi et Wellensi Episcopo Cancellario Domini Regis.
per suum J. de Sancto Dionisio.

Note.—It appears from the account of John of St. Denis (P.R.O. Accounts, etc., 249/24), that owing to the death of the Abbot of Westminster and the change of treasurers, no payments for the eleventh year of Edward I. (A.D. 1283–4) were received from the exchequer, but the allusion to the Welsh war seems to fix this document to the previous year.

XI

LES "OVERDRAGHES" ET LES "PORTES D'EAU" EN FLANDRE AU XIIIe SIÈCLE, À PROPOS D'UNE CHARTE INÉDITE PROVENANT DES ARCHIVES DE LA VILLE D'YPRES

LES nombreux cours d'eau que possède la Flandre ont été utilisés de bonne heure pour la circulation des denrées et des marchandises. Rien d'étonnant à cela, si l'on songe à l'extraordinaire activité prise dans ce pays, depuis le XIIe siècle, par le commerce et par l'industrie. Mais pour pouvoir se servir des rivières comme de moyens de transport, des travaux d'art étaient indispensables. Il fallait tout d'abord empêcher le mouvement des marées de faire alternativement monter et descendre le niveau des eaux intérieures qui, par suite de la très faible élévation de la plaine flamande, étaient soumises jusqu'à une grande distance des côtes aux oscillations du flux et du reflux. D'autre part, il importait de maintenir ces mêmes eaux à une profondeur constante si on voulait en assurer la navigabilité durant toutes les saisons de l'année. Cela était d'autant plus indispensable qu'elles furent forcées de bonne heure d'alimenter de nombreux canaux et que leur débit s'en trouva diminué d'autant.

Il suffira de rappeler ici quelques faits.

Des canaux furent creusés : en 1183, de Furnes à Dixmude,[1] en 1187, dans le territoire de Poperinghe,[2] en 1243, d'Ardenbourg à la mer,[3] en 1251, de Gand à Ardenbourg [4] et de Nieuport à Ypres,[5] en 1290, d'Ypres à Noordschooten,[6] en 1271, de Lille à La Bassée.[7]

Pour assurer à la navigation des profondeurs qui fussent toujours les mêmes, il n'y avait d'autre moyen que d'établir des barrages de distance en distance dans les cours d'eau. Mais il fallait que ces barrages pussent livrer passage aux bateaux remontant ou descendant

[1] Piot, *Cartulaire de l'Abbaye d'Eename*, No. 68.

[2] Warnkoenig, *Flandrische Staats- und Rechtsgeschichte*, t. ii., Urkundenbuch, 2e partie, p. 105.

[3] Kluit, *Historia critica comitatus Hollandiae et Zelandiae*, t. iii. p. 486.

[4] Roisin, *Franchises, lois et coutumes de la ville de Lille*, publiées par Brun-Lavainne (Lille, 1842), p. 285.

[5] Warnkoenig-Gheldolf, *Histoire de la Flandre*, t. iii. p. 279 et suiv.

[6] *Ibid.* t. v. p. 366.

[7] I. L. A. Diegerick, *Inventaire des archives de l'abbaye de Messines*, No. 147.

les rivières. On pourvut à cette double nécessité de deux manières différentes, soit par l'établissement d' " Overdraghes ", soit par celui de " Portes d'eau ".

On entendait par " overdraghe " (fl. " overdragh " ou " overdrach ") une construction en bois barrant le cours de la rivière et présentant, du côté de l'amont comme du côté de l'aval, un plan incliné. Un cabestan établi sur le rivage servait à hâler les embarcations jusqu'au sommet. Des installations de cette espèce existaient certainement dès le XIIe siècle. Les plus anciennes mentions que j'en connaisse datent des environs de 1160.[1] Depuis lors, le nombre des textes relatifs aux " overdraghes " s'accroît sans cesse jusqu'à la fin du moyen âge. L'invention des écluses à sas fit peu à peu disparaître ces encombrantes machines. Pourtant quelques-unes d'entre elles subsistèrent longtemps encore. Les archives d'Ypres conservaient un curieux dessin des environs de 1550, représentant les " Overdraghes " en usage à cette époque sur le canal de l'Yperlée. En 1827, il en existait encore un sur le canal de Loo à Furnes.[2]

Les portes d'eau (portae aquae) consistaient en un barrage constitué par des " ventelles ", c'est-à-dire par des planches épaisses superposées les unes aux autres, et engagées par leurs extrémités dans un massif de maçonnerie. Un treuil établi sur ce massif, qui le plus souvent formait voûte au-dessus du barrage, permettait de lever ces planches lorsqu'il fallait livrer passage aux bateaux. Ceux-ci se laissaient entraîner par le courant ou le remontaient grâce à la traction de cables tirés par des hommes ou par des chevaux.

Il va de soi que, pour éviter des accidents, les jours d'ouverture des portes d'eau devaient être soigneusement déterminés, les portes d'aval devant pouvoir laisser passer le flot descendant d'amont. Sur la Lys, en 1236, celles de Menin fonctionnaient les mardis et les vendredis ; celles de Harlebeke, les mercredis et les samedis [3] ; sur la Deule, celles du Quesnoy, en 1266, s'ouvraient tous les jours, de la Saint Martin à la Saint Jean (11 novembre-24 juin) et les mardis, jeudis et samedis le reste de l'année.[4]

Les portes d'eau sont certainement beaucoup plus anciennes que les " Overdraghes ". Un diplôme du roi de France Philippe Ier, dressé entre 1080 et 1085, en mentionne une à Deulemont, au con-

[1] Warnkoenig, *Flandrische Staats- und Rechtsgeschichte*, *loc. cit.* (an. 1187). Cf. une autre mention de 1169 dans l'article cité ci-dessous de Deschamps de Pas.

[2] Voir sur les " Overdraghes " L. Deschamps de Pas, " Ce que c'était qu'un overdrach " (*Annales du comité flamand de France*, t. vi. p. 210) ; Chan. Van de Putte, *Annales de la Société d'Émulation de Bruges*, 2e série, t. iv. p. 17 ; Edw. Gailliard, *Glossaire flamand de l'Inventaire des Chartes de la ville de Bruges*, p. 470. En 1783, Derival, dans le *Voyageur dans les Pays-Bas*, a décrit de visu l'overdraghe de Fintelle près de Pollinchove. L'appareil avait deux roues que les femmes du pays faisaient tourner.

[3] Roisin, *Franchises, lois, et coutumes de la ville de Lille*, publiées par Brun-Lavainne, pp. 245, 246.

[4] *Ibid.* p. 275. La restriction du nombre des jours d'ouverture en été s'explique sans doute par la moins grande abondance des eaux à cette époque.

fluent de la Lys et de la Deule.[1] Au XIIIe siècle, on les désigne parfois par le mot "sclusa" dont la signification primitive semble être celle de déversoir.[2] Le mot français "rabas", employé à la même époque et qui, en langue flamande, est devenu "rabat" ou "rabot", a été depuis la même époque appliqué aux portes d'eau.[3] Il s'explique sans doute par la chute d'eau (rabas) qu'elles provoquaient nécessairement entre le niveau supérieur et le niveau inférieur de la rivière. L'expression "Windgat" qu'elles portent aussi en flamand provient du treuil (windas) employé pour lever les "ventelles" du barrage.[4]

Il est à peine besoin de faire remarquer que les "Overdraghes" et les portes d'eau ne pouvaient livrer passage qu'à des bateaux de très faible tonnage. Les biefs qu'ils délimitaient n'avaient au surplus qu'une profondeur très minime. En 1271, celle du canal de Lille à La Bassée ne dépassait pas quatre pieds en été et six en hiver.[5] En revanche, l'activité de la navigation semble avoir été très grande. En 1297, les comptes communaux d'Ypres attestent le passage aux "Overdraghes" de la ville de 3250 "escuttes" et de 87 "marctsceipen", pendent une période de 122 jours ce qui représente un arrivage quotidien de 27 bateaux.[6]

Il est fort intéressant de constater de quelle manière on se procurait les ressources nécessaires à l'établissement des "Overdraghes" et des portes d'eau. Les finances du prince étaient incapables de subvenir à des dépenses provoquées par des nécessités d'intérêt public. Son trésor, essentiellement alimenté par les divers revenus de son domaine, était absorbé presque tout entier par l'entretien de sa cour et ses dépenses personnelles. Des tailles extraordinaires lui permettaient de subvenir aux charges occasionnelles provoquées soit par la guerre, soit par le mariage de ses enfants, soit par quelque autre évènement imprévu. Une grande partie de l'administration, confiée à des féodaux, ne lui coûtait rien et si, depuis le XIIe siècle, il avait bien à payer chaque année le traitement de ses baillis et de ses conseillers, il y subvenait grâce à l'excédent des recettes ou par des emprunts que lui consentaient ses villes ou qu'il obtenait à gros intérêts, de financiers locaux ou de financiers italiens. En dehors de cela, nulle trace de budget, nulle possibilité de disposer de fonds en vue de parer aux besoins que faisaient naître le développement et la complication croissante de la vie sociale ou économique.

L'amélioration du régime des cours d'eau ne pouvait pourtant

[1] M. Prou, *Recueil des actes de Philippe Ier, roi de France*, p. 295.

[2] Roisin, *loc. cit.* p. 246 (exemple de 1236).

[3] *Ibid.* p. 253, 280 (exemples de 1242 et 1269) ; cf. E. Verwys et J. Verdam, *Middelnederlandsch woordenboek*, t. vi. col. 939. Aujourd'hui encore, l'ancienne porte d'eau du canal de la Liève à Gand, porte le nom de Rabot.

[4] Roisin, *loc. cit.* p. 246 (exemple de 1236). Voy. d'autres textes postérieurs dans Gailliard, *op. cit.* p. 783, qui me paraît donner de ce mot une explication erronée.

[5] Roisin, *loc. cit.* p. 285.

[6] G. Des Marez et E. De Sagher, *Comptes de la ville d'Ypres de 1267 à 1329*, t. i. p. 127.

s'effectuer sans la participation du prince. Justicier suprême de sa terre, gardien de l'ordre public, protecteur des marchands, des pèlerins et des voyageurs et par surcroît possédant en vertu de ses droits régaliens, la juridiction sur toutes les rivières navigables, le comte de Flandre devait nécessairement intervenir, ne fût-ce que par un simple consentement, dans tous les travaux à exécuter sur les berges ou dans le lit des cours d'eau. L'initiative en cette matière fut prise par les intéressés, c'est-à-dire, par les marchands. Des actes assez nombreux que nous avons conservés du XIIIe siècle nous les montrent sollicitant du comte l'établissement des installations destinées à améliorer la navigabilité des rivières. En 1236, par exemple, la comtesse Jeanne décide de faire exécuter divers travaux sur la Lys: des portes d'eau à Menin et un " Windgat " à Harlebeke. Une enquête est préalablement instituée, et la charte qui nous apprend ces détails nous permet de supposer avec certitude que l'avis des bateliers fréquentant la rivière a déterminé la décision prise. Les frais incombent à la comtesse. Mais afin de lui permettre de récupérer les sommes dépensées, un droit de passage sera levé sur les bateaux. Ce droit cessera d'ailleurs d'être perçu dès que les débours se trouveront couverts: " quousque dictus custus plenarie fuerit persolutus, quo soluto, naves libere transire possunt ".[1] Un arrangement plus simple intervient en 1242 entre la même comtesse et son mari d'une part et les échevins et le conseil de la ville de Lille d'autre part. Ceux-ci reçoivent l'autorisation d'établir sur la Deule trois " rabas " " là où ils sauront qu'il soient plus utile et plus porfitant à détenir le navie, et leur avons créanté ke les cous des trois rabas devantdis reprengnent as avoirs ki par iluekes passeront ".

Comme dans le cas précédent, des taxes prélevées sur la navigation serviront donc à rembourser le coût des travaux. Trois receveurs nommés l'un par la comtesse, l'autre par les échevins, le troisième par " li marchant de la rivière " sont chargés de la perception de ces taxes. Elles cesseront du jour où la ville aura récupéré les sommes engagées par elle. Toutefois, on les remettra en vigueur chaque fois que de nouvelles dépenses seront nécessitées par la réfection des " rabas ".[2] En 1266, un débat s'étant élevé entre la ville de Lille et Jean de Quesnoit relativement à la construction d'une porte d'eau au Quesnoy sur la Deule, la comtesse Marguerite décide que la ville devra payer à Jean 508 livres de Flandre. Elle s'indemnisera par un droit de passage sur les bateaux dont le receveur sera nommé par la comtesse et dont compte sera rendu chaque année devant son bailli de Lille.[3] En 1270, une convention passée toujours entre la ville de Lille et son

[1] Roisin, *loc. cit.* p. 245.
[2] Roisin, *loc. cit.* p. 253.
[3] *Ibid.* p. 275. Cf. encore *ibid.* p. 279, un exemple analogue. Ajoutez aussi des textes de 1256 et de 1288 relatifs à une contestation entre l'abbesse de Messines et les bateliers de la Deule au sujet des portes d'eau de Deulemont, dans I. L. A. Diegerick, *Inventaire des chartes et documents appartenant à l'abbaye de Messines*, pp. 59 et 80.

châtelain décide que ce dernier établira à ses frais un canal entre Lille et La Bassée, mais que la ville lui avancera les 1500 livres d'Artois nécessaires à l'accomplissement de cet ouvrage. Dans ce dernier cas, aucune taxe sur la navigation n'est spécifiée. La commune accepte de prendre tous les frais à sa charge.[1]

Le document dont on trouvera le texte ci-dessous fait connaître avec une précision particulière la méthode employée en 1295 pour la reconstruction des " portes " de la Lys à Houplines.[2] Il appartenait à la superbe collection des chartes de la ville d'Ypres, anéantie lors de l'incendie des halles de cette ville pendant le bombardement de 1914. Je le publie d'après une copie que j'en ai prise quelques années avant la guerre.

Quoique la commune d'Ypres n'y intervienne en rien, on doit supposer qu'un exemplaire lui en avait été remis à cause du grand intérêt qui présentait pour elle la navigation de la Lys.

Le comte Gui de Dampierre y rappelle tout d'abord que les " portes " de la Lys à Houplines se trouvant en si mauvais état que les marchands " ki leur avoir menoient par là " n'osaient plus y passer, ils décidèrent de les faire rétablir à leurs frais. Trois " preud'hommes marchands " furent élus par eux à cet effet, avec l'assentiment du comte. Ils empruntèrent à intérêt les sommes nécessaires à l'exécution des travaux. Du consentement du comte, il fut décidé qu'une assise fixée suivant l'avis des marchands sur toutes les marchandises passant aux portes servirait à les rembourser. Le remboursement se fit d'ailleurs sans délai, grâce à l'affermage qu'ils firent de cette assise, pour une période de onze ans, à deux receveurs. Il fut décidé, au surplus, que si des réparations devaient être effectuées aux portes durant ce laps de temps, les receveurs-fermiers ne seraient tenus à rien d'autre qu'à la fourniture de ventelles.[3]

Rapprochée des textes allégués plus haut, cette pièce contribue pour sa part à jeter quelque lumière sur l'histoire, encore très mal connue des travaux hydrauliques dont la Flandre du moyen âge fournit tant de curieux exemples.

En la publiant ici, je n'ai pas voulu seulement mettre à la disposition des travailleurs un des très rares débris subsistant des archives d'Ypres,[4] il m'a paru aussi qu'il y avait quelque utilité à attirer leur attention sur un ensemble de faits également intéressants pour la

[1] Roisin, *loc. cit.* pp. 285, 287, 288.

[2] Commune du département du Nord, sur la rive droite de la Lys, arrondissement de Lille, canton d'Armentières.

[3] L'analyse de la charte donnée par I. L. A. Diegerick, dans son *Inventaire des chartes et documents appartenant aux archives de la ville d'Ypres*, t. i. (1853) p. 143, n'est pas tout à fait exacte.

[4] A ma connaissance, il ne subsiste qu'une seule charte originale, échappée par hasard à l'incendie de ces archives. J'en ai publié le texte dans une note intitulée: *Un conflit entre le magistrat yprois et les gardes des foires de Champagne en 1309–1310*, Bulletin de la Commission Royale d'histoire (de Belgique), t. lxxxvi. (1922), p. 1 et suiv.

connaissance de l'administration financière et de la circulation commerciale au cours du XIIIe siècle.

H. Pirenne.

APPENDIX

1295, 26 *octobre*

Lettres de Gui de Dampierre, comte de Flandre, approuvant une convention relative au remboursement des frais de reconstruction des portes de la Lys à Houplines.

Nous Guys, cuens de Flandres et marchis de Namur, faisons savoir à tous ke, comme les portes de le Lis à Houpelines fussent si malvaises et si périlleuse à passer ke li marcheant de nostre tière, ki leur avoir menoient par là, estoient en grant doutanche de damage avoir et d'encayr en péril, et pour amender le passage à leur coust et à leur fret esluisissent par commun assens et acort d'eaus trois preudoumes marchans, ki entendissent à faire rapparellier les portes en teil manière ke boines et seures fussent et demorassent par lonc tans boines et seures, c'est à savoir : Willaume de Menin, Pieron de Saint Jehan et Jakemon Ankin, nos bourghois et marcheans de nostre tiere ; et nos fust ceste besongne monstrée par ches meismes trois, et donnei à connoistre soufissaument ke, par commun acort des marcheans de nostre tière, il estoient à chou esluit, et nos requisissent chist troi, de par lor communitei, à avoir nostre grei et nostre assens à che ke il s'en entremesissent, et ke li avoir ke par les dites portes passeroient, puis que faites seroient boines et seures, payassent les frais et les coustenghes comme i aroit fais, par asise ordonée et mise sour cascun avoir par l'avis et l'acort de tous les marchans de no tière qui avoirs passe par là, à rechevoir l'assise tant et si longhement ke tout li frait et li coust del ouvrage seroient bonnement payet. Et Nous, à leur requeste, pour l'amendement et le bien de nostre tière ke nous i veiemes, et le pourfit et l'avantage des marchans, tout ensi lor otrissiens et i mesissiens nostre assens par nos lettres pendans, et soyent les dittes portes sour chou refaites et raparelliés boines et seures et de boin ouvrage et durant, si comme nous entendons ; et en ayent pour ouvrage et pour estofe li troi esluit chi desus nommei fait grande dette, liquele a montei adies par les cous et les frais, dont il ont les deniers tenus à montes, et pour celi dette et les montes payer et eskiwer les cous et les frais grans, à coi il les tenoient et ki adies montoyent, il ayent l'assise desus ditte donnée à cense à Jakemon Mulot et à Thieri Mulot sen neveu, par le grei et l'acort de tous les autres markans, à tenir par onse ans dou jour dou Noël prochainement venant, et dient ke il ne peurent trouver ki à moins d'ans le vausissent prendre. Et parmi celi cense li censisseur desus nommei ont entirement le dette, ki faite estoit pour l'ocoison del ouvrages des dites portes, payet et aquitei les trois desus dis et tout le commun des markans, et nos ayent moult requis ke nous celle cense volsissiens as censisseurs gréer et consentir et laisser lever le droiture de le ditte assise et constraindre les défalans u rebelles de payer à che k'il payècent ensi ke pour le mius l'ont assis et fait pour eaus espayer et oster de frais, ottroions boinement et volons ke li dit censisseur de le dite cense, tout le terme desus dit, tiègnent entirement et lièvent paisivlement l'assise, ke nous entendons estre celle : ke li muid de blei, de fèves, de pois, de vèche et d'orge cascun payera wit deniers ; li muid d'avaine quatre deniers ; li tonniaus de vin, d'oile, de sain et d'oint cascuns douze deniers ; li sas de laine sis deniers ; li masse de hierenc deus deniers ; li navée de piere quatre sous, et de tous autres avoirs al avenant de sis deniers pour le march. Encore ont il ordenei pour bien et pour toute fraude oster et ke li censisseur ne peussent estre decheu et adamagié, ke li dette faite pour l'ocoison del ouvrage ont de lor propre deniers payet hors le prise de le cense, et nos ont moult requis ke nous i metons nostre assens ke se aucuns, pour celle assise escamper et défrauder les censisseurs, metoit sen avoir sour tière quant il seroit venus devant les portes et le fesist cariier u mener par tière et ensi li censisseur perderoient et seroient decheu, Nous, pour toute fraude oster et pour warder les censisseurs de perte et de damage et sauver leur raison, sauve nostre droiture et le droiture d'autrui, volons ke ceste ordenanche, ki en entention de bien est faite et rewardée, soit tenue tout le terme de le cense, et commandons ke desore en avant, nus, pour escamper le dite assise n'i face fraude sour le fourfait de sissante sous, ke nous prenderiens sour le mesfaisant, et pour chou ne demorroit mie ke li censisseur n'i eussent lor droiture. Et est à savoir ke, se aucuns cous u frais eskéoit à faire as dites portes dedens le terme de le dite cense, li censisseur n'i doivent riens mettre fors ventelles seulement, si comme li troi desus nommei ont reconneu.

En souvenanche, tiesmongnage et seurtei desquels choses toutes, Nous avons fait mettre à ces présentes lettres nostre sayels, ki furent faites et données en l'an de grâce mil deus cens quatre-vins et quinze, le mierkedi devant le jour Saint Symon et Saint Jude.

(Copie de l'original disparu sur parchemin, scellé du grand sceau de Gui de Dampierre, avec contre-sceau, pendant sur double queue, côté jadis sous le No. 170 dans l'inventaire des chartes de la ville d'Ypres.)

XII

THE FINANCIAL AND ADMINISTRATIVE IMPORTANCE OF THE LONDON TEMPLE IN THE THIRTEENTH CENTURY

ATTENTION was first drawn to the financial activities of the Templars by M. Léopold Delisle. In his " Mémoire sur les opérations financières des Templiers "[1] he dealt exhaustively with the work of the French Templars, and although he tends to take too official a view of what was essentially a private and independent society,[2] his investigations show, beyond all doubt, that France owed what order and system there were in the management of her finances before 1295 to the Templars. The Temple at Paris was not only *a* treasury for the King, it was the *sole* royal treasury ; the treasurer of the Temple was the King's treasurer, and up to 1295, when the Louvre treasury was established, he was the only person who enjoyed that name. But the Temple was never, in any official sense, a branch of the royal administration. The Temple treasurer was appointed, not by the King, but by his Order, to which alone he was responsible ; he acted for the King, and undoubtedly did work which was later done by the official Treasurers of France, but he was not, as M. Delisle seems to imply, a royal minister : his Register was essentially " du Temple, non de l'état ".[3] Yet, despite the absence of any official connection, the royal treasury and the Temple treasury in France have a common history from the time of Philip Augustus until the close of the thirteenth century.

In England, where the administrative machinery was much further developed and an Exchequer treasury had long been in existence,[4] the part played by the Templars was not so striking.[5] Moreover, in

[1] In vol. xxxiii. of *Mémoires de l'Académie des Inscriptions et Belles-lettres* (1889).

[2] Some of his conclusions have been criticised on this ground by Col. Borrelli de Serres (*Recherches sur divers services publics du xiiie au xviie siècle*, Paris, 1895 and 1912, vols. i. pp. 237-48, iii. p. 5) and by M. Paul Viollet (*Histoire des institutions politiques et administratives en France*, Paris, 1898, vol. ii. p. 125).

[3] See Borrelli de Serres, vol. i. pp. 243-4. This Register, part of which (for 1295) is edited by Delisle, was continued in exactly the same way after 1295, when the royal treasury was transferred to the Louvre.

[4] T. F. Tout, *Chapters in Mediaeval Administrative History*, vol. i. pp. 74-89.

[5] Since this paper was written Mr. Bruce Williamson's *History of the London Temple* has appeared (August 1924) ; in it there is a chapter on " The New Temple as a Centre of Finance ", but this is simply a chronological account of some of the financial transactions that took place there, and does not touch on its relation to the royal administration.

the complete absence of the private records and account books of the London Temple,[1] the evidence has to be collected from scattered entries in the ordinary public records of the time, and these, it is well known, are often bafflingly uncommunicative and almost entirely lacking in human interest. They leave no doubt at all, however, as to the extent and importance of the financial activities of the English Templars. Much of the financial business of the Crown passed through their hands, and although never the sole or even the chief royal treasury the London Temple was used quite definitely throughout the thirteenth century as one of the ordinary and regular " treasuries " of the Crown, alike for the Exchequer and the Wardrobe.

To avoid confusion it will be best, at this point, to attempt some definition of that vague term " royal treasury ", as used in the Middle Ages.[2] A treasury was substantially a storehouse for articles of value, and in this sense a royal treasury is simply a place for the reception and custody of the revenue and belongings of the Crown ; but with the growth of the Exchequer a " royal treasury " came also to include the notion of the administration and distribution of the revenue, and in this sense it is perhaps better described as a " financial office ", or even as a " bank ". That the London Temple was, however unofficially, a " royal treasury " in both these senses, it is the object of this paper to make plain. In discussing its work the two meanings will be kept, as far as possible, distinct : the term " treasury ", unless otherwise qualified, will be restricted to its meaning of storehouse or place of safe-deposit ; while for the other financial and administrative functions carried out at the Temple the words " bank " or " financial office " will be used.

Like all important religious houses,[3] the New Temple,[4] London, was commonly used as " a storehouse for men's treasure . . . by such as feared the spoil thereof in other places ".[5] Of this there is ample evidence in the records of the time. Throughout the thirteenth century individual magnates, lay [6] and ecclesiastical,[7] were in the habit

[1] With the exception of the Inquisitio of 1185, now in the P.R.O. (K.R. Misc. Books, No. 16), all the records of the London Temple were apparently destroyed at the time of the dissolution in 1309.

[2] See Tout, *op. cit.* ii. 51, 52.

[3] The common reason was the protection afforded by their strong buildings and the sanctity of the Church. Cf. G. Bigwood, *Régime juridique et économique du commerce de l'argent dans la Belgique du moyen âge* (Brussels, Mémoires publiés par l'Académie royale, 1921), vol. i. pp. 16-19.

[4] Nearly always so called, to distinguish it from the " Vetus Templum " in Holborn, whence the Order removed in 1185 to the more commodious site on the Fleet, where they built the round church, dedicated in that year and completed in 1240.

[5] Stow, *Survey of London* (1908 ed.), vol. ii. p. 48.

[6] *E.g. Rot. Lit. Claus.* ii. p. 214 ; Matthew Paris, *Chronica Majora* (R.S.), iii. pp. 232, 233, 373 ; v. p. 704 ; *Cal. Pat. Rolls* (1232–47), pp. 5, 81 ; (1258–9), pp. 3, 4, 9, 12, etc.

[7] In 1278 the Bishop of Rochester's chest was sequestrated there on the plea of debt (*Cal. Close Rolls*, 1272–9, p. 447).

of storing at the Temple their chests containing money, jewels, and securities;[1] and it is not surprising that it was early used for the same purpose by the Crown, both for the Wardrobe and the Exchequer, in days when the royal household was always on the road.

The Wardrobe, being part of the Household, followed the King, but by the beginning of the thirteenth century there was need of some fixed and central treasury where the bulk of the King's private treasure might be stored, and where, in his frequent absences, payments might be made and received. When the practice first began is not clear: from 1204, however, when John entrusted to it large sums of money and the insignia and crown jewels,[2] the New Temple at London was used fairly regularly as a treasury for the Wardrobe. This is abundantly evident from the Patent and Close Rolls of the thirteenth century. There are numerous orders[3] in John's reign addressed to the Master of the Temple for the payment of large sums of money out of this treasury, either to the King's own use or to some specified person, and under Henry III. they became more frequent still.[4] In 1225–1226 the very words "garderoba domini regis apud novum Templum" are used;[5] and under the head "De denariis liberatis in garderoba in domo Templi Lond."[6] are a variety of payments, some quite small, from private persons, which seem to show that during those two years at any rate the Wardrobe office itself was temporarily established at the Temple.

Even where there is no direct allusion to the King's "Wardrobe in the New Temple", there are many entries between 1225 and 1290 where the context makes it perfectly clear that the Temple continued to act as a treasury for the Wardrobe. Thus in 1247 Peter Chaceporc, Keeper of the Wardrobe, was bidden to hand over 2000 marks deposited at the New Temple to a certain merchant named by the King.[7] From this order it would seem that the control of the Wardrobe treasure remained with the Keeper, even when its custody was in the hands of the Templars, but this appears to be a solitary instance. The rest of the evidence goes to show that the Wardrobe treasury in the Temple was directly under the control of the Temple authorities, the Treasurer or Master, whose services the King employed in the allocation and expenditure of his treasure no less than those of

[1] *P.R.* (1216–25) pp. 317, 318, 321; *C.P.R.* (1258–66) pp. 41, 656; (1266–72) pp. 281, 283, 284, 358, 474, etc.

[2] *Rot. Lit. Claus.* i. p. 139; *Rot. Lit. Pat.* p. 54b. Henry III. did the same in 1232, *P.R.* (1225–32) p. 490.

[3] *Rot. Lit. Pat.* pp. 103b, 104, 104b, 107, 108, etc.

[4] *P.R.* (1216–25) pp. 243, 319, 337, 339, 381, 383, etc.; *Rot. Lit. Claus.* i. 465b, ii. pp. 118, 126b; *P.R.* (1225–32) pp. 39, 121, 505-7, 523, 535; *C.R.* (1234–37) p. 110; *C.P.R.* (1258–66) pp. 174, 210, etc.

[5] *Rot. Lit. Claus.* ii. pp. 20, 21; cf. also i. 396b, 486b, 549; *C.P.R.* (1232–47) p. 61.

[6] *P.R.* (1216–25) pp. 505, 506, 508, 510, 538; and see *P.R.* (1225–32) pp. 8, 9, 92.

[7] *C.P.R.* (1232–47) p. 497; cf. also *P.R.* (1216–25) p. 538; (1225–32) p. 92; *C.P.R.* (1232–47) pp. 282, 287.

his ordinary Wardrobe officials. Thus, not even the Controller or Keeper of the Wardrobe could dispose of Wardrobe moneys deposited in the Temple without a royal mandate addressed direct to the Master or Treasurer, and generally specifying the purpose of the grant: *e.g.* in 1242, and again in 1245, Robert of Sicklinghall, Treasurer of the Temple, was ordered to "permit Peter Chaceporc to have access to the King's treasure . . . to dispose of it by view and testimony of the said Robert . . . according to the injunctions of the King in letters which the said Peter will show him";[1] and in 1253 the Master and Treasurer received a mandate to deliver "the whole of the King's treasure which they have, as well in gold and silver as in other jewels", to the Keeper of the Wardrobe, the same Peter Chaceporc, "to do therewith as the King has enjoined".[2] The Temple "treasury" was thus almost a "financial office" as well as a storehouse for the Wardrobe.

The close connection of the Temple with the Wardrobe is further seen in the appointment of one of the brethren as Keeper. Brother Geoffrey of the Temple, King's Almoner since 1229,[3] became in 1236 Keeper of the Wardrobe as well; but it is clear that the appointment was made on personal grounds, and the Master of the Temple refused all responsibility. This is evident from a notice in the Patent Rolls, that the King "has granted to the Master of the Temple that whatever may happen touching the said Geoffrey in the said office, the House of the Temple shall not be bound to answer the King and his heirs in anything except reasonable . . . touching Geoffrey's custody of the King's Wardrobe".[4] Brother Geoffrey's keepership lasted until February 1240.[5] It was not remarkable in any way, except as falling within a period of English as opposed to foreign control of the Household administration,[6] and it has no bearing on the use of the Temple as a Wardrobe treasury. Brother Geoffrey disappeared [7] and no other Templar ever again held his office. But the Wardrobe "treasure" continued to be kept at the New Temple, under the custody and control of the Temple treasurers, to whom Wardrobe officials were often sent

[1] *C.P.R.* (1232–47) pp. 281, 456, 457. Peter Chaceporc was keeper of the Wardrobe 28 Oct. 1241–24 Dec. 1254 (T. F. Tout, "List of Keepers", in *Eng. Hist. Rev.* xxiv. 499).

[2] *C.P.R.* (1247–58) p. 185.

[3] *C. Lib. R.* (1226–40) p. 160. His associate John was also a Templar and was acting from 11 Oct. 1231 (*C.R.* (1227–31) p. 569) up to July 1244 (*ibid.* 1242–7), p. 214, after which he seems to have become King's Chaplain (*ibid.* 1247–51), p. 423.

[4] *C.P.R.* (1232–47) p. 161.

[5] *C.R.* (1237–42) p. 172. According to Matthew Paris, Geoffrey was entirely subservient to his royal master, and lent himself as an instrument to the King in various directions (*Chronica Majora* (R.S.), iii. pp. 495, 543).

[6] Cf. Tout, *op. cit.* i. p. 251.

[7] He seems to have ceased to be King's Almoner at the same time, but he was still acting as Warden of Ospring Hospital (founded by Henry III., 1234) in August of 1240 (*C. Lib. R.* (1226–40) p. 487). In this he had been succeeded by Brother John (*C.R.* (1242–7) p. 68) by July 1243.

with royal orders to be "permitted to view our treasure deposited with you".[1] Not only money and jewels, but wax [2] for the use of the King's Chapel, herrings [3] for his larder and his alms, and books [4] for the Queen were kept in this "treasury".

When and why the Wardrobe treasury of the Temple ceased is not apparent; there is little in the shape of direct reference after about 1266, but it was certainly still in use in 1275 and 1276, in which years Brother Warin, the Treasurer of the Temple, was ordered [5] to pay money to Master Thomas Bek, Keeper of the Wardrobe, "for the expenses of the Household". With the increasing importance of the Wardrobe under Edward I., the need was probably felt of some fixed and independent treasury, and we know from Professor Tout that by 1290 two such permanent treasuries had been established, one under the Chapter House at Westminster, the other in the Tower.[6] It does not seem too much to conclude that this permanent official branch of the administration was the outcome of the "treasury of our Wardrobe at the New Temple" of Henry III.'s reign.

The Exchequer, unlike the Wardrobe, had its own treasury at Westminster, from the latter part of the reign of Henry II. Nevertheless, partly perhaps because the Exchequer officials were not always on the spot, partly because throughout the reigns of Henry III. and Edward I. "revenue flowed indifferently into either the Exchequer or the Wardrobe",[7] such use was made of the New Temple that it came to be regarded as one of the regular "treasuries" of the Exchequer, second only to the treasury at Westminster itself. Indeed, in Henry II.'s reign, before the establishment of the treasury at Westminster, we find the Temple being used by the Exchequer officials as their sole "London treasury", a convenient alternative to the treasury at Winchester for the receipt and custody of revenue.[8] And, after the disappearance of the Winchester treasury and the permanent establishment of the chief Exchequer treasury in the palace at Westminster,[9] this practice was continued. The records leave little doubt of this. In 1226 the sum of 1000 marks (received from the Cistercians) was "to be paid to the Treasurer, to be placed in the Treasury at West-

[1] *C.R.* (1237–42) p. 414; *C.P.R.* (1232–47) pp. 281, 456, 457, etc.

[2] *C. Lib. R.* (1226–40) p. 228.

[3] *C.R.* (1247–51) pp. 10, 263.

[4] In 1250 the Master was ordered to deliver to a certain Wardrobe clerk, to the use of the Queen, a "certain great book, written in French, containing old histories and romances, which is in his house in London" (*ibid.* p. 283).

[5] *C.P.R.* (1272–81) pp. 83, 99, 141.

[6] *Op. cit.* ii. pp. 51-54.

[7] T. F. Tout, *op. cit.* i. p. 51.

[8] Hall, *Receipt Roll of the Exchequer*, 1185, pp. 30, 31. In 1185 £4000 of the terminal receipt of £10,000 was placed in the treasury at Winchester; the remnant "apud nos" (*i.e.* the Exchequer officials) was deposited "ad Templum apud Londoniam".

[9] Prof. Tout suggests that "perhaps one element that brought the chief Exchequer treasury to Westminster was the increasing part which the New Temple at London was now beginning to play as a royal treasury" (*op. cit.* i. p. 98).

minster *or* to Brother Simon of the Temple, to be kept in the House of the Temple in London . . . if the said treasurer were not to be found ".[1] Again, in 1253, Hugh Bigod was commanded to pay his wife's yearly fine for the wardship of the lands and heir of her former husband, a sum of 500 marks, " yearly at the Exchequer *or* at the New Temple, London ".[2] These two instances seem to suggest that, in the absence of the proper officials or for the sake of convenience, the payment of royal revenue could always be made at the Temple, which was thus obviously in the habit of playing second fiddle to the Exchequer.

There are, moreover, numberless entries in the Patent, Close and Liberate Rolls of the thirteenth century, recording the payment and storage at the London Temple of almost every kind of tax: [3] of fifteenths,[4] twentieths,[5] and thirtieths; [6] of aids [7] and feudal dues; [8] of carucages,[9] tallages of London,[10] and of the Jews; [11] of clerical aids,[12] and of the Irish treasure.[13] Indeed, from the early days of Henry III. up to the close of the reign of Edward I., the London Temple was a regular receiving centre and storehouse of all the dues and taxes of the realm.

Did its services to the Exchequer end here? Was it simply a storehouse for revenue, or was it also, as in the case of the Wardrobe, a treasury in the administrative sense of a " financial office "? Usually the Exchequer officials, unlike those of the Wardrobe, appear to have retained direct control over the funds deposited at the Temple: the various notifications of money paid into the treasury at the Temple (addressed to the Barons) or of disbursements made at the King's

[1] *P.R.* (1225–32) p. 40. This entry bears out the first of the two causes suggested, of the use of the Temple as treasury for the Exchequer; between the three recognised sittings of the Exchequer a responsible official would probably often not be " found " (before the appointment of a treasurer's clerk to " sit at the receipt " during vacation time), and the Master or Treasurer of the Temple stepped in to do his job.

[2] *C.P.R.* (1247–58) p. 197; cf. also pp. 33, 41.

[3] From 1187 the Templars had collected and administered the various " grants in aid of the Holy Land ", and had often acted as receivers and custodians of papal subsidies as well (*e.g. Rot. Lit. Claus.* i. pp. 567, 593; *C.P.R.* (1232–47) p. 250; *Cal. Papal Letters*, i. pp. 27, 74, 170, etc.). From Holy Land and Papal subsidies it was an easy step to royal taxes.

[4] *Rot. Lit. Claus.* ii. pp. 75b, 76, 82, 84b; *P.R.* (1216–25) pp. 538, 546, 548; (1225–1232) p. 92, etc.

[5] *C.P.R.* (1266–72) p. 439; Shirley, *Royal Letters* (R.S.), ii. p. 338.

[6] *C.P.R.* (1232–47) pp. 221, 222, 275, 277, etc.; *C. Lib. R.* (1226–40) pp. 325, 326, 330, 446.

[7] *Rot. Lit. Claus.* i. p. 516; *C.R.* (1227–31) p. 593.

[8] *C.P.R.* (1258–66) p. 676; (1272–81) pp. 166, 170, 208; *C.C.R.* (1272–9) p. 943.

[9] *Rot. Lit. Claus.* i. pp. 437, 451; ii. p. 505, etc.

[10] *E.g. C.C.R.* (1272–9) p. 63.

[11] *C.P.R.* (1232–47) p. 75; (1272–81) pp. 52, 83, 84, 99, 100; *C.R.* (1247–51) p. 321; (1242–7) p. 307, etc.

[12] *P.R.* (1225–32) p. 593; *C.P.R.* (1247–58) p. 587; (1266–72) p. 493; (1272–81) p. 147, etc.

[13] *C.P.R.* (1247–58) p. 74; *Cal. Documents Relating to Ireland*, vol. i., Nos. 2871, 3013, 3189, etc.

orders (addressed to the Treasurer and Chamberlains) all point to this. A good instance of the control of the Exchequer over its treasure in the Temple is supplied in 1219, when the Treasurer and Chamberlains were ordered " to pay out of our treasury 1000 marks which are in deposit at the New Temple, London, to Brother Simon of the Temple ", to pay a certain debt owing to the Pope.[1] Again, in 1222, the same officials were ordered to pay a further sum of 1000 marks " out of our treasury which is in the New Temple in your custody ", the annual rent to the Pope; and in 1224 they had a similar order for the payment of 1400 marks to the Count of La Marche.[2]

From these examples it would appear that the Temple acted as a " storehouse " for the Exchequer and nothing more, the actual control and administration remaining with the Exchequer officials. Yet, owing perhaps to the persistent overlapping of Exchequer and Wardrobe, to the fact that revenue " flowed indifferently " into either in the thirteenth century, the King was generally able to do pretty much as he liked, and he did not scruple to use the services of the treasurers of the Temple in the direct administration and distribution of every kind of royal revenue in their charge, whatever its source.

There are endless instances of this, in connection with what are obviously Exchequer moneys. The King would order the Master, or the treasurer of the London Temple, to reserve certain sums " out of his treasure ", and expend them on his behalf in various directions; sometimes to private individuals (relations of the King, or creditors),[3] sometimes for building operations,[4] sometimes to pay up indemnities in accordance with treaty obligations,[5] sometimes simply " to the King's own use "[6]—which doubtless implies a transference from the Exchequer treasury to the more private treasury of the Wardrobe. Sometimes, indeed, the official controllers themselves, the Treasurer and Chamberlains, had to procure a mandate from the King before they could get access to their treasury in the Temple. Thus in 1214 the Master of the Temple was ordered to deliver 2000 marks in his charge to the Treasurer.[7] Further examples are seen in the time of the renowned Temple treasurer, Hugh of Stockton: he was a person of

[1] *Rot. Lit. Claus.* i. p. 396b. This is a specially clear example; it seems to indicate that the Treasurer of the Temple could not lay a finger on Exchequer moneys stored in his own house without a definite disbursement from the officials concerned. Cf. also pp. 558 and 581.

[2] *Ibid.* pp. 486b, 607; *cf.* also 124b, 141, 549.

[3] *E.g. Rot. Lit. Claus.* i. p. 514; *Rot. de Lib.* pp. 8, 54; *P.R.* (1216–25) pp. 243, 319; *C.P.R.* (1247–58) pp. 90, 100, 568.

[4] *E.g. C.P.R.* (1238–47) p. 474; (1272–81) p. 100.

[5] *E.g.* payments to the Lord Emperor (*Rot. Lit. Claus.* i. pp. 124, 179; *C.R.* (1234–37) p. 110) and to the French King (*Rot. Lit. Claus.* i. p. 465b; *C.P.R.* (1258–66) pp. 174, 210).

[6] *E.g. C.R.* (1227–31) p. 544; *C.P.R.* (1247–58) pp. 67, 119, 398, 507, etc.

[7] *Rot. Lit. Pat.* pp. 108, 108b. (For other instances see *P.R.* (1225–32) p. 105; *C.P.R.* (1238–47) pp. 61, 188.)

much importance and frequently acted, in company with the King's Treasurer, as organiser and receiver of special subsidies;[1] in 1235 the King had to ask him "to let Hugh Pateshull, the Treasurer, have the 2000 marks which he has in deposit of the King's treasure".[2]

It is clear from these various instances that the Temple treasury of the Exchequer was something more than a mere storehouse, and that its officials were very frequently employed by the King in the direct administration and expenditure of the revenue, quite independently of the Exchequer authorities.

The line between public and private was, however, extremely thin in the thirteenth century, and in all these ways the Temple was perhaps performing services for its royal patrons in their capacity as private clients rather than as kings. For the Temple, besides being "a storehouse for men's treasure", was also a bank. The rivals of the Jews and the forerunners of the great Italian merchants, the Templars, through their unassailable position as a Religious Order and their close connection with the Papacy and the Crusades, offered attractions, as bankers and moneylenders, of which men were not slow to avail themselves. It is not possible here to go into the services performed by the Temple bank in London for private individuals, but it must be remembered that there was nothing which the Temple did for the Government that it did not also do for private persons—from John's reign, when Faukes de Bréauté[3] and Hubert de Burgh[4] made large borrowings and stored their treasure there, to the beginning of the fourteenth century, when we find among its debtors and depositors, Bartholomew of Badlesmere and Stephen Burghersh (Knights),[5] and various Italian merchants.[6]

In considering the financial and administrative importance of the Temple in its work for the English State in the thirteenth century, it is important to lay stress on its character as a bank, and its independence, in this respect, of royal control. Even in France, where the Paris Temple was the sole royal treasury, the King drew on his deposits there and contracted loans as a private client,[7] and in England, where at most the Temple was a secondary and alternative royal treasury, this independence was even more apparent. Its modern counterpart is the Bank of England, rather than the Treasury in Whitehall. As such we find it conducting for the Government, as for private persons, a variety of very highly developed financial operations.[8] True, it has

[1] *C. Lib. R.* (1226–40) pp. 317, 326, 443; *C.P.R.* (1232–47) pp. 209, 212, 217, 230, 277, etc.

[2] *C.P.R.* (1232–47) p. 116. Compare with similar orders to Robert of Sicklinghall on behalf of the Keeper of the Wardrobe in 1242 and 1245 (p. 150 *supra*). See also *C.P.R.* (1232–47) p. 61.

[3] *Rot. Lit. Claus.* ii. p. 214.

[4] *C.P.R.* (1232–47), pp. 5, 81.

[5] *C.C.R.* (1302–7) pp. 444, 535.

[6] *C.P.R.* (1292–1301) p. 419; *C.C.R.* (1302–7) pp. 172, 343.

[7] Borrelli de Serres, i. 243, 244.

[8] Most of the instances mentioned above (pp. 149-153) in connection with the administration of the royal revenue might be considered equally well under this head.

been pointed out that in so doing the London Temple was often playing a part corresponding, to some extent, to that of the spending department of the modern Treasury, but this did not affect its essential character as an independent private society ; it was a bank performing, of grace, administrative business for the King ; it was not in any sense an official Government department. And as a bank it did more than merely carry out specific allocations of funds. The Templars had created, thanks to their Houses in every European country, a highly developed system of credit, by bills of exchange, by means of which payments at a distance could be undertaken without any actual transference of coin. Payments of this kind were among the most valuable services rendered by the Templars to the English Crown, and indeed to European society generally, for until the coming of the Frescobaldi and their successors there was no one else who was able to undertake them, and even these Italian merchants made good use of the Temple in their financial business at first.[1]

One of the best illustrations of the way in which payments abroad were thus effected through the London Temple is seen in Henry III.'s dealings with the Count of La Marche. In 1224 he was obliged to pay a sum of 1400 marks to the Count at Paris ; this he did by allocating to the purpose that sum at the Temple in London, against the payment of an equivalent sum to the Count in France by Brother W. Kadel, Master of the Temple, " citra montes ".[2] Again, in 1235, in an agreement with this same Count, Henry undertook, in return for the surrender of the island of Oléron, to pay the Count a pension of 800 " livres tournois " for five years ; Henry was to pay £200 sterling to the Temple at London, while the Temple at Paris was to pay the equivalent 800 " livres tournois " to the Count of La Marche.[3]

The London Temple in the thirteenth century might thus be performing in connection with any given portion of revenue three distinct functions at the same time : it might be acting as a royal treasury in the sense of a storehouse, as a royal treasury (to some extent) in the administrative sense of a spending department, and as the bank through whose operations a particular allotment out of the revenue might be used, at any given moment, to meet some obligation, either in cash at home, or by bill of exchange abroad.[4]

[1] See *C.P.R.* (1272–81) p. 375 ; (1292–1301) p. 419 ; *C.C.R.* (1302–7) pp. 172, 343. (M. G. Bigwood, in his important work already cited, makes no mention of the early use by the Templars of these " letters of credit ". Cf. vol. i. chapter v.)

[2] *C.P.R.* (1216–25) p. 439. Other good instances are seen in 1221 in connection with the payment of 500 marks required for the King's service at La Rochelle (*ibid.* p. 303), and in 1213 when John allotted 2000 marks at the London Temple to the credit of the Earl of Salisbury, then in Flanders, who was to draw upon that sum, as required, through the Temple at Paris (*Rot. Lit. Pat.* pp. 103, 141 ; *Rot. Lit. Claus.* i. 221b.).

[3] *C.P.R.* (1232–47) pp. 116, 117. There are many other examples.

[4] Sometimes, of course, the payments abroad conducted by the Temple for the English Crown were made in actual bullion, often through the agency of individual Templars (cf. *C.R.* (1227–31) p. 116, for a good example). Such services were valuable,

There remain two other important functions which the Temple performed for its royal patrons in its capacity as bank: the administration of trusts and moneylending. Of the first of these we have one early and valuable example in 1158 noted by William of Newburgh and Roger of Hoveden: they tell how when Henry II. and Louis VII. laid down the conditions of the marriage between their children Henry and Margaret, it was arranged that the dowry of Louis's daughter, which included Gisors and two other castles, should be held in trust by the Templars until the marriage took place.[1]

King John, who was in the habit of granting pensions to discontented vassals in Western France, either to his own to keep them loyal or to the French King's to make them disloyal, sent to the Treasurer of the Temple at La Rochelle in 1214 sums sufficient to insure the exact payment of some of these during a certain number of years. Thus, having promised to Ralph, Count of Eu, an annual pension of £6000, he sent to the Temple at La Rochelle £30,000, out of which the first five annuities were to be taken.[2] To take only two out of many instances of the same kind in Henry III.'s reign. In the matter of the long protracted payment of the indemnity of 6000 marks to Louis of France, the charter of promise was deposited in the Temple, where "it shall be retained until full satisfaction has been made to the Lord Louis".[3] Again, in 1228, the charter binding Roger Bigod to deposit at the London Temple two large sums to buy lands for his wife Isabel (sister of Alexander of Scotland) was lodged at the Temple "to be restored to him on completion of the said payments", which in their turn were to be kept there "until the lands are purchased as a marriage portion for the said Isabel".[4]

Even more valuable to the English kings of the thirteenth century than these highly-developed banking activities were the facilities supplied by the Temple for contracting loans. The wealth of the Templars was as proverbial as the neediness of the English Crown. Besides the capital placed in their charge by private individuals and by the Crown, large revenues flowed into their treasury from the great estates which they possessed in nearly every county in the land, and these, in the thirteenth century, were no longer forwarded to the East with the regularity and strictness of early days. The Jews were already a source of regular and systematic exaction;[5]

---

but are rather outside the banking operations proper conducted by the Temple, nor were they confined to that Order; *e.g.* Hospitallers were used in this way, as in the collection of Holy Land and royal taxes (*e.g. C. Lib. R.* i. pp. 304, 333, 334; *C.P.R.* (1266–72) pp. 439, 466, 513).

[1] W. of Newburgh (R.S.), i. p. 158; Hoveden (R.S.), i. p. 218.

[2] *Rot. Lit. Pat.* pp. 116b, 121b. There are many other examples.

[3] *P.R.* (1216–25) p. 168. For other instances cf. *C.C.R.* (1226–57) p. 438; *P.R.* (1225–32) pp. 466, 514, etc.

[4] *C.C.R.* (1226–57) p. 72; *Cal. Documents Relating to Scotland*, i., Nos. 1003, 1005.

[5] See A. M. Hyamson, *A History of the Jews in England* (1908), pp. 54, 90-91.

the Italian merchants did not come upon the scene till after the middle of the century;[1] the Templars, with their large supplies of ready money and their close relations with the Crown, were the obvious people to whom the King could turn at times of financial stress.

King John was in their debt throughout his reign. The Master of the Temple in England at that time, Aymeric of S. Maur, made him many advances, varying from the gold mark which the King borrowed in 1213 to put in the offertory on the day of his reconciliation with the Pope,[2] to sums of 1500 and 1100 marks which the Templars advanced to him in 1206 and 1215, in the first case to pay a debt to the French King,[3] in the second to pay the Poitevin troops whom he had summoned to England to fight for him.[4] In 1216 John was at his wits' end for money to pay his mercenaries, and he borrowed 1000 marks from Brother Gérard Brochard, Master of the Temple in Aquitaine, undertaking to repay the sum in London, within a specified time.[5] But his ill-fortunes and his empty treasury made the prospect of repayment very remote: before 1216 was out the Templars of Poitou were demanding something more than easy promises,[6] and John was reduced to sending an order to his seneschal in Gascony to hand over a portion of the revenues of that fief to his "beloved brother in Christ Gérard Brochard". Evidently, however, the debt was not paid in full, if at all, and it weighed heavily on the conscience of the new government. William the Marshal and Hubert de Burgh, being both pious persons, probably paid more attention to the claims of a Religious Order than to those of Jews or even of respectable and Christian merchants; at any rate, whatever the motive, and doubtless not without reminders from those concerned, definite and drastic steps were taken to pay off this debt. As early as March 1217 the Mayor and burgesses of Bordeaux were ordered to pay all the rents and revenues of the city to Brother Gérard Brochard "until full satisfaction had been made for a debt of 1157 marks sterling owed by King John to him and his brethren".[7] The order was repeated, in even stricter terms, in 1219, and by 1220 only 500 marks were still owing, and provision was made for the payment of all but 200 by Easter of the year following; and "for the rest" Brother Brochard "must receive what he can from the revenues of Bordeaux".[8] It is probable that the persevering Master, having got so much, persevered to the end.

[1] Cf. Whitwell, "Italian Bankers and the English Crown", in *Transactions of the Royal Historical Society*, New Series, xvii.

[2] *Rot. Lit. Claus.* p. 148b.

[3] *Rot. Lit. Claus.* i. p. 144; *Rot. Lit. Pat.* pp. 41b, 65, 135, 141, 190, 192.

[4] *Rot. Lit. Claus.* i. p. 194.

[5] *Rot. Lit. Pat.* p. 152b. See also pp. 141 and 177 for other sums borrowed.

[6] *Ibid.* p. 197.

[7] *P.R.* (1216–25) p. 51.

[8] *P.R.* (1216–25) p. 232. It is to be noted that in the original negotiations for the debt King John undertook to repay the sum borrowed at the London Temple. When

Although only touching indirectly on the London Temple, the story of this debt and its repayment is of importance as showing that the Templars, unlike the Jews, could compel repayment of loans even from kings, though it is doubtful if even they could have squeezed the money out of John.

Under Henry III. the borrowings continued. In 1221 a sum of 500 marks was lent by the Templars in England to help with the indemnity to Louis of France, and the issues of the manor of Godmanchester were handed over to them till the debt should have been fully paid.[1] This arrangement, which was doubtless more satisfactory to the Templars than the most solemn royal promise to pay, was repeated in 1224; Brother Alan Martel, then Master, advanced 300 marks to the King, and in return received "full seisin" of the aforesaid manor, which was to remain in his hands until "full satisfaction" were obtained.[2] There are many other such instances.[3]

With the exception of a very large debt, contracted in Syria "for the King's affairs",[4] Edward I., unlike his father and grandfather, hardly seems to have borrowed from the Templars at all, probably because the Italian merchants, the Frescobaldi in particular, were by that time established in England and supplied most of his needs. Sometimes, however, he transferred to the Templars a pressing debt to some Italian banker; thus in 1299 he arranged for the agents of "the Society of the Frescobaldi" to receive from the Temple treasurer in London 2000 marks, which he undertook to repay to the Templars within a specified time.[5]

An interesting question remains as to how the Templars indemnified themselves for their services and responsibilities as bankers and moneylenders. There are frequent notices of royal gifts to the Order, of grants of special privileges for trading in wine and wool, of exemptions from taxation; but these were mostly of long duration, and although, in a general way, they may be regarded as a return for services rendered, they cannot be held to cover specific services to individuals, whether kings or private persons. In the case of moneylending M. Delisle[6] considered that advances were made simply on security from the capital deposited with them, but we are still faced with the question as to how

---

he failed to do this, Br. Brochard, perhaps suspecting lack of pressure on the part of the English Master, who remained one of John's few loyal supporters to the end, took matters into his own hands.

[1] *Rot. Lit. Claus.* i. p. 479, "donec predictas 500 marcas perceperint de eodem manerio".

[2] *P.R.* (1216–25) pp. 453, 456; *Rot. Lit. Cl.* i. p. 612. In this instance the debt was repaid in full by the Exchequer, and the grant of Godmanchester to Brother Alan was cancelled (*Rot. Lit. Cl.* ii. p. 4).

[3] *P.R.* (1216–25) pp. 557, 537; *C.R.* (1234–37) p. 47; (1242–47) pp. 378, 504; *C.P.R.* (1258–66) p. 731.

[4] *C.P.R.* (1272–81) p. 353.

[5] *C.P.R.* (1292–1301) p. 419; see also p. 244 and *C.P.R.* (1272–81) p. 375.

[6] *Op. cit.* p. 45.

this profited them. The exaction of any payment for the use of money was regarded as a thing abominable by the whole religious feeling of the Middle Ages and was forbidden by canon law. In later days, from the close of the thirteenth century, the French and Italian merchants managed to get round the difficulty by obliging borrowers to make an additional payment if the money were not repaid within a specified time.[1] It is probable that the Templars also practised this device of " compensation for losses sustained ", and so made their profits ; this is borne out by a hint here and there in some of the entries already referred to. Thus the debt owed by John to the Poitevin Templars seems to have grown, for no apparent reason, from 1000 marks to 1157 marks on his failure to pay it at the New Temple, London, within the specified time ;[2] and in the case of the loan made by Brother Alan Martel to Henry III. in 1224, it is stated that if it is not completely repaid by the Feast of All Saints following, the Manor of Godmanchester shall remain in his hands " until full satisfaction has been obtained ".[3] A clearer instance still is supplied in 1260 : in the acknowledgement of a debt of 2800 " livres tournois " advanced by the Treasurer of the Temple at Paris, Henry III. promises " to repay the same within the month of Easter next ", and if not, " to pay the losses occasioned by the default ".[4]

Other examples might be quoted, but these are the most suggestive, and certainly seem to imply that the Templars, like the " Christian " merchants of the fourteenth century, profited on their moneylending transactions by payments " for losses occasioned by default ", which, as the specified time was always restricted, cannot have been infrequent.

Under Edward I., as has been suggested, the influence of the Templars in finance began steadily to decline. True, Edward contracted one large debt to them in 1274, and transferred to them in 1299 some pressing debts to the Frescobaldi, but instances of this sort are rare, and the connection in which they occur is of itself significant as indicating the source and cause of the decline. With the coming of the Italian merchants and the rapid growth of their societies in the last quarter of the thirteenth century, the Temple Bank was no longer the only one or even the best available, and although instances of its banking operations may be found right up to the end of Edward I.'s reign,[5] they become so rare in the last ten years as to be almost negligible.

The London Temple was still regularly used as a storehouse for

[1] Cf. Whitwell, *op. cit.* p. 185, and G. Bigwood, *op. cit.* vol. i. pp. 567-603.

[2] *Rot. Lit. Claus.* i. p. 221b, and *P.R.* (1216–25) pp. 51, 203.

[3] *P.R.* (1216–25) p. 453.

[4] *C.P.R.* (1258–66) p. 114 : " upon which [*i.e.* the amount of loss] he or his representative shall be believed ".

[5] *E.g. C.C.R.* (1272–9) p. 264 ; *C.P.R.* (1281–92) p. 244.

the Crown,[1] but this, too, with increasing rarity, doubtless owing to the development of the King's own administrative system, and especially to the establishment of the permanent Wardrobe treasuries. The Templars continued, however, to handle the taxes of Church and realm up to the very end of Edward I.'s reign ;[2] individual Templars—Masters, Treasurers, and ordinary brethren—continued to do business, financial and otherwise, for the King[3] and for private persons ;[4] and nowhere is there to be found a warmer appreciation of their services than in Edward's letter on behalf of the English Master, William de la More, written in 1304 to the Grand Master of the Order.[5]

Moreover, in this reign, for the first time the London Temple is found performing another administrative function and acting as a " record office " for the Chancery ; it was, of course, not uncommon for deeds and documents (whether of kings or private persons) to be stored there,[6] along with other valuables, but the first specific mention of the keeping there of Chancery enrolments occurs in 1289, when, after the notification of a grant by the Bishop of Worcester to the King, there follows this memorandum : " that this charter remains in a box in the chest in which the rolls of Chancery are kept at the New Temple, London ".[7] An even more interesting entry occurs in 1291. The King and the Chancellor were in Scotland, and required for reference some documents which were " in a chest of rolls of the Chancery " at the Temple ; the King's Treasurer, therefore, at his orders went to the Temple, broke open the chest, and having " examined the rolls ", extracted the two required, and sent them to the King. It is recorded further, that on the return of the King and Chancellor to London the Treasurer restored the two rolls to the Temple and supplied new keys " for the chest aforesaid ".[8]

It was, however, in the financial sphere that the London Temple made its important contribution to the English State. Throughout

[1] *E.g. C.C.R.* (1272–9) pp. 143, 264.

[2] *C.C.R.* (1272–9) pp. 21, 25, 143 ; (1279–88) pp. 279, 350 ; (1302–7) p. 61 ; *C.P.R.* (1281–92) p. 184 ; (1292–1301) p. 88.

[3] *C.C.R.* (1272–9) pp. 21, 25 ; (1279–88) p. 279 ; (1296–1302) pp. 78, 128. Guy Forest (Master, 1290–94) went to Scotland on the King's affairs in 1273 (*C.C.R.* (1272–9) p. 57) ; his successor, Brian Jay, was killed fighting for the King in the battle of Falkirk (William of Newburgh (continuation), R.S. p. 582, and *C.C.R.* (1296–1302) p. 78). Other Templars were used to audit accounts, test money, etc., and the Master was regularly summoned to Parliament from 1295 (*C.P.R.* (1272–81) pp. 277, 379, 451 ; (1292–1301) p. 88.

[4] *C.C.R.* (1272–9) pp. 54, 499, 552 ; (1279–88) p. 184 ; (1302–7) pp. 172, 343, 429, 444.

[5] *C.C.R.* (1302–7) p. 208. William was in some trouble with the Grand Master, and Edward, writing on his behalf, speaks of " the grateful and laudable services he has heretofore rendered to the King and his realm in many ways and . . . the great affection that the brethren under him are said to bear towards him, as his friendly bearing and honest conversation merit ".

[6] *P.R.* (1216–25) pp. 317, 318, 321 ; *C.P.R.* (1238–42) p. 81 ; (1258–66) p. 41 ; 1266–72) p. 656.

[7] *C.C.R.* (1288–96) p. 56.

[8] *C.C.R.* (1288–96) p. 245.

the thirteenth century it had a reputation second only to that of Paris as a royal " treasury " and " bank " ; and if it never became, as in France, the centre of the financial administration of the Crown, " le véritable trésor royal ", it was, as we have seen, very freely used by the English kings of the thirteenth century as a convenient extra treasury alike for the Exchequer and the Wardrobe, and also as a financial office and bank, through whose operations much of the royal revenue was distributed and expended. By the end of the century the Templars had the field no longer to themselves ; the foreign merchants had superseded them almost entirely as bankers and money-lenders, while in the administrative sphere the increasing efficiency of the Exchequer officials and the establishment by 1290 of the two permanent Wardrobe treasuries inevitably deprived them of most of the official royal business. In 1308 came the unexpected attack on the Order, engineered by the King of France. It is perhaps a fitting piece of irony that the sequestration of the Templar estates in England by the Crown (under papal orders) did notable service to another administrative department—the King's Chamber, whose growth in Edward II.'s reign owed much to that lucky haul.[1] Even in their downfall the English Templars played an important, if passive, part in the development of the royal administration.

AGNES SANDYS.

APPENDIX

Treasurers of the New Temple, London

Simon of the Temple .	Acting 4 Nov. 1214 (*Rot. Lit. Claus.* i. 175b).
	13 June 1224, first definite mention as " Treasurer of the Temple " (*P.R.* 1216–25, p. 443).
	June 1231 (*P.R.* 1225–32, p. 439).
Hugh of Stockton . .	Associated with Br. Simon, Aug. 1224 (*P.R.* 1216–25, p. 467) and on other occasions.
	11 Nov. 1232, " Treasurer of the New Temple " (*C.P.R.* 1232–47, p. 2).
	24 April 1242 (Issue Rolls of the Exchequer, Henry III.—Henry V., in Pell Records, London 1837, p. 18).
Robert of Sicklinghall .	22 Aug. 1239 (*C. Lib. R.* 1226–40, p. 408).
	13 Dec. 1244 (*C.R.* 1242–47, p. 277).
	28 June 1262 (*C.P.R.* 1258–66, p. 218).

[1] Between 1309 and 1314 many of the Templar estates were administered by the King's Chamber, their various " keepers " being responsible to a King's clerk, who occupied the position of " Receiver of the Chamber " (L.T.R. Enrolled Accounts Miscellaneous, Nos. 18-20, in P.R.O. ; and see Tout, *op. cit.* vol. ii. pp. 316-324).

Ralph of Brimsgrave .	1259–60. Acting as Preceptor of London (*C.P.R.* 1258–66, p. 99).
	8 June 1270, Treasurer (*C.P.R.* (1266–72) p. 439).
	10 March 1272 (*ibid. p.* 635).
Warin	25 & 30 July 1273 (*C.C.R.* 1272–79, pp. 53, 57).
	12 May 1277 (*C.P.R.* 1272–81, p. 208).
William	May 1288 (*C.C.R.* (1279–88) p. 599).
Richard of Feltham .	1 Oct. 1294 (*C.P.R.* (1292–1301) p. 88).
John of Stoke . . .	Treasurer at the time of the suppression, 1308 (L.T.R. Enrolled Accounts Misc. No. 18, m. 7).

XIII

LE STATUT "DE JUSTICIIS ASSIGNATIS QUOD VOCATUR RAGEMAN"

Tous ceux qui ont étudié l'organisation administrative et financière au temps d'Édouard Ier connaissent ce statut qui figure, par exemple, dans le recueil officiel des *Statutes of the Realm* (t. i. p. 44) à la date supposée (mais sans preuve) de 1276 (4° Edw. I). Ils savent que c'est une ordonnance ou un règlement ayant pour objet de nommer des juges chargés d' " oier et terminer les pleintes et les quereles de trespas feez . . . ausi bien des bailifs e des ministres le roy com des autres bailifs et autres gens queus qe il seient ". Mais d'où provient l'addition, dans le titre, des mots " quod vocatur rageman " et quel en est le sens ? L'original du statut n'existe plus ; nous en possédons seulement des copies exécutées à des dates très variées ; le ms. du British Museum (Harl. N°. 395), dont les éditeurs des *Statutes* ont reproduit le texte, choisi au hasard, n'est pas antérieur à la fin du XIVe siecle. Les autres manuscrits connus contiennent des variantes dont il n'y a pas lieu de tenir compte, car ce sont évidemment des fantaisies de copistes. Quant au mot *rageman* ou *ragman*, il faut l'expliquer. Étymologiquement, il signifie un homme en haillons, un loqueteux ; nos dictionnaires anglais-français le traduisent par chiffonnier. Quel rapport est-il possible d'admettre entre un chiffonnier et un juge d'enquête ? La question a été plus d'une fois posée et discutée. Il semble maintenant qu'on puisse la résoudre à l'aide d'ouvrages anglais récents. C'est ce que je vais essayer de montrer, saisissant avec joie l'occasion qui m'est offerte de rendre une fois de plus hommage aux maîtres de l'école médiévale dont le Professeur Tout est un des représentants les plus distingués.

Miss Cam, à qui j'emprunte ce que je considère comme la solution du problème,[1] nous enseigne que le mot se rencontre pour la première

[1] Helen M. Cam, *Studies in the Hundred Rolls ; some Aspects of the Thirteenth-century Administration* (vol. vi. des " Oxford Studies in Social and Legal History ", edited by Sir Paul Vinogradoff, 1921). Le paragraphe 4 est intitulé : The statute of rageman and the Placita de ragemannis. A la note 3 de la page 41, Miss Cam énumère les mss. qu'elle a vus au British Museum. Il y en a d'autres, par exemple dans la John Rylands Library à Manchester, que M. Robert Fawtier a bien voulu me signaler. Enfin, à la note 5 de la page 45, Miss Cam indique les dix-neuf " Assize rolls " conservés au P. Record Office avec l'inscription : " Placita de ragemannis " (1280–1331). Je

fois avec une date certaine dans un rôle d'assise qui existe au P. Record Office sous le No. 670 : " Placita de ragemannis et de quo warranto . . . in comitatu Notingham, in crastino Animarum, anno regni regis Edwardi octavo, incipiente nono " (1280),[1] mais comment est-il entré dans la langue administrative ? Ne serait-il pas de formation populaire, un phénomène de folklore ?

Si, laissant de côté les auteurs anciens, au premier rang desquels se place Du Cange, on consulte l'ouvrage qui, à l'heure actuelle, fixe l'état de la science pour l'histoire des mots dans la langue anglaise, je veux dire le *New English Dictionary*,[2] on y trouve de nombreux exemples rangés sous trois chefs : *ragman* 1, *ragman* 2, et enfin *ragman roll*, qui n'ajoute rien d'essentiel aux deux autres. *Ragman* 1 a désigné le Diable soit en personne soit un de ses démons, ou bien un homme vêtu de haillons (nous dirions en français un pauvre diable), ou enfin un vulgaire marchand de chiffons. L'article *ragman* 2, le plus significatif, désigne : 1° le statut de 1276, 2° toute espèce de rôle, de catalogue, de liste de noms, 3° un jeu de société, 4° un document d'archive en général. Classification peu logique, on le voit, et dont l'auteur avoue d'ailleurs ne pas être satisfait. En somme, il est plus commode de ramener ces quatre sens à deux : celui de jeu de société et celui de document d'archive ; je les examinerai successivement.

Dans le *New English Dictionary* on lit à peu près ceci : le jeu se jouait avec un rouleau muni de ficelles attachées en regard de certaines devises et que l'on tirait au hasard pour attraper la devise correspondante. On en connaît au moyen âge plusieurs types qui paraissent procéder d'un mode de divination connu en latin sous le nom de *sortes* ; ce sont les " sorts " des saints ou des apôtres. En 1880 M. Rocquain publia [3] une pièce de parchemin découverte à Cordes, près d'Albi, sur laquelle étaient écrits en langue provençale une

---

rappellerai que les " Hundred rolls " ont été édités par l'ancienne Record Commission : *Rotuli hundredorum temp. Hen. III et Edw. I* (1812–1818) ; joignez : *Placita de quo warranto, Edward I—Edward III* (*ibid.*, 1818). Cf. Charles Gross, *Sources and Literature of English History* (2e édition, 1915), Nos. 2040, 2160 et p. 481.

[1] La 8e année d'Édouard Ier a commencé le 20 novembre 1279.

[2] *A New English Dictionary on Historical Principles*, edited by James A. H. Murray, tome viii. (1910). Le rédacteur des articles relatifs à *ragman* reconnaît que l'origine et l'histoire du mot sont obscures : " in the absence of any plausible etymon, the development of senses can only be conjectural ". On peut encore consulter utilement l'ouvrage plus modeste et vieilli de J. O. Halliwell, *A Dictionary of Archaic and Provincial Words from the Fourteenth Century* (3e édition, 1887). Dans la nouvelle édition du *Middle English Dictionary* de Stratmann donnée en 1891 par Henry Bradley, l'article *ragman* remplit à peine huit lignes. Cf. deux lettres de Bradley insérées dans *The Academy*, 25 janvier et 28 juin 1890.

[3] *Bibliothèque de l'École des Chartes*, tome xli. (1880), pp. 457-74. Dans la *Revue des langues romanes*, 3e série, tome iv. (1880), pp. 152-166 et 270, Chabaneau n'ajoute rien à Rocquain à qui d'ailleurs il renvoie. Très voisins des *sortes sanctorum* sont les " sorts des apôtres " mentionnés par Joseph Anglade dans son *Histoire sommaire de la littérature méridionale au moyen âge* (1921) ; M. Anglade décrit à son tour le rouleau de Cordes, mais ne paraît pas avoir vu qu'il servait à un jeu de société (cf. A. Långfors, dans *Le Moyen Age*, tome xxiv., janvier-avril 1922, p. 124).

cinquantaine de versets plus ou moins directement inspirés des livres saints. Voici la description et l'explication qu'il en donne : dans la marge du parchemin, pendent des fils de couleur alternativement jaune et blanche ; il y a autant de fils que de versets ; le consultant touchait un de ces fils et lisait ensuite ou se faisait lire le verset contenant l'éclaircissement désiré. D'autres textes analogues, publiés par A. Jubinal et par Th. Wright [1] ont été analysés par Victor Leclerc au t. xxii. p. 177, de *l'Histoire littéraire de la France* ; un peu plus tard, Hazlitt a fait connaître un petit poème en anglais qui débute par cet incipit : " Here begynneth Ragman roelle " ; [2] puis il a exposé à son tour la règle du jeu : sur une longue bande de parchemin ou de papier on écrivait des couplets en vers ; un sceau était attaché par une ficelle en face de chacun de ces couplets ; puis on roulait la bande et les joueurs amenaient au hasard un couplet en tirant une des ficelles. On déployait ensuite le rouleau et chacun pouvait lire le couplet que lui attribuait le sort ; c'étaient soit des prédictions de bonne aventure, soit des sentences morales, soit des traits de caractère qui s'appliquaient le plus souvent tout de travers ; la lecture de ces devises suscitait des remarques amusantes, caustiques, ou même obscènes ; et de rire ! Ce " ragman roelle ", Hazlitt le rattachait tant bien que mal d'une part au Diable, que Guillaume Langland appelle en un passage " ce loqueteux qui a trompé le premier homme ",[3] d'autre part à la longue liste de prélats et de seigneurs écossais qui jurèrent fidélité au roi Édouard Ier en 1296. Plus récemment, un professeur à l'Université de Helsingfors en Finlande, M. Långfors, a réédité [4] trois petits poèmes français de la fin du XIIIe siècle composés : les deux premiers de trente-cinq quatrains, le second de cinquante, qui rentrent dans la catégorie soit des *sortes*, soit des jeux de société ou " Geus d'aventure ". Le commentaire de M. Långfors n'ajoute rien aux ouvrages antérieurs ; mais il a eu le mérite de faire, pour son propre compte, un ingénieux rapprochement entre la seconde de ces pièces, attribuée à un personnage imaginaire appelé Ragemon le Bon, et un " sermo communis " en latin rédigé, lui aussi, en quatrains versifiés. Paul Meyer, qui a découvert et publié ce " sermo communis ", avait été choqué de son incohérence ; l'illustre romaniste ne s'était pas avisé que l'auteur avait tout simplement démarqué les sentences du prétendu Ragemon le Bon en leur imprimant un caractère d'édification. Quant à chercher une suite logique dans ces

[1] Achille Jubinal, *Jongleurs et trouvères* (1835), pp. 151-157 ; Thomas Wright, *Anecdota litteraria* (1840), p. 766.

[2] W. Carew Hazlitt, *Remains of the Early Popular Poetry of England* (1864), tome i. pp. 68-76.

[3] " That ragman that first man deceivede " (*Piers Plowman*, édit. Skeat ; texte C, xix. 122). Cité dans le *New English Dictionary*.

[4] Arthur Långfors, *Un Jeu de société au moyen âge ; Rageman le bon, inspirateur d'un sermon en vers* (Helsingfors, 1920. Expressum ex Annalibus Academiae scientiarum Fennicae).

quatrains, ce serait aussi vain que d'en demander aux devises qui s'enroulent autour de nos mirlitons.

Le nom même de Ragemon, derrière lequel le rimeur français semble vouloir dissimuler sa propre personnalité, d'où vient-il ? S'il fallait en croire l'auteur, non méprisable d'ailleurs, d'un dictionnaire des termes juridiques, John Cowel,[1] il aurait existé un certain Ragimund, légat du pape en Écosse, qui, après avoir convoqué tous les possesseurs de bénéfices ecclésiastiques, les contraignit, dit-il, " à déclarer sous serment la valeur exacte de leurs bénéfices, estimation d'après laquelle ils furent ensuite taxés par la cour de Rome ". En conséquence, il proposait de corriger le titre en " Ragimund's roll ". Cowel fit ici allusion à une mission envoyée par le pape Nicolas IV en Angleterre et en Écosse pour faire évaluer en effet les revenus du clergé en vue d'une taxe pour la croisade (1288–1292) ; et le résultat de cette enquête a été consigné dans ce qu'on appelle " Papae Nicolai valor " ; mais il est évident que Cowel a confondu ce document avec un *Ragman roll* écossais compilé en 1296 et dont il sera parlé plus loin ; en outre il eût été fort embarrassé de trouver parmi les légats de Nicolas IV un Ragimond ou tout autre nom s'en rapprochant même de loin.

Quittons maintenant le domaine de l'histoire littéraire ou de la pure fantaisie pour aborder celui de l'histoire proprement dite.

On a vu plus haut que le mot *ragman* fut employé tout d'abord pour désigner les actes rédigés en exécution du statut " de justiciis assignatis " ; ajoutons qu'il en fut de même par le statut " de quo warranto ", qui est tout-à-fait contemporain ; ces actes ont été ensuite transcrits sur ce qu'on appelle les " hundred rolls ". Miss Cam a parfaitement exposé la procédure suivie alors (1274–1279) par les enquêteurs royaux : une fois nommés par le roi et son Conseil, ils devaient se rendre dans les comtés, soit pour recevoir les doléances des personnes lésées par les baillis, c'est-à-dire par les intendants des domaines royaux et seigneuriaux, soit pour constater les abus commis dans l'exercice des droits féodaux. Ils avaient pleins pouvoirs pour juger sur place et souverainement (" oier et terminer ") les délits et, d'autre part, ils devaient obliger les seigneurs à produire les titres sur lesquels se fondaient leurs droits. Un programme détaillé leur était fourni d'avance pour ces tournées (" articuli itineris "). Ils se rendaient alors successivement dans chaque centaine (" hundred ") ; là un jury local composé des délégués de chaque " villa " ou township devait répondre sous la foi du serment à toutes les questions posées par les enquêteurs. Ces réponses, dont l'authenticité était garantie par les sceaux des déclarants, étaient finalement transcrites sur des rôles de

[1] Dr. John Cowel, *A Law Dictionary, or the Interpreter of Words and Terms used either in the Common or Statute Laws of Great Britain and in Tenure and Jocular Customs* (édit. 1727).

parchemin que les juges transportaient de centaine en centaine et dont en route la masse ne cessait de s'accroître. En ce qui concerne le comté de Nottingham, Miss Cam a montré (p. 52) que, pour chaque hundred, les rôles sont formés de membranes de parchemin " dont le bas ", dit-elle, " est découpé en douze ou vingt-quatre lanières portant originairement les sceaux des jurés dont le nom est porté sur le document. Ces membranes une fois mises en forme de rôles offraient un aspect assez semblable à celui d'une pièce d'étoffe élimée, d'où l'expression de *ragman* ou de *ragment*." [1] C'est exact, à une nuance près : il est plus correct de dire que *ragman* a désigné tout d'abord l'homme, le magistrat qui portait ces paquets de sceaux pendants ; c'est ensuite seulement qu'il a pu s'appliquer à la masse des documents. Quant aux enquêteurs, n'oublions pas que c'étaient des personnages considérables, choisis parmi les plus hauts fonctionnaires de l'ordre administratif ou judiciaire ; qu'ils apparaissaient seulement de temps à autre, que leur venue devait susciter chez les plaignants de grands espoirs, chez les coupables des craintes trop légitimes, car la justice était alors en Angleterre d'autant plus dure que la royauté tirait des revenus très considérables des amendes infligées par eux. Il ne fallait pas aux gens du peuple un grand effort d'imagination pour les apercevoir sous les aspects redoutables ou ridicules de chiffonniers ou de démons. Dans tous les cas, c'est sur ces queues de parchemin que s'attachaient leurs regards, comme, dans les jeux de société, ils étaient tendus vers les ficelles révélatrices. De la langue du peuple, le mot passa enfin dans celle des agents de l'administration, qui connaissaient les documents et non les hommes ; et c'est d'eux que l'ont reçu tout naturellement les archivistes modernes et les érudits.

Mais poursuivons l'histoire de ce mot et de la chose qu'il représente.

Que *ragman* ait désigné officiellement certaines liasses, certains rouleaux scellés de nombreux sceaux, c'est ce que démontrent maints exemples souvent allégués ; j'en rappelerai seulement quelques-uns. Dans le second de ses rapports annuels (1841), le garde des archives royales (deputy keeper) a signalé " un sac étiqueté *ragman* où se trouvent plusieurs enquêtes faites en divers comtés sur des franchises (' liberties ') possédées depuis le temps d'Édouard Ier ". Dans ce sac, lit-on dans le 9e rapport annuel (1848, p. 243), se trouvent des " articuli de quibus inquirendum, scilicet *rageman* ". Il existe encore aujourd'hui au P. Record Office des " Rotuli ragemannorum " datés de 1281 et qui sont identiques aux " Hundred rolls " étudiés par Miss Cam. Il était donc assez naturel que le statut " de justiciis assignatis " fût aussi intitulé " quod vocatur Rageman ", titre, nous dit M. Hall, " emprunté à la forme de l'enquête, c'est-à-dire, aux sceaux apposés au bas du

[1] L'ouvrage de Miss Cam a été complété sur un point par M. R. Stuart-Brown qui a publié dans *English Historical Review*, 1924, pp. 83-86, un texte tiré du " Chester Eyre roll, N°. 12 ".

rôle original ".[1] Voilà la vérité ; mais cette juste observation, reléguée dans une note, peut échapper à l'attention des lecteurs ; Miss Cam nous a rendu le service de nous en fournir une preuve pour ainsi dire matérielle.

Dans l'article *ragman* 2 du *New English Dictionary*, il est dit au paragraphe 4 que le mot désigne aussi " la charte par laquelle les nobles écossais ont, en 1291, reconnu Édouard Ier pour leur suzerain ". Pour plus de précision, il faudrait dire les chartes par lesquelles le roi et les nobles écossais ont reconnu solennellement la suzeraineté du roi d'Angleterre. Ces chartes ont été publiées plusieurs fois, notamment dans les *Foedera* de Rymer aux dates du 26 décembre 1291 et du 2 janvier 1292 d'après le " Magnus rotulus Scotiae " qui contient toute la longue procédure suivie dans le Parlement de Norham. L'acte d'hommage prêté par John Balliol qu'Édouard Ier avait choisi pour ceindre la couronne écossaise, fut nécessairement revêtu des sceaux du roi et des principaux seigneurs ecclésiastiques et laïques (au nombre total de quarante-deux, le roi compris). Puis, comme chacun sait, les rapports entre le suzerain et le vassal ne tardèrent pas à s'aigrir : John Balliol, pressé par ses sujets de secouer le joug de l'Angleterre, renonça formellement à son hommage (1296) et finit par abdiquer. Édouard prit alors le parti d'annexer l'Écosse en rupture de vasselage et, pour prendre ses précautions mieux encore qu'en 1291–1292, il obligea les prélats, les nobles, les bourgeois de certaines villes ou bourgs, à lui délivrer des chartes individuelles ou collectives d'hommage et de fidélité. Ces chartes originales, qui dépassaient le nombre de deux mille, ont disparu pour la plupart, sans doute après qu'on eut pris le soin de les recopier. Il en existe en effet trois transcriptions identiques et authentiques désignées officiellement par le titre *Ragman roll*[2] ; titre qui s'explique fort bien par la ressemblance que la masse de ces actes scellés présentait avec les " hundred rolls " en service déjà depuis plus de quinze ans en Angleterre ; ressemblance tout extérieure à coup sûr et sans aucun rapport avec l'objet et la nature des documents eux-mêmes, suffisante cependant aux yeux du commun peuple qui n'a pas l'habitude d'y regarder de si près.

En Écosse, l'emploi du mot *ragman* pour désigner des liasses de chartes originairement scellées, quel qu'en fût le caractère intrinsèque, a été fréquent au XIVe et au XVe siècles. Je rappellerai seulement ceux qui sont les plus intéressants au point de vue spécial qui m'occupe ici. En 1328 eut lieu le mariage du fils et héritier présomptif du roi

[1] Hubert Hall, *Studies in English Official Historical Documents* (1908), p. 303. Cf. Giuseppi, *A Guide to the mss. preserved in the P. Record Office*, tome i. (1923), pp. 236, 340.

[2] Le "Magnus rotulus" a été analysé de près par Joseph Bain: *Calendar of Documents relating to Scotland*, sous le N°. 508 et le "Ragman roll", *ibid.* sous le N°. 823. Cf. Thomas Thomson, *The ragman rolls. Instrumenta publica, sive processus super fidelitatibus et homagiis Scotorum domino regi Angliae factis 1291–1296* (Bannatyne Club, 1834).

Robert I, David Bruce, avec une sœur d'Édouard III. A cette occasion, le chroniqueur anonyme de l'abbaye de Lanercost (qui écrivait dans les environs de 1350) [1] raconte que le jeune roi Édouard, pressé par sa mère, Isabelle de France, et par Mortimer d'abandonner les droits de suzeraineté obtenus après la grande enquête de Norham, rendit aux Écossais " unum instrumentum sive cartam subjectionis et homagii faciendi regibus Angliae, cui appensa erant sigilla omnium magnatum Scotiae . . . et a Scotis propter multa sigilla dependentia *ragman* vocabatur ". Quand en 1333 les lords écossais se révoltèrent contre ce même David devenu le roi David II, soupçonné de vouloir mettre un Anglais sur le trône, ils s'engagèrent les uns envers les autres, nous dit Fordun,[2] en échangeant des lettres de contre-assurance dites " ragmannicae litterae ".

La même terminologie se retrouve dans le même temps en Angleterre. On sait que, vers la fin du règne de Richard II, beaucoup de seigneurs, les bourgeois de plusieurs grandes villes et notamment ceux de la cité de Londres, se liguèrent pour combattre son despotisme. Dans l'espoir d'enrayer le mouvement, Richard obligea ses adversaires à lui délivrer des chartes en blanc où l'on aurait marqué des amendes arbitraires s'ils prenaient les armes contre lui. Aussitôt après le renversement de Richard, le parlement décréta que " totes les remembrances appelées raggemans ou blanches lettres nadgueres ensaelez en la cité de Londres " seraient annulées ; puis les shériffs reçurent l'ordre, par des lettres closes portant la suscription " de ragemannis comburendis ", de détruire " diversa scripta, cartas sive litteras patentes vocatas raggimans sive blank chartres, sigillis eorundem subditorum consignata ".[3]

Je n'ai pas épuisé la liste des exemples réunis dans le *New English Dictionary*, mais il faut conclure.

Le mot *ragman* a été forgé par l'imagination populaire, qu'avaient mise en branle certaines mesures ordonnées par Édouard Ier, après son retour en 1274, pour rétablir l'ordre dans son royaume ; les enquêteurs chargés de faire exécuter les deux statuts " de justiciis assignatis " et " de quo warranto ", quand on les vit transportant des liasses d'actes scellés à la mode du temps, apparurent aux yeux de gens effrayés ou narquois sous l'aspect de pauvres diables en haillons. Le contraste entre le mot et la chose était assez comique pour faire la fortune du sobriquet. Par une transition assez naturelle, le mot servit ensuite à caractériser des liasses de documents qui n'avaient

[1] *Chronicon de Lanercost*, 1201–1346, publié par Joseph Stevenson (Bannatyne Club, 1839), p. 261.

[2] John Fordun, *Scotichronicon*, xiv. p. 25. Thomson, qui reproduit les citations de l'anonyme de Lanercost et de Fordun, dit dans la préface des *Ragman rolls* que cette expression caractérise une " endenture ou tout autre acte légal exécuté sous le sceau des parties ".

[3] *Rotuli parliamentorum*, t. iii. p. 432.

plus aucun rapport avec les statuts d'origine ; il reçut droit de cité dans la terminologie usuelle de la chancellerie tant en Angleterre qu'en Écosse. Par un autre phénomène d'assimilation et dans une direction tout-à-fait différente, il fut donné à des jeux de hasard où les ficelles rappelaient plus ou moins vaguement les queues de parchemin. Si néanmoins on s'étonne que les Anglais de la " Merry England " aient eu l'idée biscornue d'établir un rapprochement quelconque entre des pièces d'archive et des amusements puérils, on la leur pardonnera en pensant au rôle joué par le dieu Hasard dans les affaires du monde, non seulement dans les " Geus d'aventure ", mais encore dans les " jugements de cour " dont souriait le bon La Fontaine.

CHARLES BÉMONT.

XIV

ARCHBISHOP PECHAM AND THE COUNCIL OF LAMBETH OF 1281

POSTERITY'S selective memory, which of necessity forgets much, is a little too apt to single out for retention such facts as are in harmony with preconceived ideas. A villain is expected to be villainous with a consistency rare in actual life, while a hero's failures are kept in stricter subordination to his triumphs than would seem natural to himself and his contemporaries. Something of this tendency, perhaps, has affected our view of the reign of Edward I. Most of its outstanding figures have their accepted shape—Edward himself, every inch a king, stern but just, frugal and self-controlled ; Eleanor, the ideal queen, wife and mother, so gentle an influence with her husband while she lived that her death meant an irreparable loss for the whole realm ; John Pecham, archbishop of Canterbury, the fussy prelate, *gestus affatusque pompatici*, trying the patience of lay and clerical colleagues to the utmost, but leashed firmly by the courage and moderation of the king. Yet any one who has examined, even cursorily, the records and writings of the time, will at once recall facts which modify these verdicts. He remembers the legacy of debt which Edward left to his son, for all the frugality of his personal tastes ; he recalls occasions when the self-control was not conspicuous, when Edward snatched a daughter's coronet from her head to throw it into the fire, as official records show,[1] or tore a son's hair out by the roots, as a chronicler asserts.[2] He marvels that an ideal mother could leave her six-year-old son [3] to bear a long illness and die alone at Guildford, when she herself was living in London, only thirty miles away, and begins to understand why Archbishop Pecham, reminding Eleanor that " the saints teach us that women are naturally more pitiful and more devout than men ", reminded her also that " there are those who say that you cause the king to act harshly ".[4]

[1] Brit. Mus. Add. MS. 7965 (Wardrobe Book, 1296–7), f. 15 v. *Ade aurifabro regis pro una magna rubeta et una magna ameraude emptis ad ponendum in quadam coronella comitisse Hollandie filie regis loco duarum petrarum que amisse fuerunt quando rex iecit eandem coronellam in igne apud Gippewicum mense Januarii.*

[2] Hemingburgh, *Chronicon* (Eng. Hist. Soc.), ii. 272.

[3] Cf. " The Wardrobe and Household of Henry, son of Edward I." in *Bulletin of the John Rylands Library*, vii. 384-420.

[4] *Registrum Epistolarum Johannis Peckham* (Rolls Series), ii. 555.

And finally, the character of that same archbishop, as revealed by the traces of his activities in his own voluminous records and those of others, shows itself a problem too complex to be dismissed by facile generalisations about officiousness and over-anxious zeal, while in the trials of strength between himself and the king the honours were more evenly divided than has sometimes been supposed.

It is with this last subject, and in particular with Pecham's actions at the council of Reading in 1279, and the council of Lambeth in 1281, that the present article deals. At both he came into conflict with the crown ; at both, in the view most generally accepted, he was defeated. At the Michaelmas parliament of 1279 the archbishop had to appear in person and declare " annulled and as though never pronounced " five of the constitutions passed at Reading in the previous July, and to promise that no prejudice should arise to the king or his realm of England in future from those which remained. Two years later, when the king had reason to suppose that doubtful questions were again to be raised in a council about to meet at Lambeth, he solemnly warned the archbishop and his suffragans against discussing matters pertaining to his crown. The contemporary historian, Thomas Wykes, who became a canon at Osney in 1282, and moved, one would imagine, in circles likely to be well informed as to matters of this kind, states definitely that Pecham thereupon gave up the idea of any fresh assertion of ecclesiastical rights. "He had intended to annul certain liberties belonging to the crown and in use for a long time past—namely, cognisance of patronage cases, and royal prohibitions in pleas about chattels and such-like which seemed to concern the spiritualty alone ", but when the king with threats " forbade him to presume to decree anything to the prejudice or depression of the king's liberty, the archbishop in terror entirely withdrew from his presumption ".[1] Most modern historians have accepted this view of the matter, among them the editor of Pecham's letters, who says in so many words, " This caution was effectual, and the statutes are concerned with nothing but ecclesiastical matters ".[2]

Now in actual fact Pecham did not withdraw. On the contrary, he proceeded to insert afresh in the legislation of the council of Lambeth exactly those points which he had been compelled to annul in the legislation of the council of Reading. These dealt, no doubt, with what to him were in a very real sense " ecclesiastical matters ", but they advanced to combat with the secular courts upon that highly debatable ground which separated lay from ecclesiastical jurisdiction, and which Edward undoubtedly had in mind when before the council met he warned the bishops to walk warily. This time, moreover, there was no subsequent recantation, and Pecham's defiance went

[1] Wykes, *Chron.* (*Ann. Monastici*, iv.), 285-6.
[2] *Reg. Epist.* I. lxvii.

entirely unpunished. So far from losing the fight before striking a blow, he fought to a finish and was left in possession of the field.

Before proceeding to examine the evidence for this statement of the case, let us pay a tribute in passing to that hot-headed but admirable pioneer of historical research, William Prynne. More than two hundred and fifty years ago, examining with eyes as keen as they were prejudiced the constitutions of Lambeth, Prynne observed in parenthesis after printing the section most vital to our argument, "The same in effect with those Clauses in the council of Reding for which he was questioned, and thereupon revoked in Parliament, yet now contemptuously revived and reenforced".[1] The immense bulk, and the comparative inaccessibility, of Prynne's great folios account for the fact that this warning escaped the notice of modern historians, but it is harder to understand why a similar statement made in a well-known book published only thirty years ago also passed unobserved. Dr. Felix Makower of Berlin, in his *Verfassung der Kirche von England*,[2] appended to his mention of the writ *Circumspecte agatis* a lengthy footnote in which he printed extracts from the controversial section of the constitutions of Reading, with the memorandum on the close roll recording Pecham's revocation, and went on to show that by the council of Lambeth the clergy were directed to publish certain excommunications, "the text of which agreed almost entirely with those published at Reading", quoting illustrative extracts. Yet in more than one authoritative work of reference which has appeared since that date, the point is ignored, Wykes' story accepted, and Pecham left to posterity's view as the blustering prelate who mouths great words but swallows them at the first hint of danger.

To understand the events of 1281, we must first recur, in rather more detail, to the events of 1279. Pecham's primacy had opened more smoothly than might have been expected when it is considered that Pope Nicholas III. had appointed him by provision, in place of Edward's friend and chancellor, Robert Burnell, elected by the monks of Canterbury. Archbishop and king first met at Amiens, where Edward may have been attracted by the enthusiasm with which Pecham adopted the correct English attitude regarding points at issue between England and France, brought to a settlement on May 23 by the treaty of Amiens. At any rate, Edward received the newcomer "courteously, benignly, and in the most friendly way", and on the day after the treaty had been signed restored to him the temporalities[3]

[1] Prynne's *Records*, iii. (1668), 257.

[2] P. 34, *n.* 71, Berlin, 1894. Or p. 32, *n.* 71, in the English translation entitled *Constitutional History and Constitution of the Church of England*. London, 1895.

[3] May 24. So Pecham told the pope (*Reg. Epist.* i. 5. My references throughout are to pages, not to the number of the letter). But the letters patent were dated at Dover on May 30 (*Cal. Pat. Rolls*, 1272–81, p. 316).

of the archbishopric, although, *nescio qua surreptione scribentis*,[1] the papal clerk had omitted to ask him to do so in the letters announcing the appointment. Edward told Pecham plainly that it was through personal goodwill that he refrained from taking advantage of this omission, and announced publicly that he was better pleased with the pope's choice than he would have been with the success of his recommendation of Burnell.

The moment Pecham set foot in England, on June 4, he expressed an earnest desire to " see the longed-for faces " of his fellow-bishops and suffragans, and summoned them to meet him at Reading, where in due course, on July 29, they assembled. The constitutions there passed [2] dealt for the most part with matters clearly within the sphere of Pecham's spiritual responsibility. One section only, *De sententiis excommunicationis publice denunciandis*, trod on debatable ground. Priests were there bidden to explain to their flocks that sentences of excommunication were incurred by eleven categories of offenders. The first were those who maliciously deprived the church of her rights by obtaining royal writs of prohibition to stop cases in progress in church courts. The last were those who in any way acted contrary to Magna Carta. The section closed with an order that copies of the charter, well and clearly written, should be posted in every cathedral or collegiate church, in some public place where they would meet the eyes of all entering, and that after twelve months the old copy should be removed and a fresh one, well written, be put in its place.[3] This order roused the king's wrath to a rather surprising degree. To the modern onlooker there seems little that is offensive in recalling public attention to a charter which, though in its origin representing the coercion of a disreputable king by his outraged subjects, had in its early reissues and confirmations under Henry III. been envisaged as the freely offered pledge of good intentions. Certainly all Edward I.'s actions so far had been taken in a law-abiding spirit. Some contemporary documents, however, such as the petitions of the clergy in 1285,[4] convey the impression that to clerical eyes the greatest clause of the charter was that opening promise—that the English church shall be free, and have her rights entire and her liberties unharmed—which from some other angles of vision seemed a formal and respectful reiteration of a general obligation, rather than the thread upon which

[1] Pecham said no more than this in his letter to the pope ; but in writing to the bishop of Tusculum he complained that the missing clause had been duly inserted in the letters referring to the elect of Dublin, *cum tamen litera sua et nostra ab eodem Benedicto, sed benedictione multum dissimili, processissent* (*Reg. Epist.* i. 6).

[2] Wilkins, *Concilia*, ii. 33-36.

[3] The order suggests some problems. Was the population, other than clerical, which went to church in the end of the thirteenth century really so literate as to read the sixty clauses of the charter, or so erudite as to interpret their many obscurities ? Yet if the posting was a mere manifesto, there was no need to stipulate that the copy should be legibly written, or renewed after wear and tear.

[4] Wilkins, *op. cit.* ii. 117-18.

the whole of the rest hung. It was significant that the petitioners in 1285 closed their requests by quoting, or rather misquoting,[1] the famous clause 39, and declaring that the rights thus secured to every free man were *a fortiori* due to the church. In the light of such an attitude, it is easier to understand why Edward took alarm at Pecham's zeal for the publication of the charter, and the punishment of all who contravened it.

Be that as it may, Edward undoubtedly objected to this and other matters in the section, and Pecham had to give way. He expressly renounced, before king and council in parliament, the clause among the sentences of excommunication referring to those who sought royal writs to hinder process in the church courts; the excommunication of royal ministers who would not lay hands on excommunicated persons, and of those who attacked the manors of clerks; Magna Carta was to be removed from the doors of churches; and nobody was to be forbidden to sell food to the archbishop of York, or to anybody else on his way to the king.[2]

Let us now turn to the events of 1281. In July Pecham issued an imperative summons for a council to be held at Lambeth on October 7. It was to include all his fellow bishops and suffragans, abbots and elective priors whether exempt or not, deans of cathedral or collegiate churches, archdeacons and proctors of chapters. By this time Pecham's activities had led him into many quarrels, and he was by no means sure of general support. The summons included a warning that no excuse of ill-health would be accepted for the non-appearance of persons who were quite able to travel about in carriages on their private business all over the province of Canterbury, and also a promise that a hearing would be given to all who had grievances.[3] On September 18, in a letter to Cardinal Matteo Orsini, Pecham declared that he was labouring his utmost, night and day, for the reformation of the English church, and finding few to help him.[4] He probably thought it additional evidence of this lack of sympathy when, in common with every other bishop or prelate about to attend the Lambeth council, he received two letters[5] issued from the royal Chancery on September 28. The first contained a brief injunction that

as you love the baronies you hold from us, do not presume to hold counsel concerning any matters appertaining to our crown, or touching our person or the state of ourselves or our realm, or to decree anything contrary to our crown and dignity. Know of a surety that if you do, we will descend heavily upon your baronies.

[1] *Attendens quod nec etiam liber homo debet deseysiri de libertate vel libera consuetudine sua, nisi per legale judicium parium suorum et per legem terre secundum magnam cartam; et multo magis ecclesia non debet nec potest suis juribus et libertatibus taliter spoliari.*

[2] *Cal. Close Rolls*, 1272–79, p. 582.

[3] *Reg. Epist.* i. 211.

[4] *Op. cit.* 227.

[5] *Foedera* (1818), i. 598; *Cal. Pat. Rolls*, 1272–81, p. 457.

The second was more detailed.

"As you know", wrote the king, "you are bound to us by an oath, according to which you ought to show all possible fealty to us in matters affecting our crown and royal dignity. Wherefore we bid you, commanding you firmly by the faith and fealty in which you are bound to us, that you devote all possible diligence to both the conservation and defence of the rights of ourself and our realm. And we strictly forbid you, all and single who are under the bond of the oath aforesaid, under pain of the loss of the temporalities which you hold from us, to procure or in any way attempt anything to the prejudice of ourselves or our realm in the same council, against us or our rights, which our predecessors the kings of England and ourselves have enjoyed by ancient and approved custom; or to give your consent to any one who wishes to procure, attempt, or decree anything of this sort. So bear yourselves in this matter that we may be obliged specially to commend you, instead of to threaten you, which God forbid."

This timely reminder must have reached the prelates just as they were about to set out for Lambeth, and would be, one imagines, very fresh in their memories when they proceeded to their discussions. Wykes seems to imply that the king's views were also actually voiced in the council itself.[1] Yet Pecham held on his way, and among the constitutions promulgated, most of them dealing with purely spiritual matters, there was once again inserted a chapter *De sententiis excommunicationis publicandis*[2] which restored nearly everything that had been deleted from the constitutions of Reading. The preamble spoke even more explicitly than that of 1279.

By the council of Oxford those were excommunicated who deprive churches of their right and who strive unjustly and maliciously to infringe or even to disturb the liberties of the same; whereby three sorts of persons are bound in the chain of excommunication—those who steal her rights from the church; those who infringe ecclesiastical liberties; and those who without infraction contentiously disturb the same. And this we understand not only with regard to the general liberties of the universal church, but also with regard to special liberties, both temporal and spiritual, against the justice of any church. Thus we hold to be excommunicated, in particular, those who by writs or laws of a lay court hinder the progress of ecclesiastical causes, which are so known to belong to the church that in no wise can they be, or are they wont to be, determined by secular judgment. This we say, not intending to confine the aforesaid sentences to such persons alone, and not approving interference with the rights of churches in other ways, but because we wish to chastise with due rigour those who are enemies of God and the church after this fashion. By the decree of this sentence, moreover, we order the denunciation, as excommunicate, of all those who by means of false exception hinder archiepiscopal or episcopal process, or evade discipline.[3]

[1] *Chronicon*, 285-6. *Rex per quosdam de suis in eodem concilio publice se opposuit*, etc.

[2] Wilkins, *Concilia*, ii. 56-7.

[3] I translate from the fourteenth-century manuscripts (especially Brit. Mus. MS. Harl. 2349 and Camb. Univ. Lib. MS. Dd. 9. 38) in preference to Wilkins' printed text.

Here then, with grave and full explanation, was restored that *clausula in prima sententia excommunicationis* which had been withdrawn at the parliament of 1279. And the remaining ten categories of offenders followed in due course, not in the exact order, but for the most part in the exact words, of the original list issued at Reading. It may have been a sop to Cerberus that the second place was given to

> those who presume injuriously to disturb the peace and tranquillity of king and kingdom, and strive unjustly to detain the rights of the king. Under this head we take to be excommunicated not only those who rouse the horror of war, but also thieves and robbers, and any who spurn the justice of the realm.

False witnesses, who had second place at Reading, now came down to the third. The fourth class were those who hindered true marriage or other cases by *exceptiones* or special pleas—a plaint which should fall into its place as an illustration of much that Maitland said in his section on Pleading and Proof, of the time when " our records became turbid with ' exceptions ' ".[1] The fifth group comprised those who maliciously imputed crimes to persons not accused by the serious and trustworthy. Sixth in order came any who when a church was vacant raised a dispute over the patronage, hoping to deprive the patron of collation for that turn at any rate. Seventh on the list were all who refused to help in the seizure of excommunicated persons. Not a word was said of the reservation made before parliament in 1279, by which ministers of the king were not to be excommunicated even if they did not obey the royal order in such circumstances. The eighth class comprised persons who accepted gifts to prevent a settlement or compromise between litigants. The ninth clause declared excommunicate those who removed anything from the houses or manors of archbishops, bishops, or other ecclesiastical persons against their will, thus ignoring the principle laid down before parliament in 1279, that in such cases the penalty imposed by the king was sufficient. To the tenth group belonged those who laid hands on any fugitive who had sought sanctuary, who prevented his being supplied with necessary food, or who stole goods deposited in churches, churchyards, or religious houses. The eleventh clause renewed the excommunication of all who contravened Magna Carta, but did not revive the order for its posting on church doors. Instead, the section closed with an admonition to the archdeacons to inquire diligently as to whether their clergy were explaining the import of all these sentences of excommunication to their parishioners.

> And as often as they find priests who are .not preaching the said moral instruction and the said sentences of excommunication to their people at the appointed times, so often shall they coerce them, and chastising them with canonical penalty, oblige them to repair their careless omission.

[1] *Hist. Eng. Law*, ii. 611-16.

Now Pecham might be prepared to argue that in promulgating this excommunications section afresh he was merely republishing accepted legislation. " In these times ", the section began, " let there be published the sentences formerly pronounced in the days of ourselves and our predecessors."[1] A reference followed to the council held at Oxford under the presidency of Archbishop Stephen Langton in 1222, and the first seven paragraphs of the section closely followed the wording of the proclamations of excommunications there made as a sort of introduction to the council's legislation.[2] Next came an allusion to the legatine council held at St. Paul's Cathedral under Ottobon in 1268, and the next three clauses contained, in much shortened form, the substance of the twelfth and twenty-seventh constitutions passed by that council.[3] If verbal precedents could thus be found in the canons of the councils of Oxford and London as well as in those of the council of Reading, in spirit the section recalled the vigorous denunciations of lay encroachments on clerical rights made at the councils of Merton[4] (1258) and Lambeth[5] (1261), in the days of that Archbishop Boniface whose " anxious labours " on behalf of the Church's theoretical position may possibly have counterbalanced to some extent that neglect of repairs of buildings which so gravely imperilled, in Pecham's eyes, the prospects of his soul.[6] When explaining to the assembled bishops the procedure to be adopted at the council of Lambeth in 1281, Pecham expressly referred to the council which had met in the same place twenty years before.[7]

All this array of precedents, however, could not alter the fact that in 1279 the king had already taken exception to some of these sentences, whatever their origin, and that Pecham had publicly annulled the offending articles. Now he was restoring the three chief grounds of offence—the threat to those who obtained royal writs of prohibition, and to those who would not help to capture excommunicated persons, and the refusal to accept the secular penalty as adequate for those who attacked the manors of clerks. Further, though Magna Carta had disappeared from the churches, it was certain that reference would be made to it when priests fulfilled their duty of preaching on the sentences, and possible that the reference would be exactly of the sort to which Edward I. objected.

This advance into forbidden ground, after the recent royal warning to trespassers, seemed so improbable that the present writer was tempted to conjecture that a variant version of this section of the

[1] Wilkins, ii. 56. [2] *Op. cit.* i. 585. [3] *Op. cit.* ii. 8. 12.

[4] *Op. cit.* i. 736-40 ; Ann. Burton (*Ann. Monast.* i.), 412-25.

[5] *Op. cit.* i. 746-55.

[6] Cf. Prof. Jenkins in the *Church Quarterly Review*, Oct. 1924, pp. 79-80.

[7] Wilkins, ii. 51. *Tertio vero recitari volumus concilium de Lamheth quod sanctae memoriae praedecessor noster Bonifacius cum fratribus et coepiscopis sui temporis noscitur salubriter edidisse.*

Reading constitutions had somehow been incorporated into the printed copies of the Lambeth constitutions. An examination of fourteen of the surviving manuscripts entirely disposed of this theory, but revealed some facts with regard to Wilkins' text in the *Concilia* which may justify, at this point, a short digression on the manuscripts and his treatment of them. He took as his basis a fifteenth-century manuscript in the Cotton collection,[1] bequeathed to the public in 1700 only, and ravaged in 1731 by the disastrous Cotton fire. Among the manuscripts which then perished, almost certainly,[2] was Wilkins' chief source for the constitutions of Lambeth, which thus disappeared six years before his book was published. He had collated this text, however, with three others, also of the fifteenth century, one at Lambeth, one at Magdalen College, Oxford, and one in the collection of Bishop Moore of Ely. The first has survived complete and uninjured.[3] The Magdalen manuscript,[4] though still extant, has had a page cut out right in the middle of the excommunications section. The Ely volume was bought by George I. with the rest of the bishop's collection on his death, and was presented to the Cambridge University library, where it still remains intact.[5]

I have examined and compared, for the purposes of this discussion, the Lambeth manuscript which Wilkins used and two others [6] in the same library; the Magdalen manuscript; the Ely volume, together with five other manuscripts in the Cambridge University library,[7] and four manuscripts in the Harleian collection in the British Museum.[8]

[1] Brit. Mus. Cotton MS. Otho A 15. In Thomas Smith's *Catalogus* (1696) it is described as Otho A 16.

[2] Mr. Gilson of the British Museum points out to me that as no fragments remain, there is a bare possibility that it was not burnt then, but was missing before.

[3] Lambeth MS. 538. Wilkins referred to it as Lambeth MS. 17. It was one of the MSS. which were taken to Cambridge during the Commonwealth, and bears on its fly-leaf the Cambridge press-mark Lθ 17. No. 17 in the *Catalogue of MSS. in the Library of Lambeth Palace* (1812), described there as missing, was an entirely different, folio, MS.; but in the manuscript catalogue of Bishop Gibson (who became Lambeth librarian in 1700 and bishop of London in 1723) the MS. 17 of the 1812 catalogue appears as 17 among the folio MSS. and the MS. 538 as MS. 17 among the octavos. It is to the kindness of the Rev. Prof. Jenkins, Keeper of the MSS. at Lambeth Palace, that I owe this explanation of a puzzling reference.

[4] MS. Coll. S. Ma. Magd. Oxon. 185. I must thank Mr. W. A. Pantin for kindly collating this MS. with Wilkins' text and transcribing the relevant portion.

[5] MS. Eliensis 235, now Camb. Univ. Lib. MS. Gg. 6. 21. My thanks are due to Dr. A. F. Kirkpatrick, Dean of Ely, who drew my attention to this volume's migrations.

[6] Lambeth MSS. 460, 778. MS. 460, of the fourteenth century, contains extracts only, and the excommunications section is not among those selected. MS. 778 may be early fifteenth century.

[7] MSS. Dd. 9. 38, Ii. 2. 28 (both fourteenth century), Ee. 6. 30, Ii. 2. 7, Ii. 3. 14 (all fifteenth century). But neither Ee. 6. 30 nor Ii. 2. 28 contains the excommunications section.

[8] Harl. MSS. 52 and 2349 (both fourteenth century), 335 and 3705 (both fifteenth century). MS. 52 makes the excommunications section cap. x. instead of cap. XIV. MS. 335 is a late copy, dates the council as November instead of October, and makes careless slips (*e.g. auribus curie* for *iuribus curie*).

The search might have been extended to nineteen other manuscripts also included in the list which Mr. Trice Martin compiled when editing Pecham's letters [1]: seven in the Bodleian library [2]; seven in college libraries at Oxford [3]; three in college libraries at Cambridge [4]; and two in the library of Trinity College, Dublin.[5] Moreover, there is little doubt that scrutiny of cathedral archives would bring to light many more, for volumes of miscellaneous collections were common possessions of a great church or a monastic house. Often they were very miscellaneous indeed. A good example is that interesting fourteenth-century volume, now in the Cambridge University library,[6] but formerly the property of Reading Abbey, which begins with the constitutions of popes, legates, and archbishops (Pecham among the rest), goes on with the rule of St. Benedict, some Reading charters, Magna Carta, and a treatise on sak and sok, and ends with a disquisition on farriery and the remark "*Explicit cirugia equorum. Qui scripsit carmen sit benedictus. Amen.*" To exhaust the whole range of such volumes in search of copies of Pecham's constitutions would be an interminable, and a profitless, business. The fourteen which have been examined may well serve as specimens of the rest, and furnish in themselves ground for some definite conclusions.

It became clear at once that Wilkins had not chosen the best manuscripts, had spent no special pains on his collation, and had introduced difficulties all his own. With fourteenth-century manuscripts available, he chose to use fifteenth-century texts. He noted few variant readings,[7] and sometimes preferred the less desirable of two alternatives. For example, where the constitutions speak of those who "by means of false exception" hindered procedure, he printed in his text *excommunicationis*, though in a footnote he drew attention to the *exceptionis* which he had found in the Magdalen manuscript. Again, he did not trouble to add from the latter words or paragraphs which he found missing in the Ely manuscript, in the Lambeth manuscript, and perhaps in the lost Cotton manuscript. This was unfortunate, for it is a curious fact that among the originals I have seen the Ely and Lambeth manuscripts alone are responsible for certain omissions. They leave out, for instance, a very important *precipue* in the clause singling out as *specially* guilty those who hinder ecclesiasti-

[1] *Reg. Epist.* III. cxxxii.-cxxxix.

[2] Bibl. Bodl. MSS. 1659 (Digby 58); 10,022 (Tanner 196); 3431 (Selden Supra 43); 4049 (Hatton 109); 11303 (Rawlinson A 423); 11965 (Rawlinson C 100); 12280 (Rawlinson C 428).

[3] MSS. Coll. Exon. 31 and 41; MS. Coll. Omn. An. 42; MS. Coll. Aen. Nas. 14; MSS. Coll. Bal. 158 and 301; MS. C.C.C. 145.

[4] MS. Coll. Pemb. 145; MSS. C.C.C. 84 and 271.

[5] MSS. 211 (formerly B5, 3) and 526 (formerly E2, 22). Both are of the fifteenth century, and MS. 211 contains constitution 9 only.

[6] MS. Dd. 9. 38.

[7] Four only in the whole of the excommunications section.

cal cases by writs of a lay court.[1] Moreover, they omit entirely the lengthy and cautious paragraph in the preamble explaining that special denunciation of such culprits does not mean that offenders of other sorts are blameless.[2] They also contain some difficult readings where the weight of manuscript authority goes to support others much easier. For example, the preamble, having stated that the council of Oxford excommunicated those who infringed or disturbed ecclesiastical liberties, went on to define these two classes precisely as those *infringentes* and those *sine fractione turbantes*. The Ely and Lambeth manuscripts read *sine ratione*, missing the point completely.[3] In a confusing passage over which many copyists went wrong, and which Wilkins printed from his texts as *quod non solum intelligimus de generalibus libertatibus universalis ecclesie verum etiam tam de spiritualibus quam de temporalibus*, he might have secured from the Lambeth manuscript 778 an intelligible version, *non solum de generalibus . . . verum etiam de specialibus tam temporalibus quam spiritualibus*. It is almost certain that to himself, not to any manuscript, were due such slips as *fides apostolica* for *sedes apostolica*, *morlalem* for *moralem*, and the like.

To return to the historical inferences to be drawn from an examination of the manuscripts. No doubt can possibly remain that the excommunications section did form part of the constitutions of Lambeth, and did in substance reproduce the corresponding section of the constitutions of Reading. One fifteenth-century copyist, indeed, unconsciously emphasised the point which concerns us, for soon after beginning the chapter *De sententiis excommunicationis* he broke off abruptly with an " *etc. ut supra* " and a reference to the constitutions of Reading.[4] With the rest, it was read aloud to the assembled prelates at the last session of the council, on Friday, October 10, 1281, and duly became law. About three weeks later, Pecham, still at Lambeth, wrote the king a letter which set the seal, as it were, upon the council's proceedings, and should be read in the closest connection with them.[5] Uppermost in his mind, and perhaps rankling, was the memory of the king's solemn reminder of the binding nature of the bishops' oaths of fealty.

" Since it behoves us to give greater obedience to God than to men," he now wrote, " we cannot by any human constitution, not even by an oath, be bound to violate laws which rest undoubtedly upon divine authority."

[1] *In quo [illos] excommunicari intelligimus [precipue] qui literis aut iuribus curie laicalis ecclesiasticarum causarum processum impediunt.*

[2] *Quod dicimus non intendentes predictas sententias ad istos tantummodo coartare nec turbaciones iurium ecclesiarum aliter approbantes, set quia huiusmodi dei et ecclesie inimicos volumus rigore debito castigare.*

[3] But Lambeth MS. 778 had the correct version.

[4] Camb. Univ. Lib. MS. Ii. 2. 7.

[5] Nov. 2, 1281. *Reg. Epist.* i. 239-44.

He went on to point out that in the past the church had been oppressed, contrary to the laws of the popes, the canons of councils, and the decrees of the Fathers, and therefore there had long been bitter dissension between the kings and magnates of England on the one hand, and the archbishops, bishops and clergy of the same realm on the other, which could never end until kings came to recognise that their laws were secondary to the laws of Christ.

Some enemy of the church may say that it is not for the supreme pontiff to lay the yoke of laws or canons of this kind upon a secular prince, but this we deny, and with us the universal church and all the saints.

From an argument on these lines, enriched with Scripture quotations, especially from Deuteronomy, Pecham proceeded to a survey of England's past history, marshalling many instances of devout and biddable monarchs of ancient times.

Constantine, who was not only king of England, but also emperor of the whole world, granted everything which we ask, and in particular decreed that clerics should be judged by ecclesiastics alone.

Wihtred, king of Kent, declared that he would obey the church's laws, as was made clear at a council held in 794. Cnut made laws about ecclesiastical persons, and as soon as St. Edward ascended the throne he swore that he would observe Cnut's laws, while William I. in his turn pledged himself to observe those of St. Edward. Thus under British kings, English kings and the early Norman kings, the church was in possession of her liberties. It was under Henry I., and above all under Henry II., with the martyrdom of St. Thomas the archbishop, that a change for the worse set in.

Since, therefore, most excellent lord, we are driven by the prick of conscience to write these things to you, as we wish to make answer in the dreadful day of judgment, we humbly beg you to deign to incline your ears to our exhortations, for by oath you too are bound to root out all evil customs from your land, and you cannot be bound by any oath whatever to oppose the liberties of the church. We freely absolve you from any oath which could in any way rouse your conscience against the church. We are firmly of opinion that neither you nor your soul will be able to prosper, nor will you be able to provide for the future security of your realm, unless you deign to hearken to our exhortation, in a cause for which so many holy fathers, and last but one Boniface of blessed memory, uncle of your illustrious mother, laboured so anxiously. We believe that the goodness of your heart will lead you to this, unless wicked counsellors deceive you. If they do, we pray the Most High that he will so afflict them with temporal penalties that their souls may be saved.

" A fine letter ! " commented in the margin the clerk whose task it was to copy this into Pecham's register ; and again, later, " Note ; A letter on behalf of the liberty of the church ".[1] Prynne's views were

[1] Reg. Pecham, f. 97.

very different when he came to read it nearly four hundred years afterwards.

> Thus doth this Papal Archprelate, instead of obeying the King's premised Writ and observing his Oath of Fealty to him, in maintaining . . . the antient Rights and Priviledges of his Crown and Realm, in this his insolent Epistle most perfidiously, trayterously, and professedly oppugn, argue, contest against them ; and by wrested, misapplyed Texts of Scripture, false suggestions, and the presidents of his most seditious trayterous predecessors Becket and Boniface, whom he highly magnifies, endeavour to justifie his and his Suffragans' Antimonarchical proceedings and Constitutions in this Council.[1]

The modern reader will hardly wax so warm, though he may well be left amazed at the letter's ingenious mixture of persuasion and threats, of Scriptural and historical argument, of admonitions based on religious obligation with appeals to family pride and personal ambition. Apparently it so far succeeded that Edward took no steps to fulfil his threats, quietly accepting the *fait accompli* of the constitutions.

There remain, however, certain further questions to be answered. What effect had the renewed publication of the excommunications upon general opinion, lay or clerical ? Did it hasten, or retard, an understanding between the opposed parties ? When the crown ultimately made some concessions to the clerical view as to the competence of ecclesiastical courts in lay causes, can any direct connection be traced with the events of 1281 ?

It is difficult to be very sure about the answer to any of these enquiries, because soon after the council of Lambeth the main current of events swept both king and archbishop into other activities. The autumn of 1281 saw new developments in Edward's anti-Angevin policy abroad ; the spring of 1282 reopened the conflict with Wales. In the subsequent campaigning, conquest and settlement, which occupied Edward till 1284, Pecham took a lively interest, and flung himself into interviews, correspondence and negotiations, first in the endeavour to persuade the Welsh rebels to submission, later in the desire to reform and organise the Welsh church. Consequently neither party to the dispute of 1281 had time to recur to it. In 1285, however, Edward returned to England, and set to work to put his house in order, as it were, in the hope of being able by the next year to go abroad to deal with pressing business awaiting him in his overseas dominions. Forthwith ecclesiastical discontent was again thrust upon his notice. Preserved in the register of Godfrey Giffard, bishop of Worcester (1268–1301), and printed by Wilkins in the *Concilia*, are three interesting documents belonging to this date. The first is a list of seventeen articles presented to the king by the bishops, together with the reply made to each by the chancellor.[2] The next gives the clergy's criticisms

[1] Prynne, *Records*, iii. (1668) 267.

[2] Wilkins, ii. 115.

upon the replies received.[1] The third contains petitions of the archbishop of Canterbury and his suffragans relating to injuries done to the church in the province of Canterbury by the royal court.[2] All three were inspired by the same sense of injury, but the expression of the grievance took quite different shape in the articles and the petitions. The former were plainly worded requests with regard to specific points of royal procedure. Each received a definite answer, and in due course each answer, satisfactory or otherwise, a definite comment. The petitions, on the contrary, took the form of a general manifesto in which particular grievances served as illustrations of the main theme, which was the unhappy condition of the church, the aggression of the crown, and the dangers arising and likely to arise from so unbecoming a conflict.

Among the seventeen articles there were several, as might be expected, touching the quarrel about jurisdiction. The very first, indeed, was a request that one or two justices, or a baron of the Exchequer, should always be at London to examine demands for writs of prohibition in doubtful cases, and should be empowered to give licence for cases to proceed despite such prohibitions, and to hand over those who had asked for the writs to the ordinaries for punishment. The chancellor's reply was that those who feared to proceed contrary to the king's prohibition might ask the advice of Ralph de Hengham, John de Geyton, William de Brompton, William de Saham, or any one of them. *Si sint mere spiritualia, procedant secure.* Criticising this response, the clergy remarked acrimoniously that advice was no use as long as public proclamation was made that the jurisdiction of the church was to be confined to will and marriage cases. This may be either a reference to an ordinance issued by the king in this year enforcing that limitation, or else to the chancellor's answer to the tenth of the seventeen articles, in which the clergy asked that in litigation before ecclesiastical courts laymen should not be aggrieved until it was known whether the case did not fall under spiritual jurisdiction, and were told: "*Curia intendit quod praelati bene sciant cognoscere quae placita sint de testamento et quae de matrimonio et super aliis non cognoscant*". Another article reminiscent of the difficulties of 1279 and 1281 was the fourteenth, which besought the king to let the charters be observed. The chancellor replied that they already were, to which the clergy retorted that if the king would look at Magna Carta he would see that they were not.

The petitions of the archbishop and his suffragans painted a very gloomy picture. The church, they said, was despoiled by the ordinance which forbade it to take cognisance of lay causes except with regard to marriages and wills; the king was claiming cognisance in many cases which properly belonged to the church; the sheriffs' officers, by

[1] Wilkins, ii. 116.

[2] *Ibid.* 117-18.

royal authority, were forbidding ecclesiastical judges to deal with tithes, violence done to clerks, defamation, breaking of oaths, usury, and other notorious crimes whose correction belonged to the church; ecclesiastical judges who had taken cognisance of cases other than those touching wills or marriages were being sought out and punished,[1] and ecclesiastical judges were being dragged after the king's court, whereas they ought to be summoned, as Magna Carta had decreed, before the justices of the Common Bench in a fixed place. From these preliminaries the petitioners went on to deduce somewhat fantastic consequences. The rich and powerful, they said, had become so glib with the assertion that the church had nothing to do with anything but marriages or wills that they could no longer be forced to contribute to the upkeep of a church. Spiritual fathers were beginning to be despised by their spiritual sons. Evil-minded persons continually demanded prohibitions, and it was to be feared that there were more persons excommunicated for this and other reasons in England than anywhere in the world. As laymen were forbidden to take oaths in an ecclesiastical court except concerning wills and marriages, it was impossible to secure trustworthy lay testimony in such matters as parish boundaries. The remaining petitions did not deal with matters directly raised in the constitutions of Lambeth, and need not be summarised here. The concluding paragraph, however, deserves quotation.

Since in all these respects the church has been disseised, we humbly beg your royal majesty that for those grievances which are new and unwonted, as clergy and people declare, you may deign to provide a remedy in God's name (*propter Deum*); bearing in mind that as no free man ought to be disseised of his liberty or free custom except by the lawful judgement of his equals and by the law of the land according to the great charter, so much the more the church ought not to be, and cannot be, despoiled after this fashion of her rights and liberties.

It was probably in answer to these petitions that in 1285, if long-standing tradition is to be believed, Edward I. issued the writ *Circumspecte agatis*, so authoritative a pronouncement upon the questions in dispute concerning jurisdiction that already in Edward III.'s reign it was being quoted in the law-courts, though not without protest, as a statute. By Coke's time it was plainly stated in the Institutes[2] that "this is an act of parliament", based on a writ devised in the parliament of Westminster, 13 Edward I. It is unfortunate that neither the original of this important document, nor any enrolment of it, has so far been discovered. As it appears in printed form in the Statutes of the Realm,[3] it bears no date and has

[1] Cf. Barth. Cotton, 166-7, *sub anno* 1285. *Eo anno fecit inquiri rex qui clerici implacitaverant quoscumque de feodo seu laicis catallis in curia Christianitatis, et de praelatis, qui graviter punierant excessus laicorum pecuniariter; et clericos, praelatos, et eorum ministros de hujusmodi* [*culpa*] *convictos graviter vinxit et incarceravit.*

[2] *Second Part of the Institutes* (3rd edn.), p. 487.

[3] i. 101.

a curious break in the middle. Addressed to certain justices not named, it bids them to act circumspectly in some matter unknown concerning the bishop of Norwich and his clergy, not punishing them if they deal in the ecclesiastical courts with pleas involving the correction of mortal sin, or penalties for the neglect of a church or churchyard, or a rector's suit for tithe, so long as it does not concern more than one quarter of the tithe due from the parish, or for a mortuary, where a mortuary has been customary, or a prelate's suit for a pension due to him, or cases of assault on clerks, or defamation, where the object is not money but the correction of sin. "In all these cases the ecclesiastical judge has cognisance, notwithstanding a royal prohibition, even if produced." With these words the document ends in some manuscript copies, but others, and the printed version in the Statutes, conclude with two more paragraphs, the first of which states that the laity ask for writs of prohibition in cases concerning tithe, oblations, mortuaries, redemption of penances, violence done to clerks and defamation, while the second embodies the king's reply, namely, that in cases of tithes, obventions, oblations, and mortuaries of the kind stated above "there is no place for prohibition", though if a clerk or religious sells his tithes, gathered in his barns or elsewhere, and is impleaded in the court of Christianity, then the royal prohibition may be used, for spiritual things have become temporal and tithes been turned into chattels.

Prynne, who made "diligentest search" without result into the origins and date of this writ, concluded that it was due, not to Edward I., but to Edward II., and was grounded on the *Articuli cleri* of 1316.[1] It is true that its later portion, from *Impetrant laici prohibicionem* onwards, corresponds closely with the wording of those articles, but, as we have seen, that portion does not appear in all copies, and the writ is perfectly intelligible and complete without it. It may be interesting to notice that the writ appears in its shorter form, in company with other documents ascribed to the year 1285, in the register of Godfrey Giffard, bishop of Worcester, who died fifteen years before the *Articuli cleri* were presented.[2] This does not, of course, by any means prove that it was issued, or was copied, during Giffard's lifetime. That portion of the register may have been written up later, and even if the handwriting corresponds with earlier entries, there is no reason why a clerk employed in the registry in the reign of Edward I. should not be still there in the reign of Edward II. Moreover, the writ is crowded in at the foot of a page, and may, perhaps, have been put into a space that happened to be blank. The marginal description, *Articuli*

[1] Prynne, *Records*, iii. (1668) 338-41.

[2] f. 237. Cf. Mr. Willis Bund's English calendar of the register (Worc. Hist. Soc.) ii. 272. Dr. E. H. Pearce, bishop of Worcester, has added another of his many services to historical studies by most kindly arranging with Canon Blake to take a photograph for me of the page concerned.

episcopis per regem concessi pro libertate et cognicione iurium ecclesie, is too vague to be a clue to date. At any rate, it is interesting to find the writ appearing in a contemporary register at the date to which all probabilities seem to point, and in the shorter form in which alone it is fully intelligible. The last two paragraphs in the printed copy seem oddly out of place. Why should a writ defining cases in which writs of prohibition are useless be followed by a statement that the laity ask for writs in exactly such suits, and that in its turn by a repetition of the royal assertion that such writs in such cases cannot be utilised? It is more natural to suppose that the first of the closing paragraphs represents a statement, made at a later date, of the persistence of the laity in disregarding the instructions of 1285, while the second embodies the promise of a later king, presumably Edward II., that the concession made to the church shall be maintained. If this is the explanation, then it is easy to see why later copyists, after recording the writ itself, might follow it by this commentary on its execution. Time, other copyists, and the editors of the early printed versions, would then gradually weld into one two things originally quite distinct.

Let us assume, then, that the writ *Circumspecte agatis* belongs to the year 1285, and represents the limit to which Edward I. was prepared to go in the matter of the jurisdiction of the church courts over lay causes. He conceded, it will be noted, much more than he was at first prepared to grant. He had hitherto maintained that suits about wills and marriages, and those alone, were on the ecclesiastical side of the boundary. To these he now added not only cases involving the correction of mortal sin, and suits about neglected churches or churchyards, but also suits concerning tithes if below a fixed value, about mortuaries, about prelates' pensions, about defamation and violent assaults on clerks. In all such cases, a royal writ of prohibition was to avail a suitor nothing, even if he had obtained and produced it. The answer to the bishops' petitions had come with astonishing speed, and much of what they had written became out of date within a few months of its drafting. The writ, it is true, referred specifically to one ecclesiastical court only, that of the bishop of Norwich, but its instructions were accepted as definitions of the course to be followed generally.

It might have been said of Archbishop Pecham, as it was said by James I. of one of Pecham's greatest successors, that he loved to "bring matters to a pitch of reformation floating in his own brain". A man, in consequence, of many enemies and many failures, he had on this occasion at least achieved considerable, if not complete, success, and that very largely through his own repeated and persistent efforts. It is impossible to read the petitions of 1285 without being at every turn reminded of the constitutions of Lambeth of 1281, while the clause referring to the numerous excommunications of those who sought writs of prohibition bears witness to the fact that the council's threats had been more than vain words. It is true that the very frequency of such sentences suggests that they did little to intimidate the church's enemies, but even if that is so, they did good work in encouraging the church's friends. Just as the supporters of the boy-king Henry III. were "specially cheered" when on Sundays and feast-days they watched the excommunication of his rival Louis,[1] so Pecham's well-wishers may have taken heart of grace when they saw him in 1281 once more unchain the thunders which in 1279 he had consented, under pressure, to imprison. A surrender excusable enough in a primate new to his work, within a few months of his arrival in England, would have seemed to the Pecham of later years a shameful betrayal of his trust. "Let all our adversaries know", Pecham wrote of himself in 1285, "that they will not find us a reed shaken in the wind."[2] In spite of the assertions to the contrary made by both contemporaries and modern writers, it seems certain that he could have quoted his conduct at the council of Lambeth in 1281 as proof of the correctness of that estimate of himself. He remained unbowed, on that occasion at any rate, beneath the driving blast of royal displeasure, and posterity should credit him both with his action and its consequences.

HILDA JOHNSTONE.

[1] Wendover, *Flores Hist.* (Eng. Hist. Soc.) iv. 3.
[2] *Reg. Epist.* iii. 889.

XV

RALPH OF HENGHAM AS CHIEF JUSTICE OF THE COMMON PLEAS

ONE of the most copious and instructive sources of information for the history of Edward I.'s time is to be found in the records of the State trials of 1289–1293, published in 1906 for the Royal Historical Society by T. F. Tout and Hilda Johnstone. The shady side of the remarkable system of administration of justice built up on the foundation laid by Henry II. is revealed with a great wealth of picturesque incidents and impassioned recriminations. The general impression produced on modern readers seems to be that although corrupt practices and extortions brought before the auditors commissioned by the King justified the drastic action of Edward I., they did not disclose any fundamental defects in the judicial organization or any widespread neglect and incompetence on the part of the judges.

This remark applies particularly to one of the leaders of mediaeval common law, Ralph of Hengham. Although he was dismissed in 1290 from the office of Chief Justice of the King's Bench, imprisoned and heavily fined, the rolls of the investigation present him in no unfavourable light. "In five out of the nine cases . . . he came out with flying colours. Possibly the accusations against him were rather the consequences than the cause of his disgrace."[1] For some ten years he was removed from the judicial body, but in 1300 his name appears in the lists of judges summoned in Parliament. In 1301 he was appointed Chief Justice of the Bench of Common Pleas, and held this office almost until his death in 1311.

It is in the course of the last period of Hengham's life that we have the best opportunity of watching his activities as a judge: it falls in years from which we have a series of reports as to the litigation conducted in the court of Common Bench. Some of these reports have been published by Horwood for the Rolls Series, but they are drawn exclusively from one MS. of the Year Books now in the Library of Lincoln's Inn. There are other MSS. containing many valuable cases omitted in Horwood's edition or reported in a different and more complete form. I may mention the British Museum MS. 31826, from which

[1] Introduction to *State Trials of Edward I. 1289–93*, p. xxx.

Professor Tout and Professor Hilda Johnstone have obtained the text of the interesting "Passion of the Judges", and the volume numbered Brit. Mus. 35116, in which an apprentice, seemingly directed by Ridinal, clerk of the Common Pleas, has inserted reports from the years 1308–1312, and also a number of instructive cases of the reign of Edward I.[1]

In this second collection direct references are frequently made to Ralph of Hengham's judgements and opinions. It appears, for example, that at the time of Hengham it was not considered necessary to summon the wife of a tenant who prayed to have aid from her in defending his case, because a wife was supposed to be always at the disposal of her husband for this purpose. The reporter of Edward II.'s time notes that in this respect the practice was different "modo", that is when William of Bereford was Chief Justice.[2] In another extract the writer of MS. 35116 refers to a judgement of Ralph Hengham delivered "in Parliament"[3] as to the operation of clause 18 of the Statute of Westminster II. (1285), which empowered a creditor to choose in satisfaction of an unpaid debt the collection of revenues from the landed estate of the debtor (up to half the entire property) (*elegit*), instead of direct execution on movables (*fieri facias*). . . . In accordance with Hengham's decision the debtor's estate was to be released if he produced the outstanding sum, even if the creditor had already obtained possession of the land by writ of *elegit*.

The most interesting opinions delivered by Hengham were given in two cases tried in Hilary Term, 1304. A report of the first of these cases, concerning bastardy, was published from the Lincoln's Inn MS.[4] and commented upon in the *History of English Law*,[5] but the reports of Brit. Mus. 35116 and Brit. Mus. 31826 are much fuller and contain characteristic details. Two questions were discussed in the trial: (1) whether bastardy could be pleaded by a demandant against the tenant in a possessory action; (2) whether long absence of the husband was a sufficient ground to rebut the presumption of the husband's fatherhood in respect of a child born in wedlock.

Alan and Margaret,[6] the demandants who had brought a writ of cosinage against Simon, contended that he was illegitimate and not entitled to succeed as nephew to Walter of Warton, because conceived when his father John was on a long voyage beyond the seas. The pronouncement of Hengham, C.J., was unfavourable as to the substance of this claim. He told the Court of a precedent: a husband had been absent three years, and on his return found his

[1] See Introduction to vol. xiv. of the *Year Books of Edward II.* (Selden Society) ed. by P. Vinogradoff and L. Ehrlich, pp. xii. ff.

[2] British Mus. Add. MS. 35116, f. 170b, II.

[3] *Ibid.*, f. 242a, I.

[4] *Year Books, 32 & 33 Edw. I.* (Rolls Series), 60, 74.

[5] Pollock and Maitland, *History of English Law* (second edition), ii. 398.

[6] British Mus. Add. MS. 31826, f. 373c. See Appendix (1) below. MS. 35116 (f. 61b) gives the names of the demandants as Walter and Mary.

wife with child and approaching confinement; a daughter was born who eventually claimed the inheritance of her mother's wedded husband in an action of mort d'ancestor. Martin of Littlebury, J., who tried the case, ascertained from the assize jurors that the facts were as stated, and yet the daughter was successful in her claim to the inheritance. In a similar case John of Metingham, C.J., had said: *We have nothing to do with the question who engendered a person; we cannot examine who entered a woman's bedroom.* Hengham himself is reported by MS. 35116 to have quoted a drastic popular saying, *Whoso boleth* [bulleth] *my kine, every calf is mine,* while Passeley, a leading pleader, put in the notorious dictum of Paulus: *Pater is est quem nuptiae demonstrant.*[1] As a result it was held that it is impossible to ascertain the degree of intimacy (*privauté*) between a man and a woman. Thus the Court favoured the contention of the tenant as regards the substance. On the other hand, Hengham supported the demandant as to the second point. In the two instances he gave from the practice of his predecessors, demandants had been admitted to assert bastardy in the person of the tenant in assizes of mort d'ancestor, an action considered even more as a standard possessory action than the writ of cosinage. In other words, the exception of bastardy could be brought by a demandant as well as by a tenant, and in a possessory action as well as in a writ of right. In the two instances quoted by Hengham assizes were called up to state the facts, and their verdicts had gone in favour of the tenants, who, however, lost through a technical mistake—failure to obtain the necessary writs in order to resummon the parties for a renewal of the trial in the King's Court after the legitimation of the tenant by the Ecclesiastical Court.

In this way the demandants in Alan and Margaret of Warton *v.* Simon of Warton gained their point in so far as they succeeded in raising the issue of bastardy. On the other hand, in the trial in question as well as in the two other cases cited by Hengham, the presumption in favour of legitimacy, carried to what might seem absurd extremes, was evidently suggested by a disinclination of the court to embark on inquiries as to intimate relations which were not, on the average, within the reach of judicial investigation—not an altogether unreasonable attitude, to judge from a *cause célèbre* of our own days. The old English saying cited by Hengham shows that it was not only the prudence of judges that prompted this resolve not to go beyond the formal test of wedlock, but also a popular tradition of old standing that made people consider the attribution of children rather as a material benefit than as a matter of fidelity or affection. There is yet another

[1] D. II. 4. 5. It may be noted that in the Roman law of the classical period it was not impossible to defeat the presumption by proof of long absence. See ULPIAN's opinion in D. I. 6. 6: Filium eum definimus, qui ex viro et uxore eius nascitur. Sed si fingamus abfuisse maritum, verbi gratia per decennium, reversum anniculum invenisse in domo sua, placet nobis Iuliani sententia, hunc non esse mariti filium.

curious point to be noted. Both in the case before Hengham and in those before Martin of Littlebury and John of Metingham, neither the verdict of the assize nor the opinion of the Royal Court on the inference to be drawn from wedlock settles the question at issue. When bastardy has been claimed and the facts of the case have been investigated by an assize, the "parol" has to be sent for examination by Holy Church. Bastardy acts as a bar to further treatment in the lay Court as long as the Court Christian has not made a pronouncement in one way or the other—in favour of legitimation or of bastardy.

This means that the royal justices did not consider the question to be formally decided by the fact of birth from a wedded wife, as the Roman and the old English sayings seem to suggest, but declined to investigate the matter and passed it on to the Ecclesiastical Court, which did not hold itself strictly limited by similar considerations.

The Church asserted firmly her right to pronounce judgement on questions of legitimacy, filiation and legitimation.[1] As the Crown maintained its hold on all trials touching inheritance, complications were bound to arise. The famous *nolumus leges Angliae mutare* of the Council of Merton was not the only pronouncement resulting in awkward dualism. One of the most celebrated canonists of the early fourteenth century, Hostiensis, devotes a long discussion to this inconvenient situation.[2]

A striking case of conflict between the two jurisdictions came before Parliament in the last year of Hengham's tenure of the Chief Justiceship of the King's Bench—in 1290. An illustration of the wider possibilities open to Courts Christian may be found in the attempt of William of Valence and Joan his wife to upset the recognition of Denise de Montecaniso as the daughter and next heir of William de Montecaniso, deceased. The King had assumed guardianship of her as the rightful heir, and the Bishop of Winchester had pronounced her to be legitimate in spite of assertions to the contrary. Thereupon William de Valence and his wife procured a Papal Bull authorizing a renewed examination by other ecclesiastical judges.[3] But the Valences were prohibited from following up this process by a strongly worded pronouncement made in the Parliament of 1290, and Ralph of Hengham, who may have been instrumental in drafting the decision, was directed to draw up a writ—obviously the prohibition to the Archbishop. It may be noted that William of Valence and his wife relied on advisers steeped in Roman law: they actually refer to a rule of the *lex scripta*

[1] *Corpus juris can.* X. iv. tit. 17, c. 5; *cf.* c. 13.

[2] *Hostiensis*, Lectura in V libros decretalium Gregorianorum, Paris, 1511. Lib. iv. 35: qui filii sint legitimi.

[3] *Rotuli Parliamentorum*, i. 16b: Et quia, Bulla illa visa, audita, et intellecta, manifeste patet quod Bulla illa finaliter tendit ad jus successionis hereditarie terminandum, cum de successione hereditaria nemo debeat cognoscere nisi Curia Regis vel Curia Ecclesiastica ad mandatum Curiae Domini Regis; et etiam si Bulla illa procederet, manifeste esset contra consuetudinem hactenus in regno usitatam.

as to appeals.[1] Hengham and the magnates in Parliament were all the more emphatic in their insistence on the rights of the King.

It is of some interest to compare the treatment of the problem in the English Courts with the practice of French Courts of approximately the same time, as illustrated by Beaumanoir's *Coutumes de Beauvaisis*. The French lawyer starts with an emphatic recognition of the authority of the Ecclesiastical Court in matters of filiation and legitimacy.[2] But he admits the possibility of disproving the presumption of fatherhood by establishing a long absence of the husband.[3] It seems almost as if the English judges were mainly interested in keeping up in this regard, as well as in connection with " subsequent matrimony ", a line of thought favourable to the traditional organisation of the family, while the French lawyers, influenced by Roman and by Canonist doctrines, were inclined to make distinctions and to abandon in some cases the presumption of fatherhood.

A second case, very fully reported in both our manuscripts, shows Hengham concerned with drawing the consequences of a royal pardon in regard to the restitution of the rights of an outlawed felon.[4] A certain John Faucillon (or Fontalon) had been outlawed for felony, but had subsequently obtained pardon from the King and returned to his native place. He stayed for a short time with his father. When the latter died, the lord Ernulf Percy entered on the estate. John claimed as son and heir, while Alice Percy asserted the right of her absent husband on the ground that the outlawed felon had forfeited his property. For some time the lady suffered John to dwell on the estate, though she kept a sergeant on it as representative and sometimes visited the house herself. Eventually Ernulf appeared on the scene, ejected John, and proceeded to cut down timber and to dismantle the house. An assize of novel disseisin was called before Henry Spigurnel and his fellow-justices commissioned to take assizes in the county.[5] It appeared among other things that John obtained

[1] *Rotuli Parliamentorum*, i. 17a: Que quidem sententia iniqua robur perpetuum obtinebit nisi predictum appellum interpositum infra annum a tempore appellationis facte sit prosecutum, secundum quod idem Wills a quibusdam discretis jura scripta scientibus intellexit.

[2] Beaumanoir, *Coutumes de Beauvaisis*, ed. Salmon, i. c. 333: Autres cas i a encore qui apartienent a sainte Eglise, si comme quant contens vient de bastardie pour debouter que li bastart n'en portent riens comme oir. Teus connoissances apartienent a sainte Eglise, ne cil de qui sainte Eglise tesmoigne qu'il est loiaus et de loial mariage ne puet pas ne ne doit estre deboutés comme bastars en court laie, ainçois convient que la justice laie croie ce que la justice de sainte Eglise tesmoigne en tel cas.

[3] *Ibid.*, ed. Salmon, i. c. 590: Li bastart qui sont né en mariage sont prouvé a la fois en la maniere que nous deismes devant en cel chapistre meisme et a la fois en autre maniere. Si comme se li maris est outre mer ou en autres terres estranges, ou emprisonnés par si lonc tans que .x. mois ou plus soient passé, et aprés les .xxxix. semaines et .i. jour qu'il s'en parti, sa famc a enfans : en tel cas il pueent estre prouvé a bastart par l'aparance du fet.

[4] Add. MS. 35116. See Appendix (2) below.

[5] The name of the county, where indicated (*Nor'*), suggests Northumberland, with which Ernulf Percy, a landholder at Kildale in the North Riding of Yorkshire, had

admission into the house from the lady on the pretext of being anxious to be present at his father's deathbed and funeral. The jurors testified that the representatives of both sides had been on the estate at the same time, and they were at a loss to say which of them had been legally seised. Spigurnel and his fellows were also unable to come to a definite conclusion, and sent up the case to the Common Bench. As reported in MS. 31826, the case opens with a narrative in Latin, which is evidently a transcript of the record forwarded by Spigurnel to the Common Bench. Hengham based his decision as usual on a review of precedents, and proceeded to analyse the effects of forfeiture and pardon. He relied by way of precedent on a case in which Roger of Mowbray had seized property held by a tenant of his who had committed felony but obtained a pardon. According to Hengham, in that case, as well as in that under discussion, forfeiture extended only to rights vested in the plaintiff on the day of his felony: he undoubtedly lost such rights through the outlawry, and the lord was entitled to seize his estates and goods on that occasion. But, on the other hand, once a pardon had been granted the pardoned outlaw resumed his full civil capacity as a freeman, and there was nothing to prevent him entering into possession of an inheritance which had accrued to him after the pardon. In the case under consideration it had been established by the verdict of the jury that John's father was alive when the said John obtained his pardon: therefore John was justified in claiming as son and heir. It would have been otherwise if the father had been dead at the time of the pardon: the estate would have been forfeited to the lord.

It may be noted that Hengham did not—at least as far as we can judge from our reports—examine the contradictory evidence as to the manifestation of seisin. The question had been obscured by the fact that both parties were simultaneously dwelling in the house and exercising certain rights of possession. The definite ejectment of John by Ernulf came too late to influence the situation as to seisin. We are faced here with one of the practical difficulties of the mediaeval doctrine of seisin. Proof rested ultimately on the actual exercise of power: in cases like the present, when the object of seisin—an estate—was large enough to admit of the coexistence of two parties asserting power, the decision as to possession was not easy to reach. Hengham's arguments, in any case, bear on the problems of rights in general, and are not restricted to the attribution of possession.

PAUL VINOGRADOFF.

connexions (*Cal. of Inquisitions*, v. 309; cf. *Calendarium Genealogicum*, Rec. Com., pp. 360, 496); but Norfolk is not excluded from possibility (*Cal. of Inquisitions*, v. 310 at foot) and is made likely by the facts (1) that Spigurnel does not seem to have held assizes in the north, but in the southern counties and especially in East Anglia, (2) that a Robert, son of John, Faucillon is found at this time in Essex (see *Cal. of Inquisitions*, iii. 390, No. 505). John had lands at one time in Mountnessing (*Gynges Monteny*; see *Cal. Close Rolls*, 1302–7, p. 451). I am indebted for this information to Professor Powicke.

APPENDIX

(1) Add. MS. 31826, f. 373, c.; Hil. 32 Edw. I.

VN Alein e Margarete sa femme porterent bref de cosinage uers vn Simon e diseint qe vn Wauter cosin Margarete fu seisi etc. E de Wauter resorti a Simon cum a vncle frere son pere Wauter De Simon a Margarete qi ore demande cum a fille. MALMESBURY: nus sumes frere e eyr memes celi Wauter e clamuns par meme la decente. ESSEBY: clamer ne poez qe son pere Wauter esposa vne Juliene qe entre eus fiz naueint autre qe Wauter nostre cosyn. TOUDEBY: il vus dit frere e eyr Wauter respoz par la. ESSEBY: assez auuns respondu entant qe nus auuns dit qe Jon e Juliene vnqe fiz naueint autre qe Wauter e vus disoms qe vus estis tut estraunge. *quo tempore per pass*(eley)[1] si deueit. ESSEBY: a meme loure sur cel estraungisement li auer nome pere. e point ne fit par quai dit, nee dens esposailles pre etc. E. HENGHAM: pus cunta vn tel conte qe vn home prist femme e pus a la outremer e illok demora iij auns e demi e en reuenant uers loutel ly fut conte a Loundres par gens de sun pais qe sa femme fut delieures de vne fille qe a sa venue a lostel nesteit qe de vn meys vel. pus morust le prodome. La fille purchaca le Mord e pleda legerement a lassise qe diseint qe el ne fut point eyr celi e pus cunterent *ut prius*. E. MARTYN DE LITTEBYRY Justice demanda par qai il lur semble qe ele ne fut point qui dixerent *pro predicta mora ultra mare* etc. Disent pur coe qe auis fut a la Justice qe nul home purreit sauer la priueite entre home e femme e poeit auer venu priuement sant coe qe autre qe ly e sa femme le scyusent si aguarda qe ele recouerat par quele emsaple aguarde fut qe Esseby respondit outre. *Cui etiam concord*(at?) *pass*(eley).[1] Pater est quem nupcie demonstrant. ESSEBY: nus vus disoms qe il est bastard. FRISKENEY: tel excepcion ne poez vser qe cest vn bref de possession e vostre excepcion est en le dreit. Mes tele excepcion bien girreit en la bouche la tenant encontre le tenant.[2] HENGHAM: en bref de Mord dancestre qe plus est si girreit ceste excepcion en la bouche le demandant. E si aueneit en tel cas qe la ou il furent mande a seinte eglise pur trier la bastardie e qe le tenant qe deusit auer sui en tel cas pur sa legitimacion en curt chrestiene e apres la curt le Rey a certe de cele legitimacion deueit auer sui vne resumuns pur auer resumuns la parole e point ne fit pur tant qe il memes fut en tenance par quai le demandant sui cum bien ly lust a resomundrer la parole a certein ior a quel ior le tenant fit defaut par quai le grant cope issit[3] e pus pur autre defaut seisi de terre et sicome[4] sant uerdit de assise. si aueit len recouire. *Et coram* J. de METINGHAM voleit le tenant auer rebote le demande par dire nent nee dens esposailles. *cui obiecit petens quod neccessa esset dicere* e engendra de dens esposailles. METINGHAM: de lengendrer nauuns qe fere qe nus ne voluns pas enqere qui entra la chambre la dame. *Item* peut estre qe il fut engendre entre la femme e sun primer barun e nee apres les esposailles entre la femme e sun

[1] pas̃s(eley). Seemingly a remark of the well-known pleader Passeley on the conduct of the pleadings by "Esseby".

[2] tenāt.

[3] *Query* conquasseit.

[4] s^e.

secund barun. *Item* par HENGHAM: dit in casu supradicto qe apres bastardie allege mande fut a seinte eglise ou le tenant encontre ky tel chose fut allege fut en tenance e deueit auer sui pur sa legitimacion uers leuesqe e pus apres auer sui la resumunce [1] e point ne fit qe le demandant fut recu a la syute fere. Et barstardie [2] troue par seinte eglise barre en le dreit cum bataille ou grant. Et postea supradicto placito mandatum fuit episcopo.[3]

(2) Add. MS. 35116, f. 5. b. i.

Lassise . . . vient e dit qe les tenements esteans en la seisine Robert Fanolon pere Ion etc., mesme celui Ion fist felonie pur la quele il fust vtlaghe. e viuant sun pere. la charte le Roi resustite a la pees issin qe bien viii jours deuant la mort sun pere sa pees fust crie e il vient a lostiel e demorra oue sun pere. R. mourust. Ion vient a la femme A. pur ceo qil mesmes fust hors du pais e lui pria qe il pureit entrer en sun heritage. La dame ne lui granta pas mes ele suffrist bien qil entrast. par qui il entra en les tenements com heire etc. Et la dame manda vn sun seriant a prendre la seisine en le noum sun Seigneur le quel demorra en les tenements en semblement oue Ion e oue sa soere quant il ne fut pas meisme tant qe a la venue Arnald en pais. Et si tost com il aperceut qe I. fust entre il vient e lui engetta e abati les mesons e arracea les arbres. Mes pur ceo qil ne sauoient dire si Ion fut seisi issi qil poeit estre disseisi il prierent descretion des Justices. Et propter dubitationem le record oue tut le proces fust mande en Bank.

[1] resum̃. [2] *sic.*
[3] The account of the case in Add. MS. 35116 (f. 61^b) concludes: Et tunc dixit Hengham Wo so boleth myn kyn, ewerc is the calf myn.

XVI

THE PERSONNEL OF THE COMMONS IN PARLIAMENT UNDER EDWARD I. AND EDWARD II.

RECENT teaching on the history of the mediæval English parliament has shown a distinct tendency to question many of the accepted opinions as to the place and importance of the Commons in the parliaments of the 14th century. The conclusions which are now becoming fashionable have been reached by various lines of study. Only one of these lines—the investigation of the personnel of the Commons in parliament—concerns us here. It has of late attracted several scholars, and has led some of them to propound a number of rather iconoclastic conclusions.[1] We are now taught that when the constituencies—particularly the borough constituencies—were ordered to elect representatives, they quite commonly omitted to do so. Even when an election was made we are told that the representatives elected often failed to appear in parliament. It is asserted, moreover, that "members were rarely re-elected".[2] From all this it is inferred that representation in parliament during the 13th and 14th centuries was regarded as a burden and was avoided as far as possible both by the representatives and by the constituencies. It is inferred, too, that the borough members, comparatively numerous on paper, were in actual fact a minority of the Commons and were outnumbered by the knights of the shire.[3] The object of the present paper is to attempt a synopsis of a few of the primary facts and to test the validity of some of the canons of interpretation that have hitherto been observed in dealing with the evidence. Consideration will be given mainly to the reigns of Edward I. and Edward II., except when lack of material from those two reigns makes it necessary to take account of the 14th century as a whole.

A word must first be said about the evidence. The main sources are the sheriffs' returns and the enrolments of writs *de expensis*.[4]

[1] Pasquet, *Essai sur les Origines de la Chambre des Communes* (1914); Lapsley, *Knights of the Shire in the Parliaments of Edward II.* (*Eng. Hist. Rev.* 1919); Pollard, *Evolution of Parliament* (1920).

[2] Pollard, p. 8.

[3] *Ibid.*, p. 319.

[4] Printed *in extenso* for the reigns of Edward I. and Edward II. in Palgrave's *Parliamentary Writs*. The enrolled writs *de expensis* are also printed in Prynne's *Fourth*

A certain amount of additional information, scattered but not insignificant, may also be obtained from the rolls of parliament and from borough accounts. There are two difficulties about this evidence. In the first place, it is incomplete. For gatherings earlier than the *colloquium* of July 1290 the surviving returns are too few and fragmentary to be of much value for the present purpose. After 1290 the evidence is more satisfactory: there are only two assemblies, those of November 1294 and November 1296, for which the names of the elected representatives are entirely lacking;[1] for the remainder, except for that of May 1300, reasonably full particulars are forthcoming.[2] Still it must be remembered that these particulars are only reasonably full: they are not complete. Thus it is only for six assemblies between 1290 and 1327 that the lists even of knights of the shire are absolutely complete[3]: during the same period there is only one constituency, York county, for which it is possible to make a list of members which (save for the meetings of November 1294 and November 1296) is quite full. Every statement made about the personnel of the Commons in parliament is therefore made subject to these numerous gaps in the evidence. The second difficulty is not so persistent, but is apt nevertheless to cause occasional embarrassment. This is the difficulty of mediæval names. Owing to the constant recurrence of the same christian names in the same family and to the careless fashion in which "senior" or "junior" or local descriptions are inserted or omitted in the returns, it is not always possible to be sure about identifications. Fortunately this difficulty does not arise as often as might be expected, and the resultant error is not likely to be serious: but the possibility of error on this score is there, and allowance must be made for it. With these reservations in mind, we may now attempt a synopsis of the primary facts in tabular form, and in doing this, it is convenient to keep the shire constituencies distinct from the cities and boroughs.

Between July 1290 and January 1327 (excluding the meetings of November 1294 and November 1296 for which, as has been said, no returns are available) there were 34 assemblies, variously styled parliaments or *colloquia*, to which the shires were ordered to send representatives. Tables A and B give a statistical summary of the shire representation.

Part of a Brief Register of Parliamentary Writs. The returns are analysed in the *Return of Members of Parliament* (*Parl. Papers*, 1878, vol. lxii. pts. i.-iii.).

[1] Except for London for 1296; Sharpe, *Cal. of Letter Books: Letter Book C*, p. 24.

[2] Returns discovered since 1878 have been entered in manuscript in the copy of the *Return of Members of Parliament* kept in the Round Room at the Public Record Office. These additions, which are not very numerous for the reigns of Edward I. and Edward II., have been noted in preparing the statistics given below.

[3] The meetings of October 1302, February 1305, September 1313, January 1315, February 1324 and October 1324. Northumberland made no election for the parliaments of January 1315 and October 1324 owing to Scottish raids.

TABLE A (Shires)

Parliaments.	Col. 1.	Col. 2.	Col. 3.	Col. 4.	Col. 5.	Column 6.									
						2.	3.	4.	5.	6.	7.	8.	9.	10.	11.
July 1290	28	64	64	..	..	..	..	..	..	..	..	..	..	..	..
November 1295	35	73	65	..	8	8	..	..	..	..	..	..	..	..	..
October 1297	32	64	55	..	9	7	2	..	..	..	..	..	..	..	..
May 1298	35	70	47	13	23	21	2	..	..	..	..	..	..	..	..
March 1300	33	66	43	15	23	14	8	1	..	..	..	..	..	..	..
May 1300	14	39	22	8	17	12	4	1	..	..	..	..	..	..	..
January 1301	35	70	16	*41	54	31	15	6	2	..	..	..	..	..	..
October 1302	37	74	39	10	35	24	8	2	1	..	..	..	..	..	..
February 1305	37	74	37	19	37	18	12	5	1	1	..	..	..	..	..
May 1306	34	68	31	19	37	15	9	7	6	..	..	..	..	..	..
January 1307	36	72	49	10	23	12	7	3	1	..	..	..	..	..	..
October 1307	34	68	34	14	34	16	10	4	3	1	..	..	..	..	..
April 1309	36	71	26	10	45	19	6	10	4	6	..	..	..	..	..
August 1311	36	72	25	16	47	23	11	7	3	3	..	..	..	..	..
November 1311	36	72	11	53	61	18	19	9	7	5	3	..	..	..	..
August 1312	28	56	30	9	26	7	7	4	5	1	1	1	..	..	..
March 1313	33	65	30	8	35	14	9	4	2	3	2	1	..	..	..
July 1313	25	50	16	18	34	16	8	3	2	4	..	1	..	..	..
September 1313	37	75	16	26	59	18	21	8	3	2	5	1	1	..	..
September 1314	33	66	45	8	21	7	4	6	1	2	..	1	..	..	..
January 1315	36	72	38	12	34	16	7	5	1	1	3	1	..	..	..
January 1316	33	57	31	9	26	12	4	3	4	..	..	3	..	..	..
May 1316	19	38	19	8	19	8	5	3	3	..	..	..	..	..	..
July 1316	36	68	23	19	45	21	9	8	2	4	..	..	1	..	..
October 1318	34	68	34	10	34	13	8	2	7	2	..	1	1	..	..
May 1319	35	70	40	14	30	13	9	2	1	4	1	..	..	..	..
October 1320	37	73	40	9	33	14	6	5	2	3	3	..	..	..	..
July 1321	36	71	28	9	43	17	7	7	4	3	4	1	..	..	..
May 1322	36	71	31	12	40	20	10	4	2	1	1	2	..	..	..
November 1322	32	64	33	11	31	11	8	6	2	3	..	..	1	..	..
February 1324	37	74	35	13	39	16	6	6	4	3	3	..	..	1	..
October 1324	36	72	42	6	30	13	6	5	2	1	..	3	..	..	..
November 1325	36	72	36	11	36	15	7	4	3	1	2	..	3	..	1
January 1327	35	70	33	7	37	18	11	4	1	1	..	..	1	1	..

* Re-elected from the parliament of March 1300.

Table A is arranged by parliaments, and gives the following information for each of the 34 assemblies to which shire representatives were called :

Column 1—number of shires known to have returned or sent members;[1]

Column 2—number of members known to have been returned or to have attended ;

Column 3—number of members returned or present for the first time known;

[1] " Returned or sent " because the names are derived partly from the sheriffs' returns, partly from the enrolled writs *de expensis*, and occasionally the persons who were actually sent were not the persons who had been returned by the sheriff : when this occurs, the names given by the enrolled writs *de expensis* have been taken in preference.

Column 4—number of members known to have been returned to or present in the parliament immediately preceding;

Column 5—number of members known to have been returned or to have attended *for the particular shire* on any previous occasions;

Column 6—an analysis of the figures in column 5, showing the numbers returned or present for the second time, the third time, etc., respectively.

TABLE B

Shires.	Col. 1.	Col. 2.	Column 3.										
			1.	2.	3.	4.	5.	6.	7.	8.	9.	10.	11.
Bedford . .	65	30	14	7	4	2	1	2	..	..	..	..	..
Berkshire . .	66	36	25	4	2	2	1	..	2	..	..	..	..
Buckingham .	66	31	14	11	2	2	1	..	..	..	..	..	1
Cambridge .	68	35	23	2	4	5	..	..	..	..	1	..	..
Cornwall . .	57	33	22	6	1	2	..	2	..	..	..	..	..
Cumberland .	55	32	18	8	4	1	1	..	..	..	..	..	..
Derby . .	58	25	11	4	7	1	..	1	..	1	..	..	..
Devon . .	64	34	19	10	2	1	..	1	..	..	1	..	..
Dorset . .	65	38	24	6	5	2	..	1	..	..	..	..	..
Essex . .	66	30	12	8	5	2	3	..	..	..	..	..	..
Gloucester .	59	35	22	7	4	..	1	1	..	..	..	..	..
Hereford . .	64	40	23	13	3	..	..	1	..	..	..	..	..
Hertford . .	60	18	3	6	2	4	..	1	..	1	1	..	..
Huntingdon .	68	33	20	5	3	1	1	1	2	..	..	..	..
Kent . . .	61	31	18	5	3	2	2	1	..	..	..	..	..
Lancashire .	56	33	19	8	3	3	..	..	..	..	..	..	..
Leicester . .	58	31	18	6	3	3	..	..	1	..	..	..	..
Lincoln . .	61	35	23	5	3	2	1	1	..	..	..	..	..
Middlesex . .	54	24	13	5	2	1	1	..	1	..	1	..	..
Norfolk . .	63	27	15	6	1	1	..	2	1	..	..	1	..
Northampton .	61	37	26	5	3	2	..	..	..	1	..	..	..
Northumberland	50	31	23	3	2	1	1	1	..	..	..	..	..
Nottingham .	56	31	19	4	6	..	1	1	..	..	..	..	..
Oxford . .	61	28	15	8	1	1	..	1	..	1	1	..	..
Rutland . .	61	37	23	8	4	..	2	..	..	..	..	..	..
Shropshire .	63	27	15	5	1	2	..	2	1	1	..	..	..
Somerset . .	67	43	30	5	6	1	1	..	..	..	..	..	..
Southampton .	64	34	19	8	3	1	2	1	..	..	..	..	..
Stafford . .	65	27	8	12	3	1	1	1	..	..	1	..	..
Suffolk . .	62	25	10	5	5	3	..	..	1	1	..	..	..
Surrey . .	59	23	12	2	3	3	..	1	..	2	..	..	..
Sussex . .	56	23	11	4	2	3	..	2	1	..	..	..	..
Warwick . .	67	36	21	5	7	2	..	..	1	..	..	..	..
Westmorland .	56	27	14	7	1	2	2	..	1	..	..	..	..
Wiltshire . .	59	33	19	8	4	..	..	2	..	..	..	..	..
Worcester .	59	29	12	9	3	5	..	..	..	..	..	..	..
Yorkshire . .	69	42	24	12	4	1	1	..	..	..	..	..	..
Total . . .	2269	1164	657	242	121	65	24	27	12	8	6	1	1

Table B is arranged by constituencies, and gives the following information for each of the 37 shires which returned members to the assemblies of 1290–1327:

Column 1—total number of returns or attendances during the period;

Column 2—total number of persons returned or attending during the period;

Column 3—an analysis of the figures in column 2, showing the number of persons returned respectively once, twice, three times, etc., during the period 1290–1327.

When we turn to the boroughs it is necessary to make a selection. During the years 1290–1327 some 175 cities and boroughs were ordered, at one time or another, to elect representatives for parliament, and from almost all these there are returns still extant. But owing to a variety of causes, the number of surviving returns is much greater from some boroughs than from others. Between 1290 and 1327 there were 28 assemblies (excluding that of November 1296, the returns for which are not available) to which borough representatives were called. From a good many boroughs returns survive for only one or two of these gatherings. From others, the series is almost complete: thus there are returns from the borough of Bedford for 27 out of the 28 meetings. The majority of the boroughs fall somewhere between these two extremes. A selection must therefore be made of those boroughs for

TABLE C (39 Boroughs)

Parliaments.	Col. 1.	Col. 2.	Col. 3.	Col. 4.	Col. 5.	Column 6.											
						2.	3.	4.	5.	6.	7.	8.	9.	10.	11.	12.	13.
vember 1295 .	33	65	65	..	..	..	..	..	..	..	..	..	..	..	..	..	..
y 1298 . .	34	68	57	11	11	11	..	..	..	..	..	..	..	..	..	..	..
rch 1300 . .	11	22	16	4	6	4	2	..	..	..	..	..	..	..	..	..	..
uary 1301 .	29	57	37	10	20	14	4	2	..	..	..	..	..	..	..	..	..
ober 1302 .	33	66	46	13	20	10	7	1	2	..	..	..	..	..	..	..	..
ruary 1305 .	39	77	48	16	29	20	6	2	1	..	..	..	..	..	..	..	..
y 1306 . .	35	64	37	18	27	17	5	4	..	1	..	..	..	..	..	..	..
uary 1307 .	36	72	52	5	20	12	6	1	..	..	1	..	..	..	..	..	..
ober 1307 .	35	70	30	6	40	16	11	7	3	2	..	1	..	..	..	..	..
il 1309 . .	35	68	42	12	26	11	7	3	2	2	..	..	1	..	..	..	..
gust 1311 .	38	76	43	9	33	16	6	8	..	2	..	..	..	1	..	..	..
vember 1311 .	34	68	21	34	47	25	10	5	4	..	2	..	..	..	1	..	..
gust 1312 .	17	34	20	6	14	6	5	2	..	1	..	..	..	..	..	..	..
ch 1313 . .	35	70	30	6	40	16	14	2	3	2	..	2	..	..	..	1	..
1313 . .	17	34	15	10	19	8	6	2	2	1	..	..	..	..	..	..	..
tember 1313 .	39	78	28	16	50	20	10	9	2	3	4	..	1	..	..	..	1
tember 1314 .	29	58	29	9	29	14	5	3	3	..	3	..	1	..	..	..	..
uary 1315 .	37	74	30	16	44	14	8	9	4	4	1	3	..	1	..	..	..
uary 1316 .	9	18	12	4	6	2	3	..	..	..	1	..	..	..	..	..	..
ober 1318 .	34	67	33	3	34	17	7	3	4	1	1	..	1	..	..	..	..
1319 . .	36	71	41	14	30	10	9	5	1	2	2	1	..	..	..	..	..
ober 1320 .	34	68	35	11	33	12	7	5	3	1	..	2	2	1	..	..	..
1321 . .	31	61	31	11	30	10	4	4	4	1	1	3	1	2	..	..	..
1322 . .	35	70	42	9	28	10	4	3	5	1	1	2	1	1	..	..	..
ember 1322 .	28	56	27	8	29	11	5	3	4	1	1	1	2	..	1	..	..
uary 1324 .	39	78	42	10	36	16	9	2	2	2	2	1	1	..	..	1	..
ember 1325 .	36	72	37	18	35	13	8	6	1	2	3	..	1	1	..	..	..
uary 1327 .	30	60	34	7	26	11	5	2	1	1	1	3	..	..	1	..	1

which the data are reasonably complete. Accordingly, attention is here limited almost entirely to cities and boroughs which can show returns for 20 or more of the 28 parliaments of the period under consideration: 39 of these borough constituencies have been taken, spread over most of the shires of England. Tables C and D give, for the 39 boroughs named, information similar to that given for the shires in Tables A and B.[1]

TABLE D

Boroughs.	Col. 1.	Col. 2.	Column 3.												
			1.	2.	3.	4.	5.	6.	7.	8.	9.	10.	11.	12.	13.
Bedford	53	28	16	6	3	2	..	..	..	1	..	..	..	..	..
Reading	46	27	18	4	2	1	2	..	..	..	..	..	..	..	..
Wallingford	42	19	9	7	..	1	..	..	1	1	..	..	..	..	..
Cambridge	46	26	16	4	2	4	..	..	..	..	..	..	..	..	..
Bodmin	37	31	28	1	1	1	..	..	..	..	..	..	..	..	..
Launceston	38	24	15	6	2	..	1	..	..	..	..	..	..	..	..
Carlisle	37	20	12	4	2	1	..	..	1	..	..	..	..	..	..
Derby	48	30	18	6	6	..	..	..	..	..	..	..	..	..	..
Exeter	47	29	19	6	1	2	1	..	..	..	..	..	..	..	..
Totness	41	21	13	5	1	..	1	..	..	..	..	1	..	..	..
Shaftesbury	42	31	25	4	1	..	..	1	..	..	..	..	..	..	..
Colchester	39	14	9	1	1	1	..	..	..	1	..	..	..	..	1
Bristol	40	29	23	3	1	2	..	..	..	..	..	..	..	..	..
Gloucester	42	24	17	3	2	..	1	..	..	1	..	..	..	..	..
Hereford	50	23	10	6	4	1	..	2	..	..	..	..	..	..	..
Huntingdon	52	28	17	6	2	2	..	..	..	..	1	..	..	..	..
Canterbury	44	26	16	5	3	1	1	..	..	..	..	..	..	..	..
Rochester	44	18	11	3	1	..	..	1	..	1	..	1	..	..	..
Leicester	46	30	19	8	1	2	..	..	..	..	..	..	..	..	..
Lincoln	44	24	15	4	2	..	3	..	..	..	..	..	..	..	..
Norwich	50	27	19	2	2	2	..	1	1	..	..	..	..	..	..
Yarmouth	49	25	15	6	1	1	1	..	..	..	..	1	..	..	..
Northampton	48	25	14	6	2	1	1	..	1	..	..	..	..	..	..
Newcastle-on-Tyne	32	16	8	3	2	3	..	..	..	..	..	..	..	..	..
Nottingham	46	25	14	5	3	2	1	..	..	..	..	..	..	..	..
Oxford	48	15	10	..	1	1	..	..	..	..	2	..	..	..	1
Shrewsbury	52	24	14	3	5	..	..	..	..	1	1	..	..	..	..
Bridgwater	50	40	32	6	2	..	..	..	..	..	..	..	..	..	..
Ilchester	40	22	17	2	..	1	1	..	..	..	..	1	..	..	..
Winchester	46	31	22	5	2	2	..	..	..	..	..	..	..	..	..
Stafford	41	19	7	6	3	2	1	..	..	..	..	..	..	..	..
Dunwich	45	20	12	2	1	3	..	1	..	1	..	..	..	..	..
Ipswich	46	21	11	6	1	1	1	..	..	..	..	..	1	..	..
Guildford	40	17	9	2	3	1	1	..	..	..	1	..	..	..	..
Appleby	42	29	21	5	2	..	1	..	..	..	..	..	..	..	..
Salisbury	52	36	26	6	3	..	1	..	..	..	..	..	..	..	..
Wilton	45	28	17	7	3	..	1	..	..	..	..	..	..	..	..
Worcester	46	30	22	3	3	1	1	..	..	..	..	..	..	..	..
York	46	28	18	6	3	..	..	..	1	..	..	..	..	..	..
Total	1742	980	634	173	80	42	21	6	5	7	5	4	1	..	2

[1] London has been omitted because the city during the latter half of Edward II.'s reign frequently elected three, four and (on one occasion) six representatives, giving power to any two or three of them to answer for the city. This practice distorts the figures for London, and makes them misleading as statistics. On the number of London's representatives see Prynne, *Brevia Parliamentaria Rediviva*, pp. 374-80.

Now these arid statistics, whatever their limitations, are at any rate quite sufficient to dispose of the theory that members were rarely re-elected. That theory may of course be understood in more than one sense. If it is taken in its most natural meaning, it does not in the least square with the facts. A comparison of the figures in columns (3) and (5) in Tables A and C will show that in almost any parliamentary assembly of the period 1290–1327 a considerable proportion of the representatives were persons who had been elected on one or more previous occasions. Taking the shire constituencies in Table A, it will be seen that in several parliaments persons who had been elected on one or more previous occasions form a distinct majority of the shire representatives: this is true of about ten parliaments, *e.g.* August 1311 (47 : 25), September 1313 (59 : 16), May 1322 (40 : 31). Slightly more numerous are the parliaments in which the knights of the shire who had been elected on previous occasions are exactly or approximately equal in number to those then elected (so far as is known) for the first time: this is true of about a dozen parliaments, *e.g.* October 1302 (35 : 39), October 1318 (34 : 34), November 1325 (36 : 36). In about eleven parliaments the knights of the shire who had been elected on one or more previous occasions are outnumbered by those elected for the first time, *e.g.* March 1300 (23 : 43), September 1314 (21 : 45), October 1324 (30 : 42): even here, however, their numbers are by no means negligible. Taking now the 39 borough constituencies in Table C, it will be seen that there are some half-dozen parliaments in which a distinct majority of the burgesses are persons who had been elected on one or more previous occasions, *e.g.* October 1307 (40 : 30), September 1313 (50 : 28), January 1315 (44 : 30). There are some half-dozen other parliaments in which the burgesses who had been elected on one or more previous occasions are exactly or approximately equal in number to those elected for the first time: examples are the parliaments of September 1314 (29 : 29), October 1318 (34 : 33), November 1325 (35 : 37). In some fifteen parliaments, however, the re-elected are distinctly outnumbered by those elected for the first time, *e.g.* October 1302 (20 : 46), January 1307 (20 : 52), May 1319 (30 : 41). It would seem, therefore, if one may generalize from the 39 boroughs taken in Table C, that re-election was rather less common in the boroughs than in the shires. Nevertheless, it was so common both in shires and boroughs that it cannot be regarded as in the least exceptional.

The point may be demonstrated in another way if we now consider the evidence by constituencies instead of by parliaments, and make use of the facts summarized in Tables B and D. These tables show for each constituency (so far as the materials allow) the total number of elections made, the total number of persons elected, and the extent to which these persons were re-elected, during the period

1290–1327. Thus for Bedford borough the total number of elections is 53: the total number of persons elected is 28; of these 28, 16 are elected once, 6 twice, 3 three times, 2 four times and 1 eight times, making the total of 53 elections. Taken together, Tables B and D are conclusive against any theory that members were rarely re-elected. They show that practically all the constituencies have examples of persons elected four times; that a good proportion of the constituencies had members who were elected five and six times; and that some of them were represented by persons who were elected as often as ten, eleven and thirteen times.[1] These statements may be illustrated by a few examples. Cambridgeshire has one member elected 9 times; Salop has one member elected 7 times and another elected 8 times; Oxfordshire has one member elected 8 times and another elected 9 times; Westmorland has one elected 7 times; Buckinghamshire has one elected 11 times. Even more surprising is the evidence from some of the boroughs. Bedford, Gloucester, Wallingford and Dunwich each have one member elected 8 times; Rochester has one elected 8 times and another elected 10 times; Yarmouth, Totness and Ilchester each have one elected 10 times; Colchester has one elected 8 times and one elected 13 times; Oxford has two members elected 9 times and one elected 13 times. It is not, however, upon these examples that the main emphasis must be laid, otherwise one might easily be deceived into thinking that Our Old and Respected Member was already a familiar flower of the constitution. The evidence of the two Tables must be taken as a whole if its full force is to be fairly shown. And its full force is greater than appears at first sight. What one sees at first sight is that in the shires there are 657 persons elected once as against 507 persons elected more than once, while in 39 boroughs there are 634 persons elected once as against 346 persons elected more than once. This, it may be urged, proves indeed that re-election was common, but proves also that the majority of members were not re-elected. That is certainly a very important truth: undoubtedly the majority of members during the period 1290–1327 were not re-elected. But that truth must not be allowed to hide another truth equally important. It is this: that in the shires, 657 persons elected once account for 657 elections, whereas 507 persons elected more than once account for 1612 elections; that in 39 boroughs, 634 persons elected once account for 634 elections, whereas 346 persons elected more than once account for 1108 elections. To get the whole truth we must not only count heads; we must also count elections. Even then, it must be remembered, we shall not have reached quite the whole truth about re-election. For the figures given above have been obtained by taking each constituency by itself and ignoring the fact that the same person might be elected at various

[1] This fact was duly noted by Prynne; *Brev. Parl. Red.*, p. 137.

times by more than one constituency, so that his first election for one constituency might not necessarily be his first election to parliament. Thus a Gerard of Braybrook was elected for Buckinghamshire to the parliaments of January 1301 and April 1309; for Hertfordshire to the parliaments of January 1307 and October 1307; for Bedfordshire to the parliaments of August 1311, November 1311 and (probably) August 1312. If, as seems likely, this Gerard is one and the same person, it will be seen that his first election for Hertfordshire was really his second election to parliament, while his first election for Bedfordshire was his fifth election to parliament. Other examples of this kind occur from time to time, at any rate in the shires. It is impossible, however, to take account of them without first establishing identifications, and this unfortunately is too lengthy a task for the present paper.[1] Accordingly these elections have had to be left out of account in compiling the accompanying Tables. If they had been included, the case against the theory that members were rarely re-elected could have been made rather stronger than it is already. But it scarcely need be pressed further. If any one is still unconvinced he might perhaps care to continue the discussion with Chaucer's Franklin. The opinions of that worthy vavasour should be interesting. For he was knight of the shire "ful ofte tyme".

So far we have taken the theory that members were rarely re-elected in its natural meaning. It might, however, be understood in another sense. It might be taken to mean that members were rarely re-elected to two or more immediately successive parliaments. Stated in this way the theory, without being wholly true, would be much more true than it is in the sense previously discussed. Column 4 in Tables A and C shows for each parliament the number of its members known to have been also elected to the parliament immediately preceding. It proves that a certain proportion of the members of any parliament were persons who had been also elected to the parliament next preceding. The proportion varies, among knights of the shire from one in twelve (October 1324) to one in three (September 1313), and among the burgesses from one in fourteen (January 1307) to one in four (November 1325).[2] These, however, are probably minimum figures. At any rate it is clear that election to two consecutive parliaments was by no means unusual, though it was not the common rule. The further question —how far members were re-elected to a series of consecutive parliaments —cannot be satisfactorily answered owing to the gaps in the evidence, but a few facts are worth noting. It would seem that election to three immediately successive parliaments, though not common, was by no

[1] See Palgrave's introduction to the alphabetical digest of persons; *Parl. Writs*, vol. i.

[2] Re-election was enjoined upon the constituencies by the writs summoning the assemblies of January 1301 and November 1311, and then the proportions are rather higher. But normally the constituencies were left to do as they pleased.

means unknown: during the period 1290–1327 there are about 60 examples to be found in the shires and about 30 in the boroughs mentioned in Tables C and D. Election to more than three consecutive parliaments was obviously unusual, but the examples available ought not therefore to be ignored. In the shires one can find 14 examples of election to four consecutive parliaments, 5 examples of election to five consecutive parliaments, 1 of election to six consecutive parliaments,[1] and 1 of election to seven consecutive parliaments.[2] In the boroughs there are 9 examples of election to four consecutive parliaments, 4 of election to five consecutive parliaments, 1 of election to seven consecutive parliaments,[3] and 1 of election to ten consecutive parliaments.[4] These examples might be slightly multiplied if complete returns were available. The fact remains, however, that re-election to a series of immediately successive parliaments was unusual under Edward I. and Edward II. Interpreted in this sense, the statement that members were rarely re-elected might be accepted: but even in this special sense it would still be subject to exceptions which, though relatively small in number, are yet sufficiently numerous to be worth bearing in mind.

Two other matters now demand consideration. Granted that constituencies which obeyed the writ of summons often re-elected the same persons, how far did constituencies ignore the summons and omit to elect at all? And supposing that an election was made, to what extent did the representatives elected actually attend in parliament?

It seems to have been unusual for shire constituencies to refuse or omit to elect: there appear to be no more than four examples between 1290 and 1327, and in each case the shire's failure to elect is explained in the return as being due to some special cause.[5] In borough constituencies, on the other hand, omissions of election are thought to have been very common. This point was first emphasized by Riess, and it has been stressed again more recently by M. Pasquet.[6] They call attention to the fact that the sheriffs in their returns frequently report that boroughs "nihil responderunt" or "nullum dederunt responsum" to the precept of election: the sheriffs say this, as Riess rightly remarks, of boroughs great and small in all the shires of England. But there is evidence that a *nullum dederunt responsum* did not neces-

[1] Richard of Chessbech for Devonshire to the parliaments of July 1321–November 1325.

[2] William of Scalebrok for Oxfordshire to the parliaments of May 1306–August 1312.

[3] William Amerose for Yarmouth to the parliaments of April 1309–September 1313.

[4] Andrew Pirie for Oxford borough to the parliaments of March 1300–November 1311.

[5] *Parl. Writs*, I. p. 60 (36); p. 176 (44); II. ii. p. 145 (66); p. 322 (27).

[6] Riess, *Die Geschichte des Wahlrechts zum englischen Parlament im Mittelalter*, pp. 17-24; Pasquet, pp. 183-92. Riess's essay is an acute and valuable study, but it is not always accurate in details, and its use of evidence is sometimes unsatisfactory.

sarily mean that a borough failed to elect. Thus Colchester made no answer to the sheriff of Essex for the parliament of February 1305, yet at least one burgess for Colchester actually attended that meeting, since a writ *de expensis* is enrolled for him.[1] Again Grimsby " nullum dedit responsum " to the sheriff of Lincoln for the parliament of September 1313, yet two burgesses of Grimsby received writs *de expensis* for that parliament.[2] Again Ipswich is returned by the sheriff of Suffolk as having made no answer for the parliament of April 1328 ; but two burgesses were as a matter of fact elected and they received writs *de expensis* for attending. An interesting letter from the bailiffs of Ipswich to the Chancery rather suggests that the sheriff did not receive their answer in time to include the names in his return.[3] That this sort of thing might easily occur is proved by one of Riess's own examples. He cites Scarborough as giving no answer for the parliament of August 1311.[4] Now the sheriff of Yorkshire certainly did enter in his return that the bailiff of Scarborough had made no answer, but Riess does not seem to have observed that this entry was afterwards cancelled,[5] and that the names of the Scarborough burgesses are actually inserted underneath. In this case the sheriff presumably received the names at the last moment and amended his return accordingly. All that a *nihil responderunt* need mean, therefore, is that the sheriff had received no answer up to the time of sending his own return to the Chancery. It may sometimes also mean that no election was made. The difficulty is to know which meaning is to be understood in any given case. *Nullum dederunt responsum* must therefore be handled with care : Riess's interpretation of it involves a dangerous argument *ex silentio*, and may easily dispose one to exaggerate the omissions of election in the boroughs.[6]

We now come to what is perhaps the most important question of all. To what extent did the representatives elected actually attend in parliament ? Recent teaching has been leaning towards the view that elected representatives very frequently failed to attend. The evidence vouched in support of this doctrine is contained chiefly in the enrolments of writs *de expensis*. The number of members for whom these

[1] *Parl. Writs*, I. p. 143 (18) ; p. 157 (47).

[2] *Ibid.* II. ii. p. 108 (39) ; p. 116 (57).

[3] P.R.O. Parl. Writs and Returns, Bundle 5, Board 4. The bailiffs' letter is printed (a little carelessly) by Prynne, *Brev. Parl. Red.*, p. 271 : they say that they have informed the sheriff of the names of those who had been elected, " et coment qe le dit viescounte eit certefiee la court de meme respounse ou noun, nous, qe prests susmes en taunt qe nous poems suffire a obeyr as maundementz de nostre seignour lige ensi qe de droit susmes tenutz, vous certifioms, sires, qe de nostre commun assent avoms eleuz nos comburgeis Geffrei Stace et Cristophre del Boys ", etc.

[4] Riess, pp. 21-2, n. 2.

[5] Palgrave indicates this by his usual sign ; *Parl. Writs*, II. ii. 46 (6).

[6] Thus Pasquet (pp. 184-5) gives Yarmouth as one of two examples of towns which " refusent presque systématiquement de répondre ". Yet returns are extant for Yarmouth for 24 out of 28 parliaments between 1290 and 1327.

writs are enrolled is nearly always considerably less than the number of persons returned by the sheriffs as having been elected: this is especially true of the borough representatives, but it also applies, though in a much lesser degree, to shire members as well, at any rate under Edward I. and Edward II. From this it has been inferred that while the number of members returned was over three hundred, the number who actually attended was commonly no more than about a hundred, the great majority of whom were knights of the shire. These inferences are sound provided that the enrolments of writs *de expensis* are exhaustive. It is thought that for the shire members, at any rate, these enrolments are exhaustive, since they usually account for all or most of the full complement of 74 knights of the shire. It is admitted, however, that they are not quite exhaustive for the burgesses: some fifteen cities and boroughs, it has been suggested, may have paid their members independently of writs *de expensis*, and were therefore actually represented in parliament though their burgesses do not usually figure in the enrolments of writs *de expensis*.[1] But apart from these few exceptions, it is thought that the number of burgesses for whom writs *de expensis* are enrolled may be taken as a fairly accurate indication of the number of borough representatives actually present in parliament. This assumption has recently been challenged by Miss May McKisack in a paper on *Borough Representation in Richard II.'s Reign*.[2] There is other evidence from previous reigns which indicates that her challenge is well founded. In the parliament of March 1340 a committee of Lords and Commons was appointed to consider certain petitions. The names of the persons chosen—who were presumably actually present in parliament—are recorded in the parliament roll. Among them are six citizens and burgesses. Yet no writ *de expenses* is enrolled for a single one of the six.[3] It is not often, however, that the rolls of parliament help in this way. But there are other sources which furnish additional tests. Specially valuable for this purpose are the borough accounts, which often record payments made for the expenses of the borough's representatives in parliament. Unfortunately these accounts have usually survived only in an imperfect condition, and very few even of those that do survive have been systematically printed or calendared. They nevertheless supply some useful instances. Thus the excerpts from the borough accounts of Reading printed by the Historical Manuscripts Commission show that representatives of the borough were actually present in at least 8

[1] Professor Pollard suggests (pp. 317-18) London, York, Bristol, Winchester, Salisbury, Southampton, Norwich, Yarmouth and the Cinque Ports. It may be worth mentioning in passing that all these boroughs (except the Cinque Ports) do occasionally appear in the enrolments of writs *de expensis*.

[2] *Eng. Hist. Rev.* xxxix. pp. 511-25.

[3] *Rot. Parl.* ii. p. 113. The names are: Thomas of Wycombe (constituency unknown), Robert of Morwode (Nottingham), Philip of Cayly (Cambridge), John of Rattlesden (Colchester), John of Preston (? Wycombe), Thomas But (? Norwich).

parliaments between April 1354 and September 1388;[1] yet no Reading burgesses are mentioned in the enrolments of writs *de expensis* for a single one of those same parliaments. Again in the excerpts from the borough accounts of Lynn printed by the same Commission, there are entries which show that burgesses received payments for attending 8 parliaments between February 1328 and February 1338; but writs *de expensis* for Lynn members are enrolled for only 2 of those parliaments.[2] Similarly, a few extracts printed from the borough accounts of Shrewsbury record expenses paid to members of 4 parliaments between August 1311 and September 1336; but the enrolled writs *de expensis* do not mention Shrewsbury burgesses in 3 of the four parliaments in question.[3] These are facts gleaned from mere scattered abstracts and unsystematic summaries of very incomplete borough accounts. It is interesting to turn to a set of borough accounts which have survived in a fairly continuous series (though there are several gaps of one or more years even here) and which have been published in a form which makes their contents pretty accurately known—the accounts of the borough of Leicester. Between 1301 and 1324 these accounts record payments to the borough representatives (sometimes one but generally two) for attending 13 parliaments: for 10 of these parliaments no writs *de expensis* are enrolled for Leicester members.[4] During the reign of Edward III., the accounts show payments to Leicester members for attending at least 23 parliaments; yet no writs *de expensis* are enrolled for Leicester for 18 of these 23 meetings.[5] It will be observed that none of the boroughs that have been adduced are among those which are supposed to have paid their members

[1] *Hist. MSS. Comm. Report XI.*, Appendix, Pt. vii. pp. 171-2. The parliaments are: April 1354, May 1368, January 1380, November 1380, April 1384 (?), November 1384, October 1385, September 1388.

[2] *Hist. MSS. Comm. Report XI.*, Appendix, Pt. iii. pp. 213-16. The parliaments are: February 1328, March 1332 (?), September 1332, February 1334, March 1336, September 1336, and two of the three parliaments of March 1337, September 1337 and February 1338. Writs *de expensis* are enrolled for the parliaments of February 1334 and September 1336.

[3] *Hist. MSS. Comm. Report XV.*, Appendix, Pt. x. p. 27; Owen and Blakeway, *History of Shrewsbury*, i. p. 546. The parliaments are: August 1311, March 1330 (or November 1330), September 1331 (?), March 1336 (or September 1336). A writ *de expensis* is enrolled for the parliament of March 1330.

[4] Bateson, *Records of the Borough of Leicester*, i. pp. 235, 246, 248, 267, 278, 296, 300, 320, 324, 328, 333-4, 339, 344, 347. The parliaments are: January 1301, May 1306, April 1309, November 1311 (or August 1312), September 1314, January 1315, January 1316, October 1318, May 1319, October 1320, July 1321, May 1322, February 1324. Writs *de expensis* are enrolled for September 1314, January 1315 and January 1316.

[5] *Ibid.* ii. pp. 11, 14, 17, 26, 41-2, 45, 46, 47, 48, 60, 75, 77, 80, 91, 108, 110, 144, 147, 148, 158. The parliaments are: September 1332 (?), December 1332, February 1334, September 1334, May 1335, March 1336, February 1338, February 1339, October 1339, January 1340 (?), April 1341, June 1344, February 1351, January 1352, September 1353, April 1354, February 1358, May 1360, June 1369, February 1371 (?), November 1372 (?), November 1373, January 1377. (Payments for other parliaments which cannot be definitely assigned will be found *ibid.* pp. 28, 141.) Writs are enrolled for the parliaments of December 1332, February 1334, February 1351, April 1354, February 1371.

without recourse to writs *de expensis*. Their example proves that we cannot rely upon the enrolled writs *de expensis* as being in any sense an exhaustive record of the borough members who actually attended mediæval parliaments. And there are other pieces of evidence which, though less definite than the facts just cited, appear to point to the same conclusion. One of these pieces of evidence may be referred to here. A parliament which met in February 1371 made a certain grant of money to the King. After the members had dispersed, the King found that it would be necessary to revise the terms of the grant. In order to save the trouble and expense of reassembling all the members, he issued a writ in April 1371 ordering the sheriffs to send from each shire one of the Knights and from cities and boroughs one of the citizens and burgesses who had come to the parliament in February, to meet at Winchester in June to revise the grant.[1] The names and respective constituencies of the members whom the sheriffs were thus ordered to send are enrolled in the Close Roll. Here then we have what purports to be a list of some of the members who " came " (*venerunt*) to the parliament of February 1371, and we may compare it with the enrolled writs *de expensis* for that parliament. Of course we must move cautiously: *venerunt* may be common form, and in the deserts of common form the unwary traveller may easily be duped by a verbal mirage. In this case " who came " may possibly mean no more than " who were elected to come ". The wording of the writ, however, appears to keep a clear distinction between the two expressions: it says that if any of the persons named " qui . . . ad dictum parliamentum . . . venerunt " are no longer alive, then " socios suos qui cum eis de veniendo ad parliamentum predictum electi fuerunt " are to be ordered to come instead of them. Again if " venerunt " meant merely " who were elected to come ", one would expect to find representatives summoned from more than two boroughs of a county like Wiltshire, where the boroughs electing representatives were at that time normally more numerous: yet two only of the Wiltshire boroughs are mentioned in these writs of April 1371. On the whole there is some justification for inclining to the view that " venerunt " here may very well mean " came ". If that is indeed its meaning, then these writs would imply that in the parliament of February 1371 no less than 83 boroughs were actually represented, though not necessarily by two members apiece in every case.[2] Yet it is for 18 boroughs only that writs *de expensis* are enrolled for the parliament of February 1371. The discrepancy is so serious that if it stood alone it might be passed

[1] *Report on the Dignity of a Peer*, i. Appendix, pp. 650-52. The persons summoned are described in the writ as persons " qui . . . ad dictum parliamentum [in February] de mandato nostro venerunt ".

[2] That is possibly the implication of the juxtaposition of " venerunt " and " electi fuerunt ". The enrolled writs *de expensis* prove that some boroughs were represented by two members each.

over. But taken with the proved discrepancies between the enrolled writs *de expensis* and the borough accounts of Shrewsbury, Reading, Lynn and above all Leicester, it cannot be lightly dismissed as incredible, and it is a warning against too hastily assuming that the citizens and burgesses were very remiss in attending and that they were a numerical minority of the Commons.

We may now turn to the shires. As is well known, the enrolments of writs *de expensis* are sometimes quite complete for all 37 shires, and in any case they always account for a greater proportion of the county than of the borough constituencies. It has therefore been supposed that for the shires, at any rate, these enrolments may be taken as exhaustive. It is very rarely that they can be tested, as the shires unfortunately had no records corresponding to the borough accounts. But occasionally a test is possible. For the parliament of March 1340, writs *de expensis* are enrolled for 61 county members drawn from 33 shires. Two of the shires for which no writs are enrolled are Oxford and Surrey. Yet at least one member was present from each of those shires, for they are mentioned in the parliament roll as appointed to serve on a committee to deal with petitions.[1] Again, it is known that Henry of Keighley, one of the knights for Lancashire, was present in the parliament of January 1301, since it was he who bore to the king the " bill " of grievances drawn up on that occasion.[2] Yet no writ *de expensis* is enrolled for him. These two examples are definite proof that the enrolments of writs *de expensis* are not necessarily exhaustive even for the shire members. The example from 1340 is especially noteworthy. An enrolment of writs *de expensis* for so many as 33 out of 37 shires might naturally be thought exhaustive. Yet it is clear that two shires which had members actually present on that occasion are omitted from the enrolment. Now the enrolments of writs *de expensis* for the shires during the reigns of Edward I. and Edward II. are often nothing like so full as that of March 1340. Thus for the parliament of January 1301 only 25 shires are enrolled, for that of May 1306 only 20, for that of October 1318 only 28, for the two York parliaments of 1322 only 19 apiece. It being certain that 33 out of 37 is not an exhaustive enrolment in 1340, one can scarcely feel confident that 28 out of 37 is exhaustive in 1318, and still less that 19 out of 37 is exhaustive in 1322. On the whole, one is forced to the conclusion that the enrolments of writs *de expensis* cannot safely be taken as exhaustive, either for the shires or for the boroughs.[3]

The foregoing considerations suggest that the evidence of sheriffs'

[1] *Rot. Parl.* ii. p. 113. Thomas de la More (Oxford) and John of Hayton (Surrey) are the two members of the committee for whom writs *de expensis* are not enrolled.

[2] Stubbs, *Const. Hist.* ii. (4th ed.) pp. 157-8. In the following June he was imprisoned for the part he had played.

[3] This conclusion was long ago reached by Prynne ; *Fourth Part,* pp. 11-12, 76, 177.

returns and enrolled writs *de expensis* may easily prove misleading unless interpreted with great caution. This is especially true when that evidence is used as an index to the contemporary attitude of constituencies and representatives towards the mediæval English parliament. There seems to be a growing opinion that mediæval constituencies were reluctant to elect, that their representatives were still more reluctant to attend, and that down to the 15th century, at any rate, this general reluctance so far prevailed that a considerable proportion of the constituencies were commonly represented in parliament only on paper, so to speak. Various facts seem to indicate, however, that these opinions need some qualification before they can be accepted with any confidence. Thus it is possible to prove, even from the enrolments of writs *de expensis* as they stand, that a good many of the members who were frequently elected actually attended a large proportion of the parliaments for which they were returned. Between 1290 and 1327, Bedfordshire returned Peter le Loring and John Morteyn 6 times; Loring was present 6 times and Morteyn 5 times: Buckinghamshire returned Robert Malet 11 times and he attended 9 times: Baldwin of Stowe was returned 9 times by Cambridgeshire, and attended 6 times: Richard of Chessbech was returned 9 times by Devonshire and was present 8 times: John Peverel was elected 6 times by Dorsetshire, and was present 6 times: Hertfordshire elected Geoffrey de la Lee 9 times and Richard Perers 8 times; Lee attended 8 times and Perers 5 times: John Waldeshef was elected 7 times by Huntingdonshire and attended every time: Lancashire returned Gilbert of Singleton, William of Slene and Edmund Nevill each 4 times, and each was present 4 times: Richard of Walsingham was elected 7 times by Norfolk and attended 7 times: Richard of Horseleye was elected 6 times by Northumberland and attended 5 times: John of Croxford was returned 9 times by Oxfordshire and was present in parliament every time: Shropshire elected Richard of Harley 8 times and he attended 8 times: Yorkshire returned Gregory of Thornton 5 times and he attended 5 times: even in the incomplete enrolments for the boroughs there are Exeter, Lincoln and Worcester each with a burgess elected 5 times and present 4 times,[1] and Bedford with William Costyn elected 8 times and present at least 5 times. But the most interesting examples from a borough come from Oxford during the period 1368–1404. Writs *de expensis* are enrolled for Oxford burgesses for every parliament except three between May 1368 and January 1404.[2] An analysis shows that Edmund Kenyon was elected 9 times and attended 9 times; that William Dagevill was elected 7 times and attended 6 times; that William of Codeshale was elected 5 times and attended 5 times; that

[1] Matthew of Crouthorne (Exeter), Henry Stoil (Lincoln), Richard Coliz (Worcester).

[2] The enrolled writs are printed by Prynne; *Fourth Part*, ss. iii.-v.

Adam River and John Hicks were each elected 5 times and were present in parliament 4 times. It may be urged that all these may have been exceptional cases which do not necessarily invalidate the inference that reluctance to attend was the general rule. It may therefore be interesting to test the members who were elected only once: among these, if anywhere, one might expect to find the persons who were reluctant. The lists for the period 1290–1327 show some 650 shire members elected (so far as is known) only once: the enrolled writs *de expensis*, incomplete as they probably are, show that at least 380 of these actually attended. For the boroughs no comprehensive test is possible: but it may be noted that in Bedford during the same period 16 burgesses were elected once, and that at least 8 of them actually attended; and that in Oxford during the period 1368–1404 19 burgesses were elected only once and 18 are known to have attended. Taken together, these figures suggest that reluctance to attend was quite possibly not a general and almost certainly not a successful attitude. The well-known case of Chipping Torrington is worth recalling in this connection.[1] It is usually quoted as proof that the men of Torrington were anxious to avoid sending representatives to parliament. But it also proves that they had not been allowed to act in the matter as they pleased—in short, that their reluctance to attend had not been a successful attitude. There are some other facts which convey a similar impression. In 1383 the burgesses of Colchester obtained a charter exempting them for five years from sending burgesses to parliament, on account of the expenses of fortifying the town; in 1394 they obtained a similar exemption for three years on the same ground; in 1404 they obtained a similar exemption for six years "provided that they keep and support all statutes and ordinances and charges made and granted in the said parliaments".[2] In 1388 Maldon obtained an exemption from sending representatives for three years in order to assist in rebuilding its bridge; in 1392 it obtained a second exemption for the same reason, this time for seven years.[3] Most interesting of all is an example from Hull: in October 1384 the burgesses were excused from sending representatives *to the next parliament* of November 1384, because of the great expense of fortifying the town.[4] These facts, while they certainly show that the three boroughs concerned were quite prepared to forgo parliamentary representation in order to further their local enterprises, also seem to show that they did not regard themselves as entirely free to neglect their parliamentary duties at pleasure;[5] they apparently thought that their

[1] *Rot. Parl.* ii. pp. 459-60; Prynne, *Fourth Part*, pp. 319-20.

[2] *Cal. Pat. Rolls*, 1381–85, p. 214; 1391–6, p. 379; 1401–5, p. 355. The proviso in 1404 suggests that the king regarded the presence of representatives as of some importance from the point of view of legal forms.

[3] *Ibid.* 1385–88, p. 508; 1391–6, p. 187.

[4] *Ibid.* 1381–85, p. 475.

[5] See also the letter of the bailiffs of Ipswich, *supra*, p. 207, note 3.

reluctance to attend had better be a chartered reluctance if it was to be a really successful attitude. Their example suggests that the reluctance of constituencies and representatives, even if it were proved, may not be the only factor to consider. The mediæval English parliament was the handiwork of kings. We must not too readily assume that those kings were always half oblivious of their handiwork; for they were strong kings and they ruled in "a small, well conquered, much governed kingdom". [1]

J. G. EDWARDS.

[1] Maitland, *Law Quart. Rev.* xiv. p. 33.

XVII

THE MEMORANDA ROLLS AND THE REMEMBRANCERS, 1282–1350

Of the many English financial records of the later middle ages the two series of memoranda rolls kept in the exchequer of account are the most important. Madox used them extensively in his studies preparatory to *The History and Antiquities of the Exchequer*, but later historians, until the present generation, have made little use of their contents. The wealth of material brought to light by Mr. James Conway Davies [1] bears witness to the value of these records, but much remains to be done before they are fully exploited. In the present paper, however, nothing more ambitious will be attempted than a description of certain characteristics of the rolls and their contents, with a view to discovering the duties of the officials who kept them. The facts were gathered during the course of an investigation of the various stages of the progress of the accounting of the assessors and collectors of the taxes upon personal property at the exchequer. As this investigation was limited to memoranda relating to such taxes, the results, except in certain instances to be noted, can obviously not cover all the duties of the officials, the remembrancers, who had charge of the rolls. This paper, therefore, forms merely an introduction to a larger subject.

A roll of memoranda was made up every year by each of the two officials of the exchequer of account, known as the lord treasurer's, or treasurer's, remembrancer and the king's remembrancer.[2] These titles were infrequently used in contemporary records ; until the close of the reign of Edward II., and, to some extent, later, it was customary for one remembrancer to refer to his colleague as " the other remembrancer ". The memoranda preserved by the remembrancers covered a wide range, for anything necessary for the elucidation of the accounts of the collectors of revenue or other persons was recorded. Of primary importance to the treasurer and barons of the exchequer were the memoranda of the appearance and accounting of the collectors of taxes. Letters sent to the exchequer and writs issued by that

[1] *The Baronial Opposition to Edward II.*

[2] Throughout the notes to this paper I have abbreviated Memoranda Roll to M.R. I have not given references to these rolls when the regnal years are mentioned in the text.

department were enrolled. There were also memoranda of matters subsidiary to the accounts, such as the appointment of attorneys and mainpernors and records of fines, days given, and respites. Under the heading *Recorda* were enrolled, *inter alia*, charters to boroughs and religious bodies, records of the trials of the tax collectors, the results of inquisitions held at the command of the crown or treasurer, and the commissions issued to the tax gatherers.

The rolls themselves consist of long and rather narrow sheets or membranes of parchment sewed together at one end, the top, so as to form a bundle or file. The memoranda kept were classified, each class forming a section of the larger rolls. These sections were subdivided by the terms of the exchequer year, and within the terms the memoranda were arranged roughly in chronological order. Under this plan the parchment sheets containing the memoranda grouped under one heading formed an independent file until the exchequer year was completed. On any day in the year a remembrancer would have at his elbow a number of small bundles of membranes each containing one kind of memoranda, and he could add new membranes and new notes to any of these as necessity required. At the close of the year these small files were assembled into a large roll, the memoranda roll.

In the attempt to learn something of the duties of the remembrancers from the records they kept, I shall first describe certain surface indications of a division of their labours. While these give results that are useful, they are set down here only as opening the way to further studies. They show, however, that the remembrancers had different ways of handling their material and different interests before the days of the great exchequer reformer, Walter de Stapledon. After the description of obvious contrasts and characteristics I shall take under consideration the contents of the classified sections of the rolls, so far as they relate to the taxes upon movable goods.

From the exchequer year 10 Edward I., arbitrarily selected for the beginning of this inquiry, until well into the reign of Edward III., there was a steady increase in the number of membranes bound up in the memoranda rolls. Whereas in 10 Edward I. the combined total of the membranes in the two rolls was 51, in 9 Edward III. the total was 533, and in 19 Edward III., 624. The contrast was due to an enormous increase in the volume of business transacted by the exchequer. A comparison of the relative size of the rolls in the two series gives results that bear more directly upon the subject in hand. In the six rolls of the L.T.R. series, dating from 10 to 15 Edward I., the average number of membranes was a fraction under 30, and in the rolls of the K.R. series a little over 20. In 20 Edward I., as a result of the reforms of William de Marchia, the L.T.R. roll increased in size to 49 membranes and the K.R. to 46, both far above the average of the earlier years. From 20 to 28 Edward I., both inclusive, the average of the L.T.R. series was about 90 membranes, and of the K.R. about 87. The rolls of the treasurer's remembrancer were, therefore, normally slightly larger than those of his co-worker, but this was not the case in the 24th, 25th, and 27th years. During the first nine years of the reign of Edward II. the pre-eminence of the series made up by the treasurer's remembrancer was clearly established. For those years the L.T.R. rolls averaged a little over 162 membranes, whereas the average of the K.R. rolls was about 135. In the years toward the close of Edward II.'s reign came the reforms of Stapledon, and with them a clearer definition of the duties of the remembrancers. An obvious result of the reforms was a striking reversal of the size of the memoranda rolls. For the 2nd, 7th, 9th, and 11th years of Edward III. the average of the L.T.R. rolls was nearly 170 membranes and of the K.R. rolls 288. The series of rolls compiled by the treasurer's remembrancer had lost the lead it had held for so many years, and that of his colleague had forged ahead. As will be seen, this change was largely caused by the delegation of the task of enrolling the *Brevia directa baronibus* to the king's remembrancer.

As the memoranda rolls increased in size the system of classifying the memoranda was expanded to meet the need of quick reference. Following the reforms of 1290 the simple classification of the earlier years gave place to temporary experiments, out of which emerged in the reign of Edward II. the classification that lasted to the end of the period selected for this study. A description of this evolution will serve to make clearer what follows.

Both of the remembrancers before 1290 were content with a few general headings at the top of the sheets of parchment upon which the memoranda were inscribed. In the L.T.R. roll of 13 Edward I. there are six classes of memoranda and in the K.R. five. The headings on the former were *Communia*, *Recogniciones*, *Precepta*, *Brevia pro rege*, *Adventus vicecomitum*, and *Visus comptorum vicecomitum*. The king's remembrancer added to this list *Affidaciones*, and omitted *Brevia pro rege* and the *Visus*. From 16 to 19 Edward I. the K.R. contained but three classes, *Communia*, *Recogniciones*, and *Adventus vicecomitum*. With the increase in the volume of exchequer business in 20 Edward I. the classification of material became more detailed. As the years passed a number of special headings were introduced. These proved in most cases to be ephemeral in character and need not be chronicled here. One change, however, took place at once ; the class of *Brevia pro rege*, previously found in the roll of the treasurer's remembrancer alone, appeared and remained in the K.R. roll. Before the close of the reign of Edward I. the development of the later system was well under way. The class *Brevia pro rege* was split in two, and writs issued by the exchequer were grouped as *Brevia retornabilia* and *Brevia irretornabilia*. Subdivisions of *Communia* were emerging: *Recorda*, *Presentaciones*, *attornati*, *dies dati et respectus*, and *Fines*, *manucapciones*, *redditus*, *affidaciones et visores*. Every heading regularly used under Edward II. and Edward III. has been found in some form on the rolls of Edward I. though in many cases irregularly.

Under Edward II. experiments ceased, and the classification of memoranda assumed the form that was to last until 1350. In the year 1307 the material on both rolls was grouped under a number of headings. First came *Adventus vicecomitum*, then *Commissiones*, *literae patentes et brevia clausa*, and *Communia* with the sub-headings, *Brevia directa baronibus*, *Fines*, *manucapciones*, *redditus*, *affidaciones*, *visores*, *Presentaciones*, *attornati*, *dies dati et respectus*, and *Recorda*. These were followed by *Brevia retornabilia*, *Brevia irretornabilia*, *Recogniciones*, *Status et visus compotorum*, and *Precepta*. This classification was used thereafter save that *Brevia directa baronibus* was later separated from *Communia* and used as an independent heading. Occasionally a special heading was used to meet a temporary need, but these were without influence upon the system. In view of the importance attached to Stapledon's reforms it may be observed here that the standardising of the classification of memoranda antedates his reforming ordinances.

Though both of the remembrancers under Edward II. classified their memoranda in the same fashion there were a few contrasts in the amount of space devoted by them to particular sections. This will account for the difference in the size of the rolls. For the first nine years of the reign of Edward II. the L.T.R. series of rolls consistently contained more material in the sections devoted to *Brevia directa baronibus*, *Brevia retornabilia*, and *Precepta*. The larger size of these sections gave to the rolls of the treasurer's remembrancer the greater part of their lead at the time.

After Walter de Stapledon's attempts to check the undue amount of duplication of material on the rolls there was, as already noted, a marked change in the relative size of the rolls. In conformity with the Cowick ordinance of 1323 the king's remembrancer took charge of the enrolment of the writs included in the class *Brevia directa baronibus*;[1] his colleague omitted these writs. On the K.R. roll of 7 Edward III. this section included 78 membranes, on that of 10 Edward III., 87, on that of 11 Edward III., 105. No inconsiderable proportion of the greater volume of records enrolled by the king's remembrancer can thus be accounted for. The lesser differences are, however, enlightening. The roll of the king's remembrancer of 19 Edward III. devoted more space to the classes of *Brevia irretornabilia*, *Recorda*, and *Commissiones*; whereas the L.T.R. roll of the same year was decidedly ahead in the number of membranes devoted to *Brevia retornabilia* and

[1] *Red Book of the Exchequer*, iii. 862-864.

Precepta. The same contrasts may be found in the rolls of the seventh year. When the contents of these divisions are examined a partial explanation of certain of these differences will appear.

The manner in which the sections of the roll were filed and then bound during the greater part of the period affords an easy method of distinguishing between the L.T.R. and the K.R. memoranda rolls and adds another to the superficial points of difference. Until after the first decade of the reign of Edward III., the treasurer's remembrancer grouped the subdivisions of the general class *Communia* by terms. To be specific, under the heading *Communia*, Michaelmas, were placed the Michaelmas *Recorda*, *Fines* . . ., and *Presentaciones*. . . . The Michaelmas *Recorda* were therefore separated from the Easter *Recorda* by two intervening sections of Michaelmas *Fines* and *Presentaciones*. In order to run down a reference to the *Recorda* of Easter it is necessary to turn first to the *Communia* of the Easter term and then to look for the *Recorda* of the same term. The king's remembrancer adopted a more logical system of filing. Under *Communia* the *Recorda* of the Michaelmas, Hilary, Easter, and Trinity terms followed each other without interruption. The other subclasses were treated in the same fashion. A searcher for Easter *Recorda* has therefore first to look up *Communia*, find the subdivision *Recorda* and then turn over the sheets of parchment until he reaches the Easter term of that group of memoranda. By 19 Edward III., at the latest, the lord treasurer's remembrancer adopted the method of filing *Communia* used by his colleague, and this distinction between the two rolls came to an end. Outside of the *Communia* the remembrancers always used one system of grouping the memoranda, that followed by the king's remembrancer with respect to the *Communia*.

A last obvious contrast between the two series of memoranda rolls remains to be described. It was the custom of the treasurer's remembrancer to jot down in the margin alongside of certain memoranda references to the Pipe Roll of the same or a subsequent year. In the place on the Pipe Roll referred to there will be found further information relating to the collectors of customs or other royal debtors. The king's remembrancer usually omitted such references. If, therefore, a memoranda roll contains many references to the Pipe Roll it is safe to assume that it was made up by the treasurer's remembrancer. These marginal notes are evidence that the remembrancer was interested in the winding-up of the accounts. In the case of the collectors of taxes upon movables no record appeared in the body of the Pipe Roll until after their accounts had been audited. If there was then a balance still due, the subsequent transactions with the exchequer were recorded on that roll. The interest of the treasurer's remembrancer in such transactions is explained by Mr. Charles Johnson's statement of one of his duties: "the Treasurer's Remembrancer was charged with the issue of process to recover the balances recorded as due on the Great Roll".[1] Since it was his duty to see to it that writs were issued to compel the payment of these balances, the marginal references to the place on the Pipe Roll where the records of the accounting were to be found would serve to remind him of his duty and to lighten the burden of keeping track of delinquent accountants.

The investigation of certain of the characteristics of the memoranda rolls, characteristics that have been termed obvious, has yielded some results that are valuable for the proper understanding of the developments in the exchequer. The great increase in the size of the rolls bears witness to the growth of the business transacted at the exchequer, for more business meant more memoranda to be recorded by the remembrancers and more sheets of parchment to be inscribed. On the same basis it is evident that there was no great amount of difference between the total amount of memoranda enrolled by the two remembrancers, and presumably in their duties, from 1290 until the reign of Edward II. Both remembrancers used the same system of classifying their material, though for a time a different plan of filing the subdivisions of *Communia*, and it was not until towards the close of the reign of Edward II. that the king's remembrancer took over one section, the *Brevia directa baronibus*, into his sole charge. The contrasts in the amount of space devoted to special classes of memoranda give a clue to the development of different duties. During the early years of the reign of Edward II. the rolls of the treasurer's remembrancer consistently contained more membranes than those of the king's remembrancer, because he enrolled more memoranda under the headings *Brevia directa baronibus*, *Brevia retornabilia*, and *Precepta*. As the two latter classes consisted largely of writs to compel the appearance of accountants at the exchequer to continue or complete their accounting, it is reasonably certain that the lord treasurer's remembrancer had a superior interest in such matters. This inference is strengthened by his marginal references to the Pipe Roll. From Stapledon's ordinances and other records of the time it is clear that the remembrancers were not merely clerks who set down memoranda for the information of the exchequer, though that was their chief function, but that they also had duties of a semi-executive character. When the treasurer's remembrancer enrolled more *Brevia retornabilia* than his fellow it may be assumed that he was not merely a more industrious copyist, but that he was especially charged with the task of seeing that certain classes of such writs were issued under the seal of the exchequer. The same conclusion may be drawn from the greater number of the *Brevia irretornabilia* enrolled by the king's remembrancer after the period of reform. What these writs were in relation to the taxes upon movables will hereafter appear. As a copyist

[1] *The Public Record Office*, 26.

of writs the king's remembrancer was, after Stapledon's time, charged with the recording of writs directed to the barons, and it was also his duty to see that the commands were obeyed. It is now time to turn to the contents of the several classes of memoranda in so far as they were connected with the taxes upon movable goods.

At the centre of the various enrolments of the remembrancers having to do with the taxes upon movables lay the records of the accounting of the taxers and collectors of these subsidies.[1] These are usually set down under the heading *Status et visus compotorum* or some similar title. During the thirteenth and fourteenth centuries there were two formal stages in accounting—the view of account and the audit of account, often abbreviated in this paper to view and audit. A view was the formal reckoning of the amount owed by the taxers and collectors after the assessment of personal property had been made; it was supposed to be held at the half-way stage in the process of handing in the proceeds of the subsidy at the exchequer. The memorandum of a view stated what the collectors owed on the basis of the rolls of the assessment presented by them, how much they had paid in and what remained to be paid. The audit was a formal and final accounting. At this stage, allowance having been made for the expenses of the collectors, for exemptions and the like, the account of the collectors was balanced. If it chanced that a sum was still owed to the crown, this amount, large or small, called the remainder of account, was noted. The subsequent dealings of the exchequer with the collectors were formally recorded upon the Pipe Roll, though the treasurer's remembrancer frequently kept what may be called informal notes of the same transactions on his roll. In addition to the memoranda of formal views and audits the remembrancer noted in the same place all sorts of facts connected with the appearance or non-appearance of the collectors. These included their appearance without their assessment rolls, the excuses they had to offer for this omission, the days given them for further accounting or payment, the writs of distraint or attachment issued to force them to appear if their delinquency continued, and anything else that might be of importance for purposes of reference. At times when the collectors were remiss the records of their accounting extended to great length, including all the facts that were needed for the information of the treasurer and barons of the exchequer.

The first reasonably complete set of records of views and audits found in the memoranda rolls is that connected with the subsidy, a ninth of movables, granted in the year 1297. No such memoranda have been found in the rolls before 1290, and after that date they were very fragmentary until the year 1298. Their condition during

[1] Examples of the various types of records hereafter referred to may be found in the Appendix contained in Number XVIII. of the *Surrey Record Society* (1923).

the latter period is probably to be accounted for on the score of the novelty of the problems facing the exchequer after the advent of William de Marchia. Before 1290 that body had had very few direct dealings with the collectors of the subsidies; after that date the connection was very close. The records of the audits of the ninth of 1297 were set down on both the memoranda rolls, but a comparison of the two rolls reveals an enlightening contrast.[1] The entries on the L.T.R. roll bear every evidence of having been written when the accounting took place: the lines are unevenly spaced and often waver; corrections are made; different ink is used for additional notes; and the sum total of the memoranda relating to one county sometimes crowds the items relating to the county that follows in the list. On the contrary, the memoranda of the king's remembrancer having to do with the same counties are in one hand and ink; the corrections made on the other roll are embodied; the spacing of the lines is clear-cut and sufficient, and there is no crowding of the accounts of the different counties. There is no possibility of evading the conclusion that the king's remembrancer copied at his leisure his colleague's record of the audits. At times, however, the copying was incomplete; in the case of several counties the king's remembrancer failed to transfer to his roll items that appear at the close of the memoranda of the L.T.R. roll. These items were in most instances references to the *Brevia retornabilia* or the *Brevia pro rege*, where certain writs were to be found. In such writs, issued to force the collectors to appear at the exchequer, the king's remembrancer lacked sufficient interest to induce him to copy the notes referring to them.

The records of later views and audits add their testimony to confirm the conclusion of copying by the king's remembrancer. A comparison of such memoranda connected with the accounting of the collectors of the subsidies of 1309 [2] and 1315 [3] bears this out. How slavish this copying could become is illustrated by a practice of the king's remembrancer in the year 1323, after the passage of the Cowick ordinance. One of the rules laid down in that ordinance was that the rolls of the taxation of personal property should be kept by the king's remembrancer.[4] When it became necessary to refer to these rolls the treasurer's remembrancer properly noted that they were "in the custody of the other remembrancer". In time the king's remembrancer copied the records of the views of account, and in a number of instances transcribed so unthinkingly that on his own

[1] *E.g.* L.T.R.M.R. 25-26 Edward I., mm. 138-139; K.R.M.R., 25-26 Edward I., mm. 97-98.

[2] The Lincolnshire view is an excellent example. It is to be found among the Hilary views on the rolls of 3 Edward II.

[3] Compare K.R.M.R., 9 Edward II., mm. 135 ff., and L.T.R.M.R., 9 Edward II., mm. 189 ff.

[4] *Red Book of the Exchequer*, iii. 866.

roll he referred to himself in the terms used by his colleague. In several cases, however, the wording was changed, and the copy was made to read "in the custody of the king's remembrancer".[1] An accommodating clerk in the year 1345 placed the matter beyond a shadow of doubt when he wrote at the bottom of the membranes of the roll of the king's remembrancer headed *Status et visus* the word "*Transcript*'".[2]

In order that the exchequer of account might be fully informed of all matters connected with the accounting of the taxers and collectors it was the duty of the remembrancers to keep track of and record various other classes of memoranda. There were the writs sent to the exchequer directing them to act, the commissions sent to the tax collectors, and the numerous writs issued by the exchequer itself to the collectors, sheriffs, coroners, and other folk. There were the memoranda of days given the collectors to account, of respites granted, of attorneys, of mainpernors, and of other matters subsidiary to the accounting. The remembrancers enrolled the records of the trials of the collectors for alleged delinquencies, and the long processes connected with claims to exemption from taxation. In short, all the details of the many-sided interests of the exchequer in connection with the taxes upon movables were carefully noted on the memoranda rolls. From these various classes of memoranda a few, the more important, have been selected for the purpose of determining the respective duties of the remembrancers.

Of the enrolled writs having to do with the taxes upon movables the first in chronological order were the commissions under the great seal issued to the taxers and collectors after they had been selected and duly sworn at the exchequer. Accompanying them were the instructions to the taxers and collectors, the so-called form of taxation. Both were enrolled among the *Recorda* after that class of memoranda emerged from the mass of *Communia*, and before that among the *Communia*, or under a special heading. No trace of commissions or forms has been found on the memoranda rolls before 1290. From that date to the year 1322 they were entered upon the rolls of both remembrancers. Then, beginning with the year 1327,[3] the king's remembrancer alone kept transcripts of them, which continued to be the practice within the period covered by this study. As the subsidy grant in 1327 was the first after Stapledon's day, his efforts to lessen the duplication of material on the memoranda rolls had in this instance an immediate and lasting effect.

Once the groups of taxers and collectors were at work in the counties it was the practice of the exchequer to send them writs under its seal

[1] Compare the views of Berkshire and Buckinghamshire.
[2] K.R.M.R., 19 Edward III.
[3] K.R.M.R., 2 Edward III., *Recorda*, Michaelmas, m. 112.

ordering them to pay cash, out of the money they had gathered, to certain persons. Such writs were first enrolled among the *Brevia pro rege* and, after that class was divided, among the *Brevia irretornabilia*. Before the year 1319 these orders to pay out money are found on both rolls, with some minor differences. When, however, in 1319 and 1320, drafts upon the collectors of the subsidy of 1319 were issued, the king's remembrancer made transcripts of more of the writs than did the treasurer's remembrancer. The former kept a record of all the writs enrolled by the latter and of a number not noted by his colleague. This difference persisted. It is safe to rely on the completeness of the memoranda of the king's remembrancer after the days of Stapledon. It may be inferred from this contrast that the king's remembrancer was especially charged with the issue and enrolment of such writs.

While this development was taking place there seems to have been a like decrease in the interest of the lord treasurer's remembrancer in all *Brevia irretornabilia* whether they related to taxes upon movables or not. During the early years of the reign of Edward II. the amount of space devoted to that class of writs was about the same in both memoranda rolls, with the L.T.R. roll slightly in the lead. In 9 Edward II., for example, there was no appreciable difference, for all the writs recorded on the K.R. roll were with one exception found on the L.T.R. roll, and *vice versa*. The difference may have been due to an error of the medieval scribe or to oversight on my part. Under the heading *Brevia irretornabilia* the treasurer's remembrancer in the Trinity term, 7 Edward III., made transcripts of but seven writs; the K.R. roll of the same class and term contains at least fifty writs. In 19 Edward III. there was a similar disparity in the amount of space devoted to this class of writs, though the exact number of writs has not been counted.[1]

Contrasted with the *Brevia irretornabilia* the *Brevia retornabilia* were writs issued by the exchequer to which an answer had to be returned. Under this heading were included orders to the sheriff to distrain the goods of the tax collectors or to attach their bodies so that they might be forced to appear at the exchequer. Within this class were also found writs to the collectors to bring in their rolls or money. The writs of distraint or attachment may be here arbitrarily divided into two types, as they dealt with delinquencies arising before or after the audit stage of accounting had been reached. The first type would, *inter alia*, be concerned with failures to bring in the rolls of taxation, slowness in the payment of the proceeds of the tax, and failures to come to the exchequer of account. The second type would deal with irregularities connected with the payment of the remainders of account.

[1] On the L.T.R. roll there are less than two membranes devoted to these writs, while on the K.R. roll there are eight.

Before the year 1323 the duties of the remembrancers with respect to the enrolment and issuance of the writs of distraint or attachment are not to be inferred from the entries on the memoranda rolls with the definiteness one might desire. The rolls of three years were selected for purposes of comparison, and the following results were obtained. On the L.T.R. roll of 25-26 Edward I. were enrolled writs of both types, that is writs relating to the delinquencies before as well as after the audit.[1] These were not found on the roll of the king's remembrancer. The L.T.R. roll of 9 Edward II. has long lists of writs of the first type, with notes of the returns made, which were not found on the K.R. roll.[2] In January and February 1320, the L.T.R. roll of 13 Edward II. contains a number of writs of the first type which were not transcribed by his colleague.[3] Under the date April 15, 1320, the treasurer's remembrancer further transcribed a writ of the same type.[4] Here it was noted that the sheriff did not return the writ, and at a later date was set down a note to the effect that no further action was taken because the execution was in the hands of the other remembrancer. There is no method of discovering when this final entry was made. It records, however, the beginning of a period of change from the old system. On the K.R. rolls of the same year, 13 Edward II., on the other hand, there are several writs of the first type which are not found on the L.T.R. roll.[5] This complicates matters. The other comparisons would lead naturally to the conclusion that the lord treasurer's remembrancer alone was interested in the enrolment, and, by inference, in the issuance of all kinds of writs of distraint and attachment, but the entries on the roll of his fellow make this conclusion impossible, for the year 13 Edward II. at least. The solution of the problem is further complicated by what happened in other years. On the K.R. roll of 25-26 Edward I.[6] were enrolled writs of the first type, and in the same series of rolls of 23-24 Edward I. were writs of the second type.[7] These entries have not been compared with those on the L.T.R., and it may be that they were copies. The example cited from the year 13 Edward II., however, would seem to indicate that the king's remembrancer could at times enrol such writs independently. The fact that the treasurer's remembrancer, during the three years noted, recorded writs of both types not transcribed by his colleague, and that the notes appended to the views referring to these writs appeared originally on his roll, point to a special interest on his part in all such writs. This I conclude to have been the case, despite the occasional

[1] L.T.R.M.R., 25-26 Edward I., mm. 116, 117, 118.
[2] L.T.R.M.R., 9 Edward II., 171, 171 d, 172, 172 d.
[3] L.T.R.M.R., 13 Edward II., m. 130 d.
[4] *Ibid.*, m. 133. Devonshire.
[5] K.R.M.R., 13 Edward II., mm., 150-152.
[6] K.R.M.R., 25-26 Edward I., m. 116. Cf. K.R.M.R., 23-24 Edward I., m. 70 d.
[7] K.R.M.R., 23-24 Edward I., m. 83. Northamptonshire.

entries on the K.R. rolls; but the duties of the remembrancer were in all probability not defined with the rigour demanded in a modern administrative office.

Whatever uncertainty there may be as to the duties of the remembrancers in the matter of distraints and attachments before 1323, there is none thereafter. Though none of these writs have been found on either roll for the Trinity and Easter terms of 16 Edward II., the records of the views and audits of the same period answer the question directly. In a few instances, when writs of the first type were noted, the L.T.R. roll recorded that their execution was in the hands of the other remembrancer.[1] On the other hand, when the delinquencies arose after the audit, the memoranda of the execution of the writs made no mention of the king's remembrancer. The records of the accounting of the collectors of the subsidies of 1327 and 1332, to go no further, embody the same distinction. In the case of the Bedfordshire collectors of the subsidy of 1327, who had been given a day to account and had not appeared, a note was added by the treasurer's remembrancer that they were distrained at the suit of the other remembrancer.[2] The Leicestershire entry in a similar case was that the goods and chattels of the collectors were distrained "as in the memoranda of the other remembrancer".[3] The memoranda of distraints after the audits on the L.T.R. roll contain no such references. The enrolment of the writs bear witness to division of labour. On the K.R. roll of 7 Edward III. there are many writs of the first type.[4] These were not recorded by the lord treasurer's remembrancer. The treasurer's remembrancer on his rolls of 7[5] 9[6] and 11 Edward III.[7] enrolled writs relating to remainders of account, the second type, and ignored those of the first. The duties of the remembrancers had, therefore, been divided along the line of cleavage afforded by the audit of account. The king's remembrancer was charged with the duty of enrolling the writs which were issued to force the collectors to appear until the audit stage of their accounting was reached, and was likewise charged with the duty of seeing that these writs were issued. The duty of the treasurer's remembrancer was then restricted to writs and processes arising out of delinquencies after the accounts of the collectors had been audited.

With the writs sent to the collectors ordering them to appear at the exchequer with their rolls or the money they had collected it is not necessary to deal at length. In the enrolment of the writs, the remembrancers, before 1323, seem to have followed the practice already

[1] L.T.R.M.R., 16 Edward II., m. 94 d, Buckinghamshire; m. 95, Berkshire.
[2] L.T.R.M.R., 2 Edward III., m. 106 d. Trinity views.
[3] *Ibid.*, m. 99. Easter views.
[4] K.R.M.R., 7 Edward III., mm. 293, 293 d, 294.
[5] L.T.R.M.R., 7 Edward III., m. 129 d. Cheshire.
[6] L.T.R.M.R., 9 Edward III., m. 117 d. Norfolk.
[7] L.T.R.M.R., 11 Edward III., m. 108 d.

described in the case of the writs of distraint and attachment. The year 1323 marks the transition from a large amount of duplication to a separation of the duties of the remembrancers. In April 1323, writs were sent to all the taxers and collectors then at work commanding them to appear at York in person on a day set with all the money they had in hand and with their rolls. These writs were entered on both rolls among the *Brevia retornabilia.* In the margin to the left of the transcripts of the lord treasurer's a note was added to the effect that the writs were vacated because the execution was in the hands of the other, the king's, remembrancer.[1] This note represents the introduction of the new system. Further mandates of the same sort of May 3, 1323,[2] were again entered in duplicate on the rolls, and bear the same note on the L.T.R. roll. Then on the 15th of June a large number of collectors were ordered to bring their money and rolls to Westminster. The transcripts of these writs, with additional notes, were made by the king's remembrancer and not by his colleague.[3] The change had come in the month of the Cowick ordinance. Later evidence supports this division of labour. Again it is manifest that the king's remembrancer, as a result of Stapledon's reforms, was charged with the care of such matters subsidiary to the accounting as arose before the accounts of the collectors had been balanced.

The last kind of memoranda to be considered here, the records of the *dies dati*, were enrolled under the heading *Presentaciones, attornati, dies dati et respectus.* The *dies dati* were days given to the taxers and collectors to account or to do whatever else the exchequer required of them. From 1290 to 1323 it was customary for both remembrancers to record the *dies dati.* The memoranda of this class on the rolls of 13 Edward II. were, as usual, irregular. Then came the year of reform, and during the Trinity term, 1323, the king's remembrancer alone kept a record of a number of days given the collectors of the subsidy of 1322.[4] In connection with the taxes granted in 1332 and 1344 no *dies dati* have been found on the L.T.R. rolls of 7 and 19 Edward III., though on the rolls of the same year made up by the king's remembrancer there are many. The records of the views on the L.T.R. roll of 7 Edward III. occasionally refer to days given *ex parte* the other remembrancer.[5] The duty of the king's remembrancer was seemingly that of enrolment, for such days were granted by the treasurer throughout the period. His records would form the basis of future decisions of the exchequer of account. I have no clear evidence in the matter of the recording of days given to the collectors after their accounts had been audited,

1 L.T.R.M.R., 16 Edward II., m. 75 d.
2 *Ibid.*, m. 76.
3 K.R.M.R., 16 Edward II., m. 157 d.
4 K.R.M.R., 16 Edward II., mm. 103, 103 d, 105, 109.
5 L.T.R.M.R., 7 Edward III., m. 160. Dorsetshire and Huntingdonshire. Compare the Surrey entry in *Surrey Record Society*, No. xviii., p. xlvi.

that is to say, of days on which they were ordered to pay the remainder of the sum due from them.

It is evident from the preceding observations that, while Stapledon's reforms were responsible for lessening the amount of duplication of material on the memoranda rolls and for a clearer differentiation of the duties of the remembrancers in regard to the taxes upon movables, certain differences existed before his day. The superior interest of the treasurer's remembrancer in returnable writs and precepts has been noticed, as also his special interest in matters relating to the winding up of accounts. It may be added here that when the formal records of the audits of the collectors of the taxes upon movables were enrolled in the series known as Enrolled Accounts, the treasurer's remembrancer became their official custodian. The beginning of this separate series dates from the tax granted in the year 1307. Throughout the period the same remembrancer was assigned the task of keeping the memoranda of the accounting of the collectors of taxes, a very important duty.

The duties of the remembrancers in relation to the taxes upon movables were, however, not clearly differentiated until Stapledon's day. Before that time, as already stated, the treasurer's remembrancer had charge of the enrolment of the memoranda of the accounting, and seems to have had a superior interest in all types of writs for bringing the collectors before the exchequer, the *Brevia retornabilia*, but it was not until 1323 that there was a division of labour worthy of the name. From then on, the king's remembrancer was especially charged with the enrolment of writs and the pursuing of processes, except the records of the accounting, up to the time that the accounts of the collectors were finally balanced. He alone enrolled the commissions issued to the taxers and collectors, the days given them to account, the writs of distraint or attachment arising before the audits, and the orders to the collectors to appear before the exchequer with money or the rolls of taxation.[1] There was some duplication of the transcripts of the exchequer writs ordering the collectors to pay out money, but the records of the king's remembrancer were more complete and more important. In line with this division of labour the Cowick ordinance provided that the king's remembrancer should be the custodian of the rolls of taxation. A direct consequence of this rule was the remarkable set of rolls preserved for the subsidies of 1327 and 1332. Relieved of the duty of watching after matters subsidiary to the accounting of the collectors before such accounts were audited, the treasurer's remembrancer was now charged with the issuance of

[1] To these general statements some exceptions may possibly be found, for I have not compared the entries on all the rolls of the period. The treasurer's remembrancer may have thought it necessary to note matters usually not within his province, but this would not invalidate the general rule.

writs and the recording of processes relating to delinquencies that arose after the audits. He still kept the original record of all stages of the accounting of the collectors ; these were as in the earlier years copied by the king's remembrancer. Both remembrancers, freed from at least a part of their previously overlapping duties, must have had thenceforth more time to deal with the increasing volume of exchequer business that came within their respective spheres.

JAMES F. WILLARD.

XVIII

THE TOWER AS AN EXCHEQUER RECORD OFFICE IN THE REIGN OF EDWARD II.

RECENT research upon the reign of Edward II. has shown that the reforms of Walter Stapleton, in addition to their effects upon the working of the Exchequer, extended even to its archives.[1] The records of both the upper and lower Exchequer, of the Treasury at Westminster and of its subordinate repository in the Tower, as well as those in the royal castles of Pontefract, Tonbridge, and Tutbury, and in the house of the Friars Preachers in London were thoroughly overhauled and " arrayed ", and at the same time two important calendars of English and Gascon diplomatic documents were compiled.[2] During this busy period the Tower, where almost the whole of this work was carried out, took on a new importance as a record office. A good deal of information can be pieced together about the actual rooms or treasuries in the Tower, where, as will be seen, a large mass of documents, brought from Westminster in the course of the sortation, was left by Stapleton when it was finished. In the next reign further large deposits were made at the Tower, and though the practice was abandoned in the fifteenth century, traces of it remain even to this day in the arrangement of the records.

Although the great " array " of Exchequer and Treasury records between 1320 and 1322 is justly associated with the name of Stapleton, the idea of such reform was already in the air, and the first steps had in fact been taken before he became treasurer. The earliest attempts at reorganisation are found in a writ of privy seal, dated October 31, 1319, addressed to the treasurer, barons, and chamberlains. This document was a comprehensive ordinance for the reform of the Exchequer as a whole. The following provision about the records was thus only one of many :

A ceo commandoms et chargeoms en la fourme susdite vous avauntditz Tresourer et Chaumberleins qe parentre vous facetz duement vostre office a

[1] I have to thank Sir Henry Maxwell Lyte for some valuable criticisms. To Mr. Charles Johnson I am indebted for much kindly assistance throughout.

[2] Tout, *The Place of Edward II. in English History*, 187-193 ; Conway Davies, *Baronial Opposition to Edward II.*, 529-531 ; Déprez, " Le Trésor des chartes de Guyenne " in *Mélanges d'histoire offerts à M. Bémont* (1913), 225-242.

la Receite et ne soufferetz la ne en nostre Tresorie nul entrer en nule manere qe par reson entrer ne y deive, ne nul a veer ne manier livres roules ne autres remembrances qe leinz sont forsqe noz juretz : et facetz totes les choses en Tresourie queles qelles soient qe charge portent veer et mettre en tiel array come appent et ce en manere qe hom peusse saver ceo qelles sont et les aver et prestement trover quele heure qe nous les voudroms aver pur nous ou pur autre qe par voucher ou en autre manere de ceo deyve estre eide.[1]

From this order we get a good idea of the defects in the keeping of the records. They had been handled by others than the Exchequer clerks (*juretz*) ; [2] the storing of them was in confusion and documents were often not to be found. The task of remedying these faults fell to Walter Stapleton, who was appointed treasurer in February 1320, some three months after the ordinance. Reform began at once ; as early as June 13, 1320, orders had been given to Walter of Norwich, the most distinguished of the barons of the Exchequer, to " array " the Exchequer records during the coming vacation.[3] The sortation was to be carried out at the Tower, which had evidently been growing more important as a record office during the reign. As early as 1312 it had been provided by Sandall, the treasurer, with presses (*almariola*) in which to store the more ancient records.[4] Sandall's work was now continued, and by the end of the month of June, John Rok, a carpenter, had been paid for fitting the White Chapel with additional presses

[1] Memoranda Roll, K.R. 93, m. 9 d. Cf. Conway Davies, *Baronial Opposition to Edward II.* 557. The ordinance provided that *certeines gentz de nostre conseil prive* should visit the Exchequer at least twice a year to report on the manner in which the ordinance was being observed. It was also to be twice enrolled, in the Great Exchequer and in the Receipt.

[2] The care of the king's treasury, which was only incidentally a record office, was in the hands of the officers of the Lower Exchequer, the treasurer and chamberlains and their clerks. The Crown had thus neither record office nor record keepers as the terms would be understood to-day ; and to this rule special officers like the keeper of Papal bulls and the two keepers of the " process of Montreuil " were not really exceptions. A certain Maurice Drawesword has been described as keeper of the king's charters (*Cal. Inq. Misc.* ii. 250), but this is an error for keeper of the king's carts. To the treasurer and chamberlains anything for preservation in the Treasury was handed over in the Court of the Receipt, often by an indenture to which was affixed the seal of the department. In the course of time the formal delivery to the treasurer and chamberlains was held to constitute deposit in the treasury, though in fact many records so received were stored by them, not in the treasury itself (the chapel of the Pyx or the Tower), but in the various rooms of their own department. Thus we hear of records delivered to the treasurer and chamberlains and preserved " in the ancient chapel of St. Stephen next to the Receipt ", " in the chest of the Tellers' chamber beyond and above the Receipt ", " in the coffer of the treasurer and chamberlains in the window behind their backs in the Receipt " (Palgrave, *Antient Kalendars*, 1, 226, 189, 161). The result was that there grew up in the Receipt a separate treasury of records, " the treasury of the Receipt ". But the term is not found in the fourteenth century, which reveals a transitional state when much is in custody that is not in the Treasury. The Wardrobe, like the Treasury, had no peculiar official to keep its records. The Chancery, on the other hand, had by the fourteenth century evolved a special *custos rotulorum*. So too the Court of Common Pleas, which seems at this time to have kept its records at St. Bartholomew's, Smithfield (Accounts etc., Exch. 332/12), had its *custos brevium*.

[3] Memoranda Roll, K.R. 93, m. 51.

[4] Accounts etc., Exch. 469/16.

for "rolls, fines, and other memoranda".[1] In August [2] there were further orders to the treasurer and chamberlains to appoint the necessary clerks to arrange by Michaelmas the records in the treasury in the Tower and at Westminster. That a bare two months were thought sufficient for the work shows it was not yet understood how much there was to be done. Actually the sortation occupied about eighteen months, from August 1320 until about January 1322. It was carried out in the White Chapel, the chief Exchequer treasury in the Tower, where James of Spain and William of Maldon, the two chamberlains, with a staff of nearly a dozen Exchequer clerks, worked in the intervals of their other duties.[3] What little we know of it is drawn from the *Issue Rolls*, which record the special payments to the clerks and to the porters carrying the records from Westminster to the Tower and thence after arrangement back to Westminster. There are payments for the large sacks (*grossis saccis*) [4] in which the various rolls and memoranda from the time of Henry II. to that of Edward I. were carried from Westminster and for the canvas in which they were packed (*imponendis*) [5] in the White Chapel. The great mass of the feet of fines preserved in the Treasury was apparently first dealt with.[6] Next perhaps came the turn of the pipe and memoranda rolls: and it is of great interest to find that some of these, doubtless the early ones, were still kept in the Treasury.[7] From the Treasury these early rolls were taken to the Receipt; thence to the king's wharf, and so by water to the Tower. This was in July 1321. Early in October these were returned to Westminster, and in December the later rolls—*magnos rotulos compotorum de Scaccario, coffros Rememoratorum et multa alia diversa*—were brought from the upper Exchequer to the Treasury, from the Treasury to the king's wharf and thence as before to the White Chapel.[8] These in their turn were sent back to Westminster in the following January. All the records brought from the Exchequer were thus, as far as we can tell, returned to Westminster. Of the records brought from the Treasury on the other hand, a great part, especially of the legal records,[9] seem after the sortation to have

[1] Accounts etc., Exch. 469/3; Issue Roll, 191, m. 3.

[2] *C.C.R.* 1318–23, 258; Chancery Warrants, i. 111/5363, *les choses qe sount en nostre Tresorie en la Tour de Loundres et aussint lestat de nostre dit Eschekier.*

[3] Issue Roll, 191, m. 8; 193, m. 4. Appendix, no. 2.

[4] Issue Roll, 195, m. 4. Appendix, no. 5.

[5] Issue Roll, 193, m. 4. Appendix, no. 4.

[6] *Ibid.* 191, m. 8. They were still in the chapel of the Pyx in 1362. Palgrave, *Antient Kalendars*, i. 194. Appendix, no. 3.

[7] Issue Roll, 195, m. 4; cf. *Dialogus de Scaccario*, ed. Hughes, Crump, and Johnson, p. 107.

[8] Issue Roll, 196, m. 9. Appendix, no. 6.

[9] Records of the two Benches and of the Wardrobe were often deposited in the Treasury upon the death of a judge or keeper of the Wardrobe, in pursuance of a writ under the Great Seal. Such an order was necessary owing to the tendency of the mediæval official or his executors to treat records as private property. Thus the rolls and wardrobe books of Walter Langton, who was keeper of the Wardrobe from 1290 to

remained permanently in the Tower. Some of them, as will be seen below, apparently remained undisturbed in the Tower from Stapleton's time until their removal to the Public Record Office in the middle of the nineteenth century.[1]

Contemporaneously with the sortation of the Exchequer records but not necessarily connected with it, went the compilation of the Calendar of documents relating to Gascony. The genesis of this calendar had a history of its own dating back to the negotiations at Montreuil (1306) and Périgueux (1311), which continued intermittently until the outbreak of the Hundred Years' War. The English commissioners were at a disadvantage throughout owing to the fact that the records at Bordeaux relating to this matter had been captured by the French during their invasion of Gascony in 1294. The whole story is told in detail in a document written by Robert of Leisseth, the constable of Bordeaux at the time.[2] Leisseth, it appears, first moved the records for greater safety to the Friars Preachers at Bordeaux: a little later he had them put on board a ship for England, to be deposited in the Tower. This ship was commandeered for the king's service, but after a time the crew, because they had not been paid their wages, left the records with the White Friars of the island of Oléron and sailed away. Soon afterwards the island was taken by the French, who plundered the friary and seized the records. As a result of this loss, transcripts had to be made from the originals and from the registers in the Wardrobe, and when negotiations began at Montreuil the work was still unfinished. Within two years the keepers of the "process of Montreuil", Philip Martel and John of Bakewell, both died, and the care of the documents already collected as well as the task of searching for others fell to the deputy of the former, a Wardrobe clerk named Elias de Jonestone. In 1315 the council at

---

1295, were only delivered into the Treasury on June 3, 1322, eight months after his death. They had remained at St. Leonard's Hospital, York, since he had ceased to be keeper of the Wardrobe (Memoranda Roll, K.R. 96, m. 81). The Chancery, it should be noted, differed from the other departments in having full and perpetual custody of its own records.

[1] Stapleton's work was continued during the following years. In 1325 Robert de Hoton, employed in 1322 in arranging the records in the royal castles, received special payment for two months' work upon the records at Westminster and the Tower (Issue Roll, 213, m. 12). The effect of these sortations was to put the keeping of the records on a much better footing. From Palgrave's *Antient Kalendars* one gathers that the chief improvements lay in the keeping of more systematic memoranda of delivery and receipt, and in the careful and often intricate arrangements for the custody of record rooms and presses. All presses, hanapers, and chests were labelled or rather marked with signs, often very quaint and aptly suggesting their contents. The two Calendars of English and Gascon charters and diplomatic documents, compiled between 1320–22, were based on this system of signs. It became customary, too, when a new memorandum or note of receipt was made, to depict against it the sign of the box in which the document was placed, and to state where the box was stored. See Hall, *Antiquities of the Exchequer*, 54-58.

[2] Appendix, no. 1. (A précis of Leisseth's report.) Cf. Dip. Doc., Exch., 1540.

Bordeaux petitioned for a register to be made from the documents in the Wardrobe in the Tower, and deposited at Bordeaux for reference.[1] It was perhaps in answer to this petition that John de Hildesle was appointed with a staff of clerks to transcribe documents in the Tower. A great deal was done in 1318–19 towards compiling this register.[2] It probably consisted of a number of volumes, of which the Wolfenbüttel MS. (No. 2311, edited by M. Bémont),[3] is perhaps the sole survivor. This is a book of *Recogniciones feodorum in Aquitania* and was evidently one of a series, for it is noted as *liber secundus intitulatus per B.* M. Bémont states that the MS. was compiled at Bordeaux between 1281 and 1294, and this dating is conclusive, if indeed it is the original register. But from the fact that the names of the scribes and the examiners, which it carefully records,[4] are all those of Englishmen, it seems more probable that it is a later transcript made in the Tower by Hildesle's clerks.[5]

In addition to transcribing the earlier registers, Hildesle's clerks rearranged and copied the Gascon documents in the Tower and in the Treasury at Westminster. This sortation perhaps suggested the plan of compiling the Gascon Calendar, which was now set on foot, for the use of the home government. The work was entrusted to Henry of Canterbury,[6] a chancery clerk, and the orders had to be repeated more than once before it was finished and the calendar delivered into the Treasury by Stapleton on November 17, 1322.[7] The Gascon calendar was a new departure, and it has naturally been supposed that Stapleton originated it. The date in particular looks significant, but it is worth noting that Stapleton's name is not mentioned in the preface, the style of which rather suggests the hand of Elias de Jonestone. The calendar was the fruit of long experience in dealing with the process of Montreuil, the difficulties of which can only have been fully understood by Jonestone. It is not

[1] Chancery Miscell. 29/8 (8).

[2] Issue Roll, 186, m. 1; Memoranda Roll, K.R. 92, Michaelmas, Recorda, m. 5 d.

[3] *Recueil d'actes relatifs à l'administration des rois d'Angleterre en Guyenne au xiiie siècle : Recogniciones feodorum in Aquitania*, ed. Ch. Bémont, 1914.

[4] *E.g.* W. de Burgh, Ed. le Blount, J. de Digby, Henry de Coventre—scribes: J. de Gellerby, Th. de Elsham, J. de Suthwelle—examiners.

[5] There is clear proof that the original homages were transcribed into registers before 1294, for in 1303–4 the Seneschal of Gascony paid 15 li. *Tournois* for the recovery of one of them, lost at Oléron (*Archives du dép^t. de la Gironde*, lv. p. 5, no. ii.). Mr. Johnson has pointed out to me that these registers were made in duplicate, one series being kept at Bordeaux and the other sent to England. The latter were apparently identical with the five volumes, lettered A-E, which are mentioned in the Gascon Calendar and which were still at the Tower in 1336 (*Mélanges d'histoire offerts à M. Bémont*, p. 232). The Wolfenbüttel MS. was perhaps copied from the second of these. See also the addendum, below, p. 247.

[6] *C.C.R.* 1318–23, 319. See Ancient Correspondence, xxxii. 77, for a *sicut alias* of this writ (October 5).

[7] Palgrave, *Antient Kalendars*, iii. 437. On December 4 it was delivered to Robert Baldok, Keeper of the Privy Seal (*Mélanges offerts à M. Bémont*, 229).

unlikely therefore that the idea of making a calendar as well as a register, was his. It is in Jonestone's favour too that the calendar was a Wardrobe enterprise carried out in the Wardrobe treasury at the Tower. Diplomatic documents were specially connected with the Wardrobe [1] through the medium of the privy seal, whose keeper was responsible for most of the king's foreign correspondence, and was normally also controller of the Wardrobe. *Liber A* and *Liber B*, the two large registers of diplomatic documents drawn up about the close of Edward I.'s reign, were Wardrobe compilations, and the Gascon calendar not only describes [2] them but even follows (with necessary differences) their general system of arrangement and reference.

The first calendar apparently suggested to Stapleton the idea of a similar work comprising general diplomatic documents. The preface of this second calendar definitely says it was done at Stapleton's instigation. In the past these documents had been transferred " from person to person and from place to place, as from the Wardrobe to the Chancery, from the Chancery to the Exchequer, and thence to the Receipt of the Exchequer, and perhaps to unsuitable persons ".[3] The intention was as much to secure better custody of the records as to make them more accessible : and to this extent it marked an advance on the Gascon calendar which had been compiled simply as a work of reference for those engaged upon the perennial French negotiations.[4] The first order to make it was dated June 28, 1321,[5] and it was finished some time in 1323. Henry of Canterbury, Elias de Jonestone, and Roger of Sheffield were mentioned in the writ as the compilers, but the first of these took no actual part in the work, which was done by Jonestone and Sheffield assisted by three other Exchequer clerks.[6] This calendar was also compiled in the Tower. The bulk of the documents for it were brought to a chamber in the White Tower called the Black Hall, which was clearly another Exchequer treasury in the Tower. Thence the documents were moved

[1] There were also, of course, large collections both in the Treasury and in the Chancery. Very solemn documents, such as treaties, were not infrequently drawn up in triplicate, so that the Wardrobe, the Treasury, and the Chancery might each preserve a copy (*e.g.* Memoranda Roll, K.R. 93, m. 83 ; Issue Roll, 213, note on the top of the roll).

[2] T.R. Misc. Books, 187, p. 190 ; Déprez, *op. cit.* p. 232, note 3. *Item duo registra magna, ligata et albo corio cooperta, signata duabus clavibus annexis de transcriptis bullarum, litterarum cartarum tangentium regnum Anglie, ducatum Aquitanie et ceteras terras dominio regis Anglie subjectas et regna Francie, Castelle, Arragonum, Norwagie et terre Flandrie, Brabancie, Hanonie, Holandie et Frisie.* That they were Wardrobe compilations is, in the opinion of Mr. C. Johnson, practically certain. See the addendum, below, p. 247.

[3] Palgrave, *Antient Kalendars*, i. 2 ; cf. *List of Diplomatic Documents* (*P.R.O.*, No. xlix.), 1.

[4] Chancery Miscellanea, 28/1 (23).

[5] *C.P.R.* 1321–24, 7. It was to be made as soon as the Gascon Calendar was finished.

[6] Issue Roll, 204, m. 4. Appendix, no. 7.

to another room (unspecified) where the examination, arrangement, and calendaring were carried out. These facts are drawn from the payments made to the porters,[1] and from further payments it appears that the documents were later moved from the Black Hall to the Chapel. It therefore seems likely that as the documents were dealt with they were returned by the workers to the Black Hall and then after the completion of the calendar the whole collection was stored in the White Chapel.

There are equally interesting details regarding the earlier Gascon calendar. The Gascon documents were kept in the treasury of the Wardrobe in the Tower, and there in all probability the actual process of calendaring was carried out. This Wardrobe treasury was the outer chamber next the Black Hall, the keys of which (four larger for the outer doors and twenty-eight smaller for the coffers within) were handed over by the keeper of the Wardrobe to the Treasurer in December 1318.[2] In December 1322, *i.e.* on the completion of the calendar, John le French of London, the joiner, received payment for two hutches which were to be filled with the Gascon documents and then stored away in the Black Hall.[3] That is to say, having been calendared in the Wardrobe treasury they were put under the custody of the treasurer and chamberlains in the adjoining Exchequer treasury.[4] The following year they were removed, along with the English calendar documents, from the Black Hall to the White Chapel.

The gradual establishment of Exchequer control over the Wardrobe after the year 1316,[5] which is the predominant administrative tendency of these years, is well illustrated by the relation of the Exchequer and Wardrobe treasuries. From this time, if not earlier, the Wardrobe treasury was subject to a degree of supervision unknown in the days of Edward I. This supervision was enforced in two ways; first, by an elaborate system of dual control of the actual "treasuries"; second, by means of periodical scrutinies of the Wardrobe treasury by the Treasurer. A complicated transaction of December 16, 1318,[6] illustrates both methods. On this occasion the keys of the Wardrobe treasury in the Tower, under the seals of John Devery (an Exchequer clerk) and Nicholas of Wellbourne, clerk of the keeper of the Wardrobe, were formally handed over to the Treasurer. They were then delivered by the Treasurer to the Chamberlains under the seals of

[1] Issue Roll, 204, m. 4. Appendix, no. 7.

[2] Memoranda Roll, K.R. 92 (12 Edw. II.), Michaelmas, Recorda, m. 8; cf. Memoranda Roll, K.R. 96, m. 59 d. Appendix, no. 8.

[3] Issue Roll, 196, m. 8. Appendix, no. 6.

[4] They were still in the Tower and under the control of the treasurer and chamberlains in 1329 (Chancery Miscellanea, 28/1 (23) and in 31 Edward III. (Palgrave, *Antient Kalendars*, i. 182, 186).

[5] Tout, *The Place of Edward II.* 189.

[6] Memoranda Roll, K.R. 92 (12 Edward II.), Michaelmas, Recorda, m. 8.

Robert Wodehouse (a baron of the Exchequer [1]) and Master John de Hildesle,[2] the king's clerk assigned to examine and transcribe documents relating to Gascony. The Treasurer and Barons next informed the Chamberlains that they, together with Robert Wodehouse and Master John, were to hold themselves in readiness to produce at a moment's notice all the Gascon process whenever the Treasurer and Barons should come to the Tower to make a scrutiny. The fact that these documents were finally transferred to the Exchequer treasury after the completion of the calendar raises a doubt whether any large collection of records was henceforth retained by the Wardrobe. Both the divided control and the periodical scrutiny,[3] at any rate, continued in regard to jewels, plate, relics, and money which the Wardrobe from its very nature continued to keep.

The rise of the new jewel treasuries in Edward II.'s reign shows that a line was beginning to be drawn between the custody of records and that of jewels, though it was a long time before the specialisation was complete. Our first information comes from an indenture of March 10, 1324, by which Robert Wodehouse, the keeper of the Wardrobe, received from Stapleton, the treasurer, and the chamberlains a quantity of jewels

> demorantz [4] en la dite Tour en toriel pres du gable de la Grand Chapele devers lest, de quel toriel les ditz Tresorer et Chamberleins ount devers eux les cliefs des huys foreins, et le dit gardein des almaries ou les ioelx sount enclos, les quex ioelx vessels . . . furent del auncien estor de la Garderobe et liverez as ditz tresorier et chaumberlains par sire Roger de Northburgh eveqz de Cestre nadgairs gardein de la Garderobe avandite.

This turret seems to have replaced the Wardrobe treasury under the Chapter House at Westminster which had been robbed in 1303.[5] At that time the jewels were under the sole control of the keeper of the Wardrobe. In 1324 the system of divided custody, by which the Treasury held the keys of the outer doors and the Wardrobe the keys of the presses, ensured ultimate Exchequer control. The actual change from the old to the new method seems to have taken place between 1315 and 1321, the years in which Northburgh was keeper of the Wardrobe.

[1] Wodehouse, though here acting as a baron of the Exchequer, was, like John de Ockham (also a baron), a clerk of the Wardrobe. Both were specially exempted from the inquiry into the number and sufficiency of the barons in 1318 (Memoranda Roll, K.R. 92, m. 27 d ; Tout, *Place of Edward II.*, 335-6).

[2] A Chancery clerk often employed on diplomatic missions. In 1323 he was one of the twelve " clerks of the first bench " (Conway Davies, *Baronial Opposition*, 577, no. 74).

[3] *E.g.* Memoranda Roll, K.R. 95, m. 68 ; 96, m. 59 d (below, p. 247).

[4] Accounts etc., Exch. 380/7.

[5] By the year 1300 the greater part of the Wardrobe jewels (but not all) and some of its records seem to have been transferred to the treasury under the Chapter House. A few jewels and, it would appear, a large part of the records remained in the " old treasury " at the Tower (Accounts etc., Exch. 357/13).

In the same indenture from which these details are taken is an early mention of the king's private or secret jewel house. One of the objects delivered to Wodehouse was

una puchea de canabo signata sigillo Walteri Exoniensis episcopi qui intitulatur sic, " clavis interioris camere iuxta aulam nigram in turri London ubi iocalia thesauri regis privata reponuntur ".

In this inner chamber next the Black Hall, the custody of which was similarly shared by Exchequer and Wardrobe, were kept the great crown and (very probably) the more precious vessels of the " ancient store of the Wardrobe ".[1] Here, too, were the " two charters of the king of Spain with golden bulls, concerning Gascony ".[2] There are many later references to it.

One other treasury at the Tower remains to be distinguished. This was the *superior thesauraria regis apud Turrim*, a treasury of the Exchequer mentioned in 1297–8.[3] To this there are only occasional references. In 4 Edward III.[4] certain of the jewels specified in an indenture are marked as *in superiori camera Turris*. In Henry IV.'s reign there were jewels in the treasury *desouz le grand sale*.[5] This *grand sale* may perhaps be identified with the *camera superior*[6] which was on the floor above the Black Hall and the neighbouring treasuries.

Of all these treasuries[7] in the Tower only one was strictly speaking a Wardrobe treasury—the outer chamber next the Black Hall. The Black Hall itself with the inner chamber adjoining, the chapel, the *grand sale* above, and the turret were all clearly under the final governance of the treasurer and chamberlains. To them the bulk of the Wardrobe documents had been delivered to be kept in the Black Hall. The jewels also were transferred to them, the most precious remaining under their permanent control, while the plate in daily or frequent use was apparently delivered back to the keeper of the Wardrobe to be kept in the turret but only under partial Wardrobe control. This loss of the Wardrobe treasury's independence was in all probability the work of Stapleton.

[1] Accounts etc. Exch. 332/26.
[2] Hall, *Red Book of the Exch.* iii. 1054 ; Palgrave, *Antient Kalendars*, i. 197.
[3] Tout, *Chapters in Med. Adm. Hist.* ii. 52.
[4] Accounts etc., Exch. 333/3.
[5] Palgrave, *Antient Kalendars*, ii. 86.
[6] Possibly, too, with the *graund tresorie* mentioned in Palgrave's *Antient Kalendars*, i. 175.
[7] In the fourteenth century the most formal documents preserved the idea of a single undifferentiated king's treasury ; *e.g.* the Pipe rolls. Cf., too, Palgrave, *Antient Kalendars*, i. 251 *seq.* But contemporaries also described the various repositories as treasuries. Thus in 1327 Adam of Orleton handed over to the bishop of Lincoln, his successor as treasurer, " the keys of the *treasuries* of Westminster and of the Tower of London " (Accounts etc. Exch. 332/26). Even the chapel of the Pyx, the treasury *par excellence*, seems to need further definition. It begins to be referred to as " the great treasury ", " the treasury in the cloister ", " the treasury under the dorter ", " the room of the king's great treasure, the key of which is in the Receipt " (Palgrave, *Antient Kalendars*, i. 194, iii. 251, i. 158 ; Accounts etc., Exch. 333/3).

The identification of these various treasuries should not be impossible in view of the fact that the White Tower has undergone no serious constructional modification and that they adjoined the White Chapel, about which there can be no doubt. The White Tower[1] is roughly square in plan: excluding the vaults there are three floors, on the second and third of which were the "treasuries". At each corner rising from the roof level is a turret. The block (inset) shows the plan of the second floor, from which the White Chapel rises to within a few feet of the main roof of the building, the gallery being on a level with the third floor. Except for a narrow passage which runs

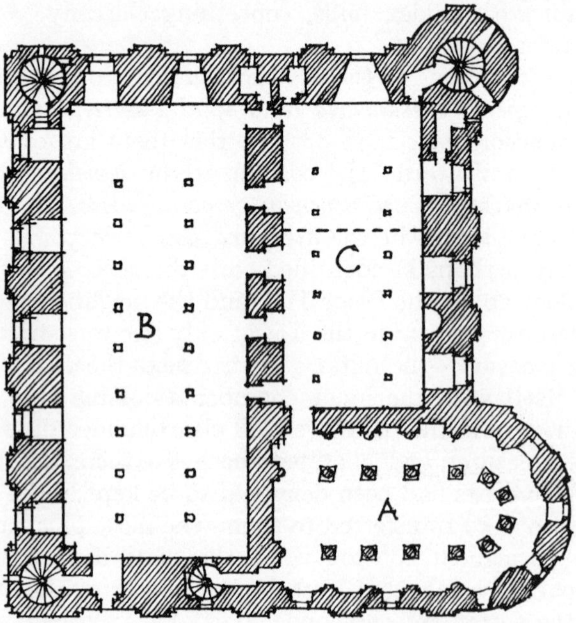

right round this story, the plan of the third floor is the same as that of the second. At the N.E. corner a spiral staircase runs the full height of the Tower. The following identifications are conjectural: but it seems likely that the larger of the two rooms on the second floor (B, now the Weapon Room) was the Black Hall and that the *grand sale* or *camera superior* was the corresponding room above, now the Horse Armoury. In this case "the inner and outer chambers next the Black Hall" occupied the site of C, now the Sword Room. It must have been divided more or less as shown by the dotted line, the outer chamber being that next the staircase and the inner that adjoining the chapel. The position of the turret (*toriel*) in which the jewels were

[1] See Bayley, *History of the Tower of London* (1821); also G. T. Clark, "The Military Architecture of the Tower of London" in *Old London* (1867), 13-139. By the kindness of Mr. ffoulkes I have had the opportunity of closely examining these rooms.

kept is defined with apparent precision as *pres du gable de la Grand Chapele devers lest.*[1] At first sight this seems to describe the turret above the east end of the White Chapel ;[2] but it is difficult to believe that so small and inconvenient a building was used as a jewel treasury. Mr. C. R. Peers, whom I consulted about this difficulty, has suggested that perhaps the description applies to the Wardrobe Tower, which lay just to the east of the apsidal end of the Chapel.[3] The Wardrobe Tower, which belonged to the original lines of the fortress before its enlargement eastward in the time of Richard I., was possibly of Henry II.'s reign.[4] Being incorporated in the king's palace, it seems to have survived the extension of Richard I., when the Roman wall against which it was built was destroyed. " It was ", says Mr. Peers, " notably smaller than the thirteenth-century ring of towers, and it was probably then, as certainly later, embedded in surrounding buildings, and would have made no great show." The fact is important, for it answers the obvious objection that to describe the Wardrobe Tower as a turret is to strain the meaning of the word. Even so, one has still to suppose that by *gable* is meant an apsidal east end, a use for which there seems to be no authority.

The men who actually examined, sorted, and calendared the records are for the most part dim figures. The chamberlains, William of Maldon and James of Spain, Roger of Sheffield, John Devery and the other Exchequer clerks were only incidentally archivists. Nearly all had their definite posts in the Exchequer and were turned on to sorting records by force of circumstances. Behind and directing them was Stapleton himself and still more probably Walter of Norwich, who during his long and distinguished career had acquired a knowledge of the working of the Exchequer such as was possessed by no one else. In a letter under the secret seal (November 27, 1323), reprehending the Barons, the king addresses him personally thus :[5]

> De vous Wauter de Norwiz enmerveilloms molt desicome vous estes plus conissaunt de noz busoignes qe nul des autres et vous avez auxint plus lungement servi.

So old and trusted a servant was very naturally first chosen " to array " the records, and it was doubtless because he was needed for more important work that others were appointed when the magnitude of the sortation was fully realised.

The only other person of note employed was Master Henry of Canterbury, a clerk of the Chancery, who was perhaps one of the

[1] Above, p. 238.

[2] Mr. Peers tells me that the four turrets of the White Tower, though greatly repaired by Wren and earlier, are part of the original scheme, and certainly all earlier than 1300.

[3] The Wardrobe Tower is shown on the plate in vol. i. of Bayley's *History of the Tower*.

[4] *Archaeological Journal*, vol. lxix. p. 175.

[5] Memoranda Roll, K.R. 97, m. 14 d.

twelve "clerks of the first bench". Together with Elias de Jonestone he was responsible for both the Gascon and English calendars, but there is no indication that he took any practical share in the work. Throughout the reign he was continually employed upon diplomatic missions, and there was scarcely a year some part of which he did not spend out of England. Elias de Jonestone, too, was a great traveller, but his journeys were exclusively connected with the search for and production of documents relating to Gascony. Elias is in fact the perfect type of the archivist of the period. For thirty years he was intimately concerned with the diplomatic documents of France and Gascony, and we still have an interesting series of his reports and memoranda upon them.[1] In the constant negotiations of the time his help and advice were sought at every turn, but except for two years (1306–8) when he seems to have been tried and found wanting, he never himself acted as a diplomat or commissioner. The brief account which M. Déprez[2] has given of him undoubtedly exaggerates Jonestone's personal importance, though not the importance of his work. He shrank even from the responsibilities of his position as record keeper and petitioned the Crown more than once to be relieved of his duties.[3] That he was induced reluctantly to continue in his post for thirty years seems to show that he was indispensable for his unique knowledge of the records and his conscientiousness in performing a thankless task.

The use of the Tower as an extension of the Treasury at Westminster, at any rate on a large scale, seems to have lasted rather less than a century. When exactly it was finally abandoned is not known. Records were still being sent there as late as 1377:[4] the diplomatic documents relating to Scotland, or one part of them, were still being kept there in 1400.[5] The fact that no evidence has come to light of the final withdrawal seems to imply that the process was a gradual one. It was perhaps connected with the extension of the palace of Westminster: it has even been suggested that it was a result of the sack of the Tower in 1381. The effect at any rate was to leave the Tower entirely to the Chancery until the foundation of the Public Record Office. After the Tower archives were transferred to Chancery Lane, it became evident that they included a considerable mass of Exchequer and legal records. Such were the *Carte Antique*, the whole of which came from the Tower. In some cases a large number of a

[1] *Lists and Indexes* (*P.R.O.*), xlix. 137-218 (Diplomatic Documents, Chancery).

[2] *Mélanges d'histoire offerts à M. Charles Bémont*, 225-229.

[3] Chancery Miscellanea, 27/11.

[4] Issue Roll, 464, m. 1. Payments for carrying books and other memoranda from Westminster to the Tower to be kept in the Treasury there. Among the Chancery Files (Tower Series) is a quantity of writs returnable in the King's Bench and Common Pleas. There is only a single small bundle for the reign of Richard II. (Chancery Files, A. 63).

[5] Palgrave, *Antient Kalendars*, ii. 62.

class came from the Tower and the rest from Westminster, for instance the Coram Rege rolls of Henry III.'s reign ; the Essoin rolls from Henry III. to Edward III. ; the De Banco rolls from Henry III. to Edward II. In other cases an odd roll or two only came from the Tower ; such were the two Pipe Rolls of 6 Richard I. and 7 John. Finally, we may note that a large number of Wardrobe records came to the Record Office from the Tower.[1]

The full solution to this problem in record history is not to be found simply in the increased use of the Tower in the fourteenth century, but the two are certainly connected. That stray documents, like the two Pipe Rolls, were left in the Tower was probably the result of pure oversight at the time of the great sortation in 1320–22. Again the White Tower apparently served as the common repository for both Exchequer and Chancery records until the year 1361, when the latter were removed to the Wakefield tower.[2] A certain number of Exchequer documents may reasonably be supposed to have got into the Chancery records during this removal.[3] The case of the larger classes —especially the legal records—suggests that when the Treasury was withdrawn from the Tower, the treasurer and chamberlains took only those rolls to which they were likely to have to refer and left or forgot the earlier ones. These may be supposed to have been absorbed into the Chancery much later, when its records spread back again from the Wakefield tower to the White Chapel.

That the Exchequer records brought from the Tower in the nineteenth century were put there by Stapleton and his successors in the fourteenth is of course not more than a hypothesis, the evidence for which lies partly in the period to which these records belong, partly in the documents he undoubtedly did deposit there, including Papal bulls,[4] and the originals of the two calendars. Such a hypothesis helps to explain Stapleton's choice of the Tower for his " array " of the Exchequer and Treasury records at Westminster, and his careful measures to secure control of the Wardrobe treasury or treasuries in the Tower. When the Exchequer records were once more concentrated at Westminster, and the Tower was left to the Chancery the

[1] *Second Report of the Deputy Keeper*, Appendix II. 1, 49, 52. The full list of the Tower records is spread over the first three *Reports*.

[2] *C.C.R.* 1333-37, 113. The rolls of the Chancery in the *Treasury* in the Tower. The Chancery records which had once been stored in the New Temple were already at the Tower in 1305 (*C.C.R.* 1302–7, 300), but were apparently removed later to the house of the Carmelite friars in London, if not also to that of the Dominicans, before they found a permanent home in the Tower in or about 1321 (*C.C.R.* 1318–23, 313). For the removal to the Wakefield tower see *Foedera*, iii. 485 (April 28, 1360). They were moved in order to provide accommodation for the captive King John of France ; and it has been reasonably conjectured (Clark, *op. cit.* 32) that the room assigned to him was that formerly called the Council Chamber (*i.e.* the *grand sale*, now the Horse Armoury).

[3] The two Pipe Rolls were stored in the Wakefield tower in 1800. See *Select Committee on the Public Records*, 1800, p. 55.

[4] *C.C.R.* 1337–39, 291.

very recollection [1] of the period when that was an Exchequer treasury perished and the provenance of these documents was no longer understood.

V. H. Galbraith.

APPENDIX

(1) *Chancery Miscellanea*, 24/2(16)

Responsio Roberti de Leisseth ad litteram domini regis dicit tantum quod antequam terra Vasconie esset liberata regi Francie omnes cistas et archas in quibus fuerunt scripta tangencia terram Vasconie fecit idem Robertus de Leisseth ammoveri et reponi in domo quadam apud fratres predicatores Burdegale et ivit postmodum idem Robertus Parisius in aresto regis Francie una cum ceteris gentibus regis Anglie arestatis et intellecto postmodum per ipsum Robertum quod negocia domini regis deterius ibant quam sperabat misit statim idem Robertus Burdegalam ad locum suum tenentem ibidem et ad contrarotulatorem castri scribendo eisdem quod predictas archas et cistas et alia bona que dominus rex habuit in custodia ipsius Roberti ponerent in quadam navi de Anglia ducenda in Angliam et liberanda custodi turris Londonie per ipsum custodienda quousque aliud haberet in mandatis : et predicto Roberto postmodum remanenti in carcere regis Francie fere per triennium nescit certe dicere idem Robertus ubi postmodum devenerunt scripta predicta. Audivit tamen dici a predictis locum tenente et contrarotulatore quod scripta et alia bona predicta posita fuerunt in quadam navi Anglie in Angliam ducenda prout eis fuit iniunctum. Que quidem navis retenta fuit una cum aliis per preceptum domini regis et ad vadia eiusdem ad custodiendam insulam Oleronis. Que quidem navis cum sibi non essent vadia persoluta exoneravit se predictis bonis et ea reposuit penes fratres minores insule predicte et postmodum recessit una cum aliis : post quarum navium recessum Gallici predictam insulam intrarunt vi et armis omnia ibidem inventa depredando et sic dicuntur esse amissa scripta antedicta et eodem modo idem Robertus amisit ibidem in quadam cista libros suos omnes quos noluit amisisse pro centum libris sterlingorum et alia bona que habuit in ducatu nec inde quicquam potuit recuperare et mortuis tam contrarotulatore quam locumtenente predictis nescit idem Robertus aliquem qui sciat veritatem nisi magistrum Eliam Everard qui fuit clericus dicti contrarotulatoris et manet nunc ut dicitur in civitate Burdegale.

(2) *Issue Roll*, 13 *Edward II.*, *Easter* (*No.* 191)

[m. 8] Magistro Iacobo de Ispania uni camerariorum regis de Scaccario assignato cum duobus clericis suis per tempus predictum [2] ad supervidendum et disponendum fines rotulos et memoranda et omnia alia in thesauraria regis et turri sua Londonie existencia et in statum competentem dirigenda recipienti denarios xxvii die Septembris per manus proprias super expensis suis per breve de magno sigillo liiis. iiiid.

[1] Arthur Agarde does not appear to have known of them. See Palgrave, *Antient Kalendars*, ii. 311-335 ; cf. Powell, *The Repertorie of Records*, 1631 (a republication of Agarde with some additional notes about the Tower).

[2] *I.e.* the months of August and September.

A like payment to William de Maldon, the other chamberlain (with two clerks), and to John Devery, Clerk of the Exchequer (with two clerks); forty shillings to John de Chisenhale, clerk (with one clerk); twenty shillings to Hugh de Bray and Geoffrey Beneit, the ushers morantibus ad Receptam per tempus predictum in subsidium et super custodia arraiamenti rerum predictarum.

(3) *Issue Roll*, 13 *Edward II.*, *Easter* (*No.* 192)

Hugoni de Braye et Galfrido Beneit hostiario de Recepta pro diversis [m. 8] minutis necessariis per ipsos emptis super arraiamento finium in Thesauraria domini regis et pro portagio et reportagio et batillagio eorundem finium tam de Turri Londonie quam de Thesauraria apud Westmonasterium recipientibus denarios xxviii die Septembris per manus proprias vs. iiid.

(4) *Issue Roll*, 14 *Edward II.*, *Michaelmas* (*No.* 193)

Duobus clericis magistri Iacobi de Ispania camerarii de Scaccario per- [m. 4] cipientibus per diem viiid. cum ipso existentibus circa arrayamentum rotulorum et aliarum rerum in capella domini regis in summa Turri Londonie a ix die Marcii anno XIIII° usque diem Sabbati proximi ante Passionem domini quartum diem Aprilis anno eodem utroque computato per xxvii dies recipienti denarios xx die Marcii per manus proprias xviiis.

Like payment to two clerks of William de Maldon, the other chamberlain, and to the two clerks of John Devery: 36s. each to William de Everdon (with two clerks) and Alexander "le Convers" (with two clerks) for the same period.

Hostiariis de Recepta pro canabo per ipsos empto pro diversis rotulis et memorandis de temporibus regum Henrici secundi, Ricardi, Iohannis, Henrici tercii et Edwardi filii regis Henrici in capella regis in summa Turri Londonie imponendis recipientibus denarios iiii^{to} die Aprilis per manus Hugonis de Bray xiis.

(5) *Issue Roll*, 14 *Edward II.*, *Easter* (*No.* 195)

Hugoni de Braye hostiario de Recepta pro denariis per ipsum solutis [m. 4] videlicet, pro diversis saccis grossis emptis pro rotulis diversis inde trussandis, portagio, reportagio eorundem rotulorum de Thesauraria usque ad Receptam et de Recepta usque aquam Thamisie ad pontem regis una cum parte batillagii eorundem cum quibusdam aliis minutis necessariis et inde usque ad Turrim Londonie recipienti denarios xxii die Iulii viiis. iiid.

Eidem Hugoni pro denariis per ipsum solutis pro portagio Magnorum Rotulorum de Scaccario et Rememoratorum de Scaccario et aliorum rotulorum de Thesauraria usque ad pontem regis et pro batillagio de ponte usque Turrim in Thesaurariam ibidem portandorum recipienti denarios xxx die Iulii per manus proprias vis. id.

Roberto le Norreys lokyere de Londonia pro serruris emendatis et [m. 6] clavibus de novo factis in Turri Londonie recipienti denarios xv die Iulii per manus proprias xiid.

(6) *Issue Roll*, 15 *Edward II.*, *Michaelmas* (*No.* 196)

Iohanni Scot pro portagio et batillagio Magnorum Rotulorum de Scac- [m. 8] cario, rotulorum de officio Rememoratorum de eodem Scaccario de Turri

Londonie usque Westmonasterium in principio mensis Octobris recipienti denarios ultimo die eiusdem mensis per manus proprias xixd.

Iohanni le Frensh juygnor de Londonia pro duabus huchiis faciendis pro instrumentis et memorandis negocia ducatus Aquitanie tangencibus imponendis et in nigra camera infra Turrim Londonie reponendis recipienti denarios xiii die Novembris per manus Iohannis de Melkesham in partem solucionis v marcarum et dimidii quas percipiet pro factura huchiarum predictarum xls.

Diversis portitoribus portantibus duas huchias de domo Iohannis le Joignur in Londonia usque Turrim Londonie in nigram cameram recipienti denarios xvi die Decembris iis.

[m. 9] Diversis portitoribus portantibus Magnos Rotulos compotorum de Scaccario coffros Rememoratorum et multa alia diversa quibusdam certis de causis de Scaccario usque Thesaurariam apud Westmonasterium mense Decembris per vices et de Thesauraria usque ad pontem regis Westmonasterii et pro batillagio et portagio rotulorum predictorum de predicto ponte usque ad Turrim Londonie recipientibus denarios xviii die Decembris per manus hostiarii Recepte iiis. id.

Item aliis diversis portitoribus pro reportagio rerum predictarum a predicta Turri et Thesauraria Westmonasterii batillagio de predicta Turri usque Westmonasterium portagio de aqua usque ad Scaccarium recipientibus denarios xii die Ianuarii per manus dictorum hostiariorum iis. id.

(7) *Issue Roll, 17 Edward II., Michaelmas* (*No.* 204)

[m. 4] Iohanni Devery assignato una cum Roberto de Chisenhale Elia de Ioneston' Rogero de Sheffeld et Iohanne de Neulond clericis ad scrutandum arrayandum et in quodam kalendari per certos titulos ponendum bullas cartas scripta et alia memoranda regnum Anglie ac terras regis Scocie Hibernie et Wallie tangencia quorum predictus Iohannes Devery percipiet per diem xiid. et quilibet predictorum Roberti Rogeri et Iohannis de Neulond iiiid. per diem et predictus Elias nichil percipiet hic quia percipit xiid. per diem in Garderoba incipientibus ad festum sancti Michelis proximo preterito recipientibus denarios xxii die Decembris per manus proprias videlicet : pro se ipso xls. : pro predicto Roberto xs., pro predicto Iohanne de Neulond xs. et pro prefato Rogero vs. quia post alios venit ad predicta facienda. lxvs.

[Details of further payments follow, and there are corresponding entries for the Easter term on Roll 207, m. 13.]

Iohanni de Devery pro denariis per ipsum solutis diversis portitoribus portantibus et removentibus diversas huchias cofros et bagas de Westmonasterio usque Turrim, de nigra camera in eadem Turri usque ad domum ubi arraiaverunt scripta et alia memoranda in eisdem huchiis cofris et bagis inventa per diversas vices recipientibus denarios xvii. die Marcii per manus proprias iiiis. ixd.

Diversis portitoribus Londonie portantibus huchias coffros et bagas cum litteris scriptis et memorandis tam de Anglia quam Scocia Hibernia Vasconia et aliis quibuscumque partibus regem et regnum sive potestatem suam tangentibus de Nigra Camera in Turri Londonie usque in capellam regis infra eandem Turrim necnon et alia diversa facientibus prout Thesaurarius et Camerarii eis iniunxerunt recipientibus denarios diversis vicibus per manus proprias xs. xd.

(8) *Memoranda Roll K.R.* 96, m. 59 d.

De clavibus tangencibus officium Garderobe liberatis Rogero de Waltham custodi Garderobe Regis.

Memorandum quod venerabilis pater Rogerus de Northburgh nunc Coventr' et Lich' episcopus venit modo hic xvii die Novembris et liberavit Rogero de Waltham custodi Garderobe domini regis xlix claves officium dicte Garderobe tangentes quas penes se habuit de tempore quo idem episcopus fuerat custos eiusdem Garderobe proximo ante dictum Rogerum de Waltham, videlicet iiii claves grossas quarum duo maiores et duo minores que sunt claves exterioris camere iuxta aulam nigram in Turri Londonie et xlv claves minutas que sunt claves coffrorum continencium munimenta et alia memoranda domini regis in eadem camera. Et sciendum quod predictus episcopus tulit hic ad Scaccarium predicto xvii die Novembris claves predictas in quadam baga sigillis magistri Henrici de Cantuaria et magistri Elie de Ioneston consignata que ibidem aperta fuit et dicte claves predicto Rogero de Waltham liberate fuerunt per predictum episcopum ut predicitur.

Postea vii die Decembris proximo sequente venit hic predictus Rogerus de Waltham et dicit se liberasse claves predictas Waltero Exoniensi episcopo Thesaurario, etc., pro scrutinio de quibusdam rebus London' faciendo : et unde dicit se habere litteram pat[entem] ipsius Thesaurarii de recepcione, etc.

ADDENDUM, on the date of the Wolfenbüttel MS., No. 2311 (see above, p. 235). That this is not a contemporary text of the *Recogniciones feodorum in Aquitania* is further suggested by the fact that the names of the English clerks responsible for it are quite different from the names of the English copyists and examiners mentioned in the two registers of diplomatic documents, Liber A and Liber B (above, p. 236), which were certainly compiled before 1296.

XIX

THE CONSTITUTION OF PROVINCIAL CHAPTERS IN THE MINORITE ORDER

THE Rule of 1223 contains only one reference to Provincial Chapters. At the end of Chapter viii., " De electione generalis ministri huius fraternitatis et de capitulo Pentecostes ", occurs the following passage:

> After the Chapter of Pentecost the ministers and custodians can severally, if they wish and it seems expedient to them, in the same year in their custodies call together their brethren once to a Chapter.

In the years which elapsed between the papal approval of the Rule (1223) and the promulgation of a body of General Constitutions of the Order (1239) the various provinces had held chapters under this vague direction. Those in Germany in 1224 and 1227 consisted of the custodians, guardians, and preachers of the province.[1] How other provincial chapters during this period were formed we do not know; but there was probably a good deal of diversity. And this may be the explanation why the General Constitutions of the Order refrained from laying down a uniform rule on the subject. The Dominican Order had already issued definite instructions as to the constitution of all its provincial chapters,[2] and the same policy was adopted later by the Carmelites,[3] and the Augustinian Hermits.[4] The Franciscan Order left to the provinces a free hand, within certain limits.

THE GENERAL CONSTITUTIONS.—The General Constitutions of 1260,

[1] *Chronica Fr. Jordani*, ed. H. Boehmer, 1908, pp. 35, 46.

[2] Capitulum autem provinciale appellamus priores conventuales cum singulis a capitulo suo electis et predicatores generales. " Constitutiones antique ord. fratrum predicatorum " (1228), ed. Denifle, *Archiv für Litteratur- und Kirchengeschichte des Mittelalters* (*ALKG.*), i. 212.

[3] Capitulum provinciale . . . ad quod omnes priores locales et vicarii priorum mortuorum, assumptorum vel absolutorum, si per conventum fuerint electi, et procuratores novorum locorum, ubi locum habemus et fratres numerum quaternarium excedentes, venire teneantur, singuli cum uno socio in suis capitulis rite et canonice electo, qui fratrum omnium vocem et auctoritatem habeat . . ., cum priore provinciali et unico ejus socio (" Antiq. ordinis constitutiones " (1324), ed. Zimmerman, *Monumenta Hist. Carmelitana*, i. 76).

[4] Cuiuslibet provincie omnes conventuales priores singuli cum singulis fratribus a conventibus eorum electis . . . conveniant ad ipsius provincie capitulum celebrandum. Constitutiones Ord. Fr. Eremit. S. Aug. (1290), cap. 32; Br. Mus. MS. Add. 38649, fol. 17; cf. fol. 15v.: Ad provinciale vero capitulum non nisi frater clericus et qui habet ad minus xxv annorum etatem pro discreto mittatur.

which were for the most part a rearrangement of "the multitude of general statutes" adopted in 1239, with subsequent additions, enacted (Rubric 10):[1]

Whereas the Rule says that ministers and custodians can in their several provinces[2] call together their brethren to a chapter, we ordain that every year in every province a provincial chapter shall be celebrated, according to the needs of each region: in which the place and day of the following chapter shall be assigned, so that those returning from the general chapter may be present. To this chapter shall come together the custodians and brethren of the province, according as it shall be ordained in the provincial chapter, provided that a multitude of persons may so far as possible be avoided.

The General Chapter of Assisi in 1269 adds:

And therefore no brother shall be sent to the chapter to receive the office of preacher (*pro predicacionis officio*) except by the advice and consent of the minister.[3]

The provincial minister presided, or, in his absence, his vicar, or the custodian in whose custody the chapter was held.[4]

The next clause in the General Constitutions of 1260 assumes that a convent elects a *discretus* to represent it in the provincial chapter:

In this chapter and in other elections friars residing in monasteries [*i.e.* nunneries of Clares] shall not for themselves have a vote; they shall, however, be admitted to the election of the *discretus* to be sent to the chapter in houses next which they reside, like the other friars of the convent. . . . This election shall be made the first day: otherwise the custodian shall appoint the *discretus*.[5]

Another clause implies that guardians did not *ex officio* attend provincial chapters:

The excesses of a guardian, which are to be sent to the provincial chapter, shall be recited to him in public in the presence of his convent if he is not going to the said chapter.[6]

The General Constitutions of 1260 also provide that the "special" visitor of a province shall complete his visitation in time to be present at the provincial chapter immediately preceding the General Chapter. He was to report to the provincial chapter the excesses of the minister and "any other things which he found difficult", but not to be present at other agenda of the chapter.[7]

Subsequent General Chapters defined more exactly the qualifications

[1] *Archiv f. Lit. u. Kirchengesch. d. Mittelalters* (*ALKG.*), vi. 129.

[2] The Phillipps MS. of the Constitutions (see *EHR.* xiii. 703) reads "singulis annis in suis custodiis" for "in singulis provinciis".

[3] *ALKG. ibid. n.* 1; *Archivum Franciscanum Historicum* (*AFH.*), vii. 479, § 4.

[4] *ALKG.* vi. 131.

[5] *Ibid.* 129.

[6] *Ibid.* 131.

[7] *Ibid.* 119, 120, 122.

and rights of electors. In an election by scrutiny a friar must give his own vote in person and could not entrust it to another.[1]

On the day appointed for the election of a *discretus* all the friars of the convent are bound by obedience to come, and the guardians are bound to notify all as far as they honestly can. . . . No friar in the same year shall have more than one vote in the election of a *discretus* to the chapter of the province or custody. Lectors (and students) lecturing or studying outside their province shall have only an active, not a passive vote in the elections of *discreti* both to the General and Provincial Chapter.[2]

These additions were apparently made by the General Chapter of Paris in 1292. The General Constitutions of Assisi in 1316 incorporated them, and added further that friars below the age of twenty years should not have a vote in the election of a *discretus* or in approving things to be sent to this chapter.[3]

Subsequent editions of the General Constitutions repeat these decrees but make no further provision as to the personnel of the provincial chapters, nor do the papal decrees on the government of the Order touch the question.

We turn now to the provincial constitutions and the documents emanating from provincial chapters.

I. Province of France.—A formula for the announcement of an election of a representative for the provincial chapter of the Province of France dating from the end of the thirteenth century exists, but the beginnings of the lines have been cut off by the binder. The letter is as follows (the words cut off and supplied are enclosed in square brackets):

[Reverendo] patri in Christo fratri N. ministro fratrum minorum in Francia ceterisque fratribus in prouin[ciali capitulo ad] talem locum congregandis Uniuersi fratres conuentus talis loci reuerenciam et [obedienciam deu]otam. Uniuersitati vestre tenore presentium facimus manifestum nos fratri N. Gar[diano . . .] fratri N. electo (a nobis, *inserted in another hand*) secundum formam constitucionis Generalis in hiis que ad nos pertinent quantum [. . . ad prou]inciale capitulum commisisse plenarie vices nostras. In cuius testimonium presen[tem litteram sigil]lo conuentus nostri duximus sigillandam. Datum anno domini millesimo cc° anno tali.[4]

There is one crucial word missing at the beginning of the fourth line between *gardiano* and *fratri*. Was it *et* or *siue*? Did the convent send

[1] *ALKG*. vi. 129, *n*. 2.
[2] *Ibid*. cf. *AFH*. iv. 518.
[3] *AFH*. iv. 518. In 1310 the General Minister, Gonsalvo, with the consent of the General Chapter at Padua, enacted a disfranchising ordinance: "Item, quod si per extrinsecas personas prestetur impedimentum amotioni predictorum excessuum [*scil*. edificiorum quoad picturas . . . vel sculpturas], locum suum sive conventum, in quo fuerint, privent [ministri] studio et potestate mittendi discretum ad capitulum provinciale; item, quod pro illo loco vel conventu nullus sit vocalis in ipso capitulo; et utraque privatio tamdiu remaneat, quamdiu remanebunt prefati excessus" (*ALKG*. vi. 70).
[4] *AFH*. vii. 488, and MS. in my possession.

both its guardian *and* an elected representative, or did it send *either* its guardian *or* an elected representative? The provincial constitutions of the end of the thirteenth century make it plain that one representative only was sent by each convent. "It is ordained that the custodians shall come to the (provincial) chapter without special companions, and from each 'place' one friar only elected for this purpose."[1] This clause is repeated in the constitutions of the Province of France drawn up in 1337.[2] And these later constitutions (like the General Constitutions) imply that guardians were not *ex officio* members of the provincial chapter: "When a guardian is not going to the Chapter" he is to be supplied with a copy of the report on his house made by the visitor.[3] According to the thirteenth-century statutes a further qualification for an elected representative is physical fitness. "None shall be elected who cannot walk (*ire*) six leagues a day."[4] This provision had dropped out before 1337. The later constitutions (1337) ordain that lepers have the right of voting in the election of a *discretus*,[5] but on the other hand they restrict the right to priests: "*Discreti* to be elected to the provincial chapter shall be elected by priests alone".[6] As provided in the General Constitutions the custodians were *ex officio* members of the chapter.

It may therefore be concluded that the provincial chapter of France consisted of the provincial minister, the nine custodians, and one representative (who might or might not be the guardian) from each of the fifty-nine convents of the province, elected by the priests of the convent. The special visitor of the province had to bring his report to the chapter immediately preceding the (triennial) General Chapter, and the inquisitors whose sphere of operations lay within the boundaries of the province were bound to attend, but were not full members of the chapter.

II. Province of Aquitaine.—The extant constitutions of the Province of Aquitaine date from about 1280, and are followed in the manuscript by a series of ordinances made by provincial chapters at the end of the thirteenth and the beginning of the fourteenth century.

The constitutions, under the heading *De modo veniendi ad capitulum provinciale*, enact (§ 2):[7]

Since it is doubtful whether guardians will be sent by the custody to the provincial chapter, to every guardian in his convent shall be read his own *visitatio* [*i.e.* the report of the visitor on his convent], in order that, if it happens that he does not go [to the chapter], he may answer by letter.

[1] *AFH.* vii. 453.
[2] *Ibid.* 499.
[3] *Ibid.* 500; cf. *ALKG.* vi. 131.
[4] *AFH.* vii. 453.
[5] *Ibid.* 500.
[6] *Ibid.* This seems to be an adaptation of Benedict XII.'s ordinance 1336 for the election of guardians, the right to vote being restricted to friars who had reached their twenty-fifth year and were in Holy Orders (*Bull. Franc.* vi. p. 38).
[7] *AFH.* vii. 476.

It is clear that guardians did not *ex officio* attend the chapter, but only if they were elected as *discreti*.

Another clause of the same section of the constitutions decrees that " not more than one *nuntius* from each custody shall come to the provincial chapter, and the multitude of those coming to the chapter shall be avoided ". An ordinance made at the Chapter of Condom, probably before 1285, introduces a modification :

We ordain that from one custody there shall never come to the provincial chapter more than two *nuntii*, one of the custodians, the other of all the guardians and *discreti* of the custody.

The ordinances made in the Chapter of Limoges (*c.* 1300 ?) provide a very different set of rules. The first clause announces that the provincial chapters shall henceforth be held at six (named) places in the province in succession : the second runs :

Provincial chapters are abolished (? amoventur),[1] and the method of coming to the chapter we ordain as follows, namely, that from the convent from which the custody takes its name the guardian *ex officio* and one *discretus* elected by the convent, from all other convents or places one only elected by the convent, shall come.

Yet the next group of ordinances, which have no date or place but are presumably later than those of Limoges, repeat with modifications the ordinance of Condom :

We ordain that to the provincial chapter there shall never come from one custody more than two *nuntii*, one of the custodians, the other of all the guardians of places where the chapter is [not] held.

If the " not " is correctly inserted, and it seems necessary for the sense, this passage supplies a clue to the meaning of the word *nuncius*. Friars coming from a distance needed a *nuncius* ; those in the convent where the chapter was held did not. The *nuncius* was not, as might at first sight appear, a *discretus* or elected representative of the chapter, but a kind of billeting officer who provided for the maintenance of the friars on their way to and from the chapter, and perhaps during the chapter. The word is used in this sense in the General Constitutions ; the passage is obscure in Cardinal Ehrle's version through the accidental omission of some words owing to *homoioteleuton* ; the omitted words are inserted in the following quotation in square brackets.

Inhibemus quoque districte, quod nullus frater in via bursarium secum ducat, sed si contingat aliquos fratres pro aliqua communi utilitate ordinis vel evidenti necessitate viam prolixam ire, in qua probabiliter videatur, quod non possint mendicando victualia necessaria invenire, per aliquem honestum nuncium, cui aliqua elemosina [modo debito committatur, cuius auctoritate

[1] The reading can hardly be correct: the editor suggests " renoventur ", " shall be reformed " (*AFH*. vii. 478).

illam recipiat et expendat, possit fratrum sic euntium necessitatibus subveniri; proviso quod huiusmodi elemosina] in honestis cibariis et aliis necessitatibus temperate et stricte, sicut decet pauperes, expendatur. . . . Nec etiam fratres venientes ad capitulum generale pueros secum ducant, si fieri poterit bono modo. Si tamen eos oporteat ducere, non ducat aliqua provincia nisi unum, cui solummodo et non aliis in ipso capitulo cibaria ministrentur.[1]

The Constitutions of Provence (A.D. 1313) speak of *famuli vel nuncii fratrum*.[2] The *nuntii*, therefore, of the Constitutions of Aquitaine have nothing to do with the constitution of the Provincial Chapter, and we return to the ordinance of the Chapter of Limoges.

According to this the chapter, if we take the number of custodies and houses given in the *Provinciale* of 1331 (ten custodies and sixty-three houses), would consist of the provincial minister, ten custodians, and the ten guardians and ten *discreti* of the ten houses after which the custodies were named, and one *discretus* from each of the remaining fifty-three houses: total, seventy-four persons.

The provincial constitutions and ordinances of the Province of Aquitaine are silent on the qualification of electors.

III. Province of Provence.—The thirteenth-century constitutions of this Province contain only one clause which throws any light on our subject:[3] "Gardianus autem absolutus in capitulo, ad quod non venerat, vicarius remaneat", until his successor is instituted.[4] This implies that guardians were not *ex officio* members of the provincial chapter. The statutes for the province issued by the Minister General in the provincial chapter at Nîmes 1313,[5] contain the curious stipulation "quod gardianus illo anno, quo fratres suos non induerit saltem de cingulis, tunicis vel habitibus, non possit ad capitulum provinciale venire".[6] The last part of these statutes, including the section *De capitulo provinciali*, is missing, and the principles on which the provincial chapter was formed remain obscure.

IV. Province of the March of Treviso.—The Constitutions of the Province of St. Anthony or the March of Treviso[7] were issued by the Chapter of Treviso in 1290. "In order that we may adjust ourselves to the General Constitutions," the friars of the Province of St. Anthony say (§ 17), "we ordain that in every place, in which there are twenty friars and more continually residing, the guardian shall come to the chapter by authority of election by us, and one other friar elected by the guardian and the rest of the friars of the convent. From other places there shall come only one friar, who shall have been elected by the friars of the place. We say the same

[1] *ALKG.* vi. 101, and MS. of the General Constitutions *penes me*, fol. 12.
[2] *AFH.* xiv. 462.
[3] *AFH.* xiv. 420-5.
[4] *Ibid.* 422.
[5] *Ibid.* 426-30.
[6] *Ibid.* 426; cf. General Constitutions of Lyons, 1325 (*AFH.* iv. 530).
[7] *AFH.* vii. 456-65.

of any place in which a lecturer happens to be residing to lecture on theology." The last sentence is obscure. It may mean that houses which had a lecturer sent two representatives, even if they had less than twenty friars, or possibly that theological lecturers *actu legentes* were members of the chapter like guardians of the larger houses. The limitation of the representation of the smaller houses to one each seems to be annulled by a concession made by the minister in the same chapter: "The minister concedes to every guardian permission to go to the provincial chapter if he wishes, even if he be not elected as a *discretus*", but perhaps such guardians were not *de corpore capituli*. Another statute (§ 19) gives the chapter a right of censorship over the elections in the smaller houses. "Whereas in elections not only the number but often rather the merit of the persons should be considered, we enact that every one elected in a place in which only one representative is to be sent to the chapter, shall bring with him in the letters testimonial of his election the names of the electors which shall be set forth in those letters, that it may be clear both to the minister and the *diffinitores* whether the election was held with the zeal of God and the common advantage." The power of supervision thus claimed by the provincial chapter in 1290, may be compared with the precept of the General Constitutions of Paris (1292), that the friars are bound by obedience, in all elections of ministers, *diffinitores* and *discreti*, to elect discreet persons having the zeal of God and the common advantage.[1]

Nothing is said about the custodians in the Constitutions of the March of Treviso. It may be inferred, however, that they were *ex officio* members of the chapter, as the General Constitutions imply. Their presence is implied in the title to a group of edicts made in the same Chapter of Treviso in 1290: "Ista sunt memorialia facta a custodibus et gardianis in eodem capitulo provinciali".[2] It would seem that the custodians and guardians exercised some legislative power in matters of discipline without the co-operation of the elected *discreti*.

The province in 1331 had only four custodies and thirty houses.

V. Province of St. Francis, or Umbria.—The ordinances of the provincial chapters between 1338 and 1343 are preserved,[3] and give definite directions as to the provincial chapter. It was to consist of all the custodians (nine in number), one *discretus* elected from every convent or place[4] in the province, one *discretus* elected in the monastery of St. Clare at Assisi, one *discretus* elected in the monastery of Pelagio (a house of Clares in the diocese of Gubbio), and two *discreti* elected

[1] *ALKG.* vi. 129 note, and 130.

[2] *AFH.* vii. 462.

[3] *AFH.* v. pp. 520-43; Documenta saeculi XIV. Provinciae S. Francisci Umbriae, ed. F. Delorme.

[4] The ordinations of the Chapter of Perugia say "every place, whether conventual or not, having a guardian": this would probably exclude hermitages.

in the convent of Gubbio. Why Gubbio is thus singled out is not explained. Inquisitors and visitors of Clares had no vote in the provincial chapter, unless they had been elected in some other capacity.[1] The chapter would thus consist of the provincial minister, nine custodians, seventy *discreti* from the seventy houses of the province, one additional *discretus* for Gubbio, and two from the friars residing in two monasteries of nuns: total, eighty-two.

The qualifications for electors and candidates are given. Every friar had an active vote in the election of a *discretus* in the house in which he resided the greater part of the year—the year being reckoned from Provincial Chapter to Provincial Chapter.[2] Further, friars returning from *studia* or from other provinces had an active vote in their native convents (apparently without the residentiary qualification).[3] The election was held within a fortnight of the meeting of the provincial chapter, and friars absent from their houses were to return for this fortnight; otherwise the election was to be held without them.[4] A friar, in order to qualify for election as a *discretus*, had to be " de familia et mansionarius loci mittentis "—residing there for the greater part of the year.[5] The same friar was not to be elected as *discretus* two years in succession.[6]

VI. PROVINCE OF BOLOGNA.—A draft letter from Anthonius de Paça of Rimini to the Minister General contains a detailed account of the election of a Provincial Minister in a chapter of this province in 1349.[7] Marianus of Perugia, Provincial Minister, having died in office, his vicar Jacobus de Signorellis, inquisitor in Romandiola, called a Provincial Chapter to Bologna to elect his successor on January 14, 1349. The chapter met " in foresteria " (guest hall ?) of the convent. Forty-two houses were represented, this number including all the houses in the Province except Carpi, whose absence is not explained. The total number of voters was 66, made up as follows:

5 custodians.
15 guardians and 15 *discreti* of the greater houses.
27 *discreti* of the other houses.
2 inquisitors, including the vicar of the minister, who voted as inquisitor.
2 visitors of the Ladies of St. Clare.

The vicar of the province did not vote.

The fifteen houses which had two representatives each were—*in the custody of Bologna*: the convent of Bologna, and the convent or monastery of St. Francis near Bologna; *in the custody of Parma*: the convents of Parma, Piacenza, and Cremona; *in the custody of*

[1] *AFH.* v. 542; cf. 531.
[2] *Ibid.* 526.
[3] *Ibid.*
[4] *Ibid.* 530, 532.
[5] *Ibid.* p. 531. The Chapter of Assisi in 1338 says " for the third part of the year " (p. 526).
[6] *Ibid.* 531, 542.
[7] *AFH.* vii. 504-7.

Ferrara: the convents of Ferrara, Modena, and Reggio; *in the custody of Ravenna*: the convents of Ravenna, Imola, Lugo, and Faenza; *in the custody of Forli*: the convents of Forli, Rimini, and Cesena. Of the fifteen *discreti* of these larger houses three happen to be mentioned in the document in other connexions; they are all three described as lectors.[1]

The presence of inquisitors and visitors of Clares as full members of the chapter is to be noticed. The General Chapter at Strasbourg in 1282 passed the following statute:[2]

Item inquisitores heretice pravitatis et visitatores monasteriorum sancte Clare in quolibet provinciali capitulo renuncient suis officiis per seipsos si presentes fuerint vel per litteras si absentes; et possint eligi ad capitulum provinciale de custodiis et conventibus ubi fuerint assignati.

But this was incorporated in the General Constitutions of Paris, 1292, with a remarkable difference: the inquisitors were left out.[3] And even as applied to the visitors of Clares, the clause would seem to mean that they were eligible as *discreti* for the custodies or houses in which they resided, not that they could *ex officio* be members of a provincial chapter. The inclusion of both these officials in the provincial chapter of Bologna illustrates the latitude allowed to the provinces in the constitution of their chapters. The letter was sealed with the seals of the vicar of the province, the custodian and the guardian of Bologna, where the election was held. These seals do not, of course, appear on the draft letter.

VII. Province of Cologne.—We possess full information about the constitution of the provincial chapter of Cologne in 1315. The provincial minister, Adolf of Stammheim, having died on November 19, 1314, Arnold, custodian of Brabant, vicar of the province, summoned a chapter to meet at Fulda in the custody of Hesse to elect a successor. The letter addressed by Arnold and the other friars *de corpore capituli* to the minister general announcing the election and asking for the General's confirmation is the source of our information.[4]

On Friday, May 9, the friars assembled at Fulda, rested, and deliberated. On the morning of Saturday, May 10, the vigil of Pentecost, they met together and sang mass; those who were not *de corpore capituli* then retired, the rest remaining. The letters testimonial of the members of the chapter were then read, and those who were disqualified by excommunication, interdict, suspension, or other lawful disqualification were not admitted. The custodian of

[1] According to Salimbene (*Chron.* ed. Holder-Egger, 593), those who had the right to elect the minister in the Province of Bologna in 1287 were "guardiani, custodes et lectores et alii discreti".

[2] MS. in my possession; cf. *EHR*. xiii. 703-8, and *ALKG*. vi. 51.

[3] *ALKG*. vi. 123 note.

[4] *AFH*. i. 88-93.

Hesse, to which custody Fulda belonged, with the advice of *discreti*, appointed the guardian of Cologne and the lectors of Trier and Fulda as tellers to take the votes. These three withdrew somewhat apart but in the presence of the assembled chapter, first took each other's votes, and then those of all the rest of the capitular fathers. Each friar as he came up said, "I, Brother —— nominate Brother —— as minister of the province of Cologne." The tellers wrote the vote down and read it out to the friar before he retired. After those of the three tellers the votes were given by custodies: first, the custodian of Cologne, followed by the representatives from the convents in that custody; secondly, the custodian of Brabant (vicar of the province), followed by his friars; thirdly, fourthly, and fifthly, the custodians of Holland, Trier, and Westphalia, followed by their friars; and lastly, the friars of the custody of Hesse, the custodian of Hesse bringing up the rear. There were in 1315 six custodies. In the Provinciale of 1331 there were seven custodies, the custody of Holland having been divided between those dates into the two custodies of Holland and Deventer. All the convents which formed the custody of Deventer in 1331 appear in the custody of Holland in 1315, except one, Falerne, which presumably was founded after 1315.

The election was not unanimous: of the 81 electors 60 voted for Thomas (of Weid), lector of Cologne, 4 for Arnold, custodian of Brabant, 3 for Romanus, custodian of Trier, 14 for William, custodian of Westphalia. All the electors from the custodies of Cologne and Hesse voted for Thomas, the lector of Cologne (except Thomas himself), and he obtained the great majority of the votes from the custodies of Brabant, Holland, and Trier. The custodian of Brabant obtained only three votes from his own custody, and the custodian of Trier only one.

All the custodians were present. All the convents in the province—forty-seven in number—were represented. Twenty-eight were represented by two persons, namely the guardian *ex officio* and a *discretus* who was in every case except two (Roermund and Maastricht) also described as lector. Nineteen convents had one representative each. In nine of these convents the representative is described as *discretus et gardianus*; in five as *discretus et lector*; in four as *discretus*. In one case (Utrecht) the single representative is described as *gardianus*, not *discretus*; this implies that the guardian attended *ex officio* and that the elected *discretus* was disqualified or absent for some reason. Consequently this house should be transferred to the class of houses which had two representatives. It is probable also that some of the nine houses which were represented only by a *discretus et lector* or by a *discretus* were really two-member constituencies, the guardian being disqualified. Aachen and Malines, both represented by only a *discretus et lector*, are perhaps instances.

It is clear that the convents in the province of Cologne were divided into two classes: the larger houses—probably those containing twenty or more friars (as in the province of St. Anthony)—were represented by the guardian and an elected *discretus* who was almost always the lector; the smaller houses were represented by one elected *discretus* who might be—and more often than not was—the guardian. The former class contained about thirty-one houses, the latter about sixteen. While the custodians attended the chapter *ex officio*, the question of additional representation of the convents which gave their names to custodies did not arise, as the custodies were for the most part named after districts not towns. The letter was sealed with the seals of the vicar of the province, the custodian of Hesse, and the warden of Fulda. No trace of them remains, the lower part of the parchment having been cut off. The seals were presumably pendent, not applied. The constitutions of the provinces have not been discovered; and we know nothing about the qualifications of electors.

VIII. Province of Strasbourg or Upper Germany.—The constitutions of this province may exist but they have not been published. Glassberger gives many acts or ordinances of provincial chapters,[1] but he was less interested in constitutional than in liturgical questions, and none of the acts which he quotes throws light on the constitution of the provincial chapters. Yet the early archives of the province of Strasbourg have survived probably in a less fragmentary form than those of any other province. They are preserved in the town archives of Lucerne, but no calendar of them appears to have been printed. They were used by Eubel in his history of the province,[2] which contains some documents from this source.

The most important for our purpose is the letter to the Minister General from the vicar of the province and the provincial chapter announcing the election of a provincial minister in the chapter of Strasbourg in 1510.[3] After the death of Conrad of Bondorf, provincial minister, on January 4, 1510, the custodian of Alsace as vicar of the province summoned a chapter to meet at Strasbourg[4] on March 3 to elect his successor. The procedure was much the same as that followed in the Chapter of Fulda (province of Cologne) in 1315, except that one of the *discreti* was appointed to act as scribe of the election in addition to the three tellers. The custodians of the six custodies were present and voted, and representatives of forty-two

[1] *Analecta Franciscana*, ii. 111, 126, 137, 179, 195, 200, etc.

[2] *Geschichte der Oberdeutschen* (*Strassburger*) *Minoriten-Provinz*, von P. Konrad Eubel, Würzburg, 1886. Statutes of the province are also preserved in MS. 106 of the Franciscan convent of Freiburg. See *AFH*. xvii. p. 239, *n*. 2.

[3] Eubel, pp. 350-53.

[4] This chapter probably met in the refectory, like the chapter of 1498 (*ibid*. p. 347).

convents ; this number appears to have included all the Conventual houses of the province—some fifteen having gone over to the Observants before 1510. Thirty-two houses sent two representatives each—the guardian and a *discretus*. Four houses were represented only by their guardians ; three of these were late and unimportant foundations.[1] It would seem that the small houses were represented by their guardians *ex officio*, not by an elected *discretus* as was usually the custom. Apart from this the method of representation was the same as in the province of Cologne. It does not appear whether the *discreti* were usually lectors. The number of electors was 86. The seals of the vicar of the province (who was also custodian of Alsace), the custodian of Swabia, and the guardian of Strasbourg were attached.

The chapter held at Strasbourg in 1498, when 88 friars under their custodians voted in the election of a provincial minister,[2] was evidently like that of 1510, and this may be considered the normal form of chapter in the province.

There is, however, evidence that a smaller chapter was frequently, and a larger chapter occasionally, substituted for the normal provincial chapter.

Of the smaller variety the earliest recorded example occurred in 1325. It is described by a contemporary chronicler, an unknown Franciscan of Bâle, as follows :[3]

Eodem anno celebratum est capitulum provinciale in Argentina post pascha dominica qua cantatur *Misericordia domini*, et ad illud capitulum de qualibet custodia venerunt septem fratres tantum ; unde de corpore ejusdem capituli fuerunt tantummodo 44 fratres. Et duravit illud capitulum XI diebus, scilicet a feria 6ª ante *Misericordia domini* usque ad feriam 2ᵃᵐ post dominicam *Jubilate* [19-29 April], et fuit provincia sine capitulo fere duobus annis, minus 5 vel 4 septimanis.

The reason for this deviation from custom was what Glassberger calls the " tribulatio ordinis " owing to the dispute with John XXII. about Evangelical Poverty.[4] The chapter seems to have consisted of representatives of the custodies, not convents. Seven from each of the six custodies would account for forty-two members of the chapter ; the remaining two would be the provincial minister and one other not identified, perhaps his *socius*.

This was clearly an exceptional measure to meet an emergency. But for about sixty years—from 1355 to 1409[5]—to judge from Glassberger's chronicle, small chapters are more frequent than the

[1] Victorsberg (1370), Heiligenbrunn (1463), and Hausach (1475). Gmünd also was represented only by its guardian, but it probably really belonged to the two-member houses.

[2] Eubel, pp. 346-7.

[3] *AFH*. iv. 686.

[4] *Anal. Franc.* ii. 134 ; cf. *ibid.* 124, " propter ministrum Generalem et socios eius ".

[5] A few occur later in the century : 1459 at Heidelberg, 1476 " convocatio capitularis " at Mainz (*ibid.* pp. 437, 461).

ordinary provincial chapters. They are called " convocationes ", or " convocationes custodum " as at Esslingen in 1355 [1] and Schaffhausen in 1402,[2] or more fully " convocatio custodum cum discretis et gardianis " as at Ulm in 1357.[3] Sometimes we get " convocatio quasi capitulum " and " convocatio et capitulum " as at Speyer in 1368 and 1386.[4] They passed ordinances (*e.g.* at Esslingen 1355,[5] Strasbourg 1384 [6]), and a convocation even elected the provincial minister at Worms in 1372.[7]

Convocations again appear frequently at the beginning of the sixteenth century—*e.g.* at Strasbourg in 1512—a " convocatio vim habens capituli ", when the reason is given " ad vitandas graves expensas et inutilem concursum fratrum ".[8]

A statute made by the provincial chapter at Ueberlingen in 1426 seems to imply that some form of custodial (as distinct from conventual) representation was usual. After prescribing the qualifications necessary for a student of the province at the University of Paris, the statute enacts that such a student on his return after completing a two-years course at Paris and fulfilling the academic duties in his own province prescribed by the ancient statutes " nondum in Discretum alicuius Custodiae eligi valeat nec poterit, nisi prius alios quinque annos in lectoratu Parisiensi vel alio Ordinis officio compleverit ".[9]

Glassberger sometimes mentions a " magnum capitulum " as distinguished both from a " capitulum " (or " capitulum provinciale ") and a " convocatio ". " Magna capitula " were held at Zürich 1375 (p. 212), Mainz 1385 (p. 215), Pforzheim 1385 (p. 216), Nürnberg 1390 (p. 220), Bâle 1401 (p. 224). What (if any) constitutional meaning the term possesses is not clear. But the chapter at Solothurn in 1502 may be a case in point. As the constitutions of Alexander VI. were to be communicated to the province at this chapter, the provincial minister summoned to it all doctors, custodians, guardians, lectors, and the leading fathers ; in all 160 friars attended.[10]

IX. Province of Saxony.—We do not know how the chapters in this province were normally constituted. But it is evident from entries in Glassberger's Chronicle that convocations were occasionally substituted for chapters and had the authority of chapters. Thus provincial ministers were elected by convocations at Erfurt in 1421, Leipzic in 1480, and Aschersleben in 1490.[11] The size of the province with its twelve custodies and eighty-eight houses must have made a full chapter a burdensome and unwieldy affair.

X. Province of Rome.—The Constitutions of this province, made

[1] Eubel, p. 340.
[2] *Anal. Franc.* ii. 224.
[3] *Ibid.* p. 183 ; cf. p. 191.
[4] *Ibid.* pp. 202, 216.
[5] Eubel, p. 340.
[6] *Ibid.* p. 341.
[7] *Anal. Franc.* ii. 209.
[8] Eubel, p. 351 ; cf. *ibid.* pp. 350, 354.
[9] *Anal. Franc.* ii. 282.
[10] Eubel, p. 349.
[11] *Anal. Franc.* ii. 274, 471, 506.

in 1316, are preserved in MS. 151 (Laing 33) in Edinburgh University Library. As these have not yet been edited, the passages relating to the organisation of the Provincial Chapter are here printed in full.

1. (f. 90r.) In nomine domini Amen. Anno eiusdem MCCCxvi° Kal. Sept. infrascripte constitutiones prouinciales fuerunt de beneplacito et assensu fratris Thome Ministri Roman' et diffinitorum ac de consilio vij discretorum singularum custodiarum per discretos totius capituli prouincialis ad hoc assignatorum in capitulo prouinciali tunc tempore Reate celebrato, aliis ab hiis penitus reuocatis, reformate.

2. (f. 92r.) In Cap. V. *De modo exterius exeundi.*
. . . Item custodes appropinquante capitulo prouinciali non mittant fratres extra custodiam nisi prius intersint capitulo sui loci, nec etiam tempore prouincialis capituli nisi urgens necessitas immineret. . . .

3. (f. 93v.) In Cap. VII. *De correctionibus delinquentium.*
. . . Item ordinat Minister de uoluntate consilio et assensu prouincialis capituli quod omnes custodie equaliter habeant diffinitores, ita quod quartus diffinitor circulariter eligatur, et in sequenti capitulo de Reatina custodia eligatur simul cum custode Vrbeuet', Campan^{e} et Maritim^{e}, que de iure habere debent ; et sic deinceps per custodias quartus diffinitor ordinarie eligatur. Et nulla custodia possit mittere ad capitulum prouinciale nisi quatuor discretos electos in custodiali capitulo [excepto g(uardiano) Romano],[1] et siquis aliter uenerit ad agenda capituli minime a[d]mittatur. Item per sanctam obedientiam inhibemus ut nullus frater singulariter [2] nominetur uel presentetur per fratres de prouincia custodie de qua diffinitor fuerit eligendus, set teneantur fratres pro(?) prouincia libere eligere discretiorem et meliorem de ipsis custodiis oriundum. . . .

4. (f. 94r.) In Cap. VIII. *De institutionibus prelatorum.*
. . . Item custodes quando uadunt ad capitulum prouinciale relinquant uicarios de consilio discretorum. . . .

5. (f. 94r.) *De capitulo custodie IX^{m} Capitulum.*
Statuimus ut de singulis locis custodie ueniat unus discretus ad custodiale capitulum, quem fratres loci elegerunt ad ipsum custodiale capitulum, et Guardianus cuiuslibet conuentus, qui Guardianus iturus ad capitulum custodie in electione huius discreti uocem non habeat : et dicimus conuentum, quantum ad hunc [huius ?] discretionis actum, in quo per capitulum lector in theologia ponitur ad legendum. Item statuimus quod inquisitores heretice prauitatis et uisitatores monasteriorum eligi possint ad capitulum prouinciale in custodiis suis tantum unde sint oriundi. (f. 94v.) Si uero fuerit aliquis in aliquo dictorum officiorum non existens de prouincia, possit eligi in custodia illa in qua se inuenit tempore prouincialis capituli, ita tamen quod uno mense ad minus in custodia illa fuerit tunc moratus.

The constitutions of the Roman province contain no heading *De capitulo provinciali.* The most important references to the provincial chapter occur under the heading *De correctionibus delinquentium,* and the whole passage (§ 3 above) is marked " vacat " in the manuscript.

[1] Added in the margin in another hand. [2] MS. sui gl'anter.

The deletion, however, probably means that the passage is in the wrong place, for we shall find that the peculiar features here revealed still characterised the Roman province more than a century later. The special mark of the Roman provincial chapter was that it contained elected representatives not of the convents but of the custodies. Every convent in a custody sent its guardian and one *discretus* specially elected for the purpose to the custodial chapter, the guardian having no vote in the election ; but a convent was defined in this connexion as a house in which there was a theological lecturer appointed by the chapter (whether custodial or provincial is not mentioned) ; the other houses were apparently not represented at all, or possibly were represented only by their guardians. Each custodial chapter (there were seven in all) then elected four *discreti* as members of the provincial chapter. The only convent directly represented was the convent at Rome, whose guardian was *ex officio* a member of the provincial chapter, and this appears to have been an addition subsequent to 1316.

Inquisitors and visitors of nunneries were not *ex officio* members of the provincial Chapter, but might be elected among the four *discreti* sent by each custodial chapter ; this probably implies that the custodial chapter was not confined in its choice to members of its own body.

The arrangement for the election of the fourth *diffinitor* of the provincial chapter from the custodies *circulariter* does not concern us here, but will be alluded to later.

According to the constitutions of 1316 the Roman provincial chapter consisted of the provincial minister, four *discreti* from each of the seven custodies, and the guardian of the convent of Rome or Araceli : total, 37.

A detailed description of the election of Master John of Tivoli as provincial minister in 1439 is contained in a letter of the Masters of Theology, the custodians, and other *discreti* of the Roman Province to the Minister General.[1]

After the resignation of the Provincial Minister, Friar Scolay de Monte Ylcino (or Scolarius de Monte Ilcino) S.T.M., " the Masters of Theology, custodians, and other discreti to whom the election of the Minister in the said province belonged," assembled in Chapter at Velletri on July 25, 1439, to elect a successor, on the summons of the Friar Scolay, then acting as vicar of the General Minister :

et ad supplicationem omnium nostrum per eum facta reformatione omnium Capitulorum Custodialium, et habilitatis ac de novo institutis omnibus Discretis qui pro vocalibus sibi fuerant presentati, ut subscripta Ministri electio rite et canonice celebraretur ; ad electionem per viam scrutinii processimus in hunc modum.

[1] *AFH.* vii. 508-10.

The vicar, with the consent of the chapter, nominated six tellers "de corpore dicti nostri provincialis Capituli" in two groups of three each, each group having one of its number as secretary. These six received and wrote down the votes. The first voters were three of the *disquisitores* (or tellers), namely, Paul de Pantaleis, custodian of Rome, Raynald de Frisinone, and Master John of Tivoli. These were followed by the guardian of Rome and four *discreti* of the custody of Rome, the custodian and three *discreti* of the custody of Tivoli, the custodian and four *discreti* of the custody of Campagna, the custodian and four *discreti* of the custody of Viterbo, the custodian and three *discreti* of the custody of Orvieto, four *discreti* of the custody of Rieti, and the custodian and four *discreti* of the custody of Velletri or Maritima. The letter then goes on to state that the total votes numbered 38, of which 37 were given to Master John of Tivoli and one to Andrew of Velletri. As a fact, however, only 35 votes are recorded in the letter. The custodian of Rieti has been apparently omitted by accident, and two of the six tellers neglected to record their votes (the last of the six, Jacobus (Cole) de Terracina, voted as custodian of Velletri). It will be noticed that five of the seven custodies have four *discreti*, and two (Orvieto and Tivoli) have only three. Probably two of the tellers were *discreti* of these custodies; and the other two, John of Tivoli (who is frequently described as "Magister") and another, may have been the "Masters of Theology" who formed one of the classes of electors, but who are not mentioned in the Constitutions of 1316. But the only one of the electors who is described as "magister" (besides John of Tivoli) voted as *discretus* apparently of the custody of Campania. One elector is described as "inquisitor", but he voted not as inquisitor but as *discretus* for the custody of Velletri. The ex-minister, who presided as vicar of the General Minister, did not vote.

The chapter, therefore, consisted of Masters of Theology, custodians, and four *discreti* from each of the seven custodies, and the guardian of Rome. With the single exception of the convent of Rome (Aracoeli), no guardian of a convent attended as such, no convent as such sent representatives. The *discreti* of the custodies were presumably elected in custodial chapter, as provided for in the constitutions of 1316; the number of *discreti* of a custody bore no relation to the number of houses in the custody; Rieti, which had twelve houses, sent the same number of *discreti* (namely four) as Campagna, which had only five houses.

The letter was sealed with the seals of the Vicar of the General Minister, the custodian of Maritima (or Velletri) and the guardian of Velletri, where the election was held. Traces of the three seals appear *in dorso*.

XI. Province of Ancona.—The Constitutions drawn up in 1478

at Montottone in the custody Fermo "for the reformation of the Province of the March of Ancona"[1] throw no light on our subject, but some documents and formulae relating to the elections in this Province (*c.* 1489) show that the custodial method of constituting the Provincial Chapter prevailed here as in the Roman Province. From these it appears that the friars of each convent elected a *discretus* to attend the chapter of the custody: the chapter of the custody then elected a number of friars to go as *discreti* of the custody to the provincial chapter.[2] The convents were represented in the provincial chapter only indirectly through the custodies. In the fourteenth century the Province had seven custodies and eighty-seven houses. The number of houses, which exceeded that of all other Cismontane Provinces and that of all Ultramontane Provinces except Saxony, would give a plausible explanation for the adoption of this system in Ancona, but the province of Rome, which, as we have seen, followed the same plan, had not this justification.

Leaving the consideration of the customs in the Observant provinces for a future occasion, we may now sum up the results which we have reached so far. The one element common to all these provincial chapters (besides the provincial minister) is the custodians, who were *ex officio* members of the chapter. From this point diversity begins. Two main classes of chapters may be distinguished: (1) those constituted on the principle of representation of houses; (2) those constituted on the principle of representation of custodies.

To the second class belong, fully, only the provinces of Rome and Ancona. It will be noticed that both were Italian or Cismontane provinces, and that our information about Ancona dates from the end of the fifteenth century. The principle was, however, operative in the Roman province from the beginning of the fourteenth century. Whether it was then a reform, and whether the method extended to other provinces which had earlier adopted the system of representation by convents, are questions to which no definite answer can as yet be given. It is, however, clear that something of the same kind was occasionally used in the fourteenth and fifteenth centuries in the provinces of Strasbourg and Saxony.

In the first class there is much variety. In the provinces of Umbria and France (and probably Provence) each house is represented by a single elected representative, but he is chosen in Umbria by all the friars of the house, in France by priests only. Aquitaine is the only province in which the head house of each custody is specially favoured by a double representation. In the March of Treviso, Bologna, and Cologne, each of the larger houses sent its guardian and elected representative, each of the smaller one elected representative only.

[1] *AFH.* xvi. 138 *et seq.*

[2] *Ibid.* pp. 147, 148.

In Strasbourg every house sent its guardian and one elected representative, except a few recently founded houses, which sent their guardians only. Some provinces show peculiar features: in the provincial chapter of Bologna inquisitors and visitors of Clares had votes *ex officio*; in that of Rome masters of theology may have sat in their own right—and perhaps lecturers in the chapters of the March of Treviso and Bologna. Friars residing in certain monasteries of Clares sent representatives to the chapters of Umbria and Bologna.

This inquiry was undertaken in order to see if it would throw light on the constitution of the chapter of the English province, about which no direct information is as yet forthcoming. Except for the presence of the custodians—and that is obvious from the General Constitutions —no inferences can be safely drawn from the diversities of customs in other provinces. The few records relating to the provincial chapters in England yet discovered tell us nothing about the constitution of the chapter. If we could find a single letter announcing the election of a friar as *discretus* of a convent or a custody, we should at least know which of the two main principles of representation prevailed in England. Or again a cryptic verse, invented to help the friars to memorise the order of precedence in a provincial chapter, might turn up and throw light on the constitution.

There are three such verses relating to the procedure of English chapters which may be given as specimens (especially as their meaning is not obvious) though they tell us nothing about the constitution of the chapter.

They occur in Bodleian MS. Lat. Th. d. 1, which contains sermons in Latin preached at various places in England by a Franciscan, Nicholas Philip, in the fifteenth century.[1] On fol. 90 (a fly-leaf in the middle of the volume) after some musical notes and the words "Script. Lichefeld. 1436" are the following hexameters:

Ordo pro diffinitoribus provincialis capituli.
Cas Wy. Bristolli Oxon Lon. Can Eboraci.

Ordo cursorum Londoniarum.
Oxon Wy. London. Can Bris. Lon. E.bor Novi London.

Circulus custodiarum pro capitulo provinciali.
Bristoll Cante Wygor. Oxonia London et Ebor.

The first shows that the four *diffinitores* or *definitores*, who formed the executive committee in all provincial chapters of all the Mendicant Orders, were chosen from the custodies in rotation. I suppose it means that the first year (say 1436) they would be chosen from the custodies

[1] The book belonged at one time (1538) to Thomas Goddard, O.F.M., and after his death to the friary of Babwell (f. 178v).

Newcastle, Worcester, Bristol, and Oxford; the next year either from those of Worcester, Bristol, Oxford, and London, or from those of London, Cambridge, York, and Newcastle, and so on. This practice of electing the *diffinitores* from the custodies in rotation appears to have been general. It is implied in the Constitutions of France 1337:

> At the instance of the provincial chapter held at Senlis at Pentecost 1309, Friar Gonsalvo, then minister general, ordained and decreed that no friar in the said province can be elected as *definitor* of any custody, unless he is a native of that custody, or has been incorporated in it absolutely and not temporarily.[1]

It is found also in the province of Umbria,[2] Rome,[3] and Tuscany[4] in the fourteenth and fifteenth centuries.

The second verse shows that the *cursor* or theological lecturer in the *studium* of London was chosen each year from the custodies in regular rotation, every third year from the custody of London.

The third verse means that the provincial chapter was held in some convent of each custody in succession. This rule was certainly not in force at the end of the thirteenth and beginning of the fourteenth centuries, when alone we have a fairly complete list of chapters. A similar custom obtained in the province of Umbria;[5] and in Aquitaine there were six convents (situated in five out of the ten custodies) in which the chapter was to be held in rotation, unless otherwise determined.[6]

Owing to the complete disappearance of the archives of the English province, the most likely places to find any scraps of information about the provincial chapters are the fly-leaves and bindings of manuscripts which belonged to Franciscan friars or to Franciscan houses in England, or to the General Minister.

A. G. LITTLE.

[1] *AFH*. vii. 499; cf. p. 501 (§ 22).
[2] *Ibid*. v. 532.
[3] See p. 262, above.
[4] Papini, *Storia di San Francesco*, i. 257 (Tabula diffinitionis, 1429); *AFH*. x. 422, 423 ("Tabula diffinitionis," 1394; "Tabula officialium," 1483).
[5] *AFH*. v. 530.
[6] *Ibid*. vii. 478.

XX

HUGO DE NOVOCASTRO OR DE CASTRONOVO, FRATER MINOR

I. HUGO DE NOVOCASTRO or de Castronovo, Friar Minor, who has obtained a notice of only a few lines in the *Dictionary of National Biography*,[1] really belongs to France, even if he was born at Newcastle-on-Tyne,[2] and came early in life—perhaps in the following of Duns Scotus—to the University of Paris. In Paris, indeed, he became Doctor of Theology and Licentiate in Decrees (or Canon Law), there he remained all his life, and there he died. He shared with John of Wales and Nicholas de Lyra the distinguished honour of interment in the church of the convent of his Order at Paris.[3]

The story of his life is wholly obscure, like that of his master, Duns Scotus, and the majority of his fellow-pupils. We know only that he took part in the General Chapter held at Perugia in June 1322 during the Generalate of Michael of Cesena, and that he then, as Doctor of Theology, joined with the Provincial Ministers of Germany, England, and France in approving two declarations concerning the question of Poverty.[4] He had thus already at that date a great position in his Order. He was further one of the faithful doctors whose figures were placed later (in 1513) as acolytes round the tomb of John Duns Scotus in the Church of the Minorites in Cologne.

II. The designation or title of honour given to him in the schools—*Doctor scolasticus* [5]—has nothing distinctive about it. His

[1] Vol. xiv. (1909) p. 317.

[2] No evidence, other than an ancient and hitherto unchallenged tradition, exists to prove that he was of English origin. There were, of course, many places called *Novum Castrum* or *Castrum Novum* in France and elsewhere, as in England.

The English Province, however, at this period supplied more than its due share of doctors of theology in the Order, and the association of Hugh with Fr. William of Alnwick (on whose works see *Miscellanea Francesco Ehrle*, i. Roma, 1924, p. 219), at the General Chapter of Perugia may lend some support to the opinion that Hugh also was a Northumbrian and came from Newcastle-on-Tyne. But it is a fact perhaps to be reckoned with that Léopold Delisle, whose every word has weight, in his *Inventaire des manuscrits latins de la Sorbonne* (Paris, 1870, p. 27), names him " Hugues de Châteauneuf ", without note of interrogation or explanation of any kind.

[3] According to the evidence of Bartholomew of Pisa, *Analecta Franciscana*, iv. p. 544.

[4] *Chartularium Universitatis Parisiensis*, ii. p. 277 ; Wadding, *Ann. Min.* vi. 396.

[5] Fr. Ehrle, *Die Ehrentitel der scolastischen Lehrer des Mittelalters* (München, 1919) ; *Franziskanische Studien*, ii. (1915) pp. 195, 197.

reputation, which was great but indefinite, was based on the following works:

On the Sentences.—Hugh was a Bachelor when he composed his commentary on the Sentences of Peter Lombard. In fact, William de Vaurouillon (Vorillong),[1] who quotes him abundantly in his own commentary, while pointing out that the opinion of Friar Hugh is opposed to the opinions of St. Bonaventura and Duns Scotus on the subject of the marriage of the Virgin, expresses himself as follows (lib. iv., d. 31):

Gravis guerra surgit inter Doctorem devotum et Doctorem subtilem, ex una, et Hugonem, ex altera, duo doctores contra unum baccalaureum.[2]

A copy of lib. ii., seen by Sbaralea "in Bibliotheca Sancti Francisci S.P.M.A." (*Sancti Petri in Monte Aureo*, S. Pietro in Montorio, at Rome, as Father L. Oliger has been kind enough to inform us), which seems to be lost, was dated "Explicit secundus liber scriptus a Gaufrido Durandi anno Domini MCCCXVII".

The commentary of Friar Hugh is found in MSS. Lat. 15864-15866 of the Bibliothèque Nationale. The first two of these were bequeathed to the Sorbonne by Master Hugues de Daours, Fellow of the Sorbonne, a native of Picardy. The incipits are: for lib. i. (the beginning of the prologue): "*Pulcritudinem candoris ejus admirabitur oculus.* Scribit beatus Gregorius" (Lat. 15864); for lib. ii.: "*Mirabilia opera tua* . . . Dicebatur in principio Sententiarum" (Lat. 15866:[3] the incipit is lacking in Lat. 15865); for lib. iii.: "*A Domino factum est istud* . . . Dicebatur in principio Sententiarum" (Lat. 15865); lib. iv. is wanting at Paris.[4]

[1] *Histoire littéraire de la France*, xxxvi. p. 312, note.

[2] This is the complete passage:

"*Si quis potest contrahere cum voto virginitatis* [*i.e.* without breaking the vow of virginity]". Dicit frater Hugo de Novo Castro q. 2ª presentis distinctionis quod sic, quod et probat tripliciter. Primo potest fieri, matrimonio contracto, ut per ingressum religionis; ergo in contrahendo, quia dissimilitudo non apparet. Secundo sic: votum honestum quod potest stare cum matrimonio potest fieri in contractu matrimonii: hujus modi est votum virginitatis; igitur . . . Tercio quia posset quis accipere uxorem sub tali pacto quod intraret religionem; ergo. Unde ex mera voluntate aut divina voluntate potest cum voto virginitatis fieri matrimonium. . . . Sed tunc gravis guerra surgit inter Doctorem Devotum et Doctorem Subtilem ex una, et Hugonem ex altera, duo doctores contra unum baccalaureum; sed ne sit guerra mortalis dicatur pro concordantia quod duo doctores sunt locuti de matrimonio ut de presenti contrahitur; et hoc modo si diceret quis: "Accipio te tamen ut me non cognoscas", negando copulam carnalem implicite et explicite, contra substantiam ageret matrimonii ut nunc currit; Hugo vero de potentia Dei intellexit".

[3] We read on fol. 80vo of this MS.: "Explicit secundus Sentenciarum secundum reportationem fratris Hugonis de Novocastro," and on fol. 82vo: "Expliciunt tituli questionum et articulorum contentorum in illis istius secundi reportati post finem Hugonis de Novocastro".

[4] Book IV. of Friar Hugh's work is quoted largely in the *In Sententias* of William de Vaurouillon; the following passage (*In Sent.* iv. 30) can furnish a convenient means of identification:

"Error dirimit, error non dirimit.—Frater Hugo de Novocastro dicit hujus distinctionis

We do not know of any other copy of Book I., which is thus very rare, except in the Library of Dantzig (No. 1969); but Book II. is found likewise at Dantzig (MS. cit.), and also, by itself, at Cambrai (No. 267, *saec.* xiv.), and at Tortosa (Chapter Library, No. 125). Books II. and III. are in the Laurentian Library at Florence, as Sbaralea has already noted (Bandini's Catalogue, vol. iv. Appendix, col. 729): Books III. and IV. are in MS. 1423 of the State's Library of Vienna;[1] lastly, Books II. to IV. are in the Antoniana at Padua (Josa, p. 154 *et seq.*), while Book IV. occurs, without the author's name, in the *Inventario* of the Library of Assisi which was drawn up in 1381 and has been edited by Leto Alessandri.[2] Further, Mgr. A. Pelzer informs us that, thanks to the description of the Vienna MS. by Denis, he has been able to identify an anonymous copy of Books III. and IV. in MS. Chigi B. iv. 96 of the Vatican.

This commentary, which is very long, very philosophical, and very subtle, enables us, naturally, to see in Friar Hugh a disciple of Duns Scotus, who is often quoted. But it would be interesting to study it (which has never been done) in order to recognise and characterise definitely the tendencies peculiar to a thinker who, as compared with those of his school, seems to have been notably original. A long-winded piece of work, which we could not undertake for this article, but which we commend to the curiosity of others. The *magnum opus* of Friar Hugh, which no one has read for centuries, had, for long, admirers. Like William de Vaurouillon, the anonymous author, who compiled in Germany, in the fifteenth century, a list of the principal doctors of the Franciscan Order, held him especially in high estimation:

> Doctor scolasticus Hugo de Novocastro pulcre manu ducit studentes ex philosophia naturali et metaphysica in augmentationem virtutis. Placuit autem mihi cum legissem de predestinatione et prescientia super I^{um} Sententiarum.[3]

We may add that the *Questiones super Sententias*, which bear the name of *Hugo* in MS. Lat. 3073 of the Bibliothèque Nationale and in MS. 178 at Bruges, have no relation to the work of Hugo *de Novocastro*.

---

questione prima: 'Error essentialis dirimit, error accidentalis non dirimit. Essentialia matrimonii sunt hec tria: posse, dare, consentire. Contra hec tria triplex error dirimit: si non habeo quam peto, si non potest se mihi dare cui me do, si non consentit in me in quam consentio, matrimonium non contraho. Accidentia sunt. . . .' "

[1] Described by M. Denis, *Codices MS. theologici Bibl. palat. Vindobonensis*, ii. 2, Vindobonae, 1800, col. 1171.

In this MS. the incipit of lib. iii. is: "Circa tertium primo queratur Utrum natura humana unita Verbo sit ypostatica sub propria ratione Verbi". That of lib. iv. is: "Circa principium quarti queritur primo Utrum in sacramentis Nove Legis sit aliqua virtus etiam influxiva ad causandum".

[2] *Inventario dell' antica biblioteca del S. Convento di S. Francesco in Assisi compilato nel 1381* (Assisi, 1906), p. 108; No. ccclxxiii., now No. 153 of the Biblioteca Communale.

[3] *Franziskanische Studien*, ii. (1915) p. 197.

There were, of course, many clerks, and even many Franciscans, named Hugh, who commented on the Sentences.

De Victoria Christi contra Antichristum.—This work of Friar Hugh was for long considered his principal title to fame. "Magister Ugo de Castronovo", says Bartholomew of Pisa, "qui luculenter scripsit in theologia et tractatum pulcherrimum edidit de Antichristo et de finali Judicio." There are a considerable number of manuscript copies,[1] and it was printed in 1471 in folio, without name of place or printer, with a fragment of Nicholas of Cues entitled *Conjectura de ultimis diebus mundi*.[2]

It was composed in 1319, for the author, trying to foretell the date of the end of the world in accordance with the calculations of Abbot Joachim, says (lib. ii. cap. 26): "Fluxerunt autem modo, scilicet hoc quo factus est ille libellus, a Nativitate Christi MCCC et decem et novem anni".

It contains two books, the first divided into 35, the second into 36, chapters.

It has nothing original, for the author warns us in his preface that, fearing to pass for a visionary or a false prophet, he has put nothing of his own into his treatise: he has simply reproduced the most authentic assertions and the most accredited conjectures.[3] Friar Hugh concludes with the final avowal that he knows neither the hour, nor the day, nor the month, nor the year, nor the century when the prophecies on the last times will begin to be fulfilled.

"Opuscule tout à fait insignifiant, c'est-à-dire digne du sujet, et plein de billevesées." Such is the judgement passed by our former colleague, Barthélemy Hauréau, in the manuscript notes which he has bequeathed to the "Commission de l'Histoire littéraire de la France". The judgements of Bartholomew of Pisa and of Barthélemy Hauréau are thus in sharp contradiction—a fact which will surprise no one.

Memorial on the Sale of Indulgences.—MS. Lat. 16089 of the Bibliothèque Nationale contains, after an acephalous and anonymous fragment on indulgences, a work on the sale of the same (Inc.: "Quia circa spiritualia majus vertitur periculum"). "Le nom de l'auteur était écrit à la marge supérieure, mais de la note mutilée par le ciseau du relieur il ne reste plus que '. . . *Castro Novo*,

[1] Bibl. Nat., Lat. 16393, fol. 134; Bibl. Palat. of Vienna, Nos. 3119, 3496, 4143; Munich, No. 18779; Erlangen, No. 314, fol. 104; Dantzig, No. 1955; Bishop Cosin's Library, Durham, No. V. ii. 5. 12. There was formerly a copy at Queen's College, Oxford: Bale's *Index Britanniae Scriptorum*, ed. Poole, Oxford, 1902, p. 172; and another in the library of the monastery of Murbach (Montfaucon).

[2] Hain, No. 8993. The Bibliothèque Nationale of Paris possesses two copies. It is from the explicit of this edition, and from that alone, that we know that Friar Hugh was not only doctor of theology, but licentiate in decrees.

[3] "Ne temerarie fingam me in hoc opusculo de temporibus novissimis Antichristi esse prophetam loquentem mendacium suisque somniis . . . adherentem, nihil in eo positurus sum quod intendo asserere nisi dicta Sacre Scripture. . . ."

Minor'." [1] Hauréau conjectured that "*Hugo de*" should be restored. This is very probable. We can for the rest only subscribe to what he adds:

Le ton de l'écrit fait juger qu'il est d'un homme considérable; pour parler de si haut aux évêques et aux officiaux, il faut avoir acquis le droit d'être écouté. . . . Les diverses pratiques des marchands d'indulgences n'ont peut-être pas été plus minutieusement exposées dans les pamphlets du XVIe siècle qu'ils le sont dans ce manifeste d'un religieux indigné [du XIVe]. C'est un document historique très instructif.

The vehement remonstrance of Friar Hugh was published *in extenso* by B. Hauréau in 1895. It can be read without difficulty. We will therefore content ourselves with pointing out that it is to be brought into connection with the great mass of English literature of the fourteenth century (of which the *Pardoner's Tale* of Chaucer is the masterpiece) against the questors, sellers of "pardons", and exhibitors of relics, who then infested the towns and still more the country districts.[2] Even in Paris, that "intellectual capital", one did not scruple, it appears, to cry in the streets that there were every day, during Lent, in various churches fifty years of indulgences to be obtained, by adding together in a wholly unauthorised manner fifty grants, each valid for one year only:

Fuit autem quandoque Parisius, occasione tali, per vicos publicos publice proclamatum quod in aliquibus ecclesiis erant in summa, singulis diebus Quadragesime, .L. anni indulgentie, nemine reclamante. Quod fuit omnino vilissimum sustinere, maxime Parisius, ubi debet fons sapientie et intellectus vigere.

The pardoners also interfere, under cover of apostolic authority, to wipe out usuries, rapines, and unjust acquisition of goods, and to authorise the redemption of vows. It is scandalous that educated men, prelates, perhaps *donis circumventi*, acquiesce in such abuses and support them by letters of authorisation.

The author, who speaks here as a canonist, is particularly *au courant* with what happens in the dioceses of Paris and Reims. Here are some very singular practices which he had occasion to observe:

De quibusdam etiam laïcis inhonestis qui, occasione quorumdam verborum que in suis litteris inseruntur ipsisque ab episcopis conceduntur, per que mandatur presbyteris videlicet quod tales in suis recipiant ecclesiis pro talibus negociis demonstrandis, ad predicandum publice in ecclesiis se ingerunt populumque communem et pauperes quorum est vivere de labore, diebus etiam non feriatis, suis omissis operibus et dietis, per dictas litteras compellentes ad ecclesias conveniri pro suis predicationibus audiendis, tot

[1] *Notices et extraits des manuscrits*, t. xxxv. i. p. 232.

[2] See Chaucer's poem and J. Jusserand, *La Vie nomade et les routes d'Angleterre au XIVe siècle* (Paris, 1884), or rather the revised English edition of this work, *English Wayfaring Life in the Middle Ages* (1892).

abusiones in sua predicacione proponunt eosque adeo labiis dolosis et lingua magniloqua verbisque procacibus et conjurationibus afficiunt . . . donec quasi per vim aliquid sibi detur . . . ; quandoque falsas reliquias deportantes, quas populo deosculandas exponunt, per quem modum quidam questores . . . pannos, vestes, pecuniam et alia fraudulenter a populo sic deluso per villas, maxime in provincia Remensi, frequenter recipere, imo verius subripere non verentur. . . .

The officials of Paris and of Reims, whom the wandering pardoners have sometimes the audacity to describe as *judices sibi dati* by apostolic authority throughout the Kingdom of France, certify and authenticate without question the so-called apostolic letters which any adventurers present to them. What does it matter to them whether they are genuine or forged, provided they get their chancery fees ?

The author concludes his treatise, which has all the appearances of a Memorandum or report, by indicating the remedies which seem to him appropriate.[1]

MSS. Lat. 16413 and 16414 of the Bibliothèque Nationale (formerly Sorbonne 1697 and 1698) of the fourteenth century contain in two volumes and twelve " books " a treatise *De laudibus Beate Virginis*, the author of which, who was on friendly terms with Cistercians, desired through humility to remain anonymous. He says in his preface :

Plures notulas pertinentes ad laudem Virginis quas multo tempore studiose coacervaveram diligenter ordinavi. . . . Et quia rogatus ab amicis meis tam monachis quam monialibus de Ordine Cisterciensium, qui speciali affectu famulari solent Virgini gloriose, non prout debui set prout potui prosecutus sum laudes ejus, ab ipso Ordine supplex exspostulo, set et omnibus quibus placuerit labor meus, ut a matre misericordie mihi miserrimo peccatori suis orationibus veniam postulent delictorum. Nomen vero meum malui subticere ne tractatus forte vilesceret cognito tractatore.

This work is found also in a very beautiful fourteenth-century manuscript of the Bibliothèque Nationale (MS. Lat. 3173), with a final chapter which is lacking in the Sorbonne version. On fol. 2 of MS. 3173 is the note in a fourteenth-century hand :

Hoc volumen est Conventus Fratrum Predicatorum Lugdunensium, quod fuit domini Hugonis, tituli S. Sabine presbyteri cardinalis, cui missum fuerat de Picardia ab auctore ejus, mediantibus aliquibus.

A fairly modern hand has written at the beginning of this volume the words " Hugo Minorita ", thus confusing apparently our Hugh with Hugh, cardinal of Saint Sabina ;[2] and it is doubtless owing to

[1] This memoir was not known to H. C. Lea, *A History of Confession and Indulgences* (Philadelphia, 1891, 3 vols. in 8vo) ; cf. N. Paulus, *Geschichte des Ablasses im Mittelalter . . . bis z. Mitte d. 14. Jahrhunderts*, vol. ii. (Paderborn, 1923).

[2] Friar Hugh de Saint-Cher (1245–1263) or Friar Hugh Séguin de Billom (†1297), both Dominicans.

this that the gilder received instructions to inscribe the name "Hugo de Novocastro" on the back of the Sorbonne copy. But this same treatise is attributed in the MS. Lat. 14561 (formerly Saint-Victor, 252) and by the binder of MS. 828 of Troyes to Jacques de Voragine. Many other copies are anonymous.[1]

The attribution to Hugh of Newcastle is clearly worthless. But it seems, however, that Friar Hugh wrote *Collationes*, of which one at least related to the Immaculate Conception, as Sbaralea states on the authority of ancient and probably well-informed writers (Daniel Agricola, Peter d'Alva, Juan de San Antonio). Again there is a *Mariale*, which is a series of sermons (and which has no connection with the *De laudibus* mentioned above), in MS. Lat. 3487A of the Bibliothèque Nationale, with the inscription "Magister Hugo". One is tempted—rightly or wrongly—to bring these data into connection with each other.

CH. V. LANGLOIS.

[1] Troyes, No. 1743; Bibl. Nat. 16498 (formerly Sorbonne, 1704), fol. 46, etc.

XXI

SOME NOTES ON BARBOUR'S *BRUCE*

Books xiv.-xvi. and xviii.

Barbour's account of Edward Bruce's campaigns in Ireland (1315–18) is one of surpassing interest for students of Irish history. Composed in 1375 and while old men could still remember the events it records, it has the value of an almost contemporary document and is, as I hope to show, despite its defects, the most reliable besides being the most picturesque account we possess of that remarkable episode. Two copies of the poem are extant, the one, MS. G. 23, in the Library of St. John's College, Cambridge, the other in the Advocates' Library, Edinburgh, both written, it would seem, by John Ramsay, the former in 1487, the latter in 1489. It was first printed apparently in 1571 at Edinburgh. Originally it formed an unbroken narrative, extending to more than 13,550 lines in MS. E., and was first divided by J. Pinkerton in his edition (London, 1790, 3 vols.) into twenty books. The best edition is that of W. W. Skeat, printed for the Scottish Text Society in 2 vols., Edinburgh, 1894. While agreeing with the general criticism of the poem offered by Skeat, I think the important thing to remember about it is that *The Bruce* is an historical romance written by a Scotsman in praise of Scotsmen. As such they are all heroes, almost always victorious even where the odds are greatly against them; seldom, if ever, do they run away from their enemies and, if they do, some excuse is generally to be found for them or the incident is omitted altogether. History is not written in this way; but historical romance is. The following notes are an attempt to place Barbour's account of Edward Bruce's campaigns in Ireland in its right historical light.

A restless disposition and personal ambition were, according to Barbour, the motives that led Edward Bruce to attempt the conquest of Ireland. To this end we are informed that he opened up negotiations with the Irish and found them willing to transfer their allegiance to him on condition that he expelled the English. In both these particulars I think Barbour is perfectly right. Of course it is quite possible that in consenting to his brother's plan Robert Bruce may have been animated by a desire to retaliate on England Edward I.'s invasion of

Scotland; but there is no reason, so far as I can discover, to believe that overtures in this direction were first made by the Irish. Having with Robert's consent and support " gaderit him men of gret bounte ", Edward took shipping at Ayr in May 1315 and landed safely with barely 6000 men in Vaveryng or Wokingis fyrth, now known as Larne Lough. Hearing of their arrival, " the lords of that cuntre "—the Mandevilles, Bissetts, Logans, and Savages—hastily collected what men they could, but hardly, I suspect, 20,000 as Barbour asserts, and prepared to withstand the invaders. Bruce, who was advancing in two divisions on Carrickfergus, learning that they were approaching, at once offered battle and, after a sharply contested field, succeeded in slaying or putting to flight " all hale the flowr of Wllister ". That, according to Barbour, was a good beginning " for newlyngis at thair ariwyng ". As a matter of fact the Scots were seasoned men and the wonder is that, taken as they were by surprise, " the lords of that cuntre " were able to put up as good a fight as they did. Pushing forward after his victory, Bruce had little difficulty in taking possession of the town of Carrickfergus; but the castle, whether it was, as Barbour says, " weel stuffit then of-new with wittel and vith men ", or not, defied his efforts to capture it, and not being prepared to lay proper siege to it, he determined " till ride forthirmar in the land ". Of a truce at this time there can be no question; but one result of Bruce's victory was that a number, " weill ten or twelf, as I herd say ", of the local chieftains submitted to him. Of these two, however, Mackfulchiane and Makartane, doubtless, as Mr. Orpen says,[1] to be identified with Mac Duilechain of Clanbrassil and Mac Artain of Iveagh, breaking their pledge,

> With-set ane place [E. a pase] in-till his way,
> Quhar him behufit neyd avay,
> With twa thousand of men with speris,
> And als mony of their archeris;
> . . . .
> Men callis that place Endwillane [E. Innermallane].

Endwillane or, better, Innermallane (?Inuermullane) appears hitherto to have escaped identification, but it clearly represents Inbhermuilean, subsequently Ballymullin and now Milltown, between Lough Erne and Lough Agher in Co. Down. The pass of Invermullane through the forest of Killultagh bore an evil reputation right down to Mary's reign, and in order to avoid it, when journeying from Newry to Carrickfergus in 1556, Sussex took another but hardly less dangerous way through the wood from Banbridge to Lisburn *via* Dromore. Apparently Bruce, relying on the adhesion of Mac Artain, preferred the more direct route; but, apart from Invermullane, the mention of Mac Artain and

[1] *Ireland under the Normans*, iv. p. 163.

Mac Duilechain proves that Bruce did not, as Mr. Orpen conjectures, proceed by way of the Six Miles Water. Having repelled the attack and refreshed his army with the cattle he had captured, Bruce pushed rapidly forward, and crossing the Bann, probably at Scarva, pursued his march to Kilnasaggart on the borders of Co. Louth. Here news reached him

> That at Dundawk wes ane assemble
> Maid of the lordis of that cuntre ;

whereupon

> His host in hy he gert aray,
> And thiddirwardis he tuk the way ;
> And neir the toune he tuk herbery.
> Bot for he wist all wtirly
> That in the toune wes mony men,
> His battalis he arrayit then,
> And stude arayit in battale
> To kep thame, gif thai vald assale.

The townsmen and " lordis of that cuntre " send out spies, and finding that the Scots were fewer than expected—not more than " half-deill ane dyner till vs here "—they advance next morning confidently to meet them. After a battle that lasted from sunrise to noon they are compelled to retreat, and the Scots entering the town together with them continue the fight till the streets run red with blood

> Of slayne men that war liand thar.
> The lordis war gottin all avay.

So the story, omitting all reference to Richard de Clare (by whom Barbour means Richard de Burgh) and the English army, who were nowhere near at the time, ought, I think, to run. With the capture of Dundalk the first part of the narrative ends ; but historians and commentators, failing to note the hiatus and overlooking Barbour's express statement that the Scots

> Syne tuk thai southwardis thar way,

make Bruce turn northwards to Kilros, or the forest of Ros, which, according to Mr. Orpen, " was presumably in the territory of Ros, somewhere in the barony of Farney, Co. Monaghan ".[1] That Bruce, after advancing as far as Ardee, where he learned that the Deputy, Sir Edmond Butler, and Richard de Burgh, having joined forces, were advancing against him with a large army, did actually retreat northward is perfectly certain ; but there is nothing in the poem to show that he took the direction indicated by Mr. Orpen. The fact is the Kilross mentioned by Barbour is not Kilros in Co. Monaghan, but Kilrush on the Barrow, near Athy in Co. Kildare, and the whole episode

[1] *Ireland under the Normans*, iv. p. 166.

(ll. 239-370), including the mysterious mention at this time of O'Dempsey, belongs to a later part of Bruce's campaign. Dundalk afforded Barbour his cue. He was anxious apparently to avoid reference to his hero's retreat, but not at the expense of omitting an account of his subsequent great victory over Richard de Burgh. Accordingly the next we hear of the Scots is that they were hemmed in between the sea and the river Bann :

The Bane, that is ane arme of the se,
That with horss may nocht passit be,
Was betuixt thame and Wllister.

How the Scots came into this perilous position there is nothing in the poem to show. But the fact that the Bann lay between them and Ulster, by which Barbour always means that part of Ulster lying to the east of the Bann and now comprising the counties Antrim and Down, clearly demonstrates that Bruce's line of retreat lay to the west of Lough Neagh. Further, as the river was not, at the point they had reached, fordable by horses, it is evident, as Mr. Orpen observes, that " they must have been below *Es Craibhe* or the cutts of Coleraine ". This is a matter, as we shall see, of great importance in determining the site of the battle of " Coigneris ". For, as we know from a description of the river by the Earl of Essex in 1574, the Bann was passable at Toome Bridge and at two fords—the one at Inishrush, the other a few miles above Ballymoney. Mr. Orpen speaks [1] of the Scots having broken down the bridge at Coleraine in order to check the approach of the Earl of Ulster. But quite apart from the fact that it is very doubtful if there was a bridge at Coleraine at this time, I cannot conceive what object the Scots could have in breaking it down and thus cutting themselves off from their base at Carrickfergus. Personally I believe the broken bridge was that of Toome. Probably it was, as the Annals of Loch Cé assert, broken down by the Scots themselves in order to prevent an attack on the part of the Earl of Ulster, who, having taken the route to the east of Lough Neagh, was advancing on them from the other side of the Bann. But this was before they recognised the real danger of their position. That position, as Barbour remarks, was one of great peril, and had it not been for the opportune appearance of that " scummar of the sea ", Thomas of Dwn, " with four shippes that he had tane ", it might have proved the end of Bruce's expedition. As it was, with Thomas of Dwn's assistance, Bruce succeeded in safely transporting his army, unobserved by the Earl of Ulster, across the Bann.

And quhen thai come in biggit land,
Wittale and mete yneuch thai fand ;

[1] *Ireland under the Normans*, iv. pp. 165, 168.

And in a wode thame herbryit thai.
Nane of the land wist quahar thai lay;
Thai esyt thame, and maid gud cher,
In-till that tyme, besyde thame ner,
With a gret host, Richard of Clar,
And othir gret of Irlande, war
Herbryit in-till a forest syde.
And ilke day thai gert men ryde
To bring wittalis, on ser maneris,
Till thame fra the toune of Coigneris
That weill ten gret myle wes them fra.

In these lines we have the situation of the two armies before the battle of "Coigneris" distinctly and, in my opinion, correctly described. The question is, where was "Coigneris"? Mr. Orpen, following the commentators, identifies the place with Connor. But this I hold to be quite impossible. For, if it were Connor, which lies as the crow flies at least thirty miles distant from Coleraine, it is hardly possible that Bruce could, as Barbour states, have made his way thither undetected by the natives. A glance at the map will make this perfectly clear. Mr. Orpen's view is that, after and in consequence of the defection of Felim O'Conor, the Earl of Ulster, feeling himself too weak to encounter Bruce alone, retired, about the time the latter succeeded in crossing the Bann, on his base (?) at Connor.[1] If he did so, then it must be admitted that he was a bad strategist. But there is no reason to suppose that the Earl did retreat. He had accomplished his purpose of hemming in the Scots behind the Bann, or rather the Scots had done the trick for him themselves, and all he had, as he thought, to do was to guard the fords and keep them where they were in order to accomplish their destruction. Unfortunately for him, Bruce, with the timely assistance of Thomas of Dwn, succeeded in circumventing his plan; but it should be noted that instead of retreating he no sooner obtained wind of Bruce's whereabouts than he advanced to meet him. As a matter of fact we have good reason to believe that when Bruce effected his passage of the Bann the Earl, with the bulk of his army, was lying at Lough Quile, where, as we learn from Athlone's account of Sussex's journey in 1556, he had built himself a castle. Ten miles or thereabouts north-west of Lough Quile, on the direct road from Coleraine to Carrickfergus, lay the little town or village of Conagher, and it was at Conagher and not at Connor, in my opinion, that the battle which followed took place. At any rate Conagher and not Connor answers the requirements of all the facts as they are known to us. The battle (10 Sept.) ended with the complete defeat of the English, and Bruce, having refreshed his army with the provisions he found in Conagher, proceeded unmolested to Carrickfergus. Arrived

[1] *Ireland under the Normans*, iv. p. 170.

there, he sent the Earl of Murray to Scotland to gather fresh recruits and, pending his return, resumed the siege of the Castle, but failing to capture it, the next we hear of him is being once more at Dundalk. Reverting to Bk. xiv. l. 241 we read that the Scots

Syne tuk thai southwardis thar way.
The erle Thomas was forrouth ay,
And as thai raid throu the cuntre
Thai mycht apon the hillis se
Sa mony men, it was ferly.
And quhen the erll wald sturdely
Dress him to thame with his baner,
Thai wald fle, all that euir thai wer,
Swa that in ficht nocht ane abaid.
And thai southwardis thair wais raid,
Quhill till a gret forest come thai ;
Kilross it hat, as I herd say ;
And thai tuk all thair herbry thair.

From the above account of Bruce's march it is apparent that the Scots proceeded on their marauding expedition through the midlands practically unopposed and that the encounter (if it ever occurred) with Mortimer at Kells, described by Mr. Orpen,[1] was too insignificant to call for even a passing notice from Barbour. All the same, Mr. Orpen is wrong in stating [2] that " Barbour in fact omits all mention of Bruce's campaign in the winter of 1315–16 ". As I have said, Kilross is to be identified with Kilrush near Athy, where long afterwards the Earl of Ormond was to inflict a crushing defeat on the Confederates. At Kilrush news reached Bruce that the " kyngis luftenand ", Sir Edmond Butler, whom Barbour mistakenly, here as elsewhere, calls Richard of Clare, having collected a large army " v battalis, gret and braid ", was in his near neighbourhood. Recognising the danger of the situation, Bruce addressed a stirring appeal to his men. The English were in great force ; but the greater the odds the greater the fame

Qif that we beir us manfully.
We are set heir in iuperdy,
Till vyn honour, or for till de ;
We ar fra hame to fer to fle ;
Tharfor let ilk man worthy be.

The Scots were on foot : the English on horseback, " sum helyt all in irne and steill ".

Bot Scottis men, at thair metyng,
With speris perssit thar armyng,
And stekit horss and men doune bar.
Ane felloune fechting wes than thair ;

[1] *Ireland under the Normans*, iv. p. 173.
[2] *Ibid.* p. 178.

I can nocht tell thair strakis all,
Na quha in ficht gert othir fall;
Bot in schort tyme, I vndirta,
Thai of Irland war cummyrrit swa
That thai durst nane abyde no mar,
Bot fled scalit, all that thai war,
And levit in the battell-stede
Weill mony of thar gude men ded.

. . . . .

Bot schir Eduard leit no man chass;
Bot with presoners that thai had tane
Thai till the wod agane ar gane,
Quhar that thair harness levit wer.

Quite so! The fight was a fiasco. Owing, as we know, to quarrels amongst the English commanders, the Scots were left in possession of the field; but Bruce was in no position to improve his victory. The English army was still intact, and he and his men were greatly distressed for lack of provisions, due to the bad harvest and his own improvident plundering of the country. At this critical moment O'Dempsey appeared on the scene, and under pretext of leading them where they could find food, inveigled the Scots across the Barrow into a dangerous position in his own country, from which they only managed to escape at the hazard of their lives. It would require more local knowledge than I possess to explain O'Dempsey's all-but-successful stratagem for the destruction of the Scottish army. But there can be no question of Barbour's inventing the episode. The idea of plugging up a lake and then, when he had got the Scots in position, withdrawing the stopper, is too extraordinary to be readily imagined by any one unacquainted with that boggy country and the ease with which a mountain tarn could be made to serve O'Dempsey's purpose. To me the chief point of interest is that O'Dempsey, the only Irishman here mentioned by name by Barbour, was, like Mac Artain and Mac Duilechain, loyal to the English.

Returning to Carrickfergus at the head of an army greatly reduced by famine and sickness, Bruce, while sending Murray for fresh recruits to Scotland, resumed his attempt to get possession of the castle. Apparently a truce had been arranged between besieged and besiegers for Holy Week 1316,

Bot apon Paske evin all richt
To the castell, in-till the nycht,
Fra Devilling come schippis xv,
Chargit with armyt men bedeyne;
Four thousand, trow I weill, thai war:
In the castell thai enterit thair.

Next morning, being Easter-day, Sir Thomas Mandeville, thinking to catch the Scots off their guard, made a sortie in force. But the Scots, though taken unawares and nearly overpowered, rallied their forces, and with Bruce at their head repelled the attack. Sir Thomas Mandeville was slain by Bruce himself, and in consequence of the drawbridge being raised all his men were killed. According to Barbour the castle surrendered shortly afterwards; but as a matter of fact the garrison, though reduced to the utmost extremities, held out several months longer. Meanwhile Bruce seems to have gone through the ceremony of having himself crowned King of Ireland on a hill near Dundalk on 1 May. Barbour furnishes no particulars, and his casual reference to

Schir Eduard, that was comonly
Callit the Kyng of Irland,

seems to show that he did not attach much importance to the event. Carrickfergus capitulated in September, and towards the end of December Robert Bruce arrived from Loch Ryan with a fresh army. After spending a short time at Carrickfergus the two brothers advanced southwards, and pursuing their way through the pass of Invermullane, they had apparently reached the neighbourhood of Ardee early in February, not May, as Barbour says, 1317, when Richard de Burgh, hearing of their progress, advanced against them at the head, according to Barbour, who is our sole authority for what follows, of 40,000 men. The Scots were marching in two divisions considerably apart from each other, the van being led by Edward, the rear by Robert Bruce. Allowing the van to pass the wood where he had ambushed his army, De Burgh fell on the rear with all his force.

Thair mycht men cruell bargane se,
And hard battal, I vndirstand.
In-till all the weir of Ireland
So hard ane fechting was nocht seyne.

Though only one to eight the Scots after a fierce tussle succeeded in utterly discomfiting their assailants. Whereupon Barbour triumphantly adds

Richard of Clare the vay has tane
To Devillyng, in full gret hy,
With othir lordis that fled him by,
And varnyst bath castels and townys
That war in thair possessiownis.
Thai war so felly fleyit thar,
That, as I trow, Richard of Clar
Sall haf no will to faynd his mycht
In battell na in forss of ficht,
Quhill King Robert and his menȝhe
Is duelland in-to that cuntre!

We know, what Barbour did not, that the Earl of Ulster on arriving in Dublin was imprisoned by the indignant citizens in the belief apparently that he was acting in collusion with Bruce. Whether they were justified in their belief is, as Mr. Orpen observes, difficult to decide. Owing to the fact that his cousin William Liath had been captured at the battle of Conagher and taken to Scotland, Ulster, in order to obtain his release, had agreed to surrender Carrickfergus. His consent may have been given in the belief that the castle could not in any case long hold out, but his diversion of some ships with provisions, sent from Dublin to the relief of the garrison, aroused the suspicions of the citizens, while the fact that his daughter was Robert Bruce's wife placed him, as commander of the English forces, in an invidious position. When Edward heard of his brother's successful encounter with the Earl he was, we are told by Barbour, extremely annoyed at the mischance that had deprived him taking part in the battle, but all the satisfaction he obtained was a sharp reprimand for his reckless conduct in losing touch with the rear.

> But the gude king said till hym than
> That it wes in his awn foly,
> For he raid sa vnvittandly,
> So fer befor, and no avaward
> Maid to thame of the reirward.
> For he said, " quha on were vald ryde
> In the vaward, he suld na tyde
> Press fra his rerward fer of sicht ;
> For gret perell so fall thar mycht."

After that the army held better together, and, passing Drogheda and Dublin without attempting to take either place, the Bruces pursued their march southwards as far as Limerick,

> Bot to gif batell nane thai fand.

At Limerick, which Barbour mistakenly asserts to be

> the southmast toune, perfay,
> That in Irland may fundyn be,

they rested two or three days

> And buskit syne agane to fare.

Here again Barbour in his *rôle* of panegyrist glosses over certain facts, which had he mentioned them, and particularly that Bruce's sudden move northwards was actually a retreat before the English forces concentrating at Ludenbeg, would not greatly have redounded to his hero's reputation. As for his statement that on their return journey the Bruces

> Throu all Irland then passit thai
> Throu Conage richt to Dewilling,

And throu al Myth and Irell syne,
And Mwnser and throu Lainenser,
And syne haly throu Vllister
To Cragfergus,

it can only be described as an exaggeration bordering on falsehood. Possibly while in the neighbourhood of Limerick or Castleconnell Bruce may have crossed the Shannon, but this was all he ever saw of Connaught. As for traversing the length and breadth of Ireland he never did any such thing, and for a very good reason. The fact is that the expedition which was intended to rally the Irish everywhere to his brother's standard proved a complete failure. Except for a few malcontents the Irish held entirely aloof from him, inwardly cursing the day he had ever come amongst them. Never in all their experience had there been such a plundering and wasting of the country as marked the route of the Scots and their Ulster allies. But if the English and Irish suffered, so likewise did the Scots. Food everywhere, owing to two successive bad harvests, was at famine prices, and it was with an army sadly diminished in numbers and efficiency that Robert Bruce reached his base at Carrickfergus, whence he shortly afterwards returned with the Earl of Murray, to Scotland. Of all this there is nothing to read in Barbour. On the contrary, if we are to believe him, it wanted only a little patience and self-control on the part of Edward Bruce to put him in complete possession of Ireland.

He was weill set now in gud way
To conquest the land all halely ;
For he had apon his party
The Eryschry and Vllister,
And he was swa furth of his wer
That he wes passit throu all Irland
Fra end till end throu strynth of hand.
Couth he haf gouernit hym throu skill,
And fallowit nocht to fast his will,
Bot with mesour haf led his deid,
That he myght haff conquerit weill
The land of Irland euirilk deill.

We may safely concede Barbour's contention that Edward's own character had a good deal to do with his failure to conquer Ireland ; but it is absurd to suppose that because he had made himself master of a corner of Ulster and had raided the country as far south as Limerick, he was any nearer accomplishing his purpose than he was on the day of his arrival. Actually there had been very little fighting. Edward himself had won a brilliant victory at Conagher and his brother had been equally successful against De Burgh near Drogheda ; but twenty such victories, even with the Irish on their side, would not have put the Scots in possession of Ireland so long as the English retained their hold on Dublin and the other seaport towns. After two years' incessant warfare all that Bruce had actually effected was the capture of Carrickfergus. During this time he had worn out two armies, and Scotland, with the war with England still raging, was too thinly inhabited to supply the necessary man power to maintain his army in efficient condition. To meet his losses he had only the Irish to fall back upon; but hitherto the Irish had displayed little enthusiasm to do more than assist in pillaging the country.

Nearly eighteen months elapsed after the return of the Scottish army to Carrickfergus, and during this time lack of provisions reduced it to inactivity. But the harvest of 1318 was both early and plentiful, and in October Edward Bruce, without waiting for those recruits, we gather from Barbour, his brother Robert was sending him, once more marched southwards at the head of two thousand Scots and a rabble of Irish.

> Bot he, that rest anoyit ay,
> And wald in travaill be all-way,
> A day forrouth thair arivyng
> That war send till hym fra the king,
> He tuk his way, furthwarde to fare
> Magre them all that with hym war.
> For he had nocht than in that land
> Of all men, I trow, twa thousand,
> Outane the kyngis off Erischry,
> That in gret rowtis raid hym by.

Arrived in the neighbourhood of Dundalk and hearing that Richard of Clare, *recte* John de Bermingham, was advancing northwards at the head, according to Barbour, of 20,000 "trappit horse", besides as many foot soldiers, Edward called a council of war. For himself he was determined to fight "thouch tryplit or quadruplit war thai", and waiving aside the advice of Sir John Stewart, De Soulis, and Sir Philip Mowbray to await the arrival of the reinforcements, reported to be on the way under Sir Walter Stewart, as a reflection on the honour of their noble name, he forced a reluctant consent from them to do as he wished. And now we are told his Irish allies when they heard of his determination to risk a battle, strongly remonstrated with him:

> And quhen thai saw he was so thra
> To fecht, thai said, "ʒe may weill ga
> To ficht with ʒon gret cumpany;
> Bot we acquyt vs vtirly,
> That nane of vs will stand to ficht;
>
> . . . . .
>
> For our maner is, of this land
> To follow and ficht, and ficht fleand,
> And nocht till stand in plane melle
> Quhill the ta part discumfit be."

Commenting on their attitude and their reasons for not taking part in the battle, Mr. Orpen asks : " How are we to account for this alleged withdrawal of the Irish forces from this crucial engagement ? It cannot have been due to cowardice. The Irish were born fighters. It is true that they often adopted Fabian tactics against the English, but it is not the fact that they never stood in plain mêlée until one side was discomfited. Only two years had elapsed since the carnage of Athenry. They may well, however, have agreed with the Scottish knights in thinking that the occasion was not a favourable one for a regular pitched battle, but we cannot rely implicitly on Barbour's account of their conduct ".[1] While admitting all that Mr. Orpen says regarding the bravery and fighting qualities of the Irish I think he misses Barbour's point, viz. that it was the habit of the Irish not to take part in a battle *between two other combatants* " until the one side was discomfited ". This was precisely the waiting attitude of Baldearg O'Donnell at a later time. The battle of Athenry, where Irish were ranged against English, is not a case in point. At Faughart we have Scots ranged against English. The Irish had promised Edward their allegiance *provided* he expelled the English. He was determined, despite their remonstrances, to risk a battle in what they regarded as doubtful circumstances. It was, in their opinion, a foolhardy decision and one for which they were not inclined to risk their lives, but yielding to Edward's request they promised, *contrary* to their usual practice, to abstain from fighting at all and to retain their position till the issue of the battle was decided.

He said, " sen that ȝour custum is,
I ask no mair at ȝow bot this,
That is, that ȝhe and your menȝhe
Wald all to-giddir arrayit be,
And stand on fer, but departing,
And se our ficht and our endyng."

What Edward hoped by their agreeing to do so was that the English, seeing the Irish posted in battle array, would be misled as to their real attitude, and this we know from the *Cath Fhochairte* was precisely what happened. The battle that followed was soon over. The Scots, as Barbour says,

war sa few, forsuth to say,
That ruschit with fais var thai ;
And thai that pressit mast to stand
War slane doune, and the remand
Fled till Erischry for succour.

Apparently many of the Scots managed to escape.

[1] *Ireland under the Normans*, iv. pp. 201-2.

Thai wencust war sa suddanly,
That few in-till the place was slayne.

But Edward and his companions fell on the field of battle. " On this wise ", moralises Barbour,

war thai nobill men
Through wilfulness all losit then ;
And that was syn and gret pite.

As for those recruits sent him by his brother Robert and for whose coming Edward would not wait,

Quhen thai herd the discumfiting,
Till Cragfergus thai went agane ;
And that was nocht forouten pane.
For thai war mony tymes that day
Assalit with Erischry, bot thai
Ay held to-gidder sarraly,
Defendand thame so wittely
That thai eschapit oft throu mycht,
And mony tymes alss throu slicht ;
For oft of thairis till thame gaf thai
Till let thame scathless pass thar vay :
And to Cragfergus com thai swa.
Than batis and schippes can thai ta,
And salit till Scotland in hy,
And thar arivit all saufly.

Such, then, was the end of Edward Bruce's attempt to wrest Ireland from England. As I have said, Barbour's account gives us the fullest and most vivid picture of that event. His narrative is disjointed, its statements often disingenuous, its exaggerations manifold ; but on the whole the facts, so far as he knew them, were as he states them to be. True, there were many things of which he was ignorant. He knew nothing of what was passing on the English side, and is even in error as to who it was that commanded the English forces in the engagements he describes. He says nothing of the general attitude of the Irish towards Bruce, nothing as to the conduct of the De Lacies, nothing on many other points upon which we desire information. His sole concern is to describe the heroic deeds of his countrymen. As to their misdeeds he is altogether silent. He has no eye for the mischief they did and the bad effect their senseless plundering had on the Irish. His poem is a romance, but reading it we obtain a clearer view of the progress of events than either the English or Irish annalists afford us. With their assistance we can control his statements and add to our knowledge, but without his guidance we should miss the main thread of the narrative.

Since these notes were written I have had the pleasure of reading Miss Olive Armstrong's *Edward Bruce's Invasion of Ireland*. According to Miss Armstrong, Bruce's invasion "was the separating line between the highest good of English rule and 'the beginning of all evil'". Personally I think the seeds of evil were inherent in the system she praises; but with this part of her thesis I am not here concerned. Her narrative of the invasion itself shows careful study of the authorities, and especially of Pembridge and Clyn; but in my opinion she has followed Mr. Orpen in all his mistakes, and where she differs from him she has gone wrong herself. To say more on this subject would be merely to repeat what I have written; but the lively interest in the invasion to which her book testifies seems to justify a more critical study of Barbour than has hitherto been attempted.

ROBERT DUNLOP.

XXII

EXCHEQUER MIGRATIONS TO YORK IN THE THIRTEENTH AND FOURTEENTH CENTURIES

THE supreme financial department of the crown was the first public office to break away from the rambling royal household to live apart in quarters of its own. The process of separation was complete by the end of the twelfth century, and the place chosen for final settlement was Westminster, whence in future the exchequer seldom moved. That it did sometimes leave its home for awhile, was due to kingly caprice or military convenience.[1]

To conduct important and costly military campaigns, the king needed plenty of ready money. Yet communication was slow, uncertain and expensive, and a commander-in-chief could not afford long to wait upon the vagaries of road transport and the whims of winds and waves. It was advisable, therefore, to have a general administrative headquarters as near to the fighting area as was prudently possible. For that purpose York was most suitable when the king was at war with Scotland. Because the king was often fighting the Scots at the end of the thirteenth century and in the first half of the fourteenth century, the administration then travelled much between Westminster and York.

The exchequer went to York six times. The first visit, of six and a half years, took place from the end of May 1298 to the Christmas vacation 1304–5 (26-33 Edward I.)[2]; the second, of five months, from September 1319 to February 1320 (13 Edward II.)[3]; the third, of a

[1] Hall, H., *Antiquities and Curiosities of the Exchequer*; *Red Book of the Exchequer*, i. xvij. Hughes, A., Crump, C. G., and Johnson, C., *De Necessariis Observantiis Scaccarii Dialogus*. Madox, T., *History of the Exchequer*. Poole, R. L., *The Exchequer in the Twelfth Century*. Tout, T. F., *The Place of the Reign of Edward II. in English History*, pp. 43-57; *Chapters in the Administrative History of Mediaeval England*, i. pp. 12-14, 93-99, 178; *The Beginnings of a Modern Capital: London and Westminster in the Fourteenth Century*, pp. 7-8, 10-11.

[2] Order to go issued in April 1298, to open session at York 2 June 1298. *Flores Historiarum*, iii. 104; *Rotuli Parliamentorum*, i. 143; Vetus Codex, p. 94 (printed in Ryley, W., *Placita Parliamentaria*, p. 225: see Madox, *loc. cit.* ii. p. 9). Order for return issued 27 September 1304, to open session at Westminster 14 January 1305. *Calendar of Close Rolls, 1302–7*, p. 220; Memoranda Rolls, Lord Treasurer's Remembrancer, 75, m. 9d; London annals in *Chronicles of Edward I. and Edward II.*, W. Stubbs, i. p. 134.

[3] Order to go issued 28 May 1319, to open session at York 30 September 1319. *Cal. C.R. 1318–23*, p. 76; Mem. Rolls, King's Remembrancer, 92, *Breuia directa Baronibus*, Trinity term; L.T.R. 89, m. 104d; Ryley, *loc. cit.* pp. 564-5; Madox, *loc. cit.*

year and three months, from April 1322 to July 1323 (15-17 Edward II.)[1]; the fourth, of two months, from October to December 1327 (1 Edward III.)[2]; the fifth, of five years and four months, from May 1333 to September 1338 (7-12 Edward III.)[3]; the sixth, of six months, from June to December 1392 (16 Richard II.).[4] All except the last were for reasons of war.

The sixth removal was a result of friction between the crown and the city of London.[5] In May 1392 the mayor, sheriffs, aldermen and twenty-four of the worthier citizens of London, were bidden to go before the king and his council at Nottingham on 25 June 1392, with plenary power to answer the charges to be made against the city, and to do what the king and council should order. Early in June, the king

---

ii. pp. 9-10; *Chron. Edward I. and Edward II.* i. p. 286, *Ann. Paul.* Order for return issued 22 January 1320, to open session at Westminster 7 April 1320. The return was made at the end of February. *Cal. C.R. 1318–23*, p. 175; *Parl. Writs*, ii. (i.) p. 239, (ii.) p. 144; Mem. Rolls, K.R. 93, L.T.R. 90, *Breuia directa Baronibus*, and *Breuia retornabilia*, Hilary term; *Chron. Edward I. and Edward II.* i. p. 288. Earlier in the reign the king, by letter of privy seal issued at Linlithgow, 28 October 1310, had ordered the exchequer and both benches to remove to York, to open session there 19 April 1311, because he was staying in Scotland. That this mandate was not obeyed is a striking illustration of Edward II.'s powerlessness then. Mem. Rolls, K.R. 84, L.T.R. 81, *Breuia directa Baronibus*, Michaelmas term.

[1] Order to go issued 11 February 1322, to open session at York 19 April 1322. *Cal. C.R. 1318–23*, p. 417; Mem. Rolls, K.R. 95, mms. 19, 69d, 124; L.T.R. 92, mms. 17, 50. *Chron. Edward I. and Edward II.* i. p. 303, *Ann. Paul.* Order for return issued 10 June 1323, to open session at Westminster 30 September 1323. Actually the exchequer was back in Westminster by the end of July. *Cal. C.R. 1318–23*, pp. 657, 665; Mem. Rolls, K.R. 96, *Breuia directa Baronibus*, and *Breuia irretornabilia*, Trinity term; Issue Rolls, E 403/202. *Chron. Edward I. and Edward II.* i. p. 305, *Ann. Paul.*; Madox, *loc. cit.* ii. p. 10.

[2] Order to go issued 18 August 1327, to open session at York 30 September 1327. *Cal. C.R. 1327–30*, pp. 160-2; Mem. Rolls, K.R. 103, m. 103d. The exchequer did not leave Westminster until 7 October 1327. Issue Rolls, E 403/231. Order for return issued 20 October 1327, to open session at Westminster 14 January 1328. The exchequer left York on 5 December 1327. *Cal. C.R. 1327–30*, pp. 324-5; Mem. Rolls, K.R. 105, mms. 6, 24, 224.

[3] Order to go issued 20 February 1333, to open session at York 31 May 1333. *Cal. C.R. 1333–7*, pp. 18-19; Mem. Rolls, K.R. 109, m. 55. Order for return issued 10 September 1338, to open session at Westminster 30 September 1338. *Cal. C.R. 1337–9*, p. 533; Issue Rolls, E 403/303; Exch. Accts. E 101/333/13, this is the original letter received by the exchequer, but it does not seem to have been enrolled there.

[4] Order to go issued 30 May 1392, to open session at York 25 June 1392. *Cal. C.R. 1389–92*, pp. 466-7; Mem. Rolls, K.R. 168, *Breuia directa Baronibus*, Trinity term. Order for return issued 25 October 1392, to open session at Westminster 14 January 1393. Mem. Rolls, K.R. 169, *Breuia directa Baronibus*, Michaelmas term. Issue Rolls, E 403/543.

[5] *Cal. C.R. 1389–92*, p. 466. *Cal. Patent R. 1391–6*, pp. 100, 125, 130, 166, 171, 226. *Cal. of Letter Books of the City of London; Letter Book H, Richard II.* pp. 377-8. Fine Rolls, 196, m. 33. Issue Rolls, E 403/538, contains an entry of £10 paid to the chief justice of the common bench, of £3 : 6 : 8d. paid to the king's attorney in the common bench, of £3 : 6 : 8d. paid to the king's attorney in the king's bench, and of £3 : 6 : 8d. paid to one clerk, for their expenses in connection with the hearing of the case. The trouble with London, and the migration of the king's courts to York, are mentioned in three chronicles: *Chronicle of the Monk of Evesham, Historia vitae et regni Ricardi Secundi*, edited by Tho. Hearne, 1729, p. 124. *Historia Anglicana* Thomae Walsingham, ii. pp. 207-11, 213. *Polychronicon* Ranulphi Higden, IX. Appendix, pp. 267-70, 272-7.

and the whole administration went to Nottingham and York. The wisdom of this step is clear. To hold the inquiry away from London would lessen the risk of a city rising, and oblige the Londoners to plead in a strange place instead of at Westminster on the threshold of their own city, where they would have been in a much stronger position and have felt more at ease. Negotiations between the king and the city went on through the summer of 1392, but by the end of September, London had been restored to favour, and in October the exchequer was instructed to return to Westminster for Hilary term 1393.

Much material remains to tell us about each migration. Preparation, journey and rearrangement of work made necessary by the absence of the exchequer from Westminster, changed but little, however, from one time to another. The removal most fully documented is that to York in 1322. Let us therefore look at it more closely.

On 11 and 23 February 1322, the first mandates were issued, some under the great seal, others under the exchequer seal. The keeper of the office of treasurer and the barons of the exchequer were ordered to take to York, at the king's expense, the exchequer with its rolls, tallies and memoranda, and the rolls of common bench, in time to begin there the Easter session on Monday, 19 April. The justices of common bench were bidden adjourn their pleas to York accordingly. The sheriff of Yorkshire, and the mayor and bailiffs of the city of York, were acquainted with the coming of exchequer and common bench and were instructed to have repaired for them the houses in York castle they had used before, the furniture and fittings of which had been left in the care of the sheriff when the administration went back to Westminster in 1320.[1] The cost of repair was to be paid by the sheriff from the issues of his bailiwick, and for money so spent allowance would be made to him by the exchequer at his next audit. That took place in 16 Edward II., and the account for those repairs, amounting to £11 : 12 : 4¼, was presented by the sheriff and passed by the exchequer in Trinity term 1323.[2] The sheriff was also asked to make known this visit, and to inform " all merchants and others wishing to sell victuals and other things " that they might " come to the said city in safety with their said goods, to receive their due payment for the same ". All the sheriffs of England received notice of the removal,

[1] One part of the indenture then made between the sheriff and the exchequer is extant, and is now in P.R.O. Sheriffs' Accounts (Exchequer, K.R.) 49/8. It is printed in facsimile and transcribed in *English Court Hand*, C. Johnson and H. Jenkinson, i. pp. 181-4, ii. plate xxiiiB. An enrolment of another such indenture made when the exchequer left York in 1393, is in Mem. Rolls, K.R. 169, *Communia* (*Recorda*), Michaelmas term.

[2] Mem. Rolls, K.R. 96, m. 88d; L.T.R. 93, m. 28. Pipe Roll, 167. Sometimes, as in 1333, the repairs were carried out under the personal supervision of an exchequer clerk sent to York for the purpose. Issue Rolls, E 403/267.

with order to make it known in their bailiwick and to go to York to do their business with the exchequer on the appointed day.[1]

Later, on 11 March, a writ of privy seal bade Walter of Norwich, keeper of the office of treasurer, first consult with some of the king's council as to how best the removal could be made, then issue the necessary warrants under the exchequer seal. In consequence Norwich, himself deputy-treasurer and chief baron of the exchequer, discussed the matter with Walter Reynolds archbishop of Canterbury, Hervey of Staunton chancellor of the exchequer, Henry le Scrope and Henry Spigurnel justices of the king's bench, William of Barford and William Harle justices of the common bench, and " others of the king's council ", and a plan was agreed upon.[2]

The journey was to be made from Westminster to Torksey in Lincolnshire by road, for which enough carts were to be gathered together in London, and from Torksey to York by water. The caravan, in charge of William of Maldon, one of the chamberlains of the exchequer, Alexander le Convers, weigher of the exchequer, and Nicholas of Acton, apposer of the exchequer, was to leave Westminster on 5 April, the Monday after Palm Sunday. Ware in Hertfordshire was to be the first stage ; the second was to be Royston, in Cambridgeshire ; the third, Huntingdon ; the fourth, Wansford, in Northamptonshire ; the fifth, Stamford, in Lincolnshire (only a short distance was appointed for the fifth day, perhaps because it was Good Friday) ; and the sixth, Grantham, also in Lincolnshire. Details of time and place for the second half of the journey, to be continued on Easter Monday by way of Newark, were to be decided by Maldon and his colleagues at their discretion. The sheriff of each county through which the exchequer would pass, was to be responsible for its safety within his bailiwick.

Writs to such sheriffs were issued by the exchequer on 18 March.[3] The sheriffs of London and Middlesex were ordered to be at Westminster on the first Monday morning, with an adequate escort of foot and horse to convoy the exchequer to Ware. With like forces the sheriffs of Essex and Hertfordshire, Cambridgeshire and Huntingdonshire, Northamptonshire, and Lincolnshire, were to meet the exchequer at Ware, Royston, Wansford, and Stamford, in turn. The sheriff of Lincolnshire was also asked to have at Torksey ready for Easter Monday, " four good strong small ships each able to bear the weight of eight winecasks ", and the necessary sailors and tackle.

For a few days before departure all was bustle and excitement at

[1] Mem. Rolls, L.T.R. 92, m. 86d. Issue Rolls, E 403/196. The writs were issued on 16 March. A different scale of payment for accounting officers' travelling expenses came into operation when the exchequer removed to York. Hall, *Red Book of Exchequer*, iii. p. 836.

[2] Mem. Rolls, K.R. 95, m. 69d ; L.T.R. 92, m. 17.

[3] Mem. Rolls, K.R. 95, mms. 125, 125d.

Westminster.[1] The exchequer had to decide which records and how much money it wished to take. Empty winecasks had to be bought, cleaned and mended, new ones made, and all lined with waxed canvas. Into the casks and certain chests and coffers, the rolls, books, tallies and treasure had to be packed and firmly secured. With these the carts, which arrived at Westminster on Friday, 2 April, had to be loaded. At last, by the appointed time, all was ready, and the procession that then set out must have been an imposing

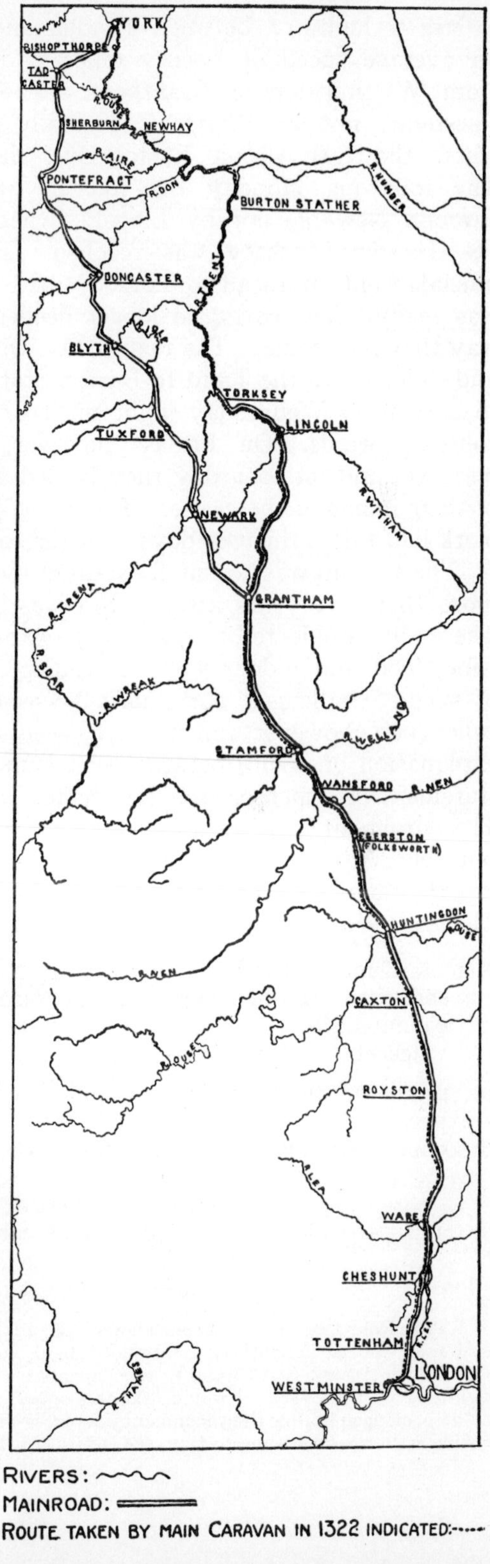

Sketch Map showing the routes used by the exchequer on its journeys between Westminster and York.

one. There were twenty-three carts, each drawn by five horses and in charge of two men.[2] There was a company on horseback, Maldon, Acton, Convers, a number of other exchequer officials, their clerks and servants, the purveyor of the carts, the purveyor of food, the crier of the bench, and grooms for the horses, fifty in all. There was the guard of foot and horse under the command of the sheriffs of London and Middlesex.

They took the road which

[1] Exch. Accts. E 101/332/12, particulars of the account for the removal.

[2] The number differs in each document and chronicle, but I have chosen this figure from the detailed account as being the final and most accurate one.

is still a highway between London and the north, and they made an average speed of twenty miles a day, taking six days to get from Westminster to Grantham. The first night was passed at Cheshunt, not at Ware as originally planned, and at Grantham where they arrived on Easter Eve, they rested for the week-end. The following Monday the journey was resumed, not, however, through Newark, but by Lincoln, where Monday night was spent. On Tuesday Torksey was reached. The next day, some of the officials went on ahead to York by road, to make sure that the castle was ready. The carts, no longer needed, went back to London the way they had come. The main body, with all the baggage, embarked and sailed down the Trent to Burton Stather. Here they were obliged to stay from Wednesday night until Friday, held up by storm and contrary winds. On Friday, however, they were able to get to Newhay, and on Saturday they landed at York, and took possession of their rooms in the castle. The whole journey from Westminster to York had taken thirteen days, and the total cost was £91 : 17 : 10.

The account was not finally audited and enrolled until 2 Edward III., more than five years after.[1] Nor was it accepted without question. The auditors objected to some of the expenses, chiefly money spent on wine, food and fodder while travelling, as being needless, and a list of such "challenged particulars" was drawn up. Maldon and his colleagues, however, must have been able to give a satisfactory explanation of them, because their sum was not deducted from the statement of expense, and the account was passed as first presented. The enrolment is, of course, only a summary of the detailed account, but there still survive, besides the enrolment, most if not all of the "particulars" of the account,[2] and the list of challenged particulars. The last I venture to give here as well for its general as intrinsic interest.[3]

Memorandum de particulis in compoto Magistri Willelmi de Maldon' et sociorum suorum nuper assignatorum super cariagio rotulorum, calumpniatis videlicet

In prima particula expense	De .xvj.d. in lauacione et mundacione doliorum.
In secunda particula	Calumpniandum est de cariagio librorum Garderobe de tempore Roberti de Wodehous', et domini Johannis de Weston' nuper Camerarij Scocie.
In tercia particula	De .xj.s. datis carectariis propter solempnitatem festi diei Pasche de Curialitate etc.
	Item de .xvij.s. vj.d. pro diuersis equis conductis

[1] Pipe Roll, 173, m. 43. Chancellor's Roll, 121, m. 3.

[2] Exch. Accts. E 101/332/12. Issue Rolls, E 403/196, 198.

[3] Exch. Accts. E 101/334/13, one membrane of thick skin irregularly shaped (14¼″ × 8⅜″ × 17½″ × 8⅜″). I would take this opportunity to thank Mr. Hilary Jenkinson for help in deciphering this document, in places almost entirely defaced, and for discussing with me from time to time the subject of this essay.

per viam per Johannem Meu pro predicto cariagio auxiliando per vices etc., eo quod dicti carectarij inuenisse debuerunt cariagium predictum suis sumptibus etc.

Item de . . . .lxiij.s. liberatis Johanni Mew ad cariagium predictum prouidendum assignato tam super expensis suis propriis et hominum suorum, quam pro expensis decem carectariorum qualibet carecta cum duobus hominibus et quinque equis venientibus London' et ibidem commorantibus per sex dies ante carcacionem dictorum doleorum vnde videtur quod idem Johannes debet inde computare antequam fiat allocacio

Expense et Custus in victualibus

Primo die Itineris videlicet die lune apud Cesterhuntere In vino . . . .ij.s. j.d.

Item . . . .ij.d. pro feno duorum equorum et . . . .viij.d. de precio vnius buselli auene, pro duobus equis superfluis, etc.

Item die martis secundo die apud Crucem Roesiam . . . In vino . . . .ij.s. vj.d. In vna Lampreda empta . . . .xviij.d.

Item . . . .ix.d. pro feno . . . et . . . .iij.s. iiij.d. ob. de precio, dimidij quarterij et dimidij buselli auene, pro nouem equis superfluis in illa dieta.

Item die Mercurii tercio die apud Huntingdon' . . . In vino empto . . . .iij.s. In pisce aque dulcis . . . .iij.s. ix.d. Item . . . .x.d. pro feno recepto . . . .iij.s. ix.d. de precio, dimidij quarterij, dimidij buselli auene, pro .x. equis superfluis in illa dieta.

Item die iouis quarto die apud Walingford' . . . In vino . . . .iij.s. x.d. In vna Lampreda . . . .xx.d. Item . . . .viij.d. pro feno, et . . . .iij.s. iiij.d. de precio dimidij quarterij auene pro .viij. equis superfluis in illa dieta.

Item die veneris quinto die apud Staunford' . . . .vij.d. in feno, et . . . .ij.s. xj.d. de precio .iij. busellorum et dimidij auene pro .vij. equis superfluis etc.

Item die Sabbati .vj^to^ die apud Grantham . . . In vino . . . .iij.s. In vna Lampreda . . . .xx.d. Item . . . .viij.d. pro feno, et . . . .iij.s. iiij.d. de precio dimidij quarterij auene pro . . . .viij. equis superfluis.

Item die dominica in festo Pasche .vij°. die. In vino . . . .vj.s. In tribus capriolis . . . .ij.s. xi.d. Item . . . .ix.d. pro feno, et . . . .iij.s. iiij.d. de precio dimidij quarterij auene pro .ix. equis superfluis. Item de duobus quarteriis frumenti emptis pro .xxviij.s. et furniatis et non inuenitur vbi expenduntur, etc.

Item die lune .viij. die. In vino . . . .ij.s. vj.d. In grossis carnibus . . . .vj.s. vj.d. In feno . . . .ix.d.

et . . . .iij.s. iiij.d. de precio dimidij quarterij auene pro . . . .ix. equis superfluis.

Item die Martis . . . .ix.die. In feno . . . .ix.d. et . . . .iiij.s. iiij.d. de precio dimidij quarterij auene, pro .ix. equis superfluis.

Item . . . .xiij.s. vj.d. in conduccione hakenettorum pro hostiariis scaccarij inter London' et Torkeseye.

Item die Mercurii .x. die . . . In vino . . . .ijs. vj.d.

Item die Jouis .xj. die . . . In vino . . . .xiiij.d.

Item die veneris .xij. die . . . In vino . . . .xix.d.

Item die sabbati .xiij. die . . . In vino . . . .ij.s. vj.d.

Item die dominica .xiiij. die apud Eboracum . . . In vino . . . .ij.s. ob.

Summa . . . .ix.li. xj.s. iiij.d. preter .xxviij.s. de precio duorum quarteriorum frumenti superius emptorum.

Summa [1] . . . .ix.li. xvj.s. vij.d.
.ix.li. xj (?, defaced). iiij.d.

Endorsed : Maldon'.

There is little doubt, even when the records are meagre, that the other migrations to York were prepared for and carried out in much the same way.[2] Always accommodation was provided in York castle,[3] the kernel being the rooms built or set aside by order of the king in 1298.[4] For the upkeep of all such premises as well as for their more particular preparation for use just before an exchequer visit, the sheriff of Yorkshire was responsible.[5] Although sometimes the caravan did part of the journey by water,[6] more often it went overland all the way.[7] In both circumstances the time taken to do the whole distance varied from ten to fourteen days.[8] So too did the expenses vary,

[1] These notes, at the extreme right-hand corner of the membrane, seem to be attempts to arrive at the total.

[2] Such differences as exist were small, as in 1319, when the sheriff of London provided the casks and twenty carts, and the sheriffs of Essex and Surrey each provided ten carts : and again in 1333, when the sheriff of London was asked to provide ten of the carts needed. Mem. Rolls, K.R. 92, *Breuia irretornabilia*, Trinity term ; L.T.R. 89, m. 159d ; K.R. 109, m. 280 ; L.T.R. 105, m. 108.

[3] Mr. Conway Davies, *The Baronial Opposition to Edward II*. p. 277, is misleading on this point, and note 4 on the same page misprints the *Calendar of Close Rolls*.

[4] Mem. Rolls, K.R. 71, m. 114d ; L.T.R. 69, m. 78.

[5] *Calendars of Chancery Rolls*, Exchequer Memoranda and Pipe Rolls, *passim*.

[6] As in 1320, 1322 and 1323. See notes p. 292, and Mem. Rolls, L.T.R. 90, *Breuia retornabilia*, Hilary term ; K.R. 96, m. 145. Exch. Accts. E 101/332/15. See map.

[7] As in 1298, 1319, 1327, 1328, 1333. See notes pp. 291-292, and Mem. Rolls, K.R. 71, m. 114d ; L.T.R. 69, m. 79 ; K.R. 92 ; L.T.R. 89, *Breuia irretornabilia*, Trinity term. Issue Rolls, E 403/231. Exch. Accts. E 101/333/9. See map.

[8] The Yorkshire accountants were expected to take only six days to get to Westminster. Hall, *Red Book of Exchequer*, iii. p. 836.

from £36 in 1298,[1] £124 : 10 : 8¾ in 1319,[2] and £76 : 1 : 3¾ in 1333,[3] to £408 for the double journey in 1392–3.[4] The exchequer and common bench generally travelled together or within a few days of each other, and in 1392 they were even accompanied to York by the warden of the Fleet prison and his prisoners.[5] Were there any attempts to escape, one wonders ?

Some of the arrangements for the return journeys were, however, different. When the exchequer went back to Westminster in 1304–5, the casks were provided by the sheriffs of Yorkshire and Lincolnshire, and the carts by the abbeys and priories of Yorkshire.[6] Again, in 1392, Yorkshire provided the carts, but then the church was specially exempt.[7] Usually the sheriff of Yorkshire was expected to see that the exchequer had everything needful in the way of casks and packing, and as a rule the carts were provided in relays by the sheriffs of the counties through which the exchequer passed, each sheriff carrying with him enough ready money to pay the expenses incurred within his bailiwick.[8]

Absence from Westminster disturbed routine and added to the delays and difficulties of transacting business, for neither all the treasure nor all the records were removed, and such records as were taken were sometimes lost by the way.[9] If the visit were short the discomfort was slight, but if the visit were long the inconvenience was correspondingly greater. Consequently, during the longer absences, exchequer officers were constantly going up and down between York and London, and a stream of messengers passed to and fro carrying letters from one exchequer official to another. Records left behind had to be consulted ; loans to the king from merchants had to be negotiated and the money taken to the king ; a new great seal made in London, had to be sent for ; or the seneschal of Gascony needed certain of the duchy's documents from the treasury.[10]

The exchequer does not seem to have left a permanent representative or branch-office at work in Westminster or London while it was away, nor does it seem that one was greatly needed, but from time to time in the longer absences, a temporary office was opened for the issue and receipt of money. During the first visit to York, the exchequer received money at the Tower of London from 25 June to 28 August

[1] Issue Rolls, E 403/102. [2] *Ibid.* 187. Exch. Accts. E 101/547/23.
[3] Issue Rolls, E 403/267, 270. Exch. Accts. E 101/333/9.
[4] Issue Rolls, E 403/543.
[5] *Cal. C.R. 1389–92*, p. 467. *Cal. P.R. 1391–6*, p. 67.
[6] Mem. Rolls, K.R. 78, m. 79 ; L.T.R. 75, m. 72. *Cal. C.R. 1302–7*, pp. 223-4.
[7] *Cal. P.R. 1391–6*, pp. 189, 191.
[8] See notes pp. 291-292, Exch. Accts. E 101/332/15. Mem. Rolls, L.T.R. 90, *Breuia retornabilia*, Hilary term ; K.R. 96, m. 145 ; K.R. 115, *Breuia directa Baronibus*, Michaelmas term ; K.R. 120, *Breuia directa Baronibus*, Trinity term. Pipe Rolls, 184, m. 49 ; 185, m. 45d. Exch. Accts. E 101/547/22. *Cal. P.R. 1327-30*, p. 176.
[9] *Cal. C.R. 1302–7*, p. 31 ; *Ibid. 1337–9*, p. 178.
[10] Issue Rolls, E 403/270, 279, 282, 288, 291, 294, 297, 300, 303, *passim.*

1298;[1] and in the next two years, in Lent, at Westminster.[2] In December 1322, about the middle of the third visit to York, the treasurer both issued and received money in London.[3] Only once in all the time spent at York from 1333 to 1338, was money issued or received elsewhere, and that was in July 1337, at London.[4]

The exact whereabouts of the exchequer and common bench could hardly have mattered greatly to London, but Westminster was not quite so unconcerned, for when the court and administration went away, Westminster lost its only means of subsistence and almost its reason for being.[5] Yet London as well as Westminster complained about such removals. The exchequer had spent much time at York between 1319 and 1323, and when in August 1327 order was again issued that the exchequer and common bench should leave Westminster, the city of London protested. Edward III. received a deputation of citizens led by Sir Richard Betton, the mayor, and listened to what they had to say, but he refused to alter his plans.[6] The harm done to Westminster became plain during the long absence of the exchequer and bench in 1333–8, for in 1337 that city found itself unable to pay its assessed taxation and a new assessment had to be made.[7]

While no doubt York throve on Westminster's loss, even York sometimes suffered unpleasant results from the presence within her walls of what was in effect an administrative capital. Lawlessness seems to have been increased, and a bad outbreak, which moved the king to reproach the mayor and bailiffs with neglect of duty, occurred in the city and suburbs in 1334. Bands of armed men went about York by day and night to attack "those coming and going to and from that city, and staying there, both the king's ministers and other lieges, and beat, wound and rob them". Nor was that all. One night a mob broke into the treasurer's house and into the king's wardrobe, and having "insulted the treasurer and the king's men", carried off what money, jewels and other goods they could lay their hands on. Happily order seems soon to have been restored.[8]

In spite, however, of all the consequent inconvenience and confusion, the king found it simpler, in those days of slow communication, to move government offices from their homes when war came, than to wait on the inevitable delays of travel.

DOROTHY M. BROOME.

[1] Receipt Rolls, E 401/143. Presumably this was the "other business" for which the treasurer went to London in August 1298. Mem. Rolls, K.R. 71, m. 50; L.T.R. 69, m. 88d.

[2] Receipt Rolls, E 401/144, 147, 148.

[3] Issue Rolls, E 403/200, 201. Receipt Rolls, E 401/241. Mem. Rolls, L.T.R. 93, *Communia* (*Recorda*), Michaelmas-Hilary terms.

[4] Issue Rolls, E 403/294. Receipt Rolls, E 401/338.

[5] Tout, *The Beginnings of a Modern Capital*, pp. 11-13.

[6] *Cal. C.R. 1327–30*, p. 165. *Cal. of Letter Books of the City of London, Letter Book E, Edward II. and Edward III.* p. 222. Sir Richard was paid £20 for his expenses.

[7] Tout, *loc. cit.*

[8] *Cal. C.R. 1333–7*, pp. 294-5.

XXIII

LA CONFÉRENCE D'AVIGNON (1344)

L'arbitrage pontifical entre la France et l'Angleterre

En 1342, Édouard III, qui depuis deux ans avait pris le titre officiel de roi de France, après avoir tenté d'envahir la France par le Tournaisis et par la Thiérache, fit campagne en Bretagne. Appelé par le prétendant Jean de Montfort contre Charles de Blois, que soutenait son suzerain, le roi de France, il avait su fort habilement intervenir dans la guerre de succession de Bretagne, dont l'histoire fut désormais inséparable de celle du grand conflit franco-anglais. C'est qu'il espérait tirer de grands avantages d'une Bretagne soustraite à l'obédience française. Car les Montfort l'avaient reconnu comme roi de France et lui avaient prêté l'hommage. La vassalité bretonne était un acheminement à la possession complète du royaume de France qu'il considérait lui être dévolu par droit successoral. L'Angleterre, pensant aux provinces perdues depuis Philippe Auguste, visait à reconstituer l'empire plantagenet. Quoique maîtresse de la Guyenne, elle ne pouvait se résoudre à n'être, dans l'Europe féodale, qu'une puissance insulaire. Le développement logique de cette politique réaliste l'amena à occuper, en 1342, la péninsule armoricaine, comme en 1346 elle occupera Calais : les ports bretons, comme ceux de la Manche et de la mer du Nord, étaient des bases continentales indispensables.

L'expédition anglaise en Bretagne dura près de trois mois du 30 octobre 1342 au 23 janvier 1343.[1] Il n'y eut pas à proprement parler de bataille décisive ; ce fut une guerre locale, une série d'escarmouches, de châteaux assiégés, de sièges levés, de dévastations méthodiques ; les deux armées—française et anglaise—s'épièrent, sans chercher à en venir aux mains. Les hostilités traînèrent tant en longueur que les patrons des nefs amarrées dans les ports perdirent patience et plusieurs sans autorisation regagnèrent l'Angleterre.[2] La mauvaise saison, la détresse financière, la peur de ne pas trouver l'argent nécessaire pour une guerre coûteuse, la crainte de se trouver sans navires de transport, en cas de repli, décidèrent le roi d'Angleterre à accepter l'armistice

[1] Débarqué à Brest le 30 octobre, Édouard III se réembarqua au port de Vannes le 23 janvier 1343.

[2] P.R.O. Privy Seals file 291, No. 15518.

proposé par deux cardinaux qu'avait envoyés le pape Clément VI, Pierre Després, cardinal évêque de Palestrina et Annibaldo de Ceccano, cardinal évêque de Tusculum.

Le 19 janvier 1343 des trêves furent signés au prieuré bénédictin de Ste. Marie Madeleine de Malestroit.[1] Elles étaient valables jusqu'au 29 septembre 1343 et renouvelables pendant trois ans. Le roi d'Angleterre devait quitter la Bretagnc. La ville de Vannes, qui avec celle de Nantes était une des clefs du duché, était remise aux cardinaux, sous forme de mandat.[2] En signant les trêves sous la médiation des deux cardinaux, les rois de France et d'Angleterre s'étaient engagés à envoyer des ambassadeurs à Avignon pour le 24 juin 1343 : les conférences en vue d'un traité devaient s'ouvrir à Noël pour un règlement définitif des questions en litige. Philippe VI s'empressa d'annoncer la bonne nouvelle au roi d'Aragon, Pierre le Cérémonieux, le 26 janvier 1343. Clément VI, pape français, était " son ami " : l'arbitrage pontifical ne pouvait manquer d'être favorable à la France.[3]

Mais les négociations qui précédèrent les conférences furent longues et laborieuses. Vingt mois s'écoulèrent, jusqu'à octobre 1344. Le retard est dû à plusieurs causes. Édouard III et Philippe VI, au lieu d'entrer en pourparlers directs, traitèrent séparément avec la papauté. Plusieurs fois, grâce à des subterfuges, des échappatoires, des supercheries même, ils se dérobèrent plus ou moins habilement l'un et l'autre. Les complications survenues en Bretagne—rébellions et conflits—comprises sous le nom d'attentats contre les trêves, compromirent plusieurs fois l'armistice.[4] Le roi d'Angleterre invoquait des arguments divers pour justifier ses précautions et ses refus de sauf-conduit ; tantôt c'étaient les cautions qu'il jugeait insuffisantes,[5] tantôt la forme même de validité des lettres[6] ; tantôt il jugeait que les plénipotentiaires ne jouissaient pas d'une sécurité complète à

[1] Malestroit, Morbihan, Canton de l'arrondissement de Ploërmel.

[2] A vrai dire Édouard laissa un lieutenant dans la Bretagne, qu'il considérait comme un pays conquis ; et il continua à occuper Brest défendue par un capitaine et une garnison anglaise.

[3] Très cher cousin, pour ce que savons que vous seriez liez du bon portement et estat de nos besoignes et de nostre royaume, savoir vous faisons que le roy d'Engleterre estoit descenduz en Bretaigne, si sommes venuz pour li contrester le plus tost que nous avons peu, et si, comme nous sommes venuz en li approchant, ses genz qui avoient prises aucunes villes en pays de Bretaigne, einsi comme il nous sentoient venir, se sont partiz et retraiz et merci dieu, il s'en est partiz à nostre honneur sanz riens conquester du nostre et avons trives ensemble de la Sant Michel prochaine venant en trois anz. Et, pour traiter des discensions d'entre nous et li, devons nous en li envoier devers le Saint Père lequel est bien nostre ami, si comme vous povez savoir.

Donné au Plermel en Bretagne le xxvi. jour de janvier.

Joachim Miret y Sans : " Lettres closes des Premiers Valois " (*Le Moyen Âge*, 2e série t. xx., 1917–1918, p. 68), d'après les Archives de Barcelone.

[4] Clément VI avait envoyé en Bretagne un de ses chapelains, Étienne de Mulceon pour faire respecter les trêves (Archives Vaticanes Reg. 215 ; De Curia, No. III., 21 juillet 1343).

[5] Arch. Vat. Reg. 137, No. 1080, 24 mars 1344.

[6] Édouard III ne voulait pas du petit sceau et exigeait des lettres de sauf-conduit scellées par le roi de France du grand sceau (*id.* Reg. 137, No. 230).

Avignon où les atteintes au droit des gens étaient parfois restées impunies.[1]

Ni le roi ni le Parlement anglais n'avaient voulu séparer deux questions très différentes, celle des provisions de bénéfices, celle de la guerre franco-anglaise. Le clergé anglais voyait d'un mauvais œil l'intrusion dans les riches bénéfices d'étrangers qui administraient fort mal et causaient des scandales. Il cherchait non pas tant à s'affranchir du Saint-Siège qu'à modérer les largesses faites en Angleterre par Clément VI à qui l'on prêtait ces paroles " Mes prédécesseurs ne surent pas être papes ". Édouard III entendait bien ne pas dissocier les deux questions. En faisant des concessions sur le terrain de la guerre avec la France, il obligeait le pape à céder sur le terrain des bénéfices, à reculer même : système de compensations réciproques qui d'ailleurs servaient plus les intérêts anglais que ceux de la papauté. Lorsque le roi retirait ses troupes de Bretagne, il signait des trêves pour être agréable au pape qui à son tour devait révoquer les collations de bénéfices ou promettre de les révoquer. Cette politique de compensations ou de dédommagements mutuels ne pouvait pas durer. Des accidents imprévus venaient briser cette harmonie apparente et rompre cette entente factice. C'est ce qui explique les brusques changements d'attitude dans la conduite du pape et d'Édouard III. Les démêlés de Clément VI et d'Édouard III retardèrent les négociations pour la paix. La diplomatie pontificale n'avait point de chance. Toujours de nouvelles complications venaient contrecarrer et compromettre l'œuvre qu'elle avait entreprise. Quand elle pensait avoir atteint le but, tout était à recommencer.

Les difficultés les plus épineuses étaient soulevées par l'arbitrage. La papauté avait cherché à s'interposer. En fait elle avait offert sa médiation. Du côté français elle était acceptée sans nulle objection. On savait qu'il y avait plus à gagner qu'à perdre. On se rappelait que jadis, lorsque Jean XXII avait voulu imposer une trêve à deux seigneurs du Midi, trêve qui contrariait les visées de la politique française, le roi de France mécontent avait dénié à la papauté le droit d'intervenir dans les litiges de ses sujets. Et Jean XXII avait affirmé son droit avec énergie.

> A coup sûr, mon fils, écrivait-il au roi de France, si tu réfléchissais avec quelque attention aux événements que peut réserver l'avenir, tu ne saurais désapprouver ni trouver dangereux pour toi-même et ton royaume l'exercice du droit qui appartient au Saint-Siège d'imposer des trêves. Car à toi ou à tes successeurs l'exercice de ces droits pourra être très utile, si les circonstances, à Dieu ne plaise, venaient à changer à ton détriment.[2]

[1] Sous Benoît XII un ambassadeur anglais, Nicolino Fieschi avait été arrêté à Avignon (*id.* Reg. 137, No. 211).

[2] Jean XXII (1316–1334). *Lettres secrètes et curiales relatives à la France extraites des Registres du Vatican*, ed. Coulon, No. 704.

Mais si la France acceptait l'arbitrage, l'Angleterre y répugnait. Elle le voulait officieux et non officiel. Le pape médiateur—et le chroniqueur Adam de Murimuth bien informé, nous le dit—devait agir en tant que personne privée et ami commun.[1] Toute l'année 1344 se passa en argumentations subtiles dont la correspondance de Clément VI nous a laissé les traces. Les lettres échangées entre le pape et la France nous montrent comment l'élu de 1328, le roi qui vient de loin, ce Philippe de Valois qu'on appelle le " roi trouvé ", c'est-à-dire le roi de rencontre, apparaît dénué de sens pratique et de souplesse. Non seulement, comme le dit Froissart, il croit " légèrement fol conseil ", mais il ignore la politique et il l'entend mal. Il perd le fil de cette diplomatie souterraine dont Édouard III connaît les secrets. Mais Clément VI, qui est un ancien maître de théologie en Sorbonne, connaît les subtilités et, en manœuvrier habile, déjoue, comme aux échecs, les plus savants calculs.

L'arbitrage pontifical porta d'abord sur un point précis et spécial : les infractions commises contre les trêves de Malestroit. La France était prête à désigner son représentant, à condition que l'Angleterre fît de même. Ils instrumenteraient et enquêteraient avec deux représentants du Saint-Siège. Édouard III déclara cette proposition impossible, inadmissible et inacceptable. Il se garda bien de donner les raisons. Mais il est facile de les deviner. Désigner un plénipotentiaire spécial pour établir les responsabilités anglaises, c'était reconnaître implicitement les torts commis du côté anglais. Édouard III, las des essais d'entente qui prolongeaient les hostilités sans régler les questions, qui éludaient les difficultés au lieu de les aborder franchement, qui les tournaient au lieu de les résoudre, voulait que de sa propre autorité le Saint-Siège entreprît de régler la question des infractions. Un échec prouverait l'impuissance et l'incapacité pontificales et l'Angleterre, forte de ce précédent, pourrait à l'avenir agir sans la papauté.[2]

Clément VI, ne s'y laissant pas tromper, refusa de s'engager dans la voie où les Anglais voulaient l'entraîner. Avant tout il se mettait en dehors du conflit et voulait bien assumer le rôle de médiateur, non pas en s'imposant aux puissances engagées, mais en recevant d'elles le mandat de régler le différend qui les divisait.[3] La France et l'Angleterre, lasses de ne pouvoir trouver seules un terrain d'entente, étaient-elles disposées à choisir la papauté comme arbitre ? Partisan de la paix, le pape voulait bien s'employer à faire cesser cette guerre funeste aux intérêts de la Chrétienté, mais ne pas être accepté par contrainte. Il voulait prêter un concours pour lequel on l'avait sollicité, mais dont il n'avait point pris l'initiative.

Après bien des tergiversations, Édouard III accepta finalement le

[1] " persona privata et amicus communis " (Murimuth, p. 136).

[2] Arch. Vat. Reg. 137, No. 988, 5 mai 1344.

[3] " non auctoritate nostra, sed ex potestate attributa nobis a partibus " (*id.* Reg. 137, No. 1083).

12 mai 1344, l'arbitrage pontifical.[1] Les ambassadeurs anglais devaient être à Avignon le 20 juin ; mais leur départ officiel ne fut annoncé que le 3 août 1344[2] : c'étaient l'évêque de Norwich, Jean d'Ufford, doyen de Lincoln, gardien du sceau privé, Hugues de Nevill, chevalier, Nicolino Fieschi, Thomas Fastolf, archidiacre de Norwich et André d'Ufford professeur de droit civil.[3]

Le 19 août Clément VI accorda leurs sauf-conduits aux plénipotentiaires anglais.[4] Deux jours après il priait Philippe VI d'envoyer les siens sans retard à Avignon.[5] Trois semaines s'écoulèrent sans réponse. Lorsque les plénipotentiaires anglais arrivèrent à Avignon le 30 septembre, la délégation française n'était ni annoncée, ni partie. Clément VI commençait à s'inquiéter et venait de dépêcher au roi de France un nouveau courrier,[6] lorsque ce dernier annonça officiellement le départ de l'ambassade française dont faisaient partie l'évêque de Clermont, le doyen de Paris, Louis d'Espagne, Louis de Poitiers et Simon de Bucy, président en Parlement.[7]

Les conférences s'ouvrirent le 22 octobre après l'arrivée de la délégation française (18 octobre), les visites d'usage et la vérification des lettres de créance. Le pape les dirigea comme personne privée et médiateur commun. Il devait être un arbitre et non un juge. Les conférences d'Avignon furent une tentative faite par la papauté pour régler le conflit franco-anglais. Mais elles mirent aux prises deux politiques inconciliables. Toute la bonne volonté de Clément VI demeura impuissante et ces pourparlers laborieux, au lieu, comme l'avait espéré le Saint-Siège, d'asseoir la paix définitive, ne servirent qu'à mettre en lumière l'impossibilité irrémédiable d'une entente.[8]

Le vendredi 22 octobre les plénipotentiaires anglais se présentèrent devant le pape qu'assistaient six cardinaux. Clément VI fit un discours sur les bienfaits de la paix et les avantages de la concorde entre les princes chrétiens. Il déclara qu'il désirait la paix " et dit en bone foy qu'il y mettroyt de sa part tote sa peine ". Les Anglais répondirent qu'ils étaient " enclins à bone pees et resonable et qu'on les troveroit en bone foi, sans fiction ".

Le dimanche 24, invités à prendre la parole, les Anglais posèrent nettement le débat sur le terrain dont ils avaient mission de ne point se départir. Entrant immédiatement dans le vif de la question, ils déclarèrent qu'ils réclamaient la couronne et le royaume de France et

[1] P.R.O. Roman Rolls, 18 Édouard III, m. 2.
[2] *Foedera*, ii. 4, 164.
[3] P.R.O. French Rolls, 18 Édouard III, m. 4.
[4] Arch. Vat. Reg. 138, No. 1086.
[5] *Id.* No. 226, 21 août 1344.
[6] *Id.* No. 285, 14 septembre 1344.
[7] Lettre de Hugues de Nevill à Édouard III, 17 oct. 1344 (Froissart, ed. Kervyn, xviii. 211).
[8] Nous pouvons suivre d'assez près la marche des négociations, qui durèrent du 22 oct. au 29 nov. 1344, grâce aux lettres que les ambassadeurs anglais adressèrent d'Avignon à Édouard III et à divers personnages d'Angleterre, grâce au Journal des Conférences (en latin). Ces pièces ont été publiés par le baron Kervyn de Lettenhove au tome xviii. des *Œuvres de Froissart*, pp. 202-256, d'après une copie de Bréquigny (Bibl. Nat. Collection Moreau, t. 699). Le ms. est au British Museum, Cotton-Cleopatra, E. II.

demandèrent à faire la preuve des droits du roi d'Angleterre. Assurément le conflit franco-anglais préexiste à la guerre et la rivalité devenue permanente des maisons de France et d'Angleterre a ses racines profondes dans l'histoire capétienne. Mais la Guerre de Cent Ans est autre chose que la continuation de cette rivalité. Elle consiste à superposer aux querelles anciennes un débat nouveau, dont la France même est l'enjeu. La Guerre de Cent Ans est une guerre de succession. Ce ne sont plus un roi et un vassal qui s'affrontent, mais deux prétendants qui se disputent une couronne. Aussi bien, le premier jour où s'ouvrirent les conférences, les Anglais répondirent-ils à Clément VI " Seint Pière, vous savets bien nostre demande, quele est assets connue, c'est assavoir le roiaume de France, comme le droit nostre seigneur le Roi ".[1]

Cette politique dynastique n'était pas neuve. Elle n'était pas la conception personnelle d'Édouard III assez énergique pour prendre l'offensive, assez heureux pour en trouver en 1328 l'occasion. Elle était traditionnelle, depuis l'avènement de Philippe V le Long. Une lettre de sceau privé d'Édouard II, dont je crois être le premier à signaler l'importance, est à cet égard singulièrement suggestive.[2] Lorsqu'en 1316–1317 Charles de la Marche, le futur roi de France Charles IV le Bel, réclama, à la mort de Louis X, sa part du royaume, Édouard II pensa exiger du fait de la reine Isabelle " sa purpartie du royaume de France ". Il était logique, après avoir réclamé une part en 1316, de réclamer la totalité en 1328 lors de l'extinction de la branche directe capétienne.

Clément VI fit observer aux plénipotentiaires anglais que la revendication successorale serait, à n'en pas douter, un fâcheux début de négociations et il proposa la disjonction.[3] Les Anglais consentirent à s'occuper des attentats commis contre les trêves et à réserver la question dynastique. Mais ils ne tardèrent pas à s'apercevoir qu'ils avaient fait fausse route. Il fallait reprendre la question dynastique et à tout prix y ramener le pape. A cet effet ils imaginèrent de laisser Clément VI proposer des solutions au problème de Guyenne et à refuser obstinément d'en proposer eux-mêmes, déclarant que c'était au pape, médiateur entre les deux parties, qu'il convenait de trouver le chemin de la paix.[4] Or les Anglais avaient bien promis de laisser dormir la

[1] Froissart, ed. Kervyn (xviii. 221).

[2] P.R.O. Privy Seals, file 97, No. 3974 (1317, 24 janvier, Brackley), Bref d'Édouard II à l'évêque de Winchester son chancelier et à Walter de Norwich son trésorier.

[3] " Et il respondist que ceo ne serroit pas a faire, à ceo que lui sembloit, car ceo ne serroit mie comencement ne voie de bone pees, eyns seroit comencement de enpescher le treté et nous dist outre que la cause de ceste guerre sourdist pur les terres de la duchee de Guyenne et que sembloyt que home dust entrelasser la demaunde du roialme et la lesser dormir a part et treter de la duchee " (Froissart, xviii. 221).

[4] " Et adonkes lui priames qu'il ceo vorroit owir et monstrer à nous tiele voie come lui sembleroit bone, esteante totesvoies nostre dite demande de roialme en sa force sauns prejudice et lui deismes que tant voluntiers treterions d'aultre duchée come de Guyenne et d'une chose apres l'autre selon sa pleisaunce. Et voloit que nous deisoms de quele

revendication dynastique, mais ils n'entendaient pas la compromettre. Toute paix conclue sous la médiation pontificale devait donc être compatible avec une discussion ultérieure des droits d'Édouard III au trône de France. Ainsi chaque proposition pontificale devait soulever infailliblement des objections tirées de ces droits que les plénipotentiaires anglais avaient promis de laisser sommeiller.

La question des attentats en Bretagne avait été ajournée parce que l'on attendait l'avis du roi de France. La question de Guyenne restait à débattre. Il était de toute évidence qu'à la veille de la grande guerre, le conflit franco-anglais se présentait avant tout comme un conflit aquitain. C'est en Guyenne que s'était surtout développée la rivalité au XIIIe siècle et au début du XIVe. La réduction systématique du fief par la royauté suzeraine tendait à jeter les Anglais à la mer. Les Anglais se déclaraient prêts à examiner toute proposition qui leur serait faite. Les Français, sur ce point, affectaient une attitude passive. De nombreux traités avaient été conclus entre les deux couronnes de France et d'Angleterre, au sujet de la Guyenne. En 1327 un nouvel acte avait été signé : ces traités, et en particulier le plus récent, telle était la base toute trouvée des négociations. Selon eux, il n'y avait rien de nouveau dans les difficultés actuelles ; il s'agissait de régler une fois de plus des désaccords survenus entre le vassal et le suzerain, comme en avaient été réglés de semblables à Amiens sous Philippe III, à Paris sous Philippe IV.[1] La diplomatie française entendait donc rester dans la tradition presque séculaire dont le principe était le maintien de la situation créée par le traité de 1259 : la paix d'Avignon que l'on se disposait à conclure devait être une convention de plus à ajouter, comme un corollaire, aux conventions précédentes ; comme celles-ci elle devait dériver du traité de Paris. Clément VI fit part de cette attitude aux envoyés d'Édouard III. Voici quelle fut leur réponse [2] :

Saint Père, nous espérions et espérons encore que l'on ouvrirait des voies

---

voye de pees nous avions penses et que nous la deisoms. Nous lui respondions que a nous ne apartint pas monstrer voye quelconque de pes, mes tant seulement esteer en nostre dite demaunde du roialme et oyer les voyes queles il mesmes nous vorroit monstrer come mediatour" (*id.* 222).

[1] "Mes une chose dient les messages de France que diverses tretees ont esté faites devant ces heures entre les deux rois et que ils vorroient que home començast de treteer sour les poyns et la fourme de la derrayne pees faite et affirmee en Gascoigne, en laquele fuist contenu que chescune des parties tendroit peiseeblement ce qu'il tynt adonkes illoques, et la partie que pleindre se vorroit, serroit oye summerement" (*id.*).

[2] "Seint Piere, nous entendoms que tant seulement tieles voies de pees deveroient estre touchees, par lesqueles nostre seignur le Roi senteroit cause de acorder a la pees et qu'il se puisse tenir pur content, eyant totefois consideration à sa dite demande. Hore est ensi que la dite pees faite en Gascoygne fuist faite pur apeiser les dissentions primerement meues par occasion des terres de la duchee entre le roi de France comme seignur cheveteyn d'une part et le duk de Guyenne come son vassal d'autre part ; mes ceste tretee en present se doit faire entre nostre seignur le roi que hore est de une part et son dit adversarie d'autre part, pur apeser, se Dieu plest, la guerre et les dissentions meues entre eux par occasion et cause du roialme de France et de la corone, par quoi il ne fait mie apeller en ceste tretee de la dite pees de Gascoigne" (*id.*).

susceptibles de conduire à une bonne paix et de convenir à notre roi, comme votre Sainteté nous l'a naguère et souvent promis. Mais cette paix passée, dont parlent les ambassadeurs français, fut faite sur des désaccords et des controverses relatives à toutes les terres du duché entre le feu roi de France, suzerain du dit duché d'une part, et notre maître de bonne mémoire, l'illustre père de notre sire le roi actuel, en tant que duc et vassal du dit roi de France, d'autre part. Or le traité à conclure ne doit pas être conclu pour le même motif, ni à l'occasion du dit duché ou de certaines terres du duché, mais pour réaliser une bonne paix, s'il plaît à Dieu, entre notre roi d'une part et son adversaire de France, d'autre part, au sujet de toutes les controverses et guerres survenues entre eux à l'occasion de la couronne et du royaume de France : c'est pourquoi en ce qui touche à la matière de paix mise en avant par les dits ambassadeurs, nous n'avons le dessein de rien dire maintenant.

Les Anglais en revenaient à leur déclaration première : ils s'obstinaient à se placer sur le terrain dynastique. Les Français leur en avaient donné une excellente occasion. Clément VI ne fut point surpris. " Certes, dit-il, j'avais bien dit aux Français que telle serait votre réponse." Le pape avait donc pénétré la tactique des ambassadeurs d'Édouard III. S'il avait cru pouvoir un instant faire réserver la question de succession, sans doute l'obstination des Anglais à attendre les propositions qui leur seraient faites l'avait éclairé sur leurs intentions. Maintenant il était évident que la revendication dynastique surgirait, au bon moment, pour faire échouer toute proposition française fondée sur le respect du traité de Paris.

Clément VI essaya d'une négociation secrète. Il prit congé des cardinaux et dirigea seul les négociations, promettant de n'en parler à " nulle alme ". Mais il n'arriva pas à triompher de l'entêtement systématique [1] des plénipotentiaires anglais.[2] Après avoir rappelé les cardinaux, il décida que la prochaine réunion se tiendrait le jeudi 28 octobre.[3] Ce jour-là, avant de convoquer les anglais, Clément VI eut avec les ambassadeurs français un entretien qui dura plusieurs heures. Puis il fit dire au doyen de Lincoln que des occupations multiples et des affaires urgentes l'empêchaient de diriger personnellement les débats. Il chargeait en conséquence les cardinaux de le remplacer auprès des parties et de le mettre au courant des éventualités ou des difficultés qui se présenteraient. Et comme il avait demandé par délicatesse si les anglais préféraient traiter avec les six cardinaux ou seulement avec les deux qui avaient jadis été en Bretagne, le doyen

[1] " Adonkes il nous dist: ensi vous vous tenes clos et les autres messages se tenent clos de lour part " (*id.*).

[2] " Et adonques comanda les dits cardinals se trere a part, et nous demanda en bone foy si nous vorrions toucher ascune voye de pees en secre et il nous dist qu'il ne la monstreit a nulle alme. Nous lui respondismes tout acertes que par nous nulle voye de monde serroit touchée ne monstrée, mes que tant seulement nous nous tendrioms en nostre demaunde du royalme de France come en demaunde de nostre droit et si nulle bonne voie de pees nous soit monstrée par mediation de sa Seinteté que nous la orroms tres volentiers et treteroms en tiel manère sur meisme cele que nous serrons trovés resonables et de volenté d'acorder a bone pées " (*id.* 223).

[3] *Id.* 240.

de Lincoln répondit que la volonté du pape serait la sienne et que d'ailleurs il n'avait pas de préférence pour un cardinal plutôt que pour un autre. Le pape s'effaçait ainsi et prenait un prétexte pour se retirer momentanément.

Les négociations se poursuivirent pendant près de huit jours entre les envoyés français et les deux cardinaux Pierre Desprès cardinal évêque de Palestrina et Annibaldo de Ceccano cardinal évêque de Frascati. Les ambassadeurs anglais profitèrent de ce répit pour écrire à leur roi, aux divers conseillers de la couronne et à l'archevêque de Cantorbéry,[1] afin de les mettre au courant de tout ce qui s'était passé depuis l'ouverture des négociations. Des cédules secrètes encloses dans les lettres fournirent à cet égard les détails les plus circonstanciés.[2]

Édouard III apprit ainsi que le traité de paix était loin d'être conclu et que la question des attentats contre les libertés de l'église, qui semblait être assoupie, renaissait plus violemment que jamais. Clément VI, voyant qu'il ne pouvait obtenir réparation, avait commencé par écrire à la reine Philippa qui venait de lui envoyer un sergent d'armes.[3] Il s'était ensuite décidé à envoyer en Angleterre deux nonces, l'archevêque de Ravenne et l'évêque d'Astorga qu'il avait chargés d'exposer ses griefs. L'excommunication ne serait lancée qu'à la dernière extrémité. Les ambassadeurs anglais lors à Avignon avaient cherché à faire surseoir l'envoi de cette ambassade. Ils voulaient encore gagner du temps et ils entrevoyaient fort bien la possibilité d'un conflit sur le terrain religieux qui ruinerait toutes les chances de paix.[4] Il suffisait en effet qu'un accueil peu sympathique fût fait aux nonces pour qu'une rupture éclatât entre l'Angleterre et le Saint-Siège. Quelle pourrait être alors la conduite des ambassadeurs à Avignon ? Ceux-ci, qui prévoyaient l'orage, essayèrent de le conjurer. Édouard III fut avisé. L'archevêque de Cantorbéry le fut également.[5] Il reçut du doyen de Lincoln une lettre spéciale avec copie des lettres adressées au roi et il y fut prié de réfléchir sérieusement aux faits qu'on lui exposait.[6] Un incident avait irrité le pape et le Sacré Collège. Édouard III, dans un bref adressé au cardinal de la Mote et à son procureur Raymond Pelegrini, s'était rendu coupable d'impolitesse à l'égard de ce cardinal. Les termes peu courtois, dans lesquels le bref était rédigé, ne laissaient aucun doute sur les intentions royales.[7] Le

[1] *Id.* 219-27.

[2] Le courrier qui les portait à Édouard III quitta Avignon le 28 octobre (*id.* 219-23).

[3] Arch. Vat. Reg. 138, No. 279, fo. 111 verso, 29 oct. 1344.

[4] " Mes certeinement jeo moy doute que les choses dount l'Église se pleint, empescheront ceo que nous avoms a faire devaunt le dit Seint Piere " (Froissart, xviii. 226).

[5] *Id.* 223. Lettre à l'archevêque.

[6] " quarum quidem continentiae sunt ponderandae et judicio meo notabiliter precavendae " (*id.* 224).

[7] *Id.* 226. Lettre à Édouard, 28 oct. 1344. " Et ore tard si est envoyé un brief de prohibition au cardinal de la Mote, dont nostre dit Saint Piere et tut le collège sount

bref avait été lu en consistoire, et le pape était tout disposé à sévir et à entamer un procès. On disait même que l'évêque d'Ely et maître Étienne de Rothbury allaient être convoqués à Avignon ; enfin Clément VI, sourd à toute prière, s'apprêtait à envoyer en Angleterre l'archevêque de Ravenne Nicolino Canali, et l'évêque d'Astorga, Pedro archidiacre de Pedroche en l'église de Cordoue.[1]

Les ambassadeurs lors à Avignon étaient vraiment inquiets de cette attitude du Saint-Siège, qui jusque-là avait déployé beaucoup de bonne volonté et de diligence.[2] Il était à craindre même que de nouveaux attentats, de jour en jour plus violents, ne finissent par entraver la marche des négociations qui se poursuivait à Avignon. Le doyen de Lincoln l'écrivait au roi d'Angleterre, en ne lui dissimulant point ses sentiments.[3] Rien n'était encore compromis : malgré l'ambassade désormais officielle de l'archevêque de Ravenne et de l'évêque d'Astorga, il n'y avait pas lieu de désespérer. Le doyen de Lincoln, qui connaissait bien la situation et pouvait donner au roi d'excellents conseils, demanda à rentrer en Angleterre, si le roi jugeait utile sa présence outre-Manche. Selon lui le conflit qui allait éclater entre l'Angleterre et le Saint-Siège pouvait avoir de très fâcheux résultats ; la guerre religieuse, disait-il, est entre toutes, celle qui est le plus à redouter.[4] Il valait mieux agir avec prudence et modération, et donner satisfaction au pape, pendant qu'il était encore temps : sinon l'œuvre de paix serait tout à fait compromise.[5]

---

esmuts et ennuyés si bien de la matere du dit brief come de la maniere du parler, en taunt que est dist en meysme le brief 'A toy Gaillard de la Mote', sauns plus cortoysement parler et hier feust leu le dit brief au consistoire et ad ordeiné nostre dit Seint Piere d'envoyer en Engleterre mult hastivement l'ercevesque de Ravennat et un evesque d'Espaigne pur requerre de par lui et de par l'Église nostre seignur le Roi qu'il face redresser et amender les injuries feates contre lui et l'Église. A ceo qu'il dist, le messagerie il ne vœt entrelesser pur rien."

[1] "pour requere de feare adrescer et amender les injuries feates contre l'église lequele envoi de messages ne pœt estre desturbé par nulle priere" (*id.* 225). Lettre à un conseiller d'Édouard (*id.* 224).

[2] "En bone foy, sire, nostre dit Seint Piere, a ceo que nous semble et pooms sentir, se monstre de bone voluntée devers nous, sire, et grant diligence met pur l'esploit de nos besoignes" (Froissart, xviii. 223). "Veuillez savoir que les bosoignes nostre seigneur le roi sount en bone comencement là Dieu mercy par mediation de nostre Seint Piere, qui met graunde travail et diligence pur trover bone voie de concorde" (*id.* 225, 226). "Et trovons nostre dit Seint Piere mult diligent et travaillant en la bosoigne pur taster et trover voie de pees" (*id.* 226).

[3] "Non dubito quin attemptata in regno Anglie in dies crescentia nostros tractatus elident, vel totaliter irritabunt, et ideo expediret quod dominus noster rex, si placeret sibi, me ad partes, re quasi adhuc integra, revocaret" (*id.* 224).

[4] "Et certe inter alias mundi guerras plus, meo judicio, ecclesiastica est timenda" (*id.* 224). "Et en bone foy jeo serroie en grant espoir de bone issue par ceste mediation du Saint Piere, se ne feussent les choses attemptees de novel contre l'Église. . . . Kar en bone foi jeo tienks la guerre de l'esglise trop perileuse en droit de ceste matere" (*id.* 225).

[5] "Adhuc sentio, sicut alias vobis scripsi, quod consultius foret, expeditius et tutius excessus notabiles, si qui sint, ut ita loquar, ad preces domini summi pontificis retrofactos ab integro reformare quam nos faciamus eos post alia rigorosa opera reformari. Vere nisi foret ista dissentionis materia, sperarem de aliorum tractatuum exitibus gratiosis" (*id.* 224).

Clément VI laissa pendant quelques jours aux cardinaux la direction des négociations. Ceux-ci essayèrent les mercredi 3 et jeudi 4 novembre de revenir sur le terrain des paix antérieures. Édouard III n'avait-il pas lui-même reconnu la paix signée en 1327 ? L'hommage n'avait-il pas été une reconnaissance du fait accompli ? Les Anglais invoquèrent les réserves de ses droits héréditaires faites par leur maître au moment de l'hommage. La cérémonie d'Amiens n'avait rien préjugé, selon eux, du problème de légitimité. Ils allèrent même plus loin : ils ne pouvaient traiter du duché de Guyenne comme revenant à Édouard en qualité de duc, sous peine d'aller eux-mêmes à l'encontre des droits d'Édouard à la couronne de France. La mort de Charles IV avait en effet créé en Guyenne une situation nouvelle : le problème juridique s'était trouvé subitement changé, et en effet Édouard ne s'intitulait plus duc, mais roi de France, et il avait pris les armes de France.

" Vous persistez donc, observèrent les cardinaux, à revendiquer le trône de France, et rien autre chose. Sur cette base, il est inutile de traiter."

Il semblait en effet qu'en présence d'une telle revendication il fût inutile de poursuivre. Mais les Anglais déclarèrent une fois encore qu'ils étaient disposés à laisser dormir la question dynastique, afin de traiter des moyens qui pourraient conduire à la paix. Ils provoquèrent ainsi une série de propositions de la part des cardinaux. Tout d'abord, quant au duché, les Anglais consentiraient-ils à revenir à l'état existant lors du premier conflit entre Édouard III et le roi de France ? La réponse fut que cette proposition ne pouvait être prise en considération, attendu que rétablir la relation de suzerain à vassal, c'était rétablir une situation telle qu'aucune paix durable ne serait possible. Mais, pour éviter tout conflit, il serait bon de laisser à Édouard le duché sans vassalité. Cette concession serait un excellent début et il serait facile ensuite de s'entendre sur le reste. Cette façon de traiter la question de Guyenne mérite que l'on s'y arrête : elle est significative. Comment la renonciation de la royauté française à la suzeraineté sur le duché pouvait-elle être un excellent début pour les négociations, sinon parce que le roi d'Angleterre, moyennant cette renonciation, se sentait disposé à " laisser dormir " ou à laisser réfuter son droit à la couronne de France ? La réponse des ambassadeurs d'Édouard à la première proposition des cardinaux ne se comprend que si l'on considère la candidature d'Édouard au trône de France, comme un moyen de déplacer le terrain de la lutte, pour arracher à la cour de France l'abandon de la Guyenne en toute suzeraineté : ce règlement de la question de Guyenne était le seul qui pût agréer à un roi actif et résolu. A vrai dire, les plénipotentiaires anglais se découvraient enfin pour la première fois ; il est essentiel de retenir à quel prix ils mettaient ce qu'ils appelaient avec complaisance " *bonum initium tractatus* ".

Les cardinaux répliquèrent qu'ils avaient songé à cette solution ; eux aussi ils pensaient qu'aucune paix durable n'était possible, tant qu'il coexisterait en Guyenne un vassal et un suzerain, témoin l'Écosse par rapport à l'Angleterre. Mais la Guyenne ne pouvait, à leur avis, être séparée du royaume de France ; le roi actuel le voulût-il, le droit s'y opposerait et les habitants eux-mêmes refuseraient d'adhérer à la combinaison ; car justement ils répugnaient à n'avoir qu'un des deux princes pour seigneur. Ce dernier argument ne convainquit guère les Anglais. Sans doute on ne pouvait démembrer un royaume ; mais la situation présente était exceptionnelle, puisque le royaume lui-même était en question. La Guyenne était anciennement un alleu : pourquoi ne le redeviendrait-elle point ? Quant aux habitants, sans doute la coexistence des deux princes faisait bien leur affaire ; mais si les princes eux-mêmes étaient d'accord, les sujets devraient bien se résigner, bon gré mal gré.[1]

Les cardinaux formulèrent une seconde proposition. Ne pourrait-on pas offrir en compensation au roi d'Angleterre les biens situés en Angleterre des Hospitaliers et autres ordres religieux ? Le pape s'arrangerait pour indemniser ailleurs ces établissements. Ainsi serait supprimée cette coexistence d'un suzerain et d'un vassal en Guyenne, germe de tout le mal. " Une telle combinaison, répondirent les ambassadeurs, n'est ni à l'intérêt, ni à l'honneur de notre seigneur le roi."

La troisième proposition fut : Que diriez-vous si le roi de France pouvait obtenir du roi d'Écosse son allié qu'il remît à votre roi l'Écosse librement, en échange d'une compensation outre-mer ?

C'était un moyen ingénieux de donner à Édouard l'équivalent de ce qu'il paraissait désirer : la Guyenne déliée du lien de vassalité. Mais les Anglais ne tenaient pas à se renfermer dans leur île pour abandonner leurs possessions continentales. Ils objectèrent que l'Écosse était vassale de l'Angleterre. Pour cette raison, et d'autres qu'il était inutile d'énoncer, il valait mieux ne pas insister davantage.

La quatrième proposition fut froidement accueillie. On donnerait au roi une forte somme d'argent pour se procurer de grands revenus ailleurs. L'attente des cardinaux, qui avaient proposé un marché, fut trompée une fois encore. " Notre roi, dirent les ambassadeurs, n'est point un bon marchand qui pour de la seule monnaie, chose vile et abjecte, abandonnerait ses droits sur une chose aussi noble que le trône de France ; en considération de ce droit, il n'était guère convenable de parler d'un tel moyen, surtout pour un début ; plus tard on pourrait s'occuper des sommes destinées à indemniser le roi d'Angleterre de ses dépens."

Enfin les cardinaux mirent en avant un projet de mariage franco-

[1] " Verumptamen si partes principales ad hoc essent concordes, incolae ducatus sustinere haberent concordiam hujus, vellent nollent."

anglais.[1] Les Anglais répondirent que c'était là une question accessoire et non essentielle. Des alliances de famille pourraient assurément cimenter l'entente des deux princes, une fois négociée, mais elles ne pouvaient rien pour fonder cette entente. Ainsi les agents d'Édouard avaient repoussé toutes les combinaisons mises en avant par le Saint-Siège : la question dynastique était devenue entre leurs mains une arme perfectionnée et ils la maniaient à merveille. Au fond ils jouaient supérieurement d'une équivoque. Il eût fallu savoir, si oui ou non la question des droits d'Édouard au trône serait disjointe de la question de Guyenne ; il eût fallu restreindre le débat actuel à la recherche d'un moyen destiné à faire disparaître cette superposition d'un suzerain et d'un vassal sur le duché. Mieux encore il eût fallu déterminer si oui ou non les Anglais voulaient faire des prétentions d'Édouard un " *casus belli* ", ou comment ils entendaient se faire payer l'abandon de ses prétentions. Une fois ces deux points précisés, c'eût été à Philippe VI de savoir s'il voulait entrer en composition avec son rival, ou le jeter hors de France. Jamais les cardinaux, jamais les ambassadeurs français n'eurent le courage de mettre aux Anglais partie en main. Le Saint-Siège se flatta jusqu'au bout de triompher à force de patience ; les Français avaient une confiance aveugle dans l'efficacité de la politique de tradition.

Les réponses faites par le doyen de Lincoln et ses collègues aux propositions des cardinaux étaient fort claires ; elles ne parurent point telles au Sacré Collège. Les cardinaux en effet, au début de la séance suivante (dimanche 7 novembre), demandèrent aux ambassadeurs ce qu'ils pensaient des " voies " dont il avait été question. Les ambassadeurs répliquèrent, non sans ironie, que si les cardinaux avaient présenté leurs propositions avec les meilleures intentions, les objections développées au cours de la séance précédente suffisaient à écarter les compensations territoriales en Angleterre, la cession de l'Écosse et l'indemnité pécuniaire. Restait le duché de Guyenne. La question du duché fut reprise à la réunion qui suivit (lundi 8 novembre). " Parlons donc, dirent les cardinaux, du dit duché, et voyons comment naquit la guerre à l'occasion du duché, quelles furent les injustices

[1] La proposition n'était pas nouvelle et elle n'était pas impolitique : elle pouvait servir beaucoup les intérêts de la France. Les cardinaux savaient de source autorisée qu'Édouard III, le 26 octobre 1344, avait envoyé maître Jean d'Ufford doyen de Lincoln, John de Thoresby chanoine de Lincoln et Raoul Spigurnell chevalier pour demander à Clément VI deux dispenses de mariage, la première pour l'union entre Édouard, prince de Galles et la fille aînée du duc de Brabant, la seconde pour le mariage projeté entre Isabelle d'Angleterre, fille d'Édouard III, et le fils aîné du duc de Brabant. Ces deux unions étaient grosses de conséquences et l'on conçoit que les cardinaux, qu'ils aient voulu veiller aux intérêts de Philippe VI ou qu'ils aient voulu tout simplement assurer la paix par un moyen plus pratique, aient songé à défaire ces projets de mariage. (P.R.O. Roman Rolls, 18 Édouard III, m. 2. 1344, 26 octobre. Westminster.) En oct. se traitèrent des négociations pour le mariage entre le fils du roi de Castille et Jeanne fille d'Édouard, on renouvela les alliances, cf. Close Rolls, 18 Éd., p. 2, m. 6 ; Gascon Rolls, 18 Éd. 3, m. 2. *Foedera*, ii. 4, 169.

commises de part et d'autre, afin de mettre les choses au point." Une fois de plus on tentait d'en revenir au point de vue juridique, aux éternelles enquêtes, en un mot à la politique de tradition. La réplique des Anglais fut nette : " la guerre ne provient nullement d'injustices commises à l'endroit du duché, mais principalement de l'usurpation du trône de France qui revient de droit à Édouard III ". Les cardinaux essayèrent de pénétrer au cœur du débat. Avant de prétendre au trône de France, le roi d'Angleterre n'avait-il pas commencé la guerre à propos du duché ? C'est après coup qu'il avait mis en avant son droit successoral, comme le prouvait la diplomatique des actes royaux, dans la formule de souscription.[1] Ainsi il était logique de rétablir la paix en prenant pour base les origines de la guerre, la question dynastique devant être exclue. Le 8 novembre les cardinaux en étaient au même point que le pape le 24 octobre. Les Anglais répondirent :

Éminences, et ne vous en déplaise, la guerre actuelle s'est déclarée à propos de la succession au trône de France, bien avant qu'Édouard III prît le titre de roi de France. La question dynastique s'était posée lors du couronnement de Philippe VI de Valois. Sur le conseil de la reine mère Isabelle et des hauts barons, alors qu'Édouard III était encore trop jeune pour gouverner, les évêques de Winchester et de Coventry avaient été envoyés en France pour protester et revendiquer la couronne de France. Mais effrayés par les menaces ils n'avaient eu ni assez de courage ni assez d'audace. La chose était connue et des actes publics, signés par des notaires, en faisaient foi.[2]

Mais, objectèrent les cardinaux à ces déclarations, n'est-il pas vrai qu'Édouard, après le couronnement de Philippe VI a prêté l'hommage pour le duché de Guyenne et le duché de Ponthieu et que subséquemment cet hommage a été déclaré lige ? N'est-il pas vrai que lors de la prestation d'hommage, jamais mention ne fut faite d'un droit successoral ? L'objection n'est pas neuve, répondirent les Anglais. Elle s'évanouira d'elle-même, si on nous laisse publiquement, devant le pape, faire l'historique de ces droits contestés. Ainsi la question se reposait toujours sur la même forme et l'on piétinait sur place.

Vous savez bien, ajoutèrent les cardinaux, que le pape vous a priés de laisser dormir pendant les conférences la question dynastique. Vous savez d'autre part que les plénipotentiaires français ne consentiront jamais à ce qu'elle soit posée. Car ils disent qu'y toucher c'est manier du poison.[3]

On revenait encore une fois à la Guyenne. Que le duché redevînt d'abord un alleu appartenant au roi d'Angleterre et l'on verrait ensuite à traiter du reste. Les cardinaux opposèrent, comme précédemment, le principe de l'inaliénabilité. Un mariage entre un fils d'Édouard et une fille de France pourrait amener un compromis : un prince anglais

[1] " Datum anno regni nostri Francie quinto, regni vero Anglie decimo octavo."
[2] Froissart, xviii. 246.
[3] *Id.* 247 : " et quod reputarent dicti nuntii Francie venenum tangi, quum tangitur positio vestra predicta de regno ".

tiendrait ainsi le duché sous la suzeraineté du roi de France. Mais les ambassadeurs eurent vite fait justice de cette combinaison. Édouard y perdrait tout ; non seulement ses prétentions à la couronne de France ne lui serviraient de rien, mais il perdrait même ses droits au duché en tant que duc. Ne pourrait-il pas dire alors qu'il avait de bien mauvais représentants ? Nous voulons bien, dirent alors les cardinaux, donner ailleurs une compensation à votre roi pour le dit duché. Cette compensation, demandèrent les Anglais, serait-elle dans le royaume ou hors du royaume ?—Les cardinaux ne purent préciser. En Angleterre on ne pouvait vraiment trouver d'autre combinaison que celle déjà proposée des biens des Hospitaliers. D'autre part donner une compensation en France, c'était se condamner à maintenir la coexistence du vassal et du suzerain. Les cardinaux demandèrent à réfléchir : ils croyaient que la question posée par leurs interlocuteurs impliquait une adhésion de principe à l'idée d'une compensation territoriale. Il fallut bien s'avouer le contraire. La compensation priverait Édouard non seulement de ce qu'il possédait effectivement en Guyenne, mais encore de ce qu'il y revendiquait. Au surplus Édouard pouvait revendiquer la Guyenne, non seulement en tant que duc, mais encore en tant que roi. C'était bien invariablement le même procédé de discussion : la question dynastique revenait à tout coup, pour mettre à néant toute proposition pacifique. On promettait de la laisser dormir, mais on la réveillait une fois par séance et à propos. Le seul point qui pût servir d'article premier à une bonne paix était la rupture de la vassalité en Guyenne. Les cardinaux déclarèrent sans ambages que jamais la partie adverse n'accepterait la rupture du lien féodal.

Du 13 au 20 novembre les cardinaux empêchés [1] ne purent présider aux conférences : la semaine entière se passa sans pourparlers. Ces loisirs permirent au doyen de Lincoln de mettre l'archevêque de Cantorbéry [2] et le roi d'Angleterre [3] au courant de la situation et de tout ce qui se passait dans les conférences et en dehors d'elles. Depuis le 28 octobre, les plénipotentiaires n'avaient point écrit à la cour d'Angleterre ; mais Édouard III avait dans l'intervalle répondu aux diverses missives reçues d'Avignon. Il avait ainsi annoncé l'envoi immédiat de plénipotentiaires nouveaux, mais sans citer de noms. Il ne se montrait pas non plus très disposé à céder à la papauté, ni sur le terrain politique, ni sur le terrain religieux. C'est ainsi qu'il n'avait point révoqué le mandement où il avait donné ordre aux maires et baillis de différentes villes et ports d'arrêter tous ceux qui portaient

[1] Il y eut alors un consistoire où Clément VI créa le 15 novembre Louis de la Cerda, autrement dit Louis d'Espagne prince des Îles Fortunées. Il y eut à cette occasion de grandes fêtes ; le lendemain 16 novembre le nouveau prince donna dans le couvent des frères Prêcheurs d'Avignon un grand dîner auquel assistèrent les ambassadeurs anglais (Adam de Murimuth, 162).

[2] Froissart, xviii. 227-229. Lettre du 12 novembre 1344.

[3] *Id.* 229-331. Lettre à Édouard III. M. Kervyn de Lettenhove l'a faussement datée du 23 novembre.

des bulles, lettres ou procès pontificaux ;[1] et Clément VI en avait conçu une vive irritation. A son tour il n'avait point voulu céder aux prières d'Édouard III. Maintes fois on l'avait supplié de différer l'envoi de l'archevêque de Ravenne et de l'évêque d'Astorga en Angleterre ; un moment il avait écouté les avis du doyen de Lincoln et acquiescé aux raisons qui lui avaient été exposées secrètement.[2] Mais il avait le 3 novembre officiellement annoncé leur départ à Édouard et à John de Stratford archevêque de Cantorbéry, sans toutefois fixer de date.[3] Une nouvelle ambassade anglaise était en route pour Avignon ; l'attitude du roi avait pu changer.

Mais on reçut à Avignon copie du mandement royal qui avait été affiché aux portes des églises de St. Paul et de Westminster. Un consistoire fut réuni et après avoir entendu par trois fois la lecture, le Sacré Collège fut unanime à déclarer que l'archevêque de Ravenne et l'évêque d'Astorga partiraient immédiatement pour Londres. La situation à Avignon était de plus en plus tendue et le doyen de Lincoln écrivait à l'archevêque de Cantorbéry " Vous pouvez bien imaginer l'issue qu'auront les négociations entamées à Avignon au sujet de la paix. Jusqu'ici on a beaucoup traité. Mais les résultats sont bien minces. J'ai été averti par une personne amie qu'un cardinal très influent avait dit hier en consistoire ' si les nonces du Saint-Siège en Angleterre sont mal reçus et s'il leur arrive d'être retenus prisonniers, nous userons de représailles et feront subir le même sort aux plénipotentiaires anglais lors à Avignon.' "[4] Une pareille perspective souriait peu au doyen de Lincoln qui effrayé demanda à être rappelé. L'émotion s'apaisa lorsqu'on annonça l'arrivée de deux envoyés anglais, le chevalier Raoul Spigurnell et le gardien des rôles de la chancellerie, John de Thoresby, que Édouard III avait désignés les 19 et 26 octobre et qui étaient porteurs d'instructions secrètes.[5]

[1] P.R.O. Close Rolls, 18 Ed. III p. 2, m. 11 dorso. *Foedera*, ii. 4, 160 : Le maire de Sandwich avait ainsi arrêté et fait remettre à Londres au chancelier Robert de Sadington certaines bulles pontificales. Le chancelier les fit déposer à l'Échiquier entre les mains de deux cameriers Jean de Houtton et Jean de Etton.

[2] " Nous avoms par diverses foits supplié à nostre dit Seint Piere, or tot la instaunce que nous poyoms, de suffrir et attendre d'envoyer ses dites messages, et lui tochames ascunes resons pour lui mover a ce feare, a lesqueles prieres il respondist une foits que ses dites messages ne se hasteroient mie taunt d'en prendre lour chemyn que nous ne pensoms oyr ascunes novelles d'Engleterre en le même temps " (Froissart, xviii. 230).

[3] Arch. Vat. Reg. 138, Nos. 391-2, fo. 115 recto.

[4] " Vos modo conjecturare poteritis qualem exitum habebimus quatinus ad reformationem attemptatorum et pacis attinet per tractatum, in quo licet multa tractata sint . . . et per multos dies tractaverimus, nichil adhuc sensimus scribi dignum. Praemunitus sum etiam per unum dominum et amicum quod unus maximus homo debuit heri dixisse in consistorio haec verba. ' Si isti praelati qui mittuntur in Angliam in ambassiata, non recipiantur et capiantur, faciemus illud idem de suis qui in curia hic existunt.' Istis consideratis videtur michi quod nec est michi benevolus, nec amicus, qui erit illius sententiae quod, ingruente guerra inter sacerdotium et regnum, in romana curia debeam tantis subici periculis et inutiliter commorari " (Froissart, xviii. 228).

[5] P.R.O. Privy Seals, file 300, No. 16428. " Edward par la grace de Dieu roi d'Engleterre et de Fraunce et seignur d'Irlaunde a nostre cher et foial Robert de Sadyngton, nostre chaunceller saluz. Come nous envoions nostre cher clerc mestre

Le 20 novembre le pape reprit la présidence des conférences. Devant les ambassadeurs français et anglais qui avaient été convoqués simultanément, il ouvrit la séance par ces paroles :

Je vous félicite de travailler avec zèle, comme nous le croyons, en vue de la paix ; mais je ne vous félicite pas en ceci que d'une part comme de l'autre, vous vous tenez trop fermés et que vous ne voulez ouvrir aucune voie précise qui puisse conduire à la vraie paix.

Clément VI se faisait donc assez peu d'illusion : il avait conscience du temps perdu en pourparlers vagues entre deux parties qui procédaient de deux politiques essentiellement différentes. Français et Anglais parlaient chacun leur langue et ne pouvaient pas s'entendre. Pourquoi donc s'obstiner à répéter toujours les mêmes propositions, à faire surgir toujours les mêmes répliques ? Clément VI fit un effort louable pour serrer de près l'objet du débat. Il invita les Français à se concerter entre eux pour lui exposer confidentiellement et nettement ce qu'ils voulaient. Il invita de leur côté les Anglais à réfléchir à la proposition faite par les cardinaux d'indemniser le roi d'Angleterre en lui cédant les biens des Hospitaliers en Angleterre. La réponse des Anglais rendue le lendemain 21 novembre, fut, comme on pouvait s'y attendre, négative.[1] Quant aux Français ils avaient limité ainsi le débat : ou le maintien de la vassalité en Guyenne, ou une compensation territoriale. Le pape proposait d'assigner cette compensation en terre d'Empire ou en Flandre. Les ambassadeurs anglais déclarèrent qu'ils devaient en référer à leur roi. Mais quelle serait la condition des terres données en compensation ? Le pape était-il certain que ce serait toujours sous la vassalité de la France ? Dans ce cas, il n'y avait pas lieu de débattre davantage et de fait les négociations sérieuses étaient désormais impossibles.

Johan de Thoresby gardein des roules de nostre chauncellerie devers nostre Seint Piere le pape pur aucunes chargeantes et secrees busoignes qe nous touchent et volons qil tigne cel office et taunqe a sa revenue face ce qappent a la garde des ditz roules par aucun clerc quel il voudra mettre en son lieu et pur qi il voudra respoundre. Si vous maundons qe vous facez receivre en son lieu pur la dite garde a son departir tiel come il vorra mettre en la forme avauntdite. Donné souz nostre prive seal à Westmouster le xix jour d'octobre l'an de nostre regne d'Engleterre disoytisme et de Fraunce quint."

Roman Rolls, 18 Édouard III, m. 2. "Pape rex, etc. . . . Dilectos et fideles nostros magistrum Johannem de Thoresby, canonicum Lincolniensem et Radulfum Spigurnel, militem, quos ad sanctitatis vestre presenciam una cum aliis nunciis nostris ad eandem presenciam pridem missis, tam super reformacione attemptatorum contra treugas initas nuper in Britannia quam super pace inter nos et Philippum de Valesio, adversarium nostrum Francie per Dei graciam ineunda sub bonitatis et rectitudinis vestre fiducia transmittimus, super intentione nostra plenius informatos, vestre clemencie votivo recommandavimus affectu, quibus, si placet, super dicendis ex parte nostra dignetur, quesumus, vestra benignitas credulam dare fidem. Conservet, etc. Datum ut supra" (26 octobre).

[1] "lequele jour nous estoit monstré par les messages vostre dit adversarie un tiel point par la bouche nostre dit Saint Piere tut en certeyn que nous ne vorrioms plus avaunt treter sauns ceo que vous nostre seignur en fussiés garnis et conseilles en droit du dit point et nous certefies de vostre entention et voluntei." Lettre au roi Édouard III (Froissart, xviii. 231).

Le doyen de Lincoln, l'évêque de Norwich et Hugues de Nevill estimèrent que leur présence à Avignon était désormais inutile et qu'une conversation avec le roi serait plus efficace ; ils demandèrent au pape l'autorisation de rentrer en Angleterre.[1] Mais Clément VI pensait que si les ambassadeurs anglais quittaient Avignon, le bruit se répandrait que les négociations étaient rompues et que la tentative du Saint-Siège était restée infructueuse. Aussi bien consentit-il seulement à laisser partir Hugues de Nevill, pendant que les autres plénipotentiaires resteraient à Avignon et que les négociations continueraient.[2] Il désigna Simon de Bucy qui de son côté irait trouver Philippe VI de Valois.

Le mercredi 24 les ambassadeurs français et anglais furent convoqués de nouveau devant le pape assisté de quatre cardinaux ; comme personne n'arrivait à s'entendre, les uns répondant toujours oui, et les autres toujours non, et comme de nouvelles lettres de créance étaient indispensables, il fut décidé qu'un ambassadeur de chaque partie irait chercher des instructions nouvelles et réglerait la question de prorogation des trêves. Les ambassadeurs anglais firent observer au pape qu'il serait peut-être inutile de dépêcher l'un d'entre eux en Angleterre ; ils étaient avisés en effet de l'arrivée prochaine de maître John de Thoresby et de Raoul Spigurnell chevalier, tous deux porteurs d'instructions secrètes. Mais le pape " demura en son primer purpos ", c'est-à-dire de renvoyer Nevill et Bucy. Le 25 novembre les deux nouveaux envoyés [3] se présentèrent devant le pape, et remirent leurs lettres ; le lendemain 26, devant l'assemblée au grand complet, maître John de Thoresby exposa les raisons pour lesquelles Édouard III l'avait envoyé à Avignon. L'objet de sa mission était double.[4] En premier lieu il était chargé de régler la question des attentats contre les trêves : car le roi d'Angleterre souhaitait d'autant plus la paix qu'il avait l'intention d'aller en Terre Sainte ; et il remit alors au pape les lettres royales conçues dans les termes mêmes que le Saint-Siège avait jadis proposés et devait faire approuver par le roi de France, sauf quelques additions intercalées par le Conseil du Roi. En second lieu Édouard III demandait que le terme prévu par les trêves de Malestroit fût prorogé jusqu'à la Mi-Carême 1345. Les cardinaux furent quelque peu étonnés de voir des revendications aussi sobres et d'entendre un langage aussi modéré : le pape préférait les voies pacifiques. Il remercia les envoyés

[1] *Id.* 232. Lettre au roi d'Angleterre : " afin que les choses monstrees par vive voys, pensons sentir vostre entention, sire, plus avaunt que par lettres et adonques nous dist nostre dit Seint Piere que ce ne suffreit il pas, quar tantost serroit dist partot que le tretee de pees en fuist rumpu ".

[2] " Et adonques nous dist nostre dit Seint Piere que lui sembloit pur le mieux que un des messages de une part et un altre d'autre retournassent ove tute haste a lur seigneurs pur sentir plus en especial lour ententions en droit des voies de bone pees " (*id.* 231).

[3] Ils étaient arrivés le 24 à Avignon (*id.* 232).

[4] Lettre de l'évêque de Norwich au roi d'Angleterre (*id.*).

anglais des bonnes nouvelles qu'ils apportaient et les pria de conférer avec leurs collègues pour se mettre au courant des négociations qui duraient depuis près d'un mois. Une réunion fixée pour le dimanche 28 novembre fut contremandée et remise au lundi 29. Les ambassadeurs anglais furent d'avis unanime qu'ils ne traiteraient pas avant de connaître les intentions fermes de leur roi, surtout depuis que les Français affirmaient très nettement que le roi d'Angleterre serait traité en vassal, pour toutes les terres qu'il recevrait dorénavant dans l'étendue du royaume de France. Il fallait donc attendre le retour de Simon de Bucy et de Hugues de Nevill qui portaient à leurs gouvernements un projet de traité. La question des attentats devait être réglée dans l'intervalle, en réalité elle ne le fut jamais.[1]

Les ambassadeurs anglais restés à Avignon commençaient à se lasser ; la question relative aux attentats commis contre les trêves en Bretagne ne recevait aucune solution [2] ; la question religieuse se posait toujours [3] ; l'archevêque de Ravenne et l'évêque d'Astorga qui avaient quitté Avignon le 21 novembre, avaient reçu des instructions spéciales et plein pouvoir pour mener à bien en Angleterre les affaires difficiles dont ils étaient chargés.[4] Édouard III et plusieurs autres seigneurs évêques ou barons avaient été officiellement informés de leur départ d'Avignon [5] : le pape n'avait écouté aucune requête et n'avait pas voulu surseoir. L'entente n'était donc désormais plus possible ni sur le terrain politique, ni sur le terrain religieux. Des ambassadeurs anglais il ne restait à Avignon que le doyen de Lincoln [6] ; celui-ci supplia

[1] " Tunc supplicavimus sibi quatinus vellet intendere reformationi attemptatorum faciendae. Ipse respondit quod loqueretur de hoc nuntiis Francie et faceret nos premuniri, quando de illa materia loqueremur, et in istis finis stat tractatus" (*id.* 256).

Les envoyés anglais expédièrent à leur roi la copie du traité en latin " pur ceo que en latin se fist ". Elle fut portée par Hugues de Nevill qui ne partit que le 29. Le pape n'avait pas voulu le laisser partir avant cette date (cf. *id.* 232).

[2] " Car en droit de la reformation des attemptats en Britanie, coment que vos lettres, sire, soient venues au pape par vos derrayns messages meistre John de Thoresby et monseigneur Radulf Spigornel, solonc la fourme de la copie quele il meisme nous bailla, nientmeyns, sire, a la fesaunse de cestes plus ne avoms riens eu certeineté, fors taunt soulement que nous fust dist de par nostre dit Seint Piere qu'il avoit parlé ove les messages de France de la matere et qu'il nous ferroit garnir quant et quele heure nous vendrions devant lui pur cele cause " (*id.* 233).

[3] " en droit des bosoignes tochauntes l'Eglise, des queaux bosoignes vos autres messages avoms asses oy de compleintes, ne pooms autre chose certeine sentir " (*id.* 233).

[4] Arch. Vat. Reg. 138, No. 467, fo. 134 verso. L'indemnité qui leur avait été allouée était de 8 florins en France, et de 15 florins en Angleterre (*id.* No. 465-66).

[5] Reg. 138, Nos. 468-92, fo. 134 verso. Le pape écrit au roi, aux deux reines Isabelle et Philippa, aux évêques de Londres, Ely, etc. Le pape avait même prié Édouard III et Jean de Stratford archevêque de Cantorbéry de ne pas laisser trop longtemps les deux nonces dans l'un des ports de la Manche, avant de leur remettre les sauf-conduits (Arch. Vat. Reg. 138, Nos. 493-94).

[6] Nevill était parti en Angleterre. L'Évêque de Norwich demandait à rentrer dans son diocèse. Nicolino Fieschi partait pour Gênes. Thomas Fastolf, que les ambassadeurs anglais s'étaient adjoint au début des conférences, avait dû être remercié " a consilio regio se abstinet et ex causa " (Froissart, xviii. 234).

Édouard III de le rappeler en Angleterre ; il alla jusqu'à écrire au Roi qu'il ne se sentait plus en sûreté.[1]

L'arbitrage pontifical était resté sans résultat. Les conférences d'Avignon se terminèrent sans rupture violente, dans l'espoir d'une entente future, que les plus clairvoyants parmi les contemporains savaient d'autant plus irréalisable et impossible que le programme anglais n'était rien moins que l'unification de l'Occident : *Anglia, Scotia, Flandria, Francia, rege sub uno.* Pour le réaliser l'Angleterre devait conquérir la France. Quand un pays a des arrières-pensées de conquête et de domination, tout essai d'arbitrage, quelle qu'en soit la forme, est voué à un échec. Le pape Clément VI, qui avait écrit un traité sur la perfection de la vie, et avait un goût marqué pour Sénèque, ne se faisait aucune illusion sur les protestations fallacieuses de paix et d'humanité. Les conférences d'Avignon, qu'il avait présidées, où il avait offert une médiation loyale, sincère, et qui aurait pu être efficace, n'avaient d'autre issue qu'une guerre acharnée, inexpiable, que Philippe VI, passif, avait laissé s'engager dans les pires conditions pour la France. Joinville rapporte que Saint-Louis disait avec l'Écriture " Benoît soient tuit li apaiseour ". Édouard III roi d'Angleterre, prétendant au trône de France, ne méritait pas cette bénédiction promise aux pacifiques. Pour satisfaire ses visées impérialistes, il était bien résolu à jeter dans la balance toutes les forces de son royaume, fidèle à la devise dont les phylactères qui ornaient les bordures de ses tapisseries nous révèlent l'éloquente teneur : " *C'est comme c'est. It is as it is.*" [2]

Cette devise, dont un rôle d'achats de la Great Wardrobe de l'année 1342 nous a conservé la mention infiniment précieuse, n'est pas anglo-normande, mais anglaise. Je suis heureux d'en offrir la primeur au grand historien de l'Angleterre au XIVe siècle. Si Édouard III n'est pas demeuré pour l'histoire, comme Philippe le Bel, une indéchiffrable énigme, ce roi majestueux et fier, silencieux et impénétrable, dont l'intimité se dérobe, a souvent déconcerté l'analyse. Sa devise apporte le témoignage de la constance de ses desseins. Avec un pareil roi décidé à poursuivre une politique d'une incontestable unité, la Guerre de Cent Ans promettait d'être, à travers des vicissitudes tragiques, un règlement général de tous les comptes accumulés entre deux dynasties rivales par trois siècles de mauvais voisinage et de compromis boiteux. Elle devait être, ce qu'elle fut, un corps à corps décisif.

EUGÈNE DÉPREZ.

[1] " car autrement, très redoté seigneur, jeo demorray en peril, come jeo sai de certeyn et suy bien garny sauns feare nul profit " (*id.* 233).

[2] P.R.O. Accounts etc. (Exch.) [E. 101] Bundle 390, No. 1. Achats faits par Thomas de Cross pour le compte de la grande Garde-robe. Année 16 Éd. III (1342-1343). " XII tapeta lanata frectata cum sermonibus regis : It is as it is."

XXIV

THE ADMINISTRATIVE CHANCERY OF THE BLACK PRINCE BEFORE 1362

EDWARD OF WOODSTOCK, earl of Chester (1333), duke of Cornwall (1337), prince of Wales (1343), and prince of Aquitaine (1362), commonly and conveniently known to posterity as the Black Prince, was, from almost the day of his birth, the nominal head of a household organisation. For a time this household was controlled by his mother, Queen Philippa, and in part by the king himself, "the governor and administrator of Edward earl of Chester", but in a few years it obtained some measure of independence. By the time Edward had reached the mature age of ten, and had twice been "keeper of England" during his father's absence abroad, his household organisation, though still somewhat undeveloped, was a vigorous instrument of government, on a footing very different from that of the nursery establishment of his brothers and sisters.[1] From this household a highly organised and centralised administrative system was gradually developed to meet the needs of increasing responsibilities and expanding territories. Once again a familiar process of evolution can be discerned; the constituent parts of the Black Prince's household tended to go "out of court" and become independent government departments, even as the component parts of the king's household had done already. By 1344, if not earlier, the Black Prince's exchequer had permanent headquarters at Westminster[2]; his wardrobe was settled in Ironmonger Lane in the city before 1346.[3] The process of differentiation had been hastened by the French wars, for the government of the prince's lands had to be carried on in the absence of the prince himself, of part of his household, and many of his councillors. Thus the same tendencies which finally completed the development of Westminster as the political capital of England can be discerned in the administrative system of the Black Prince.[4] The analogy between a subordinate and

[1] Compare his fragmentary account for 1340 (Exchequer Accounts, 389/6) with those of the king's children for 1340 and 1341 (Ex. Acc. 389/9, /10, and /11).

[2] Ministers' Accounts, 1221/5 m. 5.

[3] Miscellaneous Books of the Exchequer, Treasury of Receipt, No. 144, 23. At a later date the houses of the wardrobe seem to have extended as far as the Old Jewry (*ibid.* No. 278, 175).

[4] See Tout, "The Beginnings of a Modern Capital," p. 28, from the *Proceedings of the British Academy*, vol. xi.

a regal household is here perhaps as complete as may be found in the records of any mediaeval household, with the possible exception of that of John of Gaunt, the Black Prince's brother and rival. Points of contrast are brought out, however, as well as of comparison, and it is one such contrast which I propose to emphasise here, by examining the writing departments of the Black Prince. Limits of space make it necessary to exclude all references to his seals and secretariat after he became prince of Aquitaine in 1362, for in discussing them we should be forced to examine his feudal position in Aquitaine, and to enter into the complexities of Gascon administration.

Four volumes of the Black Prince's letters survive in the Public Record Office, and are of course of first importance for a study of his secretariats. A fragment of a contemporary title-page in one of them states that it contains "notes of letters . . . sent to Cornwall and Devonshire";[1] in the same book at least one entry was cancelled because it was wrongly entered amongst the "notes of Cornwall" instead of amongst "the notes of England".[2] The character of these volumes as note-books or registers of "letters of warrant" (as their contents are sometimes called[3]) is thus clearly revealed, and later descriptions may be disregarded.[4] The letters noted were almost all from the Black Prince, and are concerned with the administration of his lands, and, to a lesser degree, of his household. The earliest volume contains notes of letters, issued between July 1346 and January 1348,[5] which deal with every part of his administration. Increasing business, however, made some system of classification necessary, and between 1351 and 1364 one volume contains letters concerning Cheshire,[6] another concerning Cornwall,[7] and another the prince's lands in England and the affairs of his household.[8] Probably a fragment of a similar Welsh volume also survives.[9] Both charters and letters patent and close are included in the registers; they are usually recorded in full, with the omission, however, of the details of the earl's title, of the protocol, and of the ratification. Sometimes, on the other hand, a mere memorandum of the issue and contents of a letter is given. From these letters we can obtain an outline picture, with occasional detail, of the various departments of the prince's government. As the books were drawn up for practical ends rather than to satisfy the unnecessary curiosities of the student of history, they contain few direct references

[1] Miscellaneous Books of the Exchequer, Treasury of Receipt, 280.

[2] *Ibid.* 56d.

[3] *E.g. ibid.* 278, 158d.

[4] Some such descriptions are, for the Cornish volume, "proceedings before the council relative to the duchy" (Giuseppi, *Guide to the Public Records*, 212), or "The White Book of Tenures in Cornwall" (Misc. Bk. Ex. 280); for the English volume, "The Black Prince's Diary and Calendar" (*ibid.* No. 278, on the outside of the cover).

[5] Miscellaneous Books of the Exchequer, Treasury of Receipt, No. 144, henceforth cited as Misc. Bk. Ex. 144.

[6] Misc. Bk. Ex. 279.

[7] Misc. Bk. Ex. 280.

[8] Misc. Bk. Ex. 278.

[9] Ancient Correspondence, lviii. No. 35 (1354–56).

to the institution responsible for their upkeep; indirectly, however, some information may be gleaned as to the methods by which the secretarial side of the prince's administration was carried on.

Some of the letters entered in these registers are written in Latin; these include most letters of appointment, and other formal letters patent, most of the letters on ecclesiastical business, and, I think, all the charters. The majority of the entries, however, are in French; even matters of some importance may be dealt with in that tongue. It is sometimes difficult to detect why one letter should have been in the one language and another in the other; but generally the use of Latin seems to denote the maximum degree of formality. This conclusion would seem to confirm a suggestion which has been made, that the letters in Latin were issued under the prince's great seal, and those in French under his privy seal.[1] This hypothetic distinction, however, falls to the ground immediately on examination of the registers, for most of the formal letters in Latin are clearly stated to have been issued under the privy seal.[2]

At first sight the letters in the registers seem to fall into three artificial categories according to their ratification; in the first, and much the largest group, the details of ratification are obscured by the use of that comprehensive phrase "given *etcetera*", followed by the date. The omitted details may, however, sometimes be supplied by reference to other transcripts of the same letters, such as are sometimes found, for instance, on the Cheshire Recognisance Roll. In most of the letters which I have compared in this way it is clear that they were issued under the prince's privy seal;[3] occasionally they were given under "the seal".[4] In all probability, therefore, the letters in this group should properly belong to either of the other two groups, namely, that of letters clearly given under the privy seal, or the much smaller group of letters given "under our seal". In all three groups, however, the letters are written in either French or Latin, and there seems to be no difference in their form or subject-matter.

Further investigation shows that even the distinction between letters under the seal and letters under the privy seal cannot be maintained. References to "the seal" are so much less frequent than references to the privy seal that it is impossible to establish any distinction between them by the comparison of the subject-matter of the letters they authorised. Of two letters patent given on the same day,

[1] See the nineteenth-century description at the beginning of the Cheshire register.

[2] *E.g.* Misc. Bk. Ex. 278, 66 (charter), *ibid.* 68d (letters patent, with witnesses).

[3] For example, compare Misc. Bk. Ex. 144, 109 (order to the chamberlain of Chester to issue a pardon to John, son of Alexander Walley of Chester) with Recog. Roll, No. 32, m. 1, where a fuller transcript is given, the warrant also being recorded. Similarly, compare Latin letters patent appointing the first controller in Cheshire (Misc. Bk. Ex. 144, 56) with Recog. 32, m. 1d, where it is clear that this important letter is given under the privy seal.

[4] Compare Misc. Bk. Ex. 144, 151d with Recog. 32, m. 2d.

from the same place, and in the same language, one may be given by the privy seal and the other by the seal.[1] The first officer whom we know to have been in charge of a seal of the Black Prince was called "keeper of the seal", but there are indications that this seal was the privy seal.[2] Contrariwise, we find later " keepers of the privy seal " occasionally known as " keepers of the seal ".[3] Moreover, the same seal may sometimes be called " the seal " and sometimes " the privy seal ".[4] On the other hand, no two seals now exist, as far as I know, for any one date, except at times when the prince was abroad;[5] this may of course be due to the accidents of destruction and survival. Thus, although common sense may make one wish to disclaim the suggestion, and it is not possible to speak with certainty, it seems probable that " seal " and " privy seal " were different names for the same thing; no reason is apparent as to why the one term should be used rather than the other. It is clear that " the seal " does not denote a great seal, at any rate in the normal sense of the word and with its normal implications.

In the registers of the prince's letters, apart from sundry references to the secret seal and signet, there are no traces of the operations of any household seal other than " the seal " and " privy seal " which we have been discussing, and which we have seen to be practically identical. Thus from the general character of the registers we might infer that they were primarily concerned with letters of privy seal. We know, moreover, that registers of privy seal letters were kept, for a clerk was employed to write for the privy seal and register the letters.[6] The internal evidence of our registers also suggests that no others were kept simultaneously, and thus the identity of these registers seems firmly established. This identity is confirmed by an imposing heading in the margin of the Cheshire register, *De tempore domini Ricardi de Wolveston.*[7] Wolveston is known to have been made keeper of the privy seal about this time, and to have been responsible for the registration of privy seal letters.[8]

We have seen that in the four registers of the Black Prince's privy seal letters, rich though they be in administrative detail, there is no reference to his great seal before he was made prince of Aquitaine.[9]

[1] *E.g.* Misc. Bk. Ex. 278, 121.

[2] Letters of privy seal are frequent at this time, but there are no surviving letters under any other seal. Nor are there any references to the keeper of the privy seal. The inference is obvious.

[3] *E.g.* Richard Wolveston (Misc. Bk. Ex. 279, 127).

[4] *Infra*, p. 326, also p. 330.

[5] See, however, *infra*, p. 326, note 4. If seal No. 5554 (De Gray Birch, *Catalogue of Seals*) is rightly dated 1350, it is possible that two seals were in use during that year.

[6] Misc. Bk. Ex. 278, 28 (1352).

[7] Misc. Bk. Ex. 279, 108d (1352).

[8] *Ibid.* 278, 90 (1355).

[9] It is noteworthy that one reference to his great seal occurs soon after Edward became prince of Aquitaine (*ibid.* 251d), as well as a reference to " his chancellor of Gascony " (*ibid.*).

Thus, despite the best historical precedents, there are no mandates to the chancellor to issue letters under the great seal in his keeping, such as survive, for instance, on the fragmentary roll of privy seal letters of Edward of Carnarvon,[1] or such as the king so frequently addressed to his chancery. We are forced to conclude from the registers that the Black Prince had no great seal before 1362.

This conclusion seems to be compatible with our knowledge of the necessities of the Black Prince's administration, though indeed lack of information may be a cloak for many a false hypothesis. The privy seal sufficed for most of the ordinary work of government; we have seen that important commissions and grants were issued by its authority. But Edward of Woodstock had other seals also at his command. Most of the institutions of English government existed in miniature both in the ancient earldom of Chester and in the modern principality of Wales. These included an exchequer and chancery, hardly, however, distinguishable from each other, with writs and seals of their own. Although the registers of the Black Prince's letters contain no warrants for the issue of letters under the great seal, they contain many warrants addressed to the chamberlains of Chester or North or South Wales, for the issue of letters under the seals in their keeping. Such warrants usually refer to the issue of pardons and protections, seldom to the issue of commissions and appointments. Here it will not be possible to discuss the limits of the privy seal in these subordinate administrative systems, nor the scope of these local chanceries, which certainly possessed some measure of independent authority. It is clear, however, that in Chester and in Wales the local exchequer (or chancery) seals were virtually the prince's great seal. The Cheshire seal is sometimes called a "great seal"; [2] its character is indicated also by the use of white or green wax and not of red, which was so often the sign of a household seal. In Cornwall, and in the honours and other lands in England, the privy seal seems to have sufficed for all purposes. The system was certainly comprehensive, and left little scope for an additional, and still more important, seal, which would probably have usurped the position and fees of the local chanceries.

Even the evidence of those surviving seals which can be dated as before 1362 bears out our conclusion that the Black Prince had then no great seal; after that date he certainly possessed a most noble great seal, perhaps only used in Gascony, with which we are not now concerned. Most of these surviving seals are clearly small seals of various kinds.[3] Two seals, with a diameter of two inches, and similar except

[1] Miscellanea of the Exchequer, 5/2. [2] Misc. Bk. Ex. 279, 21^d, 22, etc.

[3] For a description see *Bulletin of the John Rylands Library*, vol. vii. pp. 109-117. Since writing that article I have found further information on the subject, the most interesting being a file of letters under the prince's seal as duke of Cornwall and earl of Chester (Chester, 1/1). The seal measures 1⅜ inches in diameter; its main features are an upright shield of the arms of England, probably with a label of three points, and

in details, have perhaps some resemblance to a great seal, though the wax used is red and the seals are made in one piece. The first survives, as far as I know, in a cast and a drawing only, so that speculation as to its nature is profitless. The other large seal, of similar design, in which the legend, unlike the first, omits any reference to France in the prince's title, was probably in use between the summer of 1360 and July 1362; it probably replaced its twin seal after Edward III. had renounced the title of king of France.[1] Now one of these seals, probably the former, was a privy seal, for the arc of a fragmentary impression of a seal of this size survives on a privy seal letter.[2] Elsewhere it is described as " the seal ",[3] but it was clearly not a great seal.[4]

As the Black Prince had no great seal before 1362, had he then no chancellor either? In the household of Edward of Carnarvon the chancellor had been a foremost minister. Yet in the Black Prince's registers, which teem with particulars about his servants from the greatest to the least, there is before 1362 no reference to a chancellor by name, and I have found only one to the office; this last when a groom was paid his expenses in bearing letters to " the prince's chancellor in London ".[5] There is no indication of his activity in the prince's administration, nor of his presence in the council. Other sources of information, however, are more helpful; local records of Cheshire and Cornwall supply three references to the prince's chancellor, while at least one appears in records of the king's chancery.[6]

---

a small lion rampant above the shield. The legend describes Edward as " First born son of the king of England, duke of Cornwall and earl of Chester ". The seal was still in use on 8 June 1345, more than two years after he had been made prince of Wales. A fine impression of the privy seal next used by the prince survives in Phillipps' Charters, No. 23 (John Rylands Library), and provides the only certain date for its use, that is, 13 March 1347 (see *Rylands Bulletin*, vii. No. 1, p. 111, note). I am indebted to Dr. Fawtier for a description of this seal. I can now identify seal No. 5555 (*Catalogue of Seals*, vol. ii.; *Rylands Bulletin*, vii. No. 1, p. 111) as a privy seal, in use abroad in 1360. Payment for the making of this seal (probably) is recorded in Misc. Bk. Ex. 278, 204[d].

[1] See *Rylands Bulletin*, vii. No. 1. pp. 112-114, for a description of these seals.

[2] Chancery Warrants I., File 1771, No. 7. This warrant may be dated as August 1, 1358 (*Cal. Pat. Rolls*, 1358–61, p. 89).

[3] Diplomatic Documents Exch., 1106.

[4] It seems probable that the privy seal in use in 1347 (*supra*, p. 325, note 3) continued to be used till 1353 at least, and was perhaps succeeded by the first of these larger seals, which probably continued to be used till autumn 1360. This first large seal was certainly in use in 1358 (Chancery Warrants I., File 1771, No. 7), and we know that different privy seals were in use in 1353 and 1358 (Misc. Bk. Ex. 278, 137). On this hypothesis, however, the date (1350) given in *Catalogue of Seals* for Seal No. 5554 (surviving only in a cast) would have to be abandoned. It is noticeable that the earlier method of sealing on the middle of the dorse was replaced by 1358 by the method in use for the king's privy seal letters (seal at one end, six slits).

[5] Misc. Bk. Ex. 278, 117.

[6] Ivo Glynton is referred to as chancellor in Sept. 1343 (Min. Acc. 1241/13, an account of the escheator of Cheshire); Richard Wolveston in March 1357 (Indented Receipts, File III. No. 1, in the Duchy of Cornwall Office); John Henxteworth (probably Hinxworth in Herts) in a Cornish account for 1362–63 (Min. Acc. in the Duchy of Cornwall Office, No. 15, m. 15[d]); John Hale is called chancellor in December 1346 (French Roll, 23 m. 5). An unnamed chancellor occurs in the detached address of a letter without date (Ancient Correspondence, liv. 27).

In each case, however, the men mentioned as chancellors—Ivo Glynton, John Hale, Richard Wolveston, and John Henxteworth—were keepers of the privy seal at the same date.[1] In their own departmental archives these men are never called chancellor. Too much importance must not be attached, however, to a merely nominal differentiation. It is clear that the keeper of the privy seal was the prince's chancellor, in fact if not in name, and that the office of the privy seal was the prince's chief secretarial department. Even if the obscure operations of " the seal " are taken to imply a difference from the privy seal rather than that identity with it which we have tried to prove, " the seal " would certainly have normally resided, in the same custody as the privy seal, in this central secretarial department, virtually the prince's chancery, to which we must now turn our attention.

The Black Prince's privy seal was presumably originally the seal of his wardrobe. Few of the stages of the growth of the wardrobe and the office of privy seal are known to us. The wardrobe appears very early in his lifetime, two months after his birth (September 1330) ;[2] the privy seal is mentioned in March 1334[3] if not earlier, but of its early custody we know nothing. In 1338 Edward was first made keeper of England in his father's absence, and his privy seal was then and subsequently used for national business.[4] Thus by that date it presumably had a keeper. In the spring of 1340, when the young duke of Cornwall was at Byfleet, playing at ball with John Chandos and others, and later in Suffolk, watching the departure of the king and his ships for Flanders and the battle of Sluys, his seal-keeper William Munden was in London on his lord's business, and was subsequently paid his expenses there.[5] After the king's departure the duke returned to London and its neighbourhood and the seal-keeper probably continued to reside within the household.[6] It is clear, however, that at this time the presence of the seal cannot be taken, necessarily, to imply the presence of the duke. The secretarial department was already so far developed that a clerk-subordinate was employed under the keeper of the seal ; this clerk was none

[1] The prince's keepers of the seal, or privy seal, were William Munden, acting 1340 (Exch. Acc. 389/6) ; Ivo Glynton, acting Jan. 1341 (*ibid.*), still acting March 1345 (Harl. MSS. 4304) ; John Hale, acting July 1346 (Misc. Bk. Ex. 144, 33d), still acting 10 Dec. 1353 (*ibid.* No. 279, 63[d]) ; Richard Wolveston, acting 1 June 1355 (*ibid.* 108), still acting 8 Oct. 1360 (*ibid.* No. 280, 107[d]) ; John Henxteworth, acting 1 May 1361 (*ibid.* No. 278, 236), still acting 1362–3 (Min. Acc. 15 m. 16[d], Duchy of Cornwall Office).

[2] *Foedera* (ed. 1816), II. ii. 798 ; *Cal. Pat. Rolls*, 1330–1334, 2. For the prince's wardrobe in 1332 see *Cal. Close Rolls*, 1330–1333, 517.

[3] Cheshire Plea Roll, 45 m. 19.

[4] See Chancery Warrants, Series I., Files 1532, 1533, and 1534. Also Déprez, *Études de Diplomatique*, 111.

[5] See Ex. Acc. 389/6 (part of roll of expenses of the duke of Cornwall for 14 Edward III.).

[6] Compare the places where the duke was staying, given in Ex. Acc. 389/6, with the places from which his privy seal warrants as keeper of England are dated (Chancery Warrants, I., 1534).

other than that Richard Wolveston who subsequently also became keeper.[1]

Ivo Glynton was the next keeper of the seal, and certainly acted between January 1341 [2] and March 1345,[3] if not for longer. Between these dates he is also called controller of the household.[4] This suggests that there was not as yet enough work for both a controller and a keeper of the seal, and that the two offices were combined, as in the wardrobe of Edward I.[5] or of Edward II. at the beginning of his reign.[6] By August 1344, however, they were separated,[7] perhaps in consequence of the increased business after Edward became prince of Wales. In this respect, if not in others, the wardrobe of Edward of Woodstock was already more highly developed than his grandfather's had ever been as prince of Wales.

The first surviving privy seal register begins in July 1346.[8] This contains a few letters, in Latin and without note of the warrant of issue, given at Titchfield in Hampshire in the early part of that month, which were obviously issued on the eve of the prince's departure from Portsmouth for the Crécy-Calais campaign; they are interspersed amongst later letters, usually in French and written from Westminster. The latter were normally warranted by the testimony of the archbishop of Canterbury, though notes of other warrants occur occasionally. The warrants of the archbishop were, however, written in subsequently to the entries themselves, in a different hand; they were, moreover, put in mechanically at the end of each letter, even if another warrant was already recorded. Thus these warrants seem to indicate some uncertainty as to method, or unfamiliarity with the technique of registration. It would be tempting to guess that this was the first register of the sort that was kept, and that the original intention was to record letters issued during the prince's absence. Some sort of a record of letters issued, however, was certainly kept earlier.[9]

Whether recently acquired or not, the habit of registration was probably continued, though no registers survive for the period between January 1348 and February 1351. By 1364, when they end, the registers which we possess are but the ghosts of their former selves, as is easily explained when we read that in April 1364 they were two and a half years in arrear, and that a special clerk had to be employed to bring them up to date.[10] In 1352 a clerk had been appointed by the

[1] Ex. Acc. 389/6.

[2] Ex. Acc. 389/6.

[3] Harl. MSS. 4304, p. 10d. This is the transcript of a household account for 1344-45.

[4] Viz. from 1 February 1341 (Ex. Acc. 389/13) till July 1344 (Ex. Acc. 390/3).

[5] Tout, *Chapters in Administrative History*, ii. 37.

[6] *Ibid.* 286.

[7] Peter Darran was controller in August 1344 (Harl. 4304).

[8] Misc. Bk. Ex. 144.

[9] Misc. Bk. Ex. 278, 158^{d}, which refers to a search amongst "the copies of the letters of warrant" and the finding therein of a letter dated 16 Sept. 1345, that is, nearly a year before the first surviving register.

[10] Misc. Bk. Ex. 278, 272^{d}.

prince's great council to write for the privy seal and to register letters under it, at a fee of a hundred shillings.[1] In 1355 this sum was paid to the keeper of the privy seal, presumably to hand on to the registrar, for whom he was responsible.[2]

A division of the prince's household is clearly indicated in the earliest of his registers. Part of his household remained at home, while part followed him to the wars. One seal remained at Westminster, in the custody of the keeper of the prince's exchequer there,[3] and most of the prince's letters during his absence were issued under this seal, which was usually known as the privy seal,[4] sometimes as the seal. A clerk was ordered to remain in England to write all letters under this seal.[5] Other letters were issued by the prince himself from Calais and its neighbourhood, and some of these are recorded in his register,[6] though it was presumably kept at Westminster. The seal used at Calais was also called the privy seal; [7] thus it was probably in the custody of John Hale, keeper of the privy seal, who seems to have accompanied the prince.[8] Thus the Black Prince, like his father, made special arrangements for sealing during his absence, and had one seal for use in England and another for abroad; both seals, however, were certainly privy seals. The warrants of two letters sealed at Westminster show the formalities which might attend the use of the prince's seal during his absence. A sealed bag was opened in the presence of various influential councillors, the seal applied to the documents and then returned to the bag, which was again formally re-sealed.[9] The note of this procedure seems to have been recorded because the business in hand, a licence to elect the bishop of Llandaff, was of exceptional moment, and there must be no doubt at all of its authenticity.[10]

Similar arrangements for sealing during absence were made in 1355 when the Black Prince went to Gascony. Sealing went on at Westminster in the same way as during his earlier absences.[11] A special

[1] Misc. Bk. Ex. 28d.

[2] *Ibid.* 90.

[3] Peter Gildesburgh (Misc. Bk. Ex. 144, 33d, 71d); he was certainly keeper of the prince's exchequer from August 1344 (Harl. 4304) to Nov. 1347 (Misc. Bk. Ex. 144, 131d).

[4] *E.g.* Misc. Bk. Ex. 144, 15d. After Edward's return this seal was referred to as "*notre prive seal quel nous avons use en Engleterre*" (*ibid.* 114). Gildesburgh is once called "keeper of the privy seal" (Ancient Correspondence, liv. 27).

[5] Misc. Bk. Ex. 144/38. Richard Wath was to stay in England to write those letters which were ordered to be issued under "*notre seal quel nous avoms ordeynez par avis de notre conseil a demorer deriere nous pur lesploit de nos busoignes et deliverance du poeple*". Richard was called clerk of the privy seal some months later (*ibid.* 71).

[6] *Ibid.* 23.

[7] *Ibid.* 102, cp. 33d, where letters originally given before Calais were renewed at Westminster "*sub sigillo alio privato*".

[8] *Ibid.* 33d.

[9] Misc. Bk. Ex. 144/34.

[10] Difficulties had arisen in 1345 in connection with a licence to elect issued during the king's absence (see B. Wilkinson, *Bulletin of the John Rylands Library*, vol. viii. p. 111).

[11] As no registers survive for the period 1348–51 there is little information as to sealing arrangements during Edward's absence in 1349.

seal, of which many impressions survive, was made for his use while abroad. This seal was occasionally called the privy seal but usually "the seal", or "the seal used in Gascony". Sometimes it was called "our seal pendant",[1] though it was certainly sometimes applied. This seal was deemed to have equal authority with the privy seal which remained in England.[2] Though always used in Gascony and not in England, this personal seal of the Black Prince's must not be confused with the normal Gascon seal, "the seal of the court of Gascony".

In 1346, when the Black Prince went abroad, the privy seal in England seems to have been kept at the exchequer of Westminster.[3] This practice was not continued. It was soon found necessary to have some sort of independent headquarters, and the keeper of the privy seal was paid the cost of hiring a house while the prince's business kept him in London. The cost of his boat-hire between the city and Westminster continued, however, to be allowed him.[4] In 1355–7 and 1359–60, when the prince was abroad, his privy seal letters were normally dated from London and not from Westminster. When the prince was in England the privy seal still itinerated with him; it was in Cheshire in 1353, for instance, and in Cornwall in 1354. In 1355 and 1359, when he went abroad, the privy seal accompanied him to Plymouth and Northbourne by Sandwich, the ports of embarkation. On his departure it returned to London. On his return from Gascony in 1357 the Black Prince kept his favourite feast of the Trinity in the bishop of Ely's house in Holborn,[5] and we find that the keeper of the privy seal had a chamber allotted to him there,[6] perhaps in a room over the gate.[7] At other times the temporary home of the privy seal may perhaps have been in the prince's house near the church of St. Laurence Pulteney,[8] or in the houses of the wardrobe.

Though experienced in administrative work, the keepers of the privy seal were persons of no great distinction; their names are unfamiliar, their standing uncertain. Naturally they never rivalled in prestige the lay heads of the household such as Nigel Loring and Edmund Wauncy, nor do they ever seem to have been conspicuous among the prince's councillors. The keeper of the seal was always eclipsed by John Wingfield, who was for years the most active force in

[1] *E.g.* Diplomatic Documents Exch. 1632, and *Foedera*, III. i. p. 346 (1816 edition).

[2] For an account of this seal see *Rylands Bulletin*, vii. pp. 114-16. It is called a privy seal in Misc. Bk. Ex. 278, 108.

[3] It was in the custody of the keeper of the exchequer. Letters were also sealed in "the council-chamber" at Westminster. This was perhaps the king's council chamber (Misc. Bk. Ex. 144, p. 34).

[4] *E.g. ibid.* 278, 90.

[5] *Ibid.* 118d. The temporalities of the bishop of Ely were then in the king's hands and were let at farm by him from Mich. 1356–7 (*Cal. Close Rolls*, 1354–60, p. 392).

[6] Misc. Bk. Ex. 278, 120d.

[7] *Ibid.* 279, 146.

[8] This is perhaps suggested in Misc. Bk. Ex. 278, 172d, also *ibid.* 280, 66d.

the household, and in turn steward of the prince's lands,[1] chief of the council,[2] attorney of the prince [3] and governor of his business.[4] The keepers received the not inadequate remuneration of five shillings a day as wages,[5] perhaps only for such periods as they were without the household,[6] but despite this apparently sufficient allowance Wolveston had to be paid quickly, "seeing that he has not prospered greatly and cannot support his great expenses unless he is more promptly paid ".[7] Wingfield, on the other hand, received the enormous wage of ten shillings a day,[8] and was in the unenviable position of being able to lend money to his impoverished master,[9] though later a special gift was made him to meet his debts after a prolonged stay in the city of London on the prince's business.[10] Thus we find that the keeper of the privy seal was by no means the prince's foremost minister; it is doubtful, moreover, whether there was much business with which he could deal without warrant from some other department of the prince's administration, or the personal authorisation of the prince or of members of the council.

The warrants which authorised the issue of privy seal letters are shown in the " notes of warrants " frequently given in the registers. Many of these denote a verbal order; for example, " by command of the prince himself ", " by the advice of the council "; others refer to written authorisation, as " by warrant of the signet ", " by bill endorsed by the council ". A comparison of these notes of warrants yields much information about the important elements and persons in the prince's administrative system, both when he was abroad and when he was at home; moreover, a careful study of them in connection with the subject-matter of the letters might well cast light upon the departmental powers of the keeper of the seal, to name but one possibility. The complete absence in three of the registers of any warrants " by letter of privy seal " is surely yet additional proof that they are registers of the privy seal, and not of any other more important instrument. An occasional warrant by letter of the privy seal occurs in the first register; three of these, during the prince's absence, clearly refer to his privy seal abroad; [11] the fourth, however, occurs some three weeks after his return home and is less explicable.[12] The warrants are almost as

[1] *Cheshire Chamberlain's Accounts*, 162 (Record Society of Lancashire and Cheshire, vol. lix.).

[2] Misc. Bk. Ex. 278, 20.

[3] *E.g. Cal. Close Rolls*, 1354–60, 489, 657.

[4] " *Governour de nos busoignes*," 1358 (*ibid.* 150^{d}). John Delves succeeded later to this position (*ibid.* 261^{d}).

[5] *Ibid.* 278, 63^{d}, 90, and 236.

[6] *Ibid.* 63d, also 236; Harl. 4304, 16d, etc.

[7] Misc. Bk. Ex. 278, 90.

[8] *Ibid.* 150d (in 1358).

[9] See, for example, the book of the prince's daily expenses in Gascony (1355–6), which survives in the Duchy of Cornwall Office.

[10] Misc. Bk. Ex. 278, 179^{d}.

[11] Misc. Bk. Ex. 144, pp. 30d, 38, and 100.

[12] *Ibid.* 129. One such warrant is also recorded in Cheshire Recognisance Roll 32, m. 2. The enrolment of warrants on the Recognisance Roll was not, however, carried out at all systematically at this date.

numerous in their variety as those of the king's chancery,[1] and in them we can undoubtedly trace its influence upon the Black Prince's privy seal department. The name of the clerk who drew up a letter does not as yet seem to have been used as additional authentication in the secretariat of the prince. Perhaps, however, hardly enough privy seal letters survive to test this generalisation ; on the analogy of the royal chancery, such notes would not have been recorded in the registers.

With the prince's secret seal or signet we are not here much concerned. It is not even clear whether these were the same or different seals. As soon as the privy seal began to leave the prince's person, another seal must have been needed ; by 1342 he certainly possessed a secret seal.[2] There is little indication that it was at any time the seal of that most elusive portion of any mediaeval household, the chamber ; though the Black Prince certainly had a chamber, which was more than a mere privy purse, for certain lands seem to have been associated with it for administrative purposes.[3]

These are all the related facts which I have been able to collect as to the secretarial arrangements of the Black Prince before 1362. Inevitably, the balance of the picture is destroyed by detail in one part, and by its absence in another, but the broad outlines are clear. Like the king the young Edward had a signet, secret seal, and seal of absence. He had also a small secretarial department, with the privy seal as its instrument, the keeper of the seal as its official head, and the registers of which we have spoken as its records. In these registers, comparable with the chancery rolls, in the notes of warrants which authorised the issue of letters, and in its general administrative functions, the privy seal department of the Black Prince corresponded with the chancery of the king ; and to this extent he may be said to have possessed an administrative chancery. Yet this chancery seems to have acquired but little departmental independence ; the heart of the Black Prince's administrative system was not the chancery, but the council ; and amongst the councillors the keeper of the seal was not conspicuous. In addition to the central writing department, however, the Black Prince had various local chanceries which issued letters by warrant of his privy seal, and which, within their own territorial limits, and for some purposes, filled the place which the king's chancery held in relation to the king's privy seal office. Thus in one aspect this central secretarial department corresponded to the royal chancery, in another to the office of the king's privy seal. It was in fact a veritable maid of all work, aided upon occasion by the outside help of the

[1] See B. Wilkinson, " The Authorisation of Chancery Writs under Edward III.", *Bulletin of the John Rylands Library*, vol. viii. No. 1.

[2] Min. Acc. 1241/13.

[3] There was, for instance, a " steward of the lands of our chamber " (Misc. Bk. Ex. 278, 79^{d}).

local chanceries; for all general purposes, however, its aptitude was unquestioned.

The Black Prince's single and undifferentiated central secretarial department presents an obvious contrast with the cancellarial organisation of his grandfather before his accession to the throne. Edward of Carnarvon, as prince of Wales and earl of Chester, possessed both a great and a privy seal in addition to the local seals. His chancery, however, is hardly distinguishable from his wardrobe,[1] and it is possible that the departments of his great and privy seal were not sharply differentiated. A more striking contrast is presented by his chancellor, his foremost minister, who was an infinitely more important person than the Black Prince's keeper of the privy seal. Thus the difference between the secretarial organisations of Edward of Carnarvon and Edward of Woodstock is reflected throughout the whole of their respective administrative systems. Points of contrast are somewhat less marked in a comparison of the Black Prince's secretarial office with that of John of Gaunt. The surviving registers of John of Gaunt's privy seal letters are similar to those of the Black Prince,[2] the work of his privy seal in his administrative system seems to have been much the same, and there is little indication in the published registers of the operations of a great seal other than the seal of Spain.[3] Yet the registers reveal an active chancery and chancellor, in those very words. The chancellor seems, however, to have kept the privy seal.[4] It is probable, therefore, that here, as in the Black Prince's household, there was one central secretarial department, in this case, however, with the chancellor as its head.[5] This chancellor seems to have been much more important than Edward's keeper of the seal. Thus these tentative comparisons reveal similarities and dissimilarities not only in the writing departments themselves, but in household administration as a whole; they prove that only after detailed study of each part might effective comparisons be made of the subordinate royal households of the fourteenth century.

MARGARET SHARP.

[1] Tout, *Chapters*, etc., ii. p. 178.

[2] See *John of Gaunt's Register*, 1372–76 (Camden Society, Third Series, vols. xx. and xxi.).

[3] *Ibid.* ii. 1795, which mentions "*notre plat seal de les armes d'Espaigne*". For Lancaster's seals see S. Armitage-Smith, *John of Gaunt*, Appendix VII.; this does not mention a great seal (except for Spain) before 1377.

[4] *John of Gaunt's Register*, ii. 1795. There was sometimes, however, a keeper of privy seal in England who was to make letters of presentation, etc.; this was normally a chancery matter (*ibid.* i. 323).

[5] After 1377 there was also a great seal for the duchy of Lancaster (Armitage Smith, *op. cit.* 209), but the chancellor of the duchy also kept the privy seal (*Reports of the Deputy-Keeper of the Records*, No. XL. 52).

XXV

WHAT BECAME OF ROBERT RAG, OR SOME CHANCERY BLUNDERS

ON or about the feast of the Assumption (August 15, 1367), in the forty-first year of King Edward the Third, the Abbot of Bruern took it into his head to exercise certain rights which he believed his abbey to possess in some land in Eastleach Turville. The land in question is described as lying in the field (*campo*) of Eastleach Turville, and also as adjoining the king's high road, and without a survey of the manor it is not easy to say what these descriptions mean. Eastleach Turville itself lies on the River Leach, which rises at Northleach and runs into the Thames at Lechlade. It is close to the border of Oxfordshire, in which Bruern Abbey lies, but is in the county of Gloucestershire, being indeed in the hundred of Brightwellbarrow in that county. This hundred is one of the seven hundreds which were grouped together as the seven hundreds of Cirencester, which had been granted to the Abbot and convent of Cirencester by King Richard I. by a charter [1] dated at Westminster on the 12th day of October in his first year. The jurisdiction of the seven hundreds seems to have been concentrated at Cirencester; the prison was there, the gallows were there; the hundred of Cirencester was spoken of as the chief hundred of the seven, and at the time of this story John Sergeaunt was steward of all the hundreds for the Abbot of Cirencester. It is pretty clear that the Abbot of Bruern resented the position in which he found himself; according to the statements made by John Sergeaunt in the law-suit [2] to be described hereafter, he was bound to find one tithing man from his tenants at Eastleach Turville to come with the tithing to the view of frank-pledge of the hundred of Brightwellbarrow thrice in the year; he was also bound to pay eighteen pence at each view of frank-pledge as common fine (*comynfyn*); and finally he was bound to make suit to the hundred of Cirencester every three weeks. It was over these duties that the quarrel began; the Abbot of Bruern found no tithing man, and the tithing of Eastleach did not appear at the place of

[1] *Calendar of Charter Rolls*, vol. v. p. 212.

[2] Coram Rege Roll (K.B. 27/429), Hilary, 42 Edw. III. m. 32. I owe this reference to the skill and kindness of Miss Putnam.

meeting of the hundred of Brightwellbarrow (Barrow in Hatherop), and presumably the common fine was not paid. In consequence the Abbot of Bruern was amerced, and the amercement was fixed at 6s. 8d. The Abbot of Bruern did not pay the fine, and for this refusal and other arrears of suit and dues the steward of the Abbot of Cirencester seized by way of distraint no fewer than thirteen oxen. It is true the steward only kept them one day, but in order to recover them the cellarer of Bruern had to give security, a course repugnant to the dignity of the Abbot. Moreover, in another case, where three oxen had been taken at Marsden in connexion with another dispute of the same kind, the Abbot of Bruern had not been able to recover them at all. It seems clear that the Abbot of Bruern felt that he ought to take steps to assert his independence.

Accordingly on the 15th of August he set up at Eastleach Turville a new gallows on his own ground in that place, as a visible sign that he claimed to have the right of doing justice there on all thieves taken in his land or without it, provided that they were taken with the goods stolen in his land and were taken by the owner pursuing his property; which is the definition given by John Sergeaunt himself of the liberty of infangthief and outfangthief, if I understand him correctly.[1] The appearance of the gallows was of course a challenge to the Abbot of Cirencester, and his steward, John Sergeaunt, was not slow to take it up. On the Friday after the feast of St. Faith, that is the 8th of November 1367, he held the court of the hundred of Brightwellbarrow at Barrow, and there found by inquisition the following facts. The Abbot of Bruern, said the jury, has set up a gallows in the field of Eastleach Turville where no gallows was ever seen before, and this gallows is within the liberty of Cirencester. On the same day John Sergeaunt, with Walter Haryng and William Wollpenne, John Brut and Walter Coriot, went to Eastleach Turville and threw down the offending gallows, broke them up and even cut them in pieces, if we may believe the statement of the Abbot of Bruern.[2] The next step of that Abbot was to have the gallows or rather a new gallows set up again, and again they were thrown down. No one knew by whom this second outrage was committed. None of the inquisitions taken on the matter knew the names of the guilty persons; and John Sergeaunt denied that he had been concerned in the matter. Possibly he spoke the truth. A new gallows is not likely to have been a popular institution. It may be worth noting that the jury of the hundred speak of it as a *califurcia* in the plural. The meaning of this term I do not know, but perhaps it was a gallows with two legs, as distinguished from the simpler form with one leg, and the more imposing varieties with three or four. At any rate its life was innocent, if short.

There seems to have been some further trouble after the first

[1] Coram Rege Roll, *loc. cit.*

[2] Coram Rege Roll, *loc. cit.*

destruction of the gallows. At any rate on the following day, according to the story told by the Abbot of Bruern,[1] certain of his men were assaulted and wounded by John Sergeaunt and his men, so that the Abbot lost their services for a fortnight. The exact truth of this affray does not appear, but it is worth noting as a proof of the bitterness that had grown up between the two Abbots. The Abbot of Bruern decided, it would seem, that the time had come to invoke the assistance of the law. He had an excellent legal weapon ready to his hand, in the fact that he had recently obtained letters of protection from the king, so that he could begin his action in the King's Bench and even join the king as plaintiff. In fact he seems to have started two legal proceedings at the same time. One of these was in the form of a civil action to recover damages from the Abbot of Cirencester for all the wrongs done him, which damages were estimated at £100. The other was a quasi-criminal action [2] intended to invoke on the head of the defendant any unpleasant consequences that might arise from the contempt of the king's protection. Both actions came on together at Gloucester before the court of King's Bench sitting there under John Knyvet as chief justice; and it may be noted that the court of King's Bench sitting at Gloucester was a more formidable tribunal than judges sitting as commissioners to take assizes, or deliver gaols, or hear and determine cases. There was a suggestion of the eyre about it, though the eyre itself was fallen into disuse. The record of the civil action this paper is not intended to discuss. A good many details can be found in it, and it deserves further study. Here and there it throws a dim light on the motives of the hero, and for this purpose it has been used. But in it the hero of the story never appears in person. The name of Robert Rag is not mentioned in it. It deals exclusively with the grievance of the Abbot of Bruern, and its only importance, apart from the details mentioned, is that it tells us some facts which will be set out later in this paper.

The crown case is more to the purpose, and extracts from the record of it will be found at the end of this paper. It has been stated above that this action was also due to the suggestion of the Abbot of Bruern, and probably this was the case. It is, however, quite likely that the Abbot did not quite know what he was doing when he set the legal machine in motion. On receiving the complaint the chancery issued a writ dated at Westminster on the 25th of November, not much more than a fortnight after the downfall of the gallows. This writ is addressed to John Golaffre, knight, William Hervy, John Herdewyk, and John Benet. Of these John Golaffre and John Herdewyk were local gentlemen, and William Hervy and John Benet were judges. They were only to inquire and return the finding of a jury of inquiry

[1] Coram Rege Roll, *loc. cit.*

[2] For this crown case see Coram Rege Roll (K.B. 17/431), Michaelmas, Rex, m. 39.

into the chancery; they were not empowered to hear and determine. They were to inquire into the affair of the gallows, into the taking of the oxen, and into any other wrongs done to any other persons in the county of Gloucester by the Abbot and convent of Cirencester. The sheriff is to summon a jury to assist them in the usual manner. The commissioners met the jury of inquiry at Stow-on-the-Wold on the Monday after the feast of the Conversion of St. Paul, being the 31st of January 1368, and the following finding was then drawn up. The jury found that the gallows set up by the Abbot of Bruern had been thrown down on the first occasion by Nicholas, Abbot of Cirencester, and his servants in spite of the king's protection. They made no finding as to the second removal of the gallows. They also found that on two occasions the Abbot of Cirencester and his servants had distrained the Abbot of Bruern by seizing his oxen, but they did not find that the distraint was in any way wrongful. As to other wrongs done by the Abbot of Cirencester they found that John Heywod of Cotes was a resetter of felons, and that he had received three horses and thirteen oxen which had been stolen in Berkshire. For this felony he had been taken and imprisoned in Cirencester gaol, whence he had escaped by bribing the Abbot and his servants. Apart from this scandal they found nothing to report against the Abbot of Cirencester or his servants. It will be seen that this finding left the matter of the gallows very much where it was. It was for the Abbot of Bruern to prove his right to have a gallows at Eastleach Turville, and to do this he must produce charters granting him such a right; he must show that he had a grant of infangthief and outfangthief in that manor, if he wished to establish his independence of the Abbot of Cirencester, the undoubted lord of the seven hundreds.

It will be remembered that the inquisition was to be returned into chancery. Whether this was done or not is not clear. But on the 10th of February John Knyvet, chief justice of the King's Bench, issued a writ from Gloucester, under his own *teste* and the seal of the court, ordering William Hervy to send to him all indictments found before him against Nicholas, Abbot of Cirencester, touching wrongs done by him to the Abbot of Bruern, and touching all trespasses committed by the said Nicholas against the king and others, in order that justice might be done in the matter. The civil action brought in the court at Gloucester must by this time have got towards its end. The crown case had now to be dealt with. The presiding judge must have already seen the charters produced by either side in the civil action and heard the pleadings of the parties; he also had before him the finding of the jury at Stow described above, and a presentment made in his own court at Gloucester. The names of the persons making this presentment are not given, and I have not undertaken the further search in the Coram Rege rolls which might reveal them. The presentment adds nothing to the facts already given in this paper; but it lays stress on the fact that the gallows was a new institution, and it gives the date of its first overthrow as the Friday before the feast of St. Denis, thus using a different notation for the day otherwise described as the Friday after the feast of St. Faith. The presentment professes complete ignorance as to the persons who cast down the gallows on the second occasion, and it cites in full the finding of the jury of the hundred already given. After hearing these findings the court ordered the sheriff to summon the Abbot of Cirencester and John Sergeaunt to appear and answer; and on the 14th of February, described as the Monday after the octave of the Purification, they appeared in court in person and submitted themselves to the king's grace in the matter. On the same day they also came to a settlement of the civil action. For a memorandum on the Coram Rege roll [1] records that Nicholas, Abbot of Cirencester, came before the king at Gloucester on Monday the feast of St. Valentine and granted for himself and his successors that they would observe the charter of King Richard made to the Abbot of Bruern, and confirmed by the present king, and that he and his convent would ratify that charter by their common seal, in such form as should be declared by the council, and that in future they would do nothing against the liberties therein contained. With this the Abbot of Bruern was content, as he well might be, and he allowed the civil action to drop. The crown case, however, went on to the Michaelmas term at Westminster, and on the octave of St. Martin (November 10, 1368) the Abbot of Cirencester and John Sergeaunt appeared in the court of King's Bench in person.

Whether they knew what there awaited them is a matter for conjecture; but in all probability they were not unprepared. It is pretty clear that a good deal had happened in the interval and that the council had been busy. It was probably due to the proceedings before the council mentioned in the agreement between the two abbots, that the charter of King Richard, on which the whole case of the abbot of Bruern rested, had come under inspection. At any rate in some way or other the king had become aware that in this charter produced before the court at Gloucester by the Abbot of Bruern the word "Fiffehide" had been erased, and the word "Estlech" written in its place. It will become clear that neither the council nor the chancery had ever seen the altered charter. The chancery, indeed, believed that the altered charter had been submitted to them for confirmation and actually confirmed as altered, and that it was on this confirmation that the Abbot of Bruern had sued for an allowance of his liberties in the matter between him and the Abbot of Cirencester in the court of King's Bench. And it would seem that this was the charge on which the Abbot of Bruern had been summoned before the council. On the

[1] Coram Rege Roll (K.B. 17/429), Hilary, 42 Edw. III. m. 32 B. d.

quinzain of Michaelmas the Abbot appeared and told the following story. One, Robert Rag, he said, a monk of Bruern, was the man who made the erasure and then removed the charter from the abbey, and he himself knew nothing of what had been done. Being further asked by the council whether he had any reason to give why the falsified charter and all the confirmations of the same should not be revoked and annulled, he replied that he had nothing to say. It is, indeed, not easy to suggest any possible line of defence open to the Abbot; and he cannot have been surprised that the council should have ordered him to remain in the king's court until the king should declare his will in the matter.

It was William, Bishop of Winchester, the chancellor, who himself laid before the court of King's Bench this admission of the Abbot of Bruern. And on hearing it the Abbot of Cirencester and John Sergeaunt naturally claimed that the case should be re-opened. At Gloucester they had put themselves on the king's grace; this they had done simply because they had been deceived by the falsified charter, and they urged that they ought now to be allowed to go without a day and without making any fine with the king. In due course the court gave judgement, that in view of the falsification of the charter, and on consideration of all the matters contained in the indictments and presentments before the court, nothing appeared to be laid to the charge of the Abbot of Cirencester and John Sergeaunt, and that they might therefore go without a day. The undertaking given by them in the matter of the civil action was of course disposed of by the action of the council. And so, it may be presumed, the Abbot and his steward went home, and are now out of the story.

So far our main source of information has been the roll of the Court of King's Bench. But that court took no part in the settlement of the matter of the falsified charter. The council had begun to deal with the case of the Abbot of Bruern and Robert Rag, and the council and the chancery kept it in their own hands. And a pretty mess they made of it by their own confession, not indeed without some help from the monks of Bruern. But before attempting to deal with the confusion into which they fell, it may be convenient to attempt to explain what must have been the truth of the matter. For it is pretty clear that the Abbot of Cirencester and John Sergeaunt had not understood their own charters, that the Abbot of Bruern and William de Balsham, his attorney in the civil action, had not understood their own case, and had probably relied upon Robert Rag, and that the chancery utterly failed to see through the fog so created. Whether it is possible to-day to clear up the whole confusion, may fairly be doubted, but the attempt shall be made. And to make the attempt it is necessary to settle what the charters were that were produced in court at Gloucester in the civil action. The Abbot of Cirencester based his defence on a charter of Richard I. dated at Oissel on the 20th of June in the 9th year of that king, and dated his possession of the jurisdiction over the seven hundreds from that year. In point of fact he had in his muniments a similar charter of that king dated at Westminster on the 12th of October in his first year, a fact of which at the date of the trial he was clearly ignorant. If the Abbot of Bruern was to succeed in his case, it would seem that he was obliged, or thought he was obliged, to produce an earlier charter granting to his house the liberties he claimed to enjoy in Eastleach Turville. He did this by producing two charters, one of King Richard dated in the first year of that king and the second a charter of King Edward III. confirming, with clause *licet*,[1] a charter of King Edward I., as he alleged, which confirmed a charter of King John which in turn confirmed the charter of Richard I. already mentioned. Now the date of the charter of Edward III. is not mentioned. But it may fairly be identified with a charter enrolled on the Charter Roll of 40 Edward III., on the first membrane of that roll; [2] and, as will afterwards be seen, that identification was actually made by the chancery of the time. This charter in fact does confirm, with clause *licet*, a charter not indeed of Edward I., but of Edward II.[3] dated at Westminster the 20th of February, in the eighth year of that king, which in turn confirms two charters in favour of Bruern Abbey, one dated at Westminster, 10 October, 1 Richard I., and a second, dated at Oxford, 29 March, 6 John, which is enrolled on the Charter Rolls [4] of that king. The charter of King Richard may be at once dismissed. It has nothing to do with the matter of the gallows, but it is likely enough that its existence had something to do with the confusion into which the chancery fell. The charter of King John is more important. It does not confirm the first charter of King Richard, but it is founded on it, and it does contain a grant of the required liberties in Eastleach Turville, which it calls Lech'. This grant, however, could not stand in view of the previous grant to Cirencester Abbey, and in consequence the Abbot of Bruern could only use it to support the charter of 1 Richard I. But there can be no doubt that both these charters, the charter of Richard I. and that of Edward III., were produced in court at Gloucester. And in their plea for the re-opening of the case the Abbot of Cirencester and John Sergeaunt both alleged that it was the altered charter of Richard I. that was produced in the court of King's Bench at Gloucester. But the chancery and the council had another and a more ingenious theory, which led them into trouble.

For this part of the story we must turn to the Chancery Rolls. On the Close Roll of 42 Edward III.[5] will be found the whole of the pro-

[1] This clause protected the grantee from the consequences of non-user.

[2] *Calendar of Charter Rolls*, vol. v. p. 196.

[3] *Ibid.* vol. iii. pp. 270-71.

[4] *Rotuli Chartarum*, p. 146. Also in *Monasticon*, vol. v. p. 497.

[5] Membrane, 8 d. Calendared in the Calendar of Close Rolls.

ceedings in the council in the matter of the falsification of the charter. The enrolment begins by setting out the confession (*cognitio*) of the Abbot of Bruern already described above, in the terms in which it appears on the Coram Rege Roll. Next follows the writ of the 25th of May 42 Edward III., by which the Abbot of Bruern was first summoned before the council. The note of the warrant for the issue of the writ is *per ipsum regem*; and it is a fair inference from this warrant that the king had at any rate been told that the writ was going out. In it the Abbot is ordered to be before the council on the quinzain of Michaelmas, and to bring with him the charter of Richard I. dated in the first year of that king, by which certain liberties were granted to Bruern Abbey, together with all other charters touching the liberties of the house and the confirmations of them; he is then to do and receive what the council shall decide. On the day named the Abbot appeared in person; he brought with him to the chancery the said charter of confirmation made by the present king of the charter of King Richard in which the erasure had been made, and he said that he had never seen the erased charter, but that Robert Rag had obtained the confirmation, and had run away from the monastery and taken the altered charter with him, if, in fact, it existed, so that the Abbot could in no way produce it. And so, says the enrolment, the charter of confirmation was given up, cancelled, and quashed. It is quite likely that the abbot did not know where Robert Rag had bestowed himself; it is even more likely that he did not wish to know. It is quite possible that the Abbot did not know that the charter of Edward III. did not contain any confirmation of the charter of Richard I., either with or without Robert Rag's emendation. But it seems utterly impossible to believe that the chancery should have accepted the statement of the Abbot on this point and cancelled the charter of Edward III. without discovering that it did not contain any confirmation of the charter emended by Robert Rag. But nevertheless this is what the chancery did. For the charter which was cancelled is the charter enrolled on the charter roll of 40 Edward III. on the first membrane of that roll, and there on the roll [1] is the note that this charter of confirmation is surrendered and cancelled for a falsification consisting in the erasure of one word in the original charter of King Richard contained in it, as appears by the confession of the Abbot enrolled on the dorse of the Close Roll of the 42nd year of King Edward the third. The analysis of the charter given above or a reference to the calendar will show that the statement of the Abbot was untrue and the consequent action of the Chancery absurd. But it was a misconception of long standing; in the commission to John Hervy and his fellows there is an allusion to the confirmation charter of Edward III., though it is not there stated to be a confirmation of the

[1] See *Calendar of Charter Rolls*, vol. v. p. 196.

important charter of Richard I. In the civil action the charter of Edward III. was alleged to contain a confirmation at several removes of this charter. In the proceeding before the council this was assumed to be the case by both the Abbot of Bruern and the chancery; and it is even assumed that Robert Rag first altered the charter of Richard I. and then got a confirmation of the altered charter. It is, however, impossible that this story can have had the smallest foundation. There is no reason to believe that the charter in question had ever been confirmed at all; at any rate there is no enrolment of such a confirmation on any of the chancery rolls of the reign of Edward III. But the conviction that Robert Rag had first altered the charter of Richard I. and then procured a confirmation of it as altered was so deeply imbedded in the mind of the chancery that they never succeeded in getting rid of it.

The result of the blunder was certainly hard on the monks of Bruern Abbey. It may be admitted that they deserved to lose one charter—as indeed they had already done; for even if Robert Rag returned to his abbey with the charter which he had carried off, it had been rendered useless by his machinations. But it was assuredly hard measure to lose another charter into the bargain. How the blunder was discovered we cannot guess, nor how the king was induced to set it right. But the entries on the charter roll show that the chancery was directed to correct its mistake, and that in correcting one blunder it could commit another. The first step was to cancel the cancellation of the confirmation charter of 40 Edward III. For this purpose a further note was added to the note of cancellation, and this new note states that the king, of his special grace, and because this charter had been erroneously cancelled instead of another suspected charter, had ordered Robert de Thorpe, his chancellor, by a writ of privy seal, dated 25 May in the 46th year of his reign, to renew this charter, so that the charter renewed was enrolled on the charter roll of the 46th year; where indeed it remains to this day. Nor did the king's favour stop there. He even did what he could to restore to Bruern abbey the charter which Robert Rag had taken with him. And so on the seventh membrane of the Charter Roll of 46 Edward III. there may be seen the enrolment of an exemplification of the charter which Rag had falsified. This is dated, not 10th October, but at Geddington on the 15th of September in the first year of Richard's reign.[1] A special clause was added to the exemplification, telling how a monk altered a word in this charter and then got the charter so altered confirmed and used it in a law-suit, and how, in consequence, there were proceedings in council against the Abbot of Bruern, and

[1] *Calendar of Charter Rolls*, vol. v. pp. 221-2 (May 1, 1372). This is the charter comprised in King John's charter, but not that (October 10, 1 Richard I.) confirmed, together with John's, in 8 Ed. II. and in 40 Ed. III. (see above).

how it was ordered that the confirmation should be cancelled, with a good deal more, and ending with the satisfactory assurance that all was to be as it was before Robert Rag took to evil ways. If any one enquires how it was possible to exemplify a charter, which had been stolen, which had never been enrolled, and of which no earlier text exists on the rolls of the chancery, the answer is easy. The chancery of Edward III. discovered an enrolment of the charter on the chancery rolls of King Richard I. It is perhaps unnecessary to remind the reader that chancery enrolments had not been invented in the reign of that king. It sufficed the chancery that a text of the charter had been discovered on one of the Carte Antique.[1] One would like to know how this was done; one would like to know why the chancery chose to call those mysterious documents the chancery rolls of King Richard. Perhaps it was only an artistic craving to add one more blunder to all the others committed in the case.

But it is time to consider Robert Rag and his achievements. It will be seen that it was possible in the fourteenth century in the year 1368 to alter a charter by erasing a word in it with a knife, to write a new word in its place, and by this device to deceive the advisers of an abbey, which was not without experience of litigation. It was even possible to evade the scrutiny of an eminent lawyer, then chief justice of the King's Bench and afterwards chancellor, and in the end so to confuse the officials of the chancery as to lead them into a ridiculous series of blunders. And yet any one who has ever examined a parchment document in which words have been erased and rewritten will appreciate the rashness of the attempt and the carelessness of the persons who failed to see the resulting alteration in the surface of the parchment, the increased transparency produced, not to mention the change in the writing. It is not the least part of Robert Rag's crime that he not only falsified a charter but also ran away with it, so that we can never really understand how he did it. But if the manner of his crime evades our inquiries, we can at least guess at his motives, even if we strain the evidence a little.

Let us put on one side the theory of the chancery that Robert Rag was a cunning villain who had laid a deep plot, and first falsified a charter and then obtained a confirmation of it. It rests on a series of misconceptions, which were only possible because the falsified charter had vanished with Robert Rag himself, so that neither the chancery nor the council ever saw it. Let us guess that he was the monk in charge of the muniments of Bruern Abbey, and that it was his duty to supply the charters on which William de Balsham, the attorney of the Abbot of Bruern, was to found his plea. We may even go further and suppose that the Abbot of Bruern spoke the truth when he said that Robert Rag had obtained the charter of confirmation

[1] Now numbered 17.

of 40 Edward III. already mentioned; we may even suppose that Robert Rag, when he did so, really believed that the charter of King John did confirm or repeat word for word the charter of King Richard. If this was the case, he might easily have almost gone into court without knowing that the charter of King Richard never mentioned Eastleach at all.[1] When he made this discovery he would have been in a difficulty. The charter of Richard was essential to his case; he could not at that late hour take the natural course and forge a whole charter with a definite grant of the right to have a gallows. His only chance was to amend the charter; and this he may have regarded as a more venial sin than it seems to us. After all, he would think, the word ought to have been there; why not correct a blunder? And so he took knife and pen and set to work. Now his next trouble would be to choose the point in the charter at which he would make his emendation. And here we come upon a curious fact. He picked Fifield as the name to alter. Now in the charter of King Richard the property of the abbey of Bruern in that place is described in some detail. This is, of course, natural, for Fifield lies close to Bruern itself, in Oxfordshire, and was probably the most important of the possessions of the abbey. These facts might, one would think, have suggested choosing another name in the charter to alter. On the other hand, there may have been present to Robert Rag's mind another fact, namely, that close to Eastleach Turville lies another Fifield, a small hamlet. Did he think or hope that something could be made out of this? Did he cheat himself with the argument that this made his crime less criminal? or did he see in it an opportunity for making confusion worse confounded? Perhaps he never even knew of it; and, indeed, to go further in this direction is to pass from history to fiction. Robert Rag is gone and has taken his charter with him. What became of him and it we shall never know; but the Abbot of Bruern, pronounced innocent of all knowledge of his crime, has made his own peace with the king.

One last note may be added. Nicholas of Ampney, the Abbot of Cirencester, has not left a good name as abbot; his troubles with the town of Cirencester were many and complicated. But he and John Sergeaunt seem to have got alarmed by their experiences in the suit about the gallows; and to have discovered that they had understated their case in relying upon the charter of 9 Richard I., when they ought to have pleaded the charter of 1 Richard I. For on the Charter Roll of 42 Edward III. there is an exemplification of the latter charter; and the abbey got two engrossments of it. It is well to be on the safe side, if one has to go to law.

C. G. Crump.

[1] The relation between the charter of John and that of Richard needs further study. It is possibly the source of the whole trouble.

APPENDIX

Coram Rege Roll (K.B. 27/431), Michaelmas Term.
Rex m. 39. (42 Edward III.) *Extract.*

Postea continuato inde processu coram domino Rege uersus prefatos Abbatem de Cirencestr' et Johannem Serieaunt usque ad hunc diem scilicet in Octabis Sancti Martini isto eodem termino ; ad quem diem coram domino Rege apud Westmonasterium uenerunt predicti Abbas de Cirencestre et Johannes Sergeaunt in propriis personis suis. Et super hoc uenerabilis pater W. Wyntoniensis Episcopus et domini Regis cancellarius per manus suas liberauit hic in Curia quandam cognitionem per Abbatem de Bruera factam in hec uerba. Cognitio Abbatis de Bruera facta coram Rege in cancellaria sua in quindena Sancti Michaelis anno regni Regis Edwardi tercii post conquestum quadragesimo secundo. Dominus Rex attendens quod Abbas de Bruera quandam cartam dudum Abbati et monachis dicte Abbathie de Bruera per dominum Ricardum quondam Regem Anglie progenitorem domini Regis nunc de diuersis maneriis, terris, tenementis et libertatibus in diuersis locis factam radi fecit mutando unum uerbum uidelicet hoc uerbum Fiffehida in eadem carta contenta in confectione eiusdem inserta et loco eiusdem inseri fecit hoc uerbum Estlech' et post mutationem illam cartam predictam cum illo uerbo de Estlech' in eo insertam per cartam Regis nunc confirmari optinuit et super confirmatione illa dictas libertates coram Rege in Banco suo in quodam placito inter ipsum Abbatem et Abbatem de Cirencestre pendente allocari prosequebatur, predictum Abbatem de Bruera coram Rege et consilio suo euocari fecit super premissis responsurum, qui coram dicto consilio Regis apud Westmonasterium in instanti quindena Sancti Michaelis comparens dixit quod quidam Robertus Rag' commonachus suus dictam cartam radebat et elongabat ipso Abbate penitus ignorante. Et quesito ab eo si quid dicere sciat quare dicta carta sic rasa et falsata ac omnes ratificationes et confirmationes super ipsam facte reuocari et adnullari non debeant, dixit quod non. Ideo preceptum est eidem abbati quod sub incumbente periculo a curia Regis non recedat sine mandato Regis speciali quousque dominus Rex inde preceperit uoluntatem suam. Unde iidem Abbas de Cirencestre et Johannes Seriaunt dicunt quod tempore quo ipsi de premissis posuerunt se in gratiam domini Regis ipsi decepti et omnino inde ignor[antes] fuerunt pro eo uidelicet quod carta domini Regis Ricardi de libertate tunc in curia hic prolata per quam idem Abbas de Bruera clamauit habere furcas predictas in predicto campo de Estlech' rasa fuit et falsata prout per cognitionem supradictam plene liquet per quod petunt quod ipsi absque aliquo fine cum domino Rege in hoc parte faciendo sine die recedere possint, etc. Et premissis omnibus et singulis tam coram domino Rege et consilio suo quam cur' hic ostensis et examinatis pro eo quod uidetur curie quod ex causa predicta et aliis causis in presentationibus predictis contentis non habetur aliqua materia in premissis ad ipsos Abbatem de Cirencestre et Johannem Seriaunt impetendos, ideo iidem Abbas de Cirencestre et Johannes Seriaunt eant inde sine die saluo semper iure domini Regis si quod, etc.

The other documents used in this paper are these :

Charter Roll, 8 Edward II. m. 6. This is the text of the charter of

Richard I. to Bruern Abbey, the confirmation of which was cancelled by mistake. *Calendar of Charter Rolls*, vol. iii. p. 271.

Charter Roll, 40 Edward III. m. 1. This is the confirmation charter which was cancelled by mistake. *Calendar of Charter Rolls*, vol. v. p. 196.

Charter Roll, 42 Edward III. m. 2. This is the confirmation charter obtained by the Abbot of Cirencester. *Ibid.* p. 212.

Close Roll, 42 Edward III. m. 8 d. The enrolment of the proceedings before the Council touching the forgery committed by Robert Rag. *Calendar of Close Rolls*, 42 Edward III. p. 492.

Charter Roll, 46 Edward III. mm. 7 and 6. These are the enrolments of the charters restored to the abbot of Bruern. *Calendar of Charter Rolls*, vol. v. pp. 221-2, 223.

Coram Rege Roll (K.B. 27. 427), Hilary, 42 Edward III., vol. 32. This is the record of the civil suit between the two abbots. It is not printed or calendared.

XXVI

THE ADMINISTRATION OF NORMANDY, 1420–22

On December 31, 1420, Henry V. and his queen arrived at Rouen from Paris.[1] He stayed in Normandy for about three weeks,[2] and during that time he met the Estates of the Duchy, secured a substantial grant of money, and overhauled the administrative machinery which in the last three years had gradually been constructed for the lands conquered by the English.[3] It was his first visit to Normandy since the signing of the Treaty of Troyes in the previous May. Before then, the future of Normandy had been doubtful, and it was impossible to regard the arrangements made for its government as more than provisional. But now it was settled that Henry was to rule Normandy for a time as king of England, and subsequently as king of France. While it is true that henceforth he seems to have based his claim to the duchy on the right of conquest,[4] it was implied, though not expressly conceded, in the Treaty that during the lifetime of Charles VI. he might exercise absolute sovereignty over Normandy. It was, however, categorically laid down that when, on Charles's death, Henry became king of France, it was to be reunited to the French crown.[5]

As long as Charles VI. lived, Henry would have been within his rights in administering Normandy as part of England. But it was unlikely that the French king would live long; and, all things considered, the wisest course was doubtless the one adopted by Henry—that is, to govern his conquered territory in France as a separate state, to try to make it pay for itself, and to continue, in its main features, the system

[1] Pierre Cochon, *Chronique normande* (ed. Ch. de Robillard de Beaurepaire, 1870), 285.

[2] He was evidently at Rouen on January 18, but three days later he reached Amiens on his way to England (Rymer, *Foedera*, etc. [1727] x. 49 *sq.*; *Calendar of Norman Rolls*, in appendices to Reports 41 and 42 of the Deputy Keeper of the Public Records [hereafter referred to as D.K.R.], Report xlii. 397, 398; *La Chronique de Enguerran de Monstrelet* (ed. Douët d'Arcq, Société de l'Histoire de France, 1859), iv. 24.

[3] *Rôles normands et français et autres pièces tirées des archives de Londres par Bréquigny en 1764, 1765, et 1766* (Mémoires de la Société des Antiquaires de Normandie, vol. xxiii. [1858], pp. 160, 181 *sq.*, 253; D.K.R. xlii. 397, 398; Thomas Walsingham, *Historia Anglicana* [ed. Riley, Rolls Series, 1863–64], ii. 336; *Thomae Elmham vita Henrici Quinti* [ed. Hearne, 1727], 294 *sq.*).

[4] " Come, par la grace de Dieu, par nostre Conqueste, Nous soions Paisiblement en Possessions et vraies Saisines du Duchie de Normendie et de nostre Conquest . . ." (*Foedera*, x. 56).

[5] Clauses 14, 15, 17, 18 (*Foedera*, ix. 799 *sq.*).

of administration already set up. How he meant to treat Normandy when he became king of France we cannot tell for certain. The duke of Bedford, after Charles VI.'s death, continued many of Henry V.'s arrangements, and the old relations between Normandy and the central authorities at Paris were not restored. Later, Philip the Good denounced Bedford's treatment of Normandy as a breach of the Treaty of Troyes, and used it as one of his pretexts for breaking his alliance with the English.[1] But the Treaty nowhere insisted that Normandy must revert precisely to its former position;[2] and we may well believe that Henry, who in any case was less conciliatory than his brother towards French opinion, intended that many of the institutions which he established in Normandy should be permanent.

It must be remembered that the French territory over which Henry exercised sovereign powers from May 1420 to his death, comprised more than Normandy proper. It was officially described in various ways: a form often used was "the duchy of Normandy and other parts subject to us".[3] What was covered by this and similar phrases seems nowhere to have been authoritatively defined; Henry's right to regions outside Normandy was even more vaguely treated in the terms of peace than his claim to the duchy itself, and the duke of Burgundy afterwards denied that it had been admitted at all.[4] Apparently, Henry demanded absolute control over everything which he had won by the sword before the Treaty was signed; but it seems never to have been made clear whether he meant merely the territory of which the English were in effective occupation on May 21, 1420, or whether, besides this, he claimed areas which they had once occupied and afterwards lost. Further, while it was stipulated in the Treaty that Henry's subsequent acquisitions should be to the advantage of the crown of France,[5] Gilbert Halsall, the English *bailli* of Évreux, was made captain of Dreux when that town was captured in August 1421.[6] It may be that the presence of English garrisons in Picardy in the following

[1] La Barre, *Mémoires pour servir à l'histoire de France et de Bourgogne* (1729), i. 342.

[2] Clause 18, which concerned the general relation of Normandy and the central government, stipulated that, when Henry or his heir became king of France, "ducatus Normanniae, necnon omnia et singula Loca per ipsum in Regno Franciae conquisita, erunt sub Ditione, Obedientia, et Monarchia Coronae Franciae supradictae" (*Foedera*, ix. 900). This left much to Bedford's discretion.

[3] "Conquestus de Ducatu nostro Normanniae et aliis partibus nobis subjectis" (*Foedera*, x. 142; cf. *ibid.* 103, 225); "Senescallum ducatus nostri Normannie et aliarum partium Francie nobis subjectarum" (Bréquigny, p. 159). Other descriptions are: "La duchie de normendie Et ailleurs du pays conquiz" (Exchequer Accounts [P.R.O.], 188/7, f. 1); "Normandie et autres pays de nostre conquest" (Bréquigny, 160); "Duchie de Normendie (*sic*) et . . . nostre Conqueste" (*Foedera*, x. 56); "In Ducatu nostro Normanniae et aliis locis Conquestus nostri" (*Foedera*, x. 106).

[4] La Barre, *op cit.* i. 342. Clause 14 might be taken as recognition of Henry's right to Normandy, but it says nothing about other regions already conquered (*Foedera*, ix. 899). Clause 17 admits that there are regions of France outside Normandy where Henry's rule is *de facto* accepted. Clause 18 is hopelessly ambiguous (*ibid.* 800).

[5] Clause 14, *Foedera*, ix. 899.

[6] D.K.R. xlii. 432, 437; Foreign Accounts (P.R.O.), No. 61, C.

April[1] was justified by military exigencies; but in any case it is evident that the frontier of "Normandy and the parts subject" to Henry was ill-defined and indeed variable, and it is impossible to do more than give a rough indication of it.

It was in the direction of Paris that English jurisdiction had been carried farthest beyond the limits of Normandy proper. The English *bailli* of Mantes exercised authority over the *viguerie* of Mantes and the *prévôtés* of Meulan, Poissy, St. Germain-en-Laye, and Montjoye, his sway extending to places within a dozen miles of the centre of Paris.[2] From St. Germain the frontier of the *bailliage* ran west to the Eure, which it struck not far south of Anet.[3] North of the Seine the *bailli* of Gisors had jurisdiction over Pontoise, Beaumont-sur-Oise, and Chaumont.[4] In other quarters, however, English power was not firmly established for any great distance beyond the limits of the duchy. To the north of Gournay English authority extended hardly, if at all, beyond the eastern frontier.[5] South of Alençon, it is true, English arms had on various occasions penetrated far into Maine, and at the beginning of 1421 their power extended some way south of Beaumont-le-Vicomte.[6] The English possessions in Maine were under the *bailli* of Alençon.[7] They were insecurely held, however, and were to be overrun by the dauphinists after the battle of Baugé.

No attempt was made to introduce English institutions into the regions under Henry's sovereignty. The system of local administration underwent no essential change. There were eight *bailliages*—Côtentin, Caen, Alençon, Évreux, Rouen, Caux, Gisors, and Mantes.[8] All the

[1] D.K.R. xlii. 448.

[2] Ch. de Beaurepaire, *Les États de Normandie sous la domination anglaise* (1859), 8; D.K.R. xlii. 397, 431, 448; Exchequer Accts. 188/7, ff. 5vo, 17.

[3] D.K.R. xlii. 435.

[4] *Foedera*, x. 160 *sq.*; Bréquigny, 184, 195; D.K.R. xlii. 397, 408. Nominally the *bailli* of Gisors had jurisdiction over the *bailliage* of Senlis (D.K.R. xlii. 360; the S. Lys of D.K.R. xli. 778, 779, xlii. 397, 408, 430 is evidently Senlis, which appears as Serntlyse and Seyntlyse in the account of William Philip, treasurer of war from October 1421 to the end of the reign [For. Accts. 69, F, Fvo]. But Senlis was never captured by Henry, and always had a French *bailli*. On September 21, 1421, indeed, Henry allowed the appointment of a new one (*Journal de Clément de Fauquembergue* [ed. Tuetey, Soc. de l'Hist. de France, 1903–15], ii. 27).

[5] In April 1422 there were English troops in garrison in Picardy (see above, p. 350), but this does not prove that the English were conducting the civil administration in the country around the strongholds they occupied. In the same month land at Tully in Vimeu was included in a grant made by Henry (Bréquigny, 199), but it would be rash to infer that Tully was under English rule.

[6] D.K.R. xlii. 386, 387. On the English position in Maine see R. A. Newhall, *The English Conquest of Normandy, 1416–24* (1924), 271 *sq.*

[7] Bréquigny, 161.

[8] Exchequer Accts. 188/7; Foreign Accts. 61, Fvo; D.K.R. xlii. *passim.* The term *bailli* was loosely used. The *bailli* of Dieppe, for instance, was a comparatively humble official who administered the property at Dieppe of the recalcitrant archbishop of Rouen (*Foedera*, x. 153, 195, 242; Bréquigny, 168 *sq.*, 184; Exch. Accts. 188/7, ff. 2vo, 13). Similarly, the so-called *bailli* of Eu was appointed as the king's agent in the comté of Eu while its lord, Henry Bourchier, was under age (Bréquigny, 195; *Foedera*, x. 195 *sq.*; D.K.R. xlii. 423; G.E.C., *Complete Peerage* [1887], i. 393).

baillis were Englishmen from the middle of January 1421 to the end of Henry's reign.[1] But the civil officers below the rank of *bailli* were almost all French. Of the *vicomtés* or *prévôtés* into which the *bailliages* were divided, none, so far as we can judge from the names that appear in the records, was administered by an Englishman. And scarcely an English name appears in the numerous extant documents appointing receivers, sergeants, *guernetiers*, *procureurs*, money-changers, officers of the mints, surveyors of weights and measures, keepers of seals, to mention no others.[2]

Few Normans, it is evident, would ever encounter an English civil official. And there is no sign of any attempt to anglicise the population of Normandy. A number of houses were granted to English settlers at Harfleur, Honfleur, and Caen, but not enough to be of political significance. Nor did Henry try to introduce a spiritual garrison of English clergy. Among the very numerous nominations to ecclesiastical dignities and benefices which are recorded in the rolls for 1421 and 1422, I have noted only twenty in favour of men with what seem to be English names, and but three of these were presentations to parish churches.[3]

On the other hand, the military administration of Normandy remained almost, if not quite, exclusively in English hands. Professor Newhall has carefully investigated the distribution of the English forces in the French territory under Henry's sovereignty. At the beginning of 1421, he thinks, the English garrisons numbered in all about 4000 men. On or near the important route connecting Cherbourg, Caen, and Évreux, there were approximately 1000. On the southern frontier, between Avranches and Verneuil, there might be 1400. The Seine valley required 900; the eastern boundary, from Pontoise to Eu, some 700.[4] The captains of the garrisons, royal or other, were almost all English. So were their lieutenants—an important consideration, for many of the captains were notable soldiers whose services were needed with the field army, and when this was so they were usually suffered to retain their garrison commands and exercise their authority by deputy.[5]

[1] As they had been throughout 1420 (D.K.R. xli., xlii. *passim*), with the probable exception of the *bailli* of Mantes (*ibid.* xli. 769), who for part, if not all, of that year had been on a different footing from the rest (Exch. Accts. 187/14).

[2] D.K.R. *passim*; Exch. Accts. 188/7.

[3] D.K.R. xlii. 410, 414, 422. One of the benefices in question was a chaplaincy of a garrison which consisted of English troops (*ibid.* 399). Two governorships of hospitals and eight cathedral or collegiate prebends were filled by Englishmen. So was the treasurership of Rouen cathedral and the archdeaconry of Neubourg (*ibid.* 396, 398, 410, 411, 414, 415, 420, 421, 422). There seem to have been still fewer Englishmen appointed to ecclesiastical positions before 1421.

[4] Newhall, *op. cit.* 216 *sqq.* Professor Newhall's conclusions are most interesting, but it is regrettable that he does not give detailed references to the evidence on which they are based.

[5] D.K.R. xli., xlii. *passim*; Foreign Accts. 61 Bvo *sqq.*, 69, G, Gvo. With the possible exception of Jehan Guernier (For. Accts. 61, Cvo; Exch. Accts. 188/7, f. 23), *alias* Gerner

About the central government information is scanty, and insufficient to supply answers to many questions that suggest themselves. Throughout the years 1420–22 Normandy was under civil rule, and the military, though their services were in frequent demand, were supposed to obey the civil authorities.[1] At the head of the administration was the chancellor, John Kemp, bishop of Rochester, who before Henry's death was translated successively to Chichester and London.[2] The Norman chancery was established at Rouen.[3] Kemp's staff included a keeper of the hanaper and a clerk, John Stopyndon, who had charge of the Norman Rolls,[4] but contemporary records reveal nothing else about its personnel. The chancellor was of course responsible for the great seal of Normandy,[5] but he is seldom mentioned in official documents, and it is impossible to estimate how much influence he actually exerted on the course of administration.

In organising the central government of his French possessions, Henry could not make much use of existing institutions. He did not, however, look to England for inspiration. If he consciously imitated anything, it was the administrative system of Normandy in the days of the Plantagenets. Under Henry II. the most powerful official in Normandy had been the seneschal. After the duchy had been seized by the French crown, the office was suppressed. But even before his conquest of Normandy was complete, Henry revived it.[6] At the beginning of 1421 it was apparently held by Hugh Lutterell,[7] but on January 18 he was succeeded by Richard Wydville.[8] Wydville's com-

(D.K.R. xli. 751), captain of Tancarville in 1422, all the captains of royal castles seem to have been English, but one or two Frenchmen, notably Guy le Bouteiller, captain of Rouen during the siege, were feudal tenants of castles (D.K.R. xli. 797, 800). The lieutenants were doubtless chosen by the captains, for their appointments do not appear in the Norman Rolls. We consequently do not possess a complete list of them. Further, the arbitrary orthography of the Norman chancery and treasury sometimes leaves one in doubt as to the nationality of a man named in their records. It seems likely, however, that the following were French : John Jaquemyn, lieutenant of Gisors in May and September 1421 (D.K.R. xlii. 425, 433 ; cf. xli. 772, xlii. 427) ; Thomas Gargante, lieutenant of Château Gaillard in May 1422 (Exch. Accts. 188/7, f. 17vo) ; and Peter de Lye, lieutenant of Arques in April 1421 (D.K.R. xlii. 428). But I have found no others.

1 *Foedera*, x. 107.

2 *Foedera*, x. 142, 151 ; For. Accts. 61, Cvo ; *Calendar of Papal Letters*, vii. 161 ; Le Neve, *Fasti Ecclesiae Anglicanae* (ed. Hardy, 1854), i. 245.

3 *Foedera*, x. 155 ; For. Accts. 69, F. Apart from specific allusions, the attesting clause of thousands of letters in the Norman Rolls is enough to establish the fact.

4 *Foedera*, ix. 686 ; D.K.R. xlii. 437 ; For. Accts. 69, F.

5 *Foedera*, x. 195, 216 *sq.* ; *Rotuli Parliamentorum* (1767–77), iv. 171 ; For. Accts. 69, F.

6 On the position of the seneschal before the Treaty of Troyes, see Newhall, *op. cit.* 244 *sq.*

7 D.K.R. xlii. 372, 379.

8 Not on January 8, as in Newhall, *op. cit.* 246. See D.K.R. xlii. 398 ; Bréquigny, 159 *sq.* From a summary of a document in D.K.R. xlii. 401, it would appear that John Tiptoft had been Wydville's immediate predecessor. "Normandy," however, is evidently a mistake for "Aquitaine", of which Tiptoft really was seneschal (For. Accts. 56, Fvo ; *Foedera*, ix. 914, 915).

mission made him inspector-general of all officers, civil and military, in the parts subject to Henry. He was empowered to hold musters of garrisons whenever he saw fit, and to report thereon to the treasurer-general; to enquire into the adequacy of the food and munitions in fortified places; to investigate abuses of power on the part of captains, remedying them in person unless they were serious, when he was to refer them to the Council. The seneschal was not to delegate his functions. He was to have a retinue of twenty mounted men-at-arms and sixty mounted archers, and was to receive the substantial remuneration of 13s. 4d. a day.[1] One would think that Wydville's duties as seneschal would have fully occupied his time, but until November 1421 he was also captain of Gisors and Chaumont, and he apparently took an active part in the open warfare of the year, even as far afield as Maine.[2]

The seneschal, though a great man, did not enjoy that pre-eminence which had distinguished his office in the twelfth century.[3] In particular, he had no control over finance. The Norman treasury was at Caen,[4] in charge of the treasurer-general, William Alington.[5] Alington received four *livres tournois* a day, with a bonus of £100 sterling a year, and was provided with an escort of eight mounted men-at-arms and twenty-four mounted archers.[6] He was responsible for the collection and receipt of most of the revenue of Henry's conquests.[7] He also disbursed the contents of the treasury in accordance with royal writs, but it is evident that he was allowed some discretion in the assignment of the sums due from vicomtes and other collectors of revenue, and that much of the revenue was applied to the needs of the locality where it was raised, without being sent to Caen at all.[8] A few items of Norman revenue escaped Alington's cognisance, and were paid direct to Henry's treasurer of war.[9] The sum they represent will be discussed below. Alington was assisted by a receiver-general, John Dalton, and by several tellers and clerks.[10]

The treasury was subject to the control of the *chambre des comptes*, also located at Caen,[11] the distinction between the two corresponding roughly to that between the Exchequer of Receipt and the Exchequer of Account in England. There was a permanent president of the

[1] For. Accts. 59, K. This amount seems afterwards to have been reduced to 10s. (For. Accts. 61, Bvo).
[2] For. Accts. 59, K; Bréquigny, 177.
[3] On the twelfth-century seneschal, see Powicke, *The Loss of Normandy* (1913), 70 *sq.*
[4] Rym. x. 40, 203; Exch. Accts. 187/14, 188/7, f. 25vo.
[5] Appointed May 1, 1419 (D.K.R. xlii. 318; Exch. Accts. 187/14); his appointment was renewed on November 13, 1420 (D.K.R. xlii. 381).
[6] Exch. Accts. 188/7, ff. 23vo, 25vo; For. Accts. 61, Cvo.
[7] Exch. Accts. 188/7; For. Accts. 61, Bvo *sqq.*; Bréquigny, 160; D.K.R. xlii. 429.
[8] Exch. Accts. 188/7 *passim*; Bréquigny, 184.
[9] For. Accts. 69, F, Fvo.
[10] Exch. Accts. 188/7, ff. 24vo, 25, 27vo, 28vo, 32.
[11] *Foedera*, x. 40; Exch. Accts. 187/14, 188/7, f. 10vo.

chambre des comptes[1]; and it is noteworthy that this highly dignified office was filled by a Norman knight, Louis Burgeois, who, after being taken prisoner at the capture of Caen, had soon given his allegiance to Henry.[2] Alington's accounts mention Raoul le Sage, hereditary marshal of Ponthieu, who had lands in both Normandy and Brittany,[3] and Roger Waltham,[4] described as "seigneurs de la chambre des comptes", Yves de Bordenast and Benedict Cuteller, "gentes de camera",[5] and John Brynkeley, auditor of accounts.[6] To this body Alington had to account from time to time.[7] After Henry's death it was abolished, and the fiscal officers of Normandy once more came under the supervision of the *chambre des comptes* of Paris.

At the head of the military organisation of the duchy was the king's lieutenant, Thomas Montagu, earl of Salisbury, whose authority, at first limited to regions south of the Seine, was extended over the whole of the conquered territory in November 1420.[8] His powers are not very clearly indicated in the documents appointing him to his office; but it was his duty to defend the duchy against invasion, and he was evidently permitted to make counter-attacks on enemy country.[9] As lieutenant he apparently had at his command a mobile force of some strength.[10] He was, too, captain of five castles near the southern frontier.[11] But the men of other garrisons were not subject to his orders, and if he wanted to draw upon them, he had to secure the consent of the civil authority.[12] The title lieutenant is somewhat misleading, for Salisbury, even in strictly military affairs, was much less

1 Exch. Accts. 187/14; *Foedera*, x. 32, 39. The office had existed as far back as April 24, 1419 (*ibid.* ix. 737).

2 Exch. Accts. 187/14; Bréquigny, 193. Cf. Exch. Accts. 188/7, f. 28; For. Accts. 61, Cvo. He had 200 *liv. tourn.* a year. For the relations of Burgeois to Henry in the early days of the invasion see *Rotuli Normanniae* (ed. Hardy, 1835), 195, 375; D.K.R. xli. 760.

3 For. Accts. 61, Cvo; D.K.R. xlii. 378, 381; *Foedera*, x. 2, 4, 8 *sqq.*; *Rot. Normanniae* (ed. Hardy), 198, 242; Bréquigny, 179, 180; *Inventaire des Sceaux de la Collection Clairambault* (Collection des Documents inédits sur l'histoire de France, 1885–6), ii. 161.

4 Exch. Accts. 188/7, f. 24vo. Each had a "fee" of 100 *liv. tourn.* a year, and a "reward" of 300. Cf. *ibid.* 187/14.

5 Exch. Accts. 187/14; For. Accts. 61, Cvo. They each had 50 *liv. tourn.* a year. Cf. D.K.R. xlii. 336.

6 For. Accts. 61, Cvo; Exch. Accts. 187/14, 188/7, f. 24vo; D.K.R. xli. 765. He had an annual "reward" of 100 *liv. tourn.*

7 Rot. Norm. (P.R.O.) 8 Hen. V. p. 1, m. 15 dors, 9 Hen. V. m. 4 dors.; Bréquigny, 253; Exch. Accts. 187/14, 188/7, f. 1.

8 *Foedera*, ix. 739 *sq.*, x. 29; Bréquigny, 177.

9 It appears from his report of the raid on Maine and Anjou in the early summer of 1421 that it was made on his own initiative (*Foedera*, x. 131).

10 "Ses gens darmes et archiers de ses Retenues Si bien de luy en son dit office existant comme sur la sauvegarde desdites chasteaux et villes," Exch. Accts. 188/7, f. 22. The large amounts which he received from the Norman treasury indicate that he must have had to pay many men besides those of the garrisons under his command (*ibid.*; cf. For. Accts. 61, Bvo).

11 Exch. Accts. 188/7, f. 22; For. Accts. 61, Bvo. Professor Newhall (*op. cit.* 219) estimates the total strength of their garrisons at 480 men.

12 *Foedera*, x. 99, 201 *sq.*; Bréquigny, 177, 188; D.K.R. xlii. 437.

than *locum tenens* of the king. Indeed, his authority over the English troops in Normandy was ordinarily less than that of the seneschal.

Of the admiral of Normandy, the earl of Suffolk, there is no need to say much. He was invested with all the powers which the admiral of France had possessed within the duchy [1]; but though he was responsible for the safeguard of the coast,[2] he apparently discharged his duties by deputy, for he simultaneously held very important military positions.[3]

All officials alike were subject to Henry's Council at Rouen, sometimes called the *Grant Conseil*.[4] In the king's absence it directed the administration and defence of his French territory. The chancellor was its president [5]; the seneschal and the lieutenant doubtless belonged to it, though their attendance must have been irregular; the treasurer-general, however, seems not to have been a member [6]; and the only councillors whose names appear in the records are Raoul le Sage,[7] already mentioned, and Master Thomas Brons.[8] It was apparently a small body.

A matter of some mystery is the fate of the Norman *Échiquier*. When Henry invaded Normandy, it had for some time been divided into two branches, the *Échiquier des causes* or *Échiquier ordinaire*, the functions of which were primarily judicial, and the *Échiquier des comptes*. The former was held twice a year by delegates of the *Parlement* of Paris, to which it was actually though not theoretically subordinate, while the latter was conducted by members of the *chambre des comptes* of Paris, who twice yearly received and audited the accounts of the fiscal officials of Normandy.[9] There are no records of the Norman *Échiquier* for the years 1417–22, and it has been inferred that it ceased to exist in the days of Henry V.[10] This belief has been strengthened by the fact that in the Calendar of the Norman Rolls the word Exchequer frequently appears as the designation of the financial authority at Caen, which was a very different thing from either branch of the *Échiquier*

[1] *Foedera*, ix. 753. On the admiral of France see Viollet, *Histoire des institutions politiques et administratives de la France*, ii. (1898), 444 *sqq*.

[2] D.K.R. xlii. 323, 407.

[3] He was captain of Avranches and Pontorson, and in September 1421 became governor of the marches of Lower Normandy (For. Accts. 61, Bvo; D.K.R. xlii. 434). He seems to have performed his military functions in person (Edward Hall, *Union of the Two Noble and Illustre Famelies of Lancastre and Yorke* [ed. Ellis, 1809], 108. Cf. *Chronique d'Arthur de Richemont* [ed. Le Vavasseur, Soc. de l'Histoire de France, 1890], 22 *sq.*; Morice, *Histoire ecclésiastique et civile de Bretagne* [1750-56], i. 487).

[4] *Foedera*, x. 82, 142, 157; Bréquigny, 175, 179, 184; Exch. Accts. 188/7, f. 26.

[5] *Foedera*, x. 142.

[6] "Cancellario et consiliariis nostri Magni Concilii et Scaccarii in Ducatu Normanniae, ac etiam gentibus compotorum nostrorum et Thesaurario" (*ibid.*).

[7] For. Accts. 61, Cvo; Exch. Accts. 188/7, f. 26; Bréquigny, 179; D.K.R. xlii. 414.

[8] For. Accts. 61, Cvo. He received 6s. 8d. a day for his services as councillor.

[9] On the *Échiquier normand* of the later Middle Ages see A. Floquet, *Histoire du parlement de Normandie* (1840), vol. i., and P. Viollet, *Histoire des institutions politiques et administratives de la France*, iii. (1903), 344 *sq.*, 379 *sq*.

[10] Floquet, *op. cit.* i. 220.

as it existed before the English invasion. But reference to the original documents of the time shows that the word *scaccarium* was very seldom used. In the Calendar the word "Exchequer", except when it refers to the English *scaccarium*, seems always to be a deplorable translation of *camera compotorum* or its French equivalent.[1] So far as I know, the term *scaccarium* is used of a Norman institution in only three documents of the reign of Henry V. In one of these, which belongs to December 22, 1417, it certainly seems to refer to a financial institution[2]; but it is notable that it is never used again in a similar context. And in one of the other cases, the *scaccarium* is manifestly a judicial court,[3] while in the third it is expressly distinguished from the *chambre des comptes*.[4] This last passage suggests that Henry had no desire to abolish the *Échiquier des causes*, but that, for the time being, its functions were exercised by the Council. This indeed might be represented as an approximation to the state of affairs in the early twelfth century, when the Exchequer was the *curia ducis*.[5] It is noteworthy that on June 8, 1422, James de Calez was appointed king's counsel in "notre court souveraine" at Rouen.[6] Can this be identified with any tribunal but the *scaccarium* of the two contemporary documents last cited?

It is impossible to say what part in Norman affairs Henry proposed to allot to the Estates. The Estates of Normandy and the conquered territory outside it met at Rouen in January 1421, at the first opportunity, that is to say, after the Treaty of Troyes. It is not known how many were summoned or attended, or how those present were chosen. Henry urged them to observe the Treaty of Troyes and asked for advice on the reform of the currency and the general welfare of the region represented. The Estates retired to deliberate. Some days later, in accordance with their counsel, Henry ordained that all his subjects should swear loyalty to the Treaty. To provide metal for a new coinage, it was agreed that every one, except the very poor, should furnish one mark of silver for every 100 *livres tournois* of annual income which he enjoyed, the government undertaking to pay seven

[1] This is the case in D.K.R. xli. 683, 688, 689, 715, 716, 719, 721, 748, 765, 792, xlii. 319, 320, 323, 336, 355, 372, 381, 392, 393, 437, 439, 448. I am indebted for my knowledge of the original text of these entries to my friend Mr. V. H. Galbraith, of the Public Record Office. Without such generous help as he and others have given me, work on medieval history would be impossible for the sojourner overseas.

[2] *Rotuli Normanniae* (ed. Hardy), 220.

[3] *Ibid.* 205. "Sciatis quod nos de probitate . . . Johannis Tiptoft . . . plenam fiduciam optinentes constituimus . . . ipsum presidentem nostrum tam in scaccario nostro Normannie quam aliis pro tribunalibus sedibus judicialibus quibuscunque et ubicumque infra ducatum nostrum predictum necnon thesaurarium nostrum generalem infra eundem ducatum . . ." Professor Newhall seems to have overlooked the fact that Tiptoft was appointed treasurer-general as well as president of the "Exchequer" (*op. cit.* 168, n. 112; 169, n. 118).

[4] See p. 356, n. 6, above.

[5] Powicke, *op. cit.*, 85 *sq.*; Haskins, *Norman Institutions* (1918) 88 *sq.*

[6] D.K.R. xlii. 449.

livres of good money for every mark thus contributed. The Estates complained about the disturbed condition of the country, and thus gave Henry a good opening for requesting a substantial grant. The clergy having promised two tenths, the towns offered to bring the total of the grant to 400,000 *livres tournois*. The business transacted at this meeting was of the highest moment, and the Estates seem to have been treated with much consideration by Henry. But he never summoned them again, for the money they voted had not all been collected when he died.[1]

Space forbids an examination of the efficiency of the administrative machinery described above. But a word may be added concerning the relation of Normandy to Henry's doings and ambitions in the last two years of his life. The fairly full evidence available [2] shows, as it seems to me, that its value to him at this time was mainly military: it furnished an admirable base for his operations against the dauphinists. Financially, while it supported itself—at least for the last sixteen months of the reign—it rendered him comparatively little assistance. Alington's account from May 1421 to August 1422 shows a total receipt of 388,000 *livres tournois*, and a total expenditure of 396,000.[3] In the latter sum were included 23,000 *l.t.* lost to the treasury owing to depreciation of the current coinage [4]; 32,000 *l.t.* were spent on the purchase of oxen and sheep for Henry's household,[5] and 72 *l.t.* on the safe-keeping of prisoners from Meaux.[6] Part of the 59,000 *l.t.* paid to Salisbury [7] and the 11,000 *l.t.* paid to Ralph Butler, captain of Eu and Monceaux, was doubtless spent during their operations beyond the frontiers of the conquered territory,[8] though these enterprises were largely defensive in purpose. All the rest of the money paid out was allotted to Norman needs.

It is true that William Philip, Henry's treasurer of war, received direct from fees of the great seal of Normandy, from the Rouen indemnity, and from certain transactions at the Rouen mint sums amounting in all to nearly £3000 sterling, or 20,000 *l.t.*[9] Further, an unspecified part of a sum of £5200 sterling reached him from Norman officials without coming under Alington's cognisance at all.[10] But it

[1] Bréquigny, 160, 162, 163; *Foedera*, x. 58, 85; *Thomae Elmham Vita Henrici V.* 294; Walsingham, *op. cit.* ii. 336.

[2] This includes in particular Alington's account for the sixteen months, May 1421 to August 1422 (For. Accts. 61, Bvo *sqq.*), a draft account of his, incomplete but entering into greater detail, for the last four months of the reign (Exch. Accts. 188/7), and the account of William Philip, keeper of the wardrobe and treasurer of war, which extends from October 1, 1421 to November 8, 1422 (For. Accts. 69, F.).

[3] For. Accts. 61, Bvo, D.

[4] *Ibid.* D.

[5] *Ibid.* Cvo.

[6] *Ibid.*

[7] *Ibid.* Bvo.

[8] *Ibid.* C; D.K.R. xlii. 448; Monstrelet, iv. 85; *Chronique anonyme pour le règne de Charles VI* (called *Chronique des Cordeliers* by J. H. Wylie: printed in Monstrelet, vi., appendix), 312.

[9] For. Accts. 69, F. In drawing up their accounts both Philip and Alington estimated the *livre tournois* as equivalent to 3s. sterling (For. Accts. 61, C.).

[10] For. Accts. 69, Fvo.

is hard to see how the Norman contribution to this amount can have been large. For Alington's accounts are concerned with all the important sources of Norman revenue, and Philip could not have drawn on these direct without throwing the fiscal administration of Normandy into hopeless confusion. Philip, however, acknowledges a total receipt of £55,000, of which only £11,000 came direct from the English Exchequer[1]; and it has been suggested that the balance—the so-called *Recepta Forinseca*—was drawn largely from Norman sources.[2] Now of this balance, £3000 admittedly came from Rouen, £5200 has been considered above, £4900 was derived from perquisites of war, over £9500, being unpaid debts, existed only for purposes of book-keeping,[3] and of the £21,000 remaining nearly all was received by Philip from the king's chamber,[4] to which at least £19,000 was sent across the Channel by the English Exchequer in the last year of Henry's life.[5] Further, Henry had at his disposal the revenue which the officers of Charles VI. were able to collect; he was afterwards blamed for having used it in his own interests[6]; and it can hardly be doubted that some of the money transferred to Philip by the king's chamber came from this source. In short, it seems unlikely that Normandy contributed anything to Philip's receipts save the £3000 from Rouen and perhaps £1000 out of the £5200 already discussed—a conjecture which appears to me liberal. Adding to this the amount—32,000 *livres tournois*, or £4800—which Alington spent on provisions for the king's household, and admitting (very generously) that the offensive operations of Salisbury and Ralph Butler cost the Norman treasury about £1000, we reach the conclusion that Normandy's contribution to the cost of Henry's campaigns and sieges after his return to France in June 1421 amounted to a little less than £10,000, or some 66,000 *livres tournois*.[7] It is evident that until Henry's death, the brunt of the burden of the war against the dauphinists was borne, not by Normandy, but by England.

W. T. Waugh.

[1] For. Accts. 69, Fvo.

[2] Newhall, *op. cit.* 151, 243.

[3] For. Accts. 69, Fvo.

[4] For. Accts. 69, F, Fvo.

[5] Issue Roll, 9 Hen. V. Mich. Feb. 3, 1422, 10 Hen. V. Pasch. April 20, July 29, 1422.

[6] La Barre, *op. cit.* i. 341.

[7] Alington's account for 1420–21 being lost, it is impossible to estimate how much money Henry obtained from Normandy between the signing of the Treaty and the end of the following April.

XXVII

A NOTE ON THE PRE-TUDOR SECRETARY

ADMINISTRATIVE history deals inevitably with slow transitions and gradual developments. It is seldom that a national institution or a great office of state emerges suddenly into importance, but a striking exception in this respect occurs in England with regard to the secretariat. Thomas Cromwell, by force of character and by the fact that he made the most of his chances to exert influence over the King and in council and to colour the official correspondence of the crown with his own personality, brought the office of King's secretary into a position of eminence entirely new to it. On the other hand, the increased importance of the secretary was a marked feature in all the autocratic states of the Renaissance era. The development was European not insular; both Machiavelli and de Commines stress the usefulness to a despotic prince of a trusted councillor whose duties are not too clearly defined, and the appearance of the Tudor secretariat of state is paralleled in France and Spain.

It is fairly certain then that, sudden as was Thomas Cromwell's exploitation of the office, the times must have been ripe in England for some such development. The secretaries immediately preceding him were not outstanding personalities, yet the large amount of diplomatic correspondence that was falling into their hands made them objects of suspicion to the would-be omnipotent Wolsey. The seed which came to light in Thomas Cromwell's day must have been germinating during the earlier years of the establishment of the New Monarchy in England, and since it is often asked whether the real founder of that New Monarchy was not Edward IV. rather than Henry VII., an examination of the position of the Yorkist secretary may contribute in a small way towards an answer to this question.

There are some important facts which affected the position of the pre-Tudor secretary, and distinguished him sharply from the secretary of Elizabethan times. Firstly, one should note that the increasing share taken by the secretary of state in administrative work in the later sixteenth and seventeenth centuries was very largely occasioned by the corresponding decline in the importance of the chancellor, from the point of view, not of dignity or standing, but of administrative and political importance. The work of the chancery was increasingly restricted to its legal duties and to the formalities connected with issues under the great seal; thus by the later sixteenth century it had ceased to be a general administrative department, and much of its influence passed to the newer office of the secretary.[1] In Edward IV.'s reign, on the other hand, not only was the chancellor very clearly the first minister of the crown from the political as well as the legal aspect, but the privy seal was also still of considerable importance. Indeed it seems that the keeper of the privy seal in the fifteenth century held much the same position as that occupied by the secretary a hundred years later. A comparison of letters written by Henry VI. and Edward IV. under the privy seal and the signet shows that, particularly in the former reign and to some extent throughout the period, the privy seal was often used in a missive capacity, affixed to letters expressing the King's personal wishes or commands.[2] It is also quite clear that the administrative procedure of the passage of the seals was not yet stereotyped: the privy seal was as yet far from being merely a formal stage between signet and chancery. One of the most interesting political struggles of the Lancastrian period centred round this very question, and its issue gave a new importance to the signet which was quickly exploited both by the King and the secretary. In Henry VI.'s early years the great nobles of the council had control of the privy seal, and it has been suggested that during the years 1437 to 1443 the King attempted to evade this control by an extensive use of his signet and sign manual. The council was eventually forced to recognise that the privy seal could not be refused on the production of a signet letter, although they made the reservation that the keeper of the privy seal should "have recours to the lords of the Counsaill and open to theim the matere" if he thought it to be "of greet charge".[3] Even this attempt to check the royal power was foiled, for in 1444 the King issued a final edict to the effect that all grants made since 1432 "by virtue of bills under the sign manual, signet of the Eagle, or signet at arms, as well as those signed by the Chamberlains and Clerk of the council, were as legal as if the chancellor had had a privy seal warrant".[4] It is quite impossible to say how far this struggle involved the secretary, but it is certain that the triumph of the signet was a necessary preliminary to the emergence of its keeper as an official of importance. While it is intriguing to discover that the critical years of the struggle tally almost exactly

[1] It may be noticed that the importance of John Thurloe, Oliver Cromwell's secretary of state, was immensely enhanced by the fact that both chancery and treasury were in commission during the protectorate.

[2] *Paston Letters* (ed. Gairdner, 1904), iii. 302-3; Ellis, *Original Letters* (1st Series), i. 17.

[3] Nicholas, *Proc. P.C.* vi. 316-320.

[4] This whole question is discussed at length by T. F. T. Plucknett, "The Place of the Council on the Fifteenth century", in the *Transactions of the Royal Hist. Soc.* 4th Series, i. 177-184.

with the secretaryship of Thomas Beckington, by far the most important of the Lancastrian secretaries, we must avoid the temptation to exaggerate the position of these early officials: it is the commonest thing to find household clerks, other than the secretary, witnessing signet letters, while the Council's ordinances and the royal edict which settled the dispute do not even mention the secretary, though referring specifically to the chamberlain.

Thus we are reminded of an important qualification which we must take into account in considering the position of the pre-Tudor secretary. His potential importance was as yet overshadowed by the greater eminence of other household officials, such as steward, chamberlains and controller. There can be little doubt that these rather than the secretary were the men who shared with the King that part of the work of government which was still a "household" matter. One of the main sources of the secretary's power in Tudor times was his peculiar position in the privy council: he as much as any man knew the King's mind and he was the accepted mouthpiece of the royal will. In the fifteenth century it is still the chief officers of the household who play this important part, and it is most significant that an order of Richard II. that persons "suffisantes et convenables" should be chosen to fill the offices of chamberlain, steward and privy seal, proceeds to lay down that these and these alone are to be reporters of the King's wishes between him and his Council.[1]

It is thus clear that before Tudor times the secretary was still an official of small importance, hardly yet regarded as a serious political rival by the great officers of state. Yet if we examine the career of Edward IV.'s chief secretary, William Hatclyffe, we can realise that a change is actually at work, though our knowledge is hardly sufficient to justify a generalisation as to his importance in comparison with the other household officials. One of the royal physicians, and a layman instead of the usual cleric, Hatclyffe held office as King's secretary from 1464 until his death in 1480, and it is obvious that he was no mere letter clerk or lackey. The most surprising fact is the extent to which he was employed on foreign negotiations: he began his tenure of office with a visit to Brittany which lasted from September 1464 to the following January, and his later embassies included a mission to Alnwick in 1471 and an important negotiation with Louis XI. in 1473, when he was entrusted with considerable powers. His more frequent diplomatic intercourse was with the court of Burgundy and the Hanseatic League, and one of these embassies in 1472 has been described in some detail by the herald Bluemantle Pursuivant who accompanied him.[2]

One of the immediate problems arising from these frequent embassies

[1] Nicholas, *Proc. P.C.* i. 85. Here again we see the keeper of the privy seal in the same position as the later secretary.

[2] Kingsford, *English Historical Literature in the Fifteenth Century*, pp. 379-388.

is that of the custody of the signet during such periods. Who was responsible for the drafting of the King's letters at such times, and was there in existence anything approaching an ordered office system? As far as the signet is concerned no record exists until 1480, when Oliver King, "licentiate in laws", was granted the custody of the signet whenever it might happen that "Master William Hatclyffe, the King's secretary", was absent from the King's person.[1] This provision for a deputy keeper of the signet in the secretary's absence seems to indicate an increased attention to the problem of office organisation. It comes at the very end of Hatclyffe's tenure of power, but the problem was not a new one; when Hatclyffe was absent in former years, some other official must have retained the signet, and probably exerted some influence over royal policy as reflected in the King's correspondence.

An examination of the signet letters of Edward IV.'s reign shows that there was as yet very little office organisation, for the letters were not countersigned at all regularly by the secretary, even when he was in the country; indeed Hatclyffe only signs some four times in all.[2] The signatures are those of various clerks, probably of the man responsible for the actual drafting, and it is not at all uncommon to find letters of the same date bearing different signatures.[3] The whole impression given is that of a very rudimentary office system, about which it is extremely difficult to generalise safely. Some letters are signed by the King alone, others are countersigned, and others again are signed only by clerks: some have no signature, and one at least is signed upside down. It is quite obvious that the well-organised signet office, with its formal procedure and its stereotyped forms of verification, is as yet a thing of the future; whatever Hatclyffe may have been he was no office martinet. The signet of course followed the court, and a very useful list of the royal progresses could be compiled from the dating of the letters, and when in 1475 Edward went to France, the signet accompanied the King, and thus did not form a part of the organisation built up by the King for the government of England in his absence.[4]

[1] *Cal. Pat. Rolls, 1476–1485*, p. 196. King was also appointed "coadjutor to the said William in the office of secretary during the life of the latter". This appointment is of considerable interest as it is the first trace we get of a double secretariat, though Hatclyffe's death a few months later prevented the development of this experiment.

[2] Thus of some 1800 signet warrants for the privy seal Hatclyffe signs but four. P.R.O. Privy Seal Office warrants (Edward IV.), Series 1, Files 21-55. He signs none of the signet warrants to the Chancery. Chancery warrants (Edward IV.), Series 1, Files 1377-1391. Very many of the warrants are signed by the King, with no countersignature.

[3] These may have been "clerks of the signet", but I have found no evidence that they were.

[4] Thus signet letters are dated on 26 June 1475 from Westminster, on 10 July and 6 Sep. from Calais, and again on 13 Oct. from Westminster. Privy Seal Office Warrants (Edward IV.), Series 1, File 41, Nos. 2136-2140.

The two points, then, that emerge clearly are that in Edward IV.'s reign the signet was by no means always in the custody of the secretary, and the latter was more frequently than not engaged in foreign embassies. It would almost seem from this that it is erroneous to regard the secretary as *prima facie* the keeper of the King's signet. Rather it would appear that at this time the duties attached to the office were more akin to those of the *secretarii* of the chroniclers of the thirteenth century, clerks in the counsels of the King, competent for confidential business abroad. The term thus used merely indicated a trusted servant without implying any specific official position, and although there can be no doubt that by Edward IV.'s reign the King's secretary was definitely a household official to whom alone the title was applied,[1] it is probable that his duties were still very largely of the ambassadorial type. This frequent absence of the secretary from England is in sharp contrast with later practice, and has a significance of its own apart from the question of the custody of the signet. It was, of course, one of the results of the great increase in diplomatic negotiations which marked the reign of Edward IV. and proved him to have been, at least in this respect, a fitting contemporary of Louis XI., Charles of Burgundy and the Italian princes. This new diplomacy and the numerous embassies it entailed continued in Henry VII.'s reign and affected, as we have seen, the early Tudor secretaries, but there is this great difference, that as a rule they remained at home while their Yorkist predecessors had gone abroad. If we may date the sudden rise in importance of the secretariat from the burst of diplomatic activity connected with the Renaissance and Reformation, it is equally due to this decision of the secretary to stay in England. The key to the situation was personal influence with the King ; the professional official at headquarters counted for more than the ambassador, and in no short time the secretary became the ambassador's master. Wolsey himself foresaw this danger, and was furiously angry to find that his letters to the King from Calais passed through the secretary's hands.

Thus began the intimate relation between the secretary and foreign affairs, and hence we can trace the origin of the proud, if erroneous, tradition of the Foreign Office that their chief is the senior secretary. Yet the custom by which the secretary himself went abroad as ambassador died hardly. Throughout the sixteenth century the secretary is periodically absent on diplomatic affairs, and though this soon became very unusual, we find Secretary Morton sent on an embassy to Holland in 1625, while in 1672 for a short period both secretaries were abroad. A yet more famous case occurred at the crisis of the Napoleonic wars, when Castlereagh, the foreign secretary, went abroad

[1] One should note, however, that the author of the short English chronicle describes Sir Robert Roos as the king's secretary in 1443. Roos was a member of the household but never secretary. The writer may be using the phrase in the old unspecialised sense. *Three Fifteenth Century Chronicles* (Cam. Soc.), p. 64.

with full powers, negotiated a fresh alliance and remained on the continent until the successful culmination of the campaign.

The outstanding position of the secretariat to-day makes it difficult to imagine that it might have developed along other lines. Yet a cursory examination of the position of the office in Edward IV.'s reign has shown us that at this time, when the New Monarchy was clearly foreshadowed in England, there was considerable danger lest the secretary, by his frequent absences from the country, should lose the custody of the signet, and with it that intimate relationship with the King on which the whole of his future importance was based. That danger was averted in the next century, but the secretary at Whitehall might still have been a mere nonentity : the personal greatness of Thomas Cromwell, the Cecils and Walsingham ensured a very different issue. More and more the secretary controlled the various threads of diplomatic intercourse, continually increasing his power in council by his knowledge of foreign negotiations. An effective office system and clerical staff, distinct from the signet office, was necessitated by these duties, and thus in the seventeenth century, although the secretaries were for a considerable period no longer men of high abilities or great political importance, the administrative duties performed through their office steadily increased. As the privy council declined in importance as an administrative body owing to its large numbers and the increased complexities of government, accessibility and convenience indicated the secretary's office as the most natural substitute. So eventually in the second half of the century the secretaries of state, inspired afresh by the example of Thurloe under the protectorate, emerged once again in the forefront of political life as the heads of the chief executive offices of state. It was a lengthy process, with many deviations, but its beginning can definitely be dated from the time when the secretary's duties were transferred from the courts of Europe to the palace of Whitehall.

FLORENCE M. G. HIGHAM.

XXVIII

DOCUMENTS INÉDITS SUR L'ORGANISATION DE L'ARTILLERIE ROYALE AU TEMPS DE LOUIS XI

PHILIPPE DE COMMINES dans ses mémoires [1] mentionne avec soin la particulière attention que Louis XI apporta à développer et utiliser son artillerie ; l'interpolateur du Journal de Jean de Roye insiste encore davantage ; [2] et nous savons enfin que l'armée française qui descendit en Italie en 1494 possédait une artillerie considérable, que Charles VIII n'aurait jamais eu le temps d'organiser, s'il en avait eu l'intelligence, et que les Beaujeu n'auraient jamais eu les loisirs de créer. Mais si nous trouvons dans les faits et dans les documents la preuve de l'importance de l'artillerie royale sous Louis XI, nous sommes singulièrement pauvres en données sur l'organisation de celle-ci. Les archives de l'artillerie ont disparu, les comptes de cette arme ont, sauf de rares exceptions,[3] subi le sort de tant de documents financiers conservés à la Chambre des Comptes,[4] et l'on peut dire, avec une quasi certitude, que les quelques lignes de *l'Histoire de la milice française* du P. Daniel résument à peu près complètement ce que nous savons de l'artillerie française avant le XVIe siècle.[5]

C'est cette pénurie complète qui donne un certain intérêt à une petite découverte faite par nous dans la reliure d'un manuscrit et dont nous sommes heureux de pouvoir faire hommage à M. Tout.

Le manuscrit *French* 57 (ancien MS. Phillipps 6968) de la John

[1] *Mémoires de Philippe de Commynes*, ed. B. de Mandrot, Paris, 1901–1903, in 8° (*Collection de textes pour servir à l'étude et à l'enseignement de l'histoire*), t. ii. p. 36 : " Il faisoit ses armees si grosses que il trouvoit peu de gens pour les combattre et bien garny d'artillerie et myeulx que jamais roy de France". La correspondance de Louis XI fourmille de mentions relatives à l'artillerie.

[2] *Journal de Jean de Roye*, ed. B. de Mandrot, Paris, 1894, in 8° (*Société de l'Histoire de France*), t. ii. p. 398 : " En decedant de ce monde en l'autre lessa a son fils quatre grans tresors qui sont tels. . . . Le second tresor estoit qu'il estoit garny d'un gros et merveilleux nombre d'artillerie et de l'equipage qui y falloit plus que jamais n'avoit esté roy qui fust par avant luy."

[3] Par exemple le manuscrit *Français 7881*, de la Bibliothèque Nationale contient un compte pour l'année 1489 qui n'est d'ailleurs pas un compte général. Le P. Daniel (*Histoire de la milice française*, Paris, 1721, in 4°), signale, t. ii. p. 533, un compte de l'année 1480 qui semble aujourd'hui perdu.

[4] Nous savons par l'inventaire PP. 99 des Archives Nationales que les comptes des maîtres de l'artillerie se trouvaient à la chambre des comptes.

[5] On trouve davantage dans *l'Histoire de l'artillerie française*, de L. Susane, Paris, 1872, in-12°, pp. 73-81 ; malheureusement cet ouvrage, qui n'est pas sans mérites, est absolument muet sur ses sources.

Rylands Library est un manuscrit sans grand intérêt. La chronique de France qu'il contient est dénuée de valeur et connue par d'autres manuscrits,[1] et les renseignements qu'on a ajoutés à sa suite sur l'expédition de 1494 sont purement et simplement copiés dans les bulletins de l'expédition publiés par Mlle Dupont [2] et M. de la Pilorgerie.[3] L'histoire de ce manuscrit nous est mal connue. Nous savons seulement qu'il figurait avec sa reliure actuelle dans la collection du conseiller J. B. Hautin le célèbre bibliophile,[4] et nous pouvons inférer d'une note écrite sur un des feuillets de garde que cette reliure existait déjà en l'année 1503 quand Jean Allegrin, probablement un membre de la famille parlementaire de ce nom, écrivait cette note.[5]

Or, cette reliure en veau mal tanné contenait un petit trésor. Les plats en étaient formés de feuilles de papier collées fortement ensemble qui, soumises à la vapeur, détachées et séchées, nous ont fourni les éléments suivants, réunis aujourd'hui dans le manuscrit *French 71* de la John Rylands Library :

12 feuillets du carnet de Christophe Constant, garde ordinaire de l'artillerie ;

9 demi-feuillets (partie supérieure) d'un registre du matériel de l'artillerie royale pendant la campagne de Picardie (1477) ;

2 demi-feuillets (partie supérieure) d'un registre des comptes du charroi de l'artillerie ;

enfin, cinq fragments de reçus de matériel et de cédules de paiement.[6]

Notons tout de suite que les documents les plus récents contenus dans cette reliure sont datés de 1483. Si, comme nous le croyons, les documents étaient déjà employés dans la reliure en 1503, puisque Jean Allegrin utilisait le feuillet de garde de celle-ci à cette date, nous voyons peut-être une des raisons pour lesquelles nous sommes si pauvres en documents sur les débuts de l'artillerie : les documents n'en étaient pas conservés. Peut-être les représentait-on pour la vérification des comptes généraux, mais, une fois celle-ci faite, tous les comptes particuliers étaient vendus au poids du parchemin ou du papier.

Que nous apporte donc ces fragments sauvés par la reliure du

[1] Les manuscrits *Français 5701* et *5705* de la Bibliothèque Nationale.

[2] *Mémoires de Commines*, t. iii. pp. 361-402 (*Société de l'Histoire de France*).

[3] *Campagne et bulletins de la grande armée d'Italie commandée par Charles VIII*, Paris, 1866, in 12.

[4] On trouvera des renseignements sur ce collectionneur dans *Le Cabinet des Manuscrits de la Bibliothèque Nationale* de M. Delisle, t. i. p. 365, t. iii. pp. 370 et 384. J'ai examiné les manuscrits de la collection Hautin à la Bibliothèque Nationale ; tous ont des reliures, soit plus anciennes que le manuscrit de Manchester, soit des reliures à panneaux de bois. Il existe à l'University Library à Cambridge une cinquantaine de manuscrits provenant de la même collection dont je n'ai pas examiné la reliure.

[5] C'est une reconnaissance pour la somme de 300 livres parisis à une demoiselle Jehanne Arlas (?) en date du 19 mars 1503.

[6] La reliure contenait en outre un feuillet et un morceau de parchemin sans écriture et deux feuillets de parchemin inutilisables. J'ajoute qu'un des feuillets de garde du manuscrit *French 57* est formé par un fragment, trop mutilé pour être utilisable, d'un inventaire d'artillerie.

manuscrit de Manchester ? Pour répondre à cette question, il est bon d'examiner l'un après l'autre les différents lots que nous en avons faits.

Que les douze feuillets du premier lot soient les restes du carnet de Christophe Constant c'est ce qui ne fait pas de doute. Il nous dit en effet, f° 10,[1] à la fin d'un inventaire de distribution d'artillerie : " Et sur les dites choses y a mandement patent par ce que Gobert Cadyot qui estoit maistre d'artillerie trespassa d'un cop devant Lectore [2] sans bailler mes acquitz et moy absent, ledit mandement donné le XXVIIIe jour de may M IIII^{c} LXXIII ". Or le mandement en question a été copié par le possesseur du carnet, il nous en reste la plus grande partie et la date (f° I et I v°) et il nous fournit le nom du personnage dont les " acquitz " n'avaient point été " baillés ", c'est Christophe Constant.[3] Ce personnage est mal connu, nous le trouvons désigné comme " clerc " et chargé d'affaires concernant l'artillerie en juillet 1468,[4] nous savons par lui-même qu'il remplissait des fonctions de comptable pour la même arme au siège de Lectoure, ou plutôt à l'époque de ce siège, c'est-à-dire en janvier 1473 ; un fragment d'un mandement du roi au maître de l'artillerie, dont la fin manque mais qui se date avec certitude de 1475–1476, nous fournit son titre qui est celui de " garde ordinaire " de l'artillerie royale ; [5] enfin l'un des fragments de reçus contenus

[1] Les feuillets sont indiqués par leur numérotation actuelle dans le manuscrit *French 71*.

[2] *Journal de Jean de Roye*, i. 290 : " En ce temps fu tiré de la ville de Lestaure une grosse serpentine en l'ost des gens du roy estans devant, laquelle d'un seul cop tua le maistre de l'artillerie du roy et quatre autres canonniers ". Le manuscrit *Français 20490* de la Bibliothèque Nationale contient (f° 12) un budget des dépenses prévues pour ce siège. Les frais de transport de l'artillerie s'élèvent à 937*l.* 10*s.*

[3] " (le début manque). . . . Et pour les guerres que nous avons fait fere derrierement tant es pays de Guienne que Bretaigne, Picardie, Normandie, Armignat, Roussillon, pour resister a aucuns noz reb[elles] et desobeissans [sujets], grande quantité des espe[ces] de nostre dite artillerie a esté distribuee p[our] nos afferes et en plusieurs lieux en ung mesme temps, et parceque durant icelles guerres le m[aistre] de nostre artillerie Gobert Cadyot est trespassé d'un cop devant la ville de Lec[tore], ledit Christofle absent, et n'avoit encores s[igné] les parties d'artillerie distribuees par ic[eluy] Christofle Constant ; pour quoy nous vous mandons et commandons que toutes les p[arties] de nostre dite artillerie baillees et distribuees par ledit Christofle ou ses commis qui vous appar[oistront] estre certiffiees et signees de la main de nostre cher et bien amé maistre Pierre de Willeries, contreroleur d'icelle nostre artil[lerie] vous allouez es comptes dudit Christofle Constant et rabatez de sa recepte sans aucune difficulté. Car ainsi nous plait il estre fait. Non obstant stile, rigueur de compte et que sa commission soit pl[us] expresse et ordonnances ad ce contraires. Donné a Amboize le XXVIIIe jour de may l'an de grace mil IIII^{c} soixante treize et de nostre regne le XIIe. Ainsi signé : par le roy, le sire de Crussol et autres presens : Tillart."

[4] Bibl. Nat., MS. Français 20496, f° 93 : " De par le Roy. Maistre Anthoine Raguier, trésorier de nos guerres, nous voulons et vous mandons que a Cristofle Constant, clerc, vous paiez, baillez et delivrez la somme de cinq cens livres tournois, laquelle nous lui avons ordonnee pour convertir et emploier es fraiz et despences qu'il conviendra faire pour le faict de certaine de nostre artillerie qui de present est a Falaize, laquelle avons envoiee a nostre tres cher et amé filz l'admiral. Et par rapportant ces presentes signees de nostre main nous emploierons la dite somme de v^{c} lbs. en vos rooles sans difficulté. Donné a Meaulx le XIe jour de juillet l'an mil CCCC soixante-huit. Loys. Bourré."

[5] John Rylands Library, MS. *French 71*, f° 3 v° : " Coppie d'un mandement patent pour delivrer artillerie. Loys par la grace de Dieu roy de France, a nostre amé et feal

dans la reliure du manuscrit *French 57* nous le montre en 1483 avec le titre de " notere et secretere du Roy ",[1] ce qui ne signifie nullement qu'il ait alors abandonné ses fonctions dans l'artillerie.[2] Nous ignorons ce qu'il devint après cette date. Savons-nous d'ailleurs très bien ce qu'il était avant ? Il est probable que si son carnet nous avait été entièrement conservé nous le saurions mieux mais, néanmoins, les fragments qui nous en restent permettent de voir ce qu'était ce " garde ordinaire " de l'artillerie.

Ce n'était pas un petit personnage quoiqu'il fût en dessous du maître et de son lieutenant, comme aussi de quelques autres personnages appartenant au même corps. Nous en avons la preuve dans ce fait que le roi correspondait directement avec lui. Nous trouvons en effet sur un des feuillets du carnet qui nous ont été conservés une lettre missive de Louis XI au garde ordinaire de son artillerie, lettre dont le texte était jusqu'alors inconnu et que, pour cette raison, nous croyons intéressant de publier.

" Copie d'uncs lettres missives du roy touchant l'artillerie du roy " d'Arragon.

" Christofle Constant, j'ay ordonné que toute l'artillerie qui a esté " gaignee en Roussillon, reservé les grosses bombardes, sera menee dedans " Bayonne, et escript a messire Yvon du Fou qu'il ne se joue pas d'en mener " une seule piece cheux lui ne ung seul grain de pouldre. Et pour ce, in- " continent ces lettres [veues], menez la y toute, reservé lesdites grosses " bombardes. Et si vous en avez mené aucunes menues pieces a Thoulouse, " si les ramenez audit Bayonne, et le tout par inventaire a Jehan des Vignes [3] " qui [vient (?)] de par dela a qui j'en escrips, et pour en retenir qui pourra " le mieulx servir pour la ville. Et . . . comment qu'il soit que vous y " fetes la plus gra[nde] diligence qu'il vous sera possible de la y mener [et] " qu'il n'y ait point de faulte sur tout le service que vous me desirez faire et " sur tout tant que vous craignez a me desobeir et desplaire. [Et] se vous

---

conseiller et maistre d'ostel, Guillaume Bournel, maistre de nostre artillerie, salut et dilec[tion]. Nous voulons et vous mandons bien expressement que incontinant et sanz delay vous baillez et delivrez ou faictes bailler et delivrer a nostre amé et feal consei[ller] Raoul de Walpergue, commis de par nous au gouvernement et conduicte de nostre artillerie que envoyons presente[ment] en Byscaye, les parties d'artillerie et choses qui s'ensuivent. C'est assavoir l'artillerie qui a esté gaignee ou pays de Roussillon, les deux Nerbonnois et tout le metaille qui fut ramené dudit pays tant en coullœuvrines rompues que en autres choses par nostre cher et bien amé garde ordi[naire] Christofle Constant, par l'ordonnance dudit Raoul avecques une bombarde rompue que fist maistre Nicolas le lombart, aussi nostre canonnier ordinaire, pour d'icelle bombarde et metaille fere fere des coullœuvrines et autres bastons pour la deffense de nostre dite armee, dix milliers de salpestre qui sont de present en . . . (la fin manque)."

1 MS. *French 71*, f° 26.

2 Voir par exemple le cas d'Étienne Petit qui quoique " notaire et secretaire du Roy " est aussi " contrerolleur de la thesaurerie ou recepte generale des finances du Languedoc " (*Lettres de Louis XI*, t. ix. p. 88, n. 1).

3 Ce personnage semble avoir été à differentes reprises employé par Louis XI à des opérations concernant l'artillerie ou plutôt le transport de celle-ci. Il entra ainsi en conflit avec la municipalité de Lyon en 1470. Cf. L. Caillet, "Mémoire justificatif de Jean des Vignes," dans *Bull. de la Société des Sciences et Arts du Beaujolais*, t. xi., 1910, pp. 54-73.

" estiez parti pour vous en venir par deça, revenez y tout incontinant. Et au " regard de toute la pouldre que vous avez, fectes la mener audit Bayonne, " et les dix milliers de salpestre et IIII^{m} de souffre fectes ramener par " deça. Et que [il] n'y ait point de faulte que ne faciez ce que je vous " mande. Escript a Paris, le XVIIe jour d'avril, ainsi signé dessoubz : " Loys, et contresigné : J. Mesme. Et dessus : a nostre cher et bien amé " Christofle Constant." [1]

Il semblerait donc, d'après cette lettre, que le garde ordinaire pouvait dans certaines circonstances avoir à diriger les mouvements de l'artillerie sans avoir à rendre compte à d'autres qu'au roi ou à des gens des comptes, sans faire attention aux chefs plus proprement militaires. La façon dont Yvon du Fou, lieutenant général de l'armée qui venait de conquérir le Roussillon, est mis à l'écart est à noter. Mais il est bien évident que si, dans telle circonstance spéciale et sur un ordre exprès du roi, le garde ordinaire pouvait jouer un rôle aussi actif, ses véritables fonctions devaient être d'un caractère plus sédentaire ou tout au moins plus administratif. Nous voyons en effet par les autres feuillets de son carnet qu'il est le grand dispensateur du matériel de l'artillerie. Voici à titre d'exemple ce que nous donne son carnet pour les années 1473 et 1474.

" Aultre distribucion d'artillerie fecte es annees LXXIII et LXXIIII " appert par le roole signé de Guillaume Bournel, maistre de l'artillerie, du " VIIe jour de septembre l'an M IIII^{c} LXXIIII. Et premierement :

" A maistre Phelipe Boutillart, tresorier de France, que le roy lui a donné, ars d'if : cent ;

" Item a lui, trousses de fleiches : C ;

" Item a messire Jehan de Sallezart et Guérin Le Groing, cappitaines, et que ledit seigneur leur a donné, arcs d'if : IIII^{c} ;

" Item a eulx, trousses de fleiches : III^{c} ;

" Item a este delivré a plusieurs canonniers pour faire feuz pour les guerres, salpestre vert : XXXVIII ll. ;

" Item souffres pour semblable cause : X ll.

" Item a Jacques de Reubaiz pour convertir en pouldre, salpestre vert, pois de Paris : VII^{m}IIII^{c}II ll.

" Item a lui pour semblable cause, souffre pesé a tout les fustz : II^{m}V^{c} ll.

" Item a Jehan Maulgué, pour convertir en pouldres pour la bombarde nommee Montjoye, salpestre vert : C ll.

" Item a lui souffre : XXXV ll.

" Item a plusieurs canonniers pour fere feuz comme dist est, pouldres : XIX ll.

" Item pour essayer plusieurs coullœuvrines et serpentines a esté despensé pouldres vertes audit pois de Paris : III^{c}VII ll.

" Item, plomb en plommees tirees : CII ll.

" Item boulets de fer a serpentines : III ;

" Item a esté delivré a Guillaume le Rousselet et Henry Daussel pour fere plommees : IIII^{c}LX maillets de plomb ;

[1] MS. *French 71*, f° 3.

" Nota que le roy donna audit an aux habitans d'Amyens douze des coullœuvrines neufves qui depuis ont esté reffaictes a Paris.

" Somme toute ars d'if a main : v^c ;
" Item, trousses de fleiches : IIII^c ;
" Item, salpestre vert pois de Paris : VII^m v^c XL ll. ,
" Item, souffre audit pois : II^m v^c XLV ll. ;
" Item, pouldre verte : III^c XXVI ll. ;
" Item, plomb en plommees : CII ll. ;
" Item, boulets de fer a serpentines : IIII ; [1]
" Item, maillets de plomb : IIII^c LX." [2]

Nous avons conservé les feuillets pour des distributions analogues faites à Roulet ou Raoulet de Valpergue le 17 mars 1474 [3] et en 1475 [4] et un fragment d'une autre distribution qui peut être assignée, avec certitude, à l'année 1473.[5] Ces " distribucions " sont intéressantes à un double point de vue. Elles nous montrent quelle est la véritable fonction du garde ordinaire ; il est en somme le gardien de l'arsenal ou des arsenaux royaux. Nous voyons également que le mot d'artillerie n'a pas encore pris le sens exclusif que lui accordent les modernes. Parmi les engins que distribue Christophe Constant figurent encore des arcs, des trousses de flèches, des traits d'arbalètes, des cordes d'arcs. En revanche nous constatons que Christophe Constant ne fait pas de distributions de canons, couleuvrines ou bombardes,[6] il se borne à fournir la poudre ou les éléments nécessaires à sa fabrication et les boulets. Il avait cependant aussi la garde des pièces d'artillerie. Un fragment malheureusement incomplet au commencement et à la fin nous fournit une liste de pièces d'artillerie qui comprenait au moins 51 couleuvrines de fer, 151 couleuvrines de fonte, 2 courteaux et 7 serpentines de fer.[7] Si cette liste figure dans le carnet du garde ordinaire de l'artillerie c'est évidemment qu'il a également le contrôle des pièces. Il le déclare lui-même dans une autre " distribucion " ainsi intitulée : " Distribucion de certaines pieces d'artillerie faite durant le vivant de

[1] C'est une erreur, il faudrait III.

[2] MS. *French 71*, f° 10 v°.

[3] MS. *French 71*, f° 11 v° : " Autre distribucion d'artillerie pour le voyage de Roussillon appert par le roole de Roolet de Walpergue, lieutenant de ladite artillerie, signé du XVIIIe de mars l'an M IIII^c LXXIIII . . . ".

[4] MS. *French 71*, f° 12 : " Aultre distribucion d'artillerie livree a Rolet de Walpergue, lieutenant de ladite artillerie en l'an M IIII^c LXXV, pour le voyage de Biscaye . . . ".

[5] MS. *French 71*, f° 9.

[6] Il y a cependant une exception—qui confirme la règle. A la fin de la " distribucion " pour le voyage de Biscaye (f° 12), dans le résumé de celle-ci, on a ajouté : " Item, bombardes II ; Item, canons II ; Item, coullœuvrines XIII ", ce qui est stupide puisque la distribution de ces pièces ne figure pas dans l'état de distribution. Mais on a mis un signe en marge et les mots " cy devant marché " et plus bas " in compoto ". Cette dernière mention sera examinée plus tard, elle figure à d'autres endroits. La première montre bien, comme le signe qui l'accompagne, que la distribution de pièces d'artillerie n'est pas normale.

[7] MS. *French 71*, f° 4. Il n'est pas possible, vu l'état de mutilation de cette liste, de savoir si elle concernait toute l'artillerie royale ou une partie de celle-ci.

feu messire Jaspar Bureau et avant que Christofle Constant en eut aucune charge ".[1] Cet intitulé est fort intéressant : d'abord, parce qu'il nous permet de conclure que le carnet de Christophe Constant commençait à l'entrée en charge de celui-ci, ensuite parce qu'il nous permet de préciser la date de cette entrée en charge. Nous avons vu qu'en juillet 1468 Christophe Constant n'était que " clerc " de l'artillerie, nous savons qu'en 1473 il était en fonctions comme garde, nous savons que Jaspard Bureau mourut peu après 1469.[2] Il est donc vraisemblable que c'est à la mort de ce dernier ou peu après que Christophe Constant, ayant à prendre la charge de l'artillerie, devint garde ordinaire. Mais cet intitulé nous apprend peut-être encore autre chose. Nous remarquons que Christophe Constant ne parle pas de son prédécesseur, il ne nomme que le défunt maître de l'artillerie. Ne serait-ce pas que du vivant de Messire Jaspar Bureau la charge de garde ordinaire n'existait pas ? Cette hypothèse trouverait peut-être quelque appui dans les événements des années 1469 à 1473. A Jaspar Bureau succéda comme maître de l'artillerie Helion le Groing, seigneur de la Mothe, qui démissionna peu après. Gobert Cadiot, écuyer, fut pourvu de sa charge, mais pour des raisons inconnues Helion le Groing s'opposa à sa nomination et à sa réception. Louis, sire de Crussol, fut donc chargé de l'intérim jusqu'à ce que la réception d'Helion le Groing pût être effectuée, ce que le roi ordonna par lettres du 31 mai 1472 et ce qui eut lieu le 15 juin de la même année.[3] On a donc eu une période pendant laquelle l'artillerie n'a pas eu de chef véritable. Ne serait-ce pas alors que, pour assurer la régularité du service du matériel, la charge de garde ordinaire aurait été créée pour le " clerc " Christophe Constant? Nous ne présentons bien entendu ceci que comme une hypothèse.

Cet état récapitulatif des pièces d'artillerie distribuées avant l'entrée en charge de Christophe Constant s'étendait sur une longue période. Nous y trouvons mentionné en effet les pertes d'artillerie subies à la journée de Montlhéry.[4]

> " Item furent perdues a Montléry en l'an LXV une grosse coullœuvrine de fonte nommee l'Ostesse et quatre faulcons ;
>
> " Item par Girault de Samen [5] quatre autres coullœuvrines de fonte appartenant au roy et ung des pers " ;[6]

et même des livraisons de pièces d'artillerie au duc d'Alençon en

[1] MS. *French 71*, f° 7.

[2] Anselme, viii. p. 140.

[3] Anselme, viii. p. 141 et 151. L. Susane, *op. cit.* pp. 73-74 donne une version quelque peu différente quant aux détails mais qui ne modifie pas la réalité du fait que la maîtrise de l'artillerie a fait l'objet d'une contestation et que, en attendant la décision royale, on a nommé ce que nous appellerions un séquestre.

[4] MS. *French 71*, f° 8.

[5] On sait que ce personnage, fait prisonnier à Montlhéry, passa immédiatement au service du vainqueur. *Cf. Memoires de Commines*, i. 51.

[6] La pièce fut reprise lors du siège de Beauvais en 1472. *Cf. Journal de Jean de Roye*, i. 278.

1461 et 1462.[1] Nous apprenons aussi pourquoi un contrôle sérieux des pièces était nécessaire. Les canons disparaissaient, comme ces " quatre gros canons de fer " que le canonnier Antoine le Blanc mena à Picquigny, dans la Somme, " qui depuis ont été perdus audit lieu, dont on ne scet les noms ".[2] Le plus souvent on brisait pour la fonte les pièces hors d'usage. Voici par exemple ce que l'on employa pour fondre à Orléans une grosse bombarde nommée la Réale : [3]

" . . . deux gros canons de fonte nommés les Arragonois de deux pieces chacun ;

" Item pour fondre ladite bombarde furent fondues trois serpentines de fonte nommeez la Pavye et les deux Commercys ;

" Item pour icelle treize ribauldequinz de fonte ;

" Item fut fondue et despeciee pour ladite bombarde une bombarde de fonte de deux pieces amenee de Laon, nommee la Bigneuse."

Ainsi pour fondre une pièce, on en détruisait administrativement dix-neuf. Comment le malheureux garde se reconnaissait-il dans ces états, c'est ce que l'on peut difficilement concevoir surtout si l'on veut bien considérer qu'un même nom, l'Arragonois par exemple, désignait dans la liste de Christophe Constant, une couleuvrine de fer, un courteaul de fer et sans doute plusieurs couleuvrines de fonte et plusieurs serpentines de fer.

Chargé du matériel, le garde ordinaire ne demeurait cependant pas étranger au personnel. Son carnet nous a conservé à ce sujet un document précieux, la feuille de solde d'une bande d'artillerie [4] complète, et un second document du même genre malheureusement incomplet. Nous reproduisons le premier : [5]

Canonniers soubz la bande de [6]
Bertrand de Samen par chascun an IIII^c l.t.

[1] MS. *French 71*, f° 8 v°.

[2] MS. *French 71*, f° 7. On a d'autres cas ; par exemple f° 4 v°, dans la liste des pièces d'artillerie dont nous avons parlé on trouve la note suivante : " En ce non comprises. . . . Ne pareillement sept grosses coullœuvrines de fonte amenees de Langres et de Troyes que l'on dit perdues a Dole." Il y a même plus fort. Dans les lettres patentes de commission de Raoul de Valpergue, lieutenant de l'artillerie, transcrites au f° 2, on voit que ce personnage est chargé de rassembler toute l'artillerie qu'il pourra " et par especial une bombarde nommee la cardinalle quelque part que trouver la pourra ".

[3] MS. *French 71*, f° 7.

[4] MS. *French 71*, f° 5.

[5] La question de la date de la formation de ces bandes mériterait d'être étudiée ; le P. Anselme (viii. p. 157) la place en 1477 après la mort de Guillaume Bournel. Le général L. Susane (*op. cit.* p. 76-77) donne comme date " probable " l'année 1469 pour des raisons qui sont sans valeur. En outre cet historien ne remarque pas qu'il y a eu des canonniers qui n'ont pas été mis en bande.

[6] Il y a dans le manuscrit une ligne laissée en blanc. Cela veut-il dire que la bande était sous le commandement d'un autre et que Bertrand de Samen n'en était que le lieutenant, ou faut-il au contraire ne pas tenir compte de cette ligne en blanc et lire " la bande de Bertrand de Samen ", et ne voir là qu'un artifice de comptable. Je me décide pour cette seconde lecture à cause d'une phrase du P. Anselme, *loc. cit.*, où il parle de la bande d'artillerie commandée par Jacques Galiot et appelée " la bande de Bertrand de Saman, à cause que ce Bertrand en avait été le chef ". Bertrand de Samen abandonna le commandement de sa bande en 1480 (Anselme, viii. 162).

Bertholomé de Pins	ix^{xx} l.t.
Bernard de la Fontaine	ix^{xx} l.t.
Colin Godeau	vii^{xx}iiii l.t.
Guillaume de la Lande	vii^{xx}iiii l.t.
David Pyel	vi^{xx} l.t.
Jehan Mauveau	iiii^{xx}x. l.t.
Bernardon du Bac	lx l.t.
Jehan de Berry	lx l.t.
François Rimbault	lx l.t.
Jehan de Messac	lx l.t.
Pierre Pelet	lx l.t.
Bidault de la Bastut	lx l.t.
Jehan Guiller	lx l.t.
Odin de Grant Rue	lx l.t.
Jehannin le Vasseur	lx l.t.
Jehan Petit	lx l.t.
Laurens Bichard	lx l.t.
Thomas Jamet	lx l.t.
Geoffroy Mouschet	lx l.t.
Husson Thorillon	lx l.t.
Pierre Graffin	lx l.t.
Pierre Moriet	lx l.t.
Jehan Lucas	lx l.t.
Henry Vedye	lx l.t.
Richard Heron	lx l.t.
Haguinet le Caron	lx l.t.
Simonnet de Vauchy	lx l.t.
Denis Siret	lx l.t.

La bande de Bertrand de Samen comprenait donc, outre son chef payé 400 livres tournois par an, un personnel supérieur dont la solde variait de 180 à 90 livres tournois et un personnel inférieur, infiniment plus nombreux, dont la solde uniforme s'élevait à 60 livres tournois par an. Est-il possible de saisir à quoi correspondait cette différence de solde ? Un document du fonds Bourré à la Bibliothèque Nationale nous fournit sur le second groupe un renseignement précieux. C'est un mandement du roi Louis XI qui s'exprime ainsi : [1]

" Maistre Anthoine Raguier, tresorier de nos guerres, nous avons retenus Pierre Jehan, Jehan de Berry, Guillaume Moriniau, Jehan Daviniau, charpentiers, Jehan Roullart, Guillaume Despergne, Jehan Maniau, François Rimbault, forgeurs, et Jehan Lucas, fondeur, pour nous servir doresnavant sous nostre cher et bien amé maistre Girault de Saman, maistre de nostre dite artillerie aux gaiges de cent sols tournois chacun d'eulx par moys. Si voulons et vous mandons que des deniers a vous ordonnés pour convertir au fait de nostre guerre, vous paiez et baillez a chacun des dessus nommés leurs dits gaiges a la raison de cent sols tournois par homme doresnavant par chascun moys a commencer du premier jour d'aoust prochain venant et en rapportant ces presentes signees de nostre main nous emploierons dans vos rolles tout ce que vous leur aurez paiés a la cause dessus dite sans aucune

[1] MS. *Français 20496*, f° 68.

difficulté. Donné a Estampes le XXVIe jour de juillet l'an mil CCCC soixante-sept.

LOYS. BOURRÉ.

Cent sous tournois par mois font 60 livres tournois par an, c'est bien la solde que touchent les vingt-deux derniers artilleurs de la liste précitée. Sur cette liste nous retrouvons Jean de Berry, François Rimbault et Jehan Lucas avec les mêmes gages. Il semble donc bien que cette solde soit affectée à des ouvriers d'artillerie plutôt qu'à de véritables canonniers. Les fragments du journal des dépenses en matériel de l'artillerie que nous a conservés la reliure du manuscrit *French 57* nous fournissent une confirmation de ce fait et une indication sur le personnel mieux payé de la liste de Christophe Constant. Nous y apprenons en effet que Jehan Lucas " canonnier de la bande dudit maistre Girault " [1] a touché le 8 avril 1477 cent livres de " plomb a faire plommees".[2] Jehan Lucas, le fondeur du mandement de 1467, exerçait encore les mêmes fonctions onze ans plus tard. En revanche nous voyons dans le même journal que Colin Godeau, marqué pour une solde de 144 livres tournois, sur la liste de Christophe Constant, a touché le dimanche, 25 mai 1477, quatre pics " pour faire la fosse de son baston".[3] Colin Godeau ayant la charge d'un " baston ", c'est-à-dire d'une pièce légère, est un véritable artilleur. Une bande d'artillerie se composait donc de ce que nous appellerions aujourd'hui une batterie et son échelon.

Tels sont les différents documents contenus dans le carnet du garde ordinaire, ou plutôt dans ce que nous en a conservé la reliure du manuscrit *French 57*. On voit par eux combien est étendue la compétence de ce personnage, elle est, à peu de choses près, celle qu'aura son successeur lointain, le garde général, dont l'ordonnance de 1547 fixera exactement les attributions. On peut même admettre que la compétence du garde ordinaire était plus étendue parce que, semble-t-il, moins bien définie.

Une dernière question se pose à propos de ce carnet. Pourquoi le garde ordinaire tenait-il état de ses distributions ? La réponse nous est fournie par une petite note qui revient régulièrement en marge des différents documents que nous venons d'examiner : " product. in compoto " pour les mandements ou lettres transcrits dans le carnet, " in compoto " pour les distributions. Christophe Constant se servait

[1] On s'étonnera peut-être de voir Jean Lucas qui est en 1467 dans la compagnie de Giraud de Samen, à une date intermédiaire entre 1467 et 1477 dans celle de Bertrand de Samen, se retrouver en 1477 sous les ordres de son premier chef. C'est que la carrière de ce dernier fut quelque peu agitée. Canonnier au service du roi en 1465, fait prisonnier à Montlhéry en cette année il passe au service de Bourgogne ; revenu au service du roi en 1467 il s'attache au service de Charles de Valois qu'il sert jusqu'à la mort de celui-ci en 1472 ; il revient alors au service du Roi. (*Cf.* sur ses rapports avec le frère de Louis XI, les nombreuses mentions le concernant dans le livre de H. Stein, *Charles de Valois*, Paris, 1919, in 8°.)

[2] MS. *French 71*, f° 13 v°.

[3] MS. *French 71*, f° 17 v°.

donc de ces notes pour vérifier les comptes que lui ou ses commis établissaient. Mais ces comptes ne semblent pas avoir été remis par lui directement à la Chambre des Comptes. C'est que celle-ci n'avait à connaître que de matières financières tandis que Christophe Constant s'occupait, sans avoir à s'inquieter de leur valeur marchande, des différentes parties de matériel.

Il avait en effet au dessus de lui ce Pierre de Willeries, " contreroleur d'icelle nostre artillerie " dont parle le mandement du 28 mai 1473 cité plus haut,[1] qui semble avoir été l'administrateur de l'artillerie et dont les fonctions doivent avoir été à peu près celle du contrôleur général de l'artillerie telles que les définira l'ordonnance de 1547. Nous le voyons déjà en 1473 viser les acquits du genre ordinaire, nous le trouvons de nouveau contresignant le journal des dépenses en matériel pour la campagne de Picardie en 1477 que nous a conservé la même reliure. De ce journal nous n'avons pas l'intention de parler longuement ici, notre but dans cette étude étant d'attirer l'attention sur ces documents plutôt que d'en épuiser l'intérêt. Il relate jour par jour ce qui a été distribué aux artilleurs et ce que ceux-ci ont rendu . . . quand ils ont rendu. Nous ne pouvons cependant résister au plaisir d'en citer un article qui nous a conservé les échos du compte rendu d'un capitaine d'infanterie au siège du château de La Montoire [2] en avril 1477 :

" Au capitaine des francs archers Maunoury fut delivré pour miner la muraille de ladite place L picz et tranches dont on n'en retira que x pour ce que le surplus demoura en icelle place a cause du feu qui y fut bouté incontinent aprés que par assault elle fut prise. Pourquoy icy en despence : xl."

L'auteur de ce petit mémoire s'excuse de terminer sur une note aussi belliqueuse un travail dont le sujet martial détonera peut-être dans un volume consacré à l'histoire administrative du moyen âge. Il prie les lecteurs de n'en point attribuer le choix à sa nationalité. Les raisons qui l'ont déterminé à le traiter sont plus particulières : d'abord le fait que l'histoire militaire du moyen âge a fréquemment attiré l'attention du savant professeur auquel ce volume est dédié ; ensuite le fait que les documents étudiés ont été découverts et sont conservés à la Bibliothèque John Rylands. Monsieur Tout étant un des Gouverneurs de cette institution à laquelle il n'a pas ménagé sa sollicitude, il a paru juste qu'un des manuscrits achetés sur son avis vînt contribuer à l'hommage scientifique qui lui est ici rendu.

ROBERT FAWTIER.

[1] P. 369, n. 3.

[2] Commune de Zutkerque, canton d'Ardres, arrondissement de St. Omer, Pas de Calais.

XXIX

A LIST OF THE PUBLISHED WRITINGS OF THOMAS FREDERICK TOUT

COMPILED BY MARY TOUT [1]

ABBREVIATIONS.—*B. J. R. L.=Bulletin of the John Rylands Library; D. N. B.= The Dictionary of National Biography; E. H. R.=The English Historical Review; M. G.=The Manchester Guardian; M. U. P.=Manchester University Press; S. H. R.= The Scottish Historical Review.*

1881

Review of Capt. S. H. Jones Parry's " My Journey Round the World ", *St. David's College Magazine.*

1882

THE CALENDAR OF ST. DAVID'S COLLEGE, Lampeter, edited by T. F. T. (Lampeter ; T. L. Davies and Co.).

(Reissued by the same editor in 1884 and 1886, with supplements for the intervening years.)

Review of Prof. John Rhys' " Celtic Britain ", *South Wales Daily News*, 7 Nov.

Subsequent letter on the same subject in *Ib.* 13 Nov.

1884

Numerous contributions to the *Dictionary of English History*, edited by S. Low and F. S. Pulling (Cassells). Revised edition, 1910.

The articles include : Albion ; Anglesey ; Anselm, St. ; Arthur, King ; Austria, Relations with ; Britanny, Relations with ; Britons ; Ceorl ; Church, the Early Celtic ; Councils, Civil ; Councils, Ecclesiastical ; Counties, the Welsh ; Cumbria ; Danes, the ; Damnonia ; Dunstan, St. ; Ecclesiastical Taxation ; Empire, Relations with the ; Feudalism ; Flanders, Relations with ; Free Church of Scotland, the ; Fyrd ; Galloway ; Giraldus Cambrensis ; Greece, Relations with ; Hanover, the House of ; Henry II. ; Henry III. ; Holland, Relations

[1] I have omitted many short reviews which appeared in *The Athenaeum*, *The Manchester Guardian*, and elsewhere.—M. T.

with; Howel Dda; Hundred Years' War, the; Inscriptions, Celtic; Inscriptions, Roman; Italy, Relations with; Jacobites, the; Jury, the; Justice; King; Legates, Papal; Mark System, the; Mercia; Nonconformists, the; Northumbria; Orkney and Shetland; Ostmen; Parish, the; Richard I.; Roman Roads; Romans in Britain; Spain, Relations with; Sweden, Relations with; Wales; Westminster Assembly, the.

Lectures on the Early Church History of Britain. Printed in the *Carmarthen Journal.* Reprinted separately.

(Four lectures delivered at the Old Grammar School, Carmarthen, March 1884.)

1885

Badby, John (*d.* 1410), Lollard, *Dictionary of National Biography*, ii.; Baldred, St. (*d.* 608?); Baldwulf (*d.* 803?), bp. Whithorn; Barlow, William (*d.* 1568), bishop and reformer; Barrow, Isaac (1614–1680), bp. St. Asaph; Bayly, Lewis (*d.* 1631), bp. Bangor, *Ib.* iii.; Belmeis, Richard de (*d.* 1128), bp. London; Belmeis, Richard de (*d.* 1162), bp. London, *Ib.* iv.

1886

Bilney, Thomas (*d.* 1531), martyr; Blunt, John Henry (1823–1884), ecclesiastical historian; Booth, Lawrence (*d.* 1480), abp. York, *D. N. B.* v.; Bowet, Henry (*d.* 1423), abp. York, *Ib.* vi.; Burgess, Thomas (1756–1837), bp. St. David's; Burnell, Robert (*d.* 1292), bp. Wells and chancellor, *Ib.* vii.; Byrnstan (*d.* 933), bp. Winchester; Cadell (*d.* 909), Welsh king; Cadell (*d.* 943), Welsh prince; Cadell (*d.* 1175), Welsh prince; Cadvan (*d.* 617?), Welsh king; Cadwaladr (*d.* 1172), Welsh prince; Cadwaladr Vendigaid (*d.* 664?), king of the Britons; Cadwgan (*d.* 1112), Welsh prince; Cadwgan (*d.* 1241), bp. Bangor; Cantelupe, St. Thomas de (1218?–1282), bp. Hereford, *Ib.* viii.

Review of the chapter on Roman Britain in Mommsen's *Römische Geschichte*, Band V., *English Historical Review*, i. 361-364.

1887

"Wales during the Sixteenth Century." A lecture. *Aberystwyth Observer*, 3 Dec.

Caradog (*d.* 1035), Welsh prince; Caradog of Llancarvan (*d.* 1147?), Welsh chronicler; Catherine of Braganza (1638–1705), queen of Charles II.; Cedd, St. (*d.* 664), bp. East Saxons; Charles, Thomas (1755–1814), of Bala, *D. N. B.* ix.; Charlton, Edward de (1370–1421), lord of Powys; Charlton, John de (*d.* 1353), lord of Powys; Charlton, Lewis (*d.* 1369), bp. Hereford; Charlton, Thomas (*d.* 1344), bp.

Hereford; Chishull, John (*d.* 1280), bp. London, *Ib.* x.; Comyn, Alexander (*d.* 1289), earl of Buchan; Comyn, John (*d.* 1212), abp. Dublin; Comyn, John (*d.* 1274), justiciar of Galloway; Comyn, John (*d.* 1300 ?), the elder, of Badenoch; Comyn, John (*d.* 1306), the younger, of Badenoch; Comyn, John (*d.* 1388), earl of Buchan; Comyn, Walter (*d.* 1258), earl of Menteith, *Ib.* xi.; Corbeil, William of (*d.* 1136), abp. Canterbury; Corbridge, Thomas of (*d.* 1304), abp. York, *Ib.* xii.

Contributions to *Celebrities of the Century*, edited by Lloyd C. Sanders (Cassells).

(The contributions include biographies of historians, Adolphus, J.; Alison, Sir A.; Buckle, H. T.; Burton, J. Hill; Freeman, E. A.; Froude, J. A.; Green, J. R.; Grote, George; Guizot, F. P. G.; Hallam, Henry; Lewis, Sir George C.; Macaulay, Lord; Michelet, Jules; Mommsen, Theodor; Niebuhr, Barthold Georg; Ranke, Leopold von; Stubbs, William bp. Chester. T. F. T. also wrote the articles on the following: Dalhousie, J. A. B. Ramsay, 10th earl of; Elgin, James Bruce, 8th earl of; Erskine, Thomas, lord chancellor; George IV., king; Grey, Charles, 2nd earl; Heine, Heinrich; Napoleon I., emperor; Sheridan, Richard, Brinsley; William IV., king.)

Review of C. T. Martin's "Registrum Epistolarum Fratris Johannis Peckham", *E. H. R.* ii. 555-559.

1888

"The Welsh Shires." *Y Cymmrodor*, ix. 201-226.

(The enlargement of a paper read to the society of Cymmrodorian on 7 March.)

Cunobelinus (*d.* 43 ?), British king, *D. N. B.* xiii.; Daniel (*d.* 584 ?), bp. Bangor and saint, *Ib.* xiv.; Darell, William (*d.* 1580), antiquary; David (*d.* 1139 ?), bp. Bangor; David (*d.* 1176), bp. St. David's; Davies, Edward (1756–1831), antiquary; Davies, Francis (1605–1675), bp. Llandaff; Davies, Richard (*d.* 1581), bp. St. David's; Davies, Thomas (1511 ?–1573), bp. St. Asaph; Davydd I. (*d.* 1203), Welsh prince; Davydd II. (1208 ?–1246), Welsh prince; Davydd III. (*d.* 1283), Welsh prince; Deane, Henry (*d.* 1503), abp. Canterbury; Dogmael, St. (6th cent.), *Ib.* xv.; Dubricius, St. (*d.* 612); Dwnn, Lewys (*d.* 1616 ?), Welsh herald; Eadfrid (*d.* 721), bp. Lindisfarne; Eborius (fl. 314), bp. York; Edeyrn Davod Aur (fl. 1270), Welsh grammarian; Edmund of Woodstock (1301–1330), earl of Kent; Ednyved Vychan (fl. 1230–1240), Welsh statesman, *Ib.* xvi.

Review of "Cartularium Monasterii de Rameseia" and "Chronicon abbatiae Ramseiensis" in *E. H. R.* iii. 365-367.

1889

"Owain Glyndwr and his Times." *St. David's College Magazine.*

(A lecture read before the Cardiff Cambrian Society on 7 Dec. 1888, and, later, before the English and Welsh Debating Societies of St. David's College. This lecture was repeated at Chester in an enlarged form and reprinted in the *Journal of the Archaeological Society for Cheshire and North Wales*, vi. 79-111 (1897).)

Edward II. (1284–1327), king of England; Egbert, St. (639-729); Elias, John (1774–1841), Welsh preacher; Ely, Nicholas of (*d.* 1280), chancellor and bp. Winchester, *D. N. B.* xvii.; Evans, Christmas (1766–1838), Welsh preacher; Evans, Daniel (1792–1846), Welsh poet; Fauconbridge, Eustace de (*d.* 1228), bp. London; Ferings, Richard de (*d.* 1306), abp. Dublin; Ferrers, Robert (1240?–1279?), earl of Derby, *Ib.* xviii.; Fitzalan, Brian (*d.* 1306), lord of Bedale; Fitzalan, Edmund (1285–1326), earl of Arundel; Fitzalan, John II. (1223–1267), lord of Oswestry, Clun, and Arundel; Fitzalan, John VI. (1408–1435), earl of Arundel; Fitzalan, Richard I. (1267–1302), earl of Arundel; Fitzalan, Richard II. (1307?–1376), earl of Arundel and Warenne; Fitzalan, Richard III. (1346–1397), earl of Arundel and Surrey; Fitzalan, Thomas (1381–1415), earl of Arundel and Surrey; Fitzaldhelm, William (fl. 1157–1198), governor of Ireland; Fitzgerald, Gerald (*d.* 1204), lord of Offaly; Fitzgerald, Gerald (*d.* 1398), 4th earl of Desmond, justiciar of Ireland; Fitzgerald, Thomas (*d.* 1328), 2nd earl of Kildare, justiciar of Ireland; Fitzgerald, Thomas (1426?–1468), 8th earl of Desmond, deputy of Ireland; Fitzgerald, Thomas (*d.* 1477), 7th earl of Kildare, deputy of Ireland; Fitzhamon, Robert (*d.* 1107), conqueror of Glamorgan; Fitzhenry, Meiler (*d.* 1220), justiciar of Ireland; Fitzherbert, William (*d.* 1154), abp. York and saint; Fitzroy, Henry (1663–1690), first duke of Grafton; Fitzstephen, Robert (*d.* 1183?), conqueror of Ireland; Fitzthedmar, Arnold (1201–1274?), alderman of London; Fitzthomas or Fitzgerald, Maurice (*d.* 1356), 1st earl of Desmond, justiciar of Ireland; Fitzwalter, Robert (*d.* 1235), lord of Dunmow; Gam, David (*d.* 1415), Welsh warrior, *Ib.* xix.

Reviews of Ch. V. Langlois' "Règne de Philippe le Hardi", *E. H. R.* iv. 364-369; J. B. Sheppard's "Literae Cantuarienses", *Ib.* 561-564; H. Gough's "Scotland in 1298", *Ib.* 774-775; and W. L. Bevan's "Diocese of St. David's", *Archaeologia Cambrensis*, Fifth Series, vol. vi. 164-169.

1890

A History of England, by F. York Powell and T. F. T. Part III. From William and Mary to the Present Time, by T. F. T. (Rivingtons.)

(Reissued in 1894 by Longmans. Also reissued in 1902 with

continuation 1886–1901, and in 1910 with continuation 1901–1910, Longmans.)

Giffard, Godfrey (1235?–1302), chancellor and bp. Worcester; Gilbert of St. Lifard (*d.* 1305), bp. Chichester; Gildas (516?–570?) British historian; Glendower, Owen (1359?–1416?), lord of Glyndyvrdwy, *D. N. B.* xxi.; Goldwell, Thomas (*d.* 1585), bp. St. Asaph; Gower, Henry (*d.* 1347), bp. St. David's, *Ib.* xxii.; Greenfield, William of (*d.* 1315), abp. York and chancellor; Grey, John de (1268–1323), 2nd lord Grey of Wilton; Grey, Reginald de (1362?–1440), 3rd lord Grey of Ruthin; Grey, Roger (*d.* 1353), 1st lord Grey of Ruthin; Griffith, Edmund (1570–1637), bp. Bangor; Griffith, George (1601–1666), bp. St. Asaph; Gruffydd ab Cynan (1055?–1137), king of Gwynedd; Gruffydd ab Gwenwynwyn (*d.* 1286?), lord of Cyveiliog; Gruffydd ab Llewelyn (*d.* 1063), king of the Welsh; Gruffydd ab Llewelyn (*d.* 1244), Welsh prince; Gruffydd ab Madog (*d.* 1269), lord of Bromfield; Gruffydd ab Rhydderch (*d.* 1055), king of the South Welsh; Gruffydd ab Rhys (*d.* 1137), king of South Wales; Gruffydd ab Rhys (*d.* 1201), South Welsh prince; Gwenwynwyn (*d.* 1218?), prince of Powys; Gwynllyw (6th cent.), Welsh saint, *Ib.* xxiii.; Halton, John of (*d.* 1324), bp. Carlisle; Harclay, Andrew (*d.* 1323), earl of Carlisle, *Ib.* xxiv.

Reviews of R. Sternfeld's "Karl von Anjou als Graf der Provence"; E. M. Thompson's "Chronicon Galfridi le Baker de Swynebroke"; and H. Pirenne's "La Constitution de la ville de Dinant au moyen âge", *E. H. R.* v. 773-782.

1891

A SHORT ANALYSIS OF ENGLISH HISTORY. Macmillan's History Primers.

(Reprinted in 1895, 1900, 1909, 1914, and 1920.)

Henry IV. (1367–1413), king of England; Henry VI. (1421–1471), king of England; Henry of Cornwall (1235–1271); Henry of Eastry (*d.* 1331), prior of Christ Church, Canterbury; Herewald (*d.* 1104), bp. Llandaff; Hereward (fl. 1070–1071), outlaw, *D. N. B.* xxvi.; Hothum, William of (*d.* 1298), abp. Dublin, *Ib.* xxvii.; Howel Vychan (*d.* 825), Welsh prince; Howel Dda (*d.* 950), Welsh king; Howel ab Jeuav (*d.* 984); Howel ab Edwin (*d.* 1044), South Welsh prince; Hugh Albus (fl. 1107?–1155?), chronicler; Hugh of Cyveiliog (*d.* 1181), earl of Chester; Humphrey (1391–1447), duke of Gloucester, *Ib.* xxviii.

Reviews of J. B. Sheppard's "Literae Cantuarienses", vol. ii., *E. H. R.* vi. 173-174; and S. R. Gardiner's "History of the Great Civil War", vol. iii., *M. G.* 1 Dec.

1892

"Wales in the Days of the Stuart Kings." *Transactions of the Liverpool Welsh National Society.*

Iorwerth ab Bleddyn (*d.* 1112), Welsh prince; Ireton, Ralph (*d.* 1292), bp. Carlisle; Isabella of France (1292–1358), queen of Edward II.; Isabella of France (1389–1409), second queen of Richard II.; Islip, Simon (*d.* 1366), abp. Canterbury, *D.N.B.* xxix.; Kemp, John (1380?–1454), abp. York, Canterbury, *Ib.* xxx.; Kilwardby, Robert (*d.* 1279), abp. Canterbury; Kirkby, John (*d.* 1290), bp. Ely and treasurer, *Ib.* xxxi.; Langtoft, Peter of (*d.* 1307?); Langton, Walter (*d.* 1321), bp. Lichfield and treasurer, *Ib.* xxxii.

Review of E. M. Thompson's "Adae Murimuth Continuatio Chronicarum Robertus de Avesbury De Gestis Edwardi Tertii", *E.H.R.* vii. 153-154; and W. D. Macray's "Charters illustrating the history of Salisbury", *Ib.* 746-747.

Reviews of E. A. Freeman's "Historical Essays", Fourth Series, *M.G.* 15 March; Lady Verney's "Memoirs of the Verney Family during the Civil War", *Ib.* 24 May; E. Armstrong's "Elizabeth Farnese", *Ib.* 31 May; J. H. Round's "Geoffrey de Mandeville", *Ib.* 11 June; and Sir James Ramsay's "Lancaster and York", *Ib.* 28 June.

Obituary of E. A. Freeman, *Ib.* 18 March.

1893

EDWARD I. Macmillan's Twelve English Statesmen.

(Reprinted 1896, 1901, 1903, 1906, 1909, 1913, and 1920.)

Lionel of Antwerp (1338–1368), earl of Ulster and duke of Clarence, *D.N.B.* xxxiii.; Llwyd, Sir Gruffydd (fl. 1322), Welsh hero; Llywelyn ab Seisyll (*d.* 1023?), king of Gwynedd; Llywelyn ab Iorwerth (*d.* 1240), prince of Wales; Llywelyn ab Gruffydd (*d.* 1282), prince of Wales; Llywelyn ab Rhys (*d.* 1317), Welsh rebel, *Ib.* xxxiv.; March, William (*d.* 1302), treasurer, bp. Bath and Wells; Margaret (1240–1275), queen of Scots; Margaret of Anjou (1430–1482), queen, *Ib.* xxxvi.

Reviews of "Calendar of Patent Rolls, 1327–30", "Calendar of Close Rolls, 1307–1313", *E.H.R.* viii. 135-140; A. Cartellieri's "Philipp II., August bis zum 1180"; H. Bloch's "Politik Kaisers Heinrich VI. in den Jahren 1191–1194"; and E. R. Kindt's "Gründe der Gefangenschaft Richards I. von England", *Ib.* 334-336.

Reviews of E. H. Barker's "Wanderings by Southern Waters", *M.G.* 31 Jan.; St. Clair Baddeley's "Queen Joanna I. of Naples", *Ib.* 14 Feb.; W. R. Morfill's "Poland", *Ib.* 2 May; John Skelton's "Mary Stuart", *Ib.* 24 Oct.; H. Morse Stephens' "Revolutionary Europe", 1789–1815, *Ib.* 31 Oct.

1894

"The Earldoms under Edward I." *Transactions of the Royal Historical Society*, New Series, vol. viii. 129-155.

Menteith, John de (*d.* after 1329), Scottish knight; Meopham, Simon (*d.* 1333), abp. Canterbury, *D. N. B.* xxxvii.; Mortimer, Edmund (II.) de (1351–1381), 3rd earl of March; Mortimer, Sir Edmund (III.) de (1376–1409 ?); Mortimer, Edmund (IV.) (1391–1425), earl of March and Ulster; Mortimer, Hugh (I.) de (*d.* 1181), lord of Wigmore; Mortimer, Ralph (I.) de (*d.* 1104 ?), Norman baron; Mortimer, Roger (II.) de (1231 ?–1282), 6th baron of Wigmore; Mortimer, Roger (III.) de (1256 ?–1326), lord of Chirk; Mortimer, Roger (IV.) de (1287 ?–1330), 1st earl of March; Mortimer, Roger (V.) de (1327 ?–1360), 2nd earl of March; Mortimer, Roger (VI.) de (1374–1398), 4th earl of March and Ulster, *Ib.* xxxix.

Reviews of "Cal. Patent Rolls, 1281–1292", "Cal. Close Rolls, 1313–1318", *E. H. R.* ix. 359-361; "Cart. Mon. de Rameseia", iii., *Ib.* 599; and K. A. Kneller's "Des Richard Löwenherz deutsche Gefangenschaft", *Ib.* 746.

Reviews of Mandell Creighton's "History of the Papacy during the Reformation", vol. v., *Ib.* 20 Feb.; J. H. Wylie's "History of England under Henry IV.", vol. ii., *Ib.* 13 March; Alice S. Green's "Town Life in the Fifteenth Century", *Ib.* 15 May; G. W. Prothero's "Select Statutes of Elizabeth and James I.", *M. G.* 22 May; H. O. Wakeman's "The Ascendancy of France, 1598–1715", *Ib.* 22 May; C. H. Firth's "Memoirs of Edmund Ludlow", 1625–1672, *Ib.* 3 July; H. Fishwick's "History of Lancashire", *Ib.* 16 Oct.; G. F. R. Barker's "Horace Walpole's Memoirs of the Reign of George III.", *Ib.* 20 Nov.; S. Baring-Gould's "Deserts of Southern France", *Ib.* 20 Nov.; and James Baker's "A Forgotten Great Englishman", *Ib.* 22 Dec.

1895

Ormesby, William de (*d.* 1317), judge; Osgodby, Adam de (*d.* 1316), keeper of the Great Seal; Owain Cyveiliog or Owain ab Gruffydd (*d.* 1197), prince of Powys, *D. N. B.* xlii.; Oxenedes or Oxnead, John de (*d.* 1293 ?), reputed chronicler; Pandulf (*d.* 1226), papal legate, bp. Norwich; Passelewe, Edmund de (*d.* 1327), baron of the exchequer, *Ib.* xliii.; Pelham, John de (*d.* 1429), treasurer of England; *Ib.* xliv.

Reviews of "Cal. Patent Rolls, 1330–1334", *E. H. R.* x. 150-151; and L. Toulmin Smith's "Expeditions of Henry, earl of Derby, 1390–1393", *Ib.* 569-572.

Reviews of W. H. Hutton's "William Laud", *M. G.* 15 Jan.; Lady Verney's "Memoirs of the Verney Family during the Commonwealth,

1650–60", *Ib.* 15 Jan.; and U. R. Burke's "History of Spain from the Earliest Times to the death of Ferdinand", *Ib.* 12 March.

1896

"Religious Life in England in the Later Middle Ages." *The Northern Churchman*, Nos. 87 to 95, 16 Oct. to 18 Dec.

(Nine of a course of ten lectures delivered at Owens College in Michaelmas term. The first lecture was not published.)

Peter of Aigueblanche (*d.* 1268), bp. Hereford; Phillips, Thomas (1760–1851), surgeon, *D. N. B.* xlv.; Pole, Michael de la (1330?–1389), earl of Suffolk, lord chancellor, *Ib.* xlvi.; Quivil, Peter de (*d.* 1291), bp. Exeter, *Ib.* xlvii.; Reynolds, Walter (*d.* 1327), abp. Canterbury; Richard, earl of Cornwall and king of the Romans (1209–1272); Rishanger, William (1250?–1312), monk and chronicler, *Ib.* xlviii.

Review of L. O. Pike's "Constitutional History of the House of Lords", *E. H. R.* xi. 129-132; "Cal. Close Rolls, 1318–23", "Cal. Patent Rolls, 1292–1301", *Ib.* 150-151; H. B. George's "Battles of English History", *Ib.* 550-551; P. Gachon's "Étude sur le MS. G. 1036 de la Lozère", *Ib.* 788.

Reviews of J. H. Wylie's "History of England under Henry IV.", vol. iii., *M. G.* 20 March; "Dictionary of National Biography", edited by Sidney Lee, *Ib.* 28 July; and H. Rashdall's "The Universities of Europe in the Middle Ages", *The Guardian*, 1896.

1897

Saint-John, John de (*d.* 1302), lieutenant of Aquitaine; Sandford, Fulk de (*d.* 1271), abp. Dublin; Sandford, John de (*d.* 1294), abp. Dublin, *D. N. B.* l.; L. Segrave, John de (1256?–1325), baron; Segrave, Nicholas de (1238?–1295), first baron Segrave; Segrave, Nicholas de (*d.* 1322), lord of Stowe; Segrave, Stephen de (*d.* 1333), abp. Armagh, *Ib.* li.

Reviews of "Cal. Patent Rolls, 1334–1338", *E. H. R.* xii. 159-160; F. W. Maitland's "Domesday Book and Beyond", *M. G.* 6 April; A. H. Johnson's "Europe in the 16th Century, 1494–1598", *Ib.* 22 July.

1898

THE EMPIRE AND THE PAPACY, 918–1273. Periods of European History, II. (Rivingtons.)

(Ninth Edition, 1921.)

A HISTORY OF ENGLAND, by F. York Powell and T. F. T., Part II.

From the Accession of Henry VIII. to the Revolution of 1689, by T. F. T. (Longmans.)

(Several Reissues.)

Stapleton, Brian de (1321?–1394), knight; Stapleton, Miles de (*d.* 1314), baron; Stapleton, Miles de (*d.* 1364), knight of the Garter, *D. N. B.* liv.; Taxster, John de (*d.* 1265?), chronicler, *Ib.* lv.; Thomas of Brotherton (1300–1338), earl of Norfolk and marshal of England, *Ib.* lvi.

Reviews of H. Hall's "Red Book of the Exchequer", *E. H. R.* xiii. 145-150; A. Coville's "États de Normandie", *Ib.* 569-571; C. Baudon de Mony's "Relations politiques des comtes de Foix avec la Catalogne", *Ib.* 760-762.

Reviews of J. H. Wylie's "History of England under Henry IV.", vol. iv., *M. G.* 24 May; and M. A. S. Hume's "The Great Lord Burghley", *Ib.* 15 Nov.

1899

Turberville, Henry de (*d.* 1239), seneschal of Gascony, *D. N. B.* lvii.; Ufford, Robert de (1298–1369), first earl of Suffolk of his house; Ufford, William de (1339?–1382), 2nd earl of Suffolk of his house; Umfraville, Gilbert de (1244?–1307), earl of Angus; Umfraville, Gilbert de (1390–1421), "earl of Kyme"; Verdon, Theobald de (1248?–1309), baron; Vescy, John de (*d.* 1289), baron; Vescy, William de (1249?–1297); Wake, Thomas (1297–1349), baron, *Ib.* lviii.; Walpole, Ralph de (*d.* 1302), bp. Norwich; Warenne, Hamelin de (*d.* 1202), earl of Warenne; Warenne, John de (1231?–1304), earl of Surrey; Warenne, John de (1286–1347), earl of Surrey and Sussex; Warenne, William de (*d.* 1240), earl of Warenne, *Ib.* lix.; Welles, Adam de (*d.* 1311), baron; Wells, John (*d.* 1388), opponent of Wycliffe; Weyland, Thomas de (fl. 1272–1298), judge, *Ib.* lx.

Reviews of W. Brown's "Yorkshire Lay Subsidy", *E. H. R.* xiv. 152; G. Sievers' "Politische Beziehungen Ludwigs des Baiern zu Frankreich, 1314–1337", *Ib.* 154-157; "Cal. Patent Rolls, 1305–1307", *Ib.* 350-351; "Cal. Close Rolls, 1323–1333"; "Cal. Patent Rolls, 1338–1340", *Ib.* 554-556.

Reviews of Lady Verney's "Verney Memoirs", vol. iv., *M. G.* 22 March; A. H. Beesly's "Life of Danton"; and H. Belloc's "Danton: a Study", *Ib.* 30 March.

1900

A History of England, by F. York Powell and T. F. T. New edition in one volume. (Longmans.)

(Last reissue, 1922.)

William de Fors (*d.* 1260), earl of Albemarle; William de Valence (*d.* 1296), titular earl of Pembroke, *D. N. B.* lxi.; Winchelsea, Robert de (*d.* 1313), abp. Canterbury, *Ib.* lxii.; Wykes, Thomas de (fl. 1258–1293), chronicler; Zouch, Alan la (*d.* 1270), baron; Zouche, William la (*d.* 1352), abp. York, *Ib.* lxiii.

Reviews of A. Karst's "Geschichte Manfreds", *E. H. R.* xv. 157-160; R. Holtzmann's "William von Nogaret", *Ib.* xv. 360-364; A. Cartellieri's "Abt Suger von Saint-Denis", *Ib.* 563-564; and J. Mackinnon's "History of Edward III.", *Ib.* 575-576.

1901

Reviews of E. Lavisse's "Histoire de France", t. i. 2, *E. H. R.* xvi. 355-358; J. von Pflug-Hartung's "Anfänge des Johanniten Ordens in Deutschland" and "Der Johanniter- und der Deutsche Orden in Kampfe Ludwigs des Bayern mit der Curie", *Ib.* 555-557; F. Kiener's "Verfassungsgeschichte der Provence", *Ib.* 542-546; "Inquisitions relating to Feudal Aids preserved in the Public Record Office", vols. i. and ii., *Ib.* 560-562; Ch. Bémont's "Rôles Gascons", tome ii., *Ib.* 773-776.

1902

HISTORICAL ESSAYS BY MEMBERS OF THE OWENS COLLEGE, MANCHESTER. Published in COMMEMORATION OF ITS JUBILEE (1851–1901). Edited by T. F. T. and James Tait (Longmans).

(Reissued with additional preface and index, Manchester University Press, 1907.)

The volume includes (pp. 76-136) the article "Wales and the March during the Barons' Wars, 1258–1267", with two maps, by T. F. T.

A HISTORY OF GREAT BRITAIN. Longmans' Historical Series for Schools, Book II.

(Reissued many times, with continuations up to 1919. Last edition, 1920. Also issued in two parts. Part I., from the earliest times to 1485. Part II., from 1485 to 1919.)

Map of England and Wales under Edward I. (Plate 18 with letter-press) in R. L. Poole's *Historical Atlas of Modern Europe*, Oxford University Press.

"Germany and the Empire", in *Cambridge Modern History*, i. 288-328 and 734-744.

(Germany under Frederick III. and Maximilian I., with bibliography.)

The "Communitas Bacheleriae Angliae". *E. H. R.* xvii. 89-95.

Reviews of E. Owen's "Owain Law Goch", *Ib.* 191-192; A. G. Bradley's "Owen Glyndwr", *Ib.* 192-193; J. E. Morris'

" Welsh Wars of Edward I. ", *Ib.* 557-560 ; " Social England ", vols. i. and ii., *Ib.* 756-758, and A. Molinier's ".Correspondance Administrative d'Alfonse de Poitiers ", ii., *Ib.* 773-774.

" The late Professor Adamson ", *M. G.* 11 Feb.

1903

A FIRST BOOK OF BRITISH HISTORY. Longmans' Historical Series for Schools. Book I.

(Reissued many times, with continuations up to 1919. Last edition, 1924.)

" The Fair of Lincoln and the ' Histoire de Guillaume le Maréchal '." *E. H. R.* xviii. 240-265.

" A Thirteenth Century Phrase." *Ib.* 482-483.

Reviews of E. Lavisse's " Histoire de France ", t. ii. 2, iii. 1, 2, iv. 1, *Ib.* 143-148 and 555-556 ; Ch. de Lasteyrie's " Abbaye de Saint-Martial de Limoges ", *Ib.* 342-343 ; W. Farrer's " Lancashire Pipe Rolls ", *Ib.* 550-551.

Centenary Study of the Battle of Shrewsbury, *M. G.* 21 July.

1904

AN ELEMENTARY HISTORY OF ENGLAND, by T. F. T. and James Sullivan. (New York : Longmans.)

(An American edition of A FIRST BOOK OF BRITISH HISTORY, with additions by an American collaborator.)

" Theodor Mommsen." *Cornhill Magazine.*

" The Tactics of the Battles of Boroughbridge and Morlaix." *E. H. R.* xix. 711-714.

Reviews of E. Déprez' " Les Préliminaires de la Guerre de Cent Ans ", *Ib.* 347-349 ; and E. Lavisse's " Histoire de France ", t. i. 1, ii. 1, v. 1, 2, *Ib.* 754-757.

Part of Obituary of W. T. Arnold, *M. G.* 30 May.

Professor Firth's Inaugural Lecture, at Oxford, on " The Historical Teaching of History ", *M. G.* 20 Dec.

1905

THE HISTORY OF ENGLAND FROM THE ACCESSION OF HENRY III. TO THE DEATH OF EDWARD III., 1216–1377. Vol. iii. of *The Political History of England* in twelve volumes, edited by William Hunt and Reginald L. Poole. (Longmans.)

(New edition, with corrections and additions, 1920.)

" The Study of Ecclesiastical History in its Relation to the Faculties of Arts and Theology in the University of Manchester", pp. 1-28 of *Inaugural Lectures delivered by Members of the Faculty of Theology during its First Session*, 1904–5. Edited by A. S. Peake. M.U.P.

"Some Neglected Fights between Crécy and Poitiers." *E. H. R.* xx. 726-730.

Review of J. Flach's "Les Origines de l'ancienne France", t. 1-2, *Ib.* xx. 141-143; "Recueil des Chartes de Cluny", *Ib.* 357-358; E. Lavisse's "Histoire de France", t. vi. 1, 2, *Ib.* 792.

1906

An Advanced History of Great Britain. Longmans' Historical Series for Schools, Book III.

(Numerous reissues, with continuations up to 1923. Last edition, 1923. Also issued in three parts. Part I., from the earliest times to 1485. Part II., from 1485 to 1714. Part III., from 1714 to 1923.)

State Trials of the Reign of Edward I. (1289–1293). Edited by T. F. T. and Hilda Johnstone. Camden Series of the *Royal Historical Society's Publications.*

"Schools of History." *The University Review.*

Reviews of P. Viollet's "Histoire des institutions politiques et administratives de la France", *E. H. R.* xxi. 768-772; F. A. Gasquet's "Henry III. and the Church", *Ib.* 780-782; "Willelmi Capellani in Brederode Chronicon", *Ib.* 789-790; E. Duvernoy's "États Généraux de Lorraine et de Bar", *Ib.* 795-796.

Obituaries of Mary Bateson, *M. G.* 3 Dec., and F. W. Maitland, *Ib.* 24 Dec.

Review of A. E. Medlycott's "India and the Apostle Thomas", *The Gentleman's Magazine*, Aug.

1907

"A Preliminary Estimate of the Reign of Henry III.", in *The Historians' History of the World*, edited by H. S. Williams, xviii. 356-362.

"Outlines versus Periods." Reprinted from *The University Review*, March 1907, pp. 1-16.

(A paper read at the first annual meeting of the Historical Association at University College, London.)

Review of Hans Delbrück's "Geschichte der Kriegskunst. Das Mittelalter", *E. H. R.* xxii. 344-348; E. Lavisse's "Histoire de France", t. vii. 1, *Ib.* 370-371; Lodewijk van Velthem's "Voorzetting van den Spiegel Historiael", *Ib.* 786-787; and Sir Thomas Gray's "Scalacronica", translated by Sir H. Maxwell, *Ib.* 787-788.

Reviews of L. W. Vernon Harcourt's " His Grace the Steward and Trial by Peers ", *M. G.* 15 July; and *The Cambridge Modern History,* vol. x., " The Restoration ", *Ib.* 15 July.

Review of " The Memoirs of Ann, Lady Fanshawe ", *Morning Post,* August.

Obituary of Professor John Strachan, *M. G.* 27 Sept.

Review of Dr. Max Lenz' " Napoleon ", *Ib.* 6 Dec.

Review of Albert von Ruville's " William Pitt, Earl of Chatham ", *Morning Post,* 19 Dec.

Review of T. E. S. Clarke's and H. C. Foxcroft's " Life of Gilbert Burnet, Bishop of Salisbury ", *The Saturday Review,* 14 Dec.

1908

" The Church and the New Universities." Reprinted from the *Report of the Manchester Church Congress,* 1908.

Reviews of J. W. Clark's " Liber memorandorum Ecclesie de Bernewelle ", *E. H. R.* xxiii. 129-130; Ch. Bémont's " Rôles gascons ", t. iii., *Ib.* 133-136; J. Guiraud's " Cartulaire de Notre Dame de Prouille ", *Ib.* 349-351; and E. Déprez' " Études de diplomatique anglaise. Le Sceau privé: le Sceau secret: le signet ", *Ib.* 556-559.

Article on " The University of Manchester ", *M. G.* 14 Jan.

1909

" The Chief Officers of the King's Wardrobe down to 1399." *E. H. R.* xxiv. 496-505.

Review of H. Finke's "Acta Aragonensia ", vols. i.-ii., *Ib.* 141-145.

1910

Evidence given to the Royal Commission on Public Records, printed in its *First Report,* vol. i. part iii., pp. 102-108.

Biographies of Edward I., II., and III. and Edward the Black Prince, in *Encyclopædia Britannica,* 11th edition, viii. 991-995 and 999-1000.

" An Historical Laboratory." *The Standard,* 3 Jan.

Review of R. Delachenal's " Histoire de Charles V. ", t. 1-2, *E. H. R.* xxv. 156-161.

Review of H. A. L. Fisher's " F. W. Maitland. A Biographical Sketch ", *Scottish Historical Review,* viii. 73-75.

1911

" Flintshire : Its History and its Records." *Flintshire Historical Society's Proceedings*, No. 1, pp. 1-38.

(An address to the Society, given in the County Council Chamber, Mold, 13 January 1911.)

" Firearms in England in the Fourteenth Century." *E. H. R.* xxvi. 666-702.

Review of R. Stewart Brown's " Cheshire Chamberlains' Accounts ", *Ib.* 578-579.

Review of H. A. L. Fisher's " Collected Papers of F. W. Maitland ", *S. H. R.* ix. 81-84.

1912

Bateson, Mary (1865–1906), historian, *D. N. B.* second supplement, i.; Stubbs, William (1825–1901), bp. Oxford, historian, *Ib.* iii.

Review of J. E. Lloyd's " History of Wales ", *E. H. R.* xxvii. 131-135; Chandos Herald's " Life of the Black Prince ", edited by M. K. Pope and E. C. Lodge, *Ib.* 345-349; and J. Cordey's " Les Comtes de Savoie et les rois de France pendant la Guerre de Cent Ans ", *Ib.* 552-553.

1913

" The Present State of Mediaeval Studies in Great Britain." *Proceedings of the British Academy, 1913–14*, pp. 151-166, and separately by H. Milford. A Presidential Address to the Mediaeval Section of the International Historical Congress in London, 4 April 1913.

Introduction to " The Register of John de Halton, bishop of Carlisle (1292–1324) ". In two volumes. Transcribed by W. H. Thompson. (II. i.-xliii.)

Review of " Calendar of Fine Rolls ", vol. i., *E. H. R.* xxvii. 188-189; vols. ii. and iii., in *Ib.* xxviii. 563-565.

Review of W. M. Mackenzie's " Battle of Bannockburn ", *S. H. R.* xi. 92-95.

1914

THE PLACE OF THE REIGN OF EDWARD II. IN ENGLISH HISTORY. Based upon the Ford Lectures delivered in the University of Oxford in 1913. Pp. i.-xvi., 1-422. M.U.P.

" Thomas Hodgkin, 1831–1913." *Proceedings of the British Academy, 1913–14*, pp. 503-507.

Reviews of J. H. Wylie's " The Reign of Henry V. ", vol. i., *S. H. R.*

xi. 413-415; and W. S. McKechnie's "Magna Carta", second edition, *Ib.* 427-429.

Review of E. M. Barron's "Scottish War of Independence", *E. H. R.* xxix. 755-757.

"Bannockburn and English History", *Glasgow Herald*, 9 May.

"The Sixth Centenary of Bannockburn", *M. G.* 24 June.

1915

"The University of Manchester", pp. 38-51 of *Manchester in 1915*, being the Handbook for the Eighty-fifth Meeting of the British Association, edited by H. M. McKechnie. M.U.P.

Note to the Third edition, pp. v.-vii., of *Germany in the Nineteenth Century*. A series of lectures edited by C. H. Herford. Complete edition. M.U.P.

The note was also prefixed to *Germany in the Nineteenth Century*. Second series. M.U.P.

"A Mediaeval Burglary", in *Bulletin of the John Rylands Library*, ii. 348-369, and separately. M.U.P.

(A lecture delivered at the John Rylands Library on 20 Jan.)

Reviews of J. F. Baldwin's "The King's Council in England during the Middle Ages", *E. H. R.* xxx. 117-123; and H. P. Coster's "De Kroniek van Johannes de Beka", *Ib.* 717-719.

"Magna Carta", *M. G.* 15 June.

1916

"The English Civil Service in the Fourteenth Century." *B. J. R. L.* iii. 185-214, and separately. M.U.P.

(A lecture delivered at the John Rylands Library on 15 Dec.)

"The Westminster Chronicle attributed to Robert of Reading." *E. H. R.* xxxi. 450-464.

Review of R. Delachenal's "Histoire de Charles V.", tom. iii., *Ib.* 641-644.

1917

"Mediaeval Town Planning." *B. J. R. L.* iv. 26-58, and separately. M.U.P.

(A lecture delivered at the John Rylands Library on 13 Dec. It was reprinted, with some changes, in *The Town Planning Review* (Liverpool).)

Review of C. Bémont's "Recueil d'actes relatifs à l'administration des Rois d'Angleterre en Guyenne au XIIIe siècle", *E. H. R.* xxxii. 292-295.

1918

THE CHARTIST MOVEMENT, by the late Mark Hovell. Edited and completed with a memoir by T. F. T. M.U.P.

(T. F. T. wrote Preface (pp. iii.-viii.), Memoir of Hovell (pp. xxi.-xxxvii.), and chapter xvii., The Decline of Chartism (pp. 259-312). New edition, 1925, with additional Preface by T. F. T.)

Review of W. C. Bolland's "Year Books of Edward II.—5 Edw. II.", *E. H. R.* xxxiii. 401-403.

Review of H. M. Gwatkin's "Church and State in England to the Death of Queen Anne", *History*, iii. 48-49; C. H. Jarvis' "Teaching of History", *Ib.* 57; L. J. Paetow's "Guide to the Study of Mediaeval History", *Ib.* 168.

1919

"Mediaeval and Modern Warfare." *B. J. R. L.* vol. v. 208-234, and separately. M.U.P.

(A lecture delivered at the John Rylands Library, 12 Dec. 1917.)

Reviews of "Helps for Students of History", edited by C. Johnson and J. P. Whitney, *E. H. R.* xxxiv. 270-272; Sir A. E. Middleton's "Sir Gilbert de Middleton", *Ib.* 599-601.

1920

CHAPTERS IN THE ADMINISTRATIVE HISTORY OF MEDIAEVAL ENGLAND. THE WARDROBE, THE CHAMBER, AND THE SMALL SEALS. Vol. I., pp. i.-xxiv., 1-318; Vol. II., i.-xvi., 1-364. M.U.P.

"Mediaeval Forgers and Forgeries." *B. J. R. L.* v. 208-234, and separately. M.U.P.

(A lecture delivered at the John Rylands Library, 12 Dec.)

"The Captivity and Death of Edward of Carnarvon." *B. J. R. L.* vi. 69-113, and separately. M.U.P. With appendix on "A Welsh Conspiracy to release Edward II.".

(A lecture delivered in the Chapter-house of Gloucester Cathedral on 27 Feb., and in the John Rylands Library, 10 March.)

Preface to the late Walter Short's "Pictures from France". Sherratt and Hughes.

(A tribute to an old pupil, minister of Bootle Free Church and Captain in the King's Own Yorkshire Light Infantry. Killed in France in 1915.)

Bannockburn. Historical Revisions, No. 13. *History*, v. 37-40. (Reprinted in *The Teachers' World*, vol. xxiii. No. 11.)

Reviews of W. C. Bolland's "Year Books of Edward II.—6-7 Edw. II.", *E. H. R.* xxxv. 125-127; J. Flach's "Les Origines de l'ancienne France", t. iv., *Ib.* 587-590; and G. La Mantia's "Codice Diplomatico dei re aragonesi di Sicilia, 1282–1344", *Ib.* 593-595.

Review of E. Spearing's "Patrimony of the Roman Church in the time of Gregory the Great", *History*, iv. 218; "Texts for Students", *Ib.* 218-219.

Review of "The Collected Works of Sir F. Palgrave", in ten volumes. I.-II., *S. H. R.* xvii. 52-55; Vols. III.-IV., *Ib.* xix. 60-61; Vols. V.-VII., *Ib.* 125; and Vols. VIII.-X., *Ib.* xx. 61-62.

Articles on "Making the best of brains", *Daily News*, 12 May, and "Historical Research", *Ib.* 22 May.

1921

"The Place of St. Thomas of Canterbury in History. A Centenary Study." *B. J. R. L.* vi. 235-265, and separately. M.U.P.

(A lecture delivered in the Chapter-house of Canterbury Cathedral on 7 July, and at the John Rylands Library on 8 Dec.)

"Religion in the Seventeenth Century", in *The Ancient Collegiate Church of Manchester Quincentenary Celebration*, 1421–1921, pp. 171-198. Sherratt and Hughes.

(A lecture delivered in Manchester Cathedral on 1 June.)

Reviews of J. Viard's "Les Journaux du trésor de Charles V", *E. H. R.* xxxvi. 115-119; and R. Poupardin's "Recueil des actes des rois de Provence", *Ib.* 437-439.

Reviews of "The Pilgrimage of Etheria", *History*, v. 42-43; H. L. Cannon's "Great Roll of the Pipe for the Twenty-sixth Year of Henry III.", *Ib.* v. 218-220; A. S. Turberville's "Mediaeval History and the Inquisition", *Ib.* 221-222.

1922

France and England. Their Relations in the Middle Ages and Now. Pp. viii. 1-168. M.U.P.

(Based on the Creighton lecture delivered before the University of London in 1920, and an expansion of four lectures given in the University of Rennes in 1921.)

"The Study of Mediaeval Chronicles." *B. J. R. L.* vi. 414-438, and separately. M.U.P.

(A lecture delivered in the Arts School at Cambridge on 6 Feb., and at the John Rylands Library on 9 Nov. 1921.)

Inaugural Lecture to the Potteries Branch of the Historical Association. *The Staffordshire Sentinel*, 31 Jan.

Review of Bede Jarrett's "English Dominicans", *S. H. R.* xix. 217-219.

Review of "The Cambridge Mediaeval History", vol. iii., *The Observer*, 21 May.

Review of S. H. Pearce's "Walter de Wenlok, abbot of Westminster", *History*, vii. 123-125.

Review of B. J. Kidd's "History of the Church to A.D. 461", *M. G.* 6 June.

1923

"The Place of the Middle Ages in the Teaching of History", *History*, viii. 1-18.

(The annual address before the Historical Association at Exeter on 3 Jan.)

Review of T. F. T. Plucknett's "Statutes and their Interpretation in the First Half of the Fourteenth Century", *E. H. R.* xxxviii. 271-274.

Review of G. G. Coulton's "Five Centuries of Religion", vol. i., *S. H. R.* xx. 319-321.

Reviews of C. Jenkins' "The Monastic Chronicler and the Early School of St. Albans", *History*, viii. 134-135; L. Halphen's "Eginhard, Vie de Charlemagne", *Ib.* 217-218.

"The Historical Association's Exeter Meeting", *M. G.* 8 Jan.

"Miss Burstall", *Ib.* 27 June.

1924

"Some Conflicting Tendencies in English Administrative History during the Fourteenth Century." *B. J. R. L.* viii. 82-108, and separately. M.U.P.

(An expansion of a paper communicated to the Fifth International Historical Conference at Brussels on 12 April 1923.)

"The Beginnings of a Modern Capital: London and Westminster in the Fourteenth Century." *Proceedings of the British Academy*, xi., and separately. H. Milford.

(The Raleigh Lecture read before the British Academy on Nov. 1923.)

"Mediaeval Finance." *Times Trade and Engineering Supplement*, No. 31, May.

"A National Balance Sheet for 1362–3, with documents subsidiary thereto", by T. F. T. and Dorothy M. Broome. *E. H. R.* xxxix., 404-419.

Obituary of Sir A. W. Ward. *M. G.* 20 June.

1925

"The Parliaments of Scotland." *S. H. R.* xxii. 95-100.

"The Place of St. Thomas Aquinas in History", pp. 1-31 of "St. Thomas Aquinas". Oxford: Basil Blackwell, 1925.
(A lecture given at Manchester University on 26 May 1924 and published with others in commemoration of the sixth centenary of St. Thomas's Canonisation.)

Reviews of Sir C. Oman's "History of the Art of War in the Middle Ages", vols. i. and ii., *E. H. R.* xl. 113-117; and C. W. Foster and T. Longley's "The Lincolnshire Domesday and the Lindsey Survey", *Ib.* 120-122.

INDEX OF PERSONS AND PLACES

LIST OF SUBSCRIBERS

Adair, E. R., University College, Gower Street, London, W.C.1.
Adam, Sir Frank Forbes, The Palace Hotel, Buxton.
Adams, George B., 57 Edgehill Road, New Haven, Connecticut, U.S.A.
Alexander, S., 24 Brunswick Road, Withington, Manchester.
Anderson, Mrs. R. W., Imyoka, Empangeni, Zululand.
Anderson, W. B., The University, Manchester.
Anderton, H. Agnes, 75 Frenchgate, Richmond, Yorks.
Ashley, Sir William, 29 George Road, Edgbaston, Birmingham.
Ashton, Margaret M., 591 Chorley New Road, Horwich, Lancs.
Ashton, Mrs. Mark, Heyscroft, West Didsbury, Manchester.
Aspinall, Arthur, Burrwood, Holywell Green, Halifax.
Atkinson, D., The University, Manchester.
Atkinson, R. L., The Public Record Office, Chancery Lane, London, W.C.2.

Baldick, G. S., 69 Heaton Road, Paddock, Huddersfield.
Baldwin, James F., Vassar College, Poughkeepsie, N.Y., U.S.A.
Barnes, F. R., 6 Flass Lane, Barrow-in-Furness.
Basford, Kathleen E., Lyndale, Westfield Road, Leicester.
Bass, The Rev. J. Mason, 60 Batley Road, Wakefield, Yorks.
Bateson, Nora, Legislative Library, Parliament Buildings, Toronto, Canada.
Beales, Mr. and Mrs. H. L., 6 Summerfield, Broomhill, Sheffield.
Beard, Ralph, 11 Laurel Lane, Hales Owen, Worcestershire.
Beer, Mrs., 65 College Court, London, W.6.
Bémont, C., 14 Rue Monsieur le Prince, Paris VIe, France.
Bilson, John, Hessle, Yorkshire.
Birley, Ronald, Woodside, Knutsford, Cheshire.
Boothman, Hazel E., 19A Eshton Terrace, Clitheroe, Lancs.
Boulton, H., 58 Pope's Grove, Strawberry Hill, Middlesex.
Bourdillon, Claudine, 18 Richmond Terrace, Clifton, Bristol.
Bradley, Annie, Ingledene, Junction Road, Deane, Bolton.
Bradley, Constance V., Ingledene, Junction Road, Deane, Bolton.
Bradley, His Honour Judge, 8 Balmoral Road, St. Annes-on-the-Sea.
Bridge, Doris M., 15 Sparth Road, Newton Heath, Manchester.
Bridge, John S. C., Turville Park, Henley-on-Thames.
Brierley, J. L., Grensward, Headington Hill, Oxford.
Broadbent, E. Lucy, Elmhurst, Denison Road, Victoria Park, Manchester.
Brockless, Mrs. G. F., 11 Ferrestone Road, London, N.8.
Brodie, Elizabeth, Elmslie Girls' School, Whitegate Drive, Blackpool.
Brooke, Z. N., Gonville and Caius College, Cambridge.
Broome, Mr. and Mrs. F., 37 Ashburn Road, Stockport.

Broome, Dorothy M., 37 Ashburn Road, Stockport.
Brown, Mrs. M., 12 Darley Avenue, West Didsbury, Manchester.
Browning, Andrew, The University, Glasgow.
Broxap, E., 20 Park Street, Kersal, Manchester.
Broxap, H., Pendle House, The Cliff, Higher Broughton, Manchester.
Bruce, Herbert, University College, Cardiff.
Bruton, F. A., 120 High Street, Chorlton-on-Medlock, Manchester.
Bryson, Ada, Craigton, Belfield Road, Didsbury, Manchester.
Buckley, H., 26 Cann Hall Road, Leytonstone, E.11.
Burgess, A. H., 17 St. John Street, Manchester.
Burgess, The Rev. Walter H., 4 Ladysmith Road, Plymouth.
Burstall, Sara A., University of London Club, Gower Street, London, W.C.1.
Bury, J. B., King's College, Cambridge.
Bushrod, The Rev. W. T., The Manse, Chorley, Lancs.
Butler, J. R. M., Trinity College, Cambridge.

Calder, W. M., 5 Derby Road, Withington, Manchester.
Callender, Geoffrey, Royal Naval College, Greenwich, S.E.10.
Cam, Helen M., Girton College, Cambridge.
Cane, William A., 76 Rake Lane, Clifton, Manchester.
Carlton, Dorothy, 3 Trinity Avenue, Bridlington.
Carr, J. Stanley, 10 Ambleside Road, Keswick, Cumberland.
Chadwick, Thomas, 13 Shakeshaft Street, Blackburn.
Chapman, Charles, 83 Mosley Street, Manchester.
Chapman, Sir Sydney J., The Manor House, Ware, Herts.
Charlton, H. B., Keithock, Marple Bridge.
Chew, Doris Nield, 15 Cranbourne Road, Chorlton-cum-Hardy, Manchester.
Cheyney, Edward P., University of Pennsylvania, Philadelphia, Pa., U.S.A.
Child, Myrtle, 27 Clarence Road, Barrow-in-Furness.
Chisholm, Alice T., 34 Broadway, Withington, Manchester.
Chisholm, Catherine, 34 Broadway, Withington, Manchester.
Clark, Annie M., 26 Grange Road, Barnes, London, S.W.13.
Clarke, Maude V., Somerville College, Oxford.
Classen, E., 14 Trinity Square, London, E.C.3.
Clay, Charles T., Librarian, House of Lords, Westminster, S.W.1.
Clay, Henry, Fairview, Kingston Avenue, Didsbury, Manchester.
Clayton, R. H., 1 Parkfield Road, Didsbury, Manchester.
Clemesha, H. W., County Court Offices, Preston.
Coatman, Mr. and Mrs. John, The Cottage, Abbotts Ann, Andover, Hants.
Colligan, The Rev. J. Hay, 63 Thurlow Park Road, West Dulwich, London, S.E.21.
Conway, R. S., Draethen, Didsbury, Manchester.
Cook, Francis S., Burton House, Lansdown, Bath.
Cooke, Alice M., Newnham College, Cambridge.
Coolidge, The Rev. W. A. B., Chalet Montana, Grindelwald, Switzerland.
Coopland, G. W., The University, Liverpool.
Coulton, G. G., St. John's College, Cambridge.
Cousins, The Rev. W. Phillips, Bramhall, nr. Stockport.
Cox, A. H. Gordon, The Grammar School, Manchester.
Crawford and Balcarres, The Right Hon. The Earl of, K.T., 7 Audley Square, London, W.1.

Crompton, Alice, Old Barklye, Heathfield, Sussex.
Crompton, Winifred M., The Manchester Museum, The University, Manchester.
Crump, C. G., 179 Hampstead Way, Golders Green, London, N.W.11.
Curtis, Edmund, 37 Trinity College, Dublin.
Curtis, Margaret, 19 Enmore Road, Putney, London, S.W.15.

Daniels, G. W., The University, Manchester.
Darbyshire, John A., The High School for Boys, Oswestry, Salop.
Davenport, Mrs. E. N., Roquebrun, Whaley Bridge, Stockport.
Davies, Mr. and Mrs. H. D., Haden Dene, Polefield, Blackley, Manchester.
Davis, E. Jeffries, University College, Gower Street, London, W.C.1.
Davis, H. W. C., Oriel College, Oxford.
Dawkins, Sir W. Boyd, Fallowfield House, Fallowfield, Manchester.
Deanesly, Margaret, The University, Manchester.
Déprez, Eugène, Université de Rennes, Rennes, Ille-et-Vilaine, France.
Dewe, The Rev. Joseph Adalbert, Seton Hill College, Greensburgh, Pennsylvania, U.S.A.
Dibben, Lila B., 31 Priory Road, Bedford Park, London, W.4.
Dixon, H. B., 7 Carill Drive, Fallowfield, Manchester.
Dobson, Catherine M., Brandon House, Wynne Street, East London, South Africa.
Dobson, Mrs. J. F., 11 Cambridge Park, Redland, Bristol.
Dodge, Eva, 1 Field Lane, Letchworth, Herts.
Donner, Sir Edward, Oak Mount, Fallowfield, Manchester.
Duncan, D. Shaw, The University, Denver, Colorado, U.S.A.
Dunlop, Robert, Alte Post, Golling bei Salzburg, Austria.
Dunn, John Shaw, The University, Manchester.
Dutcher, George M., Wesleyan University, Middletown, Connecticut, U.S.A.
Dymond, Dorothy, 56 Hardy Road, Blackheath, London, S.E.3.
Dyson, Taylor, King James' Grammar School, Almondbury, Huddersfield.

Eckersley, George, 16 Bertrand Road, Bolton, Lancs.
Edwards, J. Goronwy, Jesus College, Oxford.
Edwards, Mary E. I., 35 High Street, Bishop's Castle, Shropshire.
Emerson, Gladys M., Westwood, Whitefield, nr. Manchester.
Emmett, Eric, The University, Capetown, South Africa.
Ensor, Mr. and Mrs. R. C. K., The Beacon, Sands, High Wycombe, Bucks.
Entwistle, William J., The University, Glasgow.
Epstein, M., 6 Milverton Road, Brondesbury Park, London, N.W.6.
Evans, The Rev. John, 43 Deeplish Road, Rochdale.

Farrer, W., Whitbarrow Lodge, nr. Grange-over-Sands.
Farrow, Betsy, The Principal's Lodge, St. John's College, London, S.W.11.
Farrow, The Rev. W. J., Holly Bank, 175 Mossley Road, Ashton-under-Lyne.
Fawtier, Robert, The John Rylands Library, Deansgate, Manchester.
Fiddes, Edward, 173 Wilmslow Road, Withington, Manchester.
Fielding, W. R., Ierna, Galloway Road, Fleetwood, Lancashire.
Firth, Sir Charles H., 2 Northmoor Road, Oxford.
Fish, Carl Russell, 244 Lake Lawn Place, Madison, Wisconsin, U.S.A.
Formoy, Mrs. Ronald, 15 Raeburn Close, Hampstead, London, N.W.11.

Foster, Elsie, 9 Carlton Road, Burnley.
Fox, Winifred M., 331 Hungerford Road, Crewe.

Galbraith, Mr. and Mrs. V. H., 3 Raeburn Close, Hampstead, London, N.W.11.
Garside, Marion S., 59 Oak Street, Southport, Lancs.
Gaskoin, C. J. B., 14 Manson Place, London, S.W.7.
Gasquet, His Eminence Cardinal F. A., Palazzo di Calisto, Rome, Italy.
Gilbert, Leslie H., Bootham School, York.
Gill, Cecil E., Eversley, Poole, Dorset.
Gill, Conrad, 248 Bristol Road, Birmingham.
Gilson, J. P., The British Museum, London, W.C.1.
Goldschmidt, H. J., Durham House, Withington, Manchester.
Gooch, G. P., 76 Campden Hill Road, London, W.8.
Goodall, G., 35 Allison Road, Acton, London, W.3.
Gordon, The Rev. Alex., 35 Rosemary Street, Belfast.
Gorst, Isabel G., Lostock, Avondale Road, Bromley, Kent.
Graham, Rose, 12 Ladbroke Gardens, Notting Hill, London, W.11.
Grant, A. J., The University, Leeds.
Grant, M. A., Withington Girls' School, Wellington Road, Fallowfield, Manchester.
Green, Mrs. J. R., 90 St. Stephen's Green, Dublin.
Greenwood, Alice D., Capton, Williton, Taunton, Somerset.
Greg, Henry P., Lode Hill, Styal, Cheshire.
Gregory, Maud, Marrow House, Worsboro' Bridge, Barnsley.
Grieve, Alex. J., Lancashire Independent College, Manchester.
Grime, Arthur, 11 Norman Grove, Longsight, Manchester.
Gunson, Edith, 64 Westwood Street, Accrington.
Guppy, Henry, The John Rylands Library, Manchester.

Haden, Mrs. G. Nelson, Owens Cottage, Hilperton, Wilts.
Haigh, Alice, Channing House School, Highgate, London, N.6.
Haigh, Dorothy, West End, Hebden Bridge, Yorks.
Hall, The Rev. Alfred, 14 Manchester Road, Sheffield.
Hall, Hubert, 26 Old Buildings, Lincoln's Inn, London, W.C.2.
Hall, Margaret A., 4 Park Road, High Barnet, Herts.
Hall, The Rev. and Mrs. W. C., Millbrook, Todmorden.
Hannay, R. K., The University, Edinburgh.
Hargreaves, Dorothy, 1 Farrow Street, Shaw, Oldham.
Harral, Ida M., Fairholme, Barnsley.
Harrison, Mrs. G. E., Westminster Training College, Horseferry Road, London, S.W.1.
Hart, Captain and Mrs. R. C. H., The Marine Hotel, Camp's Bay, Cape Province, South Africa.
Harte, Walter J., University College, Exeter.
Harvey, Amy C., 46 Cotham Vale, Bristol.
Haskins, Charles H., 23 University Hall, Cambridge, Mass., U.S.A.
Hawcridge, Marion, 6 Prospect Road, Barrow-in-Furness.
Haworth, Mr. and Mrs. Alfred, Ravelstone, Manley, *via* Warrington.
Haworth, Frank A., Birtles Hall, Chelford, Cheshire.
Hayden, Mary T., 47 Windsor Road, Rathmines, Dublin.
Hearnshaw, F. J. C., King's College, Strand, London, W.C.2.

Hedley, Robert Moore, 29 New Cross Street, Weaste, Manchester.
Herford, C. H., 5 Parkfield Road, Didsbury, Manchester.
Hickson, Mr. and Mrs. S. J., Ellesmere House, Withington, Manchester.
Higham, Mr. and Mrs. C. S. S., 38 Mauldeth Road West, Withington, Manchester.
Hindson, Doris, 36 Arnside Street, Rusholme, Manchester.
Hodgkin, R. H., Queen's College, Oxford.
Hogg, Mrs. Hope, Ashburne Hall, Fallowfield, Manchester.
Hollings, Evangeline, Mayfield, 4 Oswald Road, Chorlton-cum-Hardy, Manchester.
Holmes, Margaret J., Rodney, West Avenue, Saltburn-by-Sea, Yorks.
Houghton, S. M., 26 Park Road, Monton, Eccles, Manchester.
Hovell, Mrs. M., Milton Cottage, John Street, Sale.
Hughes, Edward, Queen's University, Belfast.
Hughes, Helen C., The Palace, Llandaff, Glamorgan.
Hunter, May M., 29 Tantallon Road, Balham, London, S.W.12.
Hurst, Gerald B., M.P., 8 Old Square, Lincoln's Inn, London, W.C.2.
Hyde, Margaret, Scarcliffe, Worsley Road, Swinton, Manchester.

Jackson, Alice, 167 Westbourne Avenue, Bolton.
Jacob, Ernest F., All Souls' College, Oxford.
Jacobsen, Gertrude Ann, Hunter College, 68th and Park, New York, N.Y., U.S.A.
Jamison, Evelyn M., Lady Margaret Hall, Oxford.
Jenkins, The Rev. Claude, King's College, London, W.C.2.
Jenkinson, Hilary, 29 Cheyne Row, Chelsea, London, S.W.3.
Johnson, Charles, 10 Well Road, Hampstead, London, N.W.3.
Johnstone, Hilda, Moss Lea, Englefield Green, Staines.
Jones, Arthur, The Curtilage, West Hill Avenue, Epsom, Surrey.
Jones, Stanley Wilson, Malayan Civil Service, Kwantan, Pahan, Malay States.
Joseland, H. L., 6 Piccadilly Road, Burnley, Lancs.
Jucker, E. Fontana, Brockhurst, West Didsbury, Manchester.
Judson, Wilfred, 112 Coleman Avenue, East Toronto, Ontario, Canada.

Kastner, L. E., Hawthornden, Buxton.
Kay, Harold, Education Offices, Blackburn.
Kennedy, W. P. M., University of Toronto, Toronto, Ontario, Canada.
Kenyon, Sir Frederic G., The British Museum, London, W.C.1.
Kingsford, Charles Lethbridge, 15 Argyll Road, Kensington, London, W.8.
Kinsey, Elizabeth, 5 Dixon Street, Longsight, Manchester.
Kinsey, W. Warren, 5 Dixon Street, Longsight, Manchester.
Knight, E. A., The Hill, Knutsford, Cheshire.
Knott, Roger B., 3 Norfolk Street, Manchester.

Laistner, M. L. W., King's College, Strand, London, W.C.2.
Langdon, Mr. and Mrs. A., 32 Holland Villas Road, London, W.14.
Langlois, Ch. V., Archives Nationales, Rue des Francs-Bourgeois 60, Paris, France.
Lapsley, Gaillard, Trinity College, Cambridge.
Lapworth, A., 26 Broadway, Withington, Manchester.
Laski, Mr. and Mrs. Nathan, Smedley House, Cheetham, Manchester.

Laski, Mabel S., Smedley House, Cheetham, Manchester.
Laski, Neville J., 121 Lapwing Lane, Didsbury, Manchester.
Lee, Sir Sidney, 108A Lexham Gardens, Kensington, London, W.8.
Lees, Beatrice A., 8 Norham Road, Oxford.
Lees, Dame Sarah A., Werneth Park, Oldham.
Leonard, George H., The University, Bristol.
Lewis, Marjorie, Penmaen, Lancaster Avenue, Newcastle, Staffs.
Lewis, N. B., Penmaen, Lancaster Avenue, Newcastle, Staffs.
Liebermann, F., 10 Bendlerstrasse, Berlin, W.10, Germany.
Little, A. G., Risborough, Sevenoaks, Kent.
Llandaff, The Right Rev. The Lord Bishop of, The Palace, Llandaff, Glamorgan.
Lloyd, John Edward, Gwaln Deg, Bangor, N. Wales.
Lodge, Eleanor C., Westfield College, Hampstead, London, N.W.3.
Lodge, Sir Richard, Lane End, Harpenden, Herts.
Lomas, Mrs. S. Crawford, 57 Herne Hill, London, S.E.24.
Longmans, Green and Co., 39 Paternoster Row, London, E.C.4.
Low, Sir Sidney, 37 Campden Hill Court, Kensington, London, W.8.
Lowe, Mrs. J., 38 Vera Road, Fulham, London, S.W.6.
Lowe, Nancy M., In Memory of, 38 Vera Road, Fulham, London, S.W.6.
Lunt, W. E., Haverford College, Pennsylvania, U.S.A.
Lyte, Sir H. C. Maxwell, 61 Warwick Square, London, S.W.1.

MacLeavy, The Rev. G. W., 298 Middleton Road, Oldham.
Maclehose, James, The University Press, Anniesland, Glasgow, W.2.
Macpherson, Jean, 94 Park Road, Newcastle-on-Tyne.
Maltby, S. E., Friends' School, Penketh, nr. Warrington.
Manchester University History School, 1925.
Manning, B. L., Jesus College, Cambridge.
Marten, C. H. K., Eton College, Windsor.
Martin, Kenneth L. P., 51 Albert Road, Withington, Manchester.
Marx, Charles, The Cedars, Didsbury, Manchester.
Mather, L. E., Park Works, Newton Heath, Manchester.
McClymont, Jean A., 311 Dickenson Road, Manchester.
McDougall, Robert, Lerryn, Carr Wood Road, Cheadle Hulme, Stockport.
McKechnie, H. M., The University Press, Manchester.
McKechnie, Wm. S., 93 Oakfield Avenue, Hillhead, Glasgow.
McLachlan, The Rev. H., Summerville, Victoria Park, Manchester.
McNicol, Primrose, 182 Upper Chorlton Road, Manchester.
Medley, D. J., The University, Glasgow.
Melvill, J. Cosmo, Meole Brace Hall, Shrewsbury.
Mercier, Winifred, Whitelands College, Chelsea, London, S.W.3.
Merriman, Roger B., 175 Brattle Street, Cambridge, Mass., U.S.A.
Miers, Sir Henry A., Birch Heys, Cromwell Range, Fallowfield, Manchester.
Milne, E. A., Trinity College, Cambridge.
Moffet, Mr. and Mrs. S. O., 81 Heolyderi, Rhiwbina, Cardiff.
Montague, C. E., 10 Oak Drive, Fallowfield, Manchester.
Montague, F. C., 177 Woodstock Road, Oxford.
Moore, Margaret, 681 St. Helen's Road, Bolton.
Morehouse, Frances, 723 Seventh Street, S.E., Minneapolis, Minn., U.S.A.
Morris, J. E., 17 Sturges Road, Wokingham, Berks.
Morris, Mrs. F., c/o The Eastern Bank, Ltd., Baghdad, Iraq.

Morris, Wm. A., University of California, Berkeley, Cal., U.S.A.
Muir, Ramsay, 12 Cursitor Street, London, E.C.4.
Mumford, W. F., The College, Fairfield, Manchester.
Mungo, David B., The University, Glasgow.
Munro, Dana C., Princeton University, Princeton, N.J., U.S.A.
Murray, George R., 13 St. John Street, Manchester.

Neale, J. E., The University, Manchester.
Needham, Sir Christopher T., Fair Oak, West Didsbury, Manchester.
Neild, Ada, New Delph, nr. Oldham.
Neild, N., The Grammar School, Bury, Lancs.
Neilson, N., Mount Holyoke College, South Hadley, Mass., U.S.A.
Notestein, Wallace, Cornell University, Ithaca, N.Y., U.S.A.

Oldfield, Sir Francis Du Pré, 53 Palace Court, London, W.2.
O'Neill, Mrs. C. S., Ashley Road, Hale, Cheshire.
O'Neill, Mrs. H. C., 54 King Henry's Road, Hampstead, London, N.W.3.
Ormerod, Elizabeth, 23 Fenton Street, Rochdale.
Orr, John, The University, Manchester.
O'Sullivan, John M., Aberfoyle, Orwell Road, Dublin.
Owen, Joseph, 43 Mount Park Road, Ealing, London, W.5.

Page, William, Ashmere Croft, Middleton, nr. Bognor.
Pape, T., Orme Boys' School, Newcastle, Staffs.
Parish, Jessie M., 13 High Lane, Chorlton-cum-Hardy, Manchester.
Pearson, Rachel F., 6 Hartley Street, Littleborough, nr. Manchester.
Peattie, Mrs. J. D., 30 Whitefield Avenue, Cambuslang, Glasgow.
Penson, Lillian M., 31 Marlborough Place, London, N.W.8.
Perkins, Clarence, University of North Dakota, Grand Forks, N.D., U.S.A.
Petit-Dutaillis, Ch., 96 Boulevard Raspail, Paris, France.
Philips, W. Morten, 35 Church Street, Manchester.
Phillipson, S., Weylands, Wood End Green, Hayes, Middlesex.
Phythian, Mabel, 16 Cockbrook, Ashton-under-Lyne.
Pirenne, Henri, 126 Rue Neuve St.-Pierre, Gand, Belgium.
Plummer, H., Hazeldene, Fallowfield, Manchester.
Pollard, A. F., 7 St. Mary's Grove, Barnes Common, London, S.W.13.
Poole, Austin L., St. John's College, Oxford.
Poole, Reginald L., 19 Banbury Road, Oxford.
Potter, Jennie M., 16 Grange Court, Headingley, Leeds.
Powell, Olive, 6 The Park, Kingswood, Bristol.
Power, Eileen, London School of Economics, Aldwych, London, W.C.2.
Powicke, F. M., The University, Manchester.
Powicke, Mrs. W. A., Lindhurst, Knight Street, Hyde.
Previté-Orton, C. W., 55 Bateman Street, Cambridge.
Prince, A. E., Queen's University, Kingston, Ontario, Canada.
Proudfoot, The Rev. S., The Vicarage, Pendleton, Manchester.
Purves, Mrs., 81 Eaton Rise, Ealing, London, W.
Putnam, Bertha Haven, Mount Holyoke College, South Hadley, Mass., U.S.A.
Pyman, Frank Lee, College of Technology, Manchester.

Raby, Percy, 22 Moorfield Road, West Didsbury, Manchester.
Re, Emilio, R. archivio di Stato, Roma, Italy.

Redford, Arthur, London School of Economics, Aldwych, London, W.C.2.
Rees, J. F., The University, Birmingham.
Reichel, Sir Harry R., Gartherwen, Bangor, N. Wales.
Reid, James S., West Road, Cambridge.
Richardson, H. G., Fairmead, Bayham Road, Sevenoaks, Kent.
Roberts, Ellen, 41 Johnston Street, Tyldesley.
Roberts, Louisa, 348 Edenfield Road, Rochdale.
Robertson, C. Grant, The University, Edmund Street, Birmingham.
Robinson, Howard, Miami University, Oxford, Ohio, U.S.A.
Rodgers, Edith, 33 Leinster Road, Swinton, Manchester.
Rogers, Eileen, 62 Westgate, Hale, Cheshire.
Rose, J. Holland, Walsingham, 4 Millington Road, Cambridge.
Rose-Troup, Mrs., Bradlegh End, Ottery St. Mary.
Roskill, Charles, 100 Portland Street, Manchester.
Rossington, The Rev. Herbert J., Ardeevin, Cadogan Park, Belfast.
Rowbotham, Florence, Hillbrook Grange, Bramhall, Cheshire.
Royle, Dora K., Rest Harrow, Bramhall, Cheshire.
Russell, E., Verdin Technical School, Winsford, Cheshire.
Rutherford, Sir Ernest, Newnham Cottage, Cambridge.

Salter, The Rev. H., Dry Sandford, Abingdon, Berks.
Salter, F. R., Magdalene College, Cambridge.
Sandys, Agnes M., St. Hilda's Hall, Oxford.
Sargeant, F., 15 Carlton Avenue, Romiley, nr. Stockport.
Satterthwaite, W. H., Burrow Beck House, Lancaster.
Schroeder, The Rev. William Lawrence, 2 Grosmont, Grove Lane, Headingley, Leeds.
Scott, C. P., The Firs, Fallowfield, Manchester.
Scott, Ernest, The University, Melbourne, Australia.
Scott, Ethel M., Girls' Secondary School, Brighouse.
Sharp, Mr. and Mrs. W. D., 2 Lambolle Road, Hampstead, London, N.W.3.
Sharp, Phyllis, 19 Wilmslow Road, Withington, Manchester.
Shaw, Wm. Fletcher, 20 St. John Street, Manchester.
Shepherd, William R., Kent Hall, Columbia University, New York City, U.S.A.
Shipman, Henry R., 27 Mercer Street, Princeton, N.J., U.S.A.
Simmonds, Florence, Burton Grange Cottage, Clifton, York.
Simon, Mr. and Mrs. E. D., Broom Croft, Didsbury, Manchester.
Simpson, G. C., 47 Shepherd's Hill, Highgate, London, N.6.
Simpson, H. Derwent, Beechwood, Bowdon, Cheshire.
Singer, Charles, 5 North Grove, Highgate Village, London, N.6.
Skeel, Caroline A. J., Westfield College, Hampstead, London, N.W.3.
Skemp, Mrs. A. R., 20 Belgrave Road, Tyndall's Park, Bristol.
Skemp, F. W., c/o Lloyd's Bank, 9 Pall Mall, London, S.W.1.
Southam, F. A., 10 Kinnaird Road, Withington, Manchester.
Spencer, Edith, 8 Croft Street, Bacup, Lancs.
St. Davids, The Right Rev. the Lord Bishop of, The Palace, Abergwili, Carmarthenshire.
Steinthal, A. Ernest, 19 Ladybarn Road, Fallowfield, Manchester.
Stenton, Mr. and Mrs. F. M., University College, Reading.
Stephenson, Edgar, St. Anselm's Hall, Victoria Park, Manchester.
Stevenson, Lillian, 2741 S. Adams Street, Fort Worth, Texas, U.S.A.

Stocks, J. L., 22 Wilbraham Road, Fallowfield, Manchester.
Stone, C. G., Balliol College, Oxford.
Stooke, K. Margaret, Tytherton, nr. Chippenham, Wilts.
Stopford, John S. B., The University, Manchester.
Sutcliffe, Dorothy, The University, Edmund Street, Birmingham.

Tait, James, Brookdale, Hawthorn Lane, Wilmslow, Cheshire.
Talbott, Mrs., The Colonnade, Shirebrook, nr. Mansfield.
Tanner, J. R., St. John's College, Cambridge.
Taylor, Henry, 12 Curzon Park, Chester.
Taylor, Lizzie, 9 Greenwood Avenue, Mile End, Stockport.
Temperley, Harold W. V., Peterhouse, Cambridge.
Tesh, Elsie, 99 Park Avenue, Gillingham, Kent.
Thackray, The Rev. E., The Parsonage, Stand, Whitefield, Manchester.
Thomas, Mary, 22 Church Lane, Romiley, nr. Stockport.
Thornley, Isobel D., University College, Gower Street, London, W.C.1.
Titterington, Emma E., Ockbrook Moravian School, nr. Derby.
Toller, T. N., Lansdowne House, Didsbury, Manchester.
Topham, A. Margaret, Princes Drive, Borrowash, nr. Derby.
Tout, Mrs. T. F., 3 Oak Hill Park, Hampstead, London, N.W.3.
Toynbee, Margaret R., 5 Park Crescent, Oxford.
Toynbee, Paget, Fiveways, Burnham, Bucks.
Treharne, R. F., 54 City Road, Kitt Green, nr. Wigan.
Trevelyan, G. M., Penrose, Berkhamsted, Herts.
Trevor, Adelaide, Heathfield, Culcheth Lane, Newton Heath, Manchester.
Turner, H. P., The University, Manchester.
Turner, Raymond, Yale University, New Haven, Conn. U.S.A.
Tyson, Moses, Busk House, Ambleside, Westmorland.

Unwin, George, 47 Heaton Road, Withington, Manchester.
Urquhart, F. F., Balliol College, Oxford.

Veen, Gerald M. van der, 25 Owen Road, Bilston, Staffs.
Veitch, George S., 8 Brompton Avenue, Liverpool.
Vickers, Kenneth H., University College, Southampton.
Vinogradoff, Sir Paul, 36 Beaumont Street, Oxford.
Vity, Winifred, 47 Bradford Street, The Haulgh, Bolton.

Wadsworth, Mrs., Croft House, Cambasforth, Selby, Yorks.
Wales, The Most Rev. His Grace the Lord Archbishop of, The Palace, St. Asaph.
Walkden, J., Clavadel, Spire Hollin, Glossop.
Walker, Alice, Fern Bank, Delamere Road, Bowdon, Cheshire.
Walker, Curtis H., The Rice Institute, Houston, Texas, U.S.A.
Walker, I. Kathleen, 81 South Drive, Chorlton-cum-Hardy, Manchester.
Ward, Sir Adolphus William, Peterhouse Lodge, Cambridge.
Waterhouse, E., 84 Little Hallam Lane, Ilkeston, Nottingham.
Watson, The Rev. Canon E. W., Christ Church, Oxford.
Waugh, W. T., McGill University, Montreal, Canada.
Weaver, J. R. H., Trinity College, Oxford.
Weiss, F. E., Easedale, Disley, Cheshire.
Weitzman, David, 3 Paper Buildings, Temple, E.C.4.
Weitzman, Sophia, 83 Aberdeen Road, Highbury, London, N.5.

Wells, Evelyn B., 11 Gibsons Road, Heaton Moor, Stockport.
Westbrook, Mrs., Parkfield, Manchester Road, Swinton, Lancs.
Wheeler, Edith H., 1 Milton Road, Newton Abbot, S. Devon.
Wilkinson, Mr. and Mrs. B., Kilmorie, Pennsylvania Road, Exeter.
Wilkinson, H. Spenser, 99 Oakley Street, Chelsea, London, S.W.3.
Willard, James F., University of Colorado, Boulder, Colorado, U.S.A.
Williams, The Ven. Archdeacon Robert, The Vicarage, Llandilo, Carmarthenshire.
Wood, Herbert, 11 Clarinda Park West, Kingstown, Co. Dublin.
Wood, L. B., Belmont, Higher Downs, Bowdon, Cheshire.
Woodall, Ethel M., Spring Grove, East Bath Street, Batley, Yorks.
Woodcock, Mabel H. M., The John Rylands Library, Manchester.
Woods, F. U., Abbotshaw, Hard Lane, St. Helens, Lancs.
Worthington, A. H., Scotscroft, Didsbury, Manchester.
Worthington, Joseph, Sunnyside, Teignmouth Road, Torquay.
Wrong, E. Murray, Holywell Ford, Oxford.
Wrong, George M., University of Toronto, Toronto, Ontario, Canada.

LIBRARIES

Aberystwyth, The National Library of Wales (John Ballinger, Librarian).
Adelbert College Library, Western Reserve University, Cleveland, Ohio, U.S.A. (George F. Strong, Librarian).

Basel, Universitätsbibliothek, Switzerland (G. Biny, Librarian).
Belfast, The Queen's University Library (G. Gregory Smith, Librarian).
Beloit College Library, Beloit, Wisconsin, U.S.A. (Iva M. Butlin, Librarian).
Birkenhead, The Public Libraries (John Shepherd, Librarian).
Birmingham Public Library, Ratcliff Place, Birmingham, *per* Cornish Brothers, Ltd., Birmingham.
Bolton, The Reference Library (Archibald Sparkes, Librarian).
Bristol, The University Library (W. L. Cooper, Librarian).
Bryn Mawr College Library, Bryn Mawr, Pa., U.S.A., *per* E. G. Allen and Son, Ltd., London, W.C.

Cambridge, Newnham College Library, *presented by* Miss Alice M. Cooke (I. B. Horner, Librarian).
Chester, St. Deiniol's Library, Hawarden (J. C. Du Buisson, Librarian).
Clark University Library, Worcester, Mass., U.S.A., *per* G. E. Stechert and Co., London.
Colorado University Library, Boulder, Colorado, U.S.A. (C. Henry Smith, Librarian).
Columbia University Library, New York, N.Y., U.S.A. (D. B. Hepburn, Supervisor, Accessions Dept.).
Congress, Library of, Washington, D.C., U.S.A., *per* B. F. Stevens and Brown, London.
Cornell University Library, Ithaca, N.Y., U.S.A.

Dartmouth College Library, Hanover, N.H., U.S.A. (Nathaniel L. Goodrich, Chief Librarian).
Dublin, The National Library of Ireland, *per* Hodges, Figgis and Co., Dublin.
Dublin, Trinity College Library (Alfred de Burgh, assist. Librarian).
Durham, The University Library (E. V. Stocks, Librarian).

Edinburgh, Advocates' Library (William K. Dickson, Keeper).
Edinburgh, The Signet Library, Parliament Square (John Minto, Librarian).
Edinburgh, The University Library, *per* James Thin, Edinburgh.

Gand, Bibliothèque de l'Université, Belgium (Paul Bergmans, Chief Librarian).
Glasgow, The University Library (W. R. Cunningham, Librarian), *per* Jackson, Wylie and Co., Glasgow.

Haverford College Library, Haverford, Pa., U.S.A.

Illinois University Library, Urbana, Ill., U.S.A. (Phineas L. Windsor, Librarian).

Kingston, Ontario, Canada, Queen's University Library, *per* B. F. Stevens and Brown, London.

Lampeter, St. David's College Library (G. W. Wade, Librarian).
Leeds, City of Leeds Public Libraries (Thomas W. Hand, City Librarian).
Leeds, The University Library.
London, Institute of Historical Research, Malet Street, W.C.1 (H. W. Meikle, Secretary and Librarian).
London, H.M. Public Record Office Library, *per* H.M. Stationery Office.
Lund, Universitets-Biblioteket, Sweden (E. Ljunzgru, Librarian).

Manchester, Philip Theodore Haworth Research Library, History Department, The University.
Manchester, The John Rylands Library (H. Guppy, Librarian).
Manchester, The University Library (Charles W. E. Leigh, Librarian).
Manchester, Unitarian Home Missionary College Library (H. McLachlan, Librarian).
Manchester Public Libraries (L. Stanley Jast, Chief Librarian).
McGill University Library, Montreal, Canada (G. R. Lomer, Librarian).
Michigan University Library, Ann Arbor, Mich., U.S.A.

Nebraska University Library, Lincoln, Nebraska, U.S.A. (M. G. Wyer, Librarian).

Oslo (Kristiania), Universitetsbiblioteket, Norway (W. Mimthe, Chief Librarian).
Oxford, Balliol College Library (A. W. Pickard Cambridge, Librarian).
Oxford, The Meyrick Library, Jesus College (J. Goronwy Edwards, Librarian).

Princeton University Library, Princeton, N.J., U.S.A. (James Thayer Gerould, Librarian).

Reading University College Library (S. Peyton, Librarian).
Rennes, Bibliothèque de l'Université, Ille-et-Vilaine, France.
Rice Institute Library, Houston, Texas, U.S.A. (Alice C. Dean, Acting Librarian).
Royal Holloway College Library, Englefield Green, Surrey (E. G. Looker, Librarian).

Sheffield, The University Library (A. P. Hunt, Librarian).
St. Andrews University Library (Geo. H. Bushnell, Librarian).
Stockport Public Library (Richard Hargreaves, Librarian).

Toronto University Library, Toronto, Ontario, Canada, *per* E. G. Allen and Son, Ltd., London.

Vanderbilt University Library, Nashville, Tennessee, U.S.A.
Vassar College Library, Poughkeepsie, N.Y., U.S.A. (Adelaide Underhill, Librarian).

Washington University Library, Saint Louis, Mo., U.S.A. (James A. McMillen, Librarian).
Washington University Library, Seattle, Washington, U.S.A. (William E. Henry, Librarian).
Wigan Public Library, Rodney Street, Wigan (Arthur J. Hawkes, Chief Librarian).
Williams College Library, Williamstown, Mass., U.S.A. (W. N. C. Carlton, Librarian).
Wooster College Library, Wooster, Ohio, U.S.A. (F. W. Hags, Librarian).

THE END